THE ULTIMATE
SNIPER

WARNING

The procedures, drills, and techniques outlined in this book are intended for official military and law enforcement use only. It is not the intent of the author, publisher, or distributors of this book to encourage readers to perform any of the techniques or drills in this book without proper professional training and supervision. Attempting to do so can result in severe injury or death to the reader or bystanders. This book is *for academic study only*.

THE ULTIMATE SNIPER

MAJ. JOHN L. PLASTER, USAR (RET.)

AN ADVANCED TRAINING MANUAL
FOR MILITARY AND POLICE SNIPERS

PALADIN PRESS • BOULDER, COLORADO

Also by John L. Plaster
Ultimate Sniper: The Video (video)
Advanced Ultimate Sniper (video)
History of Sniping and Sharpshooting
SOG: A Photo History of the Secret Wars
SOG: The Secret Wars of America's Commandos in Vietnam
Secret Commandos: Behind Enemy Lines with the Elite Warriors of SOG

The Ultimate Sniper:
An Advanced Training Manual for Military and Police Snipers
by Maj. John L. Plaster, USAR (Ret.)

Copyright © 1993, 2006 by John L. Plaster
ISBN 13: 978-1-58160-494-8
Printed in the United States of America

Published by Paladin Press, a division of
Paladin Enterprises, Inc.
7077 Winchester Circle
Boulder, Colorado 80301, USA.
+1.303.443.7250

Direct inquiries and/or orders to the above address.

Visit our Web site at www.paladin-press.com.

Illustrations by Bradley Hopkins and Tami Anderson

Photo on back cover, bottom row, far right copyright © by Jon Hill

TABLE OF CONTENTS

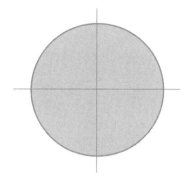

ACKNOWLEDGMENTS

*T*his second edition of *The Ultimate Sniper* is dedicated to the United States of America's military and law enforcement snipers, sharpshooters, and designated riflemen. Though few ever receive the recognition they deserve, our world is a better and safer place thanks to their great dedication, skill, and courage.

Hundreds of snipers, long-range riflemen, tacticians, optics experts, and firearms industry professionals have helped me since the publication of the first edition, sharing not only their tactics, techniques, and lessons learned but new ideas, weapons, and devices, many of which I've incorporated into these pages. Among this diverse group, first I thank my old Special Forces friend, Steve Stormoen—the first edition's mysterious "S.S."—who finally has come in from the shadows; all my colleagues and friends at Gunsite Training Center, including Dr. Richard Jee, Neal Terry, Jim "K-Bar" Kauber, Bill Jeans, Jack Furr, Bill Atkins, Eric Olds, Chris Mayer, Chris Caracci, and Ted Yost; the Marine Corps' most accomplished Vietnam War sniper, Chuck MaWhinney; Marine sniping legend GySgt. Carlos Hathcock; Department of the Army JAG, Mr. W. Hays Parks; Sgt. Darryl Schmidt, St. Paul Police Department; Sgt. Charlie Dodge, Minneapolis Police Department; Sgt. Neal Terry, Albuquerque Police Department; Agent Fred MacDonald III, Mississippi Bureau of Narcotics; MSgt. Steve Holland, 5th Special Forces Group; Tom Slowik, Arizona Crisis (SWAT) teams; George Lainhart, College Park, Georgia, Police Department; FBI Special Agent Bowen Johnson; FBI Special Agent Mike Balen; Ed Sanow and *S.W.A.T. Magazine*; Olympic rifleman Lance Peters; .50-caliber world record champion, Skip Talbot; Will Von Gal, who generously sponsored the Super Sniper Shootout competitions in the United States and Europe; Garth and Fred Choate, both serious riflemen, who helped me develop and manufacture my sniper rifle stock and the Rifle Stabilizer; Bushnell optical engineer Tim Carpenter, who explained the technicalities of laser rangefinders; Barbara Mellman-Skinner at Bushnell, for much support; Leupold's Garth Kendig, a friend and supporter; Shep Kelly of Federal Cartridge Company; my longtime gunsmith friend, Gene Mayo; Dr. B.R.G. Kaplan, M.D., for insights on wound ballistics; the Fifty Caliber Shooters Association; and fellow Green Beret vet and author Jim Morris. Additionally, I thank the cadre at the U.S. Army Sniper School, the U.S. Marine Corps Scout Sniper Instructor School, and the 5th Special Forces Group Sniper Training School for their hospitality during my visits. For the considerable amount of ammunition consumed to evaluate and test weapons, I thank Steve Hornady at Hornady ammunition, Jeff Hoffman at Black Hills Ammo, and Mike Larson of Federal Cartridge.

My original sniper school cadre, who helped launch me on this interesting journey more than 20 years ago, each contributed in his own way:

MILITARY INSTRUCTORS

Lt. Col. Gary Schraml
Sgt. 1st Class Gary Gamradt
Lt. Col. Dave Loehr
Sgt. 1st Class Blaine Nelson
Capt. Wendell Daluge
Sgt. 1st Class Michael Corrow
1st Lt. Charles Weebee
SSgt. Timothy Cole
2nd Lt. Dave Beckering
SSgt. Robert Siefert
WO1 Jeff Luikart
SSgt. Timothy Weber
CSM Dick Wagaman
SSgt. Michael Anderson
Sgt. 1st Class Darryl Brown
Sgt. Brent Henry
MSgt. Clifton Evans
Sgt. John Lepowski
MSgt. Steve Lischalk
Sgt. Michael Malterud
MSgt. Robert Payne
Sgt. Lance Peters
MSgt. Carl Peterson
Sgt. Gary Zacharias
MSgt. Daniel Purkat
Spec. 4 Brad Hopkins

LAW ENFORCEMENT INSTRUCTORS

Officer Lyle Beauchamp,
Minneapolis Police Department
Officer Lyle Delaney,
Minneapolis Police Department
Sgt. Gary Hill, Minneapolis Police Department
Special Agent Kevin Crawford, FBI
Sgt. Dan Harshman,
St. Paul Police Department
Sgt. Darryl Schmidt,
St. Paul Police Department
Sgt. Steve Campbell,
Mississippi Bureau of Narcotics
Agent Tommy Squires,
Mississippi Bureau of Narcotics
Trooper Dave Watson,
Alabama Highway Patrol

MILITARY SUPPORT PERSONNEL

SgtMaj. Robert Roschen
1st Lt. Joseph Seaquist
MSgt. James Olson

This second edition's photographers and photo technicians include my lovely wife, Gail, along with Roger Kennedy, Charles Farrow, and Doug Black. Many of Brad Hopkins' first edition illustrations have been retained, reinforced by new drawings from Tami Anderson. And finally, I thank Paladin Press publisher Peder Lund, a fellow Special Forces combat vet, and my editor, Jon Ford, for their help and encouragement.

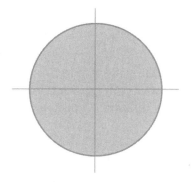

PREFACE

Though the first edition of *The Ultimate Sniper* represented the best of what was known about sniping in 1993, this art and science advanced so remarkably in the following dozen years that a second edition has become a necessity. Thanks to these updates, changes, and revisions, I believe that this new edition will help advance sniping well into the 21st century and prove as revolutionary as the original book.

And it was revolutionary. Never before had a sniper training manual addressed mantracking, for example. And though manuals cited compensation for crosswinds, they lacked the simple advice that you can neutralize the wind's effect by reducing your distance or shifting up- or downwind. Sniper training curriculum did not even address up/down ("slant") shooting. Having spent years in combat behind enemy lines and years instructing snipers, I knew that our institutional knowledge and combat experience were much greater than what was depicted in the manuals. I was concerned that this precious knowledge, paid for in blood, might be lost—only to have to be relearned, with still more blood paid.

That's why I wrote *The Ultimate Sniper*—to explain things like natural lines of drift, to provide relevant insights on ballistics, optics, shooting techniques, ammunition, human vision, parallax, smart ways to divide sectors of fire, plus the role of snipers in every type of military operation—not just the two-man, independent missions that most often come to

mind but the integral sniper role for *every* type of conventional and special operation. Until *The Ultimate Sniper* this had not been done, nor had sniper skills been clearly divided into three distinct areas—marksmanship, tactics, and fieldcraft—and addressed in the depth they demanded. Much of what I wrote existed as bits and pieces in diverse places, but no manual or book or guide had so thoroughly assembled them, focused exclusively on sniping.

And yet, *The Ultimate Sniper* equally contained original thoughts and techniques, from ballistic data cards (now often copied) to the sniper engagement sequence, the concept of "ballistic advantage" (later elaborated as countersniper "overmatching"), and even a clear definition of "accurate," to name a few.

From Croatia to Canada, from Alaska to Alabama, snipers, sharpshooters, and long-range riflemen found *The Ultimate Sniper* to be the "bible" of their craft. The Philippine Marine Corps so highly regarded it that they copied its art for their sniper unit logo, and the Karen National Liberation Army translated sections for their resistance fighters. The chapter on night operations was so authoritative that the 2nd Battalion, 8th Marines, reproduced it for all its Marines. Sgt. 1st Class Earl S. Ellis, an All-Army Sniper Champion and NCOIC of the Army Sniper School, told me he found inspiration in its pages to revise the Army's latest sniper training manual. Probably the greatest compliment came from USMC Maj. Ed Land (ret.), founder of the modern Marine sniper training program and current National Rifle Association secretary, who told an audience he'd hoped to write a book such as *The Ultimate Sniper*—but now he wouldn't have to.

Several first edition prophecies came to be. As I'd anticipated [p. 123], the M118 Special Ball round was improved into today's M118LR. Further, as I wrote in 1993 [p. 76], "The Trijicon ACOG, I think, should be on at least half the M16A2s in the USMC and the U.S. Army." That's nearly their proportion among our troops in Iraq and Afghanistan as of this writing.

Here are some new prophecies. The next leap forward in long-range shooting technology will be a Bullet Drop Compensator that's as precisely adjustable as target knobs. Not long afterward—perhaps in the next decade—we'll see an automated electronic reticle that's tied to a laser rangefinder so that, as quickly as you laze the distance, the reticle instantly resets itself for dead-on aiming. The other improvement is more mundane: a rationalizing of all sniping units of measurement—mils, yards, meters, and Minutes of Angle—so there's a simpler "yardstick" and no need to translate all these confusing figures and fractions when calculating and compensating.

What's new in this edition? Well, although tactics don't change, where and how we apply them do. Thus you will find here greater elaboration of sniping tactics and techniques against terrorists and insurgents, especially in the mountains, deserts, and urban areas of the Middle East and Central Asia. We've devoted an entire new chapter to countersniping in Afghanistan and Iraq. You'll also find new rifles, new cartridges, and breakthroughs in emerging technologies, some already applied and others that have yet to go beyond prototypes and lab principles.

Some of the recent historical accounts are drawn from my new book—which I'll hopefully finish within the next year—on the history of sniping and sharpshooting. When it's published, it will be the most detailed and complete book ever written on the subject.

And here's an important admin note: U.S. ballistic tables normally use yards, so we're using yards almost exclusively in this book. Should you need to convert yards to meters, multiple by 0.9144; to convert meters to yards, multiple by 1.0936.

As in the first edition, I urge you to support and join the National Rifle Association, and encourage your friends and relatives to do likewise. For future generations of great riflemen, we must protect this great American birthright, the Second Amendment. And finally, I ask you to join me in assisting today's U.S. Army and Marine Corps snipers on the front lines of the War on Terror via the Adopt-a-Sniper program. Founded by a Texas police sniper, Brian Sain, this nonprofit group supplies hard-to-find gear and information for our military snipers serving in remote, far-flung places. You can reach them on the Internet at www.americansnipers.org.

Maj. John L. Plaster, USAR (ret.)
January 2006

CHAPTER 1

SNIPER UNIT ORGANIZATION AND EQUIPMENT

A two-man military sniper team has two trained snipers who rotate weapons and duties at regular intervals.

SNIPER TEAM ORGANIZATION

A properly organized sniper team consists of two men, a sniper and a spotter. Both are qualified and fully trained snipers, so more appropriately it could be said a team consists of two snipers. In order to function effectively, however, one will shoot (the sniper) while his partner watches (the spotter), with each rotating these duties on a regular basis.

Also, since a military sniper is armed with a slow-firing, low-capacity, bolt-action rifle, his partner needs a high-capacity, automatic weapon—I recommend the M16A2 with an M203 40mm grenade launcher—for team defense against unexpected, short-range contacts. The two men swap weapons when they rotate roles.

Given that they are only two men, a sniper team must operate truly as a team to stand any chance of accomplishing its mission and surviving in a very dangerous environment.

Compatibility, a readiness to share, and a willingness to rotate duties without pettiness and grumbling and shirking are absolutely necessary qualities. We've listed the sniper's and spotter's duties in the box on the following page, but it must be understood that there is always a mutual contribution within a listed task; the responsible team member ultimately sees that it's accomplished, but to some degree his partner contributes to everything that's done.

Some jobs are shared, like splitting the sector so both can surveil, but even here there must be some rotation and relief or one will suffer eyestrain. And at times, one will rest while the other works, one will secure while his teammate digs, and so on. It's genuine teamwork.

The member with the most experience should be the team leader, but his primary task is to educate his partner and elevate his skills on a par with his own so they can rotate jobs completely yet suffer no decline in capability. Teamwork.

Most often, the newer sniper serves as the observer, but some authorities would argue that the more experienced of the two should spot since he

SNIPER'S DUTIES & RESPONSIBILITIES

Writes Operations Order
Coordinates with Other Units
Follows in March and Covers Rear
Obscures Backtrail during March
Leads While Stalking
Leads While Following Enemy Tracks
Selects Sniper Hide Location
Shares Hide Construction
Detects and Announces Target Indicators
Observes Half Sector with Binoculars
Adjusts Scope for Wind, Range, and Angle
Shares Range Estimates with Spotter
Decides Engagement Priorities
Engages Human and Materiel Targets
Designates Night Targets with Tracer

SPOTTER'S DUTIES & RESPONSIBILITIES

Obtains and Prepares Any Special Gear
Leads in March, May Fire Defensively
Follows While Stalking, Obscures Sign
Covers Team While Tracking Enemy
Shares Hide Construction
Draws Sketches and Range Cards
Shares Range Estimates with Sniper
Observes Half Sector with Spotting Scope
Detects and Announces Target Indicators
Identifies Targets by Priority
Estimates Wind
Times the Wind and Tells Sniper to Fire
Backs Up Sniper's Shot
Observes and Reports Bullet Impact
Operates Radio
Records Information
Vectors and Coordinates Other Teams
Operates Diversionary Devices
Sterilizes Site When Abandoning Hide

probably is better at estimating range and wind and evaluating targets.

Due to liability, police snipers do not rotate weapons—each should have a rifle assigned exclusively to himself. But police snipers must also rotate/rest/share or they won't be able to last during a protracted incident—and, face it, most incidents that eventually lead to a police sniper taking a shot *are* protracted ones.

Military units are configured according to mission, equipment, doctrine, and the terrain on which they'll fight, balanced against flexibility and simplicity to keep the unit controllable. These factors are as applicable to a sniper unit organization as for an armor division. And from these factors have evolved two basic concepts for organizing sniper elements: consolidation and decentralization.

The sniper structure most frequently found in U.S. military organizations is a consolidated one, with snipers in their own battalion-level platoon that operates directly under the S2 Intelligence Officer or S3 Operations Officer. As the chart shows, this is the sniper configuration found in U.S. Marine Corps units as well as in U.S. Army Light Infantry Divisions. In most organizations using this arrangement, the snipers also serve as battalion scouts, a good matching of skills and missions. In fact, the USMC officially calls these men "Scout-Snipers," assigned to a Surveillance and Target Acquisition (STA) platoon.

The benefits of a consolidated sniper platoon are many. First, they can train together and focus their efforts on sniping, under the control of platoon-level leaders who appreciate and support their needs. Second, since they're a battalion-level asset, their role is considered and integrated in every battalion operation.

Consolidation affords great flexibility in combat, allowing the battalion sniper employment officer to concentrate or disperse the snipers to fit the situation and the mission. For instance, all snipers can be focused along one enemy avenue of approach, massed within one company's area if the terrain best suits sniping, or split evenly, with three sniper teams attached to each company or one team for each line platoon. They also can run independent, battalion-controlled operations.

MILITARY SNIPING ORGANIZATION

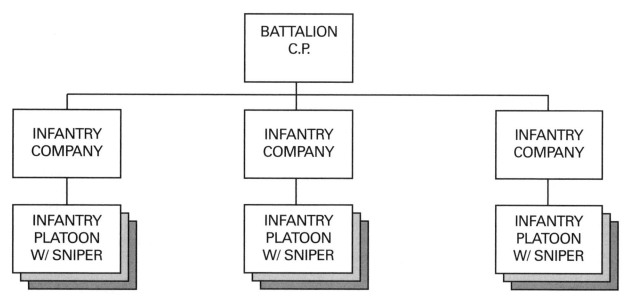

This is how a decentralized sniper configuration appears in Ranger and Reserve Component Infantry battalions.

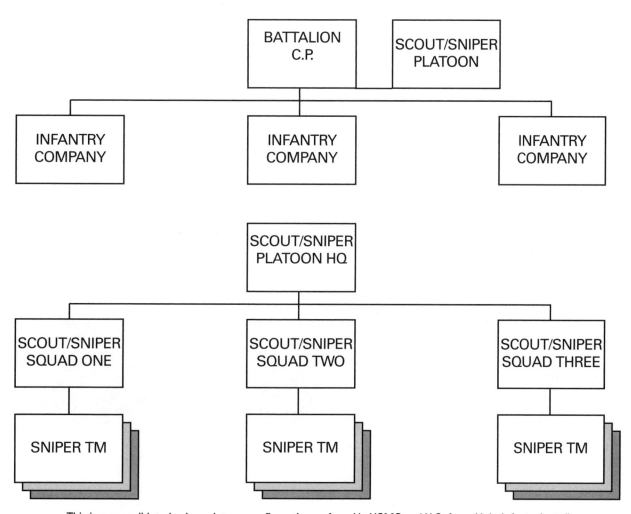

This is a consolidated sniper platoon configuration as found in USMC and U.S. Army Light Infantry battalions.

A decentralized organization is found in U.S. Army Ranger units and some Reserve Component elements. This concept, shown in the top chart on page 3, has snipers split and permanently assigned with one team in each platoon.

Given that Rangers frequently conduct platoon-size raids and ambushes—they are, after all, America's premier commando-raider force—it makes sense that they would want to integrate as much as possible at the platoon level. Building this platoon team allows all members to become accustomed to operating together, honing their tactical and skill edges in unison.

SNIPER TEAM PRIMARY GEAR

SNIPER	SPOTTER
Sniper Rifle	M14 or M16A2
w/ Bipod	w/ M203 40mm
Binoculars	Spotting Scope
Handgun	Handgun
	Laser Rangefinder

It's the company commander or platoon leader who determines how these decentralized sniper teams are employed in his operations; the battalion doesn't take snipers or sniping into account while planning.

The downside of such a configuration is that sniping emphasis may decline and snipers cannot train to as high a standard as when they're in a single platoon. But this is usually remedied by a battalion commander's oversight and directives.

Not to be forgotten is the reality that any military organization can be dramatically changed to fit the circumstances of combat, as has happened in every American war. During peacetime it seemingly takes an act of Congress to change a unit's table of organization even slightly, but in wartime, your unit leaders have tremendous latitude for adjusting to the situation. When the bullets start flying, what matters is only what works.

We've seen exactly that recently in the War on Terror. Before the attacks of September 11, 2001, the U.S. Army authorized three two-man sniper teams per battalion in Airborne and Light Infantry divisions and four teams in Mechanized Infantry battalions. Based on combat experiences in Afghanistan and Iraq, many units added a third man and a Barrett .50 caliber to each sniper team, plus a fourth non-sniper to improve security and add another pair of eyes for observation. The 7th Infantry Division tripled its sniper complement in 2004, fielding 18 sniper teams per battalion. Each 12-man U.S. Army Special Forces A-Team now seeks to cross-train at least two men as snipers. The U.S. Marine Corps, too, has boosted its reliance on snipers, adding to its traditional 17-man, battalion-level STA platoons. But the greatest precision shooting growth in both the Army and Marine Corps has been the dramatic increase in Designated Marksmen.

DESIGNATED MARKSMEN

Though the concept goes back to the earliest days of rifle-armed infantry, the early 21st century has seen considerable American interest in platoon- and squad-level infantrymen assigned the additional duty of Designated Marksmen (DM). The Marine Corps has even fielded custom-built M14s and M16A3s for these (respectively) platoon and squad sharpshooters. The Designated Marksman Rifle (DMR) is an accurized M14 that incorporates a match-grade barrel and McMillan pistol grip stock with an adjustable cheekrest. I've come upon various versions topped by the Corps' traditional Unertl 10x scope, or the Leupold Mark 4 M3, or even the day/night PVS-10 scope. Though these specially selected riflemen receive

The USMC's Designated Marksman Rifle (DMR) is a highly accurized M14, topped here with a Unertl 10x scope.

additional marksmanship and fieldcraft training, they are not sniper-qualified.

So, too, for the Marine Corps' Squad Advanced Marksmen. Armed with match-grade, heavy-barreled M16s mounting a 4x Trijicon Advanced Combat Optical Gunsight (ACOG) or Leupold scope, these sharpshooters add improved optical surveillance and precision fire to each rifle squad, though they've not yet been authorized throughout the Corps.

The Army's Stryker Brigade Combat Team includes three sniper teams under each battalion headquarters, plus an additional three-man team in each maneuver company. Like the Marine Corps, however, the Army has added a Designated Marksman to each nine-man Stryker Brigade squad, arming him with an M16 or M4 carbine and ACOG 4x scope. Though these marksmen receive specialized training, like their Marine counterparts they're not fully trained snipers. The concept for both services is that these DMs fill the capability gap between rifle-armed infantrymen and fully qualified and armed snipers—or, looked at another way, the DMs offer effective fire beyond the range of ordinary infantry (about 350 yards out to about 550 or 600 yards), giving U.S. forces an edge over their rifle-armed foes.

SNIPER SELECTION

Frederick Russell Burnham, the American explorer-adventurer who led Britain's scouts in the Boer War, described his scouts as "half wolf and half jackrabbit." What a fitting description for the sniper—and how fitting that Burnham said this. For Burnham's most accomplished recon soldiers were Scots of a Highland regiment known as Lovat's Scouts; 16 years later, these phenomenal woodsmen became the British army's first sniper unit. Yes, a sniper is a bold tempter of fate, but he also must be a wise practitioner of discretion: "He who shoots and runs away, lives to shoot another day."

This contradictory nature—as well as concerns that sniping can attract some unsuitable elements

The USMC Squad Advanced Marksman's rifle adds a heavy match barrel, bipod, and Leupold or ACOG 4x scope to an M16A3.

—requires care in selecting snipers. To this must be added reliability. "It's the only element that we tell just two men to go out and execute a mission," says Lt. Col. Michael Phillips, former chief of small arms training at the Army's Ft. Benning. "I think because so much is demanded of them, we must ensure that only those who are truly capable receive the title 'sniper.'"

What to look for in sniper candidates? Since sniping involves a triad of skills—marksmanship, fieldcraft, and tactics—I believe a sniper candidate should have experience, interest, or a demonstrated aptitude in at least one of these areas. Training solidifies this foundation and rounds him out in the other skills.

It's foolish to think you're recruiting trained men; rather, the selection process is geared to *identifying* men with the best potential, whom you then train to standard. I'm most interested in the candidate's attitude and perspective, not necessarily his knowledge, which can be expanded with training. Is this man *worth* training? That's the real question.

The World War II British army directive creating sniper teams placed proper emphasis on attitude as well as skill, requiring that the candidates be "picked men, and fit men, and proud to be such; the best marksmen, skilled in fieldcraft, confident in their self-reliance, possessed of great courage and unrivalled patience."

Marksmanship

When it comes to marksmanship, the candidate must be at least a rated expert rifleman—which he soon learns is only a starting point for sniper-level shooting.

His involvement with weapons ideally goes beyond service rifle qualification. My interest in firearms dates back to a childhood in which I was expected to handle a rifle alone in the woods by the ripe age of 8. Perhaps the candidate has been a competitive shooter, or maybe he has a deeper grasp and fascination with weapons than the average lawman or soldier. Skip Talbot, the world-record .50-caliber, 1,000-yard rifleman, thinks "long-range shooters are like bronc riders; they're born, not made."

The candidate had better like shooting, because to hone and maintain sniper-level skills he must shoot frequently. Related to this, the candidate should have an interest in firearms and technical subjects beyond the common layman, a natural curiosity about things like ballistics, bullets, and optics.

Hunting experience is especially useful because the sniper candidate already will have learned the consequences of inaccuracy or sluggish reflexes.

Fieldcraft

Fieldcraft includes the many supporting skills a sniper must develop, things such as wind estimation, camouflage, and observation. The value of outdoor sports and hunting experience cannot be understated, because how else can a young man learn such skills?

I attach more significance to those who hunt elusive game. Squirrel, turkey, or deer hunters can develop into superb snipers. Bowhunters know much about woodlore and camouflage.

But it's more than these definable skills. It's an *attitude*, a deeper level of confidence and compatibility with nature I call "close to the earth." A rural youth, especially one raised in places like Alaska, Montana, Maine, Minnesota, or Idaho—or one who was just plain allowed to roam the woods—develops his own concept about the relationship between himself and nature, the woods, weapons—about life itself.

Some outdoor sports help develop a similar appreciation, including trapping, hiking, backpacking, camping, and canoeing. These sportsmen learn to read the weather, see tracks in a natural setting, understand field maps, observe live game, move to avoid being seen—many applicable skills.

But before it seems that city slickers have no place in sniping, don't forget that *all* our ancestors once hunted day-in and day-out for sheer survival, that all these skills lie latent within us, that the least experienced city boy can learn to master the woods if he immerses and applies himself. These are forgotten, not lost, arts.

The ultimate Special Forces SOG (Studies and Observation Group) compliment was, "He's good in the woods," meaning the man had mastered the whole gamut of ancient warrior and woodsman skills demanded of jungle warfare. And the majority of SOG's jungle warriors, like yours truly, had been brought up in cities.

But within us was a natural talent, an instinct for hunting other men, just like some of our peers took readily to riding a surfboard or throwing a football. It's fascinating to watch a young soldier develop such martial skills and find, often to his own surprise, that buried within his mind and body have always been the makings of a warrior. He was always close to the earth but didn't know it.

More about Hunters

But it's been mostly hunting experience that traditionally has marked a man as a potential sniper. The Germans historically called their snipers "Jägers" or "hunters," so close is this linkage.

The Russians especially liked snipers with hunting experience. Their greatest sniper of World War II, Sgt. Vassili Zaitsev, had been a prewar hunter and trapper in the Ural Mountains.

The best Australian snipers of World War II were experienced kangaroo hunters who knew that a badly placed shot ruined a pelt, so they'd grown accustomed to making head shots at long range. Stealth and sharpshooting were their way of life.

When it comes to the United States, well, more so than any other major power, firearms and hunting are a significant ingredient of the modern American experience. The United States probably has more hunters per capita today than any other great nation.

But you need not be a hunter to be a sniper; indeed, some expert snipers have no interest in hunting. A former Green Beret friend who's a sniper with a major metropolitan police department decries the "needless" harvesting of wildlife—but would not hesitate to take out a bad guy with his McMillan rifle. He's an excellent rifle shot, a good tactician, and applies other skills well, too. Steve and I may argue about the morality of hunting, but there's no question he's a competent sniper—with no hunting experience whatsoever.

Tactics

I'm not sure how a sniper candidate can develop an appreciation for tactics other than to study military history—and read books such as this one.

The study of military history helps develop a feel for the relationships between fire and maneuver, cover versus concealment, and concentration versus dispersion. Most relevant are small unit tactics below the level of Napoleon or Clausewitz.

I strongly recommend Sun Tzu's *The Art of War*, a 300 B.C. Chinese treatise on deception and warfare that's useful for snipers. Sun Tzu wrote, for instance, "When near make it seem that you are far away; when far away that you are near." This book is required reading for CIA officers.

A nebulous quality I look for in students is "tactical sense," the ability to see tactical opportunities and threats, to be able to assess a situation with a glance and draw one's plan in the dirt. Some of this comes with experience, but much of it, I think, is a gift of God.

Serious boxers and martial artists perhaps have a better natural grasp of tactics fundamentals, as should chess players and participants in some team sports like football. I'd give a candidate extra points if he'd been a paintball competitor.

Physical Condition

I agree with Soviet Col. R. Minin's recommendation that a sniper be "physically fit and hardy with sharp vision and hearing, a good memory, and quick reactions."

A fit rifleman more steadily holds his rifle, solid muscle better withstands recoil, he bears loads without undue fatigue, and overall he stays alert longer and can go farther, faster.

Many police SWAT (Special Weapons and Tactics) units train hard and long and maintain high standards of physical conditioning. But whether your tac team does this or not, you must stay in shape or you'll begin avoiding strain subconsciously by dashing at a low trot when you should low-crawl, or walking conspicuously around a wall rather than pull yourself invisibly over it. Poor shape, laziness, and bad tactics go hand-in-hand.

The U.S. Army physical training (PT) test is adequate for police, although the SWAT teams I'm most familiar with have higher physical standards, approaching the PT levels of Special Forces and Ranger units.

As far as eyesight goes, a sniper needs at least

20-20 vision since much of his job is spotting and surveilling. Eyeglasses? Correctable vision is acceptable if the sniper has nonglare eyeglass lenses and keeps a spare set with his gear.

Smoking

It's better that a sniper candidate not be a smoker, but this is a choice best left up to the sniper, not to those who would select him. Smoking should not be used as a basis for exclusion, any more than consuming alcohol or drinking coffee, all of which affect sniper performance to some extent.

The sniper must recognize how smoking impacts his trade. In daytime his cigarettes will generate smoke and smell, while at night they create a visual signature. His marksmanship can deteriorate if he's denied nicotine at a critical moment, while his sense of smell may not be sufficient to detect odors associated with hostile activity or danger.

A pack-a-day smoker builds high levels of carbon monoxide in his blood, which reduce 20 percent of the normal night vision at sea level, an effect that increases with altitude; by 10,000 feet, he's lost 40 percent of his night vision.

I'd encourage snipers to quit smoking, but I'd also suggest that coffee drinkers switch to decaffeinated for steadier nerves.

Intelligence and Personality

To understand and apply the complexities of ballistics, adjust his rifle scope, plan missions, and just plain outsmart his foes, a sniper needs brains.

He needs wisdom, too, for his typical engagement violently teases a numerically superior foe. Like a nimble mongoose, his quick tactical parries and diversions outwit the deadly cobra. This requires coolness under stress.

The excitable adrenalin-spurting "hooh-uh" types are the exact opposite of the calm, unemotional, thinking sniper. They can adapt with great effort, but it's not easy.

These observations hold for police snipers, too. An entry team member needs to be bold and aggressive, ready to burst through doors and engage his opponent at close quarters. His whole business is smashing through risk and hitting his objective head-on. But the police sniper must be cautious, methodi-

cal, deliberate. His mission requires bypassing risk, minimizing chance, and turning odds around, not confronting or charging a suspect.

The sniper should be compatible with his teammate. I didn't say have the *same* personality, I said compatible. But they should be the same approximate size so one can pull the other out if he's incapacitated. Teaming up a Hulk Hogan with an average-size man means they'll both die if the larger is ever seriously wounded.

And when it comes to personality, the Lone Wolf type need not apply. Sniping is a *team* mission in which each man must contribute fully, not feed off the endeavors of his partner.

Patience

Special heed must be paid to patience, which World War I sniper Capt. H.W. McBride said was a sniper's most important quality. Whether he's a police officer waiting out a terrorist during a protracted skyjack or a GI calmly peering at an enemy trench for hours on end, the sniper must be as capable of taking a perfect shot 10 minutes after arrival as 10 hours into it.

The most accomplished long-range shooters I know are "slow-walkin', slow-talkin'" kinds of guys, men like Lance Peters, an Olympic-level rifleman who's won silver medals at the Pan American Games. Analytical, patient, unemotional, deliberate in their every step. Of course, these men have emotions, but they've learned to overcome them, to mentally channel stress and anxiety into oblivion.

As a determined form of self-discipline, patience enables a sniper to lie motionless in wet and cold for hours, waiting for a shot he knows most likely won't even happen. But for just a chance shot, he guts his way through the discomfort, as calm and ready as if it were a sure thing.

Psychological Screening

Most men become snipers because they're self-reliant, take pride in their skills, and want to do and be only the very best. They desire to fight as a small unit so success or failure, life or death—their very fate—is determined largely by their own exertions. In an environment often driven by unthinking violent momentum, they want to fight smart. They epitomize the American spirit.

For some peculiar reason, though, the sniping mystique can attract the wrong element—delusionary "wannabes" who think glory comes from killing. Basket cases and pathological braggarts don't last long in wartime because so-called pleasure killers usually are cowards, with no stomach for the dangers of real combat.

HUMAN NATURE VULNERABILITIES

The one quality I saw in combat that consistently got men killed or caused others to die was arrogant overconfidence—some fool thinking he knew it all. Any one of the human vulnerabilities listed below can get you killed or cause you to fail to accomplish your mission. Master these qualities and you will have mastered yourself.

Overconfidence
Inattention/Indifference
Hasty Decisions
Lack of Planning
Bad Tactical Habits
Anger/Emotionalism
Undue Curiosity
Too Easily Distracted
Laziness
Underestimating Your Opponent
Unwillingness to Train, Prepare

Those who think they're on a mission for God or who hate their mommies and daddies are quick to spot and disqualify. What's far more difficult and subtle, I think, is weeding out those who won't risk it all under fire; who, when all the chips are on the table, don't take the shot or choke up or hide instead of shoot. But the purpose of psychological screening is to exclude the crazies, not determine who has true grit.

Law enforcement agencies often have a formal psychological interview of sniper candidates and even administer diagnostic tests like the Minnesota Multi-Phasic Inventory. Given the great liability and inherent dangers of firing a high-powered rifle in a peacetime urban setting, no police agency can afford to have a man too quick to take a shot.

My greatest concern about psychological screening is that it's dependent on the subjective opinion of a psychiatrist who may not fully appreciate the stresses and realities of a sniper's environment. He could exclude the best candidates because they like firearms or seem enthusiastic.

"Bein' Willing"

In John Wayne's final movie role, that of aging gunfighter J.B. Books in *The Shootist*, he recited a memorable line that perfectly expresses the gunfighter's credo: "It isn't always bein' fast or even accurate that counts; it's bein' willing."

My greatest disappointment in Special Forces was witnessing a stateside friend become a coward in Vietnam. And a bastard coward he truly was. But at Ft. Bragg he'd seemed the epitome of a Green Beret—a lean, mean, fighting machine, witty, scoring high in tests, and so on. He could have modeled for recruiting posters. But within it all, he was a self-centered egotist whose every exertion, in retrospect, actually had been intended to bring himself recognition, including the beret cocked jauntily on his head. As we said back then, he was "90 percent show, 10 percent go."

How can you identify these types? I think attitude mirrors the soul, but the key in assessing attitude is watching what a devoted man does, not what a braggart says. Acts, not words, have true value.

Will he go on when others are quitting? Does he put his mates ahead of himself? Will he endure pain and discomfort to succeed? Does he actually give of himself, or does he only take? Will he risk himself, will he take chances? And, ultimately, will he follow orders and take the shot?

Unlike most soldiers and lawmen, it's tough to know if a sniper will engage a target that's distant and no immediate threat to himself. He may even have time to study the target and notice how much it looks like his Uncle Ralph. I've never, ever known of an incident in which a police officer or soldier found he could not shoot at a nearby bad guy who was shooting at him. The marksmanship may have been poor, the draw slow, but no moral pangs or societal taboos affected the good guy.

But something happens when a sniper looks in that optical sight and sees a pair of real eyes. It's the eyes that distinguish a living human from a target.

I've been unable to come up with a means to determine who would not take a shot, so until it actually happens, you can never be sure who's "willing." And this underscores the criticality of training realism, of making a sniper's targets so realistic that the real thing won't seem much different. Especially ensure that his targets have eyes.

POLICE TACTICAL UNIT ORGANIZATION

Law enforcement sniper teams are one component of a larger tactical unit, sometimes referred to as SWAT. Just as is true for the military, police tactical units are configured into distinct elements grouped together according to function, then mixed and matched—or "tailored"—to conduct any specific operation.

Along with two-man sniper teams, a typical police tactical unit includes the following elements:

COMMAND AND CONTROL: Normally, tac unit leaders are not heavily involved on-site during operations because they're quickly accomplished and the unit withdrawn. In most cases, leaders plan and let the subelements execute. It's only during protracted situations—such as a hostage taking—that a command post is operated on-site and the command and control element is fully utilized.

ENTRY TEAMS: Composed of four to six well-armed officers, an entry team specializes in dynamically entering a structure, quickly clearing it, retrieving hostages, and neutralizing or arresting suspects. Because these officers best understand the demands of an entry, they usually are deployed as the inner-perimeter force as well.

GAS TEAMS: The efficient employment of

POLICE TACTICAL UNIT ORGANIZATION

COMMAND AND CONTROL

MANEUVER ELEMENTS	SUPPORT ELEMENTS	OTHER ATTACHMENTS
ENTRY TEAMS	HOSTAGE NEGOT.	AIR SUPPORT
SNIPER TEAMS	COMMO ELEM.	BOMB SQUAD
GAS TEAMS	MEDIC TEAMS	

Like their military counterparts, police sniper teams contain a shooter and a spotter.

gas is a specialized function handled by two-man gas teams. Modern tactical units use gas wisely to divert a suspect's attention, deny him access to some parts of a structure, or temporarily disable him during an assault.

HOSTAGE NEGOTIATOR: This could be a department psychiatrist or an officer trained especially in negotiation skills. During protracted situations, usually involving hostage takers, a negotiator contacts the suspects and attempts to use a host of techniques to help resolve the situation.

MEDICAL TEAMS: These could be police or fire paramedics, or medics from a local hospital. What's important is that they train regularly with your unit and understand how tac team operations are conducted. Their gear and orientation are directed primarily toward trauma injuries.

COMMUNICATIONS ELEMENT: This section really comes into the fore during a protracted incident, when an on-site command post suddenly needs phones, laptop computers, fax machines, secure radios, and photographic support, not to mention technical surveillance of suspects.

There can be other attachments to the tactical team. By attachments, we mean that these sections are not organic—not actually a part of the tactical team. They're attached to the team and under the team commander's control if needed on a particular operation.

BOMB SQUAD: In addition to helping assess, remove, and possibly disable an explosive device, in many departments the bomb squad is the only section that is authorized to prepare and detonate explosive entry charges. These officers should be the local booby trap experts who can instruct snipers in detecting and bypassing devices while stalking.

AIR SUPPORT: An airborne platform facilitates command and control, reconnaissance, relay of radio messages, photographic surveys, aerial searches—a host of useful contributions to tactical team operations. And add to this the ability of a helicopter to quickly airlift officers long distances or to great heights.

The Urban Police Countersniper

The police countersniper role was created not on a whim but in proportional response to a specific threat that first emerged in the 1960s after the worst mass-killing in U.S. history.

In August 1966, a 25-year-old University of Texas student, Charles Whitman, wheeled a dolly loaded with a duffel bag and military footlocker onto his campus tower elevator in Austin. At 11:48 A.M., after barricading himself atop the 28-story tower, the husky ex-marine and big-game hunter raised a Remington 6mm Model 700 rifle to his shoulder and peered through his scope.

A few months earlier, Whitman had told a university psychiatrist that he was so upset he'd been "thinking about going up on the tower with a deer rifle and start shooting people." He now lived out that grisly fantasy.

Over the next 90 minutes, Whitman engaged people up to three blocks away, killing 13 and wounding another 31, for a staggering total of 44 casualties. But what's of most interest to us is his choice of dominating terrain and weapons, as well as how he exploited both to the detriment of responding law officers.

Within minutes of Whitman firing his first shot, more than 100 lawmen from the Austin police, Texas Rangers, and local Secret Service office swarmed to the campus, but their problem was one of ballistic and optical disadvantage. Armed only with pistols and shotguns—having an effective

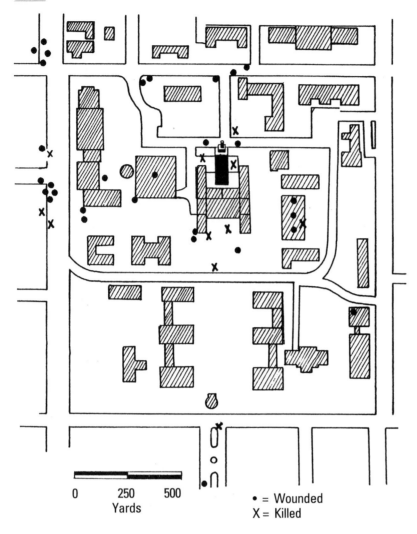

0   250   500
Yards

• = Wounded
X = Killed

AUSTIN, TEXAS, 1966. Charles Whitman killed 13 and wounded 31 from his 28-story perch, a ghastly episode of mass murder.

Whitman let loose with a .30-caliber M1 carbine.

The carnage continued for 90 minutes until finally two lawmen and a deputized civilian entered the building through a subterranean passage, climbed the tower, and rushed Whitman, riddling his body with slugs.

Following the Austin massacre, many local police departments instituted a policy of assigning one rifle-armed officer to each shift. In these early days, a police rifleman's weapon was as likely to be a .30-30 lever action as anything else, since choices frequently were based on personal preferences. I recall that the St. Louis Police Department used .30-06 BAR sporting rifles in the early 1970s. Still, rifle-armed police seemed an oddity barely tolerated by administrators, and the police rifleman remained a relatively untried, seldom-called-upon adjunct, mobilized in only the rarest of cases.

range of no more than 50 yards—the lawmen were distinctly outclassed by a man who could hit even an exposed head at six times that distance.

Whitman's tower perch was surrounded by a waist-high ledge of brick and decorative concrete columns, creating many natural loopholes through which he fired. The best countersniper weapons in Austin were the deer rifles of civilian passersby, who shot side by side with local police but to little effect against the well-entrenched gunman.

Firing from his heavily reinforced hide, Whitman dominated the flat surrounding terrain, easily hitting several police officers attempting to rush the building. When he needed more firepower,

Firing from the landing just below the clockface, Whitman proved deadly up to three blocks away.

In the 1970s, police snipers were armed with ordinary deer rifles and received little specialized training.

The 21st-century police sniper is specially trained and armed with a quality marksman's rifle.

But the lessons of Austin were pounded in again in New Orleans in August of 1974, when an ex-sailor, 23-year-old Jimmy Essex, began a killing rampage at a Howard Johnson's Motor Lodge.

A racial extremist who had vowed to kill as many whites as possible, Essex came close to equaling Charles Whitman's tally—he killed seven and wounded another 21 people. In particular, Essex hated police—of any race—and seven of his victims were responding lawmen, including Deputy Superintendent Louis Sirgo.

Essex eventually occupied a position very similar to Whitman's barricaded tower, exploiting a reinforced concrete elevator structure on the hotel roof, where he blasted away with a .44 Magnum Ruger auto carbine for 11 hours. After an entire night exchanging fire with outgunned lawmen, a USMC CH-46 helicopter finally arrived and let loose with an M60 machine gun, drilling Essex with "at least a hundred bullets," according to one press account.

Having witnessed the level of response necessitated by not responding proportionally at the very start, law enforcement administrators better realized the need for police snipers.

Some 15 years after Essex's rampage, I encountered New Orleans police riflemen among our students at a Mississippi shooting clinic and competition. I can assure you that New Orleans today is served by superb police shooters who learned much from that ghastly, tragic incident.

But it took the Austin and New Orleans massacres and a host of lesser-known outgunned shoot-outs to wash away any doubt about the need for police countersniper capabilities. And what would happen if today's properly trained and equipped police sniper encountered the likes of a Whitman or Essex? The slaughter would end with just one shot.

Here are two striking examples. On Memorial Day weekend 1999, a 22-year-old Seattle man went berserk, killing his mother and a 15-month-old nephew. Stealing his mother's car, he raced away, ran down and severely injured a motorcyclist, then beat to death an 82-year-old woman and broke the neck of another elderly woman. After wounding a responding law officer with a stolen rifle, he barricaded himself in a house, intending to kill anyone who came after him. That never happened, thanks to a single, well-placed police marksman's shot.

In Hollywood, Florida, a drunken, depressed man opened fire with an AR-15 from the 10th-floor balcony of an apartment building. Over the next hour, he fired an estimated 150 rounds, including 32 slugs into a responding police squad car, 10 of them through the windshield. By the time a police sniper positioned himself in a facing condominium tower across the street, it was almost dark and the perpetrator had left the balcony. Fifteen minutes later—apparently encouraged by more alcohol—the gunman reappeared and fired two fast shots. Honing in on his muzzle flash, the police sharpshooter fired only once. The incident was over.

Yes, police snipers have come a long way since 1966.

DIFFERENCES BETWEEN POLICE AND MILITARY SNIPERS

Perhaps the worst mistake a police sniper can make is to imagine he's a military sniper; equally, a military sniper is in grave error if he begins acting like he's a law officer.

There are considerable differences between the two, not merely the result of technical distinctions or silly concerns by officials fearing lawsuits. We must clearly examine these distinctions because they impact your tactics, organization, equipment, planning—every area of a sniper's job. And keeping these differences in mind will help you focus on the applicable data and techniques found in the following chapters.

Before drawing such distinctions, however, realize that the most fundamental sniping skills—marksmanship, fieldcraft, and tactics—are very similar for both police and military. The dramatic differences are in how a sniper *applies* them.

Legalities and Policies

The most basic difference between a police and a military sniper is how each employs deadly force.

No law officer would ever take a shot—which is deadly force—unless a suspect is a threat to himself, another police officer, a bystander, or a hostage. But quite the opposite applies to a military sniper in combat. He readily will engage a confirmed enemy soldier, and his target need not be an immediate threat to anyone. The hostile soldier's mere existence is a threat to our forces, it is understood, and the Law of Land Warfare allows engaging without warning.

Provided it is a confirmed enemy soldier and it is a time of war, the military sniper has no legal concern whatsoever. To the degree he must use judgment, it is to analyze the tactical situation and act wisely while under stress. The police sniper, however, must keep in mind that his every move must be justifiable and that he especially will have to "articulate" the threat he perceived to legitimize his shot.

Department or agency policies will vary, but it is generally recognized that a police sniper's authority to fire need not require an order from an on-scene supervisor. It should be generated by the situation itself. Ask yourself, "If I have a pistol and I am 10 feet from the suspect, can I justify using deadly force?" Should the answer be, "Yes," your only distinction as a sniper is the distance, not the justification.

As a practical matter, however, you most likely would not engage prior to the on-scene commander issuing a "green light," because the boss will have wanted to explore other options using less force or posing less danger to a hostage.

Rotating Rifles

Another liability issue for police riflemen is the rotation of rifles among officers, which can cause doubts about the weapon's current zero, its condition, and how reliably it will place a bullet exactly where intended.

Some small law enforcement agencies have attempted to economize by having officers share one or two sniper rifles, which is distinct from the military practice of *rotating* weapons between spotter and sniper. In the military, one man uses the sniper rifle while his partner has an assault rifle, which they swap when rotating duties.

Neither of these circumstances—sharing a rifle or rotating one—is suitable for the life-and-death incidents in which a police sniper may be called on to fire. In addition to liability, the officer just plain will not master a weapon that is not his own. Several times I have sent polite letters on this subject to law enforcement supervisors on behalf of their snipers, and once the issues of potential liability and effectiveness are faced, it has always led to the officers' getting the additional rifles they needed.

Indeed, some larger police agencies are now arming each sniper with both a precision-grade bolt gun and an assault rifle outfitted with a holographic EOTech sight or low-powered Leupold CQT or ACOG. This gives the responding marksman the flexibility to serve on an incident's inner perimeter with the assault rifle or to overwatch the wider scene with his sniper rifle.

Most U.S. police snipers are outfitted like this Anchorage, Alaska, officer, with a Remington 700 rifle and Leupold scope.

Two related police liability issues are sniper training and the kind of rifle the sniper is equipped with. While a competent police rifleman certainly should be able to neutralize an armed suspect, it doesn't seem wise to use him in especially dangerous situations such as a complicated hostage rescue without special training. And equipping him with a standard, off-the-rack rifle with conventional rifle scope? It's definitely worth spending a few dollars extra and getting a real sniper system.

Engagement Distances

Ever mindful that he cannot afford to miss even once, a police sniper attempts to close the distance to his target. He especially desires to be closer than 100 yards, which typically is the zero distance of his rifle. FBI statistics verify this: the national average engagement distance for a police sniper has been only 71 yards.

While some crime scenarios, especially rooftop crazies or skyjackers, could involve a much longer shot, this would be a most exceptional situation. In fact, some police agencies do not permit a shot of more than 200 yards without special approval.

But while the police sniper attempts to close with his quarry, the military sniper tries to keep him at arm's length, so to speak, somewhat like a long-armed boxer exploiting his reach advantage. I call this concept a sniper's "ballistic advantage," meaning the sniper rifle has better accuracy and lethality than the enemy's assault rifles when the sniper is more than 400 yards away. Recall that the AK-47's 7.62x39mm round has performance similar to a .30-30 deer cartridge, which most hunters would consider ineffective beyond about 200 yards, and you'll understand what I mean.

Nature of the Target

A police sniper's target is almost always a single, armed suspect who has already taken one life and probably threatened to take another. The suspect is isolated and fixed in a barricade of some sort, perhaps even shielding himself with a hostage or two.

The police sniper's challenge is to maneuver good and close for a clear, unhindered shot without the suspect's detecting him or realizing he is about to be engaged. The only threat is the suspect, and he already has been surrounded and fixed by other police officers prior to the engagement. The police sniper usually has only one target per operation, and he neutralizes that target with just one round. One "bang" and he goes home.

His military sniper counterpart, on the other hand, usually engages many targets during a single operation, perhaps even during a single engagement. The military sniper moves, spots, fires; moves, spots, fires; moves, spots, fires in a dangerous setting in which potential hostiles are all around him.

The enemy frequently has more firepower, has greater numbers, and can outmaneuver or outrun the military sniper if his position is clearly determined. Due to the ever-present danger, in addition to marksmanship and target detection, the military sniper must pay equal heed to the finer points of infiltration and exfiltration in order to accomplish his job and live to tell about it. Some police sniper missions—such as clandestine drug lab recon or remote airfield surveillance—require sophisticated infiltration and exfiltration, too.

Taking the Shot

The world does not come crashing to a halt if a military sniper misses a shot. It's merely a fact of life that imperfect range and wind estimation, sudden target movement, rough trigger release, or a host of other reasons will cause misses at great distances.

But the military sniper attempts imperfect shots at times because they're the only shots he has, or the target, if hit, is so valuable that it deserves even an "iffy" shot. When you have an enemy full colonel visible at 800 yards in a gusty crosswind, I assure you, you will attempt the shot.

Usually, these kinds of engagements involve no other friendly lives, and a miss becomes only a "learning experience" for both sniper and target alike. If a military sniper *only* attempted "sure thing" shots, he would lose a lot of effectiveness because many of the "unsure" shots would have been hits, too, and against distant or unlikely targets that would never appear as sure things at close range. Enemy colonels are far more likely to be found at 800 yards beyond the enemy's front line than at his nearest bunker.

In dramatic contrast, a police sniper must *never*

be allowed the leeway to miss. When he misses, a hostage dies, a suspect escapes, or a fellow officer loses his life, all on national television with follow-up in the newspapers.

Pressure? It's tremendous. As I wrote in an *FBI Law Enforcement Bulletin* article, a police sniper's duty places him in "the loneliest spot in the world." Lives, careers, fate, self-respect—it's all on the line and determined by exerting 3 pounds' pressure on a trigger.

Being Able to Say "No"

Related to this burdensome requirement never to miss, a police sniper—much more so than his military counterpart—must have the capacity to say "NO!"

He must have the guts to assess the situation honestly, weigh this against his rifle and his own abilities, and let his supervisor know whether the shot can be taken. Often, leaders do not fully appreciate a rifleman's capabilities; passively accommodating their desires can lead to disaster.

It could well be that the best chance for a hostage rescue requires a risky shot. Then so be it, provided everyone realizes it and less practical options have been considered and discarded. After the process, you can live with yourself even if the operation fails; you did your best.

But if you remained quiet and just went along with the flow, the result will haunt you to your grave.

The Sniper's Environment

Both police and military snipers operate in stress-filled environments, but how the stresses are generated, and how they can affect you, are quite different.

The military sniper, day in and day out, operates in great personal danger because he probably is behind enemy lines. Every single move, his tiniest act, must be modified to remain undetected, for his only true security is invisibility. When he shoots he must displace, or certain retaliation will crash upon him. He cannot relax from the moment he departs friendly lines until he returns.

The military sniper's stresses eventually reduce him to being combat ineffective. Having run many operations deep behind enemy lines, I can tell you firsthand that such 24-hour dangers will wear you down in about four or five days. In SOG, we were deadly effective at sneaking and hiding and even outmaneuvering bloodhounds and specially trained trackers, but only for less than a week.

The police officer must be able to handle the stress of being thrust, with no warning and no mental preparation, into a life-and-death situation. He could be having lunch with his fiancée one minute and 10 minutes later have a mass-murderer in his crosshairs.

But after rushing to the scene, resolved and ready, most likely he must patiently wait hours or days before being directed to take one—just one—shot. And despite years of training and many false alarms, this scenario will likely unfold only once in his entire career, if ever. But he must be ready for it every single day he's a police tac team sniper. Unlike a soldier going into combat, this engagement follows no schedule.

Mission Duration

How long a military sniper can remain in the field is dictated equally by how much food and water he can carry in with him. It works out, usually, to about five days' worth, which is the same amount of time he can keep his mind and body focused in this stressful environment.

A police sniper should arrive ready to spend eight hours in his sniper hide without further resupply or rest—at least this seems to be the current reality. Depending on the availability of relief sniper teams, you could begin rotating as soon as four or five hours, but this isn't typical.

From personal observation, I don't think a law enforcement sniper will retain the keen edge he needs for more than about four hours without a break. That break could be only an hour or two, and it's as much a mental need as a physical one. After that, he could be focused again for a few hours, but strain will set in.

After eight hours, he definitely needs rest and a complete change of pace. Elsewhere I recommend that police snipers bring enough supplies for at least 24 hours on-site, but that doesn't mean you should be staring through your scope for a full day without rest.

You must pace yourself with breaks and downtime and *real* sleep, because the history of actual incidents shows that a shot is taken either within an hour or two or not until a day or two later. If you're intense and focused at the front end, you'll burn out and won't be ready to take a shot 48 hours later.

SNIPER TEAM OPERATIONAL EQUIPMENT

Whether police or military, a sniper team requires a wide variety of equipment to accomplish its missions, much of it gear that ordinary law officers or GIs would not encounter. The sniper team's secondary surveillance role, as well as self-defense requirements dictated by operating alone, adds even more kinds of gear.

A police sniper must be equally prepared to engage upon arrival or eight hours into an incident.

This custom police sniper vest was made to author's specs by Southern Tactical Supply and features pouches for 5-round rifle speedloaders, a 20-round ammo box, and mini binoculars. (Photo credit: Fred MacDonald III)

We're going to discuss how each piece of equipment is employed, except the most critical sniping items—weapons, optics, range-finders, camouflage—which are covered in much detail elsewhere.

No matter the item, keep the threat of hostile countersurveillance in mind and ensure your gear is colored in a suitable camouflage shade. A sniper must stay invisible.

It's physically impossible to tote all the gear we're about to discuss. Therefore, it's as important for you to learn when and how to carry it as it is to recognize the basic use of it.

To start with, understand that sniper team operations fall neatly into two categories: those you plan and execute, and those initiated by the acts of a hostile. In the former case, you have time to consider using any gear, then reconfigure your rucksack and webgear to carry it. But in the latter case, there's almost no time; you're rushing to a scene with friendly lives in jeopardy.

To be prepared for either situation, you need to develop a basic load—or "alert load"—that includes the items you'd almost always need. You can grab it and dash out the door, and probably 85 percent of the time you're ready for action. Perhaps you'd pause a minute to grab another item or two, and that would cover you for 99 percent of missions.

On the other hand, when preparing for planned operations, you carefully balance an item's need against its weight and repackage based on your specific situation.

Taking this concept a step further, let's look at the kinds of containers and carriers we'd use in the context of what goes into them. In fact, this is our first category of gear.

The rear of author's sniper vest has pouches for a handy-talkie, rangefinder, spotting scope, and tripod as well as straps for a Therm-a-Rest mat. (Photo credit: Fred MacDonald III)

Cases and Load-Bearing Gear

We've prepared separate data boxes that list all the items recommended for carrying in each of the following containers and rucksacks. Here we will describe just the features and requirements for these containers. Because military snipers spend several days in the field on each operation, they'll tend to carry the large rucksack much more than will a law officer. Still, the principles here apply to both military and police snipers.

TACTICAL VEST OR WEBGEAR: Probably made of nylon, this is the one carrier that's *always* with you, no matter the tactical situation. Inside its pouches are the minimal items needed to take a shot, survive, and communicate with others. If you must strip down to the lightest possible load, you still retain your vest/webgear, which has the bare essentials needed to accomplish your mission.

DITTY BAG OR LIGHT RUCKSACK: The ditty bag is cited because many police use them, but here we *urge* law officers to switch to a light rucksack. In contrast to a ditty bag, a light ruck on your back frees you to carry your rifle in both hands, enabling you to climb, run, and shoot. When combined with his webgear, a police sniper's light rucksack contains everything he needs for eight hours on-site with no resupply or assistance. You carry this rucksack into your sniper hide position, but in a fix you could conceal it and stalk forward and still accomplish your mission with the vest/webgear contents.

LARGE RUCKSACK: This is actually your reserve stow bag, in which everything else is stored. Generally there's enough gear in here to allow 24 hours on-site with no further assistance or resupply, when combined with the contents of the small rucksack and vest/webgear. Police snipers bring

CASES AND LOAD-BEARING GEAR. The ditty bag (center) is not as useful as a military rucksack. Critical gear is stowed in vest or webgear.

this large rucksack to the scene but keep it locked in their squad or tac team van. In that few minutes he has to grab gear once alerted, a police sniper transfers an item or two from the reserve stow bag into the light rucksack he carries on his back. It's possible a police sniper could have a special mission lasting several days—like a remote airfield surveillance—which would demand so much extra gear and food that the large rucksack becomes his primary gear container. He shifts nonessential gear into the light rucksack, which he leaves behind.

RIFLE HARDCASE: Whenever being transported nontactically, your rifle should be kept in a hardcase. Although this provides complete protection, your greatest concern must be to prevent damage to the scope, the most vulnerable component of a sniping system. Any hardcase meeting airline luggage standards is acceptable, whether made of plastic or aluminum. All are foam-lined, but the addition of internal Velcro tie-downs is excellent. A larger two-gun case is preferable, I think, because you can stow and carry extra items alongside your

rifle. After opening your case in rain or high humidity, be sure to allow the foam to dry before re-storing the rifle in it. A related point: keep one or two silica gel packets in the hardcase to absorb dampness and protect the weapon from rust.

DRAG BAG OR SOFTCASE: While the hardcase is essential for shipping and storing your rifle, at times there simply won't be enough space for so large a container, such as when riding aboard a tactical aircraft or vehicle. While your scope is in a softcase, it's especially important to protect your scope with a strap-on Eagle scope cover. The drag bag is similar to a softcase, but it's heavily camouflaged and dragged behind the sniper while low-crawling. A combination nylon drag bag and softcase is manufactured by Eagle, just for sniper use.

Ammunition, Weapons, and Accessories

SNIPER RIFLE WITH SCOPE AND BIPOD: We'll deal with these items at length in a later chapter. A sniper rifle should be of .308

Eagle's combination softcase and drag bag is very popular with snipers.

bipod, and sling will weigh about 13 to 15 pounds.

SPOTTER'S RIFLE: The military spotter is armed with an M16A2 rifle and an M203 40mm grenade launcher. This high-capacity assault rifle provides enough firepower for breaking away from short-distance, unintended contacts; the 40mm grenade launcher allows firing of high-explosive and smoke rounds, which greatly assist masking and displacement following a sniping engagement. The police spotter, too, should have an assault rifle so he can add mass fire to his sniper's selective single shots and thereby give the team an antivehicle capability as well as to engage multiple armed suspects. The target-grade Spring-

caliber or larger. It should have a zoom scope or fixed-power scope with quality at least equal to that of the rifle. The bipod attaches not to the barrel but at the front swivel or to a rail beneath the fore-end, and is highly adjustable. A quality sling completes the sniping system. Combined, the rifle, scope,

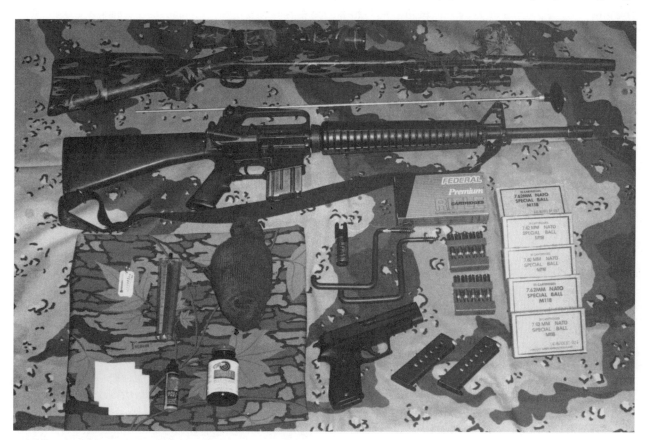

AMMO, WEAPONS, AND ACCESSORIES. These are the basic tools of the sniper's trade.

HANDGUNS. The author prefers this SIG P220 in .45 Auto, but the Beretta M92 or Glock handguns are suitable, too.

field Armory M1A (a copy of the M14/M21 system) fits this need to a tee, and by topping it with a good scope, the law enforcement spotter can back up his sniper's shot with an instant second round if required.

    HANDGUN WITH SPARE MAGAZINE: Given that the sniper most likely is armed with a bolt-action rifle having a capacity of five or fewer rounds, and realizing that his scope makes short-range engagements slow and difficult, then more so than most soldiers he needs a high-capacity automatic pistol and several spare magazines.

SNIPER'S BASIC OPERATIONAL AMMUNITION LOAD

	POLICE SNIPER		MILITARY SNIPER	
	In Vest/Total Rounds		In Vest/Total Rounds	
M118LR or Civilian Match	20–40	40–60	40–60	100–120
Barrier Penetration Ammo *	10	20	20	40
Tracer	5	10	10	20
Frangible Ammo	10	20	—	—

* Military ball, Federal Tactical Load, or Hornady InterBond TAP Barrier ammo

Having been in several shootouts using 9mm ball against bad guys and not being satisfied with the results, I am not a great fan of that caliber. The .45-caliber pistol offers much greater capability, and the .40 S&W is better still because it has ballistics similar to the .45 but allows for a larger magazine capacity. Therefore, in combat I would carry a GI .45 auto or scrounge a .40 S&W. Police snipers face similar concerns to their military counterparts, but departmental policies likely will dictate their sidearms. If you have some leeway, I again would recommend a .45 or .40 S&W, except the .45 would be a SIG-Sauer P220.

AMMUNITION BASIC LOAD: We've prepared a separate box that lists the recommended types and amounts of ammunition for carry on your vest/webgear and in your light rucksack. This is only a starting point to give you some ideas to adapt to your operational environment. Due to its potential for overpenetration, I don't think military ball is a police marksman's substitute for Federal and Hornady glass penetration ammo, although ball is excellent for penetrating light vehicles. Frangible ammo, of course, is designed to avoid overpenetration, a concern of law enforcement

ITEMS CARRIED ON WEBGEAR OR VEST (ALWAYS WITH YOU)

Rifle Ammunition	Spare Pistol Mags
Handheld Radio	Ear Protection
Small Knife	Penlight w/ Filter
Mini Binoculars	Chemical Mace
Compass/GPS	Camouflage Paste
Canteen (filled)	Strobe Light (military)
Whistle	Bandage
Insect Repellent	Plastic Restraint
Mini Thermometer	Chewing Gum
Beef Jerky	Pencil & Notebook
Alcohol Wipes	Laser Rangefinder
CamelBak	

ITEMS CARRIED IN SMALL RUCKSACK OR DITTY BAG (CARRIED WITH YOU)

Spotting Scope	Lightweight Tripod
Binoculars	Beanbag
Empty Cloth Bag	Wind Gauge
Knee & Elbow Pads	Snips
Folding Saw	Cleaning Rod
18" x 18" Canvas	Copper Solvent
Lubricant	Lens Paper
Cleaning Patches	Gore-Tex Jacket
Treesteps	Mesh Camo Suit
Spandoflage Veil	Scarf
Watch Cap	Large Flashlight
Gloves	Chemlights
Spare Batteries	Signal Panel
Signal Mirror	Map w/ Alcohol Mkrs.
Small Smokes	Parachute Cord or
Chemical Hand Warmer	Bootlaces
Cigarettes	Silicone Cement
Plastic Restraints	Facial Tissue Pkg.
Duct Tape	Canned Juices
Piddle Pack	Sunflower Seeds
Ration/MRE	

ITEMS CARRIED IN LARGE RUCKSACK (STOWED IN VEHICLE)

Body Armor	Extra Ammunition
Ground Pad	Poncho/Ground Cloth
Rappel Gear	Large Knife
Large Tripod	Full-Size Binos
Entrenching Tool	Gore-Tex Pants
Overwhites	Polypro Underwear
Wool Sweater	Thinsulate Liner
Jungle Hat	Dry Socks
Duct Tape	Camouflage Tape
Bungee Cords	Treesteps
Mini Cassette	Strobe Light
Pen Flares	Lg. Smoke Grenade
Extra Chemlights	Reflective Tacks
Luminous Tape	Ration/MRE
Piddle Packs	Chemical
Bandages	Hand Warmers
Antiseptic Ointment	Toothbrush & Paste
Insect Headnet	Iodine Tablets
Drag Bag	Medical Pills

rather than military snipers. Tracer is suitable primarily for night signaling and marking targets for friendly forces and supporting aircraft, at which it's excellent.

LASER RANGEFINDER: Every sniper team, whether military or police, needs a laser rangefinder. Compact, inexpensive Bushnell units offer ranging out to 800 yards/meters, which even under conditions that limit a laser's effectiveness will provide exact distance measurement for almost any conceivable police sniping engagement. Newer Bushnells, also reasonably priced, offer ranging out to 1,500 yards/meters. Military sniper teams may be able to get by with these devices, but ideally they should be outfitted with high-quality rangefinders, such as Leica Geovid/Vector or Swarovski lasers.

CHEMICAL MACE: This primarily is to dissuade curious animals and hostile dogs from bothering you in your sniper hide position or while stalking.

CLEANING ROD: Employed in the field to remove barrel obstructions, particularly if you've poked the muzzle into soft earth. Otherwise, used to clean jacket residue after firing each five rounds.

COPPER SOLVENT: For removing copper jacket residue after firing each five rounds.

CLEANING PATCHES: Employed with copper solvent.

SMALL BOTTLE LUBRICANT: For emergency field use.

WIND GAUGE: These are helpful but of limited value since you can only measure wind at your location, while wind at your target may be a different speed and direction.

CLIP-ON THERMOMETER: Small and lightweight, a mini thermometer is used to monitor temperature, compute any resulting velocity changes, and determine how it will affect bullet trajectory.

18" x 18" CANVAS: Lay this below your muzzle to eliminate the dust surge kicked up by muzzle blast.

EMPTY CLOTH BAG: Fill it with available sand, dirt, or gravel, close with a wire twist, and use to support your rifle forearm. I make mine from old BDU pants legs.

BEANBAG: This is an old sock, used to precisely raise or lower the butt's heel for exact, steady aiming. It's filled with dried beans or peas, or, even better, pack it with fine sand.

TREESTEPS: Invented for use by bowhunters, these are handy braces for your feet if you must fire from a peaked roof. Also, one can be screwed into a tree trunk and padded with a glove for a shooting support. Useful, too, for boosting yourself over a wooden fence or up the side of a house into a window.

Spotting and Surveillance Equipment

SPOTTING SCOPE: We'll examine these in great detail later. This is one of the basic pieces of sniping equipment, enabling the team to surveil, detect targets, read wind speed and direction with mirage, and confirm hits and adjust fire. Spotting scopes are available in fixed power or zoom. A quality spotting scope is well worth the money.

MISCELLANEOUS ADDITIONAL GEAR (AVAILABLE BUT NOT CARRIED)

Kevlar Helmet	Still Camera
Ghillie Suit	Video Camera
Gas Mask	Night Vision Devices
Sleeping Bag	Telephoto Lenses
Camouflage Netting	

TRIPOD: Used to support the spotting scope since a hand cannot hold it steady enough for long-range viewing. Tripods can be simple, folding, three-legged affairs or complicated and very adjustable with micrometer-like dials.

BINOCULARS: Used together with the spotting scope for visual overlap in both field of view and magnification power. We'll examine binoculars in depth later, but note that both mini binoculars and full-size ones serve useful purposes.

ALCOHOL WIPES: These are *not* for cleaning lenses but for wiping glass you may have to look through while surveilling. We're talking about the foil-sealed, throwaway wipes. Carry several.

LENS PAPER: Carry one package stowed in a plastic bag and use *only* lens paper to clean your rifle scope, spotting scope, and binocular lenses.

SPOTTING AND SURVEILLANCE EQUIPMENT. These are the essential "eyes" of a sniper team.

MIRROR: Used to peek around corners or over edges while searching for a hostile sniper. This can be the same mirror carried for signal purposes.

STILL CAMERA: This is not listed for carrying in any container because it's only used on special surveillance operations. Yet it's important that you train with a particular type of camera that is available for field use so you don't have to scramble at the last minute when it's needed.

VIDEO CAMERA: This is a ditto of what we've said for the still camera. Since your sniper hide is an excellent surveillance position, you easily could be tasked to video an objective prior to a hostage rescue mission or a drug raid. You need access to a video cam for training and a dedicated one for some operations.

NIGHT OBSERVATION DEVICES (NODs): These are addressed in detail later. Although military snipers should have assigned NODs that they use frequently, we're treating them as special mission gear.

NODs are available as goggles or sighting devices to be placed atop your rifle like a daytime scope.

SENSORS: Since snipers are masters of stalking and deploy in remote areas or well in advance of the main body of an operation, they could be used to emplace sensors clandestinely. They're not listed as carried in any container because they're not normally a piece of gear assigned to the team.

Edged Tools
FOLDING SAW: This is the handiest edged tool you can have, and even a moderately priced one can zip through a 2 x 4 in minutes. Used to clear a narrow field of view or firing port, improve camouflage, and perform a host of other cutting needs. Useful for both military and law enforcement snipers.

SNIPS: Small but very sharp, used to prune just a bit of grass and leaves away from your sniper hide to allow undetectable firing. Also handy for constructing and maintaining your Ghillie suit.

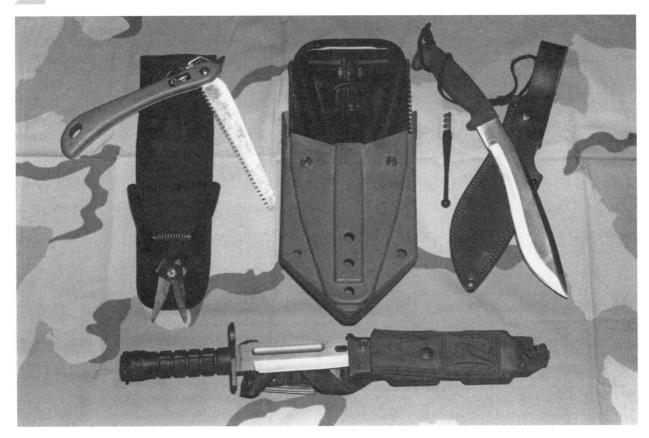

EDGED TOOLS. Any or all of these may be needed, but the author especially values the folding saw and Fiskars snips at left.

SMALL KNIFE: A small knife is useful for cutting, especially when there's a need for dexterity that a big knife cannot accomplish.

LARGE KNIFE: A large knife lends itself to hacking and chopping and should be heavy enough to give you some leverage and momentum. Yes, it can also remove an enemy sentry's head, but you'll have far greater need to accomplish more mundane work.

ENTRENCHING TOOL: A permanent sniper hide includes digging for protection against small-arms fire and enemy artillery. But a surveillance hide, too, may require digging to be totally invisible.

GLASS CUTTER: For removing glass panes in an urban sniper hide so you can fire through a window that appears to be closed.

Clothing

BASIC UNIFORM: The Marine Corps digital camouflage pattern uniforms are certainly suitable as a sniper's basic field camouflage, as is the Army's woodland pattern or desert three-color Battle Dress Uniform, or BDU. The newer Army Combat Uniform (ACU), however, appears so light colored, at least to me, that it seems best suited for a desert environment. All these uniforms have reinforced knees and elbows and lots of pockets.

GORE-TEX RAINWEAR: It's hard not to be a fan of clothing made from this high-tech material, which is derived from the same Teflon used to line frying pans. Containing millions of pores per square inch, Gore-Tex cloth is actually a membrane that allows your body heat to pass out, but the pores are too tiny to allow water to soak in. A sniper who's comfortable can remain in position much longer than can a wet, miserable man—and if hypothermia sets in, you cannot hold your rifle steady. Gore-Tex as an outer layer also shields you against wind and thus windchill. Available in several weights, the best for field use is the heavy type found on the military's Extreme Cold Weather Clothing System. The only downside is

HIGH-TECH CLOTHING. The civilian-style Gore-Tex jacket (left) is useful, but medium-weight Gore-Tex with Thinsulate liner (center) is handier. Heavyweight Gore-Tex, along with polypro T-shirt and double-layer Polarfleece liner (right), prepares a sniper even for subzero cold. The boots contain a Gore-Tex liner and Thinsulate insulation. (Photo credit: Roger Kennedy)

the audible rustle from heavy Gore-Tex, which is not too big a problem since snipers aren't in the business of sentry removal anyhow. Still, if you're concerned about rustle, you can wear BDUs over the Gore-Tex to silence it, while a special Gore-Tex Stealth Suit is available with a soft outer layer.

TORSO INSULATION: Since it contains your heart, lungs, kidneys, and liver, you should take special care to keep your torso warm and insulated. A wool sweater is excellent because wool retains most of its insulation properties even when wet. Also, a Thinsulate jacket liner works well since it provides warmth similar to down, but with much less bulk.

POLYPROPYLENE UNDERWEAR: Polypro is to underwear what Gore-Tex is to outerwear—a high-tech solution to your problems. Because it wicks dampness away from your body, polypro underwear keeps you warm without sweat accumulation and dampness. It works great in combination with Gore-Tex.

HEADGEAR: You should have a soft, jungle-style hat for warm weather because it creates an irregular, difficult-to-detect outline. For cooler temps and night, wear a wool navy-style watch cap. Remember that your body loses about 15 percent of its heat through your head.

GLOVES: Very popular among snipers are military aviator's gloves made from fireproof Nomex and leather. You need only cut off the trigger finger to adapt these snug gloves for sniper use. If you use Nomex gloves—or any other type— you must make a point of wearing them during shooting practice, too.

BOOTS: These are your option, with many types and materials available. Just be sure you don't make the mistake of using lightweight and comfortable boots when you need heavier ones. Police snipers should wear their tac team boots during ordinary uniform duty so they can deploy instantly without changing footgear and so their boots are broken in and comfortable.

DRY SOCKS: Military snipers certainly would bring dry socks to the field, but police snipers should bring them, too. If your feet get wet during an operation and they get cold, it's almost impossible to get them warm again without dry socks. Cold feet become numb and clumsy.

SCARF: I wear a triangular green field bandage as a scarf. With one quick flick, I can run it below my barrel to clear the 1/8-inch freefloat space of any twigs or crud. I also wipe my face with it, it's handy as a quick tie-down, and it can be used as a tourniquet or bandage.

PONCHO/GROUND CLOTH: As a sniper, you may have to lie prone for hours on wet ground, which can be made more comfortable with a combination ground cloth/poncho. That same poncho can be suspended above your hide to shield you and your gear from sun or rain, provided it won't compromise your location. Military-style ponchos, camouflage ones in particular, do this job well.

Camouflage Aids

PASTES AND STICKS: Designed to be applied to your hands and face, camouflage sticks and pastes take a few minutes to apply but need to be touched up several times daily. Pastes are easier to apply and wash off. We'll cover them extensively later.

VEILS: A veil camouflages your face as quickly as you can put it on, but unless it has eyeholes cut in it, it interferes with your vision. Spandoflage-type veils, though, work well. Camouflage is covered extensively in Chapter 13.

CAMOUFLAGE TAPE: Handy for covering a rifle, scope, or other equipment, camouflage tape is simple and fast to use. White adhesive tape works well in the winter.

MESH CAMOUFLAGE SUIT: This is an outstanding development that each police sniper should have. A mesh suit can be pulled right over your regular street uniform for instant camouflage. Combining this with a Spandoflage hood, a police sniper can camo himself in virtually one minute.

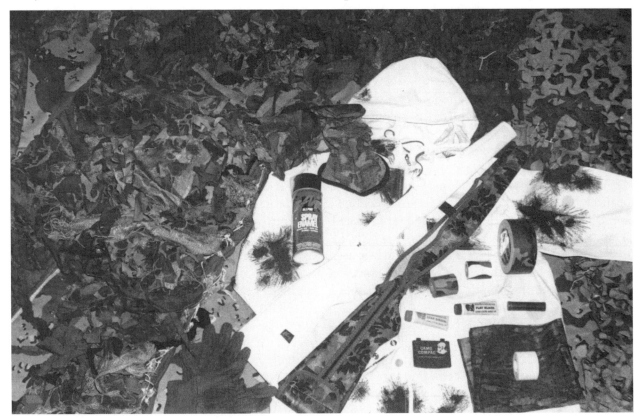

CAMOUFLAGE AIDS. The professional sniper picks and chooses the camo pattern and aids that best fit each operation.

GHILLIE SUIT: The finest sniping camouflage ever devised, a Ghillie suit allows truly invisible action. However, it's also hot and can be a fire hazard. You'll learn to make one later.

OVERWHITES: Every police sniper in the snowbelt needs overwhites, either military surplus or civilian ones designed for winter predator hunting. In a pinch you can make an expedient set, which we'll teach in Chapter 23.

CAMOUFLAGE NETTING: This is for positional camouflage or concealment of equipment. Military netting as used today is the best ever developed.

CHEESECLOTH: A piece of white cheesecloth taped or tacked on the inside of an open window pane largely eliminates outsiders from seeing in, although a sniper inside a room can clearly see and shoot through it.

Navigation Aids

MAP: For route planning, range estimation, and terrain analysis—not to mention just plain knowing where he is—a sniper needs a map. Police snipers may use a precinct, city, or county map, possibly even a U.S. Geological Survey contour interval map. Military snipers normally use a 1:50,000 metric contour interval map, although they could have aerial and even satellite photos for special operations.

MILITARY ACETATE/MAP SEALANT: Acetate is a sticky-backed but clear covering for maps that comes in rolls. A sniper cuts a piece of acetate and very carefully lays it across his map, to which it will bind instantly, for a waterproof, clear surface on which he can write with a grease pencil or alcohol marker. Liquid map sealant has the same effect, but it's brushed across the map in several layers. Acetate is more durable, although it's not usually available in civilian stores.

ALCOHOL MARKERS: These are used for writing on a waterproofed map. *Never* use red to mark a map; it won't be visible in the red filtered light you use to preserve night vision.

NAVIGATION AIDS. While a GPS is useful, a compass is essential for both military and police snipers.

COMPASS AND GPS: A sniper team may use three different compasses. A wrist compass is handy for keeping track of your direction and matching landmarks around you to your map. Better precision results from a prismatic compass, and better yet is a military lensatic. A Global Positioning System is even more precise and the fastest way to direct GPS-guided munitions—but if the battery goes out, you'll still need a quality lensatic compass.

REFLECTOR/LUMINOUS TACKS: These tacks can be prepositioned to identify drop-off or rendezvous points, especially when conducting vehicular infils and exfils in counternarcotics and low-intensity conflict operations.

Signal and Illumination Devices

RADIOS: Voice-activated (VOX) radios leave hands free to aim the rifle and pull the trigger during hostage rescue countdown shooting. They're made in headset style, as an adapter unit for ordinary police handy-talkies, and some have a microphone built into the ear mike for amazingly compact operation. Stealth/secure radios are preferable but not always available (and if you don't have a spare battery, that's when you'll need one).

SIGNAL MIRROR: Since the signal mirror is our first signal device, it must be emphasized here that such devices are either "passive"—they can be controlled so only a friendly will see it, like our signal mirror—or they're "active" and everyone in the area will notice it, which includes flares and smoke grenades. Signal mirrors come in two sizes, but the important thing is that they're good glass and have a screen hole in the center for aiming at your recipient. They're only usable in daytime with direct sunlight. Mirrors also are used for peeking around corners and over edges to look for a hidden hostile sniper.

SIGNAL AND ILLUMINATION AIDS. VOX radios and signal devices are critical tools, but they must be used passively and without detection to be effective.

GLINT TAPE: This dull black tape (or squares of it) resembles ordinary duct tape and will not reflect visible light. However, the coded IR light of an AC-130 Spectre gunship makes it brilliantly shine and flash—yet it's visible only to those viewing through night vision devices. Glint tape is sewn or glued to helmets and shoulders for instant night recognition.

SIGNAL PANELS: Another passive device for daytime use only, a neon orange panel is highly visible to aircraft and distant viewers. To make your own, purchase one yard of neon orange ripstop nylon material at a fabric store, then quarter it and tape the edges. For a first-class panel, attach camouflage material to the back. You'll have four panels for about $5 each.

SMOKE GRENADES: Useful only in daylight, a smoke grenade is visible to anyone looking in your direction. They're available as large, military-type smokes spewing lots of smoke or smaller mini smokes you can carry in your pocket that produce less smoke. One more kind is white phosphorous (WP), feared for the dangerous flaming fragments it produces but very much appreciated for the instant mushroom burst of white it exudes. The WP, though dangerous, is the best possible smoke to employ in thick jungle.

WHISTLE: A whistle works fine day or night, but it has a very limited range, useful only to signal people near you. But a whistle can be heard farther away than a voice can.

PEN FLARES: These are visible both day and night and, because they burst above trees and horizon, are useful to signal both air and ground forces. However, pen flares burn out quickly and can easily go unnoticed in daylight.

FLASHLIGHTS: Used both to signal and illuminate, flashlights can be made passive by attaching an infrared filter so only someone using a NOD can see them. Each flashlight needs a red filter so it won't degrade night vision. A spotter may use a large flashlight to illuminate a suspect up to 100 yards away for his sniper to engage. Since a large flashlight is clumsy and too easily lost if carried on your vest/webgear, stow it in your light rucksack.

CHEMLIGHTS AND HOLDER: Chemlights come in an amazing variety—a half dozen different colors, about three different light intensities, multiple-hour durations, and as visible or infrared light. Use them to mark routes and boundaries, designate where fields of fire start or end, signal aircraft, and aid in recognition. The nontoxic liquid can even be poured out to mark a surface like a vehicle top. Special chemlight holders are available that can control the amount of light seen and make it directional.

STROBE LIGHT: Generating short bursts of light in the hundreds of thousands of lumens, a strobe can be seen miles away and works great in rural areas but becomes too easily absorbed in the clutter of lights in an urban area. A strobe light primarily is employed to signal from ground to air. But be very cautious when using a strobe around inexperienced helicopter pilots, who can mistake it for hostile muzzle flashes. An infrared filter allows night strobe signaling that's not visible to naked eyes.

PENCIL AND NOTEBOOK: These should be obvious, but it's the obvious things that tend to be forgotten. Keep the notebook in a sealable plastic bag. And recall that a pencil is better for field use than a pen because it can write even on wet paper and won't freeze.

MINI CASSETTE RECORDER: It's difficult to keep notes in darkness, and the option of just remembering until dawn may not be feasible. A mini cassette recorder is an excellent solution, but if you're a police sniper, don't forget that whatever you record can be taken out of context in a future legal action, so keep your verbal notes short and factual.

RECOGNITION AIDS: These include a host of materials and devices—luminous tape, scarves, garters, chemlights, bright lettering on jackets, etc.—used to enable friendlies to instantly recognize other friendlies, which can become complicated by darkness or multiple agencies or units participating in an operation. Depending on the operation, recognition aids may extend to vehicles as well; recall that Allied vehicles in Operation Desert Storm had black-and-white Vs prominently displayed on their tops and sides. Recognition aids could be helpful in some police operations that employ unmarked cars.

Safety and Comfort Items

KEVLAR HELMET: Whether police or military, a sniper doesn't usually wear a helmet because it makes stalking more difficult and surrounds his head in a distinct outline. Police snipers usually leave their Kevlar helmets at the precinct, but it may be worth bringing along if responding to a hostile sniping incident. When accompanying a unit, military snipers should wear the same uniform, including a helmet, to avoid distinguishing themselves and becoming a target for enemy snipers.

GAS MASK: Military snipers should bring gas masks if the enemy has a toxic agent capability. Police snipers normally don't need masks because even if a location is gassed during an assault, the sniper hide will be too far away to be affected.

BODY ARMOR: Because it's hot and heavy and hard to camouflage, military snipers don't usually wear body armor. However, the frequency of improvised explosive devices (IEDs) and car bombings in today's war zones make this a sensible precaution when traveling in military convoys or while assigned to stationary security duties. Covertly emplaced snipers, who'd likely come under heavy attack if their position was compromised, could be well served by body armor, too. As a general rule, though, body armor does not lend itself to stalking and low-crawling. A police sniper would rarely have need of body armor except, perhaps, if confronted by a rifle-armed perpetrator or while supporting a raid against suspects armed with long guns.

EAR PROTECTION: A sniper must train as he will fight, so during range practice he wears unobstrusive, internal ear protection rather than clumsy earmuffs. This way he won't change his stock spotweld if he must shoot without any hearing protection in combat.

RAPPEL GEAR: Every sniper needs his own rappelling harness, gloves, carabiners, and figure eight. A rope is not necessary because in a police agency it is tac team gear and in the military it is an air assault rigger's responsibility.

KNEE AND ELBOW PADS: For low crawling and climbing over fences or kneeling in sharp gravel, a sniper needs knee and elbow pads. The best I've ever seen were made from wet suit rubber and Velcro fasteners, but any style is good provided it stays in position and is of a subdued color.

GROUND PAD: A self-inflatable foam pad is a necessity, not a luxury, for snipers. Bare winter earth will suck warmth from your prone body, and a scalding summer rooftop can preclude staying in a prone position. The Therm-a-Rest ground pad will insulate your body and make cold or heat more tolerable. I prefer the half-size because it's much more compact to carry yet still protects most of the body.

HAND WARMERS: These don't merely keep you comfortable in low temperatures, they also preserve your trigger finger's critical sensitivity. Chemical hand warmers have a long shelf life, while some are even reusable. They also can be placed inside your shirt to keep your chest and trunk area warm.

INSECT REPELLENT: Even in urban areas, mosquitoes can harass you and disrupt concentration while surveilling or aiming. Most police tac team members have no need for repellent, but of course, entry team members don't occupy a hide for hours on end.

SLEEPING BAG: In addition to its traditional use, a sleeping bag placed atop a ground pad enables a sniper to lie motionless comfortably even in subzero temperatures. Some new fillings are on a par with goose down in effectiveness.

INSECT HEADNET: Florida or Louisiana lawmen or GIs serving in a tropical climate may appreciate a headnet to keep buzzing insects away from eyes, mouth, and nose. In SOG, we never wore headnets even in the worst Cambodian swamps, but harassing insects need some getting used to, perhaps more time than you have, making a headnet worthwhile.

Adhesives and Tie-Downs

DUCT TAPE: You cannot anticipate how many ways a sniper will use duct tape. I've wrapped it around a thin tree to support a spotting scope, hemmed orange neon material with it to create a signal panel, wrapped pants cuffs with tape for quieter movement, taped over a light switch in an urban hide so no one could accidentally illuminate the room, etc. Military "100-Mile-a-Minute" tape, which is very similar, works swell, too.

PARACHUTE CORD OR BOOTLACES: Another good-for-just-about-anything item is olive-drab military parachute 550 cord. If you cannot obtain any, bootlaces can be substituted.

BUNGEE CORDS: These can hold doors open, secure a flap in the wind, become instant hangers for your hide, etc. They're all-purpose and belong in each sniper's rucksack.

ZIP TIES: These come in mighty handy as all sorts of closures and clamps. Bring an assortment for everything from cuffing hands to holding open a swinging window.

SILICONE CEMENT: Fast acting and capable of bonding dissimilar surfaces, silicone cement is the best all-purpose adhesive available. Glue silicone nubs the size of chocolate chips to boot soles for great traction on the slickest surfaces, mend tears in your Ghillie suit, reseal seams on waterproof clothing and tarps, affix rubber leaves to headgear, and so on. There are a thousand uses.

Sanitation and Medical Items

PIDDLE PACK: I first used these when flying U.S. Air Force Forward Air Control missions in the Cessna Skymaster 02A, a great little plane that lacked what was known as a "piss tube." When nature called, we urinated in a plastic bag containing a sponge. Urban snipers compelled to stay hours in a hide that lacks a toilet can do the same. A sniper with a bulging bladder can hardly take an accurate shot.

BASIC PILLS AND OINTMENTS: You'll have to determine your own needs, but these probably should include nonalcoholic cough syrup, eye ointment, a headache remedy, cold capsules, and antidiarrhetic pills.

ANTISEPTICS AND BANDAGES: An Ace wrap is a must, plus assorted bandages and cotton and tape, some Bacitracin antibiotic ointment, a burn ointment, and a cream for treating poison ivy.

ANTACIDS: I've listed these separately because they're so important. If you are under great stress,

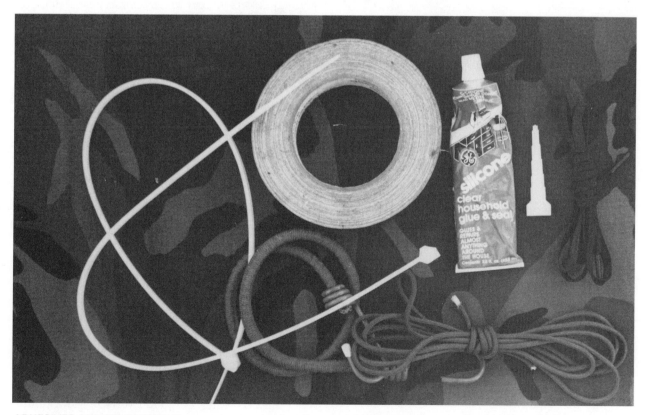

ADHESIVES AND TIE-DOWNS. Not sexy but needed for all sorts of tiny tasks, these should be in your rucksack.

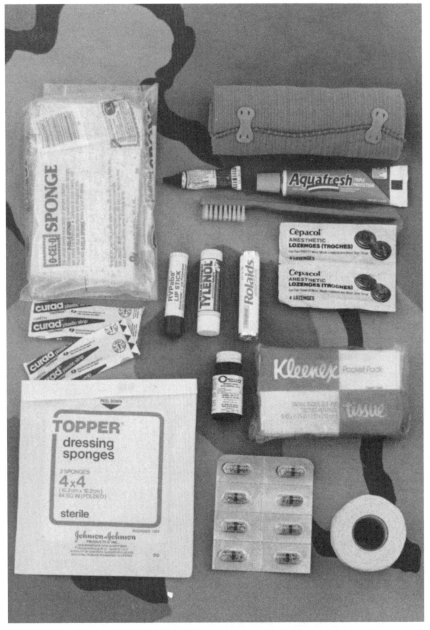

SANITATION AND MEDICAL ITEMS. These are just the minimum. Add military wound dressings, morphine Syrettes, and other useful items.

TOILET TISSUE: This is similar to the need for the piddle pack. It's easiest just to keep a sealed purse-size package of facial tissues in your ruck. If no toilet paper is available, nontoxic leaves, clumps of grass, smooth rocks, or even snow can be used.

TOOTHBRUSH AND TOOTHPASTE: You'll never risk life and limb to wash or shave in the field, but this bit of civilization can refresh you each morning. If not this, at least give yourself a Lifesaver to make your mouth livable at dawn.

Sustenance

Our recommendation is that a police sniper carry with him enough sustenance for eight hours and have additional food and water in his large rucksack for 24 hours on-site without resupply. While there may not seem much need for food, you well could find yourself in a perfect hide that you've occupied motionless for hours, then suddenly a support person walks up with a Big Mac and fries, blowing your cover completely. This has happened before, real-world.

Military snipers obviously must bring sufficient rations for the entire length of their operation.

We're also citing a need for something to munch on and dispel tension, while also passing the time. This is actually much more a psychological need than a physical one.

Meanwhile, don't forget that liquid sustenance is more important than food.

LIQUIDS: It's best that you have available a full range of water containers—1-quart, 2-quart, and 5-quart sizes—along with a CamelBak water

ate Mexican food for lunch, or just plain have an upset stomach, calmly taking a life-and-death shot becomes an extraordinary physical challenge.

IODINE TABLETS: Military snipers wouldn't go anywhere without water purification tablets, but law enforcement snipers will also need them for rural surveillance missions and some counternarcotics operations.

carrier, which you'll probably use more than any canteen. Unlike the other water vessels, you can lay in position and suck water from a CamelBak, which fits conveniently under a Ghillie suit. The other canteens will be useful to transport or store water, but most often you'll just use them to refill your CamelBak. A police sniper's canteens and CamelBak need to be cleaned regularly to avoid bacterial growth, although adding iodine tablets works, too. The lawman's light rucksack should probably contain some canned juices, which are more nutritious than mere water and have a shelf life of several years.

SHORT-TERM FOOD: To help pass time and keep mind and body alert, bring along sunflower seeds, beef jerky, and chewing gum.

LONGER-TERM FOOD: Have at least one complete meal or ration with you, either a military MRE or several cans of food that can be eaten cold, like beans and wieners. Freeze-dried foods need water, which may be in short supply.

UTENSILS: These can be plastic, metal, or wood. A wooden serving spoon with its handle cut down is the best all-purpose eating/cooking utensil, as plastic can break and metal can bang against your metal cooking cup.

CIGARETTES: If you're a smoker, prevent anxiety by ensuring you have enough cigarettes in your alert gear and water-proof matches to light them.

SUSTENANCE. Police snipers need food and liquid for at least one day. Military snipers carry enough for five to seven days.

CHAPTER 2

THE SNIPER'S RIFLE

THE SNIPER-GRADE RIFLE

Just as slight edges in many skills give a sniper his cumulatively decisive edge over opponents, so a sniper-grade weapon must be a bit better in many ways than its off-the-rack cousins to be an overall significantly more accurate weapon.

This cumulative rifle quality will dictate half the equation for determining a rifle's maximum effective range. The other half is the inherent accuracy and ballistic lethality of the weapon's ammunition. If you lack quality in either ammo or weapon, you're not capable of sniping.

We'll deal with bullet performance and match-grade ammunition in Chapter 5. Here we'll examine how a target-grade rifle is ruggedized and modified for field duty as a sniper weapon.

How Accurate Is "Accurate"?

When considering rifle quality, ultimately the question of accuracy arises, and when it does we need to specify a standard: How accurate should a sniper rifle be?

Some manufacturers promote their rifles as 1/2 MOA—one-half Minute of Angle, or producing 1/2-inch groups at 100 yards. This is really excellent, but you'll pay highly for such performance. In order to get it, you'll have to invest in a hand-built gun or special tuning of a

Hand-built by Robbie Barrkman, Gunsite's former gunsmith-in-residence, this Robar SR-90 is superb, guaranteed to shoot 1/2 MOA with match ammo.

factory rifle. I have yet to come across anyone claiming smaller groups.

At the other extreme, some bargain sniper rifles are merely standard receivers dressed up with heavy barrels and incapable of yielding even 1-inch groups, or 1 Minute of Angle. I'm not talking about Savage or Remington factory rifles but those at the lowest end of the market. While you can save hundreds of dollars acquiring such pieces, recall that in this life you usually get what you pay for, and an inaccurate sniper rifle is a contradiction in terms.

No matter what you pay, 1 MOA is the realistic minimum performance for a police sniper's rifle, given his need to place a single shot with considerable precision in hostage rescue scenarios. This 1 MOA also is a reasonable minimum standard for a military sniper's weapon, since he must engage targets at considerably longer distances—that 1 MOA group equates to 10 inches at 1,000 yards, a .308's maximum range when firing 175-grain M118LR ammunition. Any worse inherent accuracy would lead to many misses at long range.

Thus an acceptable accuracy standard is 1 MOA, but I'd say that 3/4 MOA is still a good balance of cost against performance. But when it comes to 1/2 MOA, probably 88 percent of snipers cannot exploit such accuracy, while these rifles typically are several times as expensive as 3/4 MOA weapons.

Yes, a rifle that groups 1/2 inch is desirable, but again, in many cases this is more accuracy than a shooter can exploit. Take me. On a good day, when I'm in shape and have practiced steadily, I can shoot 1/2-inch groups (or even better) with my Accuracy International AWP rifle. However, after a few months without marksmanship practice, I only shoot 1-inch groups *with the same rifle*. Unless you have sufficient opportunity to practice, you can hardly benefit from your rifle's inherent accuracy.

Still, if you're a superb rifleman and your agency can afford hand-built sniper weapons, by all means go with the best. You'll never be disappointed by a rifle that challenges your shooting ability.

The Accurate Barrel

When it comes to barrels, you should be more concerned with the quality and precision of manufacture than whether a barrel's made of stainless steel or a chrome-moly alloy, although stainless stands up longer to wear. Producers may proudly declare the superiority of their barrel-making process, but there doesn't seem to be any inherent advantage in hammer-forged or button rifling. Both techniques create stress because steel is crushed into the desired shape and the stress relieved by heat treatment. Some fine sniper rifles, including the Steyr SSG and SIG-Sauer SSG 3000, employ hammer-forged barrels.

Other makers insist that only by cutting or machining the rifling can stress be avoided and quality result—but after machining they lap their barrels, which, it can be argued, has as much to do with barrel performance as does precise cutting. Simply lapping a mediocre barrel—polishing the bore with special abrasives—won't necessarily make it a tack-driver, for too much lapping wears down crisp rifling edges, further degrading accuracy. *Quality of manufacture, no matter which process is used, is what matters most.* Larry Miller, a Wisconsin high-power rifle champion, once had me examine his Palma Match rifle's finely lapped bore through an expensive 40x bore scope. I could see that every centimeter was brightly polished. By contrast, we next looked at a factory-made varmint rifle's bore—I saw tool marks, tiny crevices, and minuscule burrs on the rifling.

Not only do these bore imperfections interfere with a bullet smoothly transiting the barrel, but they strip away tiny bits of copper jacket from the bullet. After a few rounds, this copper accumulation degrades accuracy because it slightly changes how subsequent bullets travel down the bore. *This is why benchrest competitors clean their bores every 10 rounds to preclude copper buildup.*

H.S. Precision cuts their own rifled barrels

SNIPER RIFLE BARREL LENGTHS

U.S. Army M24	24.00″
USMC M40A3	24.00″
M21/M25/M1A	22.00″
FNH/Winchester Sniper Rifles	24.00″
Remington 700 Police/PSS	24.00″
Steyr SSG PII	26.00″
Mauser SR93	27.00″
Accuracy International AW	26.00″
Savage Model 10 LE 20, 24	26.00″
Sako TRG-22	26.00″

Ballistic tables normally reflect firing from a 24-inch barrel. For each inch your barrel varies from this, add or subtract 20 fps muzzle velocity. For 300 Winchester Magnum, however, add/subtract 25 fps.

for their excellent Pro-Series rifles. When I visited K&P Barrels in Raton, New Mexico, I learned that Ken Johnson, too, cuts his match-grade barrels. Krieger Barrels also employs only cut rifling. These and a number of other barrel makers produce the highest quality match-grade barrels, with exacting tolerances of 0.0002 inch for the bore and grooves.

When manufacturing imperfections result in a barrel's less than match-grade performance, it can be improved by various coatings and treatments, the most popular being BlackStar. This process polishes the bore more thoroughly than lapping and—combined with cryo-treatment, which cools the barrel to -300°F—has been documented to improve accuracy, especially when firing moly-coated bullets. Working with K&P Barrels, BlackStar also offers cut-rifled barrels that incorporate this process.

Newer yet and very shooter-friendly is Smooth-Kote, an inexpensive, fast-drying bore treatment that molecularly bonds to metal, leaving a layer of molybdenum disulfide particles that smooth out and fill in imperfections. Smooth-Kote dramatically reduces fouling and has proven very popular

among American snipers in the dusty environment of Afghanistan and Iraq.

Barrel Twist, Weight, and Length

Most sniper rifles use four-grooved, right-hand twist rifling that makes one rotation in 10 or 12 inches. The majority of these rifles are intended to fire 168- or 175-grain bullets, so they have the faster 1:10 rate.

The heavy barrel is the rule when it comes to sniper weapons because there's less warpage as the barrel heats and thus less departure from zero. And since a wider-diameter barrel offers a larger outer surface, there's better air cooling. Remington factory sniper rifles have 3/4-inch barrels which, although heavier than standard, are not especially thick. Nor is a 1-inch diameter too thick, but by this point (and definitely by 1 1/4 inch) I'd recommend fluting or cutting shallow horizontal strips from the outer surface. This reduces weight, increases the cooling surface, and adds rigidity to the barrel. Schneider fluted barrels have a deservedly excellent reputation. Robbie Barrkman, owner of Robar and former gunsmith-in-residence at Jeff Cooper's Gunsite Training Center, incorporates Schneider fluted barrels on his superb SR-90 sniper rifle.

Externally, barrel surfaces should be parkerized or otherwise dulled to eliminate reflection and also protect against rust and corrosion.

Any barrel's muzzle must be properly crowned, which means its outer edge is beveled cleanly and evenly so there's not the tiniest possible binding or disrupting the bullet as it exits the barrel. To protect this crown against damage from bumping or falling, most sniper-grade rifles have a recessed muzzle cut back roughly 1/16 of an inch. If you're experiencing accuracy problems, check the crown for even a slight nick, which can be ground and polished to restore top performance.

Inside the barrel, accuracy can be affected by the length of the leade, which is the space between the end of the chamber and the start of the rifling. The leade allows the bullet to separate from the cartridge before it engages the rifling at the throat. In some match-grade weapons, the leade is carefully cut so the tip of a particular length bullet almost touches the rifling. My AWP, for example, has a chamber and leade cut expressly for the .308 168-grain BTHP Match cartridge, so longer or shorter .308 loads may not perform as well.

Most American sniper rifles use 24-inch barrels, which is a good compromise between handiness and still having adequate length for suitable muzzle velocity. European sniper rifle barrels often are a bit longer, usually 26 inches. As the data in the box on page 39 reveals, your rifle's ballistic performance will vary if it's not a 24-inch barrel, since this is the standard length for ballistic data. Most differences are not dramatic—probably about a 1/4 MOA click, but since you're a sniper you should know even slight variances. However, keep in mind that a .308 168-grain BTHP Match round will impact 6 inches lower at 500 yards when fired from a 20-inch barrel than when fired from a 24-inch barrel.

Though not commonly considered, barrel length also affects muzzle blast. A researcher at Ball State University, Dr. William L. Kramer, found that muzzle blast noise increases 1 decibel for each inch a barrel is reduced, which adds significantly to a sniper's sound signature.

How many rounds will you fire before your barrel wears out? Actually, it isn't the barrel's rifling that wears most but the throat—that little spot ahead of the chamber where a bullet first bites into the rifling. (That's why it's so critical *not* to use a steel cleaning rod, to prevent throat damage!) Sierra, the highly respected manufacturer of match-grade bullets, says up to 10,000 rounds can be fired accurately from a barrel if it's properly maintained. In the hands of a law enforcement sniper who practices at least monthly, I'd say this translates easily to a decade or more of shooting. A military sniper, assuming he's in combat, could shoot the same rifle accurately for years.

The Free-Floated Barrel

Never let anything touch your barrel. You'll see this advice several times in these pages, and it is repeated here with special emphasis since this is the very essence of free-floating a barrel.

Why? Think of your barrel as a tuning fork that hums when a round is fired. The vibrations emanate from the chamber area and parallel the bullet as it travels down the barrel, reaching the muzzle alongside the bullet. If your barrel is unhindered, the vibrations resonate exactly the same way each time you fire. Should something touch the barrel, it disrupts these vibrations and moves your bullet's point of impact. Remember, consistency equals accuracy. I've personally seen my Remington shift 1 MOA merely by wrapping camouflage tape on the barrel.

The simplest way to ensure that firing vibrations flow consistently shot after shot is by free-floating the barrel, which means rasping out the barrel channel in the forearm for at least a 1/8 inch gap. While there's been some debate about free-floating, the respected custom stock and rifle maker, McMillan, reports, "It has been our experience with the thousands of stocks we've installed that 98 percent of the rifles are most accurate when free-floated." Many .50-caliber rifles address the free-float issue by simply not having forearms at all, so nothing can possibly disrupt barrel vibration.

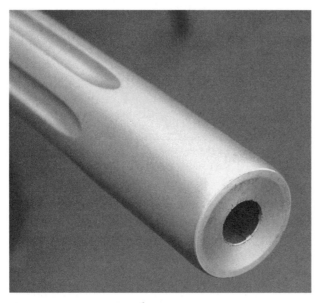

A recessed muzzle crown and fluting on a match-grade stainless barrel.

This D&L Sports accurized AR-15 boasts a free-floated match barrel, match trigger, and low-mount scope base.

Some hunting rifle manufacturers free-float all but the last 2 inches of the forearm tip, with this space called a "pressure point." This may result in suitable accuracy for hunting, but it is not appropriate for a sniper rifle.

To ensure that my barrel channel is free of bits of refuse that could touch the barrel, I run the triangular bandage I wear as a bandana down its length before firing.

The Accurate Trigger

Most sniper rifles employ single-stage triggers that the shooter gradually squeezes, applying even pressure until his shot "breaks." This is the same kind of trigger found on the majority of American hunting rifles, although the sniper's match-grade version has had its operating surfaces polished and refined for a smooth, nonbinding pull. When done well, such a "trigger job" is a piece of art and a joy to shoot.

By contrast, some sniper rifles offer a two-stage trigger in which perhaps half the slack is compressed with little pressure; then resistance increases slightly and remains uniform until the shot breaks. Having grown up with two-stage triggers, this is my preferred type. The excellent Sako TRG-22 and Accuracy International AW rifles, along with accurized M14s, employ such two-stage triggers.

The problem with many factory-installed triggers is that they're set much too heavy—often 5 pounds or more—demanding such a stiff pull that the entire rifle too easily shifts. I think most snipers would agree that setting your trigger at about 3 pounds is best, since any less makes it too easy to accidentally discharge your weapon. Further, if the trigger is set really low—say, 1 pound—some rifles are notorious for going off when they're bumped or dropped. After any work or modification to your trigger, test it to ensure it doesn't fire when the bolt is rapidly, vigorously closed, nor when it's dropped butt-down about 6 inches onto a hard surface. Conduct these tests with the safety on and off.

In contrast to most heavy, factory-installed triggers, the very impressive Savage Accu-Trigger is a smooth-pulling, crisply breaking trigger that's easily adjusted as low as 1 1/2 pounds. Even at that low setting it won't go off because—reminiscent of Glock pistols—there's a tiny lever inside the trigger that must be activated to release the sear. Like the modestly priced Savage tactical rifle on which this trigger's installed, it's a remarkably good value.

Some sniper rifles have triggers that are adjustable for length of pull. I recommend you not adjust such a trigger until you've had some experience with that rifle and have developed a natural "hold" so it's properly set.

A slip-on trigger shoe or an extrawide trigger can improve performance with a heavy-pulling, double-action revolver, but you would make a gross error in similarly modifying a rifle trigger. These actually make your trigger feel clumsy. For precision performance you need exactly the opposite—a sensitive touch trigger with maximum control.

Some European rifles incorporate "set triggers" (or "dual triggers") with a heavy trigger pulled to "set" a second, light trigger. A slight touch then fires the second trigger. Set

This Savage AccuTrigger is so good it will force competitors to improve their triggers.

This Steyr SSG's forward-set trigger can be "set" to fire with a pull of 2 to 8 ounces.

trigger advocates believe that minimal trigger pull ensures a crisp break, but I think it too easily lends itself to accidental discharges or, equally bad, a stressed sniper jerking his heavy trigger when his mind tells him to delicately squeeze his light trigger. A version of the Steyr SSG offers set triggers, but I think they're best suited to target work.

A number of aftermarket triggers are available for Remington and Winchester rifles and offer better quality than factory-grade triggers. The well-known Timney is probably the most popular, although Jewell triggers have found their way into many Remington 700 bolt guns.

The Sniper-Grade Stock

A proper stock is the foundation for precision shooting. That stock is the interface between you and the rifle's action and barrel. For absolute peak performance, it should conform to—and be an extension of—your body.

Unless you have a stock custom-built to reflect your body's size and shape—which is unlikely—the next best thing is a stock that's adjustable at the strategic points of body contact, which means the butt and cheekrest.

A butt should be adjustable for overall length and for height of the cheekpiece, both of which are critical for correct eye relief, proper eye alignment with the scope, developing a consistent spotweld, and shouldering the rifle for consistent aiming and recoil absorption.

Butt length can be adjusted in three ways: first, by employing spacers, such as those used by the Steyr SSG or the stock I designed for Choate Machine & Tool; second, by installing a

H.S. Precision's Pro-Series .308 sniping system is state of the art and reflects the company's stock-making expertise. Both the U.S. Army's M24 system and Remington Police Special rifles incorporate H.S. Precision stocks.

heights. Lacking adjustable stocks, most snipers use duct tape and Ace wraps or bandages to pad their cheekpieces and yield the desired height for eye alignment.

When your rifle butt length and cheekpiece height are adjusted correctly, you should be able to throw your rifle to your shoulder and find you have perfect eye alignment with the scope. You should neither turkey neck nor goose

Built on a specially tuned Remington 700 action and incorporating an adjustable-length H.S. Precision stock, the M24 Sniper Weapon System is topped by a 10x Leupold M3 scope. Available in 7.62mm or .300 Winchester Magnum, it's an excellent system.

rubber recoil pad; and third, as used on the Army's M24 Sniper Weapon System, with a butt that can be cranked out and locked in position. Incidentally, you can tell if the rifle butt length is improper if you find yourself "turkey necking," or moving your head backward and forward to obtain proper eye relief on your scope.

The stock's cheekpiece should be of sufficient height that your eye is aligned with the scope while your cheek is firmly held on the stock at your natural spotweld. To see if your cheekpiece height is improper, notice if you are "goose necking," or moving your head up or down to align with your scope. If you need more height, *do not* strap on a surplus M1D/C or Lee-Enfield leather cheekpiece, which was designed to shift your face sideways to align with a side-mount scope! The best solution is an adjustable cheekpiece that can be set for the height you need, like several McMillans or, as on my Choate stock, interchangeable cheekpieces of different

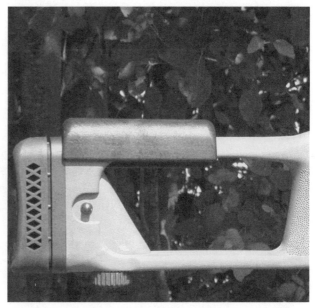

A highly adjustable buttstock. Length is tailored to shooter with spacers, while interchangable cheekrests allow correct height for eye alignment.

The stock I designed for Choate, mounted here on a Savage 110, incorporates many ergonomic features.

Frequently seen, this sniper has added duct tape, padding, and commercially available Moleskin to custom-fit his cheekrest.

neck to get a sight picture. Not only does this make for more comfortable and accurate shooting, it also improves your reaction time for a sudden life-or-death shot.

When it comes to stocks, I grew up admiring oil-rubbed wood, which was how the Winchester 70 and original Remington 700 sniper versions were stocked in Vietnam. The problem with wood is that it can swell with moisture and eventually warp, twisting and binding and causing a zero shift.

Until quality synthetic materials hit the market in the 1980s, they always seemed too light, cheap, and flimsy for serious fieldwork. That's no longer the case. McMillan, for example, produces quite strong stocks using multiple layers of 8-ounce, woven fiberglass cloth laminated under pressure with epoxy resin. While some stock manufacturers leave their stocks hollow or fill them with foam, McMillan fills its excellent stocks with solid fiberglass in the receiver area and epoxy and glass beads in the forearm. The result is a rigid, hefty stock that stands up to the roughest weather and field conditions. My Choate stock is molded of DuPont Rynite SST-35 polymer, which has more strength by weight than stainless steel. Although McMillan doesn't employ Kevlar, several other stock makers use both it and graphite for added stiffness, especially in the fore-end.

The tendency for early synthetic stocks to audibly "ping" when tapped—which could betray your position—has been solved by some stock makers, such as McMillan, by rubberizing the stock's exterior and adding layers of resin-impregnated flannel camouflage cloth.

Even fiberglass stocks must be bedded so

This Choate stock's inclined forearm allows shooters to raise or lower elevation by sliding it forward or backward on support.

that the action fits snuggly to the stock. Using a liquid epoxy that contains atomized stainless steel, quality bedding material is extremely dense and rigid. When properly installed by an expert—and only an expert should epoxy bed a sniper-grade weapon—the result is a stock that's perfectly mated to the action. Areas of particular concern are the fit of the recoil lug's back surface, proper alignment of the tang to preclude twisting during recoil, and replacement of the action screw fittings with aluminum pillars to secure the action independently of the stock. A quality bedding job includes installing Allen-head receiver screws for an accurate tension setting that varies somewhat, but usually about 60 inch-pounds. If the torque is not properly set, accuracy will decline. This is why a shooter should not disassemble a quality bedded rifle unless he has a torque wrench.

Never attempt to rasp or carve a fiberglass stock's exterior to "improve" its free-float, as if it was made of wood. You will weaken it considerably by degrading the material's structural integrity—and, I've been advised, patching it with epoxy will not restore it.

A newer bedding technique, used on the Choate stock, incorporates an aluminum bedding block machined precisely to fit Remington, Winchester, and Savage actions; this forms an extended aluminum skeleton over which the rest of the stock is molded. Installing your rifle in such a stock requires no training, just ordinary tools, yet it offers solid, quality bedding on a par with epoxy. Given how susceptible epoxy is to rifle cleaning solvents, I think ultimately aluminum block bedding will prevail.

An interesting variation on this aluminum block system is the rail gun arrangement on Accuracy International AW rifles. This involves an aluminum frame the length of the stock that's part and parcel of the receiver; the synthetic clamshell-style stock, then, screws over the full-length rail like two flaps. Thus there's no bedding to grow gummy or aluminum pillars to work loose.

The final stock feature is rough checkering or nubs on the pistol grip and forearm for positive control. When it comes to forearms, a wide, flat, semi-beavertail design reduces lateral wobble and improves stability for supported firing. The forearm bottom should be tapered so the shooter can raise or lower elevation merely by sliding the rifle forward or back on a supporting surface.

Capacity and Reloading

A total capacity of five rounds—one in the chamber and four in the fixed magazine—is adequate for a sniper rifle. Single-shot, hand-fed weapons may be suitable for benchrest competition, but they're just too limiting for sniping. Still another useful feature is a hinged floorplate to facilitate safe unloading.

The majority of sniper rifles, including the Remington in its many military and police variations, fit this bill. If I had my way, however, all sniper rifles would employ short, detachable magazines that fit close to the receiver. Not only would this speed reloading but also provide a rigid container for protecting ammo. It would also allow the sniper to segregate specialized rounds, such as tracer or barrier penetrators, which he might need on short notice.

Remington fielded rifles with detachable box magazine a few years ago, but after testing several and observing student rifles at Gunsite, I just wasn't satisfied that the magazines were rugged or reliable enough for sniper operations. The latest Remington M24A2 sniper rifle uses a much more rugged detachable magazine. Some custom rifle builders, including McMillan and Robar, incorporate 20-round or chopped-down 10-round M14 magazines on some rifles, which fits this requirement to a tee.

A number of European sniper rifles—such as the Sako TRG-41 and the Accuracy International AW—have solidly built, compact 10-round magazines. The Steyr SSG employs a five-round rotary magazine that also prevents bullet tip damage from recoil, which I like a lot. Its larger 10-round version protrudes beneath the stock and could interfere with some shooting positions, so it's probably not as practical.

Talking about protruding magazines, I urge USMC and U.S. Army Squad Designated Marksmen to scrounge old 20-round magazines for their scoped M16s. I've been in a lot of gunfights with both 20- and 30-rounders and can attest to the advantage of the shorter magazine for getting your body close to the ground. That's one of those little things that can make all the difference when someone's shooting at you.

Rifles lacking detachable magazines are still effective weapons, but I've never seen either a military or law enforcement sniper practice rapid manual reloading, and that troubles me. In fact, most live-fire range practice involves hand-feeding one round at a time. If these snipers must ever completely reload while under stress—especially the stress of hostile gunfire—they likely will move clumsily and much too slowly.

Weight

The single greatest contribution to a sniper rifle's weight is the barrel, and some shooters would argue that the heavier the barrel, the better for long-distance shooting. True enough, but sniping is not benchrest plinking, and a sniper cannot effectively stalk and low-crawl all day dragging a 20-pound rifle behind him.

Moderate weight isn't bad. It's useful for stability and can absorb considerable recoil, making even the .300 Winchester Magnum comfortable to shoot. Right off the bat, therefore, I think we can agree that untapered, heavyweight "stovepipe" barrels are not suitable for sniper rifles, but there are advantages to moderately heavy barrels.

The introduction of lightweight assault rifles such as the M16 has unfortunately given a misleading idea of a rifle's proper weight. Our excellent World War II M1 Garand, don't forget, was a hefty 9.5 pounds, but it proved handy and popular among infantrymen. And, coincidentally, it's this approximate weight—about 9 to 11 pounds—that I think is appropriate for a sniper rifle minus scope, bipod, mounts, and sling. Adding these accoutrements results in a total sniping system weight of perhaps 13 to 15 pounds, an approximation of the weight for all the weapons in this chapter. My personal preference is a medium-heavy barrel such as found on the Remington Police rifle, the Army's M24, or the Robar SR-90, so I have the accuracy, stability, and recoil absorption I want but a total system weight of about 13 or 14 pounds.

The impetus for ever-heavier barrels seems to me to be a product of the "bigger is better" school of thought. Not only do these heavy, clumsy rifles make stalking much more difficult but the weapons become so barrel-heavy that firing from the standing position becomes difficult and therefore inaccurate. A few years back, while talking to the Non-Commissioned Officer-in-Charge (NCOIC) of the Army Sniper School, MSgt. Ed Nelson, I asked his opinion on barrel weight. He chuckled and said, "Shucks, sir, if I had my way it'd be as light as the .22 I carried as a kid—then I could stalk all day long, no sweat." I couldn't have said it better. As technology and our understanding of what makes a rifle accurate improve, I think we'll see lighter rifles as accurate and capable—*maybe more capable*—than those of today.

Sling, Swivels, and Forearm Rail

Some sniper rifle stocks include a metal groove, called an Anschutz rail, beneath the forearm for positioning the bipod or installing a palm rest for offhand shooting. We put a similar rail on the Choate stock, along with a bipod quick-release, but I don't really see the necessity for a palm rest on a sniper rifle.

Swivel studs, on the other hand, are absolutely essential, both to attach the sling and to mount some varieties of bipod. Some stocks even include an extra forearm swivel stud exclusively for a bipod.

Swivels of a width compatible with your sling—usually 1 1/4 inches—are a necessity, with quick-release swivels being the most practical.

The sling primarily is a stabilizer to improve offhand, sitting, and kneeling shooting, so the best style is a highly adjustable military type. I prefer leather, but nylon is suitable provided it can be adjusted for deliberate shooting, as explained in Chapter 7 on advanced sniper marksmanship.

Bipods

More than any other accessory, the bipod has helped long-range riflemen improve their shooting performance. A bipod offers better stability and steadiness than anything except sandbags. In essence, with a bipod a shooter carries his prone support with him.

The most frequently encountered bipod, mounted on the Army's M24 Sniper Weapon System and popular among police snipers, is the lightweight, tubular one made by Harris Engineering. Attached to the front swivel stud, the Harris bipod folds its legs forward when not in use and employs spring tension to lock them down when rotated into place. This bipod weighs only 12 to 16 ounces, depending on the model.

While all Harris bipods feature extendable legs, they come in three different size ranges to reflect the shooter's desired ground clearance. These sizes—9 to 13 inches, 13.5 to 23 inches, and 13.5 to 27 inches—can support even the sitting position; however, the shortest size is best for sniping since it's considerably more rigid (and stable) than the higher ones. By far, the most useful is the L Series model since it pivots slightly, allowing a shooter to hold his rifle in correct alignment (without canting) on uneven ground.

Considerably more expensive is the Parker-Hale bipod, which originally was designed to support the World War II British Bren light machine gun. It's much more rugged than the Harris and pivots to avoid canting, but I've noticed a greater degree of flex in the Parker-Hale than in the Harris. An economically priced foreign copy of the Parker-Hale bipod is the Versa-Pod, which includes an adapter to install it on a swivel stud.

While visiting the U.S. Army's 7th Infantry

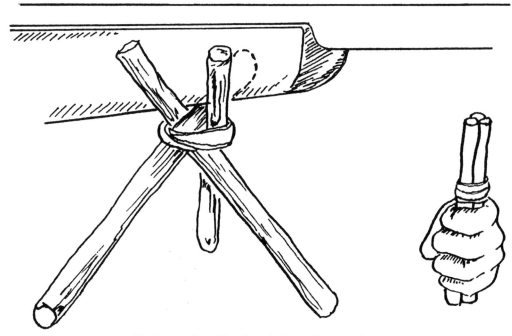

Field-expedient bipod made from three sticks.

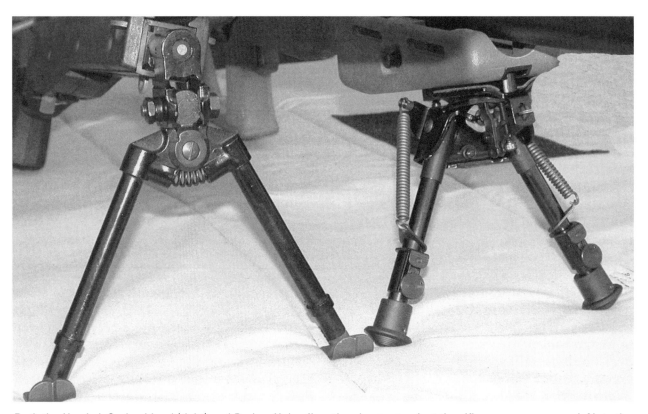

Both the Harris L Series bipod (right) and Parker-Hale allow the shooter to pivot the rifle on uneven ground. Note the wide spades on the Parker-Hale.

Division Sniper School in the mid-1980s, I found students learning to fabricate field-expedient bipods using three hand-cut sticks lashed together with parachute cord—which technically is a tripod. They used these as bipod substitutes in all shooting exercises, and they worked great.

The last bipod I'll address is one a sniper should *never* use—the old, stamped aluminum bipod issued for the M16 rifle. This spring-loaded support was clipped directly on the barrel—*horrors!*—and apparently improved shooting when firing full-auto, prone. These are still floating around, but please, be wise enough not to disrupt your barrel harmonics by clipping it on your sniper rifle.

Muzzle Brakes

I did not fully appreciate the effectiveness of a muzzle brake until repeatedly firing .50-caliber rifles. The first time I fired a .50, I was tensed up for a real jaw-shaking, something worse than a .458 Winchester Magnum elephant gun. Instead of roaring like a lion, however, that .50 purred like a kitten. The recoil was not even as strong as a .300 Winchester Magnum.

Part of the effect was attributable to the gun's weight—more than 30 pounds—though equally it resulted from an effective muzzle brake. Muzzle brakes come in an assortment of clamshell and wedge shapes or in the form of vents machined near the muzzle, but all deflect gases to "pull" a rifle forward, off the shooter's shoulder. Efficiency varies, but on average there's probably a 30 percent reduction in felt recoil. That's the good news.

The bad news is that by deflecting the muzzle blast, a brake also increases the rifle's report and generates quite a plume of dust. At Gunsite, braked rifles proved so loud (even on a .300 Winchester Magnum) that we could not position students on adjacent firing points to a brake-equipped shooter. Dr. William Kramer's Ball State University study of muzzle blasts found that adding a muzzle brake increases a rifle's acoustic energy *10 times*. Further, he learned that a muzzle brake's "initial sound"

shifts the blast to a lower 1,600 Hz pitch, a frequency especially uncomfortable for humans.

In combat a muzzle brake will increase a sniper's sound and visual signature, though these can be lessened by selecting a suitable Final Firing Position (FFP) and either wetting the ground or laying a cloth beneath the muzzle—but that doesn't always work, either. During a military firing demonstration, an instructor laid a poncho before the muzzle of Dr. Barry Kaplan, a friend and fellow Special Forces combat vet. When Kaplan fired his .50, that poncho *disintegrated* into a hundred pieces, so powerful was that muzzle blast. If I were designing a muzzle brake, I'd vent most of the gas upward. Some suppressors take this a step further and all but eliminate muzzle signature, even on heavy .50s.

Another kind of brake worth addressing is the Browning BOSS (Ballistic Optimizing Shooting System) which incorporates both a muzzle brake and a harmonic barrel tuner. Actually, the muzzle brake aspect—angled holes reminiscent of Magna-Porting—was an afterthought because the BOSS is really all about harmonic tuning. This muzzle brake—especially on low- and medium-powered cartridges such as the .223, .308, and 30.06—proved unnecessary and only made these rifles acoustically uncomfortable to shoot. To address this, Browning fielded a second BOSS version, the CR (Conventional Recoil), which lacks the muzzle brake.

The connection between barrel harmonics and accuracy has long been known though not well understood. In 1915, British sniping officer H. Hesketh-Prichard warned his men not to place bayonets on their sniping rifles "because the extra weight slows down the vibration" and would thereby "throw your shot 18 inches high at 200 yards' range." As explained concerning free-floating, upon firing a barrel vibrates like a tuning fork, which affects the bullet as it transits and exits the muzzle. Browning engineer Clyde Rose noticed that he could improve the accuracy of mediocre rifles by cutting off a bit of the barrel—and

The Browning BOSS harmonic tuner, without muzzle brake (above) and with the brake (below).

realized that, actually, he was "tuning" the harmonics. What if, he thought, you attached a highly adjustable barrel extender to a muzzle—you'd just crank it back and forth until you found the optimal harmonic length. *Eureka!*

Rose's device, the BOSS, offers micrometer-like adjustments, with 10 settings on each of 10 rotations—100 distinct barrel lengths to fine-tune harmonics. In essence, this is the opposite of what a handloader does: instead of tuning the load to the rifle, you're tuning the rifle barrel to the load. I tested the BOSS extensively and found that it worked superbly—yet it has not taken off like I thought it would. The ear-shattering reputation of the original muzzle brake version turned away some shooters, and it may be a bit too complex for others. However, I can assure you, the BOSS works.

Auxiliary Open Sights

Although the U.S. Army's M24 Sniper Weapon System includes the excellent Redfield/Palma International iron sight with 1/4 MOA windage and elevation adjustments, my personal inclination is to outfit a sniper rifle with an optical sight only. It's not that the Palma sight won't work or it's inaccurate; it's just that there's so much to learn and practice in mastering a rifle scope that I'd much rather have students not divert time from such critical training.

Some Special Ops friends would argue that optical sights can fail for a host of reasons, and they're right. But such failures are rare, and, face it, if your scope breaks you aren't going to continue your sniping mission. Either the mission will abort or you'll pick up an M16 and join your infantry brethren until another sniper rifle's available.

A police sniper, of course, would never attempt a critical shot after his scope was broken, both because of liability and the normal proximity of other police snipers who can take over the mission.

Still, I think it's just fine to have a simple fixed sight, like that on the Steyr SSG, and recognize that it's for emergency use in self-defense, not for sniping.

The Bolt Action

All things being equal, a bolt action is the most accurate action one can have on a rifle. Here's why.

In the early 1960s, I pooled money with my boyhood squirrel-hunting companions Joe Remarke and Vic Evaschuk to buy a single-shot, bolt-action .22 rifle. Our arrangement was that one of us stalked forward until he had a shot and then turned the rifle over to another. If you missed, it could be an hour before it was your turn again,

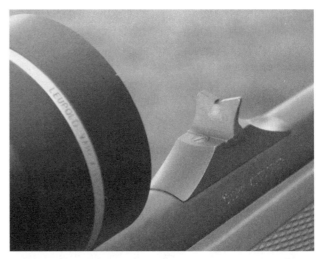

A simple fixed auxiliary sight, such as this one on a Steyr SSG, is an essential backup in case your scope's inoperable.

and any bushy-tail you saw during the interim laughed at your predicament. No unarmed boy likes being the butt of squirrel humor.

Seriously, though, shooting in such disciplined circumstances meant each shot counted and resulted in one squirrel bagged for each shot fired. It was phenomenal shooting.

A year or two later, when we all had part-time jobs, we purchased .22 automatics—Joe got a Ruger, Vic got a Browning, and I a Remington—and our shooting went to hell. We'd lost the mental focus required for one-shot hunting.

There's something psychological about bolting a rifle—a kind of finality, a bonding of spirit with task that isn't present with any other rifle action.

Bolting a rifle also results in seating a cartridge in a chamber more firmly and consistently than any other action. Think about how it feels when the locking lugs engage and your palm presses the bolt handle downward. That action doesn't just "move" into place, nor is it pushed there by spring action. No, as the bolt rotates downward, the action tenses and *locks* snugly. Provided the action is true and straight, this cannot help but lead to consistency, and remember that accuracy equals consistency and vice versa.

When it comes to the bolt being true and straight, this is one of the first areas for tuning. Quality bolt guns should have locking lugs lapped so they bear perfectly against mating surfaces. All lugs should be uniformly in contact

and the facing surfaces polished smooth. The bolt face is perfectly flat so that a seated cartridge is not wedged or twisted out of line in the chamber when its base rests against the bolt.

Behind that bolt face is the firing pin, and its performance, too, impacts directly on rifle accuracy. Lock time, which is the time that passes between your finger releasing the sear—"breaking the shot"—and the firing pin striking the primer, is a reflection of rifle quality. A fast lock time is needed so the rifle has no time to move between the instant you pull the trigger and a split-second later when it actually fires. Acceptable lock time results from bolt design and using proper lubricants. Lock times may vary from .0022 to .0057 of a second. The quality sniper rifles cited here have acceptable lock times.

AMERICAN BOLT-ACTION SNIPER RIFLES

There can be no question that America's most popular sniper rifle action is the Remington 700. In Vietnam, both Army and Marine snipers used heavy-barreled Remington 700s, a practice that continues to this day.

The USMC M40A3 represents the 700's latest evolution. Unlike its Vietnam grandfather, however, the newer version is hand-built by talented Marine technicians at Quantico's Precision Weapons Facility. Here they incorporate a Schneider match-grade stainless heavy barrel along with an epoxy-bedded

McMillan's M86 led the way for a whole field of .308 sniper rifles in the 1980s, with a composite stock, pillar bedding, and fine-tuned Remington action.

McMillan A-4 stock and Picatinny rail, which can accommodate day or night optics. The final product is 2 pounds heavier than the earlier version, with most rifles shooting better than 1 MOA.

The Army's M24 Sniper Weapon System, also based on the Remington 700, may look similar but there are many differences. To allow conversion to .300 Winchester Magnum, the Army rifle uses a long action even though most rifles are chambered for .308 (7.62x51mm). These guns, developed by Remington's John Rogers, incorporate an aluminum bedding block and an H.S. Precision stock adjustable for length. The NCOIC of the Army Sniper School, MSgt. Kurt Judson, says this rifle shoots so well that "it almost shoots itself." Remington is now marketing the M24 to police, either as a complete system or the rifle only. Recently Remington updated this rifle into the M24A2 configuration, which adds a rugged, detachable box magazine, oversize bolt knob, Picatinny rail, and optional suppressor, while also fitting it to a new adjustable stock.

Though both the Marine and Army rifles employ Harris bipods, and both systems use 10x fixed scopes with Bullet Drop Compensators (BDCs), the Army prefers the Leupold Mark 4 M3s while the Marines use the Unertl. In recent years, however, some Marine rifles have been topped by the AN/PVS-10 day/night scope as well as Leupolds.

Most U.S. police agencies I've instructed or worked with use Remington 700s—primarily

The USMC M40A3 uses the excellent McMillan A-3 adjustable stock, Harris bipod, and match-grade stainless barrel. Optics include this Unertl 10x, Leupold 10x, or sometimes the AN/PVS-10.

the company's own Model 700P (Police), although a few, like the Secret Service and U.S. Marshal's tactical team, have the more sophisticated Remington Model 40-XS tactical rifle. A standard Remington police rifle typically shoots about 1 MOA.

Many custom sniper rifle builders use the Remington 700 action—Robar, McMillan, AWC, H.S. Precision, and Brown Precision, to name a few. These rifles may resemble the "ordinary" 700, but they've been finely tuned for peak performance. Robbie Barrkman guarantees his SR-90 rifles to shoot 1/2 MOA when firing match-grade ammunition.

The only criticism I've encountered with Remington 700s concerns the extractor. Rumors abound that this thin, stamped metal blade is prone to failure, but despite owning a half-dozen 700s, shooting many others, and working with hundreds of police and military snipers, I have never encountered anyone who experienced such a failure. Still, just to ensure that this cannot happen, McMillan replaces the standard Remington bolt on its custom rifles with a Mauser-type bolt featuring a large claw extractor.

Although Marine sniper legend Carlos Hathcock accumulated his 93 kills using a Winchester Model 70 bolt-action, very few police or military snipers use this rifle today. Winchester does not market a special police sniper rifle, but a related company, FNH, recently began building a variety of high-end sniper rifles that use the Model 70 action. The FN A3G and FN A4 Shooting Systems use McMillan adjustable stocks, with the latter version selected by the FBI for its SWAT teams.

Savage Arms has developed tactical versions of its well-established 110 action, called the Law Enforcement Series. I purchased one of their early rifles in .223 and found it an honest 3/4 MOA rifle, quite an achievement for a modestly priced gun. More recently Savage has incorporated a McMillan or my own Choate stock along with their superb AccuTrigger to field a rifle that's surprisingly accurate at a very reasonable price. Though I receive no royalties, I'm delighted at this gun's performance. It was

The updated Remington M24A2 features a new adjustable stock, detachable magazine, and optional suppressor.

AWC custom-builds this copy of the USMC M40A2.

Along with a full line of custom rifles, Brown Precision produces this Tactical Elite rifle for police snipers.

The FN A4 Shooting System, used by FBI snipers, incorporates a tuned Winchester 70 action and the same McMillan stock as the USMC's M40A3.

Savage's police sniper rifle, the Model 10FPXPLEA, is acceptably accurate despite its moderate price.

recently selected as the New York State Police SWAT sniper rifle.

EUROPEAN BOLT-ACTION SNIPER RIFLES

Without question, the most prolific European-made sniper rifle is the Accuracy International AW. Not only is this excellent rifle the standard sniper weapon for the United Kingdom and a number of Commonwealth countries, it's been adopted by dozens of others, including Sweden and Spain. Designed by my friend, the late Malcolm Cooper, a two-time Olympic gold medal rifleman and nine-time world champion, this is a purpose-built sniper weapon of brilliant design. In contrast to the Remington 700, the AW action is largely squarish, which enabled Malcolm to simplify truing many inner mating surfaces. Further, the action is not bedded but permanently attached to a lengthy aluminum rail, simultaneously solving free-float and bedding issues. The clamshell stock simply screws down to this aluminum rail.

Fielded initially in Great Britain as the L96, it was upgraded after lengthy tests for the Swedish military, which led to the "AW" (Arctic Warfare) designation, though this version has become its standard model. An all-black version with a heavy 24-inch barrel, the AWP, is intended for police use. Both fire 7.62 (.308) ammunition. A similar AW rifle, the Super

The Accuracy International AW rifle in action in Iraq, here in the hands of British paras.

Magnum, is chambered for .300 Winchester Magnum, while upsized versions also exist in .338 Lapua Magnum and .50 caliber. Most of these rifles are supplied with excellent Schmidt & Bender scopes. All are tack-drivers, with my AWP shooting well under 1/2 MOA.

Somewhat similar is the Finnish-made Sako TRG-22, another .308 of skeletonized design. Like the AW, it incorporates a 10-round, detachable box magazine and two-stage target trigger. I fired its original version, the TRG-21, and found it superbly accurate, producing one ragged hole at 100 meters. There's also a larger version chambered for the .338 Lapua Magnum round, the TRG-42.

Sako's TRG-22 is a true world-class sniper rifle, yielding sub-MOA groups.

The Mauser SR93, too, is of skeletonized, minimalist design. Chambered in .300 Winchester Magnum or .338 Lapua Magnum, this sleek rifle employs a cast magnesium-aluminum frame covered where necessary by synthetic panels. Interestingly, it can be converted to fire left-handed. When I was Chief of Competition at the U.S. Military and Police Sniping Championships (the Super Sniper Shootout), a German SWAT team arrived with SR93s. They and their rifles fired impressively.

The Blaser R93 LRS2 tactical rifle is the last of our skeletonized designs. Based on the straight-pull Blaser Long-Range Sporter bolt gun, this action is extremely fast and chambered in .308, .300 Winchester Magnum, and .338 Lapua Magnum. One look tells you it's as free-floated as can be and readily adjustable for cheekrest height and stock length. The Blaser uses a five-round detachable magazine and a target-grade trigger.

Like any firearm bearing the name SIG-Sauer, the SSG 3000 is a fine, Swiss-designed weapon. Offering single- or two-stage triggers, a

The Accuracy International police variant, the AWP, mounts a heavier barrel than the AW.

A German police sniper team with a Mauser SR93 .300 Winchester Magnum rifle and (rear) Zeiss stabilized binoculars.

Blaser's LRS2 rifle offers an extremely fast, straight-pull bolt in .308 or .300 Winchester Magnum.

The Steyr SSG offers a lot of capability for its price. The SSG stock can be conveniently lengthened with rubber butt spacers.

wood-laminate or McMillan synthetic stock, and even a left-hand version, this rifle is chambered solely in .308. Like the Mauser SR93, the SIG has a black cloth heat shield above the barrel to block mirage-like thermal waves from distorting the scope's image.

When it was first manufactured in 1969, the Steyr SSG PI was the world's first synthetic-stocked centerfire production rifle. Since then, a host of SSG models have evolved, all incorporating the quality and accuracy of that first breakthrough rifle. The SSG PII, designed for police marksmen, features a larger, more easily manipulated bolt and heavier barrel. The SSG PIIK is identical, but with a shorter 20-inch barrel. The PII McMillan uses an American McMillan stock, and the PIV is especially threaded for a suppressor. The newest in the line, the SSG 04, is built on the SBS action and uses a 10-round magazine while also incorporating a Picatinny rail and adjustable cheekrest. All these SSGs are of very

high quality. What I especially like about my SSG PI is that it has the feel of a hunting rifle yet shoots 3/4 MOA or better.

SEMIAUTO SNIPER RIFLES

I have not been a great fan of semiautomatic sniper rifles, probably because of my youthful experience as a squirrel hunter. Knowing that you have a magazine full of rounds and all you have to do is pull the trigger again if you miss seems to promote what my good friend Frank Graves calls "half-assism."

This is an attitude problem, not a mechanical one, so while not blaming the weapon, we still cannot deny that the problem is real. A Special Ops friend who instructed sniping in the Mideast using the host country's Heckler & Koch PSG1 semiautos found he could best enhance student accuracy by requiring them to hand-feed each round. While instructing students armed with such semiauto

The SIG-Sauer SSG 3000 uses either this resin-impregnated stock or a McMillan. Note the tape-like heat shield over the barrel.

The Steyr SSG 04 incorporates a target trigger, Picatinny rail, adjustable stock, and SBS action.

The Steyr SSG PIV with suppressor installed.

"gas guns," I challenge them to fire one round per magazine, both to keep their minds focused and to get plenty of reloading practice. Except for exercises purposely structured to fire more than one round, I think that's an excellent habit.

But the challenge with semiauto sniper rifles goes beyond magazine capacity; it's a tuning matter as well. Because a semiauto has far more moving parts than a bolt action, gases at different pressures bled and diverted, and a host of spring tensions and sliding surfaces, it's just plain complicated to accurize one and keep it firing at match-grade quality.

The high cost of first-class gas guns—like the SR-25 or PSG1 or match-grade M1As—is not outlandish when you consider all the components it takes to squeeze that kind of performance out of so many moving parts. Still, there's been enough accumulated experience in tuning semiautos that this job is becoming better understood and more consistently achieved. One innovative step forward has been the introduction of titanium firing pins for match-grade AR-15s and SR-25s. Developed by Don Miner and made by Quality Machining of Sherwood, Oregon, a titanium firing pin—40 percent lighter than the steel pin it replaces—instantly improves lock time.

Mechanically, there are pros and cons when it comes to semiautos. On the plus side, there's an appreciable reduction of felt recoil due to the gas system and recoil springs. On the negative side, the gas system thrusts back the piston, operating rod, bolt carrier, and bolt, which suddenly shifts the center of balance rearward, then jerks it forward again, adding complexity to follow-through and recoil recovery. I think it takes a slightly different hold to control a semiauto as steadily as a bolt gun, a kind of "feel" you can only perfect through practice.

Refining these sniper versions of 7.62mm assault rifles requires all the modifications and close tolerances found in bolt guns, but with some additions. The trigger is replaced and all internal springs tuned or changed. Recoil springs are especially important since rounds must chamber with consistent pressure, just as your snugging down a bolt by hand causes consistent chambering. Further complicating accurizing is the fact that, due to the gas port and tube, many semiautos cannot be truly free-floated. The solution is to anchor anything that touches the barrel firmly so its harmonic vibrations at least are consistent.

Current Semiauto Sniper Rifles

America's Vietnam-era semiauto sniper rifle was based on the M14. Though much attention has been paid to the combat achievements of Remington 700s, M14-based sniper systems certainly have an equally impressive record.

In the open, flat expanses of the Mekong Delta, the U.S. Army's most accomplished Vietnam War sniper, Sgt. Adelbert F. Waldron III, exclusively used an XM21 System to account for a confirmed 113 enemy kills. The war's top Marine sniper—with 103 enemy KIA, 10 more than Carlos Hathcock—my longtime friend, Sgt. Chuck MaWhinney, often used an M14 with Starlight scope for night operations, during which he achieved more than 30 percent of his kills. One night Chuck used a PVS-2

Sgt. Adelbert F. Waldron III, the U.S. Army's top Vietnam sniper, takes aim with the XM21 with which he killed 113 enemy.

night scope on an M14 to pick off an entire file of North Vietnamese troops crossing a river, shooting 16 of them exactly as renowned World War I rifleman Alvin York had done—*back-to-front*—so the approaching enemy could not appreciate the deadliness of his fire.

It was an updated version of the XM21 system—the M25—with which Delta Force sniper MSgt. Gary Gordon engaged untold numbers of assaulting Somalis in Mogadishu in October 1993, killing "an undetermined number of attackers until he depleted his ammunition," according to his posthumous Medal of Honor citation. His spotter, Sgt. 1st Class Randall Shugart, went down shooting beside his sniper team leader, firing his M4 carbine to the bloody end.

M14-based sniper systems are found today in both the Army and Marine Corps. The USMC version is a basic M14 upgraded by Corps precision gun builders with a match-grade barrel, McMillan stock, plus fine-tuning to become the

The U.S. Army's Designated Marksman Rifle in Iraq. This model has a resin-impregnated stock and Leupold Mark 4 M3 scope, identical to the M24 system's scope.

The USMC Designated Marksman Rifle uses a McMillan synthetic stock and the same Leupold optic as Army sniper rifles.

Designated Marksman Rifle (DMR). There's one DMR-armed rifleman per infantry platoon.

The Army's version can be found either as an M21 or M25 system, with the latter adding a stainless match-grade barrel and synthetic stock. The original M21 uses a dense, resin-impregnated wooden stock. The ART scopes on both models have been replaced, either by the Leupold Mark 4 or AN/PVS-10.

Springfield Armory continues to build a high-quality version of the M21 based on their Super Match Rifle. Using a Hart, Krieger, or Douglas match-grade barrel and a stock featuring an adjustable cheekpiece, this rifle is employed by police agencies and military Special Ops units worldwide.

Whether a military-built gun or Springfield Armory product, I believe the DMR/M21/M25 is an ideal spotter's weapon because ballistically it matches the sniper's .308 bolt gun round;

adds a high-magazine capacity, rapid-fire capability to the team; and allows both shooters to share range and windage "dope." Further, I think it's just as suitable for police sniper teams as military ones.

That variety of semiauto 7.62mm sniper/spotter rifles certainly includes the excellent SR-25, manufactured by Knight's Armament. Designed by the legendary Eugene Stoner, the company guarantees the 24-inch-barreled SR-25 for 1 MOA accuracy. In recent years several updated SR-25 versions have evolved, with the 20-inch-barreled Mk 11 Mod 0 rifle adopted in 2000 by the U.S. Navy SEALs. To achieve high accuracy with this shorter, free-floated barrel, company engineers had to improve or change the

Springfield Armory's M25 rifle uses match-grade components and an adjustable synthetic stock.

The U.S. Army's latest M14-based rifle incorporates a Picatinny rail and telescoping stock.

firing pin, extractor, ejector, and buffer and re-engineer all moving parts. Like all SR-25s, the Mk 11 Mod 0 uses an Obermeyer match barrel. Knight's latest iteration, the Battle Rifle, incorporates an even shorter 14.5- or 16-inch barrel with chromed bore and chamber, a muzzle brake, and four-position M4 carbine-style buttstock. One variation replaces the standard 16-inch barrel with a match stainless one.

Knight's Armament is a serious contender for the U.S. Army's XM110 Semi-Auto Sniper

System (SASS) program, which calls for a match-grade, magazine-fed, 7.62mm weapon. The winning contractor will supply 30 rifles for evaluation, with an ultimate potential buy of 1,200 weapons, all destined for elements of the Special Ops community.

Remington, too, is competing for the SASS contract with a custom-built 7.62mm, semiauto designed by its military/law enforcement director, Michael Haugen. A retired Special Forces sniper school commandant, Haugen assembled the finest components from a number of subcontractors into a sophisticated gas gun that carries the Remington label. Considering these two entries, it's going to be a close competition. Haugen also contributed to his company's major updating of the M24 Sniper Weapon System.

Until Federal introduced its Tactical Load barrier-penetrating ammunition, I thought the

Designed by Eugene Stoner, the .308-caliber SR-25 is built by Knight's Armament.

The Navy SEAL version of the Knight's Armament SR-25, the Mk 11 Mod 0, with suppressor.

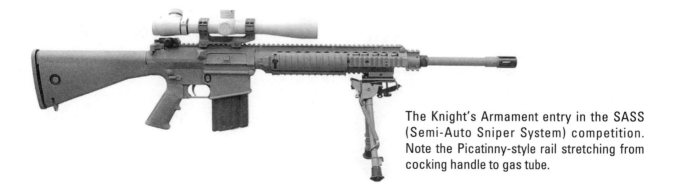

The Knight's Armament entry in the SASS (Semi-Auto Sniper System) competition. Note the Picatinny-style rail stretching from cocking handle to gas tube.

Remington's entry into the SASS competition is this skeletonized rifle that features components from a host of high-end manufacturers.

.223—although accurate—was too light for police snipers. That load, along with a great .223 ammo variety from Federal, Hornady, and Black Hills, has changed my mind. Recent advances in accurizing accessories and techniques—such as free-floating and true match-grade barrels—have given new life to AR-15-based sniper rifles. Virtually all these sniper-grade semiautos remove the front sight post and feature a flattop with a Picatinny rail. This lowered scope mount not only enhances stock-eye-scope alignment but brings the scope axis closer to the bore, thereby reducing parallax and improving the bullet's trajectory coincidence with the shooter's line of sight. To appreciate this, notice how little you must move a flashlight to follow your eyes when held to your cheek versus the dramatic shifts required if it's held at your waist. Dave Lauck of D&L Sports, a custom AR sniper rifle builder, provided the data in the box at right, which shows how profound is this improvement.

Sniper-grade ARs are built by a host of companies, including, of course, Colt, along with Olympic Arms and DPMS, to name a few. Colt particularly markets its free-floated, flattop

Accurized Rifle to law enforcement agencies.

European semiauto sniper rifles are not as numerous as a decade ago for a number of reasons, mostly having to do with the Continent's armies shifting to a new generation of bullpup-size assault rifles that don't do well as sniper variants. One major exception is the Swiss-designed SIG SSG 550 Sniper, chambered in 5.56mm. Adopted by the Swiss army and several European police agencies, the SSG 550 Sniper has a finely tuned action, match-grade barrel, adjustable stock, and two-stage target trigger.

The only semiauto .300 Winchester Magnum sniper rifle I've encountered is the Arms

---

AR-15 BULLET PATH COMPARISON *

Distance	Handle Mount	Flat Mount
100 yds	+3.0"	+1.0"
150 yds	+4.9"	+0.9"
200 yds	+5.6"	-0.4"

* 69-gr. Sierra MatchKing bullet

The Colt Accurized Rifle features a stainless, match-grade, free-floated barrel, target trigger, and Picatinny-type flattop.

The SIG SSG 550 Sniper is a match-grade, highly tuned .223/5.56mm rifle. It's used by a number of European police agencies and the Swiss army.

This .300 Winchester Magnum semiauto from Arms Tech, the Super Match Interdiction Rifle, is built on the Browning BAR rifle action.

Tech Super Match Interdiction Rifle. Custom-built in Phoenix, Arizona, it incorporates a highly modified Browning auto action, heavy match-grade 26-inch stainless barrel, and McMillan A-2 stock. The resulting weapon, with scope and bipod, weighs more than 13 pounds. This rifle saw combat action in Somalia in 1993 and was well regarded by the

Special Ops shooters who used it. The great thing about this rifle is that it fires that powerful .300 Winchester Magnum round to sniper-quality accuracy, and it's quick for follow-on shots. I particularly like that it employs a sturdy, detachable magazine.

TAKEDOWN SNIPER RIFLES

My personal experience with takedown sniper rifles is the Sauer 200, a high-quality German bolt gun no longer available. This rifle typically showed a bullet impact shift of 1/4 MOA (surprisingly good) when reassembled, but that was a brand-new rifle having all its mating edges still crisp.

A Special Ops sniper friend I deeply respect shared with me his opinion of takedown rifles, of which he had more experience. He suggested that eventual wear must degrade the exact mating of threads and surfaces and tensions. We speculated about the differences in barrel harmonics, as well as the recoil effect on hex screws imperfectly torqued. All that's required to shift point of impact 0.7 MOA is a hair-thin 0.001 inch (one-thousandth of an inch!) variance between your crosshair and the bore. Just realize that such variances become *cumulative* when you reinstall a barrel and reattach a scope, and each time it's assembled/disassembled/reassembled the edges must wear a bit.

Our conclusion was that any takedown rifle inherently involves some accuracy trade-offs, but the key is focusing on its special-purpose rationale, such as a counterterrorist operation in which a sniper's presence must not be disclosed prior to taking the shot. In this respect, high-quality takedown rifles, such as those shown here, can be a mission-essential weapon. As with most exotic weapons, just remember that a takedown rifle is a supplement—not a substitute—for its more conventional equivalent.

The H.S. Precision Pro-Series Take-Down rifle kit contains interchangeable .308 and .300 Winchester Magnum barrels and bolts in a custom, high-impact, mil-spec case. Like all H.S. Precision rifles, it's an accurized Remington 700 action built on one of the company's excellent adjustable-length stocks.

Accuracy International offers a takedown version of its superb AW .308 rifle—the Covert—so compact that it fits in an ordinary-looking airline case. With the Covert's integral suppressor, is it any wonder that it comes from the land of James Bond?

The AWC Model 91 BDR (Breakdown Rifle), too, is supplied with its own luggage case. It incorporates a quality McMillan stock that disassembles at the pistol grip so that the barrel need not separate from the scope or action.

H.S. Precision's takedown rifle is a well-engineered special-purpose weapon.

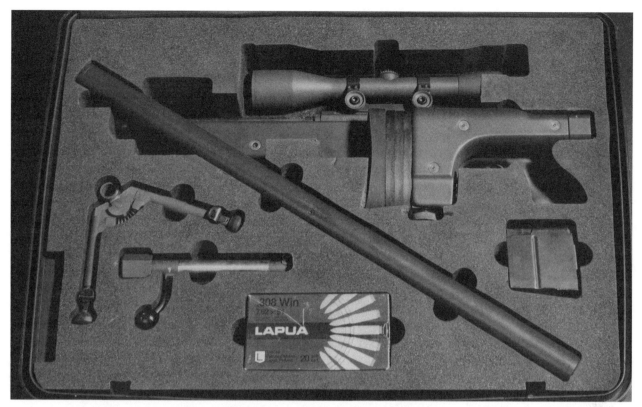

Fitted snuggly into its case, this AW Covert rifle has a barrel-length suppressor.

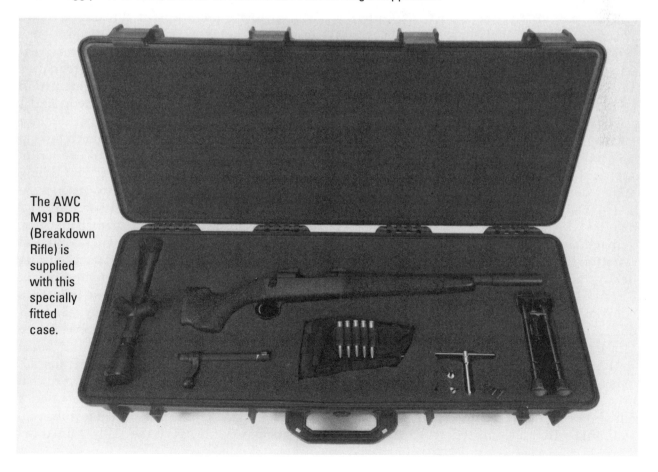

The AWC M91 BDR (Breakdown Rifle) is supplied with this specially fitted case.

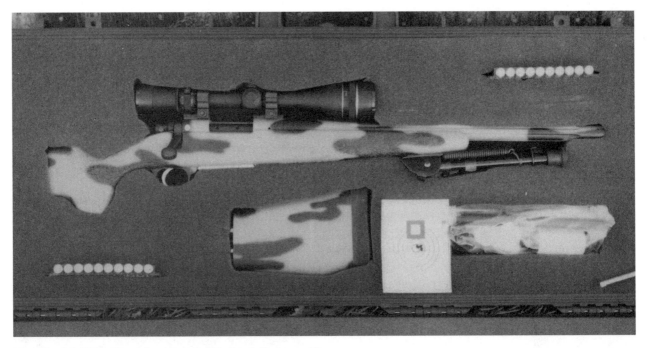

Dave Lauck (D&L Sports) custom-builds this takedown rifle.

Dave Lauck at D&L Sports of Gillette, Wyoming, builds a similar takedown rifle, easily stowed, with a 20-inch barrel. Like the AWC rifle, it ensures zero retention by not separating the action or scope from the barrel.

SUPPRESSED SNIPER RIFLES

The only time I ever shot a man with a suppressed weapon was in April 1969. Our SOG recon team, RT Illinois, had been inserted in Cambodia 30 minutes after one of the heaviest B-52 strikes of the war to assess damage to the enemy's secret cross-border sanctuaries. The target was the suspected headquarters of the NVA 27th Infantry Regiment. This was part of the "secret bombing" for which Henry Kissinger was later criticized. Of course, I thought it was a splendid idea and still do.

The North Vietnamese soldiers who managed to survive this aerial bombardment, however, thought it a terrible idea, and— Kissinger and the B-52 crews not being available—they attempted to convey their feelings to we members of RT Illinois. The ensuing firefight was horrific.

While our team leader, Ben Thompson, led two badly wounded Vietnamese mercenaries and the rest of the team toward an extraction landing zone, teammate George Bacon and I delayed the assaulting North Vietnamese in a series of short ambushes. In addition to tossing grenades, George and I took turns peppering our pursuers with small-arms fire, he riddling them with 5.56mm from his CAR-15 and me "ppfff-fff-tt-ting" at them with a suppressed 9mm Karl Gustav Swedish K submachine gun. When George fired, the NVA sought cover and slowed down, but when I let loose, it had no effect. They had no idea I was shooting at them. This lack of muzzle blast proved a psychological disadvantage, but my weapon's ballistic shortcomings soon proved even more hazardous.

As we finally burst across our extraction LZ to rejoin the team, our exfil aircraft arrived. No sooner was our perimeter complete when a North Vietnamese soldier appeared less than 20 yards from me, his AK at the ready. I lifted my

This AWC M92 rifle is fitted with a Spectrum 2000 suppressor.

Factory-suppressed version of the AW rifle.

Swedish K and let him have it with a full burst of 9mm ball. I was absolutely certain I hit him, center-chest. He collapsed unnaturally, falling forward in knee-deep grass.

Moments later a Huey slid into the LZ, and I rushed forward to secure the clearing while our wounded were hurried aboard. In particular, I was careful to cover the spot where the NVA had fallen and ran almost directly over it—and found to my horror that he'd crawled away, even taking his AK with him.

Fortunately we escaped through moderate groundfire, but I had learned an important combat lesson: avoid employing a specialized weapon for a purpose other than that for which it was intended. I'd brought along the Swedish K in hopes that if we came upon a small party of disoriented or injured bombing survivors, I could dispatch all but one and we'd take him prisoner. Accurate, dependable, and outfitted with an effective suppressor, the Swedish K was ideal for that role. But a suppressed 9mm submachine gun is a terrible choice for a running gunfight, especially taking into account its degraded terminal ballistics.

This observation applies equally to suppressed sniper rifles: they have a definite place in military and some law enforcement arsenals, but their usefulness is limited and their employment must be weighed in light of their restricted capabilities.

Current Suppressors and Suppressed Rifles

Some truly excellent suppressors and suppressed sniper rifles have been perfected in recent years and are much finer devices than those we used on covert operations in Southeast Asia. True, we had effective suppressors for our pistols and submachine guns, but suppressing a pistol-size round was not nearly so challenging as silencing a powerful assault rifle cartridge. (Note that no device actually silences a weapon; hence we say they're "suppressed" to some extent rather than silenced.) In the 1960s, a suppressor effective enough to quiet an assault rifle would have exploded from the tremendous pressure generated by these cartridges. We tested a few such devices, but none proved effective at quieting a .308 weapon.

Another traditional problem with rifle suppressors was their clumsy size, adding 15 inches or more to a barrel—it felt like you were carrying a spear. Further, mounts or adapters sometimes worked loose, shifting the zero for no obvious reason.

Those problems are a thing of the past.

This AWC Spectrum 90 suppressor can be fitted to a host of rifles, from .22LR to .300 Winchester.

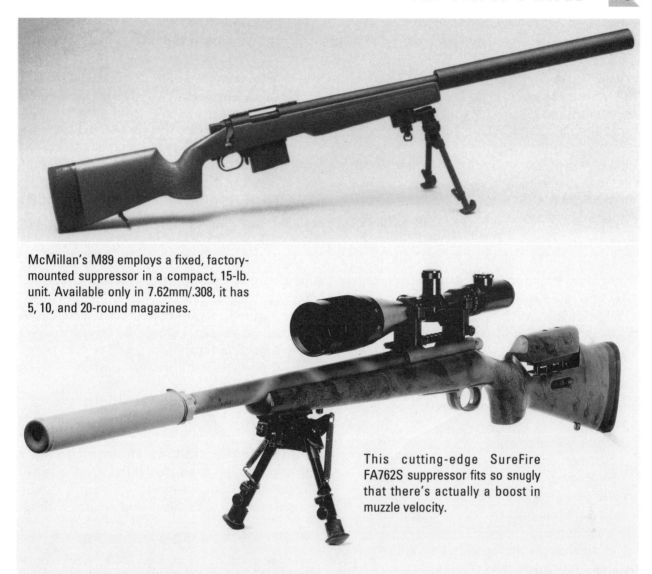

McMillan's M89 employs a fixed, factory-mounted suppressor in a compact, 15-lb. unit. Available only in 7.62mm/.308, it has 5, 10, and 20-round magazines.

This cutting-edge SureFire FA762S suppressor fits so snugly that there's actually a boost in muzzle velocity.

Modern designs have reduced suppressor size even as they have boosted their efficiency. Arizona-based AWC offers a line of compact rifle suppressors for bolt guns and semiautos, including the M14/M21. I fired these AWCs extensively at Gunsite and found them of very high quality. Gemtech's Tactical Precision Rifle Suppressor is designed specifically for the .308/7.62mm, offering either a threaded mount or Gemtech's own Bi-Lock quick-detach mounting system.

New to this high-end suppressor business is SureFire, the respected makers of tactical lights and gear. Its FA762S Fast Attach suppressor is cutting edge, with a fit so snug that it actually boosts muzzle velocity by 30–50 fps. Depending on how these suppressors attach, all offer the possibility of improving harmonics and thereby potential accuracy. Of equal interest, these compact units—8 to 10 inches long—pretty well eliminate muzzle flash.

How effectively do suppressors reduce muzzle report? The chart on page 70 cites the results of a firing test of several suppressors by Al Paulson for *S.W.A.T. Magazine*. To fully appreciate what Paulson's decibel (dB) readings mean, understand that, like earthquakes, decibels are measured in orders of magnitude: a 70 dB sound is not twice as loud as 35 dB—but *a thousand times* louder! Therefore, the

DECIBEL READINGS FOR SUPPRESSED SNIPER RIFLES

Rifle/Suppressor	NATO Ball Normal/Suppress	Fed. Match Normal/Suppress	Sako Subsonic Normal/Suppress
McMillan M89 w/ AWC	168 dB/136 dB	168 dB/136 dB	156 dB/122 dB
Remington M700 w/ Ciener	168 dB/138 dB	168 dB/138 dB	157 dB/126 dB
Vaime SSR Mk2	168 dB/149 dB	168 dB/149 dB	157 dB/135 dB

SOURCE: Al Paulson, *S.W.A.T. Magazine.*

McMillan 89's suppressed measurement of 136 dB, a reduction of 32 dB, was only 1/1,500th the noise originally heard. When subsonic ammunition was fired the reduction was even better, cutting the report to 1/2500th the sound of a normal 7.62mm shot.

To put these decibel levels in perspective, compare them to common sounds:

Light Whisper	30 dB
Normal Voice	60 dB
Jet Engine	100 dB
.22 Pistol	148 dB
12-ga. Shotgun	156 dB

Note that all three rifles and suppressors generate much less noise than even the .22 LR pistol, with about 100 times less noise for the AWC system.

While a suppressor reduces muzzle report, it has long been realized that a truly quiet weapon must fire subsonic ammunition. In order to eliminate the bullet's sonic boom—heard as a loud "crack" downrange—it must have a muzzle velocity less than 1,080 fps, the speed of sound at sea level. Jeff Hoffman, president of Black Hills Ammunition and a former SWAT officer, has extensively tested his subsonic .308 loads—the only factory subsonic rifle ammo made in America—and concluded that a 1:8 barrel twist best stabilizes these projectiles.

However, by eliminating the bullet's crack and firing it through baffles that bleed off gases, you've changed your rifle's performance. Indeed, a good friend observed, "A suppressed sniper rifle is an oxymoron—a contradiction in terms."

Ballistically, as we'll see, he's correct.

Isaac Newton Was Right

When Isaac Newton observed, "For every action there's an opposite but equal reaction," he could have been talking about installing a suppressor on a sniper rifle. You cannot effectively reduce something so physically dramatic as a rifle's blast and report without

Subsonic loads are required for truly quiet suppressed fire, with Black Hills the only U.S. maker of this specialized ammo.

some kind of trade-off, in this case significantly reduced ballistic performance. Bluntly put: you will not be able to shoot as accurately, nor with nearly the terminal ballistics, nor as far as with a normal sniper rifle.

To start with, even if you're firing full-power ammunition—not subsonic—the combination of a shorter barrel and suppressor will degrade accuracy and reduce the bullet's kinetic energy. The marvelous SSG, for instance, will lose about 200 fps velocity due to the shortened barrel, with a resulting energy decline of 15 percent, or 373 foot-pounds. This slower initial velocity will cause the bullet to plunge earlier and more drastically than otherwise, changing your ballistic tables and knocking any Bullet Drop Compensator (BDC) out of synch with the bullet's true trajectory. For instance, a Federal .308 Match 168-grain fired through a 16.5-inch barrel will hit a target 10 inches lower at 500 yards than will the same bullet fired through a full-size SSG.

Equally important but less objectively measurable are the effects on accuracy of firing a match-grade round through a suppressor. Installing a suppressor adds variables to your rifle: the way in which the bullet travels down the suppressor, as contrasted with how it travels down the barrel; internal ballistic issues on bullet acceleration and stability from a short barrel; and changes in how the suppressor handles blast/gas as carbon and heat transform it internally the more you shoot it. Having not tested these factors myself, I'm hesitant to cite an acceptable standard except to say that a suppressed sniper rifle that fires 1 MOA or better would be a most impressive weapon.

But what about firing subsonic ammo? It should be obvious that reducing a 168-grain bullet's velocity from 2,600 fps to 1,050 fps will degrade the round's trajectory, while the slower speed dramatically reduces the round's muzzle energy from 2,521 foot-pounds to a mere 390 foot-pounds.

To visualize what this means, realize that this terminal effect is similar to that of *a .45*

automatic pistol! That's right, your 168-grain subsonic bullet's trajectory, energy, and penetration are comparable to handgun performance. This means your maximum effective range while firing subsonic ammo is probably 100 yards for head shots, with energy now below 300 foot-pounds. At that distance, you will not be able to penetrate an opponent's body armor.

"Well," you tell yourself, "then I'll just fire full-velocity ammo and accept that there will be a supersonic crack." That's not really a solution either. Lacking subsonic 5.56mm ammo, Medal of Honor recipient Franklin Miller and I experimented with a suppressed M16 in SOG because we'd been told that despite this crack, the suppressor would still confuse the enemy about a firer's location. The only place that proved true was behind the weapon; from anywhere within 45 degrees of the shooter's front, that high-velocity crack told us his approximate location. Neither of us ever carried it on a mission.

A 1992 Finnish government study scientifically confirmed our experiment. Firing full-velocity loads at 128 meters from a .308's muzzle, it was found that "suppressed and unsuppressed [decibel] levels in front of the rifle were rather close to each other," although "to the side the sound levels were significantly reduced." I think had we and the Finns continued this testing at greater range—over 300 yards, perhaps—we'd have found it more difficult to discern the shooter's location.

SSK Guns and Whisper Ammunition

Facing these ballistic limitations, it occurred to J.D. Jones that instead of bemoaning the lowered lethality of subsonic ammo, the solution was to make beefier projectiles. His company, SSK Industries, developed a special cartridge, the .300 Whisper, that propels a heavy, 240-grain bullet just below the speed of sound. It may be subsonic, but that heavy slug crashes into a target like the proverbial thrown brick, while its overall case length is short enough to feed in a modified M16/AR-15 action.

J.D. Jones of SSK Industries designed these Whisper cartridges for tremendous impact despite subsonic velocity. (L-R) The .300 Whisper with 240-grain bullet, .300 Whisper with armor-piercing bullet, and .338 Whisper with .300-grain bullet.

Thus, instead of a suppressed sniper rifle delivering .45-caliber pistol performance, SSK's subsonic .300 Whisper, Jones says, "delivers more energy more accurately than any existing subsonic round at 200 yards." His rifles shoot 1 MOA, with a suppressed .300 Whisper M16 upper so compatible that a sniper can convert an ordinary M16 and be ready to fire in moments. Cor-Bon Ammunition offers a variety of subsonic and high-velocity SSK loads.

With the success of his .300 Whisper, Jones has expanded the SSK line to include larger cartridges in .338 and .50 calibers, which will be addressed in Chapter 9 on heavy rifles.

Suppressed Rifle Employment

For all its ballistic shortcomings, there are still tactical situations in which a suppressed sniper rifle is a welcome tool. The most obvious use is eliminating sentries, especially during a hostage rescue, such as when Americans were held in Iran in 1979–1980. Had Delta Force reached the U.S. Embassy compound in Tehran, suppressed sniper rifles could have removed gate guards without alerting other terrorists until the rescuers had penetrated the embassy grounds. There were usable firing positions in facing buildings within 150 yards so that even subsonic rounds could have been used.

A more conventional military role involves precisely but quietly eliminating all kinds of terrorists and their helpers while concealing the presence of friendly snipers, whether taking out roadside bombers, lookouts near a terrorist training camp, or trackers following a recon team in the Hindu Kush. In all these scenarios, though, I don't think I'd want a fixed suppressor but rather a removable one to employ with subsonic rounds only when needed.

It's difficult to imagine a law enforcement situation in which a suppressed sniper rifle would be a benefit. A hostage rescue or recapture of a key facility from terrorists such as a nuclear plant may require eliminating foes silently. But the elite lawmen who would execute such an exotic operation—the FBI Hostage Rescue Team or special counterterrorist teams under the Department of Homeland Security— certainly have every piece of gear you can imagine, including suppressed weapons. Some local or state law enforcement agencies may choose to add such rifles to their arsenals, but I doubt they'd have much need for them.

But here's the major exception: suppressed rifles in .22LR caliber. It's not uncommon on high-risk warrant operations at drug residences to encounter attack dogs purposely positioned to delay the entry team and alert the drug dealers so they can flush or destroy evidence. A .22 rifle with suppressor can really do the trick here, silently depriving the bad guys of their "early warning" system. Perhaps even more

Firing a suppressed .308, I was impressed by this AWC device's compact size—fewer than 8 inches.

Bernalillo County, New Mexico, Deputy Erik Little's suppressed Ruger 10/22 generates less noise than snapping your fingers.

As quiet as it gets: an AWC-suppressed Ruger 77/22 bolt gun. Unlike a semiauto, no gas escapes through the action.

often, there could be a need to eliminate street lights to conceal the approach of an entry team, and again, a suppressed .22 could do that with minimal concern about overpenetration or lack of a backstop to catch the bullet.

I'm aware of several police agencies that have acquired .22-caliber rifles with suppressors, mostly installed on Ruger 10/22 semi-autos and 77/22 bolt actions. Reportedly these rifles have a suppressed noise level of about 124 dB, compared to 148 dB for an unsuppressed .22 pistol.

Ultimately, I believe that *every* military sniper will have a suppressor of some kind on his rifle, both to confuse the enemy as to his location and to allow him to engage targets without alerting other nearby hostile forces.

RIFLE MAINTENANCE

When it comes to maintenance of a sniper-quality rifle, you'll find more "don'ts" than with any other weapon. It isn't that sniper rifles are fragile; it's just that seemingly minor factors in lubrication, cleaning, and general maintenance can degrade the fine accuracy that distinguishes a sniper-grade weapon. As in so many other areas, your extra attention to detail yields superior performance.

Here's the most important "don't": unless you have a torque wrench, do not remove the receiver/barrel from the stock or attempt to fiddle with the torque screws holding it together. The precision shooting platform we call a sniper rifle fits together so exactly that even a few inch-pounds of torque may shift a bullet's point of impact.

Cleaning Tools

The U.S. Army has been issuing segmented steel rifle rods since World War I, which implies that these are suitable tools for cleaning any rifle. But that hard steel on a segmented rod should *never* be used on a sniper rifle because its hard edges can nick the throat, that spot just forward of the chamber where a bullet first bites into the rifling. Instead, use a one-piece rod of polymer, fiberglass, aluminum, or nylon-coated, which is softer than the steel of your bore. Flexible cable pull-through rods are not suited to military operations since they cannot force an obstruction from your barrel. Carry to the field a segmented aluminum rod to remove blockages.

Even when using a soft rod, employ a bore guide, a hollow polymer device that fits in your receiver when your bolt's removed. It will correctly align your rod so it strokes smoothly across the throat and into your bore, precluding damage to the front edges of your rifling.

To clean your chamber, use a .45-caliber copper brush and, likewise, use relatively soft .30-caliber copper brushes on your bore. Stainless steel brushes unnecessarily wear the throat and bore. Watch how a brush wears, and replace it as soon as the front bristle tips become mashed, as these are the bristles that do 90 percent of the cleaning. Some solvents may dissolve copper brushes, which can be stopped by rinsing them with rubbing alcohol after use. It's acceptable to use an eyehole rod tip to hold your patches, although rifle purists prefer a jag-style tip.

A good toothbrush, pipe cleaners, and a dentist's pick complete your cleaning tools.

Lubricants and Solvents

Epoxy-bedded rifles require special concern while cleaning because solvents can seep into the receiver area and transform that iron-hard material into a gummy mess. Thus, when cleaning the bore on an epoxy-bedded rifle, keep the muzzle lower than the receiver so any excess solvent runs out the barrel, not into the bedding. Some shooters go a step further and brace their rifles upside down during cleaning, making it impossible for solvent to come in contact with the lower receiver. This is not an issue for rifles having aluminum block bedding, such as the Army's M24.

Rifle maintenance involves three different kinds of liquids: solvents to remove powder and leading and copper; lubricants to allow mating surfaces to slide smoothly; and rust preventatives primarily for external, nonworking surfaces. Several products claim to do all of these tasks, and some shooters swear by them. The only substance, I think, that comes close to that is Break Free, and even it does not remove copper.

A few old-timers I respect advise using only one substance for each of these tasks and then ensuring it does it well. For instance, to clean carbon and gunk from your bore, use a really good bore cleaner such as Hoppe's #9. To remove copper and gilding metal residue, there are several ammonia-based cleaners, with Sweet's 7.62 and Shooter's Choice the most common brands.

For a lubricant, I personally like one that has bits of Teflon or graphite in liquid, of which there are several brands. Just ensure you have a true

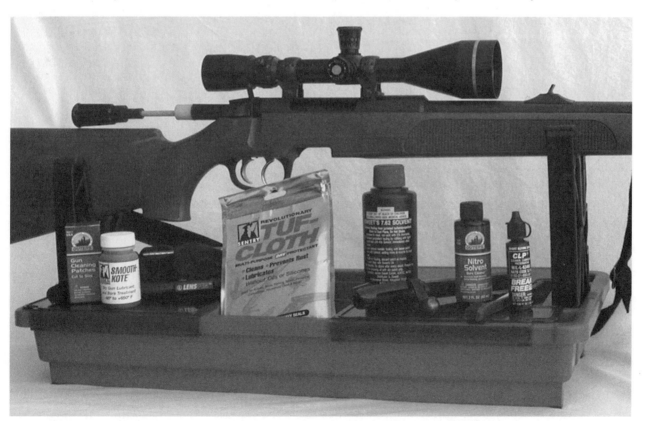

The variety of solvents and lubricants that maintain a sniper-grade rifle. Note bore guide and one-piece rod.

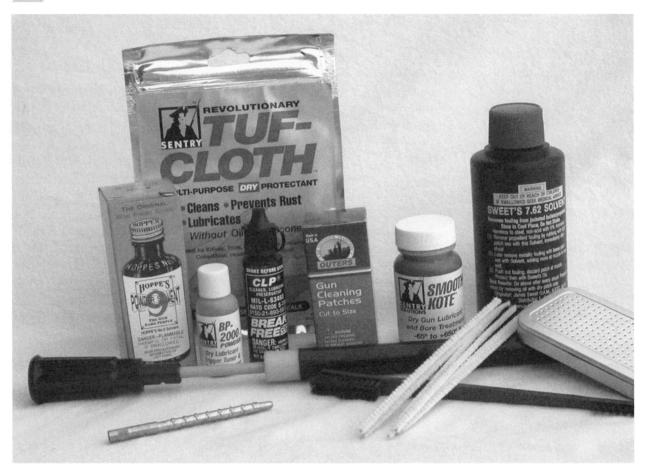

Along with high-tech moly-coating lubricant and a patch jag (foreground), a sniper needs copper solvent, such as Sweet's 7.62 (right).

lubricant, not a combination solvent and lubricant. However, any quality gun oil, such as Rem Oil, will do this job. That high-quality oil serves as a rust preventative, too. In fact there are many good rust inhibitors, natural and synthetic.

In the dry desert and dusty climes of Iraq and Afghanistan, powder-fine dust is an everyday hazard. Probably the best dry lubricant I've come upon is Smooth-Kote and its related cloth applicator, Tuf-Cloth. They're suited for sub-zero cold, too, because they're all but immune to thickening at low temps. What's especially impressive is that Smooth-Kote molecularly bonds to metal, leaving a layer of molybdenum disulfide particles that lasts a long time, almost permanently. Smooth-Kote and Tuf-Cloth work so well that they belong in every sniper's kit.

The only item I'd add is a packet of granulated silica gel for insertion in your rifle case. This packet pulls moisture from the air and helps protect your rifle against damage from dampness. The best types are those that can be reactivated by drying them in an oven. But I warn—do *not* store your rifle in its case. That sponge-like foam cushioning too easily retains moisture and can quickly rust a quality firearm.

Cleaning Techniques

To begin, clear the barrel channel, that 1/8-inch gap around the barrel, by sliding a cloth down it somewhat shoeshine fashion. All you're doing is ensuring that no debris is in contact with the barrel. Follow by wiping the synthetic stock with a damp cloth until it's clean. If it's necessary to use detergent, rinse and wipe that away completely, too.

Next, remove the bolt. At least once a year detail-strip the bolt and clean all components, then treat with Smooth-Kote as an effective, dry lubricant. If you've never disassembled your bolt, have an armorer talk you through it. This annual cleaning is important to prevent dirt or gummy lubricant from degrading your bolt's lock time.

During ordinary maintenance, wipe the bolt clean and pay special heed to its face, where grit and tiny bits of brass can accumulate. Pay close attention to the extractor and use your toothbrush to get behind it.

Before cleaning the chamber and bore, position an epoxy-bedded rifle so solvent will not seep down into the lower receiver. Then use a .45-caliber bore brush dipped in powder solvent—Hoppe's #9 is perfect—to clean the chamber. Rotate the brush *sideways*, not back and forth, a good eight or 10 turns. Be sure to get into the locking lug recesses in the receiver ring. Use patches to remove the solvent.

Next, insert the bore guide and begin cleaning the bore with a .30-caliber copper bore brush on a one-piece plastic, aluminum, or fiberglass rod. Emphasis here—do not damage the throat, where your bullet first encounters the rifling. *Always* insert the rod from the breech, through the bore guide. And be sure to pour powder solvent on the brush instead of dipping the brush in the bottle to avoid contaminating the solvent.

The U.S. Marine Corps recommends 20 strokes to clean carbon from a bore, adding more solvent if necessary. Be sure that the brush completely protrudes from the muzzle before pulling it back during each stroke. Now you're ready to run patches.

Now we get tricky. Run patches *only one way*, from the chamber to the muzzle—the same direction the bullet travels—and each time the patch exits the muzzle, *remove the dirty patch*, pull the empty rod back, attach a new patch, and repeat. Why? To ensure that all the gunk, carbon, and solvent are pushed completely out

the bore, with none inadvertently dropped into the receiver. Keep running fresh patches until one comes through clean.

Although it seems your bore is clean, it still contains traces of bullet jacket copper. Using a patch soaked with Sweet's 7.62 or another copper solvent, stroke the entire bore several times, then allow 10 minutes for it to dissolve the accumulated copper. Now run patches chamber to muzzle, just like before. On these patches you'll find tiny, almost microscopic bits of copper or vague green stains. Keep running patches until they come through clean. Finish by removing the ammonia with a patch containing Hoppe's #9, then one more patch containing light oil or Break Free.

A special note on copper solvents: some competitive shooters, as well as custom rifle builders, recommend cleaning copper after every five or 10 rounds. This involves only a patch with copper solvent and a few strokes, then running clean patches until one comes through clean, and one more patch with Hoppe's #9 to remove the ammonia residue. Follow this regimen and you'll get peak performance from your rifle.

End your routine by thoroughly cleaning the receiver interior using patches with powder solvent or Break Free, and wipe until all carbon is removed. Here's where pipe cleaners and that toothbrush will come in handy, especially if the rifle is a semiauto with many nooks and crannies.

Sometimes a rifle bore seems to resist coming clean, especially if it's coming out of storage or has gone a long time without proper maintenance. That's when a USMC three-day cleaning regimen suggests cleaning it each day as cited above, then plugging the muzzle with a cork and leaving the chamber soaking in powder solvent overnight. That's as clean as a bore can get.

Lubrication and Rust Protection

When last we looked at it, your bore was totally clean but dry. Now, run one last clean patch with oil down it, chamber to muzzle, leaving a thin coat of oil inside. This is for protection against rust.

Indeed, to add one final touch of consistency—especially for police snipers—when you depart for the field or arrive on-scene during a call-out, run one more dry patch down the bore, both to remove any accumulated dust and ensure there's uniformity in your cold-bore (first) shot from the rifle.

To treat a bore with Smooth-Kote, begin with a clean, dry bore. Further degrease it with rubbing alcohol, running patches until they come clean. Put Smooth-Kote liquid on a patch, thoroughly coat the bore, and then allow it to dry for two hours. The manufacturer says this long-lasting, submicron coating of molybdenum disulfide will fill imperfections, making your bore so "slick" that future cleaning is dramatically easier, with less copper buildup. Though not quantified, usually there's some accuracy improvement as well. I don't think there's enough experience yet for firm guidance on this, but snipers who've served in Iraq tell me Smooth-Kote works great, although a few "old hands" think the resulting reduction in fouling encourages riflemen not to clean their bores often enough.

To lubricate internal working surfaces, always use the minimum because it will attract dust like a magnet. Every mating, sliding surface needs lubrication.

For rust protection, wipe a thin layer of oil on all external metal surfaces, so thin that it does not feel wet to the touch. Or you can protect exterior surfaces with a moly-impregnated Tuf-Cloth, which dries in a few minutes.

Follow these procedures and your rifle won't merely operate trouble-free, it will also stay a tack-driver for 10,000 rounds.

CHAPTER 3

SNIPERSCOPE BASICS

THE SNIPER'S RIFLE SCOPE

Some serious shooters desire every bit of proven technology that can be packed into one scope, an attitude I won't criticize unless you're trying to substitute technology for good training. You cannot buy ability no matter the size of your checkbook.

On the other hand, some of my Special Operations friends vehemently declare that to be reliable, a scope must be stripped of everything but the most fundamental features. The more gizmos you add, the more things there are to break or malfunction.

There's no absolute answer to this controversy, just the need to recognize that there's more than one school of thought, and you should carefully consider every feature you want in a rifle scope.

Magnification: What Power?

While it may seem advantageous to use a powerful rifle scope—say, 20x—realize that disadvantages accompany higher magnification. After about 12x mirage can be a problem, especially for afternoon shooting when thermals start to shimmer on the earth. Instead of clearly seeing your target, it flickers in rippling waves of light.

Another problem with high magnification is the accompanying narrower field of view. At 50 yards, a 20x scope offers only a 3-foot field of view, so narrow that if you had to fire close-range in self-defense you probably couldn't even find your foe. A 10x fixed power scope—as found on U.S. Army and Marine Corps sniper rifles—yields twice that field of view, or 6 feet at 50 yards. Target clarity in low-light conditions, too, suffers with a high-magnification scope.

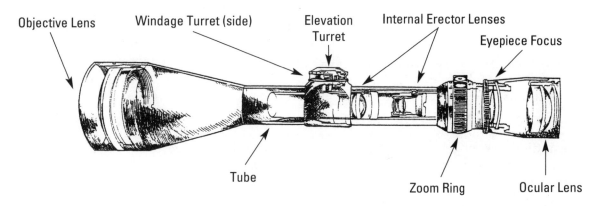

A typical modern scope, the Leupold Vari-X III.

Thus, if you're outfitted with a fixed-power scope, 10x is probably the lowest magnification required for long-range shooting, while it's still not so high that you're overly vulnerable for short-range engagements and lose low-light capabilities.

Zoom vs. Fixed Power

The single greatest sniperscope controversy is the reliability of a zoom versus a fixed-power scope.

A fixed-power rifle scope is solid and dependable due to its simpler design. The tube is stronger than a variable because it doesn't need all those cuts to accommodate the more complicated zooming apparatus, and overall there are fewer moving parts and thus fewer things to go wrong and fewer places where dust or dampness can penetrate.

My personal experience over four decades is that most zoom scopes are reliable and adequately rugged for hunting situations. Having worked with many law enforcement agencies in recent years, I have yet to encounter reports of a zoom scope failing in a situation where a fixed-power would not equally have failed. The great majority of police snipers use zoom scopes, mostly 3.5-10x.

Where I have seen rifle scopes "break," it has been almost exclusively broken reticle wires, along with a few bent objective lens bells when a rifle was dropped. In the latter cases, these were thin-tubed civilian hunting scopes on police sniper rifles.

If kept to the mechanics of scope design, the arguments for fixed power would appear compelling. It's only when you consider the capabilities of a variable-power rifle scope that benefits really come to the fore.

The disadvantage of a fixed-power scope is that you're locked into one magnification—you cannot adjust to changing circumstances, engagement distances, target sizes, and available light. In particular, police snipers and counterterrorists often need high magnification to facially identify a suspect, but 20x magnification isn't suited for the typical law enforcement

sniper's engagement distance of 70–75 yards, where he'll only have a 4-foot field of view. This limits him to covering one window or one door. If something happens beyond that narrow confine, he won't be able to see it, much less engage it. A close-range moving target, too, is almost impossible to track with a high magnification scope.

Instead, I think he should have a variable scope: crank it to high power to visually ID a suspect's face, then crank it down to a suitable power for that engagement distance. You must shoot in low light? Reset the magnification to yield the best exit pupil, as explained in Chapter 22.

The strongest argument for a zoom scope, I believe, is the ability to turn it to low power so you can shoot defensively at short range. A zoom scope set at 3x has a 17-foot field of view, more than three times wider than a 10x scope. While I don't want to "cheap shot" those critical of zoom scopes, I don't think they fully appreciate how tough it is to get off an accurate snap-shot in short-range, chance shootouts. Having narrowly survived some horrific short-range gunfights myself, I think these honest men don't realize how critical it is to be ready for sudden, unexpected close-range encounters.

The bottom line: a zoom scope with a minimum 3x or 4x and a maximum of 9x, 10x, 14.5x, even 20x—and higher when shooting a .50-caliber at extreme range—is perfectly fine if it's a real sniperscope, not a thin-skinned hunting scope. Neither a zoom nor a fixed-power scope has a monopoly on suitability; this is one of those honest-men-with-honest-differences issues.

Tube Diameter

Many riflemen don't realize that scope tubes are not necessarily the same diameter. While the great majority of high-power scope tubes are 1-inch (25mm) wide, an ever-growing number are 30mm, a reflection of the influence of European designs, which frequently employ the wider tube widths. Schmidt & Bender and Zeiss have developed even wider 34mm tubes for scopes intended for .50-caliber rifles.

The 30mm tube (right) allows more light passage than a 1-inch tube.

The benefits of a wider tube are threefold. First, because the transmitted light need not "bend" so much when traveling down the tube, there will in theory be less distortion around the edges and a crisper image. Second, the wider internal lenses will allow the unhindered passage of more light, with a brighter view reaching the shooter's eye. Third, a wider tube allows more elevation MOAs for long-range shooting.

All these are true to some degree, but not necessarily enough to make a lot of difference in performance. For example, there must be a boost of at least 10 percent in light before the human eye can detect any difference. And a good-quality scope should have very little peripheral distortion anyway.

Still, if your budget can handle it, these 30mm tubes are better and worth having.

Objective Lens Size

Think of that front objective lens as a funnel, a gatherer of light; within reason, the bigger it is, the better for long-range shooting. And this is especially useful in the reduced light of night or in the shadows of a jungle's heavy canopy.

Furthermore, the higher the scope's magnification, the larger the objective lens must be in order to have sufficient light for most shooting situations. As is covered elaborately in the section on optics, the exit pupil of any optical device, including a rifle scope, ideally should be between 5mm and 7mm, so the cone of light projected from its

rear coincides with the diameter of your eye's pupil at low light. The exit pupil is computed by dividing the objective diameter by the scope's magnification. Thus a 40mm objective with 9x has a 4.4 exit pupil.

As a minimum, a sniperscope probably should have a 40mm objective lens. A maximum diameter of 56mm, found on several quality European scopes, may be more than you need, but it's still quite acceptable. The latest Zeiss .50-caliber scope features an enormous 72mm objective lens.

Don't become overly impressed by a scope purely because of an enormous objective lens, though. As you'll see later, you should be more concerned with lens quality than lens size. Some cheap scope manufacturers deviously attach oversize objective lenses on otherwise average scopes, knowing that only about 60 percent of that wide image is actually being transmitted. Don't buy "bargain" scopes!

Adjustable Objective Lens

By adjustable, we mean the objective lens can be focused, which not only allows for a clearer target image but, as a by-product, also reduces or eliminates completely any parallax. (Other concerns about parallax will be addressed later in this chapter.)

Some scopes with adjustable focus use a ring on the objective lens. Most modern sniperscopes, however, put this adjustment in a knob on the left side of the scope, opposite the windage knob. Having used both types, I think the side-mounted knob is a bit better because it's easier to reach while you are lying in your sniper hide, but both styles work adequately.

Coated Lenses

Quality scopes have coated lenses, which can be recognized by tipping the glass until you see a purple, blue, or even yellow reflection.

Both sides of each lens are coated with a metallic fluoride so thin that it is measured in millionths of an inch and applied microscopically with an ion gun. This coating, which reduces reflection, enhances the passage of light and thus significantly improves how much we can see when looking through it.

Prior to the development of optical glass coating techniques—perfected by Zeiss during the 1930s—each lens that light passed through would reflect a bit, perhaps up to 5 percent. If, as in the case of a modern zoom scope, the light had to pass through eight lenses, the final image that reached your eye could have lost 40 percent of its original brilliance.

But quality molecular coatings—especially multicoatings—reduce reflection to as little as 1 percent per lens, a difference so dramatic that you can recognize it instantly if you compare a coated and uncoated scope side by side.

Multiple coatings done under rigidly controlled quality control are not cheap. It's one reason that the very best scopes may cost much more than similar scopes of even identical magnification and objective lens size.

Positive Clicks and Sub-MOA Adjustments

Until fairly recently, most scope windage and elevation adjustments were accomplished on plates held in place by friction. Spring resistance to rotation was all that maintained your zero; if you wanted to record that zero, you could be no more precise than merely noting where a plate's indicator lines were set. This meant you couldn't be very precise at all.

Many quality scopes have replaced simple friction plates with very precise adjustments that audibly "click" with each sub-MOA increment. One click, which you can both hear and feel, moves the reticle an exact and predetermined amount.

There's no guesswork if you understand how to interpret reticle changes and Minutes of Angle, a subject we'll address in depth. But even more importantly, these positive click adjustments are *repeatable*; you can add 10 clicks of elevation, take a few shots, then come down 10 clicks, and you're back exactly where you started.

The size of these increments, too, has become much more precise. Nearly all the scopes in this book employ 1/4 MOA positive click adjustments, which are twice or even four times more exact than were adjustments in the past. It should be noted that a few of the German and Austrian scopes use 1/3 MOA increments, a product of their metric system.

Range Estimation Capability

To some degree, any scope having a duplex reticle can be used for range estimation since it contains several exact widths and heights that will subtend predetermined measurements at distances you can then estimate. Indeed, Leupold explains how to do this with literature that accompanies its scopes, and we teach you these techniques in the range estimation section.

Some scopes come with special range estimation devices, such as the mil dot reticles in Leupold and Unertl military sniperscopes. Range estimation is a worthwhile feature in a sniperscope, with mil dots slightly edging out other types because they're fast to use and do not add any moving parts to the scope.

Finish

Obviously, a sniperscope should have a matte finish, either bead-blasted, anodized, or some kind of parkerized/acid dulled. None of these is especially superior to the others for reducing reflection, but the harder, thicker finishes offer more protection against rust.

But even if your scope has a high-gloss finish, you can just wrap tape and camouflage cloth around it and that will eliminate reflection. Or, better yet, spray paint your scope and rifle to fit the coloration in your area of operations. Just be sure to tape the dials and witness marks and cover the lenses.

RETICLES

A scope reticle is one of those little things riflemen use but don't give a second thought to—not recognizing that like any other piece of gear, obtaining the most suitable reticle and employing it correctly can dictate a shooter's long-range effectiveness.

One of my instructors was so taken with my

new Leupold 50mm Vari-X III that he, too, ordered one. But no sooner was it mounted atop his Steyr SSG than he knew somehow it was different. I had to look through his scope a couple of times before I realized it had a heavy reticle; in fact, it was about twice as wide but otherwise identical to my Duplex reticle. While it was suitable for hunting in heavy brush, this crosshair was much too wide for engaging man-size targets eight football fields away.

Leupold was happy to replace it with the thinner reticle the instructor had wanted but failed to order correctly; my point is that even a reticle's width—not to mention its style— impacts on a sniper's performance. These seemingly "little" things are worth noticing.

Reticle Styles

While you may find 10 or 12 reticles listed for some scope brands, they are only variations of about three or four basic designs, which we'll consider here for sniping suitability.

Probably the oldest reticle style is the post, shown at the top of our illustration. This was the favored reticle for World War I scopes, and it was used also for the U.S. Army's M1C/D sniper rifles in World War II and Korea. It was popular as well in civilian scopes in the late 1940s and early 1950s, a preference, I think, based on its resemblance to a rifle's front sight blade.

Unfortunately, the post design lends itself to instinctive shooting errors because it feels so natural to aim through the spot where the thick vertical post intersects the thin horizontal reticle. Many of our Reserve Component military students had M1Ds with post reticles, and we had unending problems because these novice shooters did not correctly use the *top* of the post, which if you look closely, protrudes a bit above the horizontal reference crosshair. Yes, I said that the horizontal line was *only* for reference to prevent canting. It should never be used as an aiming point. The *top* of the post, on the other hand, is a very precise spot that you can split mentally for even more exact shooting.

The post design is accurate—I've taken

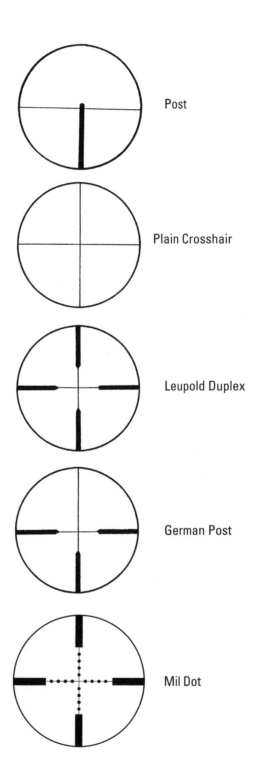

Post

Plain Crosshair

Leupold Duplex

German Post

Mil Dot

many deer with an old Weatherby Imperial post reticle scope my father left me—but the design has two serious shortcomings. The most concrete is that the wide post can completely cover your target if you must hold high, a serious concern for long-distance shooting. And second, there is that instinct problem of using the horizontal reference line as if it were a crosshair, which I must confess I did myself a few years ago when taking a fast shot at a running buck. While luckily I dropped him, I unintentionally had aimed high because in a rush I'd fired instinctively.

On the other hand, because the post reticle is so thick, it allows for excellent aiming in dense brush and low illumination. But I still would not recommend it for sniping.

Our next candidate reticle is the conventional, unadorned crosshair, which, if it is of sufficient width, certainly will do the job. It's important that I emphasize here, before the reticle becomes more complicated, that a crosshair's horizontal line is always the visual means you use to avoid canting.

The only problem with a plain crosshair is that it must be thin enough to allow precise aiming but not so thick that it covers or obscures your target. While you can reach somewhat of a compromise, it won't do either job well. And that's why the next reticle, the duplex, was devised.

The duplex crosshair was a godsend, the perfect compromise. The outer portion of each reticle is very thick, so a rifleman can make it out in low light and see it against a complex background. But the center area of the crosshairs, the portion the shooter actually uses for aiming, is very thin so that he can shoot with precision.

Not only this, but the duplex design—the term was first coined by Leupold in the 1950s—causes your eye to gravitate to the center and, unlike the post reticle, encourages you to instinctively use the correct aiming point.

Understandably, the duplex reticle has become the sniper's and ordinary hunter's favorite, and it's now offered by all major scope makers, who use the following trade names:

A mil dot reticle inside the Leupold Mark 4 M3 scope.

Leupold – Duplex	Nikon – Nikoplex
Weaver – Dual-X	Zeiss – Z-Plex
Pentax – Penta-Plex	Burris – Plex
Bushnell – Multi-X	Steiner – 7B

As an indirect result of the duplex reticle's design, it also can be used for range estimation. This is because the reticle contains several distinct but measurable areas that subtend certain measurements. The range estimation section will deal with this at length, but I cite it here as still another point favoring the duplex design.

The only reticle competing with the duplex is the German post, which actually is just a duplex whose upper vertical crosshair is as thin as the reticle center. This is to allow the shooter a clearer field of vision for spotting targets.

The German post design is very popular in Europe, although it's sometimes found on American scopes, too. Both Swarovski and Steiner offer German post reticles in their sniper-quality rifle scopes, a design they call the 4A.

Another duplex variation which we'll cover in detail elsewhere is the mil dot reticle, a design that superimposes ultrathin dots over the narrow duplex lines. These dots allow excellent range estimation as well as holds for distance and leads for wind and moving targets.

We didn't even illustrate one style among these reticles because the absent design—the dot—has no suitability for sniping. The problem is, a dot thin enough for precise aiming is so thin that you can't see it in low light or brush. The dot reticle is a popular design for target shooting because it contrasts well against an unobstructed, white target and can be held nicely on a black bull's-eye. But a sniper seldom shoots in such conditions. Thumbs down on dot reticles.

Illuminated Reticles

When first introduced a decade ago, illuminated reticles amounted to on/off lights that backlit your crosshairs so that, theoretically, you could shoot in low-light conditions where your reticle otherwise became indiscernible. Problem was, many glowed so bright that they could degrade your night vision at the very spot in your eye that most intensely was trying to see your target. And since they were battery-powered, it seemed that here was just another gadget to break and suck up batteries.

My thoughts began to change when higher quality, rheostat-controlled illuminated reticles eventually followed. Because you can set these

The Leupold illuminated mil dot reticle. Note fine "+" at reticle center.

for a host of light levels—more than a dozen on some models—you can fit reticle illumination to available ambient light to see targets without washing away night vision. With an illuminated reticle, then, you have a real advantage for about 15 minutes at dawn and dusk, when it's still too bright to use a night vision device. Often this is the most critical time for a sniper's fire, because winds tend to calm and enemy soldiers get sloppy, thinking its already dark enough (or still dark enough) to move about, or chancing to have one last cigarette before dark or the first cigarette at dawn.

An illuminated reticle is a worthwhile feature on a sniper rifle, but only if it's controlled by a rheostat-type adjustment.

Reticle Dimensions

You may have heard that spider silk is used for crosshairs. Well, spiderwebbing only 1/5000 of an inch wide and amazingly strong was used for all kinds of military and scientific optics until the 1940s, when processes were perfected for making the ultrathin metal wires that replaced them. Today we use reticle wires made of steel or brass alloys that withstand shock and heavy recoil much better than the spider silk of olden days.

When it comes to modern scopes, the most critical reticle dimension is the width of the crosshairs where they intersect, that exact spot you use as an aiming point. If these crosshairs are too thin, you'll find that they "disappear" in low light or thick brush or while tracking a moving target. On the other hand, if they're too thick they'll completely cover a distant man and, at short-range, lead to sloppy shooting.

Crosshair dimensions are described in fractions of a Minute of Angle (MOA), which, recall, equals almost exactly 1 inch at 100 yards, 2 inches at 200, 6 inches at 600, and so on.

If your reticle's crosshair is 1 MOA, it covers 1 square inch at 100 yards—much too thick. How can you shoot half-inch groups when your reticle is twice this wide? At the other extreme are superfine target crosshairs that are sometimes only 0.05 MOA wide and can only be seen against a white, clear target background.

About halfway between these extremes are the most suitable crosshair widths. But since modern zoom scopes magnify the image and reduce the field of view at higher powers, you'll actually have a thinner reticle, relatively speaking, at higher powers. The recommended crosshair widths listed below, therefore, are linked to your fixed-scope power, or its setting if it's a zoom:

Power Setting	Suitable Width
3x	.75 MOA
9x	.25 MOA
10x	.20 MOA
12x	.18 MOA

Realize that these figures are for the intersection point of the actual crosshairs only, not the thicker edges found in some reticle styles, such as the duplex or German post.

A final but important fact is that most European zoom scopes place the reticle in the first sight plane, at the forward end of the scope. The effect is that, unlike most American scopes in which the reticle stays the same relative size when you increase magnification, the reticles in these European scopes proportionally increase as you zoom. That would be a problem if the reticle magnified until it became so thick that at high power it covered the target; knowing this potential, however, European designers use a reticle that at low power is so thin that even when fully magnified, it's about the same size as your American reticle. Thus, it's not a problem.

The benefits, however, are notable. First, placing the reticle in the first sight plane means it can be etched or laser electroscribed onto a lens, doing away with a breakable wire reticle. Further, of great interest to snipers, since a first sight plane reticle expands proportionally as the power zooms, you can use a mil dot reticle that's valid at all magnifications. (By contrast, a variable scope with a wire-type mil dot reticle in the second sight plane is only accurate at one setting, with most scope makers synchronizing it for the highest magnification.) Due to these benefits, the latest Leupold Mark 4 Long Range/Tactical scopes put the mil dot reticle in the first sight plane.

TARGET KNOBS

The most precise way of aiming at a target is to hold your crosshairs directly and squarely upon it, which implies the ability to adjust a scope's elevation for each engagement. Reflecting the technical advancement of sniper-grade optics, all the scopes in this book are trajectory-adjustable, either with a Bullet Drop Compensator (which we'll see later) or target knobs.

Sometimes also called "target turrets," target knobs are windage and elevation knobs that rotate to offer micrometer-like increments of consistent reticle movement. In most cases, these increments are a fraction of a Minute of Angle, which we cover thoroughly in the next chapter. (A Minute of Angle is handy because it equals almost exactly 1 inch at 100 yards.) Most often, a sniperscope having target knobs will rotate at 1/4 MOA per click. Metric-based European scopes operate similarly, but typically move a bullet's impact 1 centimeter at 100 meters, which equates to about 1/3 inch at 100 yards per click. Actually, if a sniper went *totally metric*— that is, he used meters for laser ranging, centimeters for calculating elevation/windage

Leupold's alternate-style target knobs on a Vari-X III 3.5-10x50 scope.

SNIPERSCOPES WITH TARGET KNOBS

Model	Maximum Elevation
Nightforce NXS 5.5-25x56	100 MOA
Nightforce NXS 3.5-15x50	110 MOA
Leupold Mark 4 M1 10x	90 MOA
Leupold Mark 4 LR 3.5-10x	65 MOA
Leupold Mark 4 M1 16x	140 MOA
Nikon Tactical 4-16x50	85 MOA
Burris Xtreme Tactical 3-12x50	90 MOA
Burris Xtreme Tactical 10x50	90 MOA
Bushnell 10x40	45 MOA
Swarovski 6-24x50 P	43 MOA
Swarovski PV 4-16x50 P	65 MOA
Swarovski AV 6-18x50	45 MOA
Zeiss VM/V 6-24x56	60 MOA
Zeiss Diavari V 6-24x72	63 MOA

Note: The Bushnell and Swarovski AV scopes have 1-inch tubes; others have 30mm. Not all Leupold or Nightforce tactical scopes are listed here.

adjustments, and a centimeter-increment scope—he'd operate at higher efficiency than a counterpart using a combination of mils, meters, and Minutes of Angle.

Nightforce has addressed this issue somewhat by developing an optional elevation knob on its NXS scopes that employs mils as increments—0.1 mil per click and 5.0 mils per rotation. Interestingly, NVEC has a 0.2 mil elevation knob on its 4x Raptor Gen. III night weapon sight. These mil adjustments make possible fast, precise fire adjustment.

What should a sniper look for in target knobs? Although some target scopes offer 1/8 MOA per click, that's so fine that it takes forever to make elevation adjustments. I think 1/4 MOA is ideal for a sniping target knob.

As a rule, I would advise police snipers—*not* military snipers—to use scopes with target knobs. Why? Law enforcement snipers must deliver high-precision fire at close range, with 99 percent of their shots placed at less than 150 yards. Especially when firing around and between hostages, target knob adjustments allow the most precise kind of aiming, the degree of discretion expected of a lawman's use of deadly force.

By contrast, a military sniper usually is making "area shots," as Carlos Hathcock used to describe center-mass aiming. Because the military sniper must be ready to engage multiple targets with quick response, he doesn't have time to fiddle with target knobs so he uses a Bullet Drop Compensator—with one major exception. Long-range .50-caliber shots must be ranged exactly and aimed precisely to hit a target, pretty well requiring the use of target knobs.

Some scope makers, such as Leupold and Zeiss, offer both target knobs and BDCs on their sniper-grade optics, while others offer one or the other. The custom shops at Burris and Leupold will even retrofit target knobs on their high-end scopes, which I've done several times and always with great satisfaction.

BULLET DROP COMPENSATORS

A Bullet Drop Compensator (BDC) is a dial mounted atop the scope that can be rotated to certain preset distances. After zeroing, just set your BDC to the indicated range, which moves the elevation to the correct height; then, aim dead-on and fire. Since the sniper doesn't have to consider a lot of ballistics or compute his elevation change, he can detect a target and engage faster than a rifleman using target knobs and more accurately than a rifleman using holdover.

Some BDC-equipped scopes, such as Leupold's M3A military and Long Range line, have an entire family of interchangeable BDCs, each synchronized to a particular load—such as Federal's .308 175-grain BTHP Match—in either meters or yards. Indeed, Leupold's custom shop will even build a one-of-a-kind BDC to fit a customer's favorite load, and at a very reasonable price.

A second kind of BDC, as found on the Zeiss

A Bullet Drop Compensator (BDC) allows for fast elevation adjustments but lacks the precision of target knobs.

Diavari V 6-24x50 T, offers a variety of seven BDC trajectories. You select the one that best fits your load, and Zeiss installs the corresponding cam. Though well-built, this BDC has limited sniper usefulness since its maximum range is only 300 meters.

The downside of all BDCs is that they incorporate an "average of averages" for tracing a bullet's trajectory. The "dope" that created it is no different than the average ballistic table, which assumes a 24-inch barrel, a scope reticle 1 1/2 inches above the bore, sea-level elevation, and 59°F temperature. It's far more accurate than old-fashioned "Tennessee elevation," or holdover, when you just held high to compensate for distance, but it's not as accurate as a finely adjusted target knob. A U.S. Army or Marine sniper—each of whom employs a BDC in his scopes—knows to test that BDC at an assortment of distances and carefully record (and apply) any discovered variations.

But that fine-tuning itself cannot be as meticulous as a target knob because the Army's M3A BDC uses 1 MOA elevation increments. This means that if a sniper wants to raise his

The BDC on this Leupold Mark 4 M3 allows engagements from 100 to 1,000 meters or yards, with interchangeable compensators for assorted calibers, even custom made for specific loads.

This Hensoldt BDC adjusts elevation in synch to the .308 168-grain BTHP Match trajectory.

bullet impact 4 inches at 700 yards, he'd may as well leave it alone since *one click equals 7 inches* and one click would put his bullet 3 inches high!

Why do these scopes have 1 MOA increments? That Unertl or Leupold scope is designed to engage targets anywhere from 100 to 1,000 meters, with all those various ranges found in one rotation on the BDC. It's a compromise, and there's a factor of imprecision, but it's *fast*—and engaging fast outweighs a host of other considerations for a military sniper. With practice, he'll learn his rifle so well that he knows how to hold a hair

here or there and when to apply a click or two to yield cutting edge accuracy. After all, it's not all about the hardware. Still, quite a number of veteran snipers from Iraq and Afghanistan have urged the Army to modify that BDC, so we may eventually see finer, 1/2 MOA or even 1/4 MOA increments.

FIXED MAGNIFICATION SNIPERSCOPES

Both U.S. Army and U.S. Marine Corps snipers use fixed-power 10x scopes, with the Army opting for the rugged and optically excellent Leupold Mark 4 M3A. In its latest version, the M3A's Bullet Drop Compensator displays the elevation as distance, with numerals indicating hundreds of meters, while below this, parallel witness marks display elevation as Minutes of Angle, so the sniper can fine-tune and record his settings. In one rotation, the sniper can adjust elevation all the way to 1,000 meters. Like many current sniperscopes, the M3A has a focus knob on its left side, opposite the windage knob, so the sniper can focus without his eye leaving the reticle.

The Marine workhorse, the Unertl 10x, has proved itself in a dozen conflicts, big and small, as a reliable, accurate instrument. What I particularly like about this scope is its fine-focus knob, akin to the fine-focus on quality spotting

SNIPERSCOPES WITH BULLET DROP COMPENSATORS

Model	Maximum BDC Range	Comments
Leupold Mark 4 M3	1000 yards/meters	1 MOA elevation, 1/2 MOA windage
Leupold LR/T	1000 yards/meters	1 MOA elevation, 1/2 MOA windage
Unertl 10x	1000 meters	1/2 MOA elevation & windage
AN/PVS-10	1000 meters	U.S. military's day/night scope
Kahles 10x ZF 95	800 meters	Optional cams available
Schmidt & Bender	600 meters	Cams available for specific loads
Hensoldt 10x	800 meters	Cams available for specific loads
Zeiss Diavari V 6-24x50 T	300 meters	Seven different cams available
Zeiss VM/V 3-12x56	600 meters	.308 168-gr. cam, 1/2 MOA elev.

Note: All listed scopes have 30mm tubes except the Kahles, with a 1" tube.

The USMC's long-favored sniper optic, the Unertl 10x. Note the mount built into the forward scope ring for a Simrad night vision device.

Built on a 1-inch tube, this Kahles 10x ZF-95 scope offers multiple BDCs for specific bullets.

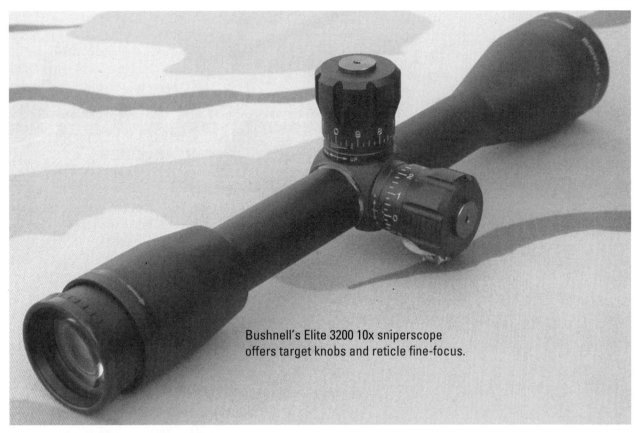

Bushnell's Elite 3200 10x sniperscope offers target knobs and reticle fine-focus.

scopes. Like the Army scope, it incorporates a mil dot reticle and BDC that reaches out to 1,000 meters in a single rotation, but with 1/2 MOA per click. When the widow of John Unertl Jr. sold the company in 2000, U.S. Optics contracted to support the USMC's Unertls and developed an improved version.

The latest U.S. military sniperscope, found in the hands of both soldiers and marines, is the AN/PVS-10, a convertible day/night scope with a BDC and mil dot reticle. Its two versions offer either a 125mm objective lens and 8.5x magnification or a 178mm lens with 12x magnification, the latter weighing a full 5 pounds. On the plus side, this is quite an innovative development—for the first time ever, a sniper can use a single zero for day and night engagements. The downside (beyond added bulk and weight), veteran snipers tell me, is that its daytime optics are not as keen as those of the Leupold scope it replaces. We'll examine the AN/PVS-10 in more detail in Chapter 22.

Hensoldt, a division of Zeiss, builds two

excellent 10x sniperscopes, the ZF500 and ZF800, outfitted with BDCs that allow shooting, respectively, to 500 and 800 meters. The ZF500 has 1/4 MOA elevation increments, while the longer-range ZF800 has 1/2 MOA adjustments. Both incorporate mil dot reticles and a cam specifically tuned to the .308, 168-grain load.

Kahles, the military scope company owned by Swarovski, has a 6x and a 10x version of its ZF-95 scope. Built on a 1-inch tube, these offer exceptional clarity and incorporate both a BDC and mil dot reticle. I have one on my Sako 7.62mm rifle.

Bushnell, which formerly offered a 30mm tube, 10x sniperscope, incorporated its best features into a moderately priced 1-inch version. The only fixed-power scope in Bushnell's Elite 3200 line, this 10x40mm scope has target knobs and a mil dot reticle to make an extremely good buy for its capabilities.

The Burris Xtreme Tactical line includes a quality 10x50 sniperscope, outfitted with target knobs and mil dot reticle in a 30mm tube. The

This Burris Xtreme Tactical scope has 10x magnification and target knobs.

rugged tube and posi-lock help it stand up well to tough recoil and field conditions. Its internal gears boast steel-on-steel adjustments.

VARIABLE MAGNIFICATION SNIPERSCOPES

Burris also makes a 3-12x50 variable version of its Xtreme Tactical scope. Like its 10x cousin, this scope has 1/4 MOA target knobs and a ballistic mil dot reticle inside a heavy 30mm tube. And like Leupold, the Burris custom shop will retrofit target knobs on many of its scopes.

This Burris 3-12x50 Xtreme Tactical scope incorporates 1/4 MOA target knobs and a ballistic mil dot reticle.

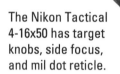

Nikon offers two tactical scopes, each with a 30mm tube, target knobs, adjustable focus,

The Nikon Tactical 4-16x50 has target knobs, side focus, and mil dot reticle.

Mounted atop a Sako TRG-22, the high magnification Nightforce NXS 5.5-25x56 sniperscope.

and mil dot, glass-etched reticle in the first sight plane. Available in 4-16x50 or 2.5-10x44, they incorporate fine, 1/4 MOA adjustment increments.

The relatively new but highly regarded scope maker Nightforce produces nothing but variable-powered scopes with 30mm tubes. Its NXS Nightforce Extreme tactical line includes six different models offering maximum magnifications of 22x, 32x, and even 42x, these higher powers allowing for long-range, 2,000-yard shooting with .50-caliber rifles. Using reticles etched into the first focal plane and a variety of mil and ranging reticles, all these Nightforce variables are excellent for sniping.

Leupold, by far, offers the greatest variety and options in variable magnification tactical scopes, with the Mark 4 line recently expanded to embrace 15 scopes, each somewhat overlapping police, military, and special operations requirements. These include target knob and BDC versions, with many based on the superb Ultra, a variation of which is the U.S. Army's M3A rifle scope. It's hard to beat Leupold's rugged 30mm tube and those solid M1 target knobs. Even Leupold's police line has become beefier by putting Vari-X III innards inside Ultra-style 30mm tubes, both for improved elevation controls and to add more MOAs of adjustment. Leupold's great variety of BDC dials synchronized to specific loads—including the Federal 175-grain BTHP Match and 168-grain BTHP Match in both yard and meter versions—have made this manufacturer a tremendous influence in the long-range shooting industry.

European sniperscope development has kept apace with America's. It's hard to beat a Schmidt & Bender variable, which is why Malcolm Cooper selected these scopes for his superb Accuracy International rifles. My AWP is topped by a Schmidt & Bender 3-12x50 having a 600-meter BDC, mil dot reticle, and step-style optical rangefinder. It's a challenge for me to shoot up to the capabilities of this scope and rifle. Though this has a 30mm tube, Schmidt & Bender recently developed a 5-25x56 scope with a 34mm tube for extreme long-range shooting.

Swarovski offers two variables with 30mm tubes and metric target knob adjustments, and one "Americanized" variable with a 1-inch tube. The metric variables—the PV 4-16x50 P with 65 MOA of elevation, and PV 6-24x50P with 43 MOA—have a mil dot or Swarovski's own TDS-4 "Christmas tree" ranging reticle.

This Leupold scope places Vari-X III innards in a 30mm tube to create an excellent 3.5-10x magnification, BDC sniperscope.

Their target knobs raise elevation at clicks of 1 centimeter per 100 meters. The Americanized scope, the AV 6-18x50, moves 1/4 MOA per target knob click, and like all Swarovski scopes uses high-quality lenses.

European lens quality is embraced, too, by Zeiss, which fields several variable magnifi-cation sniperscopes. Perhaps their finest current instrument is the VM/V 3-12x 56, dubbed the Tactical Marksman. Featuring BDCs synchronized to the .308 and .338 Lapua Magnum round—and with 0.5 MOA elevation and 0.3 MOA windage adjust-ments—it incorporates 65 MOA total elevation. Like all Zeiss high-end scopes, it has a 30mm tube. The even more powerful Zeiss Diavari V 6-24x72—with the largest quality objective lens I've come upon in a sniperscope—will be covered in Chapter 9 because it so perfectly fits long-range heavy rifles such as the .50 caliber, .338 Lapua Magnum, and CheyTac .408. More down to earth is the Zeiss Diavari V 6-24x56 T, available with either BDC or target knobs, which offer 0.5 centimeters per click.

Other foreign developments suggest great future potential for sniperscopes. The Swarovski LRS laser-ranging rifle

Schmidt & Bender's excellent 3-12x50 sniperscope with BDC on an AWP sniper rifle.

Available with target knobs, this Swarovski PV 6-24x50 scope has a fine-focus objective lens.

The Zeiss Diavari V 6-24x56, available with BDC or target knobs.

scope, which put a quality laser rangefinder right in the rifleman's scope, was a bit too expensive and ahead of its time to be commercially successful, but it blazed a path that other scopes inevitably will follow. More recently, the Canadian-based firm Elcan broke similar new ground with the world's first digital rifle scope—that is, like a video camera, the scope records an image and superimposes on it a variety of reticles that the shooter changes by pushing a button.

I've personally examined both scopes and concluded that they offer such enormous potential that we will eventually see these features incorporated into sniperscopes, though the technology and its efficiency must be further refined. The day is not far in the future where all this technology will be integrated, and as quickly as a sniper lazes his distant target, his reticle automatically will reposition itself so that *real-time*, he simply ranges-aims-fires. Won't that be an incredible capability!

ASSESSING SCOPE QUALITY

Not long ago, one of our NCOs spent two days trying to track down national standards for optical glass so we could evaluate scope lenses. He learned there were no hard data standards for comparing lenses.

I tried to find some kind of comparative assessment of scopes, kind of a *Consumer Reports*, but no such comparison exists. While I could do an assessment myself, it wouldn't be a detached and scientific study without thousands of dollars worth of equipment, much beyond my already overstressed Visa card.

Therefore, instead of providing answers, I'll give you the questions to ask and factors to take into account when selecting a scope.

Lens Coatings
Multiple lens coatings will lead to better light passage than a single coating or no coating. High-quality scope lenses have three to seven coatings, each of which is a complicated, expensive process.

The quickest way to recognize quality lens coatings is to take the scope outdoors and appreciate the brilliance of its image. A quality scope will most likely impress you by how bright its image looks.

Peripheral Distortion
A high-quality lens has no visible distortion on its edges, where the image should be just as crisp and clear as the center.

Acuity
Acuity is the ability of an optical device to resolve an image so that its tiniest details are visible. To check acuity, take the scope outside and look at a detailed, contrasting image, such as an auto license plate, perhaps a block away. We've published a resolution chart on page 97 to help you do this. You may have to compare several different scopes of equal magnification to appreciate the superior resolution of the best one.

Exit Pupil and Twilight Factor
Chapter 11 explains these ratings, but I think they've been much overstressed.

You can have a cheap, poor-quality scope with an oversized objective lens and manipulate exit pupil and twilight factor ratings. You're stuck with third-class lenses, ground not nearly so well as another scope that didn't rate as high.

The Leupold Mark 4 is a good example. Its M3 military version has an exit pupil of four, which seems barely adequate, but the lenses are so well ground and coatings are of such high quality that it performs superbly in low light.

Exit pupils and twilight factors are only a guide and probably should not even be applied to cheap scopes.

Internal Windage and Elevation Gears
Simply put, these gears should be steel so they won't wear and begin to wander from true values of 1/4 MOA. When you hear that positive "click," it should mean exactly one increment of movement, not approximately one increment.

Some manufacturers use aluminum, brass, and even nylon gears. Since a sniper changes windage and elevation frequently, such soft gears soon lose their precision.

Point of Aim While Zooming

This was mentioned in the zeroing section as a check for wear, but indeed, it is a problem with some brand-new scopes.

Use a boresight (or collimator) to see if the crosshair wanders even slightly when you change the magnification on a zoom scope. I tested several new scopes and found one that traveled a few MOAs when shifted from 9x to 6x. That's not good enough for a sniperscope.

The more expensive scopes, I found, stayed true and did not shift around while zooming.

Optics Test Pattern

We've designed the chart on the next page so you can evaluate optics and determine which binoculars, rifle scope, or spotting scope gives the best resolution. Purchasers of this book are authorized to copy this chart for their own or agency use, provided they do not remove the credit line and don't reproduce it for sale.

The pattern's as wide as it is high, consisting of three distinct stripes. Copy it and post it at least 25 yards away—or beyond the optics' minimum focus distance.

Start by observing the largest pattern and adjust the focus so it's crisp and clear. Then, see which of the smaller patterns is the smallest in which you can still see whether the stripes are vertical or horizontal. At some point, a pattern just looks like a black square; the next larger pattern becomes the finest resolution this lens allows you.

Take a competing optical device *of the same magnification* and repeat this process, first focusing on the biggest pattern and then seeing which is the smallest pattern you can distinguish.

The device that allows you to see the smallest pattern has better resolution, but this is only valid when comparing devices of equal magnification.

When comparing zoom rifle or zoom spotting scopes, compare them only at one equal setting—usually the highest magnification—and brace yourself so vibration doesn't give you false results.

Parallax

Parallax is like radioactivity in that it is feared mostly because it isn't understood. For all the overly complicated articles I've read that warned me about its mysterious effects, it was finally Leupold that cut through the hocus-pocus with one uncomplicated declaration: "Don't worry about parallax."

Here's why: if you're using a quality rifle scope that's been factory-set to be parallax-free at 150 yards, *the worst possible parallax error* is only 1.3 inch at 500 yards! Unless you're wearing an Olympic Gold Medal for long-range shooting, that's too little potential error to reduce your accuracy in any significant way.

Further, if you've properly focused your adjustable objective lens—a feature worth having—it reduces potential parallax problems even more. And if you have developed a spotweld so you consistently place your shooting eye at the exact same spot time after time, you have reduced it still further. I would guess these two additional factors probably cut potential parallax error to a half-inch or less at 500 yards.

And indeed, an adjustable objective is important for scopes of 10x or larger since the higher magnification scopes are a little more prone to parallax problems. Still, though, you should understand parallax so you can argue coherently over a beer with fellow snipers.

The problem with rifle scopes is that the entire reticle sits in one spot; unlike open sights, a scope has no rear aiming point to align precisely with a front aiming point. Imagine that you had a rifle with only a front blade for aiming; unless you placed your shooting eye at exactly the same spot on the stock, you could not have consistent accuracy. You realize that even using extreme care in placing your cheek at precisely the same spot for each shot, you'd still be a little off sometimes. The sight picture would look just the same, but you know that to

Duplicated from *The Ultimate Sniper* by John Plaster,
copyright 1993, 2006 by John Plaster. Published by Paladin Press.

a tiny degree it can look right and still have your eye slightly to one side or the other. This is what parallax is: the apparent sideways shift of a crosshair caused by the shooter's eye being able to focus through it, although slightly off center.

Here's another way to look at it. If you stand on a scale and look down to see your weight, let's say you can read 180 pounds. But you can lean to the right and, behold, you see that you weigh only 150 pounds! This is the same off-center principle at work.

But don't get excited about it. Parallax is not a significant problem with modern, quality scopes, and an adjustable objective lens eliminates parallax almost completely. Still, if you're having accuracy problems, you should be able to check your scope for parallax. It's a simple process.

Place your rifle on a steady table or bench and sandbag it so it won't move even a hair. Now, adjust the rifle so you're aiming at a 1-inch spot 100 yards away. Brace the rifle again so it won't move, then carefully lift yourself away. Now, go back and look through the scope without touching it. To the degree that the crosshair is no longer pointed at the 1-inch spot, you are experiencing parallax. Repeat this to make sure you've done it correctly and not shifted it in any way. Your crosshair should be well within 1 inch of where you'd originally positioned it. If you're sure it has moved noticeably, send the scope back to the manufacturer or replace it.

SNIPERSCOPE ACCESSORIES

The most vulnerable component of a sniping system is its optics. *Protect your scope!* Whenever your rifle's not in your hands or a hardcase, make a habit of protecting your scope with a padded scope cover, even if you must make your own field expedient with paracord and foam

Scope accessories include this Eagle padded cover and (L-R) protective lens caps, polarizing filters, KillFlash shade, field-expedient aperture cover, and commercial sun shade.

rubber. Eagle makes a suitable cover, moderately priced. It belongs in every sniper's kit.

By now you've come to appreciate how critical your lenses are to long-range shooting and realize how important it is to protect these precision-ground surfaces. But there are right and wrong ways to accomplish this. The *worst* way is using see-through plastic covers. This intervening layer of low-quality translucence reduces your scope's clarity, negating the fine acuity your lens offers. Rubberized scope caps held on by elastic bands can do the job, but they're likely to be lost, and you'd never carry them in the field.

The best lens protection is provided by flip-up covers, the most common type being those made by Butler Creek, which interpose no layers of plastic. You can pop them open in a heartbeat, and they work.

A lens hood or sunshade is a worthwhile investment. Appreciate that the undoing of Nazi Germany's supersniper at Stalingrad, Major Koning, was the glare off his objective lens. As World War I veteran British Lt. Col. N.A.D. Armstrong warned in a 1942 British sniping pamphlet, "More observation posts have been given away by the light shining upon the glass than in any other way."

As our illustration shows, a conventional hood must be at least as long as your objective lens is wide. If you have a 40mm objective lens diameter, you need a hood at least 40mm long. Then sunlight cannot reflect off your lens unless the sun is visible in your field of view. Burn this into your memory: *If the sun's in your field of view, you are reflecting its light in the direction you're looking, and thus compromising your location!* Scope makers offer factory-made hoods, but you can fashion one yourself from plastic or metal tubing. Just be sure it's

blackened on the inside and does not touch your barrel.

Probably the best means to eliminate reflection is by installing a KillFlash shade on your objective lens. The KillFlash is standard issue in the U.S. Army and Marine Corps. Originally developed by my friend Peter Jones to reduce reflection off military Steiner binoculars' laser-reflective coating, this fine honeycomb design eliminates a scope's reflective glare, although it's less than 2 1/2 inches long.

Peter's company, Tenebraex, has also perfected polarizing scope filters that penetrate the reflective glare off windshields and

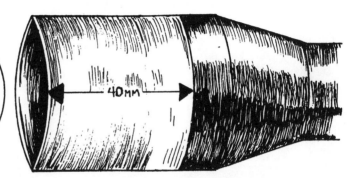

A hood must be at least as long as your objective lens is wide to prevent visible reflection.

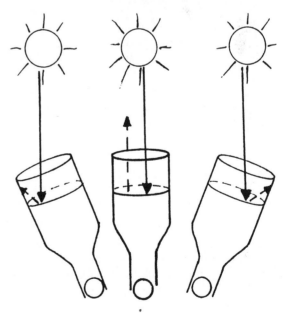

OBJECTIVE LENS REFLECTION. When a hood is properly installed, no light reflects unless the sun is in your field of view.

The fine honeycomb mesh on the KillFlash eliminates a scope lens reflective glare.

This polarizing filter allows a sniper to see through glaring windows.

windows. Though of interest mostly to police snipers, there have been enough shots through glass in Iraq that this polarizing light capability may be worthwhile for military snipers, too.

When operating in the glaring light of snow or open desert, your scope often conveys too much light to your eye, degrading your vision. Just as you'd wear sunglasses to cut such blinding glare, you can reduce light transmitted through your scope by attaching an aperture to your objective lens. All this really means is reducing light transmission by partially covering the lens—just be careful *not* to let tape or adhesive touch the lens surface! I use slide-on expedient covers made from tape and plastic scrap and painted camouflage. It doesn't need to be fancy to work.

SCOPE MAINTENANCE

Unlike your rifle, your scope is relatively maintenance free. You should never disassemble it, so the cleaning and oiling requirements concern only external surfaces.

To fully appreciate the care needed when cleaning lenses, think of it not as a scope but as an expensive camera. Except for field emergencies, use only quality lens paper and camera lens cleaning liquids on lenses. When you use ordinary window cleaner and toilet tissue, you will gently reduce metallic fluoride coatings through abrasive action. I have seen scope lenses wiped free of any coating due to "diligent" cleaning by a proud rifleman.

Before wiping the lens with lens paper, carefully blow any grit or sand off it. It's best to use a small rubber squeegee brush to do this, but breathing on it is okay if you wait until any vapor evaporates before wiping. Substitute cleaners could be acetone, pure alcohol, or even clean water. In a pinch you could use good quality facial tissue, but don't make a habit of it.

I keep lens paper in a plastic bag in my rifle hardcase and a bottle of lens cleaner in my ditty bag. In combat I would carry both to the field.

Even handier is the LensPen. This pen-sized lens cleaning kit contains a soft, retractable brush on one end and a chamois buffer impregnated with lens cleaning compound on the other. Just brush away any dust or grit, then polish the lens with the buffer. It's compact and works great.

The scope's metal outer surfaces can be kept rust free with a thin coat of any firearm-quality oil. Do *not* use solvent-type cleaners such as

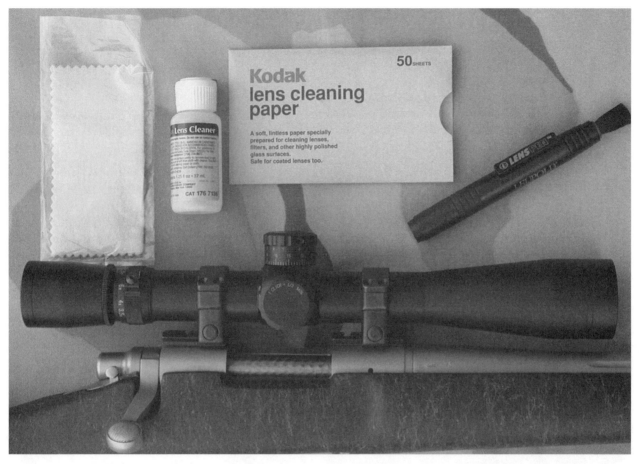

Protect your lenses! Clean with special flannel cloth, lens paper, lens liquid cleaner, and the handy LensPen.

WD-40 on a scope, since they may penetrate to the interior and cause fogging.

Check the turret covers to ensure they're tight and the O-rings intact, since this is the primary avenue for dampness to invade a scope. And check the hex screws on the mount and rings to confirm they are snug.

Under no circumstances should you disassemble a scope. If you do, the dry nitrogen inside will leak and your scope will become prone to fogging. Such moving parts as a zoom ring, BDC, or adjustable objective are factory lubricated and need no field maintenance.

As part of your annual maintenance program, you should test the BDC to ensure its gear teeth are not so worn that you've lost repeatability. Also, test the zoom for any crosshair wandering at different magnifications.

SCOPES ON ASSAULT RIFLES

Though assault rifles are not sniper weapons and the recent proliferation of scopes on them cannot make snipers of regular infantrymen, this combination has nonetheless had quite an impact on small-unit combat in Iraq and Afghanistan.

U.S. Special Operations forces for the past decade have placed the Aimpoint sight on many M4 carbines, which dramatically improved close-quarters and low-light shooting. Using an electronic dot of light instead of a crosshair, these operators achieved faster target acquisition and higher hit probabilities than with open sights.

An especially impressive red dot sight, the EOTech 551/552 projects its reticle dot into a holographic viewer. No matter where your eye is—off-center, close, far—so long as you can see

Thousands of Aimpoint sights have seen service in Iraq and Afghanistan.

This EOTech sight (R) is mounted forward of an AN/PVS-14 for night firing.

This 4x ACOG is the "Day Optical Sight" to the U.S. Army and the "Advanced Combat Optic" to the Marine Corps.

Leupold's CQ/T sight offers low magnification (1-3x) for close-quarters and medium-range shooting.

that dot and put it on the target, your shot will go there. It's not just parallax free—parallax cannot exist in this sight! I've fired my EOTech extensively and find it the fastest and finest close-quarters sight I've ever used. My inclination toward the EOTech is driven as much by its wide field of view as by its impressive rheostat settings—22 different intensities.

Both the Aimpoint M2 military sight and EOTech 551/552 are compatible with Generation II and III night vision devices, allowing you to use them in tandem with an AN/PVS-14. It's possible to view them through PVS-7B goggles, too, but it's pretty tough to contort your neck for a proper sight picture. I don't recommend it.

Unlike these assault rifle optics, which do not magnify an image, Trijicon's ACOG (Advanced Combat Optical Gunsight) is a fixed 4x scope contained in a rugged cast body. The U.S. Army calls its ACOGs the Day Optical Sight, while the

Jerry-rigged but it works, an American GI's scoped M16A4 in Iraq.

USMC has dubbed it the Advanced Combat Optic. Fitted with a quick-ranging reticle and holdover lines, these ACOGs have been quite popular in Iraq and are found on thousands of flattop M4 carbines and M16A3s.

On its own initiative, Leupold has developed a specialty assault rifle optic, the Mark 4 CQ/T, which, unlike the ones cited here, offers variable magnification from 1x to 3x so it can be used both for close-quarters and medium-range engagements. The CQ/T is designed to fit a Picatinny rail.

Meanwhile, many GIs in Southwest Asia, just like their fathers and grandfathers in Vietnam and Korea, have taken to scrounging their own scopes and mounting them atop M16s, which can make for a difficult spotweld with the scope so high above the cheekrest. While not enabling precision shooting, these riflemen are finding even these jerry-rigged optics accurate enough to hit man-size targets out to 300 yards with high probability, and it gives them an edge on al-Qaeda, Taliban, and Iraqi "mujs."

While the recent proliferation of scopes on assault rifles enhances the accuracy of ordinary riflemen, it ultimately cannot increase their effective range, which is limited by the ballistics of their 5.56mm ammunition. As a 7.62mm-armed sniper, this means you sometimes avoid engagements of less than 400 yards, in which the optical odds are becoming a bit too even. Your "ballistic advantage"—a concept I harp on—begins at 400 yards. That's one of the few edges you have, especially with so many optical sights nowadays.

The EOTech 551 and 552 holographic sights have proved popular and effective in combat.

CHAPTER 4

USING A SNIPERSCOPE

MASTERING YOUR SCOPE

To realize the full capabilities of the wondrous optical device mounted on your rifle, you must carefully examine it and use it in a wide range of circumstances during training.

Know the MOAs

What's the full range of MOAs up/down in your scope, and how many clicks does this equal? By heart, do you know the comeups to go from 200 to 500 yards? In an instant, can you say what one click equals at 300 yards?

LEUPOLD MARK 4 RIFLE SCOPES

	M1/10x	M1/16x	M3/10x
MOA Up/Down	45/45	65/65	60/10
MOA Right/Left	27/27	20/20	30/30

And what about windage MOAs? Do you know the full range of right/left MOAs? Can you compute in your head the necessary clicks to compensate for a 15 mph crosswind at 400 yards? And how about the number of clicks to lead a walking man at 725 yards?

If you have target knobs, can you say exactly how many MOAs there are per complete rotation?

Know the Center

Knowing your scope's mechanical center—the MOA center for up/down elevation and right/left windage—will save you time and effort when you have to recenter the reticle before zeroing.

After zeroing, this information allows you to know the remaining up/down clicks after adjustment and can indicate the need for a shim if there's not enough elevation to go to maximum range.

Know the Reticle

The reticle should be crisply focused, but you also need to know the exact MOA measurements in your reticle so you can use it for range estimation.

On a duplex reticle, the distance from the crosshair to the start of the thicker reticle portion is probably about 10–15 MOAs, which equals 10–15 inches at 100 yards, twice that at 200 yards, three times that at 300 yards, and so on. This is explained further in the range estimation section in Chapter 12.

Should your reticle have mil dots, you must master how to use them for range estimation, moving-target leads, elevation holds, and wind compensation.

Fine-Tune Your BDC

Actually fire at each indicated distance on your Bullet Drop Compensator and record even slight differences. On another day, again fire at each of these 100-yard increments, applying the fine-tuned differences you noted earlier and see if you're now dead-on, as you should be. If not, refine again and test again.

Essential for protecting the lenses, these lens caps can be popped open in an instant.

You also should know the exact MOA increment on the BDC so you realize exactly what one click does to the elevation. This can come in mighty handy when you need to fine-tune for up/down shooting. For example, I realize my Leupold Mark 4 M3 has 1 MOA incremental clicks.

Low-Light Capability

Elsewhere I recommend that 40 percent of practice fire be at night, a realistic percentage given the high incidence of both police and military action after dusk. During this firing, you must learn how far you can make a shot when the only illumination is a four-cell flashlight, a car's brights, and full or half moonlight. These distances will vary according to scope quality and magnification and shooter eyesight.

Muscle Memory

Just as Old West gunfighters practiced quick drawing, a modern sniper practices throwing his rifle to his shoulder so perfect eye relief results. Exact eye relief will nearly eliminate parallax, give you the fullest field of view, enable the fastest possible shooting, and benefit your eye with the maximum available light.

ELEVATION AND WINDAGE ADJUSTMENTS

Every rifle scope has a limited number of adjustments for elevation and windage, expressed as a total number of Minutes of Angle, or MOA. Whether your scope adjusts at increments of 1/4 MOA, 1/2 MOA, or 1 MOA, the maximum adjustment is cited as its total Minutes of Angle. The Leupold Mark 4 M3A scope, for instance, allows up/down total elevation of 75 MOA, while its right/left windage is 52 MOA.

Your greatest MOA concern when selecting a scope is ensuring that it has enough elevation to adjust for shooting long-range with your cartridge. How can you determine what "enough" is? We have calculated elevation requirements for the primary sniping loads—the .308 175-grain BTHP Match (the U.S. military's M118LR round); the .308 168-grain BTHP Match (the primary police sniping round); the Federal .223 69-grain BTHP Match; and the .300 Winchester Magnum 190-grain BTHP Match (the so-called "Navy load") out to 1,000 yards—along with their elevation comeups, which we'll explain shortly.

As you can see, 45 MOA squeaks you by on all these loads, but clearly, you're better off with 50 or even 60 MOA since your mount may "eat" two or three MOAs of elevation while zeroing. When it comes to a .50-caliber rifle and extreme range shooting, of course, you'll want even more elevation, which we'll address in the chapter on heavy rifles. The mounting section will deal with it in more depth, but you should know that wafer-thin shims and inclined mounts can help you gain more elevation should your scope need it.

Most scope bases include sufficient windage adjustment for zeroing so you can preserve your

**SCOPE ELEVATION REQUIRED
TO REACH 1000 YARDS ***

.223, 69-gr.	BTHP Match	40.5 MOA
.308, 168-gr.	BTHP Match	44.0 MOA
.308, 175-gr.	BTHP Match	41.75 MOA
.300 WinMag, 190-gr.	BTHP Match	30.25 MOA

* Assumes 100-yard zero, varies by mount and base.

scope's internal windage for fine-tuning and, if you choose, to "dial your dope" for windage compensation or moving target leads.

MOUNTS AND MOUNTING

The same exacting standards of quality demanded in a sniper-grade rifle and scope must be found in its mount, too. It's the height of foolishness to acquire a $1,700 rifle and an $800 scope and connect them with a $15 mount and rings.

Mount quality results from close tolerances during machining; some mounts not only have poor tolerances, but they aren't even machined—they're stamped out of soft alloys. And because these soft alloys have a different hardness and density than a rifle receiver's steel, they'll expand and contract at a different rate, leading to your scope ever so slightly twisting away from zero. Even if a cheap mount is constructed of decent steel, its low tolerances will not mate it tightly to the receiver, leading to acute recoil vibrations that will shake it loose.

Beyond this, a poor-quality mount will not align straight and true with your rifle and therefore consumes an inordinate amount of your scope's internal adjustments for zero.

Redfield requires that its mounts mate with any rifle manufacturer's receiver dimensions to a tolerance of +/-.003 inch, an acceptable standard that you should demand of a mount suitable for a sniper rifle.

Different Mounts and Rings

A mount consists of two components: the squarish base that attaches to the receiver, and the rings, which hold the scope to this base.

The most often encountered base on U.S. military sniper rifles is the Picatinny rail, military standard 1913, intended to accommodate a variety of optics, lights, lasers, and night vision devices. All major base and ring manufacturers have modified their products to be compatible with this rugged but very precisely designed mount. For example, the Nightforce two-piece base, although machined to a slight upward taper of 20 MOA (to allow longer-range shooting), is built to the Picatinny standard. Leupold's superb steel Mark 4 Tactical Mounts, found on most military and police sniper weapons, incorporate a Picatinny-style rail.

Provided the rings are of high quality and match the scope's matte finish, they're acceptable. You need only be concerned that the ring height will match your scope since the larger your objective lens, the higher you must mount it for adequate clearance. Rings typically are available in three heights. You should keep your scope as low as possible so it's less prone to being bumped or dragged and damaged.

See-through rings, which lift your scope so high that you can see beneath them to aim it, may be fine for deer hunting but they have no place in sniping. Not only do these rings make your scope more prone to damage, they lift the scope so high from the bore that long-range elevation adjustments will vary from "book" values. Such tall rings can degrade the calibrated accuracy of an excellent Bullet Drop Compensator.

Bases are manufactured essentially as one- or two-piece. A one-piece base is about 5 inches long and straddles the ejection port on its left side. A two-piece base screws into the same receiver holes and attaches only the rings themselves to the receiver. I could cite a number of pseudoscientific claims in favor of one- or two-piece bases, as argued by various shooters, but when it comes right down to it, either base style will do the job, so it's an issue of personal preference.

The military standard 1913 Picatinny rail and quality steel rings are found today on most U.S. sniper rifles.

In most mounts, the base is adjustable for windage so that when bore-sighting you can adjust the mount and thereby preserve maximum internal windage for zeroing. It's a feature worth having.

Tip-off and quick detachable bases, like see-through rings, have no place on a sniper rifle. While in theory these mounts allow you to remove a scope and then return it without loss of zero, they usually only come *close* to the zero, not back to the very precise zero a modern sniper demands. Probably the most frequent interest in such mounts is to enable the sniper to use a night vision device in darkness, then return to his daytime scope at dawn. Despite all sorts of fancy dovetails and torque screws, I have yet to see any manufacturer make toler-

ance guarantees for such mounts, and I doubt any of them restore zero consistently closer than 2 to 5 MOAs.

The last category of mounts are "integral," a term that means the rifle manufacturer machined special grooves in the receiver that mate with their own special rings so that no other mount is needed. The mount is integral to the rifle, with the benefits of simplicity, lighter weight, and fewer intervening pieces to be shaken by recoil. Sako, Ruger, and Steyr use integral bases, and, having owned or used all three, I can say they work just fine.

But no matter the type of bases or rings you use, I strongly recommend replacing your conventional screws with hex screws, which can be torqued snugly.

Mounting the Scope

Before installing anything, clean all screws and screw holes with acetone or alcohol to eliminate any oil or grease that could reduce tightness. If you're remounting this scope or it previously was on another rifle, you should take time here to restore the crosshair's mechanical center, a procedure explained on page 113.

Begin mounting by attaching the base using hex screws, upon which you have applied a thin coating of Gun-Tite, a special adhesive made by Loctite, to anchor them in place. When you've snugged them down, rap each screw once sharply and you'll probably be able to rotate it another half-turn.

Into the front mount, insert the ring with the dovetail at its bottom using a 1-inch or 30mm dowel or pipe (*not* the scope), as appropriate, to rotate it in line with the barrel's axis. To fine-tune the front ring's alignment, install the rear ring and manipulate the pipe or dowel until there's no binding between the two.

Now, remove the tops of both rings and insert the scope, screwing the rings down, but not so tight that you cannot slide or rotate the tube. You're ready to adjust the distance between the scope eyepiece and your shooting eye, known as "eye relief."

Adjusting Eye Relief

Since most military and police sniper rifles are handed down from previous users, there's a hesitancy for the inheriting marksman to change anything that has "worked" in the past. This attitude is not entirely wrong—"if it ain't broke, don't fix it"—but when it comes to eye relief, it's a big mistake. Whether you're mounting or remounting a scope or you've just been issued a sniper weapon, you *must* adjust the eye relief.

Excuse my harping, but I must emphasize: correct eye relief is critical to properly employing a scope. If you have correct eye relief, you can shoot very fast since the instant you throw your rifle to your shoulder, you can see through the scope. If you have correct eye relief, your entire field of view is visible, yielding the maximum benefit from your optics. If you have correct eye relief, you've largely eliminated parallax. If you have correct eye relief, you'll see the maximum brilliance from your scope, with your eye at just the right exit pupil distance. If you have correct eye relief, your natural stockweld will become an even stronger "muscle memory" and make for better shooting. These are not inconsequential benefits.

On the other hand, if you don't have correct eye relief, you'll find yourself "turkey necking"— bobbing your head back and forth until you find the scope's focus. This is slow and leads to inconsistent shooting.

Interrelated to eye relief is ensuring that your rifle's cheekrest is the correct height so that your eye aligns with the center of the scope and you aren't bobbing your head up and down to find the image, a bad habit I've dubbed "goose necking." Your cheek should be firmly planted on the cheekrest in a natural stockweld and not craned up when eyeing through the scope.

Once you've installed the base and rings, look through the scope and push it as far forward as you can and still see the entire field of view. You'll find that there's about a half-inch margin of vision, and you want to begin with the eye relief as far forward as possible. You start here so your fine-tuning will leave a maximum gap with less chance of the scope striking your eyebrow during recoil.

Now, raise the rifle to your shoulder several times with your eyes closed; when your cheek feels naturally positioned, open your eyes and check the eye relief. Don't try to focus on anything, just check and see if the field of view is at its maximum and you have a clear scope picture with the image filling the glass. Fight the temptation to slide the scope back the tiniest bit more than is absolutely necessary, remembering that recoil will thrust it back during firing.

Once satisfied, tighten the screws a bit more, but leave them loose enough that you can rotate the scope with thumb pressure. Now you're ready to adjust the vertical and horizontal crosshair alignment to prevent canting.

Canting

Canting is the slight misalignment of a scope's crosshairs, when the vertical line is not exactly vertical and the horizontal line is not exactly horizontal. The scope is turned slightly right or left and must be rotated back to the center.

If your scope is canted, you'll tip your rifle while firing and dump bullets right or left, with the effect increasing with distance. For example, you could find that for each six clicks in elevation, the canted crosshair pulls you one click to the left, a situation that hardly lends itself to precision shooting. Even a tiny 1-degree cant will shift your bullet one-half inch per hundred yards.

We've shown a simple way to check canting in the accompanying illustration. Extend your bipod and place the rifle on the ground while holding its butt up at arm's length. If you look carefully, you can actually see the magnified crosshair through the eyepiece.

Now, imagine there's a line running from the heel (bottom) of your buttstock right through the scope to the exact center of its top. The vertical crosshair should coincide with this imaginary line. Rotate the scope until it does, and recheck it at arm's length. (Be careful not to disrupt the eye relief you've just finished setting.)

So, having set the eye relief and checked for canting, you may finish tightening the hex screws, again rapping them to torque them good and tight.

Should you later have problems with the scope slipping inside the rings due to recoil—a real possibility on heavy magnums and .50-caliber sniper rifles—you can anchor the tube to the rings with 3M Scotchkote Electrical Coating, a technique developed by Ross Seyfried, a gun writer and fancier of especially powerful rifles.

Focusing the Eyepiece

Although the scope's eyepiece focus should be factory-set for 20/20 vision, don't assume it's properly set, since someone could have futzed around with it or maybe you're inheriting the scope from a previous shooter with slightly different vision.

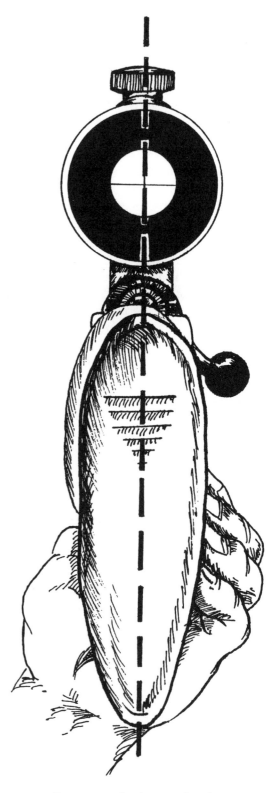

Prevent canting by ensuring that the vertical crosshair truly is vertical.

I'm talking about focusing on the *reticle*, not the ability to see objects through the scope. An in-focus reticle with crisp edges and crosshairs enhances precision shooting. Depending on your scope, you'll find that the rear eyepiece or a threaded ring directly in front of it is rotated to adjust eyepiece focus.

The trick to adjusting reticle focus is to aim your scope at a neutral background, such as the sky or a white wall, so you concentrate purely on focusing the reticle itself.

Also, while adjusting, *make sure* you don't look through the scope too much or your eye will adjust itself and fool you into thinking the reticle's in focus. Only check the focus for a few seconds, then pull your head away, adjust, then look again—but only for two or three seconds.

If you've taken the time to focus correctly on your reticle, you will have greatly reduced later problems with your target being in focus but your crosshairs appearing fuzzy. After reaching age 40, most riflemen experience a subtle decline in close-distance vision, making it imperative to refocus the reticle at least annually for crisp aiming.

Boresighting

The final step before zeroing your rifle is to boresight it, which will save considerable time on the range.

There are two ways to boresight a rifle, with the first requiring that you literally sight down the rifle's bore. To do this, take out your bolt and firmly sandbag or prop your rifle so it's pointing at a small object about 100 yards away. Remove the scope's turret caps so you can adjust the windage and elevation.

Now, look down the rifle's bore and, through the rifling, pick out that small object, then adjust the sandbag so it won't move. Very delicately, lift your head and look through the scope to see how close the crosshair's pointing at the same spot. Make a bold adjustment on windage and elevation to move the crosshair to the object. Then, again look through the rifle's bore and reconfirm that it's pointing at the tiny spot, and again see if the crosshairs are on it.

You may have to repeat this several times, but once you've adjusted the crosshairs for the exact spot where the bore is pointing, crank up 2 1/2 MOAs—10 more clicks—of elevation so you'll mechanically have compensated enough to be "on paper" at 100 and 200 yards. Now you'll be close enough to start zeroing.

A more technical and exact boresight results from a collimator, an optical device you insert at the muzzle with a stud the same size as your bore. When you look through your scope, you'll also be looking through the collimator's grid at the muzzle, with each square representing a few MOAs, usually four or five. Like a target, the collimator grid contains a bull's-eye at its optical center, to which you adjust the windage and elevation. Laser boresights, too, save range time when zeroing a rifle and operate similar to a collimator, allowing you to make rough adjustments before live-firing.

Should your rear base be adjustable for windage, use this base, *not* the scope's internal windage, while boresighting. The internal windage is later used for the live-fire zero.

Elevation is adjusted using only the scope's internal adjustments. Once your crosshairs are aimed directly at the collimator's bull's-eye, you'll be shooting accurately enough at least to be on paper.

Shims

A shim is a very precise, thin wafer of brass used to raise or lower a scope suffering from enormous elevation adjustment problems. If your scope is having problems—such as requiring 10 MOAs from the mechanical center to reach boresight—you may have consumed so many MOAs that you cannot later adjust the scope for dead-on aiming during long-range firing.

By inserting a shim between the rear scope base and receiver, you can raise the point of impact and greatly increase "up" MOAs. A shim placed beneath the front base will lower point of impact and increase the "down" MOAs. These shim widths and resulting MOA changes are:

Shim Thickness	Changes by X MOAs
.005"	3.5 MOA
.010"	7.0 MOA
.015"	10.5 MOA
.020"	14.0 MOA

The importance of preserving elevation MOAs of adjustment becomes clear with a specific example. Let's say your scope has 30 MOAs total elevation and you have a .308 rifle with a 300-yard zero. After zeroing, you find you have 10 MOAs down and 20 MOAs up, but in order to engage targets at 100 yards you need -5.25 MOAs, and to fire at 800 yards you require +23 MOAs. You need three more up MOAs to adjust for 800-yard shots.

Therefore, by inserting a .005-inch shim under the mount's front, you will have in effect "shifted" 3.5 MOAs and can now adjust elevation almost perfectly from 100 through 800 yards. That's quite a result for a paper-thin piece of brass!

You won't know for sure what the final up/down MOAs will be until after you've zeroed, and this means you may have to completely remount the base in order to insert a shim, then boresight again and rezero. It's time-consuming but worthwhile.

On the other hand, this should verify the importance of having a scope with plenty of up/down elevation MOAs for your round's trajectory so you have enough margin to make adjustments and don't even need shims.

Another option is offered by Burris, the Pos-Align Offset Insert Kit, which contains shim-like inserts that fit inside the company's Signature scope rings. These scope ring inserts precisely shift elevation or windage, depending on how they're installed.

RECENTERING A RETICLE

Each time a scope is remounted on a rifle, then fine-adjusted for an exact zero, an inevitable by-product is that a few clicks of windage or elevation have been shifted from the scope's mechanical center.

After several remountings, a significant amount of internal adjustments—especially elevation—may have been consumed, reducing the potential outer adjustment limits and therefore the maximum distance at which you can click in to engage a target dead-on.

Restoring a reticle to its factory-set mechanical center is very simple if there are an equal number of up/down or right/left MOAs. All you need do is turn the adjustment all the way to one end, then come back in the reverse direction and count the number of clicks. Now that you know the total clicks, divide by half and turn the knob back that far.

If you have an unequal number of MOAs—such as 45 up and 15 down elevation—it's a bit more complicated but no problem using the following technique.

Cut two Vs of similar height in a narrow cardboard box so it can hold your scope, as shown in the top illustration on page 113. After removing the elevation and windage turret covers, place the box and scope on a flat surface like a bench and tape it down.

Now, aim the crosshairs at a precise spot 50 yards or farther away. Starting with the elevation turret up, and being very careful not to move the box, rotate the scope while watching the crosshairs.

You will see that the crosshairs will trace an elongated circle or elliptical path as you com-

Elevation and up/down compensation use the vertical mil scale.

Regardless of the technique you use, recentering should be done before a scope is remounted and boresighted.

MINUTE OF ANGLE SIGHT ADJUSTMENTS

When using target knobs or zeroing a scope, you'll be fine-adjusting your elevation and windage to apply corrections. As well, when shooting, your spotter will help you adjust fire at various distances, and here, too, you'll need to know precise ways of applying such corrections to your scope.

Already we've observed that a Minute of Angle is an angular width that equals almost exactly 1 inch (1.047 inch) at 100 yards and spreads out enough to equal 2 inches at 200 yards, then 3 inches at 300 yards, and so on.

The Minute of Angle measurement is especially handy for shooting because we describe bullet trajectories in inches, and the

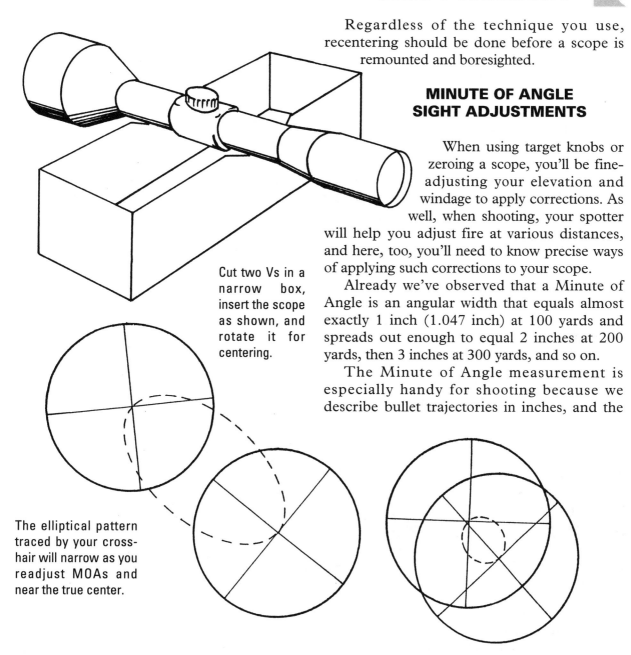

Cut two Vs in a narrow box, insert the scope as shown, and rotate it for centering.

The elliptical pattern traced by your cross-hair will narrow as you readjust MOAs and near the true center.

pletely rotate your scope, as seen in the drawing above.

To restore a mechanical center, you must adjust the elevation or windage to reduce the wide elliptical shape into a very narrow circle. You may have to rotate/adjust/rotate several times to achieve this. Reducing the elliptical path to a few MOAs should be acceptable, a circular pattern of about one-fourth your field of view, around the reticle center.

windage and elevation increments on scopes are fractions of an MOA, with 1/4 MOA commonly found on sniperscopes. All this means is that it takes four clicks to equal 1 MOA.

And how do we use this wondrous measurement? I think some examples will explain all. While zeroing your rifle at 100 yards, you fire a shot that your spotter reports hit 3 inches low. You know you must raise the elevation 3 inches—a snap because at 100 yards, 1 inch equates to 1 MOA. No conversion's required. Since your scope has 1/4 MOA adjustments, that means you must come up 12 clicks (3 inches = 12 clicks @ 1/4 MOA). That was simple.

Now, though, you're firing at a target 500 yards away, and your spotter reports your round hit 6 inches high. You stroke your chin. Let's see, an MOA at 300 yards equals 3 inches, at 400 yards it would be 4 inches, and at 500 yards 1 MOA equals 5 inches. So, to lower the point of impact by 6 inches at 500 yards, I'd have to go down 1 1/5 MOAs. My scope has 1/4 MOA clicks, and therefore I go down 5 clicks to be as close as possible (5 clicks = 6.25 inches).

Next let's compute a windage change. Your bullet has impacted 4 inches left at 700 yards. How many clicks in what direction do you adjust? (Answer below.)

MOA Equivalents at Various Ranges
Distance in Yards

	100	200	300	400	500	600
1 MOA	1"	2"	3"	4"	5"	6"
1/4 MOA	1/4"	1/2"	3/4"	1"	1 1/4"	1 1/2"

The lower line of 1/4 MOA equivalents tells you what one click equals for the indicated ranges. To remember it, just recall that it starts as 1/4 inch at 100 yards—which is identical to the 1/4 MOA increments of your scope—then grows by 1/4 inch each 100 yards. It's an easily understood progression, and if you keep it straight in your mind, you'll avoid a lot of confusion later.

What does one click equal at 300 yards? That's easy—3/4 inches. (You remembered the progression: 1/4, 1/2, then 3/4 for 300 yards.)

A faster way used by long-range target shooters is to fractionalize the 1/4 MOA equivalents, so that 100 yards = 1/4, 200 yards = 2/4, 300 yards = 3/4, 400 yards = 4/4, 800

yards = 8/4, and 1,000 yards = 10/4. As these old-timer shooters compute the clicks, though, they say it out loud as, "Why, 400 yards, that's four-quarters of an inch, or one full inch," meaning one click will equal an inch of movement. "And 700 yards, that's seven-quarters of an inch, or one and three-quarters movement per click."

My good friend Jim "K-Bar" Kauber, a retired Navy SEAL Master Chief and former Gunsite precision rifle rangemaster, has his own handy formula for determining sight changes at various distances. Let's say you've fired a shot at 300 yards and your spotter reports it hit 15 inches low. Here's Jim's formula for calculating the correction in Minutes of Angle:

$$\frac{\text{Correction (in inches)}}{\substack{\text{Distance} \\ \text{(in hundreds of yards)}}} = \text{MOA correction}$$

Let's try it with the numbers from our example:

$$\frac{15\ \text{(inches)}}{3\ \text{(hundreds of yards)}} = 5\ \text{MOA correction}$$

It doesn't matter so much which way you mentally compute MOAs and clicks, but you must have *one* way and practice it. After a while, you'll find yourself clicking in changes about as quick as your spotter calls your shot.

The solution to the windage compensation, above, is two clicks *right*. Recall that at 700 yards 1 MOA equals 7 inches, and each 1/4 MOA click will move the strike of the bullet 1 3/4 inches (seven-quarters, according to an old-timer). Two clicks at 1 3/4 inches each equals 3 1/2 inches, which is as close as you're going to get.

USING TARGET KNOBS

Most police rifle scopes adjust elevation not with a BDC but with target knobs, and for good reason. A military-style Bullet Drop Compensator allows quick elevation dialing for a rapid engagement, but the trade-off is a decline in precision. Recall that in the last chapter, it was noted that the Army's Leupold Mark 4 M3A scope raises elevation at 1 MOA per click, while the USMC's Unertl has 1/2 MOA increments. Thus, a police sniper's realistic engagement distances—perhaps 50 yards out to 200 yards—would allow only two to four clicks of BDC variation, which is not nearly the degree of precision expected of a law enforcement rifleman.

The lawman's target, too, is often much smaller—a single head among four hostages, a half-exposed face, a forehead peering over a window sash—and an occasional miss is not an acceptable standard. No, the police sniper must achieve precision with his aiming, his shot placement, and the degree to which he can adjust his scope. All this leads to using target knobs, with those found in this book offering 1/4 MOA per click, a much smaller, more precise adjustment than a BDC.

Zeroing a target knob-equipped scope is fast

Target knobs, like these atop a Leupold Mark 4 scope, allow very precise elevation adjustments and exact aiming.

and easy. Remove the sling and bipod to create a clean forearm, then rest your rifle snuggly upon sandbags. Support the heel—that is, the bottom of the butt—with a sand-filled sock which your nonshooting hand can squeeze or release to slightly raise or lower the butt. Interspersed with plenty of dry-fire to remain calm and focused, fire a five-round group at 100 yards, applying the basic marksmanship techniques cited in Chapter 6. Analyze the group, then apply the required correction on the windage and elevation knobs. Continue to fire five-round groups and make corrections until you're satisfied that it's firing absolutely dead-on.

This will vary somewhat with the brand and model of scope, but you next loosen the windage and elevation knobs until they turn freely without further engaging the internal adjustments. Now turn each knob clockwise or counterclockwise to *perfectly align* the knob's "0" with the center of a facing scale or witness

RIFLE SCOPE SHORT-RANGE FIELDS OF VIEW

Power	@ 50 yds	@ 25 yds
12x	4.5'	2.25'
10x	5.5'	2.75'
9x	7.0'	3.50'
6x	9.0'	4.25'
3x	16.0'	8.00'

mark. Carefully retighten the knob, keeping that "0" in perfect alignment. Be sure to note which indicator line is immediately below the target knob because this tells you the rotation. In the case of a Leupold Vari-X III, this usually aligns the 100-yard zero elevation at the center of the target knob's second rotation. This makes the 100-yard zero true only when the "0" is aligned with the "2" line. Remember, your scope has several rotations, with 15 MOA per rotation on a Leupold Vari-X III. If I mistakenly align my knob's "0" on the wrong horizontal line, my shots could impact 15 MOA high or low.

USING ELEVATION DATA WITH TARGET KNOBS

Elevation Settings, .308 168-gr. BTHP Match

Yards	MOA Settings*	Inches +/-
50	———	———
75	———	———
100	zero	zero
125	———	———
150	———	———
175	———	———
200	2 MOA + 1 click	-4.4"
225	———	———
250	———	———
225	———	———
300	5 MOA	-16.1"

* Assumes 1/4 MOA per click.

Here's a handy way for a police sniper—or any long-range rifleman—using target knobs to record and refine his elevation knob settings. First, draw up a 3 x 5 card with increments of 25 yards, from your minimum to maximum engagement distances, depicted here as 50 yards out to 300 yards. Then, using your round's data, enter the "book" trajectory and elevation knob settings. Since you're using a 100-yard zero, at 200 yards a .308 168-grain BTHP would impact 4.4 inches low (-4.4"), thus requiring a knob setting of UP 2 MOA plus 1 click. Enter the 300-yard data, too. Now, with a solid zero on your scope, carefully test-fire it at each 25-yard increment, using a laser rangefinder to confirm these distances. Learn exactly what the knob setting should be at each distance and enter it on your card. You'll find that the book settings will be a little off because of tiny differences in your rifle/scope/ammo and the book assumptions. It's especially important to test-fire at less than 100 yards (recall, the average police engagement is about 70 yards) because "funny" things happen during that short-range trajectory. At 75 yards (firing with that 100-yard zero) you may well find your round impacting a bit high, perhaps one click. That's because your bullet path rises slightly above your line of sight. And at 50 yards (firing with the knobs set on the 100-yard zero) you'll probably impact about an inch low because your scope reticle is 1 1/2 inches above your bore. Don't worry about the technical explanation— just test-fire at 50 and 75 yards and then adjust your knobs and record these settings so you know exactly the correct elevation. Duplicate this card, cover it with plastic tape, and keep it in your rifle case. Every time you case your rifle, make a habit of returning the knob to its zero on the correct rotation, and recheck the zero every time you uncase it. Think of it—just fill out this card and you'll be dead-on for firing each 25 yards all the way to 300 yards. Though our sample implies a maximum range of 300 yards, I recommend that a police sniper eventually refine his elevation settings all the way to 500 yards, just in case.

COMEUPS

The concept of comeups can be credited to the military service that has paid more heed to rifle marksmanship and shooter development than any of its American rivals, the U.S. Marine Corps.

Going back at least to the M1 Garand (and probably the 1903A3 Springfield), the idea of comeups was to *know* the exact Minutes of Angle a rifleman needed to raise his sights to go from one distance to another at 100-yard increments. I recall a scene in the epic film *The Sand Pebbles* in which Steve McQueen cranks up his sights, counting the clicks carefully, then places a shot exactly on target at about 400 yards. He had used comeups with an open sight, but the concept can be applied equally to a rifle scope.

A scope-equipped sniper uses comeups either with target knobs or even just an elevation ring to count off 1/4 MOA clicks as he cranks to another elevation. Comeups are calculated for each specific round—based on its bullet weight, velocity, and resulting trajectory—so you must match the particular comeup table here to the round you fire.

Also understand that these comeup tables work *regardless* of your zero range. In essence, they tell you how much to go up or down from one zero so you'll be zeroed at the next range. Of course, there will be tiny but notable variations between these tables and your rifle's performance, so test-fire these comeups and modify them a bit before using them real-world.

THOSE MARVELOUS MIL DOTS

Most modern sniperscopes use a special reticle containing tiny dots atop the stadia lines.

TARGET KNOB COMEUPS: .308 168-gr. BTHP Match
(from a 100-yard zero)

	Actual MOAs	Rounded MOAs	Cumulative Rounded	Leupold Knob Settings *
100 to 200 yds	2.26	2.25	2.25	Zero Rotation: 2 MOA + 1 click
200 to 300 yds	3.1	3.0	5.25	5 MOA + 1 click
300 to 400 yds	3.55	3.5	8.75	8 MOA + 3 clicks
400 to 500 yds	4.15	4.25	13.00	13 MOA
500 to 600 yds	4.70	4.75	17.75	Next UP Rotation: 2 MOA + 3 click
600 to 700 yds	5.24	5.25	23.00	8 MOA
700 to 800 yds	6.11	6.0	29.0	14 MOA
800 to 900 yds	6.9	7.0	36.0	Next UP Rotation: 6 MOA
900 to 1000 yds	7.9	8.0	44.0	14 MOA

* Assumes 1/4 MOA per click, 15 MOA per rotation, as on Leupold Mark 4 LR scopes.

TARGET KNOB COMEUPS: M118LR .308 175-gr. BTHP Match
(from a 100-yard zero)

	Actual MOAs	Rounded MOAs	Cumulative Rounded	Leupold Knob Settings *
100 to 200 yds	2.2	2.25	2.25	Zero Rotation: 2 MOA + 1 click
200 to 300 yds	3.0	3.0	5.25	5 MOA + 1 click
300 to 400 yds	3.45	3.5	8.75	8 MOA + 3 clicks
400 to 500 yds	3.95	4.0	12.75	12 MOA + 3 clicks
500 to 600 yds	4.52	4.5	17.25	Next UP Rotation: 2 MOA + 1 click
600 to 700 yds	4.97	5.0	22.25	7 MOA + 1 click
700 to 800 yds	5.67	5.75	28.0	13 MOA
800 to 900 yds	6.47	6.5	34.5	Next UP Rotation: 4 MOA + 2 clicks
900 to 1000 yds	7.23	7.25	41.75	11 MOA + 3 clicks

* Assumes 1/4 MOA per click, 15 MOA per rotation, as on Leupold Mark 4 LR scopes.

TARGET KNOB COMEUPS: .223/5.56mm 69-gr. BTHP Match
(from a 100-yard zero)

	Actual MOAs	Rounded MOAs	Cumulative Rounded	Leupold Knob Settings *
100 to 200 yds	1.8	1.75	1.75	Zero Rotation: 1 MOA + 3 clicks
200 to 300 yds	2.46	2.5	4.25	4 MOA + 1 click
300 to 400 yds	3.0	3.0	7.25	7 MOA + 1 click
400 to 500 yds	3.6	3.5	10.75	10 MOA + 3 clicks
500 to 600 yds	4.24	4.25	15.0	15 MOA
600 to 700 yds	5.93	6.0	21.0	Next UP Rotation: 6 MOA
700 to 800 yds	5.0	5.0	26.0	11 MOA
800 to 900 yds	6.85	6.75	32.75	Next UP Rotation: 2 MOA + 3 clicks
900 to 1000 yds	7.79	7.75	41.75	10 MOA + 2 clicks

* Assumes 1/4 MOA per click, 15 MOA per rotation, as on Leupold Mark 4 LR scopes.

TARGET KNOB COMEUPS: .300 Winchester Magnum 190-gr. BTHP Match (from a 100-yard zero)

	Actual MOAs	Rounded MOAs	Cumulative Rounded	Leupold Knob Settings *
100 to 200 yds	1.54	1.5	1.5	Zero Rotation: 1 MOA + 2 clicks
200 to 300 yds	2.28	2.25	3.75	3 MOA + 3 clicks
300 to 400 yds	2.69	2.75	6.5	6 MOA + 2 clicks
400 to 500 yds	2.99	3.0	9.5	9 MOA + 2 clicks
500 to 600 yds	3.28	3.25	12.75	12 MOA + 3 clicks
600 to 700 yds	3.68	3.75	16.5	Next UP Rotation: 1 MOA + 2 clicks
700 to 800 yds	4.2	4.25	20.75	5 MOA + 3 clicks
800 to 900 yds	4.5	4.5	25.25	10 MOA + 1 click
900 to 1000 yds	5.18	5.25	30.5	Next UP Rotation: 0 MOA + 2 clicks

* Assumes 1/4 MOA per click, 15 MOA per rotation, as on Leupold Mark 4 LR scopes.

Arrayed outward in all four directions from the center are four evenly spaced dots called "mil dots," but that's a slight misnomer: *it's the space from center dot to center dot that measures one mil, not the dot itself.*

A typical sniper's first impression of these mil dots is, "At least they're small enough not to interfere with my aim." Once you learn to use these dots, however, and realize that short of a laser, there's no more accurate range estimation device—and that these dots help you precisely lead moving targets, hold off for wind, and compensate for uphill and downhill targets— well, you'll agree that these dots are just plain marvelous. And the simple beauty is that you can do all these things without ever taking your eye from your scope or your sight picture off your target. Fast, simple, and no moving parts.

What's a Mil Dot?

A mil is an angular width, just like a Minute of Angle is an angular width, except the mil is a little wider. Recall how 1 MOA represents 1 inch at 100 yards, 2 inches at 200 yards, 8 inches at 800, etc. The mil dot concept is similar, except it primarily has been used to measure distances when adjusting artillery fire. As any artilleryman or mortar gunner can tell you, 1 mil equals 1/6400 of a circle. Much more importantly to us, however, this same 1 mil angular width equates to 1 yard at 1,000 yards or 1 meter at 1,000 meters. This proportional relationship makes possible a simple formula to calculate distances:

$$\frac{\text{Measured Object's Height or Width in Yards (or Meters)} \times 1000}{\text{Same Object's Width or Height in Mils}} = \text{Range in Yards (or Meters)}$$

THE STORY OF MIL DOTS

Remember those World War II submarine movies where the captain ranged an enemy ship through his periscope? Actually, he was measuring the ship's length in mils—and since whole classes of ships were built to the same dimensions, he already knew its length in yards. Thus, in the same way we range today with a mil dot reticle, he could range that ship, then accurately launch torpedoes to intercept it. This mil system for ranging goes back at least to World War I, when artillery forward observers used the mil scale in binoculars to adjust artillery fire. The problem is that binoculars and periscopes use 10-mil increments—equaling 10 yards at 1,000 yards—much too large for ranging man-size objects.

In the late 1970s, U.S. Marine Corps Capt. Jack C. Cuddy was challenged to find a more exact way for Marine snipers to estimate range. After experimenting with

USMC Capt. Jack C. Cuddy (R), developer of the mil dot reticle, speaks to Marine Corps Commandant Gen. Robert Barrow at the 1979 Interservice Rifle Championships.

various ways to use the mil system in a rifle scope, Cuddy settled on the system we see today, found not just in the USMC's 10x Unertl but in many other scopes all around the world. Despite the development of laser rangefinders, the mil dot reticle remains the sniper's mainstay because it adds no moving parts or bulk or weight to his scope, and it's unaffected by weather, but it yields precise ranges unmatched by anything but a laser.

Yet mil-ranging inherently involves a bit of compromise. To reduce fractions and simplify calculations, the U.S. military says a 1-mil angular measurement equals 1-6400 of a circle. Actually, a circle contains 6,175 mils, which means the U.S. system accepts a 2 percent error, equating to 10 yards at 500 yards or 20 yards at 1,000 yards. The Russian mil measurement, too, is a compromise, but they round their circle down to 6,000 mils, causing a slightly larger error of about 3 percent.

Let's try a couple of examples.

Several blocks away, you spot an insurgent sniper atop a roof about to engage a friendly patrol. Through your mil dot reticle, you see a light pole just below the hostile sniper. Being a complete professional, you know that this style of Iraqi light pole is 9 feet tall, which means 3 yards high. In your reticle, the pole measures 8 mils. Your spotter taps out the formula on a handheld calculator:

$$\frac{3 \text{ (yards)} \times 1000}{8 \text{ mils}} = \frac{3000}{8} = 375 \text{ yards}$$

We'll try one more. This time while covertly observing the Baghdad Airport Highway, you detect a pair of electric wires running from a dog's carcass back to a low wall, behind which sits a man watching for an American convoy. Knowing that terrorists have used donkey and dog carcasses to conceal improvised explosive devices, you place your mil dot reticle on that wall—which is the same height as the wall where your team is hiding. The wall is 1 1/2 yards high. It measures 5 mils high. Again, your spotter taps it into the calculator as quick as you announce your readings:

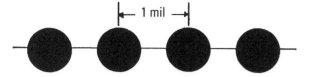

A mil is actually the distance from one dot's center to the next dot's center.

$$\frac{1\ 1/2\ \text{(yards)} \times 1000}{5\ \text{mils}} = \frac{1500}{5} = 300\ \text{yards}$$

You dial your BDC to "3," squeeze off one shot, and scratch one would-be bomber.

Please keep this in mind because it's important: the mil formula works equally well for ranging in meters or yards, but don't mix the two. Measure the object in yards to find the distance in yards, and use meters to yield distances in meters.

A Closer Look at the Mil Dot Reticle

As you may have noticed, all mil dots are not shaped identically. The mil dot in a USMC Unertl scope looks like a miniature football because it's made by wrapping a superfine wire around the stadia line, then tapering it off. Other mil dots are perfectly round because they are etched or laser cut into the lens of the first focal plane. No matter the dot style, the distance *between* dots is always one mil.

The mil dot reticle scale, as shown in our

The wire-wrapped, tapered mil dots in this USMC Unertl scope look like tiny footballs.

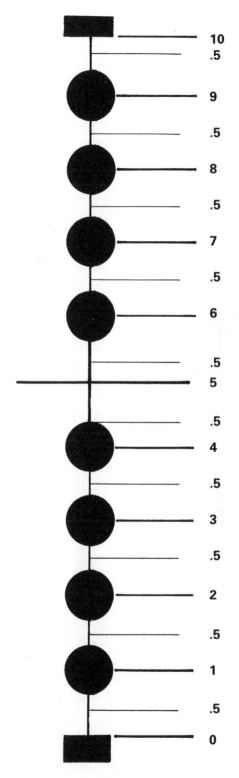

FINE-TUNING THE SCALE FOR RANGE ESTIMATION. We've indicated the exact halfway points so you can mentally split it even finer (right).

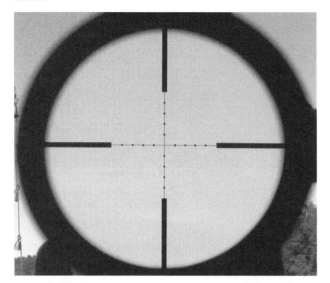

Round mil dots in this Leupold Mark 4 LR scope have been etched into the first focal plane.

illustration, is actually 10 mils high and 10 mils wide, because the very center dot was left out—had it been there dead-center, it would have interfered with your aim. Notice that the crosshair intersection point is at the exact center of where this missing dot would have been. When counting mils, just pretend this dot is there and count it.

Also look carefully at where the thick stadia lines start on the reticle outer edges. Notice that instead of these outermost mils starting or stopping at the middle of a dot, they start/stop at the edge of a thick line. Therefore, you can see 10 mils of right/left width and 10 mils of up/down height.

A Closer Look at Mil-Ranging

A mil dot reticle is a lot like a quality rifle—it offers great precision, but it can be no more accurate than the man using it. To begin with, don't be casual about how you hold your rifle when mil-ranging. Aim the reticle just as steadily and as well supported as when you're using that reticle to take a shot.

Second, be precise when it comes to the object you're measuring, and I mean that two ways: both for knowing or estimating it's real dimensions in yards or meters, and how exactly you measure it in fractions of mils. *Know* that a

VIEWING THROUGH A ZOOM SCOPE

Unlike its fixed-power cousins, a zoom scope can have its magnification changed to fit the specific demands of your situation and needs. This feature requires some emphasis because most snipers set a zoom scope on its highest magnification and never exploit this capability.

When spotting through a rifle scope, give your eyes frequent rests to prevent strain.

Close-Quarters Self-Defense Shooting

3-5x Reduce magnification to low power when marching or stalking through woods and jungle, where contacts of less than 100 yards are likely. You should practice rapid-fire drills against targets at 25–50 yards, with your scope set on low power.

Observing/Searching for Targets

6-7x Unless the area you're scanning is very far away—say 700+ yards—you should use only about 6x, so you have a wide field of view. Your spotter complements this by using a 20x spotting scope or 10x binoculars. Once you have found something worth a closer look, you just zoom up to higher power.

Engaging Distant Targets

9-12x When you or your spotter confirms a target, zoom up to highest power. You should always prefer to shoot with this maximum magnification since this was the setting you originally used when zeroing and should provide the most exacting accuracy.

light pole is 9 feet high, or that a fence post is 4 1/2 feet (1 1/2 yards) high. To put yourself in the correct mind-set, use decimal-point fractions of a yard, then ask yourself, "Is that 4.5 yards or actually 4.6 yards?" And when you measure it, use *tenths of a mil* if possible.

Your reticle is not divided more finely than the dots themselves, but almost immediately you'll be able to split the distance between mils mentally so you can measure half mils, too. With practice, you'll be able to mentally split these measurements into quarters and, eventually, tenths of a mil.

Here's a simple exercise. Along with several sniper buddies, do your best mil-ranging against distant targets and check the results immediately with a laser rangefinder. To the degree that your estimate was erroneous, analyze why, then do it again, repeating the process. Maybe run a few side bets or rib the sniper with the least accurate estimate. That's how you develop an "eye" for seeing those tenths of a mil.

One great development has been the installation of mil dot reticles in some spotting scopes, particularly the Leupold Mark 4 12-40x60. Think of it—at 40x (four times the magni-fication of an Army or Marine rifle scope)—the spotter can measure an object with incredible exactness. At Gunsite we found mil dot reticle spotting scopes great not only for mil-ranging but also for adjusting a sniper's fire because both the spotter and the sniper could keep their eyes on their optics and use the same mil increments for shifting fire. It was fast and very precise.

While U.S. military sniperscopes use mil dot reticles at fixed, 10x magnification, several variable-magnification rifle scopes also incorporate mil dots. Like spotting scopes, these offer higher magnification for ranging, but here's a major consideration: most of these scopes put the reticle in the second focal plane—which means the mil dot size is only in synch for one magnification, usually the highest. Quality European scopes, such as the Schmidt & Bender—along with some Leupold Mark 4 LR zoom scopes—have the mil dot reticle in the first focal plane so it stays in synch at all magnifications.

Note that my previous examples did not range on men but on objects near them. Mil-ranging off a human body is inherently inexact because there's no standard size. Further, as shown in our illustration below, a sitting man or kneeling man is not actually half the height of an upright man. And a kneeling man is considerably taller than a sitting one—about 50 percent taller.

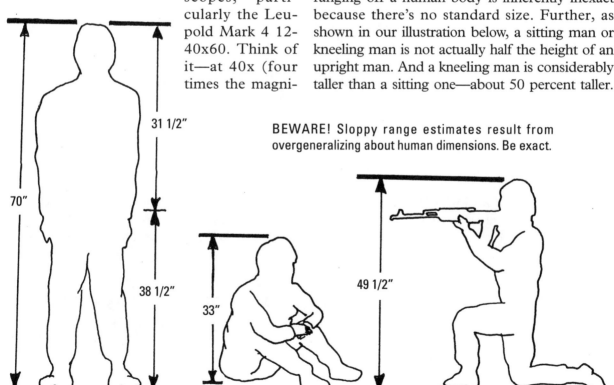

BEWARE! Sloppy range estimates result from overgeneralizing about human dimensions. Be exact.

31 1/2"

70"

38 1/2"

33"

49 1/2"

Examples of 36-inch (1 yard) range indicators when using mil dot reticles.

Likewise, notice that a man's waist is not the halfway point of his height—a spot about halfway between his crotch and his waist is the more accurate mid-height point. With practice, you may learn to estimate a man's height according to how large he looks compared to the SVD or AK or RPG he's carrying.

It's well worth the effort to find common objects in your area of operations that exactly measure yards/meters or fractions of them. Man-made objects usually are best because they're likely to be of uniform size. These could be doorways, windows, cars at the front axle, or road signs. Oil drum capacities and dimensions vary, but they're usually a standard size inside a particular country. Enemy equipment, too, is of standard dimensions, everything from truck widths to the height of a tank—for example, a Russian-built T-72 is almost exactly 1 yard from its bottom track to the base of its turret.

Windage Holdoff and Moving Target Leads

We've included a table that lists 1-mil width equivalents from 100 to 1,000 yards (actual and rounded off) so you can calculate how many mils to hold right or left when firing in a crosswind or engaging a moving target, and to compensate when firing at targets uphill or downhill from you. These shooting techniques and their required holds are explored fully in later chapters, but here's where you get an appreciation for what your mil dot reticle can do.

As you can see, the required leads and holds increase with distance, *but so does the relative width of a mil.* Look carefully and you'll see that a 2-mil moving target lead for a walking man is almost perfect from 100 yards all the way to 600+ yards. Calculate your own holds and test them live-fire.

The real beauty of a mil dot reticle and BDC is that you can first rotate the BDC to the exact range, then use the mil scale for a split-second to fine-tune your aim—for wind, target movement, or up/downhill compensation—and then, using a dot or an imaginary "hold" between two dots, fire with great exactness. True, it would be even a bit more precise to "dial your dope" for fine-tuned windage or compensation, but that takes a few extra seconds and requires you to remove your eye from the scope. That

Wind compensation and moving target leads use the horizontal mil scale.

MIL WIDTH EQUIVALENTS FOR COMPENSATED SHOOTING
M118LR (.308 175-gr. BTHP Match)

Distance Yards	1 mil Actual	1 mil Rounded	Walking Target * Lead	10 mph Crosswind	45 Degree Up/Down Comp
100	3.6″	4″	7″	0.6″	0.7″
200	7.2″	7″	13″	3.0″	3.3″
300	10.8″	11″	21″	7.0″	7.8″
400	14.4″	14″	29″	12.7″	15.0″
500	18.0″	18″	37″	20.8″	24.0″
600	21.6″	22″	46″	31.4″	37.0″
700	25.2″	25″	56″	44.3″	54.0″
800	28.8″	29″	68″	60.1″	75.0″
900	32.4″	32″	80″	79.1″	102.0″
1000	36.0″	36″	93″	101.1″	135.0″

* Assumes 3 mph walking speed.

target could be long gone by the time you renew your aim. If there's plenty of time, with your target lax and unconcerned about your possible presence, by all means, dial all your dope and take that picture-perfect shot. But quite often you'll find that a well-placed shot, fired quickly, is more certain of success than a perfectly planned shot fired a little later.

Mil-Ranging Shortcuts

Here are a few ways to speed up your mil-ranging. First, get your spotter a small hand-held calculator, so he can tap out the mil formula data as quickly as you read it through your scope. He tells you the indicated range, you dial your BDC, and "bang!" It gets a little more complicated in darkness, but you can figure your own way around that challenge.

Another shortcut is the Quick Mil Dot Calculations chart we've printed on page 126. Copy it, cover it with clear tape or acetate adhesive, and use it in the field. Every distance solution is right on the mark, but, as you can see, it condenses a lot of data, especially when it comes to the longest distances. This originally was published by the Austrian military scope maker, Kahles, but I've modified the format to make it easier to read.

A third shortcut is to scrounge a set of laminated cards that contain all the possible solutions for mil-ranging, in tenths of a mil, out to 2,000 yards. These cards have been floating around in the U.S. Special Ops community for at least a decade, but I don't know where they're available commercially. Any major military sniper school probably has a set on-hand.

Finally, an ingenious device called the Mildot Master was recently developed by New Mexico rifleman and engineer Bruce Robinson. Operating like a slide rule, it allows you to quickly compute mil ranges, bullet drop, and up/down angled shooting and works so well that it's now standard issue to U.S. Army snipers. I'm sure it can be ordered through the Internet, and it's well worth it.

QUICK MIL DOT CALCULATIONS

Actual Object Height or Width

Meters	.20	.30	.40	.45	.50	.55	.60	.81	.91	1.50	1.67	1.75	1.80
Inches	9	12	16	18	2	22	24	32	36	60	66	69	72
Yards	.250	.333	.444	.500	.558	.611	.667	.889	1.00	1.667	1.833	1.917	2.00
3/4	333	444	593	666	741	815	889	1185	1333	2223	2444	2556	2667
1	250	333	445	500	556	611	667	889	1000	1667	1833	1917	2000
1 1/4	200	266	355	400	445	489	534	711	800	1334	1466	1537	1600
1 1/2	167	222	396	333	371	407	445	593	667	1111	1222	1278	1333
1 3/4	143	190	254	285	318	349	381	508	571	953	1047	1095	1143
2	125	167	222	250	278	306	334	445	500	834	917	959	1000
2 1/4	111	148	197	222	247	272	296	396	444	741	815	852	889
2 1/2	100	133	178	200	222	244	267	356	400	667	733	767	800
2 3/4	91	121	161	182	202	222	243	323	364	606	667	697	727
3	83	111	148	167	185	204	222	296	333	556	611	639	667
3 1/4	77	102	137	154	171	188	205	273	308	513	564	590	615
3 1/2	71	95	127	143	159	175	191	254	286	476	524	548	571
3 3/4	67	89	118	133	148	163	178	237	267	445	489	511	533
4	63	83	111	125	139	153	167	222	250	417	458	479	500
4 1/4	59	78	104	118	131	144	157	209	235	392	431	451	471
4 1/2	56	74	99	111	124	136	148	197	222	370	407	426	445
4 3/4	53	70	93	105	117	128	140	187	210	351	386	404	421
5	50	67	89	100	111	122	133	178	200	333	367	383	400
5 1/4	48	63	85	95	105	116	127	169	190	318	349	365	381
5 1/2	45	61	81	91	101	111	121	162	182	303	333	349	364
5 3/4	43	58	77	87	97	106	116	155	174	290	319	333	348
6	42	56	74	83	93	102	111	148	167	278	306	320	333
6 1/4	40	53	71	80	89	98	107	142	160	267	293	307	320
6 1/2	38	51	68	77	86	94	103	137	154	256	282	295	308
6 3/4	37	49	66	74	82	91	99	132	148	247	272	284	296
7	36	48	63	71	79	87	95	127	143	238	262	274	286
8	31	42	56	63	70	76	83	111	125	208	229	240	250
9	28	37	49	56	62	68	74	99	111	185	203	213	222
10	25	33	44	50	56	61	67	89	100	167	183	192	200

MEASURED HEIGHT/WIDTH IN MILS

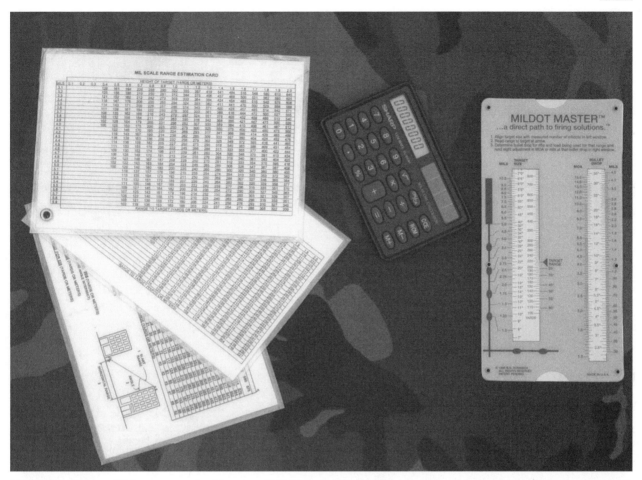

The Mildot Master (R) is now standard issue to U.S. Army snipers, while mil dot cards (L) are useful, and a hand-held calculator essential.

BULLETS AND BALLISTICS

THE SNIPER'S BULLET

One bullet is not the same as the next. This is the simple statement with which I begin ballistics classes because it is critical that a sniper acquire an appreciation for even slight differences in bullet performance.

Consider the data in the chart, "Bullets Are Not the Same." Say we're hunting mule deer in Wyoming, and you suddenly discover you've misplaced your .30-06 ammunition. Luckily, I also have a .30-06, so you ask to borrow a few rounds. "For sure." Since you're a more attuned shooter than the next rifleman and know that you've zeroed your scope with 150-grain

bullets, you ask if my ammo, too, has 150-grain bullets. Again I reply, "For sure." Great!

But wait. Despite even the same bullet weight, there's a tremendous variation in the performance of different bullet types, different powders, and different loads. Indeed, looking at the box you'll see some bullets with a 50-percent greater kinetic energy at 500 yards, an extreme trajectory difference of 13.6 inches at 500 yards, dramatically different wind drift, and so on.

And these all are .30-06, 150-grain rounds. Think of how much more inconsistent things could become if these bullets were of different weights.

My point: the first step in achieving con-

BULLETS ARE NOT THE SAME
.30-06 150-gr. Bullet Performance at 500 Yards

CARTRIDGE	Energy in ft-lbs.	Velocity in fps	Drift from 10 mph wind	Drop from 100-yd. zero
Federal Hi-Shok	876	1620	31.0"	-66.9"
Federal Prem. BTSP	1212	1907	21.3"	-58.7"
Hornady Spire Point	975	1711	27.0"	-65.6"
Hornady BTSP	1065	1788	24.3"	-63.6"
Norma BTSP	970	1706	28.9"	-58.8"
Remington Core-Lokt	876	1622	30.9"	-66.8"
Remington Bronze Point	1047	1773	25.6"	-62.2"
Winchester Power Point	716	1466	37.5"	-72.3"
Winchester Silvertip	876	1622	30.9"	-66.8"

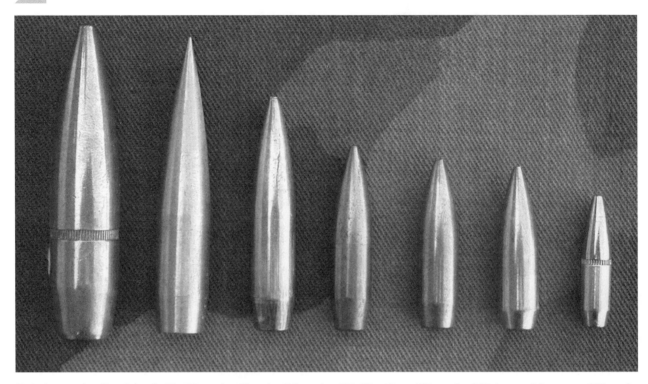

Relative projectile sizes (L-R): 750-grain .50-cal.; 419-grain .408 CheyTac; 300-grain .338 Lapua Magnum; 190-grain .300 Winchester Magnum; 175-grain .308; 168-grain .308; and 69-grain .223.

sistent performance is by always shooting the exact same kind of round. And by exact, I mean *exactly* the same round.

Boat-tails Are Better

Returning to that box, notice that generally the slowest bullets with the greatest drag and widest wind drift—the Federal Hi-Shok and Winchester Power Point—are stubbier, round-nose types. It's not that they're bad bullets; it's just that they're designed to cause more damage against a target at close range, as so-called "brush busters." That's their job.

But one load—the Federal Premium—has a significantly better trajectory, retains more energy, and stays truer through wind than the others. This is a boat-tail bullet, a sniper's best friend.

The boat-tail design is called such because its silhouette resembles the outline of a boat, with a thin tip and a tapered base. This design retains more velocity than others due to an aerodynamic shape that both improves wind resistance and reduces drag by cutting down the

size of its base—the area affected by the vacuum a speeding bullet generates. Military rifle ranges must add 10 percent more distance to impact areas when troops are firing boat-tail rounds because of such enhanced performance.

A boat-tail isn't necessarily the best round for hunting, but it so improves ballistic performance generally that it indeed is the best round when it comes to long-range accuracy. And accuracy is a sniper's greatest concern—remember, accuracy equals consistency and vice versa. Well, the consistency part of this bullet equation is provided by firing not merely boat-tail bullets but *match*-grade boat-tail ammunition, manufactured to the closest of tolerances for exactly the same performance, shot after shot.

Match-Grade Ammunition

Although several brands of match-grade bullets are available, the first was Sierra's 168-grain MatchKing bullet. Federal Cartridge loads this Sierra bullet in its popular .308

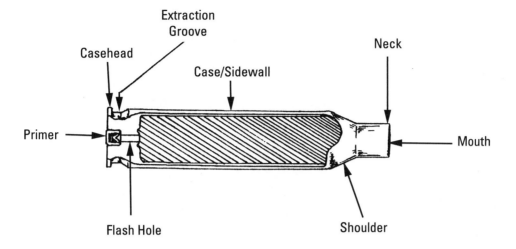

A typical modern rifle cartridge.

BTHP Match ammunition (as do several mainstream companies), and it's this ammo I've seen in the hands of police snipers much more so than any other.

First produced in the late 1950s, Sierra's 168-grain MatchKing bullet proved its superiority at its first outing, capturing first place at the 1959 Pan American Games. This bullet remains very popular in 200- and 300-yard rapid fire competitions, while heavier Sierra MatchKing bullets have won more than 20 Camp Perry Wimbledon 1,000-yard matches.

Sierra ballistician David Brown says this phenomenal bullet's tolerances are very close; in fact, an entire lot is rejected if a randomly selected sample will not attain a five-shot, 100-yard group no greater than 1/4 MOA using a machine rest. Each bullet's weight must be

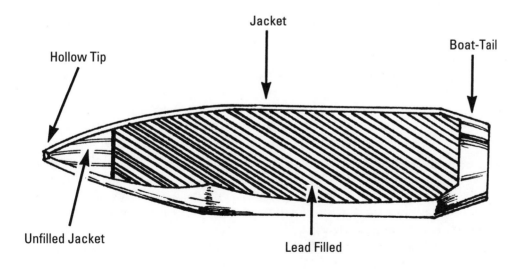

Sierra's renowned BTHP MatchKing bullet.

within 2/10 of a grain, and jacket wall concentricity has a fine .0003 of an inch maximum tolerance.

Brown helped me put to rest one myth about this bullet. "The hollowpoint design is a by-product of our production process, not for expansion upon impact," he said. Formed jackets are fitted into a precision die upside down; the lead is pressed in at a carefully controlled rate until all but an exact, small space in the tip is filled. Now, in order to extract the finished bullet from this tight die, a thin, wirelike punch is pushed through, right into a narrow hole left in the tip for this purpose. Out pops the bullet, which now has a tiny hole and slight unfilled space in the tip.

This is not a true hollowpoint; indeed, it tends to break or bend upon impact, not expand in any traditional sense. As an added benefit, this design "eliminates any point deformation in flight," according to Sierra.

Match bullets also are manufactured by Hornady, Speer, Lapua, and Nosler. Lapua uses superb Scenar 168-grain hollowpoints or 170-grain FMJ BT bullets in its .308 Match rounds. Quality is the byword in all these bullets and cartridges.

Lots and Lots of Lots

Remember: Accuracy equals . . .? Yes, *consistency*, and there's yet another way to add a bit more consistency to our ammunition performance, and that's by using rounds only from the same manufacturer's lot.

In the same lot of ammunition, all the primers were made on the same equipment, with the same compound, probably by the same person, and likely on the same day. The powder came from the very same batch, which was mixed at the same time, shipped on the same day, stored in the same way and for the same period of time, then loaded into the cartridges by the same machine. The brass came from the same stock, it was extruded and shaped at the same time and on the same machines, and it was sized and finished on the same day. The bullets, too, were made in a single lot, from the same machines and the same components and by the same people. Then, finally, all these came together into one lot of loaded ammunition that was made at one time, in one place, on one machine, and by the same persons.

So, you take the rounds from this lot, just this lot, use it to zero your rifle, then find a secure place to store all the ammo you'll need for perhaps the next six months, and use only this ammo for practice and real-world applications. When this lot is gone, rezero your rifle for another lot of match-grade rounds and again store an ample supply in a secure place.

Moly-Coated Bullets

In recent years there have been many claims that coating a bullet with molybdenum disulfide increases velocity and improves long-range accuracy. Without question, a thin layer of "moly" makes the bullet slicker, reducing friction as it travels down a bore. As an added benefit, the bullet slightly coats the bore, leaving it cleaner and somewhat impervious to powder fouling, and thus easier to maintain.

Whether applied as a liquid that dries into a film coating or impact plating using a tumbler and wax sealant, this moly coat is so thin that it doesn't change a bullet's outer dimensions.

Before his untimely death, I spoke with NECO founder Roger Johnston, who developed the impact plating process, the most-used means for moly-coating bullets. When done in combination with BlackStar barrel treatment (see Chapter 2), Johnston reported that moly-coated bullets yield a 13 percent decrease in chamber pressure but only a 3 percent decrease in velocity, suggesting that the powder load could be modified to yield much flatter trajectory without exceeding a rifle's maximum chamber pressure. That offers remarkable ballistic possibilities that have yet to be fully realized.

There's no question that moly-coated bullets help a bore better withstand powder and copper fouling. Black Hills Ammo owner Jeff Hoffman, a competitive shooter and former SWAT sniper, used to clean his bore every 20 rounds. But now, he reports, "I shoot all day long, typically 80 to 100 rounds, then clean at the end of the day. Cleaning is easier than before, even after [firing] four to five times as many rounds." Hoffman's company offers America's widest variety of loaded, moly-coated match ammo, some 14 high-quality loads in .308, .223, and .300 Winchester Magnum.

Walt Berger—a longtime champion rifleman and president of Berger Bullets—is also convinced of moly-coating's efficiency. "I have shot 1,193 rounds of moly-coated bullets," he says, "without having to use a bore brush once—and a high of 73 rounds before using a patch saturated with solvent." Berger now moly-coats a variety of his commercial match bullets.

While developing the M118 Long Range round, the Lake City Army Ammunition Plant included several tests using moly-coated bullets, which "all shot better than control cartridges in 600-yard accuracy tests." Interestingly, these loads also demonstrated a "measurable reduction of chamber pressures." However, by the time the distance reached 1,000 yards, the moly-coated rounds performed no more accurately than other loads. Had these test rounds been loaded to higher velocity—which the reduced chamber pressure could allow—they may have scored better at 1,000 yards, too.

One long-range shooter who boosted his powder load to exploit that reduction in chamber pressure claims a phenomenal 5 MOA reduction in bullet drop at 1,000 yards. Another reports a marked improvement in shot-string consistency—that is, unable to clean his rifle every 5 or 10 rounds, he nonetheless finds consistent accuracy from his 15th or 20th or 25th rounds due to less bore fouling, so his bullets impact consistently. Previously he'd found his groups open up after about 10 rounds.

I don't think there's any question that moly-coated bullets have a beneficial impact on long-range shooting accuracy. But clearly defining, measuring, and standardizing that impact, and understanding the dynamics of how it all fits with powder load and rifling and resulting velocities, is still something of the future, which perhaps we'll see reflected in the next generation of sniper ammunition.

.308 WINCHESTER: THE SNIPING WORKHORSE

Beyond any doubt, the .308 Winchester (7.62mm NATO) is the world's most popular military and law enforcement sniping cartridge, and for good reason.

This bullet is powerful enough to penetrate most media a police or military sniper would encounter, yet it's not a heavy magnum round that generates punishing recoil. And it packs sufficient lethality for even the most drug-crazed suspect with one well-placed shot.

Unfortunately, by contrast I know of several stateside police sniping engagements in which

An abundance of ammo—all .308 Winchester 168-grain BTHP Match.

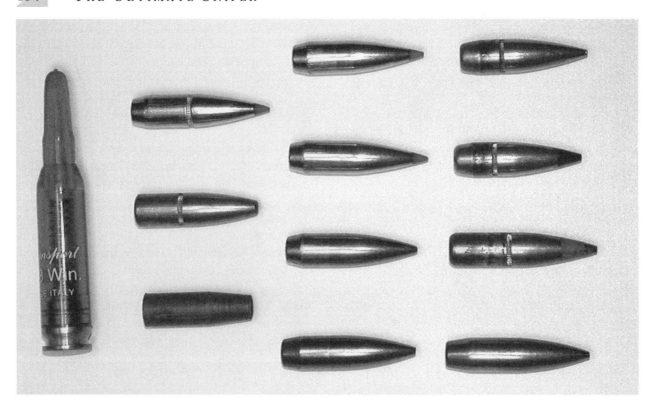

.308 SNIPING PROJECTILES: (left column, top to bottom) Hornady TAP 165-grain barrier; Federal 165-grain Tactical; Longbow frangible; (middle column) Hornady TAP 155-grain A-Max; Hornady TAP 168-grain A-Max; Sierra 168-grain BTHP; Black Hills moly on 175-grain Sierra BTHP; (right column) M80 147-grain ball; M993 military armor piercing; military tracer; M118 Special Ball 173-grain (obsolete). At left is a Snapcap for dry-firing.

suspects were solidly hit with .223 bullets but went on to kill hostages or police before being incapacitated. If you compare the data we've provided, you'll notice that the .308 packs considerably more energy, holds up much better in a crosswind, and retains superior velocity at long distance. Due to its faster initial velocity, the .223 has a bit better trajectory than the .308, the only area in which it can even compare to the 7.62mm round.

Through its extensive use, we know a great deal about the .308, and there's an adequate variety of match-grade or premium bullets for almost any application. Our ballistic data addresses both the civilian Federal .308 168-grain BTHP Match and the military M118 Long Range round, since there are minor but significant variances between these two bullets, despite the fact that both leave the muzzle at

2,600 fps. The slightly better performance of the military match reflects a 7-grain heavier bullet.

Indeed, as I hope to impress upon you, the essence of precision long-range shooting is recognizing and taking into account even minor differences whenever encountered.

The .308 Winchester Ballistic Advantage

A term cited repeatedly in this book is "ballistic advantage," the great benefit you have over potential opponents due to your .308's performance. I coined this term so snipers could clearly understand that at ranges beyond about 400 yards, their rifles are inherently more accurate, more powerful, and more lethal than the assault rifles carried by their adversaries. At shorter ranges, an assault rifle's large magazine capacity and high rate of fire give an opponent the advantage.

BALLISTIC COMPARISON: .223 vs. .308

FOOT-POUNDS OF KINETIC ENERGY

		Distance in Yards				
	Muzzle	200	400	600	800	1000
.223 69 gr. Match	1380	925	475	375	235	170
.308 175 gr. Match	2625	1975	1460	1060	765	560

BULLET DRIFT IN 10 MPH CROSSWIND

		Distance in Yards				
	100	200	400	600	800	1000
.223 69 gr. Match	0.9"	3.7"	16.3"	41.3"	82.2"	140"
.308 175 gr. Match	0.6"	3.0"	12.7"	31.4"	60.1"	101"

BULLET VELOCITY

		Distance in Yards				
	Muzzle	200	400	600	800	1000
.223 69 gr. Match	3000	2460	1980	1560	1240	1060
.308 175 gr. Match	2600	2260	1940	1650	1400	1200

TRAJECTORY FOR 100-YARD ZERO

		Distance in Yards				
	100	200	400	600	800	1000
.223 69 gr. Match	Zero	-3.2"	-28.3"	-89.4"	-207"	-405"
.308 175 gr. Match	Zero	-4.5"	-34.9"	-103"	-222"	-415"

Therefore, think of yourself as a long-armed boxer who keeps your foe at arm's length, where you can pound him and exploit this great advantage. Equally, realize that allowing your foe to come within close range brings mortal danger.

Since this is an advantage inherent with the ballistics of these respective rounds, let's examine these relationships exactly. Our first data box compares .308 Federal Match bullet energy against the energy of Soviet Type PS 7.62mm 123-grain and 5.45mm 53-grain rounds fired from an AKM assault rifle. (A foot-pound is the amount of energy needed to lift 1 pound, 1 foot.)

From the muzzle, the .308 has approximately two times the energy of its competitors—meaning it will strike with twice the force, penetrate media to about twice the depth, and so on. But as we go farther out, the advantage of the .308's heavier boat-tail bullet actually becomes even greater. By the time we're at 600 yards, it's hitting with about *four times* the force. To keep this in perspective,

BULLET VELOCITY
Distance in Yards—Velocity in Feet per Second

	Muzzle	100	200	300	400	500	600
7.62x39mm SOV	2340	2080	1836	1606	1388	1190	1051
5.45x39mm SOV	2953	2663	2387	2130	1889	1662	1447
.308 168-gr. Match	2600	2420	2240	2070	1910	1760	1610
.308 175-gr. Match	2600	2420	2260	2090	1940	1790	1650

BULLET DROP/TRAJECTORY
Distance in Yards—Path in Inches

	100	200	300	400	500	600
7.62x39mm SOV	-3.5	-14.9	-37.0	-72.4	-126.5	-106.9
5.45x39mm SOV	-2.1	-9.2	-22.4	-43.2	-74.1	-117.7
.308 168-gr. Match	-2.5	-11.0	-26.4	-49.9	-82.9	-127.2
.308 175-gr. Match	-2.6	-11.0	-26.4	-49.8	-82.5	-126.3

10 MPH WIND DRIFT COMPARISON
Distance in Yards

	100	200	300	400	500
7.62x39mm SOV	1.5"	6.4"	15.2"	28.7"	47.3"
.308 168-gr. Match	0.8"	3.1"	7.4"	13.6"	22.2"
.308 175-gr. Match	0.6"	3.0"	7.0"	12.7"	20.8"

FOOT-POUNDS OF ENERGY
Distance in Yards

	Muzzle	100	200	300	400	500	600
7.62x39mm SOV	1485	1172	913	699	522	384	299
5.45x39mm SOV	1026	834	671	534	420	325	246
.308 168-gr. Match	2520	2180	1870	1600	1355	1150	970
.308 175-gr. Match	2625	2285	1975	1705	1460	1245	1060

realize that the AKM rounds generate much less energy at 600 yards than a mere 9mm does at the muzzle, which is about 350 ft-lbs. (You must respect a 9mm, too, as a lethal round, but don't forget that your sniper hide should give you protection against direct small-arms fire.)

Next, consider the drift advantage you have when it comes to a 10 mph crosswind, shown in the next box. Again, the advantage is immediate but becomes more profound with distance. By the time the AKM 7.62mm round has traveled 400 yards, it has blown fully two body widths off target. Imagine your foe hopelessly "guesstimating" when firing 500 or more yards into the wind or shooting against a stiffer crosswind.

THE LEGALITY OF OPEN-TIPPED MATCH BULLETS

At first glance, it would appear that hollowpoint match bullets—such as the Sierra and Hornady 168-grain and Sierra 175-grain MatchKings—violate the Hague Convention of 1907, which forbids "projectiles or material calculated to cause unnecessary suffering." In the past, this clause has been found to encompass so-called "dumdum" bullets that mushroom or expand violently and break apart. Civilian ammo boxes describe match loads as "BTHP," meaning "boat-tail, hollow-point." Does that mean these rounds are illegal? Is it a war crime to use them?

U.S. Army Special Operations Command requested a formal finding on sniper use of match-grade hollowpoint bullets, which led to a study by W. Hays Parks, the Department of the Army's highest-ranking civilian Judge Advocate General (JAG) officer. A Vietnam combat vet and reserve Marine colonel, Parks is an accomplished high-powered rifle shooter and handloader, so there could not have been a better technical and legal expert to examine the issue. Here is his study's conclusion:

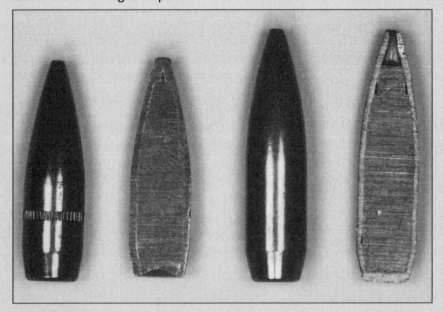

This cutaway view of Sierra BTHP Match (R) discloses that it's not a true hollowpoint and inflicts tissue damage similar to military ball (L).

"The purpose of the 7.62 mm 'open-tip' MatchKing bullet is to provide maximum accuracy at very long range. Like most 5.56 mm and 7.62 mm ball bullets, it may fragment upon striking its target, although the probability of its fragmentation is not as great as some military ball bullets currently in use by some nations. Bullet fragmentation is not a design characteristic, however, nor a purpose for use of the MatchKing by United States Army snipers. Wounds caused by MatchKing ammunition are similar to those caused by a fully jacketed military ball bullet, which is legal under the law of war, when compared at the same ranges and under the same conditions. The military necessity for its use—its ability to offer maximum accuracy at very long ranges—is complemented by the high degree of discriminate fire it offers in the hands of a trained sniper. It not only meets, but exceeds, the law of war obligations of the United States for use in combat."

Thanks to Colonel Parks' study, a similar opinion was issued by the U.S. Navy's JAG, which applies to Marine and Navy SEAL snipers, too.

A round's bullet path tracks its descent from the instant it exits a muzzle aimed parallel to the earth and indicates the amount a shooter must hold high when firing at longer distances. Here the advantage over a 7.62x39mm is obvious, but the higher velocity 5.45x39mm maintains a trajectory comparable to the .308 Match round.

Our final comparison is velocity, and here the long-distance .308 advantage clearly shows, despite the initial superiority of the 5.45x39mm bullet. Because the heavier .308 better maintains momentum, it overtakes the 5.45mm bullet at 400 yards, and by 600 yards it's decisively superior to either AKM round.

Now let's combine these ballistic effects. The .308 Match bullet strikes with considerably more energy, an advantage that increases with distance; it shoots truer and straighter in a crosswind; it is much flatter shooting than the 7.62x39mm and approximately similar even to the 5.45x39mm; and the .308 considerably exceeds these rounds'

velocity beyond 400 yards. Overall, this is a decisive ballistic advantage.

Put this together with the considerably higher quality of a sniper's match ammunition, the greater accuracy of his rifle, the superb optics of his scope, and, cumulatively, there's a tremendous advantage to the sniper when engaging targets more than 400 yards away.

THE M118 LONG RANGE ROUND

When I began instructing sniping in the early 1980s, America's military sniper round was the M118 Special Ball, a 173-grain, 7.62mm (.308) cartridge. Though it incorporated an excellent Lake City Army Ammunition Plant brass case and it was more accurate than the standard military M80 ball round, the M118's accuracy could not compare to civilian match ammo. At my request, Lance Peters, an Olympic-level rifleman, extensively tested the

TRAJECTORY TABLE, .308 168-GR. BOAT-TAIL HOLLOWPOINT (MATCH)
Trajectory by Yards, Expressed in Inches

Zero Range	100	200	300	400	500	600	700	800	900	1000
100 yards	Zero	-4.5	-15.9	-35.5	-64.6	-105	-159	-228	-315	-421
200 yards	+2.2	Zero	-9.15	-26.5	-53.3	-91.5	-143	-210	-295	-400
300 yards	+5.3	+6.1	Zero	-14.3	-38.1	-73.2	-121	-185	-267	-369
400 yards	+8.9	+13.3	+10.8	Zero	-20.1	-57.6	-96.3	-157	-235	-333
500 yards	+13.0	+21.5	+23.1	+16.5	Zero	-27.0	-67.6	-124	-198	-292
600 yards	+17.5	+30.5	+36.6	+34.5	+22.9	Zero	-36.1	-87.8	-157	-247
700 yards	+22.6	+40.7	+51.9	+54.9	+48.4	+30.6	Zero	-47.0	-112	-196
800 yards	+28.4	+51.4	+69.3	+78.1	+77.4	+65.4	+40.2	Zero	-59.4	-139
900 yards	+35.0	+65.5	+89.1	+105	+110	+105	+86.4	+52.2	Zero	-72.4
1000 yards	+42.2	+80.0	+111	+133	+147	+149	+137	+110	+65.2	Zero

TRAJECTORY TABLE, M118 LONG RANGE 175-GR. MATCH
Trajectory by Yards, Expressed in Inches

Zero Range	100	200	300	400	500	600	700	800	900	1000
100 yards	Zero	-4.5	-15.8	-34.9	-63.0	-103	-155	-222	-308	-415
200 yards	+2.3	Zero	-9.0	-26.0	-52.0	-90	-139	-204	-288	-392
300 yards	+5.2	+6.0	Zero	-13.8	-37.0	-72.0	-118	-180	-261	-362
400 yards	+8.7	+13.0	+10.4	Zero	-20	-51.0	-94.0	-152	-230	-328
500 yards	+12.7	+21.0	+22.2	+16.0	Zero	-27.1	-66.4	-121	-194	-288
600 yards	+17.2	+30.0	+36.0	+34.0	+22.6	Zero	-34.8	-85.0	-154	-243
700 yards	+22.1	+39.8	+50.7	+53.7	+47.5	+29.8	Zero	-45.1	-109	-193
800 yards	+27.8	+51.1	+67.6	+76.3	+75.6	+63.6	+35.0	Zero	-58	-137
900 yards	+34.2	+64.0	+87.2	+102	+108	+102	+84.7	+51.7	Zero	-72.3
1000 yards	+41.5	+78.5	+109	+131	+144	+146	+185	+109	+65.0	Zero

M118 for consistent bullet weight, consistent powder charge, case concentricity, seated bullet straightness, and jacket concentricity. Except for case concentricity, the M118 took a back seat to Federal's .308 168-grain BTHP Match. To ballisticians and ammunition specialists this was no great discovery, but, like many other studies, it demonstrated the need to develop an improved military sniping round.

U.S. Special Operations snipers and, later, Marine and Army snipers began firing a military version of the civilian 168-grain Match round, designated the M852. Though this significantly improved sniper accuracy, at longer ranges—especially when the 168-grain bullet went subsonic at about 900 meters—that accuracy could not hold up. What was needed, the U.S. Marine Corps explained in a letter to the Smallarms Division at Picatinny Arsenal, was "7.62 mm Sniper ammunition having the capability of one Minute of Angle accuracy at 1000 yards." Further, this new round would have to parallel the trajectory of previous .308 sniper ammo to fit elevation adjustments on Bullet Drop Compensators.

Thus began a cooperative project involving the USMC, the Army's Picatinny Arsenal, Winchester/Olin's Lake City Army Ammunition Plant, and Sierra Bullets. Headed by Picatinny Arsenal's Paul Riggs, the project included Marine Program Officers Capts. Jay Tibbets and Fred Callies, Mark Resetich of Rock Island Arsenal, Gary Hoeflicker of Lake City Army Ammunition Plant, and Olin engineers Jim Bourdlais, Ed Bray, John Hall, Tim McFarland, and Steve Goldschmidt. The new load they were developing was designated the M118 Long Range.

First, Sierra designed a new 175-grain, boattail, hollowpoint match bullet that was slightly more streamlined and 2 grains heavier than the old M118 and 7 grains heavier than the M852 Match load. According to Sierra's senior

The civilian version of the 175-grain M118 Long Range .308 is offered by Black Hills, IMI, and Federal.

ballistician, Kevin Thomas, this new bullet is essentially a 155-grain Palma Match bullet to which 20 grains were added, then it was stretched for a higher ballistic coefficient to approximately .500. It uses the same boat-tail as the M852, but the circumference at the base is tighter. The new jacket is 95 percent copper.

Next, Lake City's excellent brass case was examined to see where it could be modified to be even more consistent or better contribute to accurate bullet seating and release. This led to a new match-grade primer, modified case taper tooling, and more precise forming and loading procedures. Experiments were conducted to determine the ideal bullet seating depth. The standard 7.62mm NATO overall cartridge length had been 2.830 inches

.308 168-GR. BTHP MATCH
Distance in Yards

	Muzzle	100	200	300	400	500	600	700	800	900	1000
VELOCITY	2600	2420	2240	2070	1910	1760	1610	1480	1360	1260	1170
ENERGY	2520	2180	1870	1600	1355	1150	970	815	690	590	510

M118 LONG RANGE 175-GR. MATCH
Distance in Yards

	Muzzle	100	200	300	400	500	600	700	800	900	1000
VELOCITY	2600	2420	2260	2090	1940	1790	1650	1520	1400	1300	1200
ENERGY	2625	2285	1975	1705	1460	1245	1060	900	765	650	560

PROBALITY OF HIT

		Original M118 173-gr.	M852 168-gr.	M118LR 175-gr.
600-Yard Targets:				
10" Target	USMC Quantico	0.981	0.991	0.999
	Army Sniper School	1.000	0.999	1.000
15" Target	USMC Quantico	1.000	1.000	1.000
	Army Sniper School	1.000	1.000	1.000
20" Target	USMC Quantico	1.000	1.000	1.000
	Army Sniper School	1.000	1.000	1.000
800-Yard Targets:				
10" Target	USMC Quantico	0.840	0.934	0.954
	Army Sniper School	0.776	0.907	0.950
15" Target	USMC Quantico	0.982	0.998	0.999
	Army Sniper School	0.964	0.994	0.999
20" Target	USMC Quantico	0.999	1.000	1.000
	Army Sniper School	0.997	1.000	1.000
1000-Yard Targets:				
10" Target	USMC Quantico	0.592	N/A	0.759
	Army Sniper School	0.417	0.516	0.796
15" Target	USMC Quantico	0.867	N/A	0.955
	Army Sniper School	0.681	0.803	0.972
20" Target	USMC Quantico	0.972	N/A	0.955
	Army Sniper School	0.850	0.943	0.998

maximum, but tests showed that accuracy improved as overall length increased, so 2.855 inches became the new load's final length, which still allowed feeding from magazines into semiauto weapons. Interestingly, it had been found that lengthening the cartridge improved accuracy because it reduced the distance the bullet had to "jump" from the chamber to the rifling (across the leade), enabling a truer, straighter entry into the bore.

With the bullet, the brass case and the load now refined, extensive live-fire tests followed, pitting the new M118 Long Range against the two rounds it was intended to replace, the 168-grain M852 and the original M118 Special Ball. Above are some of those comparative results, fired by Marine and Army sniper instructors, in which 1.0 equals a 100 percent hit probability.

Reviewing this data, it's clear that the superior accuracy of the 175-grain load does not emerge until after 600 yards, becoming very noticeable at 800, then decisively superior at 1,000 yards. In a Lake City Army Ammunition Plant test using machine rest barrels, the M118 Long Range's extreme spread at 1,000 yards was only 12.09 inches, compared to 15.32 inches for the M852 and 18.25 inches for the M118 Special Ball.

Part of this superior performance is drawn from the 175's higher retained velocity, cited in an accompanying box. Note how at 900 and 1,000 meters, the 175-grain bullet is more than 100 fps faster than the M852 and how it remains supersonic beyond 1,000 meters.

Unsurprisingly, the entire U.S. military has switched to the 175-grain M118 Long Range, and no longer even procures the M852 or M118 Special Ball. To distinguish the M118 Long Range from other 7.62 NATO loads, an "LR" code is stamped on the cartridge base.

The primary government contractor for M118 Long Range ammo is Federal Cartridge, which also offers a civilian match version. Black Hills Ammunition, too, loads the 175-grain Match round, using both uncoated and moly-coated MatchKings, while Israeli Military Industries (IMI) markets a 175-grain load in America. I'm not sure about the IMI load—which I've fired but not tested—but the Black Hills 175-grain performs superbly, giving me consistent sub-MOA groups in a variety of rifles. The Federal load, too, has shot to the highest of accuracy and is, in fact, a challenge to shoot to the edge of its envelope.

LONG-RANGE VELOCITY COMPARISON
168-gr. and 175-gr. Loads

	M852 168-gr.	M118LR 175-gr.
Muzzle	2600 fps	2600 fps
600 meters	1539 fps	1648 fps
700 meters	1399 fps	1515 fps
800 meters	1276 fps	1394 fps
900 meters	1173 fps	1286 fps
1000 meters	1092 fps	1193 fps

OTHER .308 MATCH LOADS

Despite the military's switch to the 175-grain load, the 168-grain BTHP Match continues to be the most popular police sniping cartridge in the United States and much of the Western world. That's because the 168-grain performs as accurately as the 175-grain at 600 yards or less, and most police sniper engagements take place well under 100 yards. The longest U.S. police sniper shot that I've ever heard of was 275 yards, which, extreme as that was, still fell far under the distance at which it would make any difference to use the 175-grain bullet. Thus, there's little reason to switch to the heavier load.

Occasionally the 168-grain Match bullet has been criticized for its terminal ballistics—that is, it does not mushroom and induce a wide wound channel upon impact. Instead, as shown in ballistic gelatin tests, the tip tends to break off, tumbling the slug or fragmenting it. When police snipers have not placed a round into a vital area (covered later), there have been incidents where suspects have not been immediately incapacitated. The solution, I think, is proper shot placement, not abandoning match-grade projectiles. The day will come, I'm certain, when accurate, match-quality bullets offering as much terminal effect as a mushrooming slug will replace our current ammo. Until then, police snipers need the most accurate ammo available—match grade.

There's quite a variety of high-quality .308 168-grain Match loads available. Federal led the way in the 1980s, but many other ammo makers have followed and offer extremely high-quality loads. Black Hills even offers regular or moly-coated bullets, while Hornady has fielded an impressive array of TAP (Tactical Application Police) Precision .308 cartridges, with the 168-grain load in both a hollowpoint and Hornady's famous A-Max tipped bullet. When I was the Chief of Competition at the NRA Whittington Center for the 1998 U.S. Military and Police Sniping Championships, competitors fired nothing but Hornady 168s, and they performed superbly. Hornady TAP also includes an A-Max in 155 grain.

THE LONGEST SHOT IN IRAQ

Attesting to the improved long-range accuracy of the M118LR round is its performance in combat in Iraq. On 11 November 2004, USMC Sgt. Herbert Hancock, chief Scout-Sniper with the 1st Battalion, 23rd Marine Regiment, engaged a 120mm mortar crew firing on Marines from Fallujah, across the Euphrates River. Hancock and his teammate, Cpl. Geoffrey Flowers, climbed to a rooftop to spot the mortar crew. Just as they brought Marine mortar fire on the insurgent position, Hancock laid his crosshair on one black-robed crewman, dropping him. He ran his bolt and got a second insurgent, too. The others were pounded by Marine mortars.

Later, when his two one-shot kills were confirmed by a ground party, the distance was measured—an impressive 1,050 yards. Thus far, that seems to be the record for a .308 rifle in Iraq, but equally, it's verification of the wisdom in developing the M118LR round.

USMC Sgt. Herbert Hancock, a police officer from Bryan, Texas, shot two Iraqi mortar crewman at 1,050 yards, the longest shots yet recorded there.

European ammo quality is excellent as well. I extensively tested Sellier & Bellot's 168-grain Match and found it comparable to the best American loads, so good that I approved it as the standard competitor's round for the 1997 Super Sniper Shootout in the Czech Republic because we had difficulty bringing in American ammunition.

Additional match-grade loaders include PMC, Winchester, and Remington, though they don't seem to make a special effort to market this ammo to police snipers.

Other specialty ammo—including glass-penetrating and frangible rounds—give today's police sniper such a variety that it's almost like carrying around golf clubs, ready to fit the club to the shot, giving him impressive flexibility and precision.

SUBSTITUTING OTHER 7.62mm AMMUNITION

Ideally, a sniper fires only match-grade ammunition from the same lot. But what happens when, in a pinch, no match ammo is available?

Although there will be a decline in accuracy, your rifle is capable of firing any NATO-standard 7.62x51mm cartridge. These Western military rounds display a special interoperability circle-and-crosshair symbol on their base, which should be easy for a sniper to remember. Also note that several European countries describe boat-tail bullets as "streamlined," a term found on some ammo packaging.

Beyond interoperability, you also must take into account that these bullets are not the same weight as yours, and they'll fly at a different velocity, resulting in a different trajectory.

Take the U.S. M80 7.62mm ball, for example. It was designed for the M14 rifle and comes

INTEROPERABLE 7.62mm ROUNDS

Country	Type Ammo	Bullet Wt.	Velocity
USA	M80	147 grs.	2750 fps
Belgium	SS71/1	143 grs.	745 fps
Germany	BT Ball	145 grs.	2784 fps
Portugal	BT Ball	143 grs.	2741 fps
U. Kingdom	L2A2	144 grs.	N/A
S. Africa	BT Ball	143 grs.	2784 fps
Sweden	10PRJ	144 grs.	2718 fps

packed in five-round stripper clips. While your M118 Long Range rounds weigh 175 grains, this weighs only 147 grains. The M118 exits a muzzle at 2,600 fps, while M80 ball has a faster muzzle velocity of 2,750 fps. Since the M80's bullet is lighter and travels faster, it will hit higher on a target than M118 Long Range. So will most of the other rounds we cite.

This means not merely that you'll have to reconsider holds, leads, etc., but that your BDC will be totally out of synch with this ammo.

Should you be compelled to use substitute ball rounds, ensure that the rounds you select are boat-tail, then test several lots for accuracy. Use only the best lot, and set it aside in a secure place.

SNIPING WITH THE .223

One of my strongest objections to law enforcement snipers using a .223 rifle was a lack of suitable ammunition, a shortcoming that has been more than filled in recent years by an impressive array of match rounds and specialized loads.

The first such round was the 69-grain BTHP Match, which has been popular enough that it's the load we're using for all our extended ballistic data and calculations. This and nearly identical loads are available from Federal and Black Hills, with the latter also offering a moly-coated version. Of even more interest are the heavier Hornady TAP 75-grain Precision load and Black Hills 77-grain BTHP Match, whose shapes are so streamlined that they're practically VLDs, or very low drag bullets. These efficient projectiles assure improved long-range accuracy with the .223 cartridge, as well as a greater delivery of energy and improved penetration. Though not yet as popular a police sniper round as the 69-grain, I think that will change in the future, though some rifles will need to be rebarreled with proper rifling to accommodate these heavier bullets.

When it comes to barrier penetration, both Hornady and Federal offer special glass-penetration rounds, with (respectively) 62-grain and 55-grain bonded bullets.

Hornady offers additional .223 loads with

The family of .223 sniper loads includes match, bonded barrier-penetrating loads, and moly-coated from Black Hills.

BALLISTIC PERFORMANCE DATA, .223 69-GR. BOAT-TAIL HOLLOWPOINT (MATCH)
Distance in Yards

	MUZZLE	100	200	300	400	500	600	700	800	900	1000
VELOCITY (fps)	3000	2720	2460	2210	1980	1760	1560	1390	1240	1130	1060
ENERGY (ft-lbs.)	1380	1135	925	750	600	475	375	295	235	195	175

TRAJECTORY TABLE, .223 69-GR. BOAT-TAIL HOLLOWPOINT (MATCH)
Trajectory by Yards, Expressed in Inches

Zero Range	100	200	300	400	500	600	700	800	900	1000
100 yards	Zero	-3.20	-12.2	-28.3	-53.3	-89.4	-140	-207	-295	-405
200 yards	+1.6	Zero	-7.4	-21.9	-45.3	-79.8	-129	-194	-280	-389
300 yards	+4.0	+4.8	Zero	-12.3	-33.3	-65.4	-112	-175	-259	-365
400 yards	+7.1	+11.0	+9.1	Zero	-17.8	-46.8	-90.2	-150	-231	-339
500 yards	+10.6	+18.0	+19.6	+14.1	Zero	-25.8	-65.7	-122	-199	-299
600 yards	+14.9	+26.6	+32.5	+31.3	+21.2	Zero	-35.6	-87.7	-160	-256
700 yards	+20.0	+36.8	+47.8	+51.7	+46.7	+30.6	Zero	-46.9	-115	-205
800 yards	+25.8	+48.4	+65.2	+74.9	+75.7	+65.4	+40.7	Zero	-62.4	-147
900 yards	+32.7	+62.2	+85.9	+103	+110	+107	+89.0	+54.7	Zero	-77.0
1000 yards	+40.4	+77.6	+109	+133	+149	+153	+143	+116	+69.0	Zero

lighter bullets in 40, 55, and 60 grains. These rounds, I think, lend themselves more to entry team operators armed with M4 carbines than snipers.

The .223 family also includes military ball rounds, either the original 55-grain bullet that served in Southeast Asia or, more recently, the 62-grain bullet that offers deeper penetration and improved range. Military tracer, too, can be quite useful in some situations as a day or night signal aid, especially for coordinating with aircraft. (I left the waterproof sealant on the tracer bullet in the accompanying photo so you could see how firmly seated and sealed is a military round. Though this protects from the elements, it unevenly releases the bullet, partially explaining the inaccuracy of some military ammo.)

Finally, I've also depicted Longbow's frangible .223 projectile, which genuinely fires

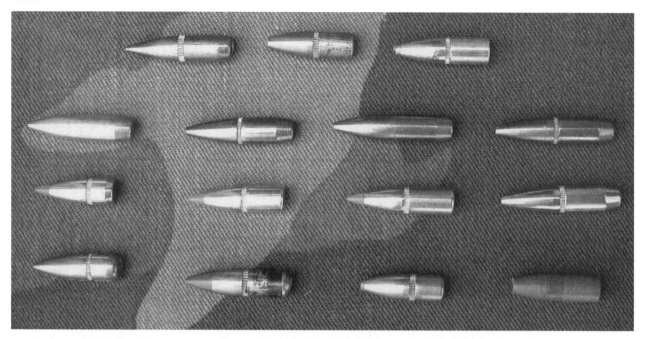

.223 PROJECTILES: (top row, L-R) .62-grain M855; Federal Tactical 55-grain; Hornady 62-grain TAP Barrier; (second row, L-R) Sierra 69-grain Match; Black Hills 68-grain moly; Black Hills 75-grain moly; Black Hills 77-grain moly; (third row, L-R) Hornady 40-grain TAP; Hornady 60-grain TAP; Hornady 55-grain TAP; Hornady 75-grain Precision Match TAP; (bottom row, L-R) military 55-grain ball; military tracer; 55-grain Federal softpoint; Longbow frangible.

match-grade and parallels the 69-grain bullet's trajectory to 100 meters. It's designed to be totally consumed inside a suspect with no exit.

Overpenetration and the .223

The dynamic little .223 bullet, especially in softpoint, tends to splinter and fragment and consume itself upon impact, reducing any overpenetration danger almost to nil. While I'd still urge a police sniper to align himself so there's a positive backstop beyond his target, there's an excellent probability that significant missiles would not fly beyond the target.

I once had coffee with a law officer who'd "taken the shot" against a knife-wielding madman who'd seized a hostage. He fired one round of .223 commercial softpoint at a distance of about 100 yards. The bullet "virtually exploded" when it penetrated the subject's head and struck his spinal column, creating so many bullet splinters that a later X-ray "looked like a picture of the night sky," he reported. No significant bullet fragments exited from the suspect.

That's the good news about the .223. The bad news is that shot placement becomes much more important because the .223 will not penetrate a human as deep as a .308, nor will it create as wide a wound channel to inflict tissue or organ damage. I'm aware of one recent incident in which multiple .223 wounds to a suspect's torso did not incapacitate him before he murdered a hostage. The .308, I believe, is more forgiving of such imprecise marksmanship.

As well, at the relatively close range of only 300 yards, the .223 55-grain bullet produces just 465 ft-lbs. of energy, which is inferior to most .357 Magnum loads point-blank and barely squeaks by the FBI's minimum ballistic gelatin penetration criterion of 12 inches.

Other Considerations

At a sniper course I instructed in Arizona, two USMC security detachment students armed with scoped M16s barely qualified because a relatively light wind almost pushed their .223 bullets completely off the target. At

400 yards, a mere 10 mph wind drifted their bullets 15 inches, while the .308 police snipers on either side of them had their bullets carried only 7.4 inches. That's a big difference.

But a legitimate argument can be made for police snipers using both calibers and fitting their choice to a particular set of circumstances. Some departments are doing this today.

On a practical level, however, it must become cumbersome to master two rifles, maintain both with their ammunition, keep them packed in your squad car, then tote both of them to each incident and, like a bag of golf clubs, draw the most compatible rifle for any given shot.

If it's realistic to settle on only one rifle, I'm an advocate of the .308 because it can do everything the .223 can, but deeper, farther, with less wind drift, and with more energy delivered into the target. But I won't be preachy about it since others can honestly and informedly differ with me. And that's why we're including all the data on .223s—we may disagree, but we don't have to argue about it.

MILITARY 5.56mm: BULLETS AND BARRELS

Considerable confusion and a seeming decline in accuracy have accompanied the adoption of the heavier-barreled M16A2. Adding to the confusion has been adoption of the Belgian SS-109 62-grain bullet as the U.S. M855 round, which replaces the original lightweight 55-grain M193.

We'll sort through this below, but keep one thing clearly in mind: use the original, lightweight 55-grain round in the original, lightweight M16/AR-15 and performance will be fine. Likewise, fire the heavier round with the heavier M16A2 to avoid problems. Simple enough.

Now here's the explanation. Although it took two decades to face it, the U.S. military finally recognized that the 5.56mm round lacked sufficient energy and penetration for midrange shooting. The M16A1 was considered to have a maximum effective range of only 460 yards.

The solution was immediately apparent:

increase bullet weight by 10 percent and you'll increase performance by 10 percent. The Belgians already had perfected such a bullet, which proved to fit the bill perfectly. However, because this bullet was heavier and a hair longer (4/10 of a centimeter) than the 55-grain round, it did not stabilize properly in the M16A1 barrel, which has 1:12 rifling.

How bad was this mismatch? In U.S. Army tests, a six-round, 100-yard group firing the heavy Belgian-designed bullets through an M16A1 measured 12 inches across—*12 inches!* When the proper 55-grain ammo was fired through the same rifle, that group instantly tightened up to 3 inches.

It was found that the heavier, longer, 62-grain rounds worked best when fired through a barrel having very fast 1:7 rifling, which is the rifling used in the M16A2.

Keep this sorted out and you shouldn't have any problems.

THE MAGNIFICENT .300 WINCHESTER MAGNUM

Though the 175-grain M118 Long Range cartridge has pushed an additional 100 or so yards of effective range out of the .308, realistically this round runs out of a lot of "oomph" after flying 1,000 yards. By then it has slowed to only 1,200 fps, generating 560 ft-lbs. of energy, only about half of what it possessed at 600 yards, which reduces its penetration and lethality. Further, its declining trajectory has become such a sharp arc that even a minor range-estimation error can cause a clean miss.

There is a way to boost that long-range performance and attain more effective velocity and terminal effects at 900 to 1,100 yards—by employing the cartridge king of long-range shooting, the .300 Winchester Magnum. This powerful cartridge traditionally has dominated .30-caliber, 1,000-yard shooting at the NRA's annual Camp Perry matches. It was because of the .300 WinMag's impressive performance that the U.S. Army's M24 Sniper Weapon System was designed to be readily convertible from 7.62mm to the heavier round.

The .300 WinMag, 190-grain BTHP Match is loaded by Federal and Black Hills, the latter also offering a moly-coated version.

Before looking at the ballistic data, let's appreciate just how far 1,000 yards truly is.

The .300 Magnum Environment

One readily can concede the obvious, that 1,000 yards equals 10 football fields laid end-to-end, or that it's 3,000 feet, which makes it about three-fifths of a mile.

If you had a 36-inch stride and took one step per second—an ambitious pace—it would take more than 16 1/2 minutes to walk 1,000 yards. That's a long, long way.

But now imagine this. At 1,000 yards—where you'd have trouble even seeing a man without optical assistance, where it takes a .308 bullet nearly two seconds to travel that far—the .300 Winchester Magnum still has more kinetic energy—more so-called "knockdown power"—than a .44 Magnum pistol does *point-blank*.

This .300 Winchester Mag is the uncontested king of the long-range shooting realm. But this wonder-cartridge has much more going for it than just impressive energy.

Pretenders to the Throne

In the original *Dirty Harry* movie, Clint Eastwood selected a .458 Winchester Magnum rifle—a virtual elephant rifle—supposedly to outgun his Zodiac Killer opponent. Though anyone knowledgeable about high-powered rifles would advise against such a cartridge, this kind of "bigger is better" silliness can creep into even law enforcement circles. The fact is, when it comes to long-range shooting, there's no American magnum rifle that performs better than the .300 Winchester Magnum. Just look at the data in the chart on page 149.

Despite all these heavy magnums producing more energy at the muzzle, not a one can compare to the .300 Magnum at merely 500 yards, and this superiority is clearly evident when it comes to wind drift and trajectory, too. True, they all start "hotter" than the .300 Magnum, but these big, ponderous bullets quickly decelerate and become ballistic embarrassments.

More so than its .308 Winchester little brother, the .300 Magnum produces significant recoil, but it's manageable with practice. American military snipers outfitted with .300 WinMags—mostly in the Special Ops community—use a 190-grain match-grade load developed by the Navy's Surface Warfare Center at Crane, Indiana. Known as the "Navy load," it generates 2,900 fps muzzle velocity. This is the round we're using for all our .300 WinMag ballistic charts and data. Equivalent civilian .300 WinMag loads are manufactured by Federal and Black Hills, which both use Sierra 190-grain MatchKing bullets, although Black Hills also offers a moly-coated version.

SPECIALTY AMMUNITION

A sniper usually fires match-grade ammunition, but he must be familiar with other types of rounds so he can selectively employ the most

TRAJECTORY TABLE, .300 WINCHESTER MAGNUM 190-GR. BTHP MATCH
Trajectory in Inches, Distance in Yards

Zero	100	200	300	400	500	600	700	800	900	1000
100 yds	zero	-3.0	-11.5	-26.0	-47.5	-76.8	-115	-165	-227	-303
200 yds	+1.5	zero	-6.8	-20.0	-40.0	-67.5	-105	-153	-213	-288
300 yds	+3.8	-4.6	zero	-10.8	-28.4	-53.8	-88.5	-135	-193	-265
400 yds	+6.5	+10.0	+8.0	zero	-15.0	-37.6	-69.7	-113	-169	-238
500 yds	+9.5	+16.0	+17.0	+12.0	zero	-19.7	-48.7	-90	-142	-208
600 yds	+12.8	+22.5	+27.0	+25.1	+16.4	zero	-25.8	-63	-112	-176
700 yds	+16.5	+30.0	+38.0	+40.0	+34.8	+22.0	zero	-34	-79	-138
800 yds	+20.7	+38.3	+50.5	+56.6	+55.8	+47.2	+29.4	zero	-41	-97
900 yds	+29.7	+47.2	+64.0	+74.6	+78.3	+74.3	+60.9	+36	zero	-52
1000 yds	+34.9	+57.6	+79.6	+95.3	+104	+105	+96.4	+77	+47	zero

COMPARATIVE MAGNUM RIFLE BALLISTICS

	MUZZLE DATA			500-YARD PERFORMANCE		
Cartridge/Load	Vel. fps	Energy ft-lbs.	10 mph wind	200-yd zero	Vel. fps	Energy ft-lbs.
.300 WinMag 200-gr. Fed. Prem. BTSP	2830	3560	14.9"	-40.5"	2110	1970
.338 WinMag 250-gr. Fed. Prem.	2660	3925	33.6"	-60.2"	1500	1245
.375 H&H Mag. Fed. Prem. 250-gr. BTSP	2750	4200	26.7"	-52.1"	1690	1580
.458 WinMag Federal 510-gr. SP	2090	4945	56.8"	-116.2"	1080	1320
.416 Rigby Federal 410-gr. SP	2370	5115	42.3"	-93.6"	1280	1485
.470 Nitro Express Fed. 500-gr. SP	2150	5130	50.6"	-105.3"	1140	1435

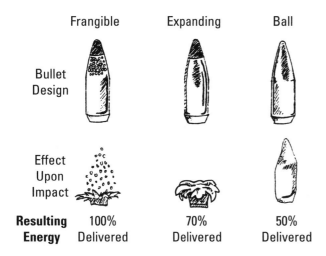

A bullet's design dictates what it does to a target.

appropriate one as the target and situation dictate—or when it's the only ammo available.

The three most basic types of bullets are ball, expanding, and frangible, as we've illustrated.

Ball Ammunition

The hard outer surface on ball rounds causes them to retain their shape and dimensions after impact and, due to nonexpansion, convey the least amount of energy into a target. Although it's not scientific, I've estimated that a ball round conveys roughly 50 percent of its energy and loses half its velocity while transiting a human target.

Ball ammo tends to have the deepest penetration because it maintains an efficient, dynamic shape, but this also causes an overpenetration danger due to its relatively high velocity after exiting the target. This danger can be significant: a .308 bullet traveling at half its normal speed still has kinetic energy comparable to a .357 Magnum bullet at full velocity.

When firing ball, a police rifleman must always consider the need for a positive backstop or a perimeter with sufficient depth to protect even distant bystanders.

Ball ammunition includes flatbase spitzer rounds, which are typical for assault rifle bullets, and streamlined boat-tails like the M118 Special Ball bullet. Due to its gilding metal

jacket, the ball round also is called full metal jacket (FMJ) or hardball. Some people call it "military" ammunition.

Expanding Bullets

Our next category, expanding bullets, include softpoint, mushrooming, and hollowpoint rounds, all designed to increase in diameter after impact and thus deliver far more energy into the target than a ball round does. These rounds also are called hunting or dumdum bullets.

In the illustration at left, I've noted that an expanding bullet delivers roughly 70 percent of its kinetic energy and loses that much velocity, resulting in less danger of overpenetration. And because this wider projectile presents a larger surface passing through the medium, the resulting permanent wound channel inflicts more damage and has a greater likelihood of passing through critical organs or nerve tissue.

Expanding bullets were ruled illegal for use in war by the Hague Convention of 1907, although they may be used in counterterrorist and law enforcement operations.

The wound ballistics section addresses the Sierra Match bullet's terminal performance, but we must note here that it is not a true hollowpoint and thus breaks up on impact but does not expand.

Frangible: Ultimate Dumdum Bullets

The ultimate expanding bullet is a frangible one that totally shatters or vaporizes on contact and thus delivers 100 percent of its energy instantly into its target.

Strong U.S. law enforcement interest in frangible rounds began in the early 1970s when armed U.S. Air Marshals were placed aboard American jetliners in reaction to an epidemic of hijackings. (A Special Forces SOG friend—who'd also participated in the Son Tay POW camp raid in 1970—was one of our nation's first air marshals.) These marshals soon identified a significant problem: if they had to fire, their rounds could penetrate the jetliner's skin and cause catastrophic decompression.

Several special bullets were designed that would deliver a lot of punishment into a "soft" human target but would neither ricochet off nor penetrate even a thin metal layer. One design used a thin serrated jacket filled with hundreds of tiny #12 shot suspended in liquid with a plug in its nose.

The most famous of these bullets became a commercial success as the Glaser Safety Slug. It's available in .308, and I've fired several rounds which, while producing awesome punishment into a medium, does not match the trajectory or accuracy of a match bullet. Still, I can imagine a scenario involving a nuclear or chemical facility in which overpenetration is such a concern that a frangible bullet is the best answer.

What should be realized when using frangible bullets, however, is that their devastating effect is very shallow and, despite impressive surface injuries, the bullet may not neutralize the subject. Further, even the thinnest cover can protect your target from any effect at all.

U.S. military frangible rounds include the M160 in 7.62mm, which uses a 108.5-grain bullet made from Bakelite plastic and powdered lead, fired with a muzzle velocity of 1,320 fps. Despite this speed and bullet weight, however, it will not penetrate even an anchored 3/16-inch Dural plate at 25 yards.

Picatinny Arsenal's Joint Service Small Arms Program—the same element that developed the M118 Long Range ammo—has been working on a frangible 5.56mm round called the CPA, or Controlled Penetration Ammunition. Although this experimental projectile matches the trajectory of the standard 62-grain M855 to 100 meters, and it penetrates enemy body armor at close range, it will not exit ordinary building walls after transiting a hostile's body. Thus far, however, this prepressed metal powder bullet does not achieve the standard minimum ballistic gelatin penetration of 12 inches, which we cover later. Still, that's pretty impressive performance.

Equally impressive is Longbow frangible ammunition, developed by former Special Forces officer and fellow SOG veteran John Mullins. This match-grade projectile of metal powder and

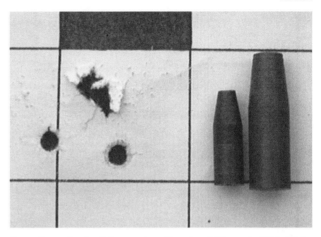

Longbow frangible projectiles in .223 and .308. This group was fired from 100 yards, using zero for heavier 69-grain Match.

inert material vaporizes almost on impact yet retains integrity long enough to neutralize a suspect. Offered as both .308 and .223 loaded rounds, it was developed for police and Special Ops sniper use. I've tested the Longbow ammo and achieved .223 groups as small as 0.537 inches at 100 yards—definitely match-grade. As shown in the accompanying photo, there was a slight zero shift when I switched from 69-grain Match to the lightweight Longbow projectile. (Of course, an adept sniper would know this and fine-tune his rifle when he switched ammo.)

Custom ammo maker Cor-Bon offers a lightweight .223 round that's so explosive on impact that essentially it's a frangible round. The Cor-Bon Tactical 40-grain load screams from a muzzle at 3,800 fps, firing flat and so fast that it's consumed by its target, with no exit. Promoted for use in urban environments, like all frangible rounds it's great only so long as your target lacks cover. Further, given its light weight (and greater susceptibility to crosswinds) along with its rapid deceleration, I don't think it's realistic for a sniper to employ this or any frangible round at more than 100 yards.

A commercial .223 frangible round called Rhino Shock employs an aluminum-tipped hollow bullet with a tellurium solid-copper base that, when fired at its 5,000 fps muzzle velocity, vaporizes on contact. This round likely lacks match-grade accuracy and may not be suitable for sniping, but it could prove very useful for entry teams.

The big three ammo makers—Remington, Federal, and Winchester—all manufacture frangible rounds, but they're designed to reduce lead particulates on firing ranges, not to reduce or eliminate overpenetration. Some of these rounds may have utility for sniping, but none of these companies promotes its frangible loads for lethal situations.

Various exploding bullets have appeared over the past decade, but I have yet to learn of one that is both dependable and accurate. Most, like the round that would-be assassin John Hinckley pumped into President Ronald Reagan, do not detonate—thank God in this case—unless they impact against a hard object.

Tracer Rounds

A sniper employs tracer rounds to signal and direct the fire of others. While it's probably true that tracer will wear a quality barrel much faster than will other bullets, it should be no problem firing tracer as 1 to 2 percent of your annual practice.

You need familiarity with firing tracers because they perform different ballistically than other rounds. In addition to their faster speed (2,750 fps) and lighter weight (141 grains)—which causes them to hit higher than heavier match bullets—they are inherently less accurate.

Official U.S. military standards require that a 10-shot pattern of M62 tracer rounds be no wider than 36 inches at 550 yards. That's a very large group, *three times* wider than the acceptable standard for M118 Long Range.

But this kind of group is desirable for machine gun performance, in which moderate bullet dispersion is desirable. The M62 tracer's trajectory is further complicated by the burning subigniter and igniter, which change its weight and balance in flight. The trace element burns out at 900 meters, or 1,000 yards.

Designed for machine gun use, the orange-tipped M62 tracer normally is found belted in a ratio of 1:5 with ball ammunition.

Despite the 7.62mm SLAP's impressive armor penetration, it does not fire accurately through a bolt-action rifle.

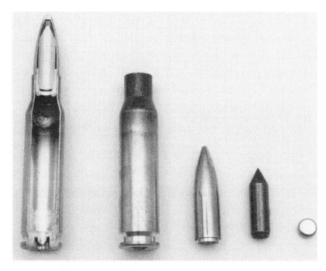

The M993 7.62mm armor-piercing round.

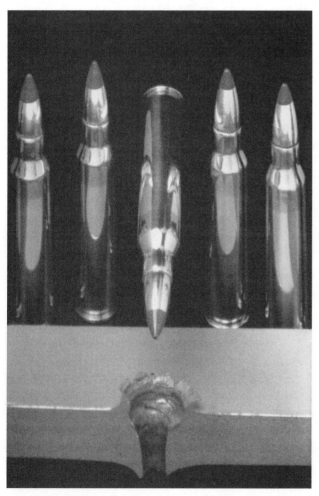

The post-Vietnam, 62-grain 5.56mm M855 round contains a tungsten core that penetrates thin-skinned vehicles.

A newer kind of tracer especially useful for snipers is the 7.62mm M276 Dim Tracer, which burns an infrared compound that's invisible to the naked eye but glaringly bright to night vision devices. Originally developed for Special Ops units, it's now a standardized round available throughout the U.S. military and identified by a green tip surrounded by a ring of pink.

Barrier-Penetration Rounds

Although the U.S. military 7.62mm SLAP (Saboted Light Armor Penetrator) offers impressive armor penetration—up to 3/4 inch of case-hardened steel—it has proved terribly inaccurate in the M24 Sniper Weapon System. At Ft. Benning, a sniper school instructor told me he'd test-fired this discarding-sabot round, and at best it yielded pie plate-sized groups at 100 meters, which we thought likely resulted from how the sabot entered the rifling throat. This round is available as a tracer (M959) or plain saboted round (M948).

More accurate apparently are the M993 (7.62mm) and M995 (5.56mm) armor-piercing (AP) rounds that were designed with rifles in mind. Initiated in 1992, they were tested against Russian-made BRDM-2 armored cars, which their tungsten cores successfully penetrated. According to "the book," these tungsten penetrators can breach up to 12 millimeters (1/2 inch) of steel if fired at 90 degrees obliquity to the surface.

This issue of obliquity needs special emphasis. To achieve maximum penetration, all these AP rounds must strike a surface perpendicularly, which is not an easy matter if your target's moving or—like an armored vehicle—it's purposely designed with deflecting curves and angled corners.

Today's basic 5.56mm issue round, the 62-grain M855, incorporates a tungsten core that penetrates deeper into dense and thin media than the earlier M193 55-grain bullet. (See the gelatin comparison on page 159.) This is true generally for all military hardball rounds compared to the hollowpoint bullets employed in match loads. If you need to shoot through media, the solution may be substituting ordinary hardball ammo.

More specialized penetration rounds have been developed in recent years, especially for police snipers. Federal offers its Tactical Load in both .223 (55-grain) and .308 (165-grain), which use bonded bullets that mushroom but penetrate deeply because they retain most of their mass. Hornady, too, offers special TAP barrier-penetration loads in .223 and .308, likewise using bonded bullets. All these specialized loads will be explored later, particularly concerning their glass-penetration capabilities.

PENETRATION AND OVERPENETRATION

An advantage and a disadvantage when employing a high-powered rifle in a law enforcement situation is the ability of the bullet to penetrate media.

I'm a strong advocate of the .308 for police work partly because it can penetrate commonplace media such as car doors and windows while usually retaining sufficient bullet weight and velocity for lethal effect on a suspect.

On the other hand, there are well-founded concerns about overpenetration, which is the hazard that results from a bullet passing completely through a subject and endangering hostages, bystanders, or other law officers. If a .308 slug exits a body, after having lost even half its velocity, its kinetic energy is still comparable to a full-power .357 Magnum bullet, which is no small danger. Having once had a friendly bullet penetrate a wall and miss my head by 3 inches sensitizes me to the issue.

One solution advocated by some law officers is to employ a .223 for sniping since its bullet typically fragments and has less chance of overpenetration. While their opinions are as valid as mine, I hate to see us limiting our potential due to a rarely encountered safety problem; I've never heard of anyone in this country struck by a police sniper's bullet that had passed through a suspect. As far as that goes, there's also a danger of bone fragments injuring a hostage or a bullet deflecting. Let there be no doubts about it: hostage rescue shooting is wrought with genuine dangers—this is one hot kitchen.

My personal recommendation is to consider a positive backstop beyond your target—by which I mean a thick material that will stop a

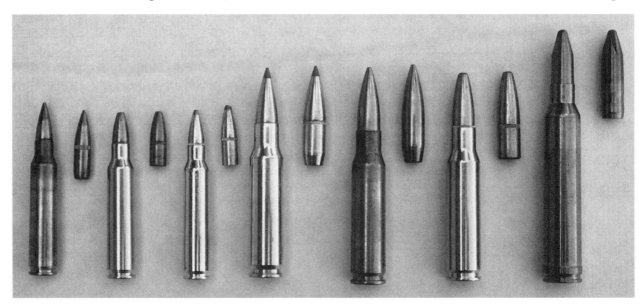

A variety of barrier-penetrating rounds (L-R): M855 5.56mm; Federal and Hornady .223 glass-breaching rounds; Hornady 165-grain .308 TAP barrier round; 7.72mm hardball; Federal 165-grain .308 Tactical Load; and German .300 WinMag copper solid.

5.56mm M193 BALL PENETRATION DATA

Distance	Concrete	Pine Boards	Sandbags
25 meters	1.4"	10.5"	1.4"
100 meters	1.3"	22.4"	2.5"
200 meters	1.2"	25.0"	3.7"
400 meters	0.8"	14.9"	8.8"
600 meters	0.5"	6.7"	7.6"

flying bullet—and even reposition yourself to exploit such a backstop.

The other aspect of media is learning exactly what kind of penetration you can achieve when engaging a barricaded enemy or suspect. We have U.S. Army data from several ballistic tests, fired both for the 5.56mm and 7.62mm NATO rounds. Keep in mind that these are full metal jacket military rounds, not softpoint or hollowpoint.

It's important to observe that the 5.56mm is a most peculiar bullet that penetrates *deeper* into media like pine boards and sandbags at longer range than at close range. This is because the bullet initially flies so fast that it fragments on impact and loses its momentum. According to this same test, the 55-grain M193 bullet will penetrate a military flak vest at up to 700 meters and pierce a helmet with liner at 550 yards. All these results are a bit better than some tests one of my NCOs, SSgt. Gary Gamradt, and I conducted a few years ago, which we'll cover momentarily.

Another U.S. Army test, this of the M80 147-grain 7.62mm ball round, was fired at 200 meters (220 yards) and had the following effects:

- Penetration of pine boards: 50 inches
- Penetration of loose sand: 10 inches
- Penetration of solid concrete: 3 inches

I interpret these results as meaning I could engage a hostile who'd taken cover behind even a sizable softwood tree by shooting ball ammo

directly through it. We'll have more data on penetrating concrete and sand from the next test, but I hope you are starting to note that different tests don't necessarily yield identical results, a significant concern for media penetration. Inconsistencies can create an uncomfortable level of unpredictability.

Our next data includes 7.62mm M80 ball fired as five-shot bursts from an M60 machine gun, with the recorded penetration that of the deepest bullet. Since some but not all of these projectiles benefited by following a round into the medium, there's a degree of random chance that's too random for me.

100-YARD 7.62mm BALL AND .30 ARMOR-PIERCING DATA

Medium	7.62mm Ball 5-rd. Bursts	.30-06 Armor-Piercing Single Shots
Soil: Wet	28"	28"
Dry	19"	19"
Sand: Wet	19"	28"
Dry	16"	19"
Clay: Wet	35"	35"
Dry	24"	24"
Wood/Boards	19"	UNK
Log Timbers	28"	48"
Rubble (soil, concrete, etc.)	12"	14"
Brick Wall	14"	UNK
Stone Masonry	9.5"	UNK
Concrete	9.5"	7"
Aluminum	UNK	2"
Soft Steel	UNK	1"

INFORMAL MEDIA PENETRATION TEST

Target	5.56mm M193 Ball	7.62mm M80 Ball
Military Sandbags	100 yards—Fail	100 yards—Fail
Helmet with Liner	200 yards—Max	400 yards—Easy
Concrete H-Block	200 yards—Max	300 yards—Max
4″ Layer of Pine	400 yards—Barely	400 yards—Easy
1/8″ Sheet Steel	100 yards—Max	300 yards—Easy
1/4″ Boiler Plate	100 yards—Max	200 yards—Max
Car Door, '68 Dodge	300 yards—Barely	400 yards—Easy

Recently I tested a variety of sniper rounds against living trees to measure their penetration, to help you determine both the cover they offer and what it takes to punch through one when a hostile is firing from the other side. After only a few firings, I found that my results did not parallel those in the preceding paragraphs. Unless you find yourself in a lumberyard shootout, it's unlikely that penetration data dealing with pine boards is very relevant. And one tree is not the same as another of the same diameter, as any forester will tell you, especially hardwood versus softwood. Even pine trees, for instance, vary in their sap content and bullet resistance.

Here's my bottom-line conclusion: all this penetration data amounts to interesting yardsticks that you should consider, but you should test *your* ammo against the likely barriers *you* will encounter in *your* area of operations. In Iraq, where a lack of wood means most homes are built from mud-brick, you should know how well your variety of sniping rounds penetrate this medium. Afghan mountain villages, by contrast, often use stacked natural rock. Palm trees, I'd imagine, offer almost no resistance to a .308 bullet, but you should know that for sure if you're serving in Iraq. A police sniper should recognize the difference between engaging a suspect who's behind a hollow wooden door in a house and a metal door in a commercial building and know the penetration capabilities of his ammo for both scenarios.

What's far more predictable is the accompanying information on .30-06 armor-piercing, a black-tipped round that performs about 10 percent better than its 7.62mm AP counterpart. (See data box, page 155.) I have great confidence in its accuracy and effectiveness at media penetration. Especially worth noting is that this round pierces 7 inches of concrete and that wet soil generally is much easier to penetrate than dry soil, sand, or clay.

Our last data is from a test Staff Sergeant Gamradt and I shot a few years ago, which, while not controlled enough to be called scientific, still yielded interesting conclusions. The most surprising one was that no bullet penetrated a simple military sandbag wall, even at 100 yards. As can be seen, our helmet proved much more resistant to 5.56mm ball than did the Army test. Also, one curious observation was that while some of these media were, indeed, penetrated, the bullet had lost so much "oomph" that I doubt it would have had much lethality left. When that 5.56mm bullet exited 4 inches of pine boards at 400 yards, it had almost no velocity left.

It's *this* kind of result that must be measured, for no current data tells us how much velocity remains *after* a bullet transits such media. Theoretically, if a bullet exits and drops harmlessly to the ground, it "succeeded," even if it's not capable of inflicting injury.

And indeed, any media shooting must be

considered an iffy proposition, and especially dangerous when it involves nearby friendlies or a hostage rescue. While it's just fine for military use, media shooting is a desperate technique for law enforcement, and its use should be dictated only by necessity.

SNIPING WOUND BALLISTICS

Not many years ago, rifle bullet effectiveness typically was demonstrated by shooting water-filled vessels, such as plastic milk jugs, and observing the explosive results. While visually

Dr. Martin Fackler, wound ballistics authority, with the author at a national SWAT conference where both were guest speakers.

dramatic, such demonstrations featured just one terminal ballistic effect—temporary cavitation—which actually is the least significant effect. Yet so impressive was it that many shooters thought this was how high-powered rifle bullets inflict damage into a target.

In the real world, though, everyone could see that bullets do not cause humans to explode like milk jugs—something was wrong. Arguments abounded over concepts like "knockdown power" and Relative Incapacitation Index, the deadliness of bullet styles, and what foot-pounds of energy really meant.

Between anecdotal evidence and autopsies, gunshot wound ballistics gradually evolved into the truer science of today so that at last we're starting to understand what bullets do and we can methodically compare some very precise effects.

Much of this must be credited to Dr. Martin Fackler, a U.S. Army physician with the Wound Ballistics Laboratory at Letterman Army Hospital. Equally, though, I must thank Indiana lawman Cpl. Edward Sanow, whose extensive research with a former Detroit homicide detective, Evan Marshall, led to their seminal work on pistol bullet ballistics, *Handgun Stopping Power* (Paladin Press, 1992).

During this research, Corporal Sanow also conducted a series of rifle bullet tests, and he was generous enough to share both data and photographs with the author.

What Bullets Do

Bullets crush, compress, and tear away flesh, leaving a circular tube or path of destruction called a "permanent wound channel." Depending on whether the bullet is full metal jacket or expanding or a hollowpoint, this wound channel may be somewhat wider than the initial bullet diameter.

The ultimate determinant of damage to a target is where this permanent wound channel passes through it, otherwise known as "shot placement." Should the channel cut a swath through fleshy thigh muscles, the subject likely will not be completely or rapidly incapacitated. If the shot is placed so that the channel

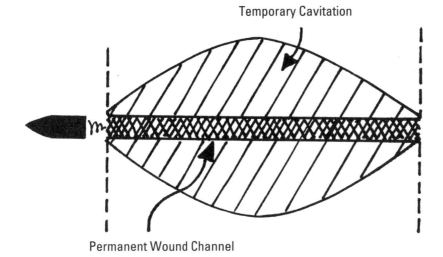

WHAT BULLETS DO. Most damage results from the permanent wound channel.

The other terminal ballistic effect is what happened to those milk jugs, now called the "temporary wound cavity." The shock wave that accompanies bullets causes a wild but temporary inflation of human tissue, lasting only a split second and having little incapacitating effect if the projectile is a slow-moving pistol bullet. The photographs you've seen of impressive cavities carved by bullets into clay or duct sealant were images not of bullet damage but of temporary wound cavities.

But before we probe the subject much deeper, we first must take a closer look at human physiology.

tears through center-chest, quite likely the subject will have lethal damage to the heart, spine, major arteries, and/or lungs, resulting in rapid incapacitation.

The issue of minimum penetration is critical when comparing pistol bullets, but most rifle rounds significantly exceed the FBI's minimum penetration depth of 12 inches so that bullets can pass through an arm or shoulder and still reach the vitals.

Effects on a Human Body

The concept of "rapid incapacitation" evolved from a 1987 study by the FBI Weapons Advisory Committee. This study concluded that to be stopped quickly—"rapidly inca-

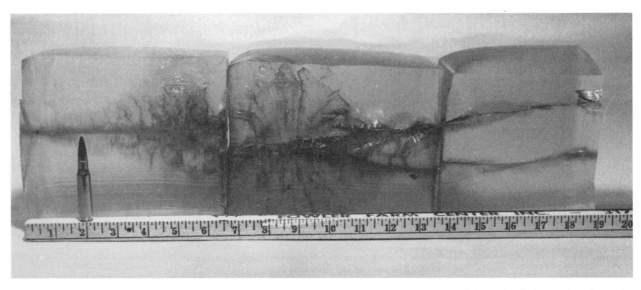

.308 FEDERAL MATCH GELATIN TEST. Note massive permanent wound channel and then dual channels where tip and rest of bullet split. (Photo credit: Ed Sanow, *S.W.A.T. Magazine*)

pacitated"—a subject must be wounded in the central nervous system (CNS) or suffer a dramatic, swift loss of blood.

Severe blood loss can induce unconsciousness in 10 to 15 seconds from oxygen depletion to the brain, while the subject should experience degraded vision and declining dexterity a few seconds earlier. This short but significant delay in effects explains the often heard hunting stories about deer running 50 yards despite a totally shattered heart.

Such severe blood loss in humans is induced by wounding the vascular (blood system) organs, such as the heart and liver, or cutting major blood vessels, such as the femoral arteries of the groin or the carotid arteries in the neck.

An effective CNS wound should impact the spine above the shoulder blades, at the brain stem (medulla oblongata), or into the brain's neural motor strips. When properly executed, this shot results in *instant* rather than rapid incapacitation, and the subject goes down as

precipitously as if you'd flicked a light switch. For all CNS shots, the rule of thumb is the higher on the spine, the better. I've twice hit big game high in the spine, and in both cases the animals collapsed and never moved so much as a hair; it was as if their bodies had turned to liquid.

When it comes to temporary cavitation, the effects supposedly are not as predictable and therefore should not be considered, although it's known that temporary caviation inflicts injury to nonexpanding tissue such as the liver, brain, and kidneys as well as liquid-filled organs like the bladder. The least cavitation injury is to tissues that readily stretch, such as the lungs, muscles, skin, and ordinary blood vessels.

Bone hits probably should not be assessed because they're too unpredictable and just as likely to cause worse wounding due to secondary bone missiles as to reduce injury by deflecting a bullet.

Much of the current ballistic theory is based on pistol bullets, although rifle bullets usually

BALLISTIC GELATIN COMPARISON: .308 168-GR. vs. PISTOL BULLETS

	.308 169-gr. Match	.45 Auto Silvertip	9mm 147-gr.
Permanent Wound Channel Depth	16.5–22"	10.2"	15"
Permanent Wound Channel Diameter	0.7"	0.75"	0.60"
Maximum Temporary Stretch Diameter	6.4"	3.2"	3.3"
Muzzle Energy in Foot-Pounds	2520	411	360

BALLISTIC GELATIN COMPARISON: .308 vs. .223 AND 7.62x39mm

	.223 69-gr. Match	.223 55-gr. FMJ-BT	.223 62-gr. FMJ-BT	7.62x39mm 123-gr. FMJ	.308 168-gr. Match
Perm. Wound Channel Depth	13.2"	10.7"	12.2"	16.2"	22.0"
Perm. Wound Channel Diameter	0.45"	0.4"	0.5"	0.6"	0.7"
Max. Temp. Stretch Diameter	3.3"	2.9"	3.5"	2.7"	6.4"
# of Significant Fragments	8	1	1	4	3–5
Muzzle Energy in Foot-Pounds	1380	1280	1325	1445	2520

inflict much more damage and possess five or even 10 times the kinetic energy.

Ballistic Tests of Rifle Bullets

It was Dr. Fackler who found that gunshot wounds into swine flesh could be reproduced and calibrated in a mixture of 10-percent ordnance gelatin when maintained at 40°F. Thus a bullet that penetrated 7 inches in living flesh would equally penetrate 7 inches in Dr. Fackler's gelatin mixture, making ballistic tests much simpler and more valid.

Cpl. Ed Sanow of the Benton County, Indiana, Sheriff's Department used this gelatin mixture to conduct a series of rifle bullet ballistic tests in 1991, generating data and the photographs we're using here. All shots were fired at 10 feet.

Our greatest interest certainly is the .308 HPBT Match gelatin test, depicted in the photograph on page 158. Sanow found that the Sierra hollowpoint bullet snapped in two at the stress point where the lead filling ended, spawning two large projectiles that tumbled base-over-tip and carved an incredible wound channel, then followed separate paths until the heaviest fragment came to a halt 22 inches into the gelatin. The lighter hollowtip penetrated 16 inches of gelatin.

As the charts on page 159 note, this 6.4-inch temporary stretch is double that of pistol bullets, as well as other .223 and 7.62mm rifle bullets. Given this dramatic result, it's worth considering what happens when a bullet tumbles in a target.

By simple mathematics, we can determine that a .308 bullet having a muzzle velocity of 2,600 fps, when fired from a rifle having a 1:10 rifling twist, exits the barrel with a spin of 187,200 rpm—far more than most riflemen would ever guess. Rotating with more rpm than many gyroscopes, and flying supersonically nose-forward with an aerodynamically sleek boat-tail shape, it impacts. Then, suddenly, it's twisted sideways into a buzz saw blade fighting its own yaw and spinning more than 3,000 times per *second*. It twists and tears, and both pieces bounce against each other, like two supersonic razors hacking their way through tissue at the rate of the wildest whipsaw ever seen.

A split-second later, the two largest fragments split into separate paths. The recovered bullet base diameter was .59 inch, nearly double its original size, while Sanow found there had been a total of three to five significant fragments amounting to about half the bullet weight.

Thus, the Federal .308 HPBT Match bullet

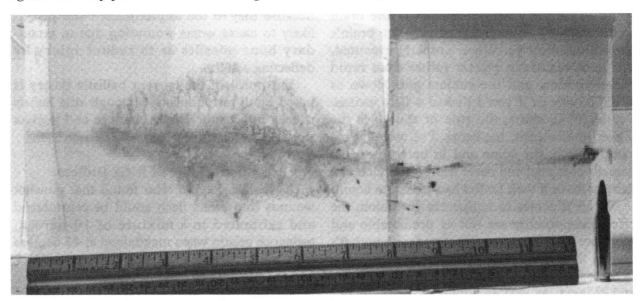

5.56mm, 69-GR. MATCH GELATIN TEST. The lightweight, zippy bullet shattered, losing much energy and thereby lacked much penetration. (Photo credit: Ed Sanow, *S.W.A.T. Magazine*)

ENERGY COMPARISONS OF SNIPING BULLETS (FT-LBS.)

	300 yards	500 yards	600 yards	1000 yards
Federal Match .223 69-gr. BTHP	750	475	375	170
Federal Match .308 168-gr. BTHP	1600	1150	970	510
Fed. Prem. .300 Mag. 200-gr. BTSP	2520	1970	1890	995

inflicted dramatically more damage into the target and penetrated much deeper than did the AK or any of the .223 rounds, with much of this damage due to fragmentation and tumbling.

Sanow was surprised by how poorly the .223s penetrated ballistic gelatin, with all rounds barely meeting the FBI minimum standard of 12 inches. After about 75 yards, Sanow found that the 55-grain military FMJ .223 bent slightly on impact into a crescent-shaped "banana" and ceased fragmenting. Surprisingly, it was the Federal Match HP that consistently penetrated deepest rather than the FMJ rounds, and it also generated the most fragments.

The largest .223 wound channel resulted from the newer M855 FMJ bullet, which usually tumbled in the gelatin. "The 62-grain M855 snaps off clean at the base of the penetrator core," Sanow said. "This is true out to about 150 yards."

The traditional 7.62x39mm AK round performed somewhat better than the .223s, undoubtedly because its bullet weighs more than twice as much. This underlines the ballistic significance of a heavier bullet, which maintains more momentum during penetration and usually goes deeper.

And this brings us back to the .308 Match round, which weighs about triple the weight of the .223s and about 25 percent more than the AK bullet. Packing about twice the kinetic energy of these other bullets, the heavier .308 Match understandably can better smash through bone and intervening media such as glass or car doors and still deliver lethal energy into the target.

Anecdotal Evidence of Incapacitation

But there still are knowledge gaps and opinion chasms when it comes to rifle bullet effects. Corporal Sanow and I once discussed the subject at length, swapping personal observations and experiences. It was Sanow's view that rifle bullets having a remaining velocity of more than about 1,200 to 1,300 fps would cause injuries through temporary cavitation as distinct from wound channel damage. I share his belief that a rifle bullet's cavitation pulse becomes so sharp, so sudden, so violent, and so large that it can tear flesh from bone, hemorrhage or bruise blood-rich organs, and even sever veins and arteries.

Dr. B.R.G. Kaplan, M.D., has told me that, beyond question, hypervelocity bullets (more than 3,000 fps) induce significant tissue damage through cavitation, a belief widely recognized in the wound ballistic community. Current concepts explain part but not all of what's happening—too many contradictions and exceptions exist for one pat theory.

For instance, I was reliably informed of a Mideast sniping incident in which a counter-terrorist marksman—presumably Israeli—drilled a hostage taker with a .300 Winchester Magnum center-chest. Instead of a mere wound channel, the terrorist's entire chest cavity "was filled with a mush of organs and tissue and blood so convoluted that it looked like Jello," I was told by an expert on the subject. Much of that damage resulted from a violent, massive cavitation.

My personal observations, too, tend to support the "there's more happening here than a mere wound channel" opinion. After witnessing more than 30 rifle gunshot wounds, all inflicted by 7.62x39mm rounds at less than 100 yards, I can say beyond any doubt that even the moderate-velocity AK round nearly always inflicts much more than simply wound channel damage.

It was while working on the first edition of this book and recalling such shooting incidents that an unusual research approach arose: informally interviewing gunshot victims to determine to what extent they could continue to resist despite their injuries. This way, we can project the kinds of effects rifle wounds will have on hostiles, especially enemy snipers struck by our fire.

I must thank several old friends who relived incidents they'd rather forget so that you could benefit from their knowledge.

Our first subject, Greg K., had been hit twice in the thighs by 7.62x39mm rounds, breaking one leg and initially losing considerable blood. Greg told me that after he'd stopped the bleeding, he was quite capable of continuing to shoot his M16, although he could no longer walk without assistance.

Larry P., our second subject, took an AK round though the upper left arm, which tore away much flesh and caused heavy bleeding, although it didn't break the bone. He, too, was certain he could have continued to fire, even though he was in pain and feeling some shock. The situation was similar for a Vietnamese member of my team, Hai, who took an AK round high in his right arm; he was in no mood to fight, but could have shot in self-defense at close range. In neither case, however, could they have delivered precision fire.

Our next subject, Larry W., had been hit in the stomach, most likely by a 7.62x39mm round. He told me only a year after being wounded that he'd felt as if the wind was sucked from his lungs, and he could not breathe without great effort and pain. Between the pain and shock, he was not capable of handling a weapon. The same was true for a Vietnamese teammate who'd taken an AK hit to the stomach. We all but had to carry him back to an extraction helicopter landing zone; I doubt he could have done much more than hold a rifle in his lap.

Another subject, John S., took an AK wound in his left ankle, which broke the bone. He was in tremendous pain and not capable of aimed fire and required morphine in order even to walk with assistance.

This last subject's experience raises the issue of pain and its debilitating effects that cannot be measured objectively. From personal observation, I'd say that, mercifully, the most severe wounds seem to generate the least pain—perhaps great shock pops a nervous system "circuit breaker"—although attendant shock causes disorientation and reduces motor skills. The worst gunshot wound agony I ever observed was caused by a bullet punching through a man's hand, shattering a dozen tiny bones in the process.

Now, considering that a .308 generates 50 percent more energy with a bullet weighing 30 percent more than an AK round, we can reasonably extrapolate some conclusions.

First, any wound inflicted by a high-powered rifle bullet is serious and greatly reduces a subject's effectiveness. This is an important lesson for a friendly sniper who mistakenly awaits a "perfect" shot against a hostile sniper. As I advise elsewhere, it's seldom that you'll get a truly perfect shot at a sniper, and it's much better to wound him—even with a limb shot—than it is to hope for a better opportunity. Merely wounding him will reduce him from an offensive threat (capable of maneuvering and firing deliberately) into a defensive threat (no longer able to move and only capable of firing in self-defense at short range).

My second conclusion is that limb wounds—arms or legs—will incapacitate though not kill a target, at least to the extent of converting an offensive into a defensive threat.

My third conclusion is that—unlike a pistol—any torso hit with a high-powered rifle will either kill or totally incapacitate a target. As distinct from a limb wound, he probably won't even be a defensive threat; although not dead, he's completely out of the fight.

Our fourth and final conclusion is that these wound ballistics demonstrate that shot placement is as critical a consideration for police, hostage rescue, and counterterrorist snipers as it is for a uniformed law officer firing a pistol.

SHOT PLACEMENT

Because society quite rightly imposes a taboo on the taking of human life, our paper targets usually are abstract and lacking in enough detail to understand where or why we're placing a shot. I've never seen a silhouette target that identifies the location of the brain, spine, heart, kidneys, liver, and major arteries; though, in fact, these are our true targets, not a simple silhouette or vague center mass.

The concept of shot placement has become well developed for pistol engagements, so we're refining already researched issues and upgrading them so we can rationally estimate when an intended shot will incapacitate instantly, rapidly, or not at all.

A sniper needs to learn the exact position of these intended impact points so he can place his shot properly, especially in the case of hostage-rescue operations. Equally, you must know where to place a shot against a subject who's partially concealed or protected by body armor—and be able to judge knowledgeably whether to take a shot or wait in hopes of better target exposure.

These issues are especially important for police and counterterrorist snipers, although a military sniper usually can achieve his purpose merely by wounding a target.

How Instant Is "Instant" Incapacitation?

Almost any rifle shot that penetrates the cranial cavity will kill, but it's a question of how quickly. Note that I said cranial cavity, not a head shot; that's because about two-thirds of the head consists of tissues and bone that, despite severe injury, will not necessarily lead to even rapid incapacitation, much less the anticipated instant incapacitation. But bullets that actually breach the cavity usually lead to catastrophic results.

Brain tissue is relatively malleable and liquid, an ideal medium for transmitting cavitation shock. Because the cranium is a sealed vessel, it's the only part of the human body that may violently explode just like those plastic milk jugs. This is a grisly but true observation.

Fine-tuning such head shots, however, reveals aiming points for the quickest possible effect, faster than so-called rapid incapacitation, which I'm distinguishing by terming it "instant incapacitation." But how instant is "instant"?

It's faster than the suspect's brain can decide to fire and the resulting neural impulse reach the index finger. Think of your bullet as interdicting this "message" by cutting the nervous system pathway. We can even compute how quickly this happens.

It takes a .308 bullet only 0.12 seconds to travel 100 yards to a suspect, then an additional

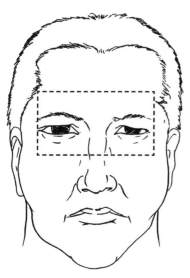

CRANIAL CAVITY, FRONT

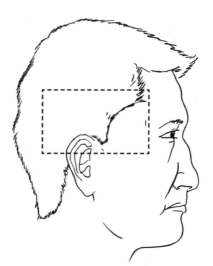

CRANIAL CAVITY, SIDE

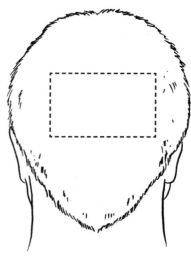

CRANIAL CAVITY, REAR

0.0000516 seconds (approximately one-half millionth of a second) to snap the suspect's 1.5-inch spinal pathway. Contrast that to the 10 to 15 seconds a suspect could retain consciousness after even a perfect heart shot.

An effective CNS shot requires a hit in the spine above the shoulder blades, through the brain stem, or into the cranial cavity.

The illustration on page 163 shows three head views that highlight the cranial cavity impact area. Imagine that this is a 3 x 5 card—which, indeed, it approximates—that, in front, overlaps the suspect's eyes. When it comes to the side of a suspect's head, note that it's wider—as is the brain inside—and flatter, reducing the likelihood of bullet deflection. Here the bottom edge of the imaginary 3 x 5 card is centered on his ear. The back of a suspect's head lacks reference points so it's a center-mass shot, but you can still imagine a 3 x 5 card over its center. It's well worth your while to study your own head in a mirror to see how these imaginary impact points overlap a head.

While the cranial cavity is the single best impact point for instant incapacitation, also keep in mind that it's the one part of a suspect's anatomy that is most likely to move—even when he's otherwise still. Notice how quickly people turn their heads and how this would affect an aimed shot. A startled person will spin his head 45 degrees in less than a second. It's not as easy a shot as it may first appear.

Realistically, what's the maximum range to attempt a cranial cavity shot? Ask yourself, how far away can you reliably hit a 3 x 5 card? Forget about the "5" because we have to consider the smaller likelihood that your round could impact high or low—that means 3 inches. Your rifle and ammo, as you've demonstrated numerous times during practice fire, is capable of 1 MOA or less. That would imply 300 yards, accepting an occasional miss.

But adding the complications of no spotting round, firing from an improvised field position, a bit of suspect movement, a minor error in range estimation, and a hostage or bystander present and I would urge only the most superb marksman to attempt that cranial shot at more than 100 yards. If you find yourself farther away, do your best to stalk closer. If that's not an option, accept the possibility that your hit will not result in instant incapacitation and have a backup shooter ready to follow your shot, or even simultaneously engage with a second sniper.

Rapid Incapacitation Shot Placement

As the illustration on page 165 well shows, a center-chest shot will impact into "a target-rich environment" that induces at least rapid incapacitation.

Overlapping layers of vulnerable targets are clustered around the torso center, to include the heart with its major arteries, the spine just behind the heart, and the liver found just at the bottom of the rib cage. Please note that the heart is *not* located center-chest but slightly to the subject's left side.

A hit to the heart obviously will cause severe blood loss and lead to unconsciousness and likely death in 10 to 15 seconds. A spine hit, which isn't as certain, is a CNS shot with instant incapacitation and possible death, but it cannot be relied on to prevent the subject from firing a weapon unless it impacts higher than the shoulder blades.

A rifle wound to the liver will induce dramatic and rapid blood loss, having an effect similar to a heart shot. Soft liver tissue is especially vulnerable to damage from temporary cavitation, meaning even a near miss can inflict serious injury.

Moving farther down the torso, we see the kidneys, probably the most susceptible organs to crippling pain from even the slightest wound, which can incapacitate the subject. Like the liver, the inelastic kidneys are readily injured by temporary cavitation.

Major blood vessels, too, make good targets, especially the femoral artery in the groin (not illustrated) and the carotid arteries in the neck. Because the neck also contains the spine, it can prove an especially productive impact point.

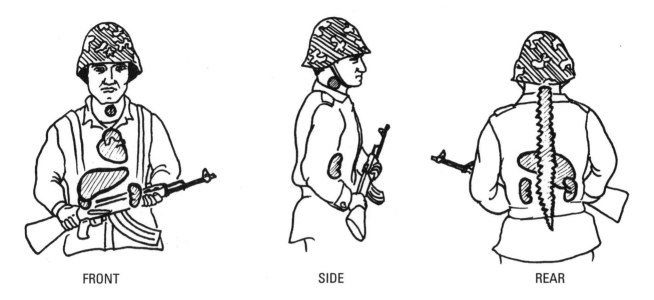

FRONT   SIDE   REAR

Torso aiming points for rapid or instant incapacitation.

Shots taken against the side of a subject are a special case, since the arm bones can reduce penetration—especially with the .223—or deflect bullets away from most of the torso. This could be a suitable situation for a neck or kidney shot if these areas are unobstructed, but since a side view creates such a thin target, it may be better to hold your fire in hopes the subject turns and faces you, presenting a much higher likelihood of hitting a vulnerable point.

Lung shots won't necessarily cause significant bleeding or lead to unconsciousness, although breathing difficulties will limit mobility, and pain may reduce effectiveness. Like other elastic tissues, the lungs readily stretch and thus have little vulnerability to temporary cavitation.

While bone hits may cause pain and immobility, these effects are too unpredictable to intentionally take such shots unless a bone shot is the only one you have.

SNIPER BALLISTIC DATA CARDS

Obviously, there's a lot of critical ballistic data a sniper needs to know and apply when shooting—much more than the average rifleman. It is the correct, exact utilization of this information that makes all the difference in long-range accuracy.

But how's a sniper to keep this all straight, all these tables and factors and formulas?

I struggled with this problem years ago, until one night a light bulb went off in my head. Eureka! Just plot it all down on a 3 x 5 card, then memorize it. Or, even slicker, slip it into a transparent holder pasted to the left sleeve of your Ghillie suit so you can see it with your left eye while keeping your right eye at the scope. And by having it so handy, you can study it until you've memorized it.

We've provided two versions of my ballistic data cards, both for the .308 Federal Match 168-grain BTHP round, which contain all you need to compensate for range, windage, target movement, and up/down elevation.

The first version should be used with a scope having a BDC and includes space to note any fine-tuning you've developed for precise adjustment at each distance. The second version is identical except it's set up for target knobs. Notice the left column top lists these settings for my scope, which has "1/4 M/C or 15M/ROT"— this means, "1/4 minute per click or 15 minutes

Card 1

ELEVATION BDC Fine Tuning	MOVING TARGET LEADS	WIND DRIFT (in inches)

ELEVATION — BDC Fine Tuning

100
200
300
400
500
600
700
800
900
1,000

308M 168-GR

MOVING TARGET LEADS

Walking (3 MPH)

7"	13"	21"	29"	37"
100 Yds	200 Yds	300 Yds	400 Yds	500 Yds
12.6"	26.4"	40.8"	57.0"	73.2"

Running (6 MPH)

REMEMBER: Oblique movement is 1/2 Value!

UP/DOWN COMPENSATION

(data for 45 degrees Up/Down angle)

0.8"	3.4"	8.0"	15.0"	25.0"
100 Yds	200 Yds	300 Yds	400 Yds	500 Yds

REMEMBER: Always compensate by aiming LOW!

WIND DRIFT (in inches)

	5 mph	10 mph
100	0.4	0.8
200	1.5	3.1
300	3.7	7.4
400	6.8	13.6
500	11.1	22.2
600	16.7	33.3
700	23.6	47.1
800	32.0	64.1
900	42.1	84.2
1000	53.7	107.5

REMEMBER: Oblique wind = 3/4 value!

Card 2

ELEVATION

Trajectory in inches	Comeups 1/4 MOAs
100 +5.3"	
	9 Clicks
200 +6.1"	
	12 Clicks
300 Zero	
	14 Clicks
400 -14.3"	
	16 Clicks
500 -38.1"	
	18 Clicks
600 -73.2"	
	20 Clicks
700 -121"	
	23 Clicks
800 -185"	
	26 Clicks
900 -267"	
	29 Clicks
1000 -369"	

308M 168-GR

MOVING TARGET LEADS

Walking (3 MPH)

7"	13"	21"	29"	37"
100 Yds	200 Yds	300 Yds	400 Yds	500 Yds
12.6"	26.4"	40.8"	57.0"	73.2"

Running (6 MPH)

REMEMBER: Oblique movement is 1/2 value!

UP/DOWN COMPENSATION

(data for 45 degrees Up/Down angle)

0.8"	3.4"	8.0"	15.0"	25.0"
100 Yds	200 Yds	300 Yds	400 Yds	500 Yds

REMEMBER: Always compensate by aiming LOW!

WIND DRIFT (in inches)

	5 mph	10 mph
100	0.4	0.8
200	1.5	3.1
300	3.7	7.4
400	6.8	13.6
500	11.1	22.2
600	16.7	33.3
700	23.6	47.1
800	32.0	64.1
900	42.1	84.2
1000	53.7	107.5

REMEMBER: Oblique wind = 3/4 value!

Card 3

TGT KNOB
(1/4 M/C or 15M/ROT)

1st ROT
100	0
200	2MIC
300	5MIC
400	8M3C
500	13M

2nd ROT
600	2M3C
700	8M
800	14M

3rd ROT
900	6M
1000	14M

308M 168-GR

MOVING TARGET LEADS

Walking (3 MPH)

7"	13"	21"	29"	37"
100 Yds	200 Yds	300 Yds	400 Yds	500 Yds
12.6"	26.4"	40.8"	57.0"	73.2"

Running (6 MPH)

REMEMBER: Oblique movement is 1/2 value!

UP/DOWN COMPENSATION

(data for 45 degrees Up/Down angle)

0.8"	3.4"	8.0"	15.0"	25.0"
100 Yds	200 Yds	300 Yds	400 Yds	500 Yds

REMEMBER: Always compensate by aiming LOW!

WIND DRIFT (in inches)

	5 mph	10 mph
100	0.4	0.8
200	1.5	3.1
300	3.7	7.4
400	6.8	13.6
500	11.1	22.2
600	16.7	33.3
700	23.6	47.1
800	32.0	64.1
900	42.1	84.2
1000	53.7	107.5

REMEMBER: Oblique wind = 3/4 value!

per rotation." Below that, we've listed the knob settings for each 100-yard increment, starting with "0" at 100 yards. At 200 yards, the entry "2M1C" means "2 minutes + 1 click," which I found in the comeup tables in the previous chapter. The terms "1ROT" and "2ROT" and "3ROT" signify that knob settings are on the first, second, or third rotations, which also is found in the comeup tables.

If you're shooting a different round—say the military M118 Long Range or the 190-grain .300 Winchester Magnum—just look up the data in this book and prepare a similar ballistic data card.

But be cautioned: all of this is "book" data, which, while generally accurate, may be slightly different from the results obtained when *you* fire *your* rifle with *your* scope and *your* ammunition. A term I've used to describe this special, unique relationship is *personality*, meaning there's just enough difference between your combination and that of anyone else's rifle, ammunition, scope, and shooting style to constitute a distinct pattern of performance.

To determine your performance "personality," start with this book data, then supplement it with information you record during shooting practice, noticing such things as, say, taking only 15 clicks to come up from 400 to 500 yards, or the need to compensate 9 inches low at 300 yards for up/down shooting instead of the indicated 8 inches. These things won't be apparent immediately, and I'd recommend against changing the data card until a variance is confirmed during several practice sessions.

A Step Further

Although to many it would seem that these cards offer all the ballistic "dope" you need for shooting, you still haven't fine-tuned your elevation enough for long-distance "threading the eye of the needle." I recommend that you turn that 3 x 5 card over and jot down at 25-yard increments all the distances from 50 yards to 1,000 yards, then at each 25 yards enter target knob settings or BDC fine-tuning. This will become especially important past 500 yards, where you begin to see considerable

elevation variance from each hundred-yard distance to the next.

For example, notice on the target knob card that at 700 yards you set the elevation at 8 MOA and, just 100 yards later, at 14 MOA. *That's a 6 MOA variance, 24 clicks in just 100 yards!* I think you'll want to know exactly where to set the elevation knob for a 765-yard shot, given that at this distance 1 MOA equals 7 inches. Through practice on known-distance ranges or in open country where you can accurately laze your target, you can build up this kind of point-of-aim/point-of-impact verification until you have all those 25-yard blanks filled.

Still another style of ballistic data card was taught to me by Olympic Gold Medalist Malcolm Cooper, founder of Accuracy International. Working with the 22nd SAS, Malcolm had helped design a graph with arcs. The graph's left side was measured in 1/4 Minutes of Angle, while the bottom was distance-to-target at 25-meter increments. Every time an SAS sniper fired practice, he put a dot where he'd confirmed his dope at an exact lazed distance. In between these confirmed points, the sniper drew a line to "connect the dots" and fill in the other distances and MOA settings. Eventually he had a complete arc, with dots all the way to maximum range, and all he had to do was look at his card to see what his elevation should be in MOAs at any given distance.

Taking even that a step further, Malcolm explained, he showed the SAS snipers how to plot a *second* arc on that same graph, this representing another round with a different trajectory that he might have need to fire. Now here's what's important to remember: this second arc *began* by noting its 100-meter zero, relative to the zero for the sniper's normal round.

Say our sniper normally fires M118 Long Range—that would be his "hard" zero—and perhaps the second round is the Longbow .308 frangible. With the M118 zero on his rifle, the sniper fires and adjusts his knobs to zero for the Longbow ammo—*but he doesn't loosen and rotate the target knobs!* He simply jots down where that Longbow zero is, then likewise develops Longbow elevation settings at 25-yard incre-

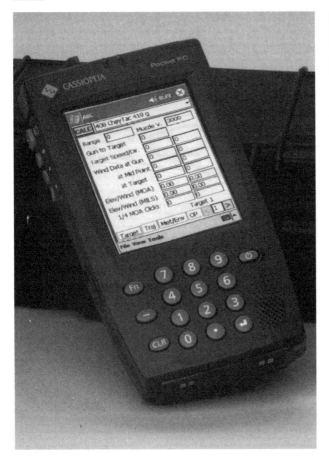

CheyTac's ballistic program incorporates dozens of variables to enhance extreme-range shooting.

The Nightforce ballistic program offers settings and corrections as MOAs, mils, and centimeters per hundred meters.

ments and jots these down, too. He posts these Longbow settings as dots on his card alongside the M118's dots and develops a second arc, which, likewise, will tell him what his MOAs of elevation must be at any distance. *And at any point he can switch back to his original M118 ammo without re-zeroing* because it's all based on the M118's zero. Think of it—he can now track with great precision two different rounds, off the same graph.

Using this system of arcs, Malcolm told me, some SAS snipers keep track of the elevation settings for up to three different rounds. Malcolm may be gone, but his brilliant mind and his AW rifles are still helping snipers around the world.

BALLISTIC COMPUTERS

Given the great amounts of ballistic data a sniper must consider, and the variances of wind, altitude, and temperature and their effects on a long-range shot, it should not be a great surprise that software programs have been designed specifically for sniping. Actually, the first time I ran across such a program was in the early 1990s, in a discussion with an old Special Forces friend then serving in a "black" Spec Ops unit. While I calculated elevation settings with a stubby pencil, he laughed and told me about his handheld Hewlett-Packard that included every possible consideration that could affect a long-range shot, to include uphill/downhill angles. His Hewlett-Packard's program was restricted to a tiny number of Spec Ops snipers, but that same capability has since become available to every police and military sniper.

Nightforce, maker of high-quality rifle scopes and mounts, offers sophisticated ballistic calculation software for handheld PCs that produces settings and corrections as Minutes of Angle, mils, or centimeters-per-hundred-meters. Using this program, you can print graphs, charts, and data cards and plot exact holds on your reticle.

CheyTac, the cutting-edge builder of the .408 CheyTac heavy sniper rifle, has its own ballistic software for handheld PCs that offers amazing possibilities. This program not only considers wind—at the gun, at the target, and in-between—but also temperature, humidity, barometric pressure, latitude—even the Coriolis effect and rotation of the earth, which affect extreme-range, 2,000+ yard shots. The CheyTac program serves up corrections for every small-arm caliber from 5.56mm to .50 and varies the results according to the precise height of a reticle above the center of the bore.

While I welcome all these impressive capabilities, when it finally gets down to taking the shot, it's still marksmanship fundamentals that count the most. And that's what we're covering in the next chapter.

CHAPTER 6

BASIC SNIPER MARKSMANSHIP

SNIPER MARKSMANSHIP

A sniper practices shooting to develop consistency. Keenly attentive, he looks for ways to introduce consistency into his every little task because he knows that consistency equals accuracy and accuracy equals consistency. If his rifle is tuned for consistency, and with his every shot he uses the same scope sight picture, trigger pull, breathing, and body position—and a dozen other tinier subskills—the inevitable result will be accurate shooting.

To make the difference between "all right" shooting and superb performance, you must hone the skills and shooting techniques taught in this chapter. Whether you learned to shoot a rifle in the service or never fired one until joining your department's tactical team, you'll still benefit from what's covered here.

A Shooter's Attitude

About half of achieving superb performance is your attitude. It can either help you or hinder your development.

The few problems I've had coaching riflemen were due to their egos. You can take pride in what you do and how well you do it, but when it reaches the point that it masks errors or closes your mind to further progress, it's no longer pride but blind ego. A sniper's surest, fastest route to hell is to become oblivious to his own shortcomings. As Dirty Harry once said, "A man's got to know his limitations," if he's to correct them.

Amazingly, some men have convinced themselves they can be "natural" master shooters with little or no practice. Maybe they overdosed on John Wayne movies as children. By contrast, I've found that women make excellent shooting students since they have no hang-ups about how accurately they "naturally" should shoot. Never forget that rifle shooting is a perishable skill and can only be developed and maintained by live-fire practice.

The first forward step in attitude is to dismiss any emotional reaction to your shooting. Become a detached, objective observer of your own performance who can analyze errors and diagnose correct solutions. Be honest with yourself. The Olympic-level rifle shooters I know are "slow-walkin', slow-talkin'" kinds of guys who don't get shaken but think before they act.

Accept the contradictory realization that your entire shooting career will be spent striving for perfection but absolute perfection is unobtainable. Never exaggerate your own performance; look not at nine perfect hits but at the one miss and figure out what caused it, then apply this to the next shot. Competition is great, and I applaud all match winners, but as soon as you start thinking you're the "best," you'll begin that downhill slide to Lucifer. Continually ask yourself, "What can I do better?" Compare your performance not to anyone else's—compare it only to your own.

Competitions, such as this match at the NRA Whittington Center, help police and military snipers hone their skills.

Log a lot of detail in your record book, study it between shooting practices, and use it to plan how you shoot in subsequent practice sessions.

The Spotter's Role

Whenever you fire, your spotter should be lying beside you, observing and coaching. The converse is true when he's firing and you become the spotter. The two of you are a sniper *team*.

The spotter's role is not one of emotional support. While you're firing, he's 100 percent occupied in specific spotting tasks, to include estimating range and wind, reading mirage, detecting and assessing targets, observing fire, confirming hits, and suggesting corrections.

But since this is practice fire, the spotter also serves as your coach. He assists recoil and trigger-pull drills, watches your breathing, sees if your position is solid and consistent, and so forth. As a coach, he must be honest but diplomatic, patient, and understanding. This builds mutual trust and instills in him a keener focus on his own body position, breathing, trigger control, etc., since he must sensitize himself to these in order to coach you.

At times you'll have to fire in practice without your teammate, but whenever possible it's better to have him with you.

Techniques to Improve Shooting

The quality of your practice will never exceed the quality of what you put into it. To start with, never fire practice with anything but match-grade ammunition—military or commercial—or you're just wasting your time. You should occasionally fire ball and tracer ammo, but that's for familiarization, not for serious practice firing.

If you keep some ammo loose for alert purposes or return from the field with loose ammo, these are the rounds you fire in practice. This way you rotate your operational ammo and keep it fresh. Of course, both practice and operational ammo are from the same lot.

Focus yourself mentally and physically on just one shot at a time, a concept I call "this is the first shot of the rest of my life." Later we'll cover techniques for developing a focus on these one-shot kills. Related to this, make an effort to call each shot, estimate where it impacted, and log it in your record book even before your spotter announces the exact point of impact.

That record book will do wonders in helping you understand your rifle, your scope, your ammo, and how you perform with them under varying conditions. Maintain the book stead-

Zero your rifle with high-quality, match-grade ammo and then use only this load for all practice fire.

fastly and record every shot. Use the resulting information to develop a 3 x 5 sniper data card, which was covered in the last chapter.

Dry-fire as much as possible—it's the most convenient, inexpensive, and time-efficient way to improve your shooting.

I must insert here a special plug about the value of known-distance firing versus unknown-distance firing. The former takes place on a range laid out with well-marked distances and target arrays typically on line at 100, 200, 300 yards, etc. An unknown-distance range has targets at irregular distances, usually concealed or of the pop-up type, with no indicator of how far away they are. A sniper needs both kinds of firing practice.

Known-distance practice confirms how accurately the BDC is performing, develops certainty and confidence in range estimation,

and prepares the shooter for unknown-distance shooting. Obviously, unknown-distance shooting hones target detection and range estimation, which are critical sniper skills. *Both* types of practice are important and needed.

Bull's-eye-type practice, which starts each shooting session, should take place on a known-distance range. The subsequent drills, which add realism and stress, should take place on an unknown-distance range.

During Practice Firing

Since you cannot focus on every single aspect of shooting all the time, it's good to feature just one aspect for each practice session, like trigger control, breathing, follow-through, and so on. Rotate this special emphasis for each session and involve your spotter in coaching you on it, too.

The FBI recommends that police snipers

practice at least monthly to maintain an acceptable level of shooting skill, which is a good minimum. If you can fire more frequently, by all means do so. I have never known a competitive rifleman who had a decline in performance from too much practice.

Once you've learned the fundamentals, you won't need to fire more than about 20 rounds per practice session. Fire it slow and make each shot count—just as you would in real life. Never allow yourself to slide into mindless banging away.

Spend half your range time on actual marksmanship practice on a known-distance range, firing at bull's-eye targets. The second half of each shooting practice session is devoted to drills that—along with accurate shooting—challenge a sniper's patience, judgment, and self-discipline. You must never be allowed more than one shot at a target in these shooting drills.

The box on pages 228–229 details recommendations for many categories of shooting practice, such as day and night, various body positions, types of targets, and so forth. These are not the final word on practice fire but illustrate the detailed thinking required for a true training program.

Even if your scope has an excellent BDC, you still should occasionally use holds to compensate for distance. This is because it's much faster to engage multiple targets at various ranges using holds rather than constantly changing the BDC setting. Military scopes that have a mil dot reticle allow excellent hold compensation, but since these also have BDCs, this feature is seldom, if ever, exercised. The ballistic tables in this book show the exact holds required for a host of popular sniping rounds, including .223, .308, and .300 Winchester Magnum.

Practice as You'll Operate

Your practice fire will not be very useful unless it accurately reflects how you actually operate in the field. Rolling out a comfortable shooting mat and pulling on your custom shooting jacket have as much to do with sniping as with an expedition

to Mars. But there are some other practices, less obvious, that are just as unrealistic.

I've seen some snipers don strap-on recoil pads on the firing range. Would they really have such pads in the field? And what about earmuffs? It's better to use hearing protectors that insert in your ear so you don't develop an odd spotweld from practice fire—and you'll actually have the same hearing protection with you in the field.

Wearing street clothes instead of your tactical uniform with full gear is unrealistic, too. How will your body armor—or your webgear, for that matter—affect body position unless you practice with it during range firing?

Long-Range Police Shooting

Since the average real-world police sniper shot is less than 100 yards, and his environment is an almost exclusively urban one, is there any need for law enforcement snipers to practice shooting at long distances?

I say absolutely yes. In the first place, long-range shooting magnifies errors that are not even apparent at 100 yards and therefore cannot otherwise be diagnosed and corrected. Equally, though, the police sniper needs to explore his own and his rifle's full spectrum of capabilities. The bulk of police students have been amazed to shoot beer-can-size groups at 500 yards—their close-range groups dramatically tighten because they practiced firing at long range.

And even though the majority of real-world shots are close-range, a police sniper must prepare for less likely but real long-range threats. It's conceivable he might have to engage a rooftop crazy letting loose on Christmas Eve at a city's busiest shopping mall, or cover a skyjacked commuter plane when he cannot stalk closer to within 400 yards of it. So, although the recommendations suggest 75 percent of police firing at less than 200 yards, the other 25 percent extends all the way to 600 yards.

Due to urban sprawl and a decline in nearby high-powered rifle ranges, some police snipers have acquired heavy-barreled, small-

An excellent training rifle is this .22-caliber Krico Super Sniper with heavy barrel, target trigger, and birdcage flash suppressor.

caliber rifles—such as .22 Long Rifles or Hornady .17-caliber Magnum Rimfires—that offer good practice at 50-yard ranges. To be useful, such a training rifle must be of similar quality and heft to the officer's normal sniper rifle. By no means can this substitute for regular, live-fire training with his duty weapon, but it does make it possible for the law enforcement sniper to get in more range time, and that's unquestionably beneficial.

THE INTEGRATED ACT OF SHOOTING

Actually firing a rifle, and firing it with great accuracy, requires the simultaneous application of many component skills. These generally can be divided into the areas of breathing, trigger control, correct scope picture, and solid body position. With each shot you take, time after time, you synchronize this whole range of components until they combine to form the single integrated act of shooting.

Breathing

When you breathe, your chest expands and contracts. This cyclical movement is transmitted to your rifle, causing it to rise a bit, then fall a bit with each breath.

By learning to control your breathing, you'll impose a short calm, during which the rifle is rock-steady, when you can get off an accurate shot. All that's really meant by breathing control is holding your breath in perfect synch-

ronization with the other integrated components of firing. But it's easier said than done.

The problem is that you can only hold your breath a few seconds before oxygen deprivation starts to degrade vision and imposes a slight shake worse than if you'd never held your breath in the first place. To experience this effect, look at a distant object and hold your breath; within about eight seconds you'll find it difficult to see it clearly.

There's a definite technique to proper breathing. First, surge the oxygen content in your blood by taking one or two deep breaths. No matter which of the breathing patterns you use, it should begin this way.

Now let's get more complicated. Note that a normal breathing pattern has a cycle of about four or five seconds. Now, pay close heed to your own breathing for a moment. Feel the cycle of it, in and out, in and out. It's calm, not forced.

If you're especially conscious of it, you'll notice a very short pause just after you exhale but before you inhale. This two-second pause—known as the natural respiratory pause—is the steadiest point in the entire breathing cycle, and a shot taken here should be the most stable. But since the pause lasts only two seconds, it may be too short to aim and fire. Therefore, a precision rifleman extends the pause by holding his breath just as he finishes exhaling. This "empty lung" technique is shown in the illustration on the next page.

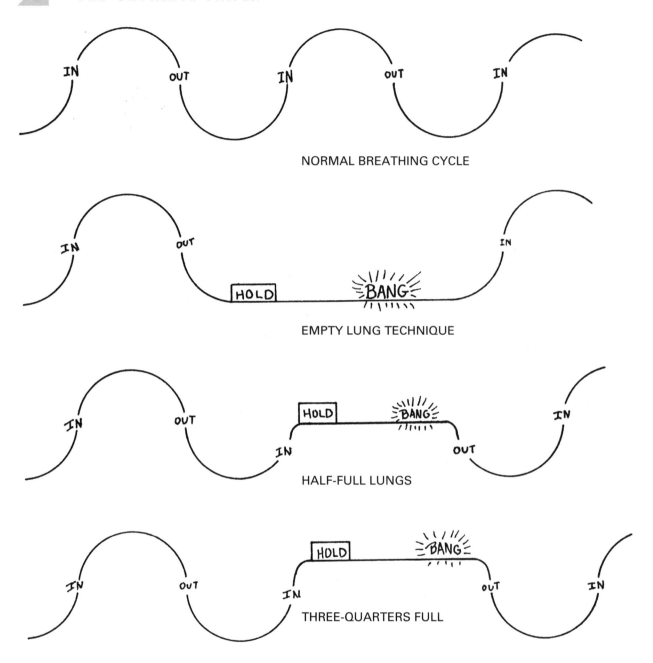

NORMAL BREATHING CYCLE

EMPTY LUNG TECHNIQUE

HALF-FULL LUNGS

THREE-QUARTERS FULL

Breathing cycles and shot release.

Putting it all together, then, first take a couple of deep breaths to build up oxygen in your blood. Next, exhale normally, then hold your breath. Now, while totally calm and steady, squeeze off the shot. Competitive rifle shooters use this breathing technique for each shot they take because it makes possible the steadiest hold.

But as a sniper you may not have enough time before a shot for several preparatory breaths or even to blow out your breath before a shot. Several special shooting situations require you to fire on command or at the instant a target appears—ready or not.

Therefore, you need to practice shooting while holding your breath with your lungs half-full and three-quarters full as well as empty. We've graphed all these breathing cycles. They're almost as steady as the empty lung technique, but what is lost in steadiness is gained in flexibility. I've found my best shooting results from holding a half-breath and getting my shot off within about four seconds.

As quickly as he detects a target, an experienced sniper begins deep breathing so he's ready to fire when his rifle reaches his shoulder. I've also found while hunting big game that this deep breathing helps to calm me before taking the shot.

A novice shooter typically takes too much time for about every other practice shot and must repeat the cycle. If you couldn't get it all together during one breathing cycle, blow it out and start again; *don't* just go ahead and shoot anyway! It's the correct repetition during practice that will enable you to do it correctly under stress.

Scope Sight Picture

The second component of the integrated act of shooting is a correct scope sight picture, which must be just as synchronized as any other element.

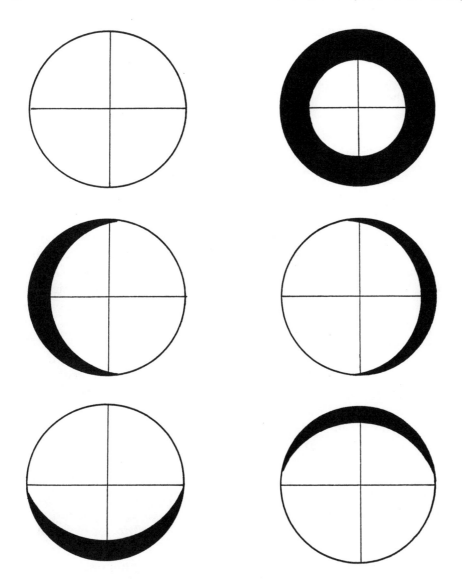

Only the upper left is a correct scope picture. The others result from incorrect eye relief or bad spotweld.

The most critical aspect of a consistent scope picture is perfect eye relief—holding your eye at the exact same distance from the eyepiece, shot after shot. This will minimize any possible parallax, yield the most light, and allow you to see the widest field of view.

The spotweld, which is the place where you hold your cheek against the stock, should become a muscle memory habit so that your eye is automatically at the correct distance and you can fire as quickly as the rifle reaches your shoulder if necessary. Gary Schraml, the retired officer and master shooter who works on my rifles, even goes so far as to slightly concave his custom stocks so the shooter's cheek cannot help but achieve a good spotweld.

On page 177 we've illustrated correct and incorrect scope pictures. Notice that the key indicator of any error is the presence of shadow within the scope's image. If you have a good spotweld, you'll have good eye relief, and this will result in a correct scope picture.

Whether you close the nonshooting eye is your own preference. Some competitive shooters will take me to task on this, insisting that the only way to fire is with both eyes open, noting that the closed eye's pupil will dilate and thereby disrupt the open eye, etc. That's scientifically correct, but I've known too many superb riflemen who close one eye—especially self-learned natural marksmen—to declare that both eyes open is the "only" acceptable way to fire. I think untrained sniper students should learn the two-eye method and experienced marksmen should try the two-eye method, but no one has a monopoly on this issue.

Leaving both eyes open while waiting out a concealed bad guy, however, is absolutely essential to prevent eye fatigue. Your vision will degrade a bit even if you stare too long through your scope. To keep your vision fresh, move your eyes around and even completely lift your head away from the scope if the situation allows it.

The way you use the crosshairs to aim is important, too. Elsewhere we illustrate how to quarter an obscure target or select a tiny point within a larger target so that your mind and eye can focus with precision. Related to this is consciously focusing on the crosshair at the instant of firing for the most exact aim possible. Also, this final focus will enable you to "call" your shot. With practice, you can learn to synch your trigger pull to the instant you mentally focus that final time on the crosshair.

If you can convince your mind "*that's it*" when the crosshair's in focus that final time, and it's precisely on the intended point of impact, truly incredible accuracy can result. This melding of mind, vision, and trigger, with practice, will enable you to shoot when it "feels" right, a higher mental plane of muscular and cerebral exactitude.

Proper Grip

Grasp the rifle at the pistol grip using a handshake grip—firm but not so tight that it induces any tremor. Lay your thumb beside the stock rather than across it so it allows you to keep your shooting hand in line and trigger finger free to pull the trigger directly back. Thumbhole and through-the-stock grips—such as the Russian SVD, the Accuracy International, and my own Choate stock—are designed to keep the shooter's hand in line, as if he's shooting a pistol for undistorted, natural aiming.

When firing prone or off support, turn your nonshooting hand back, under the butt, to hold it into your shoulder while also squeezing a sand-filled sock that supports the heel. This squeeze or release slightly raises or lowers the butt to hold it steadily on the target.

It's very important to keep that butt snug into the shoulder, or it can cause considerable recoil pain. As you prepare to fire, go out of your way to use the baby finger of your shooting hand to pull back on the pistol grip and keep steady pressure as you squeeze off the shot. Practice this so you don't inadvertently tense your trigger finger during that final squeeze.

Trigger Control

As you should realize by now, trigger control is an important component of this integrated act of exact shooting. But trigger control is

Make a practice of holding your thumb along the stock to avoid shifting the rifle.

especially important because, more so than any other factor, an improper trigger pull will lead to inaccuracy or complete misses.

Simply put, correct trigger control is the ability to release the firing pin without imparting any movement to the rifle. All trigger pull problems are caused by flinching or jerking the trigger, which usually results from anticipating the instant of firing—reacting from the shock of recoil even before any recoil is felt. The shooter has found the dreaded blast and push of recoil so painful that he unconsciously jerks his finger when he thinks the rifle's about to fire.

To overcome this, conventional infantrymen are taught to become oblivious to trigger release and be surprised by the instant of firing. This technique may work for ordinary riflemen firing assault rifles having a trigger pull of 6 to 10 pounds, but it will never do for snipers.

Quite the contrary, a sniper *sensitizes*

himself to the feel of his trigger and learns to know when it will fire so he can consciously plan that instant of shot release. Indeed, the ability to fire at a predetermined split second is the essence of hostage-rescue shooting.

Beyond mastering dry-fire, a sniper also learns to handle recoil so well that it's not a cause of discomfort and doesn't inspire jerking. The best way to absorb recoil painlessly is by properly seating the rifle in your shoulder, although we have included an entire section later in this chapter on reducing felt recoil.

Most American bolt-action sniper rifles have single-stage triggers offering a constant, consistent resistance, suggesting that you fire it with a steady pull. Some European bolt guns, such as the Accuracy International AW and Sako TRG-22, have military-style, two-stage triggers, with a light initial pull, then more resistance as it nears breaking. I think it's easier

THE INTEGRATED ACT OF SHOOTING

	READY	**AIM**	**FIRE**	**FOLLOW-THROUGH**
BODY POSITION	Natural POA, comfortable, muscle tension, butt in shoulder	Final fine adjustments, taking slack out of sling, grip beanbag, bipod steady	Steady, stable, firm	Absorb recoil, continue steady hold, eject cartridge, reload
SCOPE PICTURE	Scope picture is clear, fills the eyepiece, target visible	Slight reticle movement due to beathing, focus back and forth at target and reticle	Crosshair exactly on target, in focus at instant of firing	Continue focus on target, observe results, call shot
TRIGGER CONTROL	Safety is off, finger lightly on trigger	Take slack out, pull directly back, just to edge of release	Straight, clean pull; breaks clean, too	Leave finger lightly on trigger
BREATHING	Normal cycle	Deeper inhale/exhale	Inhale half, HOLD	Back to normal

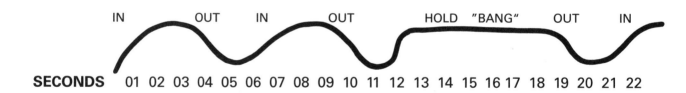

IN   OUT   IN   OUT   HOLD   "BANG"   OUT   IN

SECONDS 01 02 03 04 05 06 07 08 09 10 11 12 13 14 15 16 17 18 19 20 21 22

"jerk-firing" a two-stage trigger—that is, instead of a steady pull, just one quick jerk to fire—especially in an emergency. But no matter single- or two-stage, all that really matters is mastering that trigger for a clean breaking shot.

How you finish this final release will be dictated by the situation. If you have unlimited time, such as during range firing, and the target is stationary, you can squeeze off the shot at leisure. A snap-shot against a suddenly appearing, moving target, on the other hand, requires a release almost as quick as taking in the slack. Having developed an "educated" trigger finger, however, allows you to vary release to fit your target and shooting situation.

And when it comes to the actual pressing of finger to trigger, only the fingertip should be in contact. The tip is far more sensitive than any other finger area, although that trigger seems almost intended for wrapping around it the crease of the first knuckle—the *worst* point for contact.

The fingertip should be at least two-thirds of the way down the trigger to take advantage of leverage and to allow it the maximum arc while taking up slack. Once you've determined where to place your finger comfortably, do it this way consistently.

Other than its tip, your finger should not touch the rifle so that your pull is straight and unhindered and does not push the stock in any way.

Body Position

Now we come to the last component of our integrated act of firing, the correct and consistent assumption of a solid body position.

Which position you use for any particular engagement will be dictated by your target, ground clearance, and available support. As a sniper, you'll *always* exploit any kind of support within reach, whether you use a standing, kneeling, sitting, or prone position. Support may be enhanced, too, by using your sling.

The steadiest position is prone, followed by sitting, then kneeling. The least stable position is standing. Obviously you'll prefer the prone, but you'll have to use whichever position best fits the circumstances.

All positions, though, have several principles in common. First, understand that your bones are the foundation for holding your rifle, *not* your muscles. The muscles add cushioning and allow you to grasp the rifle firmly, but it's mostly the bones that will keep the rifle in place.

Second, you must make yourself comfortable in your position. This means deviating the position to fit your body and adjusting slightly to fit the surroundings. If you're comfortable, you'll hold the rifle steadier and can remain alert but motionless longer.

Third, you'll fire best by reshifting your body to fit your natural point of aim. To determine this natural point of aim, close your eyes and point the rifle in the general direction of your target. Now, open your eyes and see if you're properly aligned. Shift your body around as required; then close your eyes and try again until you point at the target naturally. You can find a natural point of aim for each position and each engagement.

Having said so much about proper body position, I cannot be honest and realistic unless I add a bit of heresy. Much too much has been

written about assuming a body position that is just so and how the long-distance shooter must check and recheck this and that for steadiness, and so forth. I am guilty of this, too, but perhaps these few words will help redeem me.

Recall the warnings of the World War I sniping expert H.W. McBride, who observed that a sniper must be able to react *fast* or he may never get off a shot. To this sound advice I add that a sniper often will find circumstances dictating that he fire from lopsided, uncomfortable, and even "unacceptable" positions into which he must contort his body to even *see* the target.

Anyone can fire consistent X-rings on a fine day and from a prone position with the sandbag propped up just so. As a sniper, though, you'll take pride in being able to achieve excellent results while lying in mud, slightly above freezing, and with a cramp in your neck.

Granted, you'll strive to improve so difficult a locale, but reality is that perfect results must be yielded from even imperfect settings. The only variable in such conditions, ultimately, is *you*, the sniper.

Follow-Through

This is an essential part of each shot you take, not for what you do during it but what you *prevent* by going through the act of follow-through.

First, a definition. Follow-through is a process by which the shooter maintains continuous concentration and nonreaction after firing a shot so he develops a mental and physical habit of allowing no disruption whatsoever at the instant of shooting. It's as if he didn't even fire a shot.

The significance of follow-through becomes more apparent when you realize that .022 of a second passes between the trigger releasing the sear and the firing pin actually striking the cartridge's primer. And a further .002 second will pass while your .308 bullet travels down the 24-inch barrel. If there's any slight movement of the rifle during this period, the crosshairs will no longer be exactly on target as the bullet exits the muzzle.

One friend has urged me to bring this point home to my students by having them fire a black powder rifle, in which the delay between pulling the trigger and the weapon firing is much longer and the movement effect far greater. His point is well taken, though I doubt we'll don our buckskins and fire Kentucky long rifles to prove it.

What helps me to maintain myself right through follow-through is thinking about the target and lying very still after firing, then regaining focus in the scope. I don't even ease the trigger forward until then. It's like I'm frozen in time.

Although the chart on page 180 suggests that the shooter eject his cartridge and rebolt the rifle during follow-through, it's more exact to say this comes a second later. The same goes for calling the shot to your spotter, which trails follow-through by a second.

Follow-through wraps up all the steps and components of the integrated act of shooting, which by now you should respect as a whole complex set of things to remember and apply during practice fire. To apply these in the correct place, and in perfect synchronization, is the mark of a precision rifle shooter. They're used for every shot you fire, time after time.

During each practice fire session, I emphasize one shooting component for special attention, such as breathing. I'll pay particular heed to breathing during each shot and ask my spotter to observe and coach my breathing. Any other detectable errors are diagnosed and corrected, too, but this heavy emphasis in one area helps me hone that skill.

To ensure you have a real program of honing the integrated act of shooting, we've created a special place to log each session's emphasized skill right on your record book page.

SHOOTING WITH A BIPOD

Since snipers rarely can carry along sandbags to the field, the next best support they have is a bipod, which is second only to sandbags for providing steadiness and stability.

Turn this knurled knob to adjust pivot tension on a Harris L Series bipod.

More than any other accessory, the bipod's ability to raise and hold a rifle above the ground has helped long-range riflemen improve their shooting performance. Mind you, a bipod will not make up for poor marksmanship—it's simply another means of supporting your rifle. All the techniques for precision shooting—from breathing to trigger control to follow-through—must be meticulously applied while shooting with a bipod just as with any other kind of shooting support.

While under way, many a sniper stows the bipod in his rucksack to reduce his rifle's weight and lessen the chance of the folded legs getting hung up on something. However, if there's a chance of hostile contact and the bipod would be needed immediately, it's better to keep it mounted. When zero-firing on sandbags or otherwise firing off a solid support, remove the bipod since its folded frame won't stabilize your rifle as steadily as the bare forearm.

While using a bipod, the most important thing to keep in mind is the subtle way it can cause you to cant your rifle, tipping it slightly right or left and thus causing you to dump your rounds right or left at your target. Try to place the legs on a firm surface or anchor them deeply in soft soil so they don't shift or tip sideways.

Even if you begin firing with the bipod legs

positioned properly, you may start canting if rushed or when you shift laterally from one target to another, which can pivot the bipod. The best way to prevent canting is to mentally double-check the horizon on some flat surface—such as water or a distant road or a man-made vertical line, such as a telephone pole—to reestablish perspective. If you have a Harris L Series bipod, which allows pivoting, set the knurled resistance knob fairly stiff, just loose enough to pivot.

For the best stability, keep the legs set as short as possible and try pushing your rifle slightly forward to put isometric pressure on the legs, which will actually stiffen them.

USING A RIFLE SLING

Most advertisements you see for rifle slings actually are for carrying straps, which are not the same thing.

A carrying strap allows you to tote your rifle on your shoulder or across your back so that you don't have to bear its heavy weight in your arms. While it's very handy, a carrying strap will kill you in combat since you become lazy and have your rifle on your shoulder rather than in your hands when you need it. I guarantee you, a man with his rifle at the ready will always "outdraw" an opponent whose rifle foolishly is slung. Every time.

A sling is designed to brace yourself for steadier, more accurate shooting. Snipers need slings, not carrying straps.

Sling Designs
While leather slings have been around longer and have more high-power competitor fans than newer nylon designs, either type works acceptably. All that really matters is that the sling has enough width and the right kinds of adjustments for serious shooting.

Whether nylon or leather, it should be 1 1/4-inch wide and dark enough to blend into your environment. Of course, you need 1 1/4-inch swivels to match, with the quick-release type being most suitable.

The competition-type leather slings tend to have better and more adjustable keepers and hooks, with perforations instead of just a sliding buckle as a stop. Although my purist friends will criticize me for admitting it, the nylon slings can be adjusted more easily.

Hasty and Deliberate Slings
The "hasty sling" position is called such because it can be assumed rapidly. It will significantly improve your steadiness, but not as well as the "deliberate sling," which we'll cover momentarily.

As the illustration shows, the hasty sling requires only that you slip your nonshooting arm through it once, then, up close to the forearm, slip just your hand through a second time. By flexing your biceps and pushing slightly with your hand, you can take out all the slack until you're in a very firm and stable position. I'd guess that a hasty sling position takes less than two seconds to assume but improves steadiness by 40 percent.

To take up a deliberate sling, you must first release the swivel at the butt, then form a loop large enough to slide your nonshooting arm into it, as shown in the illustration on page 184.

The "hasty sling" is wound around the arm once and tensed for stability.

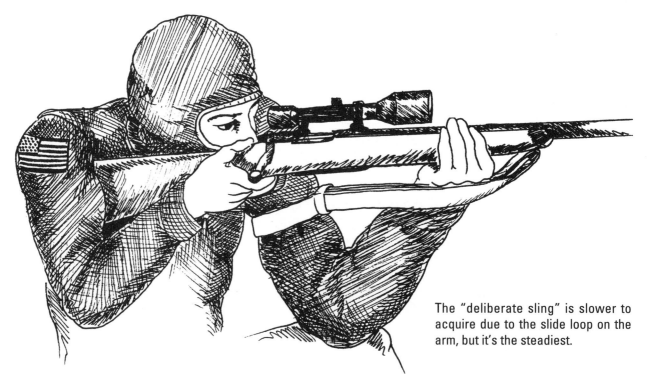

The "deliberate sling" is slower to acquire due to the slide loop on the arm, but it's the steadiest.

Next, place the loop just above your biceps and push down the keeper or buckle until it's snug around your arm. You'll have to experiment with this to learn the exact spot to achieve it, but the result should be that once this loop's in place and you insert your hand between the sling and forearm, your position will be rock-steady, with considerable leverage bracing the rifle in place. When used correctly, a deliberate sling position will improve steadiness by perhaps 60 percent. With practice, you can learn to assume a deliberate sling in about 15 to 20 seconds.

But I must note a need for caution. In bracing too hard, you could pull the stock against your barrel and even pull the barrel off zero. This is not as perverse as it sounds. The U.S. Army found that heavy pulling on the M16's front swivel caused point of impact to shift almost 4 inches at 100 yards. Part of this effect undoubtedly was due to the M16's lightweight design, but hefty pulling could affect other rifles, too.

If your rifle forearm has double swivel studs, you could use a third "very hasty" technique, as developed for Jeff Cooper's famous Scout Rifle. The developer, Carlos Widmann of Guatemala, installed a simple leather loop between the two forward swivels. As shown in the illustration on page 185, slip your arm through only once, like with the hasty, and then take slack out with hand pressure. This technique's almost as steady as the deliberate sling, and it's even faster to assume than the hasty, while due to the swivel locations, the stock's pulled down and away from the barrel with less likelihood of binding. The only significant drawback is that when not in use, it flops around and can get caught in foliage.

Usually a sniper will assume a supported firing position rather than employ his sling because it's faster to get into, easier to maintain for long periods, and quicker to displace from. There is probably too much emphasis on sling shooting due to the influence of competitive marksmen, who fire in many events in which their only support is a sling. You should always attempt to use a bipod or expedient support, but lacking this, you'll find your sling a good second choice for stability.

I must admit that a sling is also a means by which you can carry your weapon, but only for short periods if the situation demands, such as

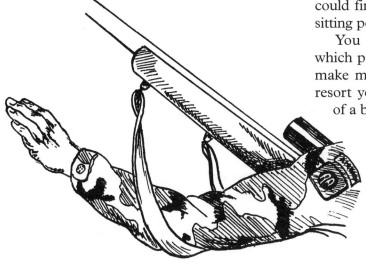

This short loop is the "very hasty" technique for stablized shooting.

could find cover against hostile return fire for a sitting position but not a kneeling one.

You must *always* seek support, no matter which position you employ. Think, "How can I make myself steadier, more stable?" As a last resort you carry support with you in the form of a bipod and highly adjustable sling.

Years ago, there was only one acceptable way to assume any position, and it was up to you to force your body to comply with it. In recent years, it has finally been realized that a shooter who can adjust himself and modify his stance will be more relaxed and probably form a much more stable position. Therefore, you're encouraged to shift and modify if it improves your performance. The proof is in the pudding.

The pros and cons of various positions are based on several criteria, which we've listed in the box below. Note that some positions are better than others, but there's no such thing as a "best" position. Each advantage has a trade-off. (Incidentally, by "protection" we mean presenting as small a target as possible to small-arms fire.)

when you need your hands free to drag a wounded comrade or to climb. About the silliest you could ever feel is to find your hands empty when there should be a gun there.

SHOOTING POSITIONS

The shooting position you assume in the field is dictated by what's available around you and the location of your target.

Clearly, you'd always prefer the great stability of a prone position, but ground-level foliage or intervening terrain may not allow it. As well, you

The Standing Position

Also known as the "offhand position" to competitive rifle shooters, the standing position is the least stable but fastest to assume.

If you must fire standing, reduce magnification to eliminate the "wobble" you see in your

PROS AND CONS OF VARIOUS SHOOTING POSITIONS

	FIELD OF FIRE	STABILITY	PROTECTION *	SPEED TO ASSUME
STANDING	Best, Wide	Poor	Hazardous	Fastest
KNEELING	Fairly Good	Mediocre	Still Dangerous	Very Fast
SITTING	Restricted	Better	Better	Fair
PRONE	Worst, Narrow	Best	Best	Slowest

Protection from enemy fire.

scope. You'll find it much easier to stay on target.

Most likely, you would fire standing only if you encountered a target while you're on the move, probably firing in self-defense. It's important to keep the supporting arm tucked beneath the rifle and your elbow pressed to your rib cage. Breathing is critical.

More so than any other position, standing is affected by wind, requiring that you fire between wind gusts.

The Prone Position

On page 187 we've illustrated two versions of the prone position—with the leg on your shooting side extended or pulled forward to relieve some pressure off your chest. For some people, the latter reduces breathing movement and improves steadiness. Still another way to do this is to place that foot across the back of your other knee.

Steadying your breathing this way helps you do things like confirm alignment for your natural point of aim. Just look at your reticle and verify that the crosshair rises and falls vertically across the target.

The prone position has so much going for it that, other things being equal, it is the one you'll assume whenever possible.

The Hawkins Position

This is a modification of the prone, purposely intended to be the lowest you can possibly lie and still shoot. Your body hugs the ground so close that no profile can be seen.

Your rifle butt is not on your shoulder—it is dug slightly into the ground. And you probably will have to twist your head to get eye relief and see through the scope.

The forearm, too, is as low as possible, propped right on the ground if you have soft soil. You also can grasp the forward swivel with your left hand as support and reduce recoil by keeping the left arm extended and taut.

The Hawkins position is used in thin cover, such as that found in a desert.

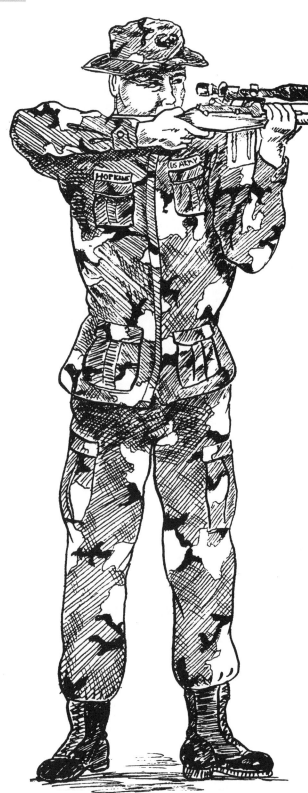

STANDING. Note position of elbows.

STEADIEST. The prone position with sandbag.

HAWKINS POSITION. Heel of rifle is recessed into ground; forearm is on ground or anchored by hand on sling.

Relieve pressure on chest by pulling leg forward.

The Kneeling Position

During my old SOG days, I preferred the kneeling position when reacting to sudden contacts. You presented a much smaller target than when standing, and it was not too hard psychologically to get yourself moving again through enemy fire. It was really fast to get into it and instinctive since the first thing you want to do under fire is get down.

But for sniping it is fairly unstable, almost as bad as standing. Most people can't kneel very long before fatigue sets in. You can prolong your time by leaning into a tree or corner of a building. Be sure to keep your elbow forward of the knee for best stability.

KNEELING. This Army sniper in Iraq steadies his M25 rifle with a good kneeling position.

SQUATTING. A solid squatting position requires feet flat on the ground, buttocks resting on the ankles, and elbows on the thighs.

Though there are several ways to position the right leg, I think the best stability results when you have the rear foot extended flat on the ground and your buttock resting directly on it.

The Sitting Position

Although there are several variations on the sitting position, we've illustrated two common types.

The difference is in how you place your feet. The steadiest and probably the lowest is having your legs extended with feet flat on the ground. Turn your toes inward for isometric tension against your elbows. A second technique is to cross the legs about halfway up the shins, or you could cross only your ankles.

Try both and use the one that best fits your body and yields the best stability. Be sure to

SITTING. Open legged, feet flat on the ground.

SITTING. A solid, cross-legged sitting position. Note elbows are inside the knees.

place your elbows inside your knees for good muscle-to-muscle contact.

The sitting position is second only to the prone in stability, while its higher elevation can give you a much wider field of fire and field of view.

REDUCING FELT RECOIL

During preliminary marksmanship training, we watch sniper students closely to identify those experiencing painful recoil. It's critical to alleviate this before it degrades marksmanship development.

No matter the rifle caliber, realize that painful recoil results when the rifle butt is not being held snugly against the shoulder. If the butt's held properly, recoil is conveyed automatically into the body's upper trunk, where it's ab-

sorbed comfortably. Pain will likely result, however, if the rifle is held loosely, even if you're only firing lightweight rounds such as the .308 Winchester.

The best solution is prevention—learning to handle recoil by properly seating your rifle in the pocket of your shoulder. On page 190 we show how first to hold the rifle pointed upward and away as you initially position the butt, a maneuver that opens the pocket wide so it's easy to find. Then, rotate the rifle forward and down and you're ready to fire. Although competitive shooters use this technique whenever they shoulder a rifle, it requires too much movement for sniping; practice it only to accustom yourself to finding the pocket.

I've developed a simple drill to help shooters handle recoil, depicted on page 191. The student assumes his firing position and bolts his

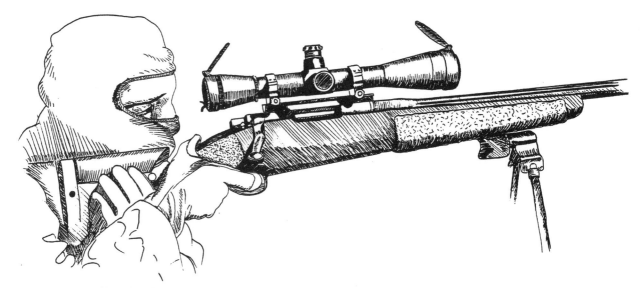

Nonshooting hand seats butt in shoulder and applies gentle pressure during firing.

Seating rifle in shoulder reduces felt recoil and enhances stability.

rifle on an empty chamber while his coach kneels and grabs the barrel firmly. As the shooter dry-fires, the coach roughly thrusts the rifle into his shoulder, simulating enough recoil that the shooter can self-diagnose any errors, but not so much to induce significant pain. In one school, I used this technique over and over with one lawman, with a bit of interspersed live fire, and solved his recoil problems in 30 minutes.

Another recoil-reduction technique I discussed with a national-level competitive rifle shooter is muscular development; that is,

This recoil drill corrects problems and builds shooter confidence.

frequently encountered problem is the arrangement of gear dictated by a military unit's SOP—which sometimes is drawn-up by rear-echelon "experts" who've forgotten that soldiers need their shoulders clear so they can fire their rifles.

Adding Recoil Butt Pads

The simplest weapon modification to reduce felt recoil is the addition of a thick rubber pad on the rifle butt. Many heavy caliber rifles come standard with such recoil pads.

Any competent gunsmith or armorer can install a recoil pad, but in the process some of the butt, too, must be removed or the butt will become too long.

Adding Weight

The old solution for reducing recoil in elephant guns was to drill a sizable hole in the butt and fill it with lead. This really works.

The problem with this solution, however, is that it also makes the rifle heavier to carry and clumsier to manipulate. Unlike the past century in Africa, a modern sniper has no gun bearer; he must consider carefully anything that may add weight to his basic load or reduce his weapon reflexes.

Mercury Recoil Reducers

These are the high-tech evolution from adding lead to the butt. They increase weight somewhat but also use momentum to reduce recoil.

One or more mercury-filled cylinders are installed in the butt, which add less weight than lead. These reducers help stretch out the duration of recoil because the sharp recoil will have already passed before the dense mercury even begins to move inside its cylinder. So, instead of, say, 50 pounds of recoil impacting in

improving muscle tone and depth of your shooting shoulder through bench presses, curls, and push-ups. Since muscle absorbs shock better than flab, and its firmer resiliency better resists pressure, it makes sense that exercise could be beneficial.

Beyond these, there are a host of recoil-reducing devices and techniques, discussed below. I must warn you, though, that using any of these in training commits you also to use them in action. You can hardly expect, say, to wear a recoil pad at the range but not in the field and yet have consistent accuracy. You *must* train as you will operate.

Keep Shooting Shoulder Clear

To shoot accurately and with minimal recoil pain, your shooting shoulder should be clear of anything that interferes with the solid positioning of the rifle butt against your shoulder. Not only should you not have gear cluttering up your webbing but your suspenders should be slid completely off so nothing comes between that natural pocket and the butt. I once fell victim to this myself when my pin-on major's leaf slid between a .300 Magnum's butt and my shoulder—my yelp could be heard halfway down the firing line. A far more

1/10 of a second, 35 pounds pushes backward for 3/10 of a second.

Recoil Shoulder Pads

Several varieties of rubber and sponge recoil pads are available either to be worn over other clothing or as a fixed feature of jackets and even T-shirts. The PAST company has a wide line of recoil pads and clothing.

We have also had students glue foam sponges inside their Ghillie suit shoulders and cover them with rubber or Naugahyde. This works, too.

But again, you *must* ensure that if you use a recoil pad in practice, you will use it during real operations. If you don't, you will find that your eye relief and spotweld will have changed, hardly the thing you want to discover when "taking the shot."

ZEROING A SNIPER RIFLE

I once borrowed a dozen M24 Sniper Weapon Systems from a military unit so we'd have enough on hand for our students. While these were cheerfully provided, I chuckled to hear that some unit snipers had grumbled, "There go our zeros."

It was humorous because these novice riflemen mistakenly saw their zeros as permanent, one-time, unchangeable adjustments. I don't think your zero is an airplane altimeter and needs tuning for each use, but it does require regular verification and adjustment, as cited in the the sidebar on page 195. Further, you should be so familiar with your scope and its adjustments that zeroing is an ordinary, easily accomplished task.

Cold Barrel vs. Warm Barrel

Recognizing that consistency equals accuracy and vice versa, a sniper constantly looks for ways to increase his shooting consistency and diagnoses any causes of inconsistency.

Variations in rifle barrel temperature lead to variations in where a bullet impacts because a hot or even warm barrel will warp at least slightly. How much it warps, how quickly it warps, how differently it warps according to different kinds of ammo—these add more variation and lead to still more inconsistency.

The easiest way to reestablish consistency is to zero according to where your round impacts when fired through a cool barrel, the so-called "cold-barrel zero." As a general rule, fire slow enough that your barrel never warms—perhaps one round per two minutes to a max of three rounds, then pause for five minutes before starting this cycle again. Use some common sense, pacing your fire according to ambient temperature, especially when it's very cold outside and each round potentially raises the barrel temperature. By pacing your shooting so there's no temperature increase, you'll impose a very high standard of consistency, which yields superb accuracy.

Counterterrorist and police snipers use this cold-barrel zero since theoretically they fire only one round per situation, and each shot must be of almost machine precision, possibly even placing a bullet in a hostile's brain stem at 100 yards despite the subject encircling himself with hostages. There's no room here for average groups or compensatory holds between cold- and warm-barrel zeros.

Today's military sniper, outfitted with a precision bolt-action rifle, adjusts his zero for a cold barrel, too. If you're engaging targets correctly, you won't "warm up" with several sloppy shots and then all of a sudden get serious and accurate. No, your very first shot is perfect—then, after a pause to observe results, displace, and prepare to fire yet again, you take another cold-barrel shot. A sniper shoots a series of cold-barrel shots.

Conventional infantrymen fire so many rounds in practice that they unknowingly zero assault rifles for a warm-barrel zero's group and see the cold-barrel shot as an errant "flyer" that should be disregarded. That's fine if you're firing hundreds of rounds per engagement, but the military sniper builds his whole being around that very first round's impact, which may seem to others to be a "stray" but to him is a one-shot kill.

The most difference I've ever noticed between my cold and warm shots is about .75 MOA, enough to be worth noticing but not enough even to cause a miss on a torso shot. Any difference in warm- and cold-barrel zeros must be recorded for your own particular rifle since it affects even identical rifles to different extents. In that rare event that you must fire quickly against a host of hostiles, you apply any variation you've noticed between warm- and cold-barrel zeros so you can always anticipate where your rounds will impact. A sniper knows his rifle.

Zeroing a BDC-Equipped Scope

In Chapter 4 we covered zeroing a scope fitted with target knobs. Zeroing a BDC-equipped scope isn't much

Save your 25-yard group target to test zero later.

different. Remove the sling and bipod to create a clean forearm; then rest your rifle snuggly upon sandbags, preferably in a prone position. Support the heel—that is, the bottom of the butt—with a sand-filled sock, which your nonshooting hand can squeeze or release to slightly raise or lower the butt.

Already your scope should have been boresighted using a collimator or—the old-fashioned way—by removing the bolt, looking down the bore to some distant point, and gently turning the windage and elevation until your crosshairs point to the same point. Either way, this boresight will save time because it should put your reticle close enough to cut paper with your first shots.

Ideally, so the wind does not become a factor, you will zero your rifle on a calm day, preferably before 10 A.M., before heat builds

and thermals start moving the air around.

If you have a variable-magnification scope, set it to the highest magnification for the best possible target clarity, and, if you have adjustable focus, fine-tune the focus. The first zero rounds you fire should be at only 25 yards so you're certain to cut paper and see where you're hitting. Even if you only fire one shot, by beginning at 25 yards you'll cut zero time and the number of rounds you must fire.

Making initial adjustments from that 25-yard firing, then continue zeroing by focusing first on windage at 100 yards. I know some BDCs ideally require zeroing at 200 yards, but that's more so for elevation. (It's worth lazing the distance before you start firing. I've found several old military known-distance ranges that were several yards long or short! An imprecise zero will yield cumulative error at long range!)

It's really important to get a hard windage zero with little or no crosswind influencing it, so I think you're better off to get a hard windage setting at the shorter distance. Interspersed with plenty of dry fire to remain calm and focused, fire a five-round group at 100 yards. Analyze the group, then apply the required correction on the windage knob. If there's any wind present, only fire during the calms between gusts so it has no influence. It's okay if you turn the elevation, too, but the final adjustment will come later, at 200 yards. Continue to fire five-round groups and make corrections until you're satisfied that the windage is absolutely dead-on—at least to the extent possible, since military Leupold and Unertl scopes only allow 1/2 MOA windage adjustments.

This diamond bull is the best style for zeroing a scoped rifle.

Incidentally, I think the ideal zeroing target is a diamond-shaped bull's-eye with thick horizontal and vertical lines over which your crosshairs can be placed precisely, which we've displayed. To help you zero, the background grid contains 1-inch squares, so you can make MOA corrections. But make sure it's stapled straight and those lines are absolutely horizontal and vertical to coincide with your reticle.

Now, if it's suitable for your BDC, fire at 200 yards to fine-tune your elevation, again interspersing plenty of dry-fire and fire a five-round group. Any corrections should only be elevation changes because you already zeroed the windage at 100 yards. Again, if any wind is present, fire in calms between gusts so wind does not become a factor.

Once you're satisfied with the elevation, it's time to "set" the zero on your knobs. This will

Final BDC zeroing step—loosen BDC knob, then realign for zero distance and retighten hex screws.

vary somewhat depending on your scope, but first loosen the hex screws on the windage until it turns freely without further engaging the internal adjustments. Now rotate it clockwise or counterclockwise to *perfectly align* the "0"— meaning *zero windage*—and carefully retighten the screws, keeping that "0" in perfect alignment. Next, do the same with the BDC elevation knob, but here be certain to align it so it's set on the distance at which you zeroed. For example, with a Leupold M3A, if you zeroed at 200, make sure the "2" is aligned to the horizontal witness line below the BDC, then carefully tighten the screws.

That's it—you're ready for action!

Checking Your Scope's Zero Consistency

When you've achieved and recorded an

MONTHLY CERTIFICATION FIRING

Many law enforcement agencies require that their snipers fire for certification monthly, usually during the tactical team's monthly training day. This certification demonstrates the officer's marksmanship and his weapon's accuracy, verifying that he and his weapon are ready to "take the shot."

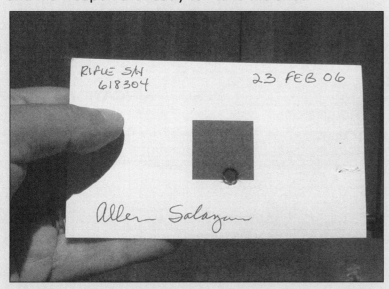

All that's need to document monthly certification firing—one cold-bore shot fired into a 3 x 5 card.

A simple but realistic way of accomplishing this was passed along to me by an FBI sniper friend and past student, who served on the Bureau's regional SWAT team.

All he and his FBI colleagues did was put a 1-inch black target paster on a 3 x 5 card and then use it for a 100-yard, cold-bore shot. Think of the simplicity: as we observed in Chapter 5, a 3 x 5 card approximates the size of a suspect's instant incapacitation areas, and certainly that's a sufficiently small target for a center-torso shot, too. This keeps the shooting standard realistic rather than launching arguments about acceptable group sizes, benchrest versus offhand groups, and so on.

Though the FBI sniper aims at the black paster, his cold-bore shot's impact anywhere on the 3 x 5 card is sufficient accuracy to hit these vital areas, which is their team's certification standard. The FBI sniper makes it a practice to fire this certification as his first shot when he arrives on the range.

Afterward, the sniper dates and signs the card, jots down his rifle's serial number, and puts it away until the next monthly practice session. Should he be required to take a real-world shot, that 3 x 5—which my friend used to call "the Grand Jury card"—is on file and attests that he and his rifle were ready.

acceptable zero, your work's not done. Now you must test your scope to see if it shifts when you change magnification or elevation or operate the Bullet Drop Compensator.

Since you zeroed a zoom scope at its highest magnification, now you'll check it at lower powers. Fire a 3.5-10x scope at 6x and 3.5x and carefully compare the point of impact to the initial 10x impact. If there's any variation, record it; if it's 1 MOA or more, replace the scope.

(I once used a collimator to test four different scope brands for drift from the grid's zero when they were zoomed. Several stayed right on dead center, but one wandered about 3 MOAs when I shifted from 9x to 6x, and it surprised the hell out of me. The excellent scopes were more costly.)

Next, test-fire the Bullet Drop Compensator at each 100-yard distance on its knob. Unless the BDC is expressly designed for shooting with your exact load, there will be at least a bit of variation between the indicated range and where you must set it to strike dead-on at that range. On some scopes, for example, I must click one or two increments up or down at most distances to be exactly on bull's-eye. This is the most time-consuming part of zeroing, but learning such exact fine-tuning brings tremendous confidence to your long-range shooting. Record these slight variations.

Should you have target knobs, test the comeup data we've provided for accuracy at appropriate ranges. Fire these at 100-yard increments, fine-tuning along the way so they're exactly on the mark. Record any variations, which will be slight, from the indicated values.

The final test I've dubbed "repeatability," which only means that your elevation or windage will go back exactly to where it was if you've changed it rather than back to the original setting. The simplest way to check it is to fire a three-round group at 100 yards, then click up a given number of clicks, fire another three-round group, then dial back down the same number of clicks and see if the next group places exactly where the first one did. Do not fire the test so quickly that you heat the barrel abnormally. Do the same thing for windage and see if there is any shift.

A shift of even 1 MOA would alarm me because what you're really testing is the consistency of the scope's internal gears, which means you could have a very significant problem at greater ranges. What's not commonly recognized is that scopes wear out due to their internal gears, not usually to scratches on the lenses or dings on the tube. A heavily used scope, especially having soft brass gears, eventually will wear enough that it no longer can be changed incrementally with consistency.

Should you experience repeatability problems, try the test again. If you have similar results, replace the scope.

Zero Verification

Your rifle's accuracy is only as dependable as your zero. If, unknown to you, something has

---

ZERO VERIFICATION

A sniper should verify his weapon's zero in the following situations. These are listed in order of importance, but ideally all require verifying:

- Any hint scope was knocked, knobs turned

- After separating action from stock

- After unpacking from shipping

- Cheekrest height or butt length changed

- Switching to a new lot of ammunition

- Temperature change of +/- 20 degrees

- Altitude change of 1,500 or more feet

- Before each planned operation

- During a critical incident

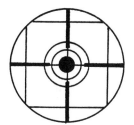 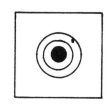  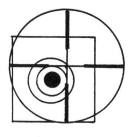

ONE-SHOT ZERO (L-R): Aim carefully and fire one shot; note its impact point; wedge rifle to hold steady at original aim point; crank crosshairs to the impact point.

caused your zero to move, disaster is certain. You'd may as well not even fire.

Under certain circumstances (listed in the box on page 196), you automatically should verify your zero by test-firing your weapon. But the bottom line is this: if you have the slightest doubt about your zero, verify it. Just the psychological impact of such doubt degrades shooting confidence.

The ideal is to verify your zero on a full-size range with no time constraints. But an old elk hunter's trick could save the day if no full-size range is available. Here's how it works: when you finish a full-fledged zero, take out another target and fire your rifle into it at only 25 yards. Obviously your rounds will strike high above the point of aim, but record this height *exactly*. In a pinch, you can now verify your zero by shooting only 25 yards and confirming that the point of impact is the same height above point of aim.

While preparing to be part of a unit defense—and before the enemy arrives—you can verify your zero quickly by having your spotter observe while you fire a round into any material that shows visible effect when struck. Standing water, a dirt mound, or a brick wall should do the job.

The One-Shot Emergency Zero

There's one last zero technique to consider, and it's accurate enough for an emergency but not for true precision shooting. It's *very* fast and could mean the difference between life and death.

Carefully aim at a target or any surface that leaves a visible mark where you hit it. You should aim at a precise point. Now fire one round.

Wedge your rifle into a rigid, solid position with sandbags or other supports so it won't move even a bit. Remove the turret caps so the elevation and windage dials are exposed. Then, realign the rifle, looking through the scope so you're pointing the crosshairs exactly at your *original* point of aim. Make sure the rifle won't move.

Very, very carefully, so as not to move the rifle even a bit, turn the windage and elevation dials so the crosshairs shift to the point where your bullet impacted. You've made the point of aim the point of impact. This is a zero, and you're now ready for action.

SNIPING TARGETS

Sniper training requires an assortment of targets and an understanding of how best to employ them for challenging training. Marksmanship practice falls into two wide areas: practice fire for skill maintenance and shooting drills, in which stress and realism are injected to teach tactical skills and judgment on top of marksmanship.

For practice fire, conventional paper bull's-eye targets are just fine, but a much wider target array should be used for shooting drills.

No matter the overall shape or dimension of a target used in drills, your intended point of impact must be small enough to be challenging. This means that even if you're shooting at a full-size silhouette, your designated point of impact is

THE VALUE OF DRY-FIRING

The easiest, most convenient means to maintain your skill is dry-firing. Since no recoil or muzzle blast is present to mask your reaction, dry-firing enables you to diagnose and overcome tiny problems with jerking, breathing, etc. Just be sure to use a Snapcap so you don't unduly stress your firing pin.

Assume a stable, supported shooting position, place your reticle on a tiny target, and squeeze the trigger so smoothly that the reticle doesn't move when the shot breaks. Ensure you also practice follow-through; then rebolt the weapon and reacquire the target. This routine is the habit you must develop—only then have you completed a shot.

It's a challenge to dry-fire a rifle without dropping a coin balanced on its barrel.

My secret for accurately firing someone else's rifle is to dry-fire before taking my complimentary shot. For this kind of familiarization, close your eyes and concentrate solely on your finger and its interplay with the trigger. Relax and don't be analytical—just let your finger adapt so it's comfortable with the trigger.

When it comes to your own rifle, you want much more than mere familiarization. Close your eyes and see how long you can take to break a shot, purposely taking as long as possible. Smoothly, consistently, delicately taking up the slack and breaking the shot could easily take 20 seconds or more. Again, focus mentally on your finger and let your mind float free.

Here's a great trigger exercise I learned at Ft. Campbell, Kentucky, many years ago. Get into a solid supported position, then have your spotter balance a coin on your barrel just behind the muzzle. If your dry-fire release is smooth and solid, the coin won't fall—and if you're really solid, it won't wobble at all. Dime-size coins are tougher than quarters.

Another dry-fire technique is to watch your reticle movement as you prepare to fire. Breathing will cause it to rise and fall vertically across and above your target; if there's any lateral or horizontal movement, readjust your body position and reposition the rifle on its support. At the instant you fire, of course, you'll be in your natural respiratory pause, so ideally there should be no movement.

Your spotter can help a lot by closely observing your dry-fire, especially your trigger finger. Any trembling, jerking, or twitching will be obvious to him, and he can see if your finger smoothly pulls, then pauses during follow-through. Ideally, your finger should pull through the shot-break, then pause slightly at the trigger stop. If your finger quivers or lifts away too quickly, it means you've allow the sound of the shot or feel of the recoil to break your concentration. You're not thinking about *this shot* but already thinking about the next shot, or you're bolting your weapon, etc.

The eye is the window to the mind—and by watching a sniper's dominant eye, a spotter can see how effectively he's concentrating. From 20 feet away I can tell if a rifleman's jerking merely by noticing whether his dominant eye blinks when his shot breaks. A more accomplished marksman probably won't blink, but your spotter will notice, lying beside you, whether your pupil dilates or contracts at any point during dry-fire. If your mind is truly locked on the target—if you are in your "bubble," as Carlos Hathcock used to put it—your eye stays focused on the target.

Another dry-firing technique works great at the range to help a shooter overcome jerking problems induced by recoil and muzzle blast. Here the shooter dry-fires about 10 times; then while he looks away, the spotter slips a live or dummy round into the chamber and has him "fire" again. The shooter has no idea whether he's about to face real recoil or just another dry-fire. What works best, I've found, is to repeatedly feed him the dummy round—10 times or so—to overcome any anxiety, then slip in a real round, followed by many repetitions with the dummy round. All the while, of course, the spotter/coach is closely observing to detect and diagnose any continuing problems. Using this technique, I've had students completely overcome jerking problems in as little as 15 minutes.

but a tiny spot highlighted in contrasting color. To start with, 3 Minutes of Angle (or 3 inches at 100 yards, 6 inches at 200 yards, etc.) is acceptable. Then, when your skills improve, the point of impact should be reduced to 2 MOAs.

The more realistic you can make your shooting drill targets, the better. Dressing a silhouette in complete uniform or civilian clothes is highly effective, as is pasting on a Xerox copy of a face. If nothing else, you can add white pressure-sensitive labels trimmed to resemble eyes; there's nothing like a target that looks back at you.

Paper Targets

COMMON BULL'S-EYE: The humblest of targets snipers use, it's employed for about half of all live-fire practice. A sniper warms up on the bull's-eye target, then goes on to other types for shooting drills.

DIAMOND BULL'S-EYE: This is best for zeroing a rifle because it allows precise alignment of crosshairs at the diamond tips. It can also be used for practice fire.

DARK SILHOUETTE: Lacking any features, this could be a military Type D or an IPSC Official Practice Target. Dress it up and add a reactive feature at the intended point of impact (e.g., tape a clay pigeon or 3 MOA balloon on its chest). Glue a Xerox face on its head.

DETAILED SILHOUETTE: This could be a Duelatron or Realistic target, which contains complete human features. These are ready to use except for a designated point of impact, which you just draw on or add a small reactive subtarget.

DAZZLE: To challenge sniper competitors at international matches, I devised a special kind of target I called the "dazzle." The concept was drawn from the weird camouflage schemes painted on World War I ships, with lots of bizarre lines and shapes, intended to confuse a U-boat commander's range estimate through a periscope. We're showing one that has a jumble of triangles in a sea of black dots, but as the sniper is

Realistic targets must challenge snipers. These full-size faces demand correct facial ID before engagement.

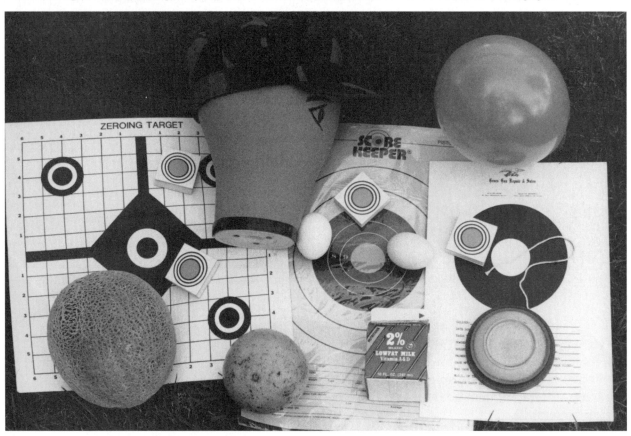

Variety keeps shooting interesting, especially with reactive targets.

instructed, *only one* triangle is his target. Furthermore, he may not fire until commanded, which may occur any time in the next 30 minutes, but he must engage within 5 seconds of the command. It's intended to visually and mentally challenge in addition to being a marksmanship challenge. You can make your own just by mounting a strange array of 1-inch black pasters on a target or any number of things.

Reactive Targets

I'm a great fan of reactive targets because they make shooting fun and draw on a shooter's concentration in ways a paper target cannot. Constantly look for ways to integrate these into your shooting drills.

BALLOONS: Inexpensive and very flexible, balloons can be inflated to predetermined diameters, then sorted by color to represent hostages and captors, etc. Helium-filled balloons tethered to bushes and stakes can transform any open meadow into a shooting gallery.

CLAY PIGEONS: Since they're 4 inches in diameter, clay pigeons should not be employed closer than 200 yards. The best way I've devised for attaching them to other targets is by gluing a string to the back with silicone cement, then stapling the string to the target face.

STYROFOAM HEADS: A police sniper friend introduced me to these, although mannequin heads were used by British snipers during World War II. Styrofoam heads, however, are relatively cheap at less than a dollar apiece and can be hit several times. Paint them a flesh pink or black tone, accent eyes and hair, etc., for the most realism.

EGGS AND GOLF BALLS: These are fun targets we've used at the end of sniper courses for old-fashioned shooting contests, but note that they're approximately the same size as a human brain stem. It's realistic to shoot them at 100 yards, although we've also shot 'em up at 200.

FALLING METAL PLATES: These can be made to order in any small shop. The beauty of metallic silhouettes is that, like helium balloons, they can make any meadow a shooting gallery.

EXPLODING TARGETS: Measuring 2 x 2 inches, these cost about $1 apiece. They're fun to shoot and a real challenge at 100 or more yards. Their pressure-sensitive adhesive backing allows fast attachment, say, to a silhouette's forehead. When these go "bang," you know it.

MILK CARTONS: Half-pint milk cartons make good targets for 200 or more yards, and, unlike glass containers, these are environmentally safe. A great sniping range can be prepared in minutes by half-concealing 10 milk cartons per shooter on a hillside 200+ yards away and letting spotters and snipers have at 'em.

MELONS: We've used these primarily for terminal ballistic demonstrations and simulated blood splatter, although they can be used more

A Ft. Benning sniper school instructor poses with a steel "Iron Maiden" that audibly rings when struck by a bullet.

Self-sealing targets from Newbold (R) and Just Shoot Me withstand thousands of hits. In back, one of the author's "dazzle" targets.

generally as reactive targets. For best results, let the melon sit in full sunlight for a couple of days to let the pulp get especially mushy.

SELF-SEALING PLASTIC: Newbold makes these circular, bright orange plastic targets, in diameters from 1 to 12 inches. They can screw onto target frames or tree limbs in a flash and take lots of punishment. I've shot the pictured targets with both .308 and .223 and there's hardly a smudge on them. I'd guess each target is good for thousands of bullet impacts. However, you really need a spotter observing the target because often the bullet passes through with hardly any sign of its impact. Just Shoot Me makes similar self-sealing plastic targets, including a 4-inch orange cube for USMC sniper training (M-STC-4), which the company says can take 30,000 hits.

CHAPTER 7

ADVANCED SNIPER MARKSMANSHIP

CONSISTENCY EQUALS ACCURACY

A precision shooter realizes that accuracy only results from consistency and vice versa. If you can consistently place shots in one spot, all that is left is to adjust your crosshairs to that spot. There's a degree of consistency in everything you do and every piece of gear or component for your weapon.

It is the *totality* of consistency that results in accuracy. By continuously looking for ways to increase consistency, you automatically will develop better accuracy. Accuracy equals consistency, and consistency equals accuracy.

Equipment Consistency

You strive to use the same components in the exact same way, shot after shot. This means that ideally you should not swap rifles with your teammate, but each of you should have your own exclusively. In the case of law officers, who tend to shoot more so in hostage-rescue scenarios, this exclusiveness is especially important, both for shooter confidence and liability. Military snipers may have to share a single sniper rifle, but they heighten consistency by using a single zero and firing the rifle individually as much as if the rifle was assigned only to one man.

Consistency is also achieved through ammunition by firing only match-grade rounds, ensuring that operational ammo and practice ammo are from the same lot. When you change lots, you rezero your rifle for the new batch of ammunition.

If you have a zoom rifle scope, you should prefer to fire both practice and real-world at the same magnification—usually the scope's highest. And you zero your scope set at its maximum power, too.

I don't know any military or police snipers who use earmuffs on real operations, and therefore I don't think you should use this type of hearing protection during practice. The larger muff types can cause you to develop a peculiar spotweld and possibly cant during range fire, which you could overcome with modified technique. But since you wouldn't have muffs in the field, your point of aim/point of impact could shift slightly. It's more realistic to use ear protectors that fit entirely in your ear, of which there are several effective brands, so that even if you forget them or choose not to use them in the field, there will be no disruption of consistency.

This consistency extends to the use of a beanbag to support the rifle's heel for exact aiming. If you use one in practice, you should use one on real operations, too.

Practice firing both with sandbags and bipod so you'll know the slight differences in results. I can shoot a group about 1/4 MOA tighter with a sandbag rest.

Shooter Consistency

The habits you develop in practice—which I call a shooter's "style"—must be the same on a

Use a beanbag (a sock filled with sand) to raise or lower the rifle butt with your nonshooting hand for steady, micrometer-like adjustments.

range when punching paper as it is when you're on a rooftop plugging bad guys.

Let's start with your scope picture. You should see your full field of view, with no distortion on the edges. The relationship between proper field of view and eye relief, parallax, and maximum exit pupil is cited in detail elsewhere. Repetition of a good scope picture in practice and in action can only lead to consistent results.

Leaving the nonshooting eye open during firing has pros and cons, as does closing it. But whichever of these you choose, do it consistently day and night, with available light or artificial illumination, during offensive or defensive firing exercises.

A spotweld, by definition, is the consistent placing of your cheek on the rifle butt, which is a major contribution to correct eye relief, field of view, and so on, as cited earlier.

All the factors that contribute to the integrated act of shooting—trigger control, aiming, breathing, body position, and follow-through—must be done not just correctly but *consistently* as well. If you cock back one leg to reduce pressure on your chest for easier breathing, then you must do this for every prone shot.

Combining equipment consistency, then, with a consistent shooting style inevitably results in great accuracy and a sensitizing to even tiny variances. When you have become so confident of your shooting that, for instance, you consciously plan on slight compensation for a 15-degree uphill angle, or a mere 3 mph oblique wind, you will have become a truly crack shot.

MAKING EACH SHOT COUNT

Many years ago, while training Southeast Asian mercenaries, I'd challenge a student to assume his sexiest "assault" stance and riddle a nearby silhouette with full-auto fire. Gleefully, he'd tuck his M16 or AK-47 beneath his armpit and, "brt-t-t-t-t-t," 30 rounds would rip through the air—but go only God knows where. The amazed students, upon examining the intact silhouette, could see that, despite sound and smoke, a lot of bullets carelessly sprayed will hit nothing. My point exactly.

In order to become a superb sniper, a rifleman must zoom in his consciousness from having had none while blasting at full-auto to having a bit of focused attention at semiauto to being able to concentrate keenly on each round fired as a sniper. Each round.

A sniper does not fire patterns or groups or average shots. He fires *one shot* over and over and over, and develops certain one-shot habits during practice fire that will carry over to real-world shooting.

The sniper conditions himself to regard each round fired in practice as a single, final event with an exact beginning, a definite end, and a precisely measured result.

During range fire, he removes each round individually from its box, loads it individually, fires it as a single event, calls it to his spotter, observes the results of that one shot with a spotting scope, then records its exact point of impact in his record book.

He analyzes the results of each shot so even the slightest inaccuracy is correctly attributed to a bit of wind, breathing, trigger control, and so

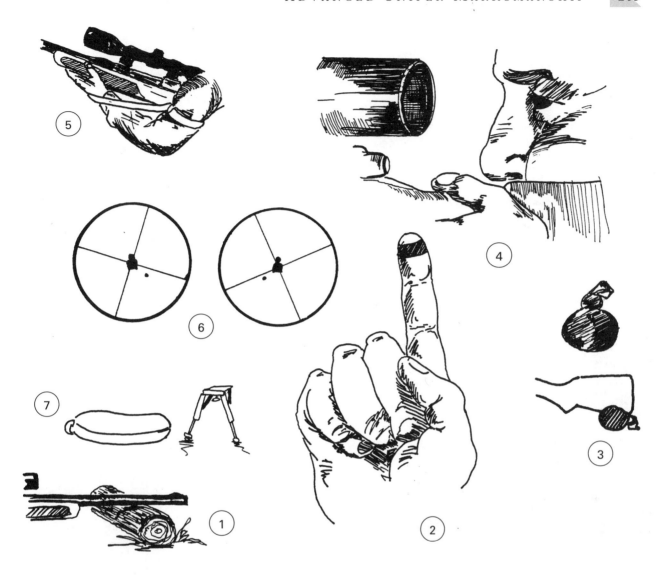

MARKSMANSHIP TIPS. (1) Never let your barrel touch anything; (2) use only the most sensitive portion of your trigger finger; (3) place a beanbag below butt for precise hold; (4) maintain correct eye relief for a consistent sight picture and to eliminate parallax; (5) time allowing, improve stability with the sling; (6) stay conscious to the danger of canting; and, if available, (7) choose the support of a sandbag over that of a bipod.

on. Ego has no impact; the sniper and spotter honestly and objectively diagnose the shot. Then the shooter plans his next shot and applies what he has just learned to improve the results.

It also may be useful to dry-fire between each live-fire shot, a habit that has helped me a lot.

No more than five rounds should be fired into a single impact point to better focus the shooter's concentration. This also prevents confusion about which hole resulted from which shot.

Finally, during any practice session don't let yourself slide into mindless "banging away," even if you have plenty of ammo available. Indeed, most law enforcement snipers I know fire no more than 20 rounds per monthly training session—but each shot is a quality shot.

THE RIFLE STABILIZER

Choate Machine & Tool manufactures a portable shooting support I designed that incorporates a length-adjustable arm that attaches to a rifleman's hip. After extensive testing by a variety of shooters, we've found that it consistently cuts groups in half, whether fired offhand, sitting, or kneeling.

The Rifle Stabilizer—as I've dubbed it—essentially is a tripod leg with a wide cradle that's hinged at your hip so when not in use it lies flat against your left side, out of the way. The Stabilizer offers a steadying effect similar to shooting sticks—almost as much as a bipod—but it adds no weight or bulk to the rifle and keeps the shooter's supporting hand clear to manipulate his weapon when not in use. It's quick to employ and works best for the very position that most needs support, offhand shooting. It's the only portable shooting support I know of that's fast enough for snap-shooting.

When not in use, the Stabilizer arm rotates out of the way to the shooter's side.

The Stabilizer works by shifting the rifle's center of balance to the supporting hip for improved skeletal support while also reducing muscular tension and the destabilizing effects of breathing and heartbeat. Further, because much of the weight has been shifted, it reduces muscle fatigue, allowing a rifleman to steady his weapon two or three times longer. The heavier the rifle, the better it works because these are the rifles most difficult for shooters to steady for an extended period.

The Stabilizer fits on a belt, including military webbing and Molle systems, and weighs 7 1/2 ounces. Though its design appears no more complex than a safety pin, it took me 12 years to develop it.

The Rifle Stabilizer improves accuracy by shifting support to the shooter's waist and skeleton.

SUPPORTING YOUR SHOOTING

No matter whether sitting, standing, lying prone, or kneeling—and no matter what kind of target he has—a wise sniper *always* seeks a location having support or adds support to a location that lacks it.

The difference in shooting performance with or without support is so profound that every experienced shooter has learned this. The only time a sniper fires unsupported is when he suddenly encounters a close-range enemy and must fire instantly in self-defense.

The steadiest support results from placing a hard surface against a soft one. Remember this: soft to hard or hard to soft. What does this

SUPPORT COMES IN MANY FORMS. A bipod, rucksack, sling, bag of dog food, or sandbag steadies shooting. When using a treestep or log (bottom left and right), be sure to emplace an intervening soft layer.

mean? To start with, understand that your rifle forearm—fiberglass or wood—is hard. If you attempt to support it against a log or wall, it won't be very steady because something hard wobbles or slides against another hard surface. You must put something soft between your hard forearm and that hard log—say, your field jacket—to become stable. Get what I mean now?

You need something soft that will conform, that "gives" a bit against that hard forearm, for the steadiest, stablest support. Your flesh is relatively soft and gives enough to be worth placing your hand between the rifle and a hard supporting surface. A sandbag is soft support, too, but also adds weight and density for better steadiness.

But hard to soft also enhances accuracy by damping the violence of recoil. If you've ever made the mistake of balancing your rifle on a fence post or a bare log and fired, you know what I mean; the recoil bounced your rifle wildly about, an effect that can begin even before your bullet exits the muzzle. This is begging for inaccuracy.

Most supported firing situations can be enhanced even further by employing a properly adjusted sling, but this isn't always suitable or possible. Due to the time required to adjust it and the occasional difficulties of fitting in a shooting location while using a sling, I think of a sling as the "support of last resort." The major exception is shooting while standing, which dramatically improves with a sling.

What about bipods? No question, a bipod is an excellent means of support when you have a flat, relatively stable surface beneath it. But you must stay alert to the danger of canting when using a bipod. And even when the bipod is folded forward, be careful to use the forearm and *not* the bipod bottom as the surface in contact with your support.

This Marine's sniper rifle fits snugly in his spotter's shoulder for a sitting-supported position.

The steadiest support you can use, though, is a sandbag. Most likely you're shooting prone if you're employing a sandbag, but any way you can work one into another position will improve your shooting. It's worth carrying an empty sandbag in your rucksack, at least a half-size one made from a cutoff BDU pants leg. Fill it on-site with any available dirt, gravel, or sand.

Your rucksack, too, is a handy support which I've had students use extensively in sniper training courses. Usually, a rucksack that's not quite full works better than a stuffed one since it can conform more easily.

Note how the spotter braces his body to support the rifle.

All kinds of furniture can be reconfigured to use as shooting support. Tables obviously fit the bill, but chairs are easier to move around. We've illustrated the two-chair technique on page 210 so you'll see that the supporting chair back has a winter coat thrown over it—remember, hard to soft—and canned goods or heavy books are stacked on it as a counterweight.

When firing in an inhabited area—as police snipers must do—field-expedient substitutes for sandbags usually are all around you. A dog food bag works well, as would large sacks of flour or rice or even charcoal briquettes. Best results come from fine-grained, heavy materials. You can even make a support bag by half-filling an ordinary plastic trashbag with whatever material is at hand.

One novel shooting support found in almost any American home is an ironing board. It works so well that—despite being the source of unending jokes—some tactical units keep an ironing board in the team's call-out van.

The archery hunter's tree-step, cited earlier as an anchor for rooftop shooting, makes a great support when attached at sitting or kneeling levels on a tree. To create a soft layer, slip your hat or glove over the tree-step before laying the rifle forearm on it.

When U.S. Cavalry engaged Plains Indians, they sometimes accomplished especially long-range shots by employing a novel support—another cavalryman sitting very still. This "body-support" technique is taught today at U.S. Army and Marine Corps sniper schools and includes standing and prone support, in addition to sitting support. As shown in the accom-

TWO-CHAIR TECHNIQUE. Note the soft padding and counterbalance.

panying photographs, the rifle is placed in the natural padding of a muscled area of the neck, the shoulder, or thighs, which offer the greatest degree of steadiness. Then the supporting person braces himself to remain both motionless and in solid support. This works fine and safe if the support man is wearing hearing protection and keeps his eyes closed when his teammate fires. (A special note from my attorney: do this at your own risk.)

The proper way to support your rifle by hand-cushioning it against a tree or corner is shown at right. Note that it's actually the hand that's supporting the rifle, and the forearm is separated from the hard surface by the soft hand.

An unusual supported position that I developed myself enables you to use the flat surface of a wall for excellent stability. As demonstrated by our DEA sniper on page 211, stand with your back to the wall and both your heels about 12 inches away from it. Now, lean back, off balance, with your shoulders solidly into the flat surface. You should have anywhere from 40 to 55 percent of your weight in your shoulders and the rest in your feet. I've found this position quick to assume and a remarkable improvement over the standing position. It works against trees, too.

Expedient support can be added to many

Corner support has rifle touching hand, not corner.

places simply by stringing a rope, a line, or even a tow strap that's taut enough to support your rifle. Even if there's no place to tie a line, you can pound nails into two walls and string the support line between.

One technique used by African plains

Wall support has both shooter's shoulders on the wall, with a percentage of his weight distributed between his shoulders and feet.

African tripod allows long-range precision in grassland.

hunters is a chest-high, field-expedient tripod. Cut from available saplings, this support is lashed together with parachute cord and allows long-range shots across flat, open country, such as that found in grasslands and desert. The only shortcoming is that this tripod is clumsy and inconvenient to carry—and you're standing up in open country while firing, in front of God and everybody. But this technique can give you a decisive edge over an opponent you're tracking through deep grass or shrubs that preclude his shooting from a prone position; you'll be able to hit him at a great distance, but he shouldn't be able to hit you.

Serving the same purpose but with fewer shortcomings is the monopod, which can double as a walking stick. Note in our illustration at right that the shooter places his hand *atop* the monopod so he can accomplish a correct soft-to-hard contact.

A monopod is easy to carry.

SHOOTING WITH A TRIPOD

While visiting the Marine sniper school at Quantico, Virginia, and the Army's school at Ft. Benning, I watched instructors teaching students how to employ tripods to support precision rifle fire. Every single student had a shooting tripod.

The great value of a tripod is the flexibility it gives in selecting a Final Firing Position (FFP). Unlike shooting at a firing range, a lot of real-world terrain and ground foliage make it almost impossible to see great distances from a prone position. But equally often, you won't find suitable support for sitting, kneeling, or offhand firing.

A shooting tripod is notably more stable than a large bipod or shooting stick because it puts three points of contact on the ground, and, as a rule, the more contact you have with the ground, the steadier the resulting support. It also leaves your nonfiring hand free to steady the rifle rather than merely hold a shooting stick.

Modifying a tripod for shooting is not difficult. Select an ordinary photographic tripod of suitable minimum and maximum height—for me that's 57 inches at the high end (since that's my forearm height when I'm standing) and a minimum of 23 inches to support sitting fire. Spray paint it in camouflage colors and fabricate a cradle of bent metal or woven wire that attaches at the "shoe" base normally used to attach a camera. Pad the cradle with foam and tape. Finally, attach a rifle sling for carrying it over your shoulder.

An important accessory is a small sandbag that fits in the cradle and adds stabilizing weight. I make my own field bags from old military fatigue pants legs, cut off and sewn at one end, with a twist-tie for the other. Conveniently, they're already camouflaged.

Here are some tips to get the most from a shooting tripod:

• Extend the wider legs first, because the thinner legs are less stable.

For every position above prone, a tripod improves stability.

This tripod may appear unbalanced on uneven ground, but it gives great stability and support.

Note the intervening sandbag on this Army sniper's tripod.

- Extend the tripod legs as little as possible to minimize wobble.
- To improve stability, hang a sandbag inside the tripod, beneath its head.

Don't *balance* your rifle on the tripod because that creates a kind of see-saw effect. For most shooters, there's better stability to pull the rifle closer to you, leaving just the forearm in contact—especially if you have a small sandbag in the cradle. If the legs are not of uniform length or not adjusted exactly for uneven ground, don't worry too much—with practice you can learn to lean your body forward or back a bit for a kind of equilibrium akin to isometric tension.

It's tough to quantify, but from using one myself I'd estimate that a tripod doubles your realistic effective range compared to firing in these positions without support.

SNAP-SHOOTING

A snap-shot is fired as quickly as you can throw your rifle to your shoulder, usually in self-defense against a relatively close target— perhaps 50 yards or less. That reduced distance demands a faster reaction time because a slow shot could well be no shot.

Your scope puts you at a close-range disadvantage against a hostile having open sights because your field of view, especially with 10x fixed magnification, can make target acquisition difficult—thus the need for practice.

If you have a variable scope, set it at its lowest power, both to expand the field of view and to increase the focal depth of your eye relief—which means you don't have to hold your eye exactly at the correct eye relief to see a full scope sight picture. To see what I mean, throw your rifle to your shoulder at 10x, then at 3.5x, and notice how much easier it is to acquire a target at the lower magnification.

As taught at Quantico and Ft. Benning, keep both eyes open and carry the rifle muzzle-low, butt-high. As you shift your eyes, track with your muzzle so that when a target suddenly appears the muzzle already is aligned with the line from your eye to the threat. When shouldering your rifle, *don't* swing the muzzle— *push it* toward the target, leaning your shoulder into it and even slightly pushing the butt forward. This stabilizes a barrel-heavy sniper rifle for the one-second window to take your shot. Forget about carefully aiming—it's faster and more instinctive to let the *outline* of the target guide you to its center and then break your shot.

Snap-shooting requires practice, but a lot of it can be developed through dry-firing.

SIMULTANEOUS ENGAGEMENTS

In certain situations, it's useful for several snipers to simultaneously engage the same target or multiple targets. Police snipers may

Snap-shooting is fast, not fancy. Just quarter your target, then fire center-mass, like this Gunsite student.

need to neutralize several suspects simultaneously during a hostage rescue, to double the odds of neutralizing a subject behind glass or to support a sniper-initiated assault. Realizing that enemy personnel will disappear or jump to cover with the first sniper's shot, several military snipers may want to engage simultaneously against multiple targets. Or, as I've documented as far back as the American Revolution, several sharpshooters can fire at once to double or triple the odds of hitting a distant or moving target. This technique was used extensively by sharpshooters in the American Civil War. Our illustration of World War I Army snipers is based on a real incident in which three sharpshooters took out a German who was theoretically well beyond a Springfield rifle's effective range.

No matter its purpose, a simultaneous engagement is a kind of command fire—that is, at least two snipers fire at once, on command, against a single or multiple targets.

First, all the snipers must confirm that they're on-target and ready to fire by a verbal notice. Then, to synchronize firing, a countdown is employed, which varies somewhat. I recommend a numerical countdown because that adds pace to the command, but that's my own preference. I believe in reverse order, "Three, two, one," with the snipers firing exactly when they hear the "N" in "one." Ideally, in dry-firing you only hear one "click" from their firing pins or, live-fire, only one "bang."

Albuquerque Police Department sniper trainer Neal Terry—with whom I've instructed several courses—advocates the word com-

A simultaneous engagement by multiple snipers can dramatically increase the likelihood of a long-range hit.

mands, "Standby . . . ready . . . fire," using three distinct words that are unlikely to be mistaken during the stress and confusion of a real-world engagement.

Ideally, the command countdown is given by a spotter or sniper employment officer. Things get a little tougher when the countdown must be given by a sniper who's also firing. I call this position the "base sniper" because the rest synch their shots to him. His challenge, then, is to control his breathing so well that he can talk even as he's squeezing his trigger. What works best, I've found, is to speak in a dull monotone so there's no variance in exhaling. This process works really well if the snipers are outfitted with voice-activated radios.

No matter how the countdown is given, the shooters must hone their ability to "jerk-fire"— that is, instead of squeezing steadily and not even realizing the shot's about to break, they feel it coming and time it to break exactly in unison. This takes some practice, with dry-fire of great assistance.

It's especially important for police snipers to have a clearly understood codeword to halt the countdown if some emergency or change arises. You can select your own word, but make sure it does not sound even remotely like "one" or "fire."

Before making a real-world simultaneous engagement, I strongly suggest several dry-fire rehearsals just to get things honed and everyone ready.

AMBIDEXTROUS SHOOTING

Both police and military snipers must practice firing from both shoulders. Soldiers learn ambidextrous shooting so they can take advantage of every target opportunity that presents itself as well as grab the best cover that's available.

A law enforcement sniper attempting a hostage-rescue shot prefers to relocate his hide rather than fire from his "weak" shoulder—especially considering liability and legal overtones. When firing in self-defense, however, even a lawman needs to be able to exploit available protection from hostile fire, and that's why he learns ambidextrous shooting.

Still, peculiarities of hide location and target location could make a weak shoulder shot the one shot a police sniper has—but this would be very unusual.

As the illustration below shows so well, attempting to fire from cover that better fits your opposite shoulder pushes you dangerously away from protection. Not only does it expose you to fire but it makes you far more prone to being spotted. The middle of our three shooters puts

DANGER! The center figure shows what happens when a right-handed shooter fires from a left-hand corner.

himself in this predicament by firing right-shouldered from left-shoulder cover. The men on either side of him show how to match firing shoulder to available cover and demonstrate the advantages of proper matching.

The greatest difficulty in weak-shoulder firing is properly seating the rifle in your shoulder and keeping it snugly there to prevent excessive felt recoil.

Maintaining correct eye relief can be difficult, too, and requires some getting used to. Both eye relief and proper seating can be greatly improved through lots of dry-fire practice—but this must lead to live fire, too, or you'll have problems if you ever attempt to fire ambidextrously in a real-world situation.

I've found it easiest to fire from my weak shoulder in a prone, supported position, so this is probably the best position to practice until gaining confidence. The hardest position is standing, unsupported, which is what you should work your way toward. In a separate section I've recommended firing 5 percent of your rounds from your weak shoulder.

EXACT AIMING TECHNIQUES

My father once told me a yarn about a duck-hunting friend who fired box after box of shells but never dropped a bird because he aimed at entire flocks instead of individual ducks. His point was that no matter how hard you try, your shooting can never be more exact than your aiming.

Aiming is merely another kind of concentration, another way in which a sniper's superior attention to detail yields better results than those of an average rifleman.

That average rifleman is taught only to aim at his opponent's center-chest—a vague, wide area—but given the width of his front sight blade, it's still a realistic matching of target width to width of aiming device. Because of such wide latitudes, the ordinary rifleman's accuracy limitations are apparent.

But when we have a sniper equipped with a far more precise optical aiming instrument, amazingly he's sometimes merely taught to aim center-chest, just like an ordinary rifleman. I assure you, if you practice sniper marksmanship against full-size silhouette targets and simply aim center-chest or center-mass, you will never realize even half your marksmanship potential. Sloppy 3-inch groups fired at 200 yards will become complete misses at 700 yards.

To focus your eye and your mind, you must hone in on your target and pick the exact spot you wish to hit. As shown in the illustration on page 218, a sniper doesn't aim at the side of a head, he aims at the tip of an ear. When it comes to a more nebulous target, shown here as a balloon but it could be an enemy partially obscured by brush, mentally divide the target into equal portions with the crosshairs, or "quarter" it. And even when you're taking a center-chest shot, you aim at some precise point such as his top button.

A rule-of-thumb approach recommended by an old Special Forces sniping friend is to pick an impact point on the target the same size as your bullet, an excellent mental and visual focus technique. Just don't get so fancy about a tiny spot that you delay your shot. Shoot exactly but quickly.

Another aspect of exact aiming is understanding the relationship between your eye, the reticle, and the target. In theory, a properly focused reticle allows you to have both the target and the crosshair clearly visible at the instant of firing—but it doesn't always happen just this way. If you cannot focus simultaneously on both target and crosshair, consciously choose to focus on the crosshair when your rifle fires.

The final issue of exact aiming is whether to close the nonshooting eye or leave both eyes open. The benefit of closing one eye is to eliminate visual distractions while shooting; the benefit of leaving both eyes open is to reduce eyestrain and enhance comfort. Either way works fine, but using *both* ways works terribly. Remember that consistency in everything you do has an impact on accuracy; therefore, decide on one eye open or both eyes open, then shoot that way consistently.

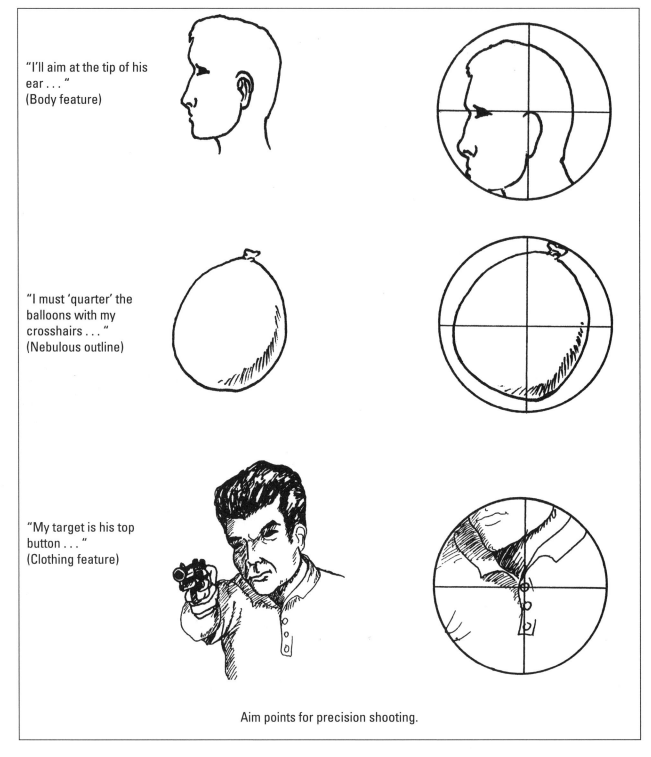

"I'll aim at the tip of his ear . . . "
(Body feature)

"I must 'quarter' the balloons with my crosshairs . . . "
(Nebulous outline)

"My target is his top button . . . "
(Clothing feature)

Aim points for precision shooting.

Talking about eyes, some German police snipers taught me a simple way to improve target clarity. As demonstrated in the accompanying photo, lay a dark cloth over your head and the scope to block bright light. This dilates your pupils so you can see more detail in distant targets.

Improve target clarity by covering head and scope with a dark cloth.

THE SNIPER MARKSMANSHIP RECORD BOOK

A sniper maintains detailed records on his rifle's and ammo's performance to discover even tiny variances from "book" values. This data is logged in your marksmanship record book, where it's updated and continually reassessed. How many rounds have gone through your barrel? Check the record book. Notice a decline in accuracy since last month? That's when you switched to another ammo lot—you'd better dump this ammo and start again. How well can you engage moving targets traveling left to right? Check the record book. Yes, it's also a history of *your* shooting performance so you can trace growth, decline, and plateaus and find fundamental problems that need special training focus.

The record book, over time, becomes the best analytical tool you have, but it's only useful if you keep exacting, complete information. This detail helps you discover how your rifle performs a bit differently from any other, how it has its own distinct "personality," and how you can get the most out of it. It's how you determine the need to make changes on your sniper rifle data card.

Police snipers should assume that their record books eventually will be subpoenaed by a grand jury, so keep this in mind when recording information. Both police and military snipers will find this data handy when discussing their weapon with an armorer.

Our Gift to You

Although various record book formats have been around for 50 years, we developed these three versions especially for sniping. We allow purchasers of this book the privilege of repro-

PREFIRING CHECKLIST

Most of the following prefire actions are so obvious that any shooter automatically remembers to do them, right? Wrong. At one time or other, I've forgotten every single one of them.

Copy this checklist, keep it in your record book, and use it during each range firing session.

- AMMUNITION OF SAME LOT NUMBER?
- AMMUNITION CLEAN AND SERVICEABLE?
- BORE CLEAR?
- ANYTHING TOUCHING THE BARREL?
- SCOPE SCREWS TIGHT?
- SCOPE LENSES CLEAR/CLEAN?
- ANY BRUSH OR CAMO MATERIAL OBSTRUCTING VIEW?
- SANDBAG OR SUPPORT ADEQUATE?
- BIPOD FIRMLY IN PLACE, ON STABLE SURFACE?
- SCOPE CANTING IN THIS POSITION?
- SCOPE OBJECTIVE LENS FOCUSED/ADJUSTED?
- BULLET DROP COMPENSATOR SET FOR DISTANCE?
- ESTIMATED RANGE ACCURATELY? COMPENSATED?
- ESTIMATED WIND ACCURATELY? COMPENSATED?
- RECORDED INITIAL WIND AND RANGE IN RECORD BOOK?
- SHOOTING SHOULDER CLEAR OF STRAPS, HARNESS?
- POSITION ADEQUATELY COMFORTABLE?
- EARS ON?

CHECKLIST FOR FIRING EACH SHOT

The following actions should occur during each shot fired in practice, and almost all are used in real-life combat or police incidents, too.

Through repetition, these should become habits so you apply them while under stress and thereby achieve superb shooting despite pressures.

- BODY POSITION CORRECT?
- RIFLE GRASPED PROPERLY FOR COMFORT?
- RIFLE GRASPED PROPERLY TO ABSORB RECOIL?
- CANTING?
- BREATHING CORRECTLY?
- BEANBAG SNUG UNDER RIFLE BUTT?
- CORRECT EYE RELIEF
- CORRECT SCOPE SIGHT PICTURE?
- TRIGGER CONTROL "FEELS" RIGHT?
- SHOULD I TRY A DRY-FIRE FIRST?
- USE A PRECISE POINT OF AIM?
- DID SHOT IMPACT AS CALLED?
- FOLLOW-THROUGH WAS SMOOTH, NATURAL?
- RECORDED SHOT IMMEDIATELY IN RECORD BOOK?
- PLANNED NEXT SHOT?

ducing and using these blank forms, provided you don't sell or commercially duplicate them, only use them for official agency business, and leave the source line intact.

Log this information as you shoot, shot by shot. This will occupy you long enough to keep your barrel from warming and also help you develop patience and pace between shots. You'll start to see each shot properly as a distinct, one-time event.

Always use a mechanical pencil; not only does this mark you as a competitive shooter, but it makes for easy erasure and writing even when the paper's damp.

Two versions here are very similar, with one designed for recording shots at stationary targets and the other for moving targets. The bull's-eye target page is new for this edition of the book. We'll consider how to log data in the stationary record book first.

Sheet 1

DATE	LOCATION	RIFLE SER # AND SCOPE		BDC ELEVATION		WINDAGE	
				INITIAL	CORRECTED	INITIAL	CORRECTED

AMMO WITH LOT #		TODAY'S TNG EMPHASIS	

TEMP	PRECIP	WIND 12	TOTAL RDS FIRED/TODAY

ZERO CHANGE:

UP/DOWN: 9 — 3

RT/LEFT: VEL   TOTAL RDS FIRED/BARREL

DRILL: 6

SPOTTERS

MY POS

CALL

TIME

EST/ACT

REMARKS:

36 27 18 9   9 18 27 36
27 +   +   +   +   +   +   27
18 +   +   +   +   18
9   +   +   +   +   9
0   0
9   +   +   +   +   9
18 +   +   +   +   18
27 +   +   +   +   27
36 27 18   0   18 27 36

Duplicated from *The Ultimate Sniper*, copyright 1993, 2006 by John Plaster. Published by Paladin Press.

Sheet 2

DATE	LOCATION	RIFLE SER # AND SCOPE		LEAD	MILS LEFT	MILS RT	LEAD

AMMO WITH LOT #		TODAY'S TNG EMPHASIS	

TEMP	PRECIP	WIND 12	TOTAL RDS FIRED/TODAY	MOVEMENT 12

ZERO CHANGE:

UP/DOWN: 9 — 3

RT/LEFT: VEL   TOTAL RDS FIRED/BARREL   9 — 3

DRILL: 6   VEL   6

MY POS

DIR

CALL

TIME

EST/ACT

REMARKS:

        6   3   0   3   6
9   +   +   +   +   9
6   +   +   +   +   6
3   +   +   +   +   3
0   0
3   +   +   +   +   3
6   +   +   +   +   6
9   +   +   +   +   9
        6   3   0   3   6

Duplicated from *The Ultimate Sniper*, copyright 1993, 2006 by John Plaster. Published by Paladin Press.

DATE	LOCATION	RIFLE SER # AND SCOPE		BDC ELEVATION		WINDAGE	
				INITIAL	CORRECTED	INITIAL	CORRECTED

Form table:

AMMO WITH LOT #		TODAY'S TNG EMPHASIS	

(Elevation/windage plot grid with values 36 27 18 9 | 9 18 27 36 and plotted + marks, concentric circles for target, WIND compass 12/9/3/6 with VEL, TOTAL RDS FIRED/TODAY, TOTAL RDS FIRED/BARREL, SPOTTERS, rows: TEMP, PRECIP, ZERO CHANGE:, UP/DOWN:, RT/LEFT:, DRILL:, MY POS, CALL, TIME, EST/ACT, REMARKS:)

Duplicated from *The Ultimate Sniper*, copyright 1993, 2006 by John Plaster. Published by Paladin Press.

The Stationary Target

DATE: The date you're shooting.

LOCATION: Record not only the town or post but the specific range you're firing on.

RIFLE SERIAL NUMBER AND SCOPE: This ties the data directly to one rifle and scope.

AMMO AND LOT NUMBER: Note the exact type of ammo, to include bullet style and weight. Get the lot number off the box.

TODAY'S TRAINING EMPHASIS: I urge you to single out one marksmanship aspect for each shooting session—things like follow-through or breathing. Ask your spotter to coach you.

TEMP: You'll probably see differences in trajectory between hot and cold days.

PRECIP: Note whether it's raining, snowing, misting, or foggy.

DRILL: If you're shooting a drill instead of ordinary practice, note which kind of drill it is, such as surgical shooting, a follow-up shot, etc.

ZERO CHANGE: Once you've fired some

spotter rounds, you may choose to change your current zero. If so, record the changes here according to 1/4 MOA clicks.

WIND: Draw an arrow indicating wind direction and log in the velocity. Recheck it and adjust at least each half hour.

TOTAL ROUNDS FIRED/TODAY: Enter this at the end of firing.

TOTAL ROUNDS FIRED/BARREL: This is your running total. Add today's total rounds fired to the total from the last page.

SPOTTING ROUNDS: You may choose to fire a few rounds to confirm zero before practice fire or drills. Plot spotters here and save the other spaces for subsequent firing.

MY POS: For each shot, note whether you were sitting, standing, kneeling, lying, etc. This helps you assess positional shooting.

CALL: Immediately after follow-through, place a small "x" where you *think* your round impacted, with *one box representing one shot*, and only 10 shots recorded per page. You'll compare the call momentarily to where your spotter tells you it actually impacted.

TIME: If a time limit or target exposure time was involved, note it here. Especially note if you blew the time limit!

EST/ACT: When firing on an unknown-distance range, record your range estimate in the upper half. Compare this later to the actual range, obtained after firing, in the lower half.

REMARKS: This is where you record any other pertinent data, to include: group size; night observation device serial number; reminder to change your sniper rifle data card to reflect new data; type of support used, such as a bipod or sandbag; amount and type of artificial illumination; uphill or downhill targets; special point of aim for anti-body-armor drills so you'll later realize the throat or femoral artery shot was purposely targeted; weak shoulder shots; smoke or special situations; and so on. Here, too, is where you diagnose any problems or declare the system combat-ready.

BDC ELEVATION—INITIAL and COR-RECTED: If you must deviate from the indicated initial setting, note the change here.

WINDAGE—INITIAL and CORRECT-ED: Again, start with it set where it should be true and record the correction if you change it.

INCHES LEFT/INCHES RIGHT: Earlier you plotted the "call" shots where you *thought* the rounds should impact. Here, plot the real impact points, designating them with the numerals 1 through 10. If you missed the silhouette, plot each miss according to inches it is from dead-center, with each crosshatch indicator representing 9 inches apart, allowing you to plot misses up to 36 inches in any direction.

The Moving Target

We'll only note the few differences on the moving target page.

MOVEMENT: Draw an arrow to indicate the moving target's direction and log in its estimated velocity.

DIR: When engaging multiple moving targets, indicate whether each one is moving right-to-left or left-to-right by drawing an arrow

for each target. This will help you identify and diagnose arm-swinging problems.

CALL: Again plot where you think your round impacted, but note that it's now a thin silhouette, the same shape as the "mover." Don't plot the intended lead—plot where you expect the bullet to hit and compare this momentarily to where it really hit.

LEAD/MILS LEFT—LEAD/MILS RIGHT: Enter the lead or mils you've computed, but correct them if necessary.

FEET LEFT—FEET RIGHT: Not only is our "mover" silhouette unisex, he's unidirectional so it can be used for targets moving either right or left. And since long-range leads may be several feet, these crosshatches represent 3 feet. Be sure to plot your bullet's impact point, not the lead, in this space.

The Bull's-Eye Target

This record book page is essentially identical to the stationary target, except it allows you to enter bullet impact points on a miniature, circular target.

BOLTING A RIFLE INVISIBLY

At times the danger of being detected may be so great that you dare not move, especially following a shot and with intense enemy observation directed your way. For such times, practice bolting your weapon using one of two techniques that minimize visible motion.

The first one simply requires that you keep both elbows planted where they were when you fired and your eye at the correct eye relief. You move only your right hand to operate the bolt. This technique, with practice, also allows very fast follow-up shots.

We have illustrated the second technique on page 224 since it is more complicated. Here you're concerned that the enemy could possibly see your expended brass if it is flipped in the air.

First (1), rotate the rifle to the right so the ejected round falls directly to the ground. Next (2), lift the bolt handle very slowly, and (3) pull the bolt to the rear until you meet resistance. Then

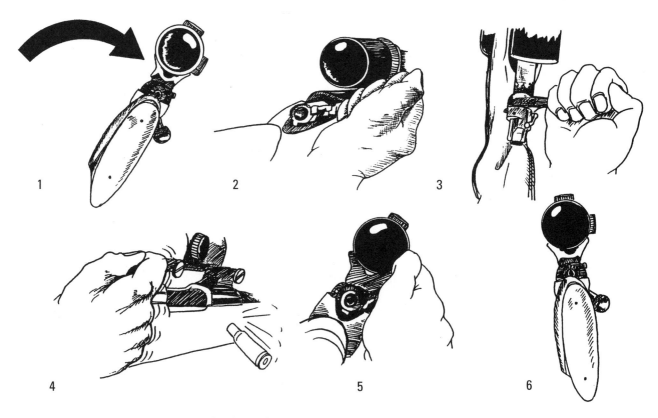

Bolting a rifle invisibly is a six-step action.

(4) smartly tap it that last quarter inch, which will pop the brass from the extractor onto the ground. Ease (5) the bolt forward, ensuring it has picked up a fresh round, and rotate it down. And finally, (6) return the rifle to the upright position and reacquire your sight picture.

The drill is a good concurrent training subject during sniper courses or while waiting your turn on a firing line.

RAPID RELOADING TECHNIQUES

Although he trains to fire deliberately and all his actions are methodical, a sniper nonetheless must reload quickly. The problem, however, is that his bolt-action sniper rifle is not designed for rapid reloading unless it has a detachable magazine.

Aware of these problems, I developed the following reloading techniques, which aren't the only way to skin this cat, but at least these offer a practical solution.

First, the Reload Carrier

Rather than struggling to grasp one round, you should grab five, the entire number you will load. This is done by cutting down a Federal 10-round .308 plastic cartridge carrier so it holds only five rounds. I call this a "reload carrier."

A standard military first-aid bandage pouch can hold two of these reload carriers for a total of 10 rounds, or two reloads, per pouch. You should have two such pouches on the right side of your pistol belt, assuming you're a right-handed shooter.

Another way to make a reload carrier is to find old 7.62mm stripper clips, which also carry five rounds. Just substitute the military ball with your match ammunition. However, I've found that it takes more time to strip rounds off a stripper clip than it takes to pluck them from my cut-down Federal reload carrier.

The only further improvement would be to

line the inside of the pouch with Gore-Tex to protect the ammunition from rain. I'd leave a small flap at the top to be folded over underneath the snap, which should keep water out and prevent any condensation problems.

The Reloading Drill

Now let's see how you'll use this setup to reload quickly and simply. First, after firing your last round, ensure that you leave the bolt pulled well to the rear so there's plenty of upper receiver access.

Next, switch the rifle's weight entirely to the left hand, which cradles it just forward of the receiver. As quickly as your left hand grabs it, your right hand should be going for your ammo pouch. If you're in the prone position, you'll probably shift somewhat onto your left side for easier access to the pouch.

Flip the pouch open and withdraw one reload carrier of five rounds. You should have placed that carrier in the pouch so that when you removed it and lifted your hand, the cartridge bases are up and ready to grab for fast removal.

As your right hand gets close to the receiver, shift the weight of the rifle from the left hand to the left forearm and slide that left hand a bit under and around the receiver, just enough so it can hold the reload carrier.

Now, place the reload carrier in your left hand and with the right, pluck those rounds and place them in the rifle. You'll prevent hang-ups and delays by ensuring each cartridge base is snug against the rear of the magazine well before trying to load the next cartridge.

If you're in a real hurry, only load as many rounds as the magazine well can hold—which is one less than maximum capacity—and slide that bolt forward ASAP. If you're not under heavy pressure, however, push the fifth round into the chamber and slightly shove down on the fourth loaded cartridge as you bolt forward, above it.

With some practice, you'll be able to reload in less than 10 seconds—a far sight faster than any of the techniques I've seen attempted by many students.

Practice rapid reloading using the five-round holder developed by the author.

THE SNIPER ENGAGEMENT SEQUENCE

Professional soldiers train for combat action by practicing battle drills, a set of specific steps they execute when suddenly thrust into dangerous situations, similar to football special teams mastering quarterback sacking and punt blocking. These drills are thought out carefully so each action happens in correct sequence and contributes to the overall engagement.

After wrestling with all the actions a sniper must accomplish—many of them critical but easy to forget or do out of order—I devised a battle drill especially for snipers that combines fieldcraft and marksmanship skills, which I call the "sniper engagement sequence." The engagement sequence equally applies to police snipers, who would follow these steps in a modified way after getting a "green light."

Practice this sequence over and over until you can do it in correct order, automatically.

1. NOTICE TARGET: You are not certain it's a target; you or your spotter just notice there's something worth checking closer.
2. SEEK STABLE POSITION: If you're already in a hide, just confirm the bipod is solid or support is stable. If you're moving, select a position that offers the best cover and/or concealment and occupy a prone or sitting position, preferably with support.
3. ESTIMATE RANGE: You can do this several ways; what really matters is that you're accurate and you apply the data to your BDC or target knobs. *Remember:* incorrect range estimation is the primary cause of long-range misses.
4. CLARIFY THE TARGET: You and your spotter employ optics to confirm the nature of your target. You focus your scope at the target, which automatically eliminates parallax. If there are multiple enemies visible, you establish target priorities. Police snipers use this step to confirm their suspect's identity. This also is a good time to

start deep breathing in preparation for firing, which can help calm you, too.

5. ESTIMATE WIND: Since you should still be watching the target through the scope, your spotter should estimate wind, then tell you the result, which you use to adjust your windage knob or to compensate by holding right/left. While the spotter's checking the wind, you determine whether the target is moving and compute the leads, which you then apply.
6. AIM AND FIRE: This will be fairly easy if you have a BDC and windage knob; if you don't, you should talk out loud as you adjust the target knobs for range, wind, and movement, verifying their correctness as you talk. And then you perfectly perform the integrated act of firing, with your eye focused on the reticle at the instant you shoot.
7. FOLLOW-THROUGH: You follow the shot with no movement, no change in body or mind. Your spotter watches the target and observes where your bullet impacted. If it missed, he tells you exactly where it hit—data you use to adjust for a perfect shot.
8. RELOAD: Actually, the follow-through step is so short that you probably bolt the rifle as your spotter announces where the bullet impacted. Don't wait for information from him; just reload as quickly as possible after follow-through so you're ready for another shot.
9. ENGAGE OTHER TARGETS: Elsewhere we debate how many shots to fire in one engagement, which is a judgment call. What's important here is that you practice this drill so you're ready for whatever you decide or whatever circumstances allow you.
10. DISPLACE: Don't hang around to admire your handiwork. When the engagement's finished, displace to another hide or leave the area.
11. REPEAT THE SEQUENCE: So long as you're in the field, you'll just keep repeating this sequence over and over, every time you detect a potential target.

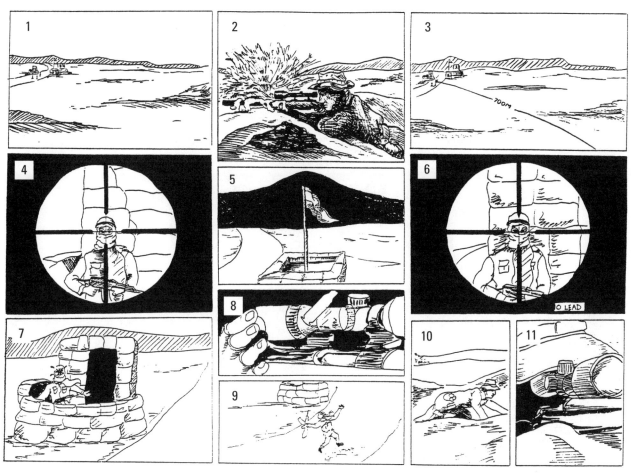

The sniper engagement sequence.

RECOMMENDED MARKSMANSHIP PRACTICE

You should balance and integrate your annual shooting schedule so that in a year's time you've practiced all the following situations and techniques in the proportions indicated. This practice does *not* include shooting drills, which should consume half your firing time.

These figures are just a starting point, so adjust them to fit your shooting environment. For example, Arizona law officers need not fire 40 percent of their practice in rain or snow. Also, if there's any chance whatsoever that you'd need to shoot in the presence of CS or other chemical agents, you should wear a gas mask during at least one training session a year.

TACTICAL SHOOTING DRILLS

I divide practice firing into two categories. The first is bull's-eye shooting, in which the sniper fires off a bench or prone-supported, diligently recording each shot, confirming his zero, and preparing himself for the more realistic firing that follows.

Tactical shooting drills—the second category—challenge not just accuracy but also the qualities that make a sniper, such as concentration, patience, discipline, and confidence. Each drill simulates an important teaching point or some aspect of a real-world engagement, while also inducing some physical and psychological stress. Such shooting drills are especially important for police snipers because they cannot be expected to learn from error,

AMBIDEXTROUS FIRING

Strong Hand	Weak Hand
95%	5%

RANGE TYPE

Known Distance	Unknown Distance
60%	40%

SHOOTING TIME

Marksmanship Practice	Tactical Shooting Drills
25%	75%

SHOOTING POSITIONS

	Police	Military
Prone with Sandbag	15%	10%
Prone with Bipod	25%	25%
Prone without Support	10%	10%
Benchrest	5%	0%
Sitting Supported	15%	15%
Sitting without Support	5%	5%
Kneeling Supported	10%	10%
Standing Supported	10%	15%
Standing without Support	5%	10%

SHOOTING DISTANCES

Police		Military	
75–100 yards	40%	<100 yards	10%
100–200 yards	35%	100–500 yards	50%
200–600 yards	25%	500–900 yards	40%

except in training. The ultimate goal is to transform the mechanical act of shooting accurately into a mechanical act of shooting accurately under pressure.

To underscore further the emphasis of one-shot kills, in a tactical shooting drill the sniper has only one round for each exercise. If he misses, he cannot engage again, which helps him recognize the finality of his every shot. For realistic variety, fire these kinds of drills in daylight and at night under artificial illumination.

When designing your own drills, induce stress by the pressure of time limits, and add physical exertion so the shooter must contend with controlling his respiration and heartbeat while firing. I like to add a degree of uncertainty

TARGET MOVEMENT

Stationary Targets	Moving Targets
90%	10%

TARGET EXPOSURE

Fleeting Target	Exposed Target
25%	75%

LIGHTING CONDITIONS

Daylight	Night
65%	35%

FLAT GROUND VS. UPHILL/DOWNHILL

Flat Ground	Up/Down
85%	15%

SHOOTING DURING PRECIPITATION

Dry Weather	Rain/Snow
60%	40%

TEMPERATURE

Cold	Warm	Hot
25%	50%	25%

TYPE OF AMMUNITION FIRED

	Mil M118 Long Range	Civilian Match	Standard Mil Ball	Barrier or AP	Military Tracer
Military Sniper	92%	—	4%	3%	1%
Police Sniper	—	90%	4%	5%	1%

or change while the drill's under way so the shooter is forced to think through the situation and employ judgment as well as fire his rifle.

Noise and light distractions are useful, too, such as exploding firecrackers, flashing lights, smoke, a screaming woman's voice, or a squad car's siren. (At Gunsite I sometimes added a nice touch by pouring ice water on a sniper's back or playing a boom box with his most-detested music. Twangy country-western does the trick for urban-raised African-American officers, while rural white lawmen haven't much time for thumping rap music.)

Here are two good examples of tactical shooting drills:

The Fleeting Target

This is a police sniper's most frequent exercise because it best duplicates reality. The sniper is authorized and prepared to engage and knows generally where the suspect is, but he must wait until the target exposes himself, which will only be for a few seconds.

At the start of the exercise, the sniper is allowed to see his target and "lock on," readying himself and his rifle for what could be a long wait. Then the target is lowered or rotated out of sight. At some point over the next 30 minutes, the target reappears only once. A new sniper starts with a 10-second exposure; as his skills improve, exposure time lessens to 5 seconds. This exercise helps develop patience and concentration. To boost stress, "tease" the shooter by occasionally exposing the target for just 1 second before finally giving him the full 5-second exposure.

On ranges lacking rotating targets, the same simulation can be achieved by a range officer using a stopwatch. While pacing back and forth behind the shooters, the range officer suddenly shouts "green light" and slaps a particular shooter's leg. Five seconds later, the range officer blocks that sniper's objective lens, ending his time window. This continues randomly until all the snipers have fired.

The Surgical Shot

This timed exercise elevates the complexity of hostage rescue shooting. Down range are five facial portraits juxtaposed on a target. At the start of the exercise, the sniper and spotter are 25 yards from the firing line and allowed 5 seconds to study the hostage-taker's mug shot. Then, they dash halfway to the firing line, snatch one round, low crawl the final 12 1/2 yards to the grounded rifle, load it, spot the correct suspect, engage, and dash back to the finish line with the expended cartridge. The timing starts from the instant the shooters see the mug shot. The exercise is a "no go" if a shooter fails to hit the suspect, mistakenly hits a hostage, or fails to bring back the expended cartridge. This exercise emphasizes the importance of facial ID instead of relying on the suspect's attire, while also putting the sniper under physical and psychological stress.

Photographs of similar-looking people increase the difficulty. For example, use all white males with short hair wearing sunglasses, as on our sample target on page 200. When firing from more than 150 yards, this becomes a team event that requires both a sniper and a spotter with a spotting scope to ensure correct identification.

Imagination and lessons from real-world engagements can provide an unending flow of challenging tactical drills. Accuracy, I'm sure you agree, is not the sole determinant of a sniper's performance—concentration, discipline, confidence, and patience must be honed, too.

CHAPTER 8
SPECIAL
SHOOTING
SITUATIONS

ENGAGING A MOVING TARGET

Normally a sniper avoids engaging moving targets because the likelihood of a first-round hit declines precipitously after 400 yards, as the probability data box on page 233 demonstrates. These estimates are based on my observations at schools and practice sessions. Therefore, it's usually better to wait and engage your target when he pauses momentarily. Should he not cooperate—and a moving target is the only shot you've got—then apply what we cover here.

Calculating Target Movement and Leads

All the data published here reflects a target moving 90 degrees to the path of your bullet, that is, moving directly right or left, which is *full value*. Look at the illustration at right.

Should the target move oblique right or left, whether toward or away from you, use one-half the value, since in rela-

tive terms he's crossing your front at half the speed. When he's heading directly toward you or away from you, there're no value and no movement compensation or leads at all. Aim dead-on.

The quickest way to determine if a man's moving obliquely is to note whether you can see both arms. A man traveling perpendicular will have one arm masked by his body, while an oblique mover has that opposite arm at least partly visible.

Using data for .308 168-grain Match, determine how much to lead an oblique walking target that's 400 yards away. Do that now.

The answer is 14.5 inches, which is half the value for a man walking right or left at 3 mph. When I prepared these tables, I went with 3 mph as the speed a man travels when he's actually going somewhere; a cautious or tired man moves slower. The 6 mph figure represents a jog or slow trot or a soldier running with full webgear. And the dash speed I thought should be 10 mph.

Should you act-

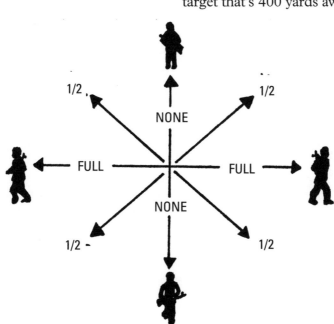

Target movement will dictate full value, half value, or no compensation.

MOVING TARGET LEADS

.308 168-gr. Match and M118LR 7.62mm
Distance in Yards

	100	200	300	400	500	600	700	800	900	1000
Walk 3 mph	7"	13"	21"	29"	37"	46"	56"	68"	80"	93"
Trot 6 mph	13"	26"	42"	57"	74"	92"	113"	135"	158"	185"
Dash 10 mph	21"	44"	68"	95"	122"	154"	187"	224"	264"	306"

BULLET TIME OF FLIGHT

.308 168-gr. Match and M118LR 7.62mm
Distance in Yards, Time in Seconds

100	200	300	400	500	600	700	800	900	1000
0.11	0.24	0.38	0.53	0.70	0.87	1.06	1.27	1.50	1.75

ually carry all this data in your head and apply it to each shot? Nope. I memorize the 3 mph leads, then double it for a trotting man and triple it when he's at a dead run. Mentally I can halve any one of these if the target's moving obliquely.

The easiest way to remember .308 lead distances is to count in sevens—7, 14, 21, 28, 35, 42—and you'll have the correct walking leads almost perfectly for 100, 200, 300, 400, 500, and 600 yards. This technique's even closer for military M118 ammo.

Moving Target Leads

It's just fine for a precision shooter to calculate a moving target's compensation down to the closest half inch, but it's tough to actually shoot this way. A simpler means of applying moving target compensation goes all the way back to the days of musketry and is called, appropriately, using "leads."

Our forefathers knew that it was hard to estimate what an inch looks like against and in front of a distant target, especially a moving one. So these frontiersmen applied Yankee ingenuity and decided that a man was 12 inches wide—1 foot—when looked at from the side, as we've illustrated. This became one "lead."

Looking at our .308 168-grain/M118 data, therefore, instead of leading a 100-yard walking man by 7 inches, I use half a lead, which is measured from the *center* of his body. My aim point becomes the edge of his body in the direction he's moving, which means although a perfect lead should be 7 inches, I'm using only 6 inches and will be 1 inch off—a tiny compromise to make considering how clearly my mind's eye can tell me to aim at the leading edge of his body. If he was walking at 500 yards, I'd hold 6 leads ahead of his center, equal to 36 inches.

12"

A "lead" equals a man's width of 12 inches.

MOVING TARGET COMPENSATION

.300 Winchester Magnum 190-gr. Match
Distance in Yards

	100	200	300	400	500	600	700	800	900	1000
Walk 3 mph	6"	12"	19"	25"	32"	41"	49"	58"	68"	79"
Trot 6 mph	12"	24"	37"	50"	65"	82"	98"	116"	136"	158"
Dash 10 mph	19"	40"	61"	84"	108"	137"	162"	194"	227"	264"

.223 Match 69-gr. BTHP
Distance in Yards

	100	200	300	400	500	600	700	800	900	1000
Walk 3 mph	5"	7"	13"	20"	24"	17"	43"	56"	68"	83"
Trot 6 mph	10"	13"	26"	41"	47"	33"	87"	111"	137"	166"
Dash 10 mph	18"	21"	44"	68"	79"	110"	145"	186"	229"	276"

PROBABILITY OF FIRST-ROUND HIT ON A WALKING TARGET

100 yds	200 yds	300 yds	400 yds	500 yds	600 yds	700 yds	800 yds
95%	90%	80%	75%	60%	50%	35%	20%

Let's combine our counting by sevens with leads to see just how closely we could actually hit targets using our ancestors' leads technique.

.308 168-GR. AND M118LR LEAD COMPARISON

Distance	Walk 3 mph	Count by 7s	Leads	Lead Width
100 yds	7"	7"	1	6"
200 yds	13"	14"	2	12"
300 yds	21"	21"	3.5	21"
400 yds	29"	28"	4.5	27"
500 yds	37"	35"	6	36"
600 yds	46"	42"	7	42"

Can you see why Daniel Boone and Davy Crockett were such fine riflemen? Although my preference is the "counting sevens" technique—which I double for a trotting target and/or halve when it's oblique—you could just as well memorize leads and do the same thing: 1, 2, 3.5, 4.5, 6, and 7. Whatever works best for you is the most appropriate technique.

Another technique uses a rifle scope's mil dot reticle for very exact moving target compensation, which we've covered extensively in that section; the mil dot technique seems the most appropriate for the Army's M24 Sniper Weapon System and the USMC's M40A3.

Moving Target Firing Techniques

As a former military State Marksmanship Coordinator, I receive the NRA's excellent monthly competitive marksmanship magazine,

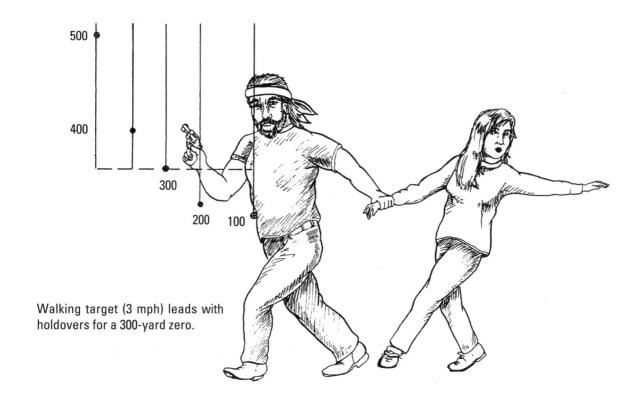

Walking target (3 mph) leads with holdovers for a 300-yard zero.

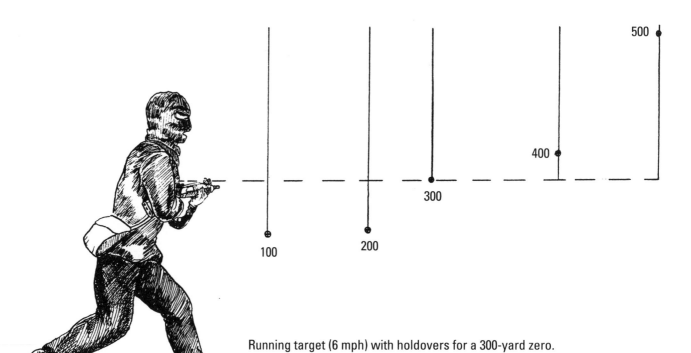

Running target (6 mph) with holdovers for a 300-yard zero.

Shooting Sports USA, and absorb its many tips and techniques, some of them from Martin Edmondson, the National Running Target Coach for our Olympic-level U.S. Shooting Team.

As Coach Edmondson notes, the key to engaging a moving target is keeping the rifle firm in a weld with eye and shoulder and pivoting only the waist—or, in our case, leaning slightly into the bipod. Keep body movement as limited as possible. You should have a smooth swing that catches up with the target, slightly passes him enough for the lead, holds for another second, then follows through as the shot's squeezed off.

By following this sequence and swinging up from behind him, your mind will have acquired his pace and speed as your crosshairs overtake him. Then, when you get the right lead, wait another second so it "feels" good, then release the shot and follow it through. Think about how smooth and natural that will feel and how choppy and disconnected it is to try to throw your crosshairs in front of him, figure out his pace, get the right lead, etc.

Much military shooting literature says there are two moving target techniques: "trapping," which has you holding the crosshair stationary and waiting for the approaching target to position itself for the right lead, when you shoot; and "tracking," which has you panning with him. I think the best technique uses aspects

of both, as does the swing-from-behind one I just detailed.

As distinct techniques, tracking works well at close range where a wide swing is necessary, while trapping traditionally fits best at long range where the field of view is larger and only a tiny pivot is required.

The trapping technique, however, is very suitable for engaging a fleeting runner, which is a man who dashes to cover, pauses out of sight, then suddenly emerges to dash to the next bit of cover. To dust this kind of opponent, anticipate his next cover destination so you can determine where he'll burst forth from his present cover. Trap him by placing your crosshairs at waist-level, about one pace away from the cover. Holding it very steady, let the shot go as soon as there's even the first blur of movement.

And talking about shot release, one of the problems novice snipers have with moving target shooting is jerking the trigger, which is solved with plenty of dry-fire practice between live-fire rounds.

Some rifle instructors recommend increasing the lead—even doubling it—for right-handed shooters engaging targets moving right to left (or the reverse for lefties) due to the body's "natural hesitation" when pivoting this way. While this is a concern for novices, I think the solution is extra practice and dry-fire, not adopting two ways to take the same shot. But whatever works for you is right.

TRAPPING. Hold steady and
allow target to move into correct lead.

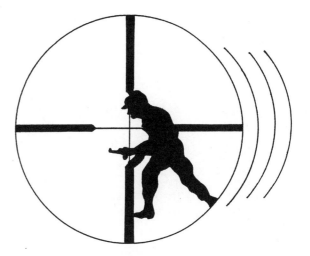

TRACKING. Swing with
target to achieve correct lead.

UP/DOWN COMPENSATION

Here's the problem: you zero your rifle on flat ground so that the arc of your bullet cuts into bull's-eyes perfectly—then you get into mountain country or an urban area and engage a target that's significantly uphill or downhill and those bullet arcs get all confused. The arc your bullet traced to hit a bull's-eye on flat ground is very different from the one you create when aiming significantly up or down.

How much difference is there? When shooting .308 168-grain Match at a target only 300 yards away, the same trajectory that allows an exact bull's-eye on flat ground leads to a shot that's 7.8 inches *high* if your target is 45 degrees uphill or downhill. And the problem gets worse with distance.

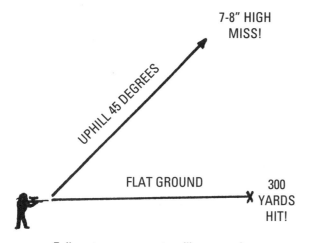

Failure to compensate will cause misses.

Before we get into explanations and solutions, *lock these facts* in your brain:

- Up and down shooting *both* require compensation, with the same amount needed for 45 degrees up as 45 degrees down, etc.
- You must always compensate by *aiming low!* I remember this by visualizing a limbo dancer—*always go low!*
- Your zero distance has no effect: the amount of compensation is determined solely by up/down angle and distance to your target.

USMC snipers practice downhill shooting on a mountain slope.

- The amount of needed compensation increases significantly with range and steepness of angle to a maximum of 60 degrees.

Why We Need Up/Down Compensation

After wrestling with this complex problem for years, I finally came up with an understandable illustration that explains it—I think.

You zeroed your rifle on flat ground, at zero degrees, by aiming somewhat high, which caused the bullet to rise then fall just enough to hit the bull's-eye. This established a certain exact height between the bull's-eye and your sight setting—or line of sight—which we've shown as a dashed vertical line.

Now, when you aim uphill (or downhill) 30 degrees, gravity pulls your bullet at the same rate, so your sight's still the exact same height

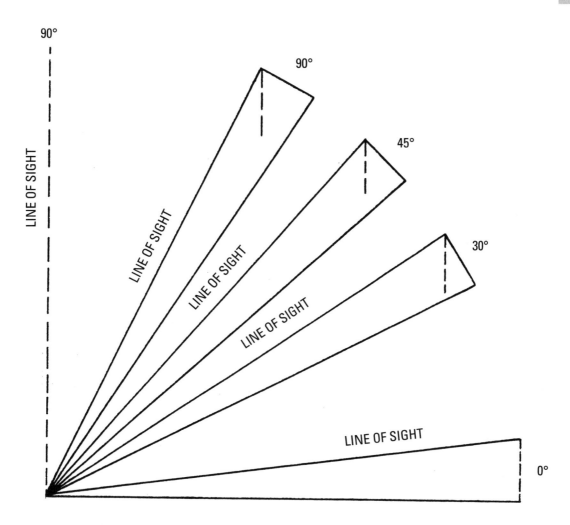

With your rifle zeroed to hit the bottom of the dotted line, the bullet's path "climbs" ever higher as you aim up or down. You must compensate low.

above the bullet's path—*but* that vertical drop is now causing your round to impact a bit *high*. Notice how the dashed line is the same length and hangs vertically from your line of sight—just like on flat ground—but there's now a gap between it and the bull's-eye you're aiming at. Remember, the bullet impacts the bottom of the dashed line.

When you raise the angle to 45 degrees, this gap becomes much more apparent. By the time you're aiming at a target 60 degrees up or down, there's a considerable gap between where you're aiming and where your bullet hits. And it's here at 60 degrees that the effect is greatest, because by the time you're shooting straight up—90 degrees—there's no longer any effect since gravity's pulling at the bottom of the bullet and the dashed line is the same as your line of sight.

How to Compute Up/Down Compensation

Keep in mind that up/down compensation is quite separate from compensation for distance, even though it similarly increases with range.

Our starting point is finding "bullet drop," which is the ballistic measurement of how many inches a bullet falls when a rifle barrel is perfectly parallel to the earth. Each cartridge

Angled up/down compensation is required for rooftop shooting, such as demonstrated here atop the Pentagon.

has its own particular bullet drop data, which we're providing for .223 and .300 Winchester Magnum in the adjacent charts—and, of course, with more elaboration for the .308 168-grain Match, which is so close ballistically to the M118LR that we're using the same data for both. (For example, at 500 yards, these two bullets are within *1/10 of an inch* when compensating for a 45-degree shot. Even at 1,000 yards and 60 degrees, there's only 1 percent compensation variance.)

To find the required compensation, take this bullet drop data and multiple it by the factors shown in the "Computing Up/Down Compensation" box at right. Note that the factor changes by 5-degree increments and maxes out at 60 degrees, which is where up/down compensation itself maxes out. Compute this: find a .223's compensation for 45 degrees up/down, when the target distance is 400 yards; 36.3

COMPUTING UP/DOWN COMPENSATION

5 Degrees:	Drop inches x .004
10 Degrees:	Drop inches x .015
15 Degrees:	Drop inches x .034
20 Degrees:	Drop inches x .060
25 Degrees:	Drop inches x .094
30 Degrees:	Drop inches x .134
35 Degrees:	Drop inches x .181
40 Degrees:	Drop inches x .235
45 Degrees:	Drop inches x .293
50 Degrees:	Drop inches x .357
55 Degrees:	Drop inches x .426
60 Degrees:	Drop inches x .500

SOURCE: Sierra Reloading Manual

UP/DOWN COMPENSATION
.223 69-gr. BTHP Match

	100	200	300	400	500	600
Bullet drop	-2.0"	-7.2"	-18.2"	-36.3"	-63.3"	-101"
30 Degrees	0.3"	1.0"	2.4"	4.9"	8.4"	13.5"
45 Degrees	0.5"	2.1"	5.3"	10.6"	18.5"	29.5"
60 Degrees	1.0"	3.6"	9.1"	18.2"	31.6"	50.5"

UP/DOWN COMPENSATION
.300 Winchester Magnum 190-gr. Match

	100	200	300	400	500	600	1000
Bullet drop	-2.2"	-9.3"	-21.9"	-40.5"	-67.0"	-102"	-347"
30 Degrees	0.2"	1.2"	2.9"	5.5"	9.0"	13.6"	46.5"
45 Degrees	0.6"	2.7"	6.4"	12.0"	19.7"	29.7"	102"
60 Degrees	1.0"	4.6"	11.0"	20.5"	33.6"	51.0"	174"

bullet drop inches x .293 = 10.63 inches that you must hold *low* to hit perfectly.

We computed the data for the three most general up/down angles of 30, 45, and 60 degrees for each cartridge just so you could get a better feel for the effect and as a reference we'll use shortly to show *how* to compensate. But let's try one more example first: find the required compensation for a .223, when the target is 50 degrees up/down at a range of 500 yards.

You multiply 63.3 bullet drop inches x .357 = 22.5 inches of low hold. (Remember: always compensate by aiming low.)

Since the .308 Federal Match 168-grain BTHP is of great interest to us, we computed all this compensation data for you. By reviewing it, some points should leap off the paper at you.

First, see how we shaded it to highlight compensation of 4 inches or more. It's starkly apparent how compensation grows with the steepness of angle and distance to the target.

Second, note how significant this compensation may be even at moderate distances and gentle slopes. For example, a 20-degree slope demands 5 inches' compensation at 500 yards;

that's a lot on top of any compensation you're already taking for wind, range, and target movement.

Third, appreciate how significant the differences are for an angle of 30 degrees versus 45 degrees: think about how easy it is to snap-think a slope is 45 degrees when it's actually much less. Hold your arm up at a 45-degree angle—make *sure* it's really 45 degrees—and register how truly steep that is. When you're in mountains or an urban area, similarly use your arm while estimating angles to keep your conclusions accurate.

And last, while operating in urban areas, keep in mind how quickly angles increase as a hostile's position gets higher above ground. By the time he's four to five stories or higher and you're across an average downtown street, he's probably already 40 degrees up. Recall the Texas tower gunman, Charles Whitman, whose 28-story perch must have been about 50 degrees up from most lawmen, who typically fired from cover 300 yards away. This means their uncompensated shots probably hit about 10 inches high!

.308 168-GR. MATCH AND M118LR UP/DOWN COMPENSATION
Distance to Target (Yards)

Degree Slope	100	200	300	400	500	600	700	800	900	1000
5 Degrees	.01"	.04"	.10"	.20"	.33"	.51"	.74"	1.0"	1.4"	1.8"
10 Degrees	.04"	.16"	.40"	.75"	1.2"	1.9"	2.7"	3.9"	5.2"	6.9"
15 Degrees	.09"	.38"	.91"	1.7"	2.8"	4.3"	6.3"	8.7"	12"	16"
20 Degrees	.16"	.67"	1.6"	3.0"	5.0"	7.7"	11"	15"	21"	28"
25 Degrees	.25"	1.0"	2.5"	4.7"	7.8"	12"	17"	24"	33"	43"
30 Degrees	.30"	1.5"	3.5"	6.7"	11"	17"	25"	34"	47"	62"
35 Degrees	.48"	2.0"	4.8"	9.0"	15"	23"	33"	47"	63"	84"
40 Degrees	.62"	2.6"	6.3"	12"	19"	30"	43"	60"	82"	108"
45 Degrees	.70"	3.3"	7.8"	15"	24"	37"	54"	75"	102"	135"
50 Degrees	.90"	4.0"	9.6"	18"	30"	46"	66"	92"	125"	165"
55 Degrees	1.1"	4.8"	11"	21"	35"	54"	79"	110"	149"	197"
60 Degrees	1.3"	5.6"	13"	25"	41"	64"	92"	128"	174"	232"

REMEMBER: Always compensate by aiming LOW. (Shading = 4 inches or more)

Short-Range Advantages

The simplest solution to up/down confusion—and the one most police snipers apply—is to keep the distance as close as they can, say no more than 100 yards. Look at the chart showing this short-range information.

No matter whether you're firing .308, .223, or .300 Mag. or the suspect's at 30 degrees or 60 degrees, by virtue of your short range, the maximum possible error is only about an inch when you aim dead-on.

Already we've cited stalking forward as one way of reducing the effect of a heavy wind, so this only reinforces the concept.

But in many law enforcement instances—and in most military situations—100-yard shots are simply not feasible and are wrought with hazard. So you must compensate instead.

Up/Down Compensation: Holding

The most fundamental way of applying up/down compensation is simply to hold your crosshair low by the required amount on your target.

Let's say your target is 500 yards away at an angle of 45 degrees, and you're firing .308 or M118LR, which computes to 24 inches low. Therefore, after setting your BDC for 500

SHORT-RANGE ADVANTAGES
100-Yard Up/Down Shooting Compensation

	.308/7.62mm	.223 Match	.300 WinMag
30 Degrees	0.3"	0.3"	0.2"
45 Degrees	0.7"	0.5"	0.6"
60 Degrees	1.3"	1.0"	1.0"

MIL EQUIVALENTS AND INCHES FOR UP/DOWN 45-DEGREE SHOOTING

Yards	Full Mil Width	Inches for 3/4 Mil Dot	Required Compensation .223	.308	.300 WinMag
100	4"	3.0"	0.5"	0.7"	0.6"
200	7"	5.2"	2.1"	3.3"	2.7"
300	12"	9.0"	5.3"	7.8"	6.4"
400	14"	10.5"	11"	15"	12"
500	18"	13.5"	18"	24"	20"
600	22"	16.5"	29"	37"	30"
700	25"	18.7"	45"	54"	—
800	29"	21.7"	65"	75"	—
900	32"	24.0"	92"	102"	—
1000	36"	27.0"	125"	135"	—

.308 168-GR. MATCH AND M118LR
Minute of Angle Compensation for a 45-Degree Slope

Yards	Compensation	MOAs	Closest 1/4 MOA Clicks
100	0.7"	0.70	3 (0.74 MOA)
200	3.3"	1.65	7 (1.75 MOA)
300	7.8"	2.60	10 (2.50 MOA)
400	15.0"	3.75	15 (3.75 MOA)
500	24.0"	4.80	19 (4.75 MOA)
600	37.0"	6.10	24 (6.00 MOA)
700	54.0"	7.70	31 (7.75 MOA)
800	75.0"	9.37	37 (9.25 MOA)
900	102"	11.30	45 (11.25 MOA)
1000	135"	13.50	54 (13.50 MOA)

REMEMBER: Compensate by aiming LOW.

yards or otherwise compensating for range, you aim at his crotch and squeeze off your shot. It impacts center-chest.

Up/Down Compensation: Mil Dot Reticle

The mil dot section on page 125 explains how to use the Leupold Mark 4's mil reticle to compensate for uphill/downhill shooting, and in this function mil dots really shine.

We've published a chart of mil equivalents in inches so you could see how well they coincide with needed compensation at 45 degrees for our four primary cartridges. Further information is found in the mil dot section.

Up/Down Compensation: Minutes of Angle

We've published a special chart with .308 and M118LR information for 45 degree up/down compensation and compared it to MOAs and 1/4 MOA clicks so you can see how to apply this data to a BDC, target knobs, or an elevation ring.

Now we're getting ready to start cookin', so pay close attention. Our first leap in logic: set in your brain that 45 degrees is the only data you truly must learn. Forget about the long lists in 5-degree increments, etc. Just learn 45 degrees and apply this compensation full-value on a slope of 45 degrees. Use half this compensation value when the target's at 30 degrees.

First, let me prove how valid this is by referring you to the .300 Winchester Magnum up/down compensation box. The .300 WinMag at 600 yards at 45 degrees requires 29.7 inches compensation; half that for 30 degrees is 15.4 inches, which is very close to the 13.6 inches actually required.

Some precision fanatics are cringing because this generalizes, but appreciate how much *faster* you can compute things in your head and engage—and remember Captain McBride's warnings about slow reactions yielding nothing. While, indeed, this technique ignores 60-degree shooting, it's very, very close for 30 and 45

degrees, and seldom would even mountain and urban shots ever exceed 45 degrees.

That seemed fairly simple, but I've actually saved the easiest way for last—and it's so quick to both compute and apply that I'm calling it the quick fix.

Up/Down Compensation: The Quick Fix

I cannot take credit for inventing this brilliant means of up/down compensation since I picked it up from the FBI. But their formula wasn't mature, and it took some work to refine it, so it no longer can be called the FBI Technique, either. I've dubbed it "quick fix" because you can calculate it all in your head and adjust your scope—especially a BDC—about as quick as it took you to read this sentence. It's not micrometer-precise, but it's so fast that it's really deadly. Captain McBride would be very proud of us.

Here's how it works: you see a target that's 45 degrees up or down at 500 yards. Set your scope at 0.7 of that distance and shoot. That's all. Set it at 0.7 the distance of any range and you'll hit a target that's 45 degrees up or down.

It means cranking your BDC to 350 yards

QUICK-FIX 45-DEGREE UP/DOWN COMPENSATION ON A BDC (.7 Distance)

Actual Yards	200	300	400	500	600	700	800
@ .7 Distance	140	210	280	350	420	490	560
Effect of .7	2.5"	5.2"	11.7"	21.0"	33.4"	49.5"	70.0"
Needed Hold	3.3"	7.8"	14.7"	24.4"	37.4"	54.0"	75.0"
Error	0.8"	2.5"	3.0"	3.4"	4.0"	4.5"	5.0"

QUICK-FIX 30-DEGREE UP/DOWN COMPENSATION ON A BDC (.9 Distance)

Actual Yards	200	300	400	500	600	700	800
@ .9 Distance	180	270	360	450	540	630	720
Effect of .7	1.0"	3.0"	6.0"	8.5"	13.0"	27.0"	34.4"
Needed Hold	1.5"	3.5"	6.7"	11.1"	17.0"	24.7"	34.4"
Error	0.5"	0.5"	0.7"	2.5"	4.0	4.7"	4.4"

(0.7 of 500 yards), aiming dead-on, and letting rip. Look at the chart showing 45-degree quick-fix compensation, which shows the actual yards, what 0.7 of these distances equal, how low you'll be holding in inches, and the amount of error you've accepted.

When your target is 30 degrees up/down the process is the same, except now you use 0.9 so that when you're shooting 600 yards you set your BDC at 540 yards and aim dead-on, etc. Again, you're accepting some error, but it's relatively tiny at most distances.

The only warning I must add is to *never* use quick-fix or any of my angle-generalizing techniques for hostage-rescue shots. That's time to get out your notebook and calculate the precise, exact hold you'll need and apply it meticulously.

ENGAGING A FLEETING TARGET

A fleeting target is a stationary hostile who exposes himself for only a few seconds, then ducks back into cover and concealment until he again exposes himself. Examples include an artillery forward observer in an observation post or a soldier concealed behind a log and occasionally peering over its top—or an enemy sniper attempting to spot you. This is the most realistic suspect activity for police sniping situations, too.

Essentially, engaging a fleeting target is a game of patience and preparation. You've located and identified your target but cannot engage him because he won't stay exposed long enough to raise your rifle, spot him through your scope, breathe correctly, and squeeze off one shot.

The solution is to complete all these preliminary steps before he reappears—that is, get into a good prone-supported position and adjust yourself and your rifle so there's no need to readjust at the split-second of firing. Wedge clothing or a sandbag under the heel of your rifle, adjust and anchor the bipod, etc., so your rifle is perfectly "locked-on" your target's location. All you do is wait for the target to reappear.

Adjust your body and make your position as comfortable as possible. You should be able to lie motionless with the rifle so well locked-in that no movement is needed to shoot.

Eye fatigue is a potential problem if you stare with one eye through the scope for a prolonged period. Preclude this by keeping both eyes open and watching the enemy's position with your left eye while resting the right eye. From time to time shift focus to your right eye just to confirm that the crosshair's still aligned and ready and you have correct eye relief.

When you see the enemy reappear with your left eye, shift focus to your right eye, confirm the scope crosshairs are on him, and squeeze off a shot.

How long must a target be exposed to be engaged? Consider the following data:

FLIGHT TIME, .308 168-GR.
Match HPBT Bullet
(Yards and Fractions of a Second)

100	200	300	400	500	600	700	800
.11	.24	.38	.53	.70	.87	1.06	1.27

Obviously, the closer your target, the sooner the bullet reaches him, which means (for him) it's far more dangerous to expose himself for 1 second at 100 yards than at 500 yards. Add to these times the amount of time it would take you to spot him, shift focus to one eye, look through the crosshairs, and squeeze off a shot. With practice, you should be able to engage a target that exposes itself for 1.5 to 2 seconds.

The snipers I personally train exercise their ability to engage fleeting targets more so than any other shooting technique.

SHOOTING THROUGH GLASS

The medium through which a sniper most often could be required to shoot is glass. Unlike other barriers, you can actually observe and verify a target through glass, and this would seem a reasonable shot to attempt. But placing an effective, neutralizing shot through glass is no simple matter, for it's more complex than it appears.

Consider the glass itself. It can be 1/8-inch, soda-ash glass in an old urban house, so brittle a BB gun would penetrate, or a multilayered, half-inch, laminated door at a supermarket. A car windshield's safety glass is a sandwich of glass holding a layer of Butacite PVB, yet the same car's side windows are thin safety glass that shatter to bits when struck by a bullet. Newer snowbelt homes have double-layer glass windows with the space between filled by inert gas as an insulator. Then there's tempered glass, heat-treated to make it stronger, which also gives it a harder surface. And how about so-called, "bulletproof" glass, made from Lexan polymer? All these can have varying thicknesses, too.

Here's the first rule of thumb in glass penetration: do not plan on using a hollowpoint, match bullet. Many tests have been conducted—including my own tests at Gunsite and shots I've observed with the Minneapolis Police Department—that leave no doubt that this round is not suitable because it's likely to break up or deflect due to its bullet design. The 168- and 175-grain BTHP Match bullets offer superb accuracy, but they were never intended to penetrate glass or barriers.

I used to advise the same when it came to glass shooting with any .223 bullet, but the fielding of new penetration ammo has persuaded me otherwise. I've personally tested the Federal .223 Tactical Load at the factory, live-firing it through a windshield into a gelatin block at 100 yards. As shown in the accompanying photos, this 55-grain bonded bullet retained 99+ percent of its weight (54.5 grains) and deflected less than 1 MOA when fired 90 degrees into the windshield. My second shot, fired at a more ballistically challenging 45 degrees into that laminated glass, retained 29.5 grains, then penetrated a gelatin block some 10 inches.

Both Federal's .223 load—also available in a 62-grain version—and its bigger .308 Tactical Load use a special bullet that's molecularly

This bullet hole through a glass window in Ramadi, Iraq, marks where U.S. Marines shot an insurgent sniper. Note HMMWV through bullet hole.

bonded to the jacket so that, even though it mushrooms, the lead core remains nearly whole after impact.

At Gunsite we tested the .308 Tactical Load extensively, requiring that each law enforcement student fire it cold-bore using the same zero as his normal 168-grain Match. About half our students experienced some degree of zero shift (almost never more than 1 MOA), and they found their groups opened up to about 1 MOA. Thus, each student learned, he could switch

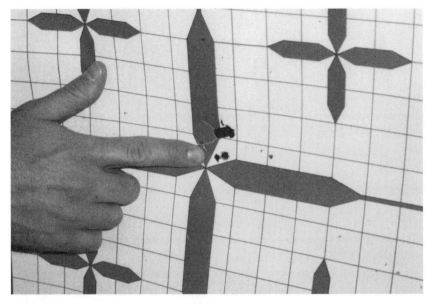

The two lower holes mark where the author's two rounds impacted after penetrating an auto windshield—a slight deflection from dead center. (Upper hole was torn by a secondary projectile.)

Despite penetrating the windshield, the author's .223 slug slammed some 10 inches into this gelatin block.

instantly to a bonded bullet, but he'd trade off some precision and have to take into account this potential zero shift.

Firing at 100 yards against the kinds of glass found in homes and autos, our students never failed to penetrate and impact a facial target in the designated 3 x 5 target area. We also went on to test these bullets against heavier glass, to include airliner passenger and pilot windows and "bullet-proof" glass from a bank. Not all were penetrating shots, but I don't think it would be responsible to disclose the exact results here. Instead, I suggest that law enforcement readers contact the National Tactical Officers Association for very detailed test results from a variety of U.S. agencies and police snipers.

More recently, I've tested excellent Hornady barrier-penetration ammo that also uses bonded bullets and impressively penetrates glass. Available as a .308 165-grain InterBond TAP Barrier load and a .223 load in 62-grain, I found a slight zero shift, depending on the rifle. But as with the Federal ammo, that's to be expected if you're switching to a different bullet weight and style. What's important is that you test-fire the ammo, know whether there's any shift, then apply it if you must take a glass shot. With both the Federal and Hornady .308 glass-penetrating loads, the trajectory was so close to 168- and 175-grain Match

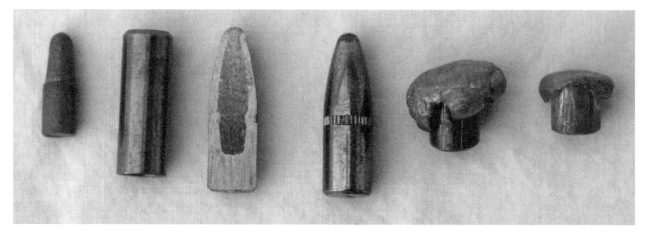

Federal's 55-grain .223 bonded bullet, showing (L-R) lead core, jacket, cutaway view, assembled bullet, and two rounds the author fired through a car windshield.

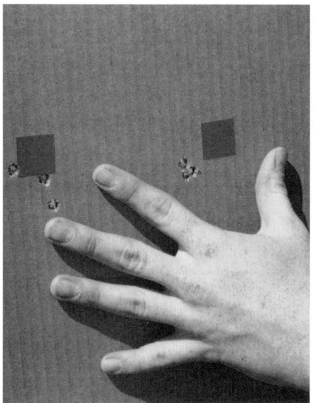

At Gunsite, about half our students saw a zero-shift when switching from 168-grain Match (right group) to 165-grain Tactical Load (left group). Note larger group, too.

Police sniper Chris Mayer and the author inspect results of firing a 165-grain bonded bullet into an airline passenger window.

Federal and Hornady offer special glass-penetrating, bonded bullet loads in .223 and .308.

that—after taking into account the zero shift—it didn't vary from the match more than 1/2 MOA out to 300 yards.

One interesting glass-piercing load I received from a German police sniper is a .300 Winchester Magnum with a 155-grain solid-copper alloy bullet with grooves cut into the tip, sort of like a drill bit. There's nothing like it in America. Another interesting European bullet is Lapua's Forex, available in a 185-grain .308 load and a 260-grain .338 Lapua Magnum round. The Forex bullet is precision-machined on a CNC lathe and incorporates a hollowed base to ensure it flies nose-heavy to reduce deflection when it hits glass.

Actually, all the barrier-penetrating rounds covered in Chapter 5 offer glass-penetrating capability, especially the military ball rounds. Additionally, however, ball ammo raises the issue of overpenetration, which may endanger hostages or bystanders beyond your target.

When a bullet impacts glass as an angled shot, police sniper tests reveal, it tends to turn somewhat inward into the same angle it was traveling instead of being deflected. Theoretically, one edge of the bullet touches first, which probably causes friction and pulls the

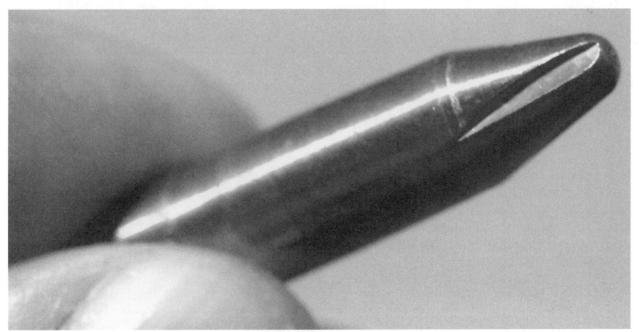

This German .300 WinMag, 155-grain copper alloy solid has drill bit-like grooves cut into its nose.

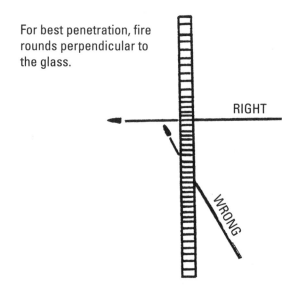

For best penetration, fire rounds perpendicular to the glass.

RIGHT

WRONG

least two simultaneous shots. The first breaks glass—losing much of its lethality, it's theorized—while the second projectile passes through cleanly to neutralize the suspect. The only problem is that it depends on the kind of glass—great against a car windshield and probably ordinary window glass in a home, but not as certain for the thicker glass in a commercial building, which can vary considerably.

Actually, when it comes to penetrating glass in commercial buildings, multiple snipers ready to back a sniper's initial shot with *instant* follow-up shots may be the surer strategy. Perhaps this is the second point I should emphasize: a sniper taking a shot through glass should, whenever possible, be backed up by at least one more sniper.

bullet slightly inward. To minimize this effect, it's best to shoot dead-on, as close to perpendicular to the glass surface as possible.

Another suggested technique is to employ at

A Special Ops friend familiar with overseas incidents brought to my attention the very real danger of secondary missiles—glass shards and pulverized fragments—that can injure or kill

A high-speed camera captures the instant that a Federal Tactical Load bullet pierces this plate glass. Hazards of secondary shards and pulverized glass are very clear.

hostages. Recent tests have found that these secondary missiles generally follow the path of the bullet and must be taken into account when planning a hostage-rescue shot. I recall a live-fire training exercise with the Minneapolis Police Department's Emergency Response Unit, where a sniper fired a round into a condemned house's living room. Though his bullet flew true, a jacket fragment penetrated 1 inch into a sandbag quite a distance laterally—which could have caused a serious or lethal soft-tissue wound.

According to the U.S. Marine Corps, a 7.62mm ball round generates a shotgun-like cone pattern of fragments and shards after penetrating glass. Elaborate tests determined that the bullet's copper jacket rips away, while the lead core remains largely intact and continues generally on the same path after penetration.

My knowledgeable sniper friend Neal Terry believes that in addition to firing perpendicular to the glass surface and aiming for the largest target area on the suspect, it's best to shoot when the suspect is as close to the glass as possible, both to reduce the possibility that deflection could cause a miss and to lessen the danger to hostages from secondary missiles.

Before attempting a shot through glass, I'd recommend that you know exactly what kind of glass is involved and experiment with similar material so you can anticipate the likely results. I've found that local glass suppliers often will provide samples gratis for such worthwhile experiments.

Should a police sniper attempt a shot through glass? If hostages are at risk and there's no better solution, absolutely. My recommendation is not that you avoid such shots; it's only that you understand the risks and idiosyncrasies when forced to shoot glass so that, to the degree possible, the odds are with you.

HOSTAGE RESCUE SHOOTING

This section must be brief and pointed, because disclosing too much here could benefit any hostage taker who got his hands on this book.

Hostage-rescue shooting is the most psychologically and physically demanding kind of sniping. There's not the slightest room for error, nor is there opportunity for spotter rounds or second chances. Everything depends on one trigger squeeze.

Here are some things to consider:

- Don't attempt a shot beyond your ability.
- Don't allow superiors or others to rush you.
- Employ at least two sniper teams per suspect to increase the likelihood of a clear shot.
- Multiple targets require multiple sniper teams, firing in unison.
- Reconfirm your zero if time permits; maybe even rezero for the exact distance you must shoot.
- Use military ball or barrier-penetrating ammo if you must shoot through glass.
- Employ a diversion if possible.
- Softpoint and hollowpoint ammo may legally be employed by military snipers in counterterrorist situations.
- Complex situations require a sniper coordinator at the command post.
- A positive backstop minimizes overpenetration concerns.

ENGAGING MATERIEL TARGETS

A sniper's ability to place shots precisely into vulnerable points gives him the capability of degrading and destroying materiel targets in addition to human ones. It's only a matter of knowing where these Achilles' heels are located and how best to impact them.

First, understand that you'll always achieve the deepest penetration and least likelihood of ricochets by having your bullets impact at 0 degrees obliquity—that means impacting perpendicular to the target's surface. As our illustration on page 250 shows, a 1-inch medium becomes 50 percent thicker (1.5 inches in relative terms) if your bullet hits it at 45 degrees.

Second, for most materiel targets you're better off using black-tipped armor-piercing ammunition. The U.S. M993 (7.62mm) AP round's

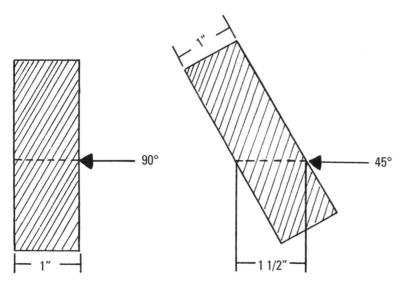

The angle of your bullet matters. Shoot perpendicular to the materiel's surface.

tungsten penetrator can pierce up to 1/2 inch of steel if fired at 90 degrees obliquity to the surface, and even the green-tipped 62-grain M855 5.56mm round incorporates a tungsten core.

If you can use a .50 caliber, all the better yet.

Materiel Aiming Points

Armored vehicle vision blocks can be cracked by 7.62mm fire. Although crewmen can change blocks, they'll be blinded at least temporarily, which can help your comrades engage them with antitank missiles. The laser range-finder, located on a tank turret in a squarish 6-inch mount, is

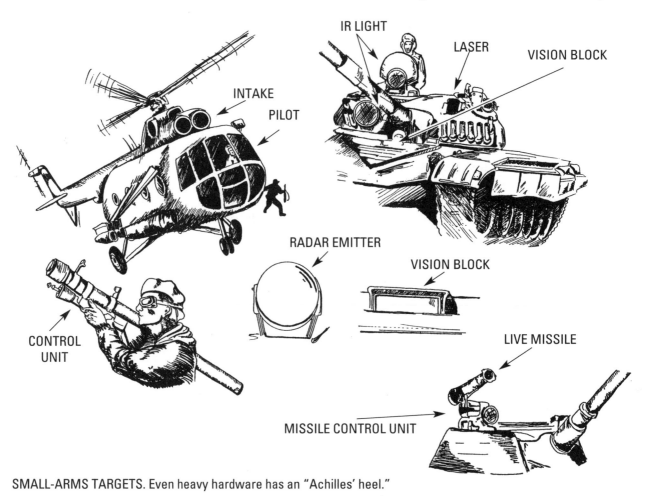

SMALL-ARMS TARGETS. Even heavy hardware has an "Achilles' heel."

susceptible to small arms fire, as are the commander's and driver's infrared searchlights. Soviet and Chinese forces traditionally teach their tankers to pause momentarily to fire; this is the best time for you to shoot, too. Helicopters hover for a second or two while soldiers disgorge, the perfect time to head-shoot the pilots or destroy the turbine engines with shots into the front air intake or back exhaust stack.

Antiaircraft missilemen are easily replaced, but their guidance units are not. Aim just above and forward of the handgrip to hit the infrared tracker unit. Similarly, any weapon system that uses optical sights can be degraded by focusing your fire on the optics; a massive artillery piece is ineffective without its shoebox-sized sight.

This principle is true for modern electronic control units, too, such as the antitank missile launcher shown on a Soviet BMP armored fighting vehicle. One round through the box-shaped control unit and that missile is little more than an expensive noisemaker.

Radar dishes themselves aren't harmed by rifle fire, but in the center of the dish is the system's emitter, a microphone-sized device susceptible to even slight damage. Knock this out and, for example, a ZSU-23-4 antiaircraft system loses much of its effectiveness.

THE SNIPER'S DEMOLITION AMBUSH

A sniper's single bullet can inflict mass casualties if it's used to trip a long-range demolition ambush. Depending on how you construct the target—and your marksmanship abilities—you easily could be hundreds of yards away at the instant of detonation. And at that range, the detonation blast masks your muzzle blast, precluding the enemy from even hearing your shot.

The Electrical Circuit "Gate"

All you're really doing is setting up an electrical circuit with a "gate" that you close mechanically with your rifle bullet. This gate is

a gap in the circuit between a battery and an electrical blasting cap. This blasting cap, in turn, is inserted in the first of a series of claymore mines. The other claymores are linked together by det cord, each of which has a nonelectric blasting cap crimped at each end. By setting it up this way, when the first claymore goes, the others instantly follow. You could link two or 200 claymores this way.

Laying the Ambush

Align your claymore series to cover an ambush kill zone, perhaps on a trail or edge of a road used by the enemy. Be sure to conceal the claymores! Run the electric wire behind a tree or rock, with the positive wire running up to the gate. For safety's sake, don't connect the interrupted circuit to the battery unless you're sure no friendlies are in the kill zone, and make sure you aren't too close to the backblast area. If all is well when you make the connection (i.e., it doesn't detonate), then withdraw to your hide.

Detonating the Ambush

Located high in the tree is your actual target—the gate you'll close with one bullet. Your hide could be 400 to 600 yards away, depending on the target's size and your marksmanship abilities. When the enemy enters the kill zone, fire one well-placed shot to detonate the entire claymore series. Since your muzzle blast will be masked by the detonation, you can safely wait to engage an enemy relief force or call indirect fire.

On the next page we've illustrated several styles of mechanical gates, to include metal screens and metal plates, that can be closed with a full metal jacket bullet. These would have the current actually pass through the bullet jacket, while the third clothespin device is detonated by shattering glass falling away from the clothespin, which allows electrical connections to meet.

I've tested other devices that worked perfectly. Gate designs can be as varied as your imagination.

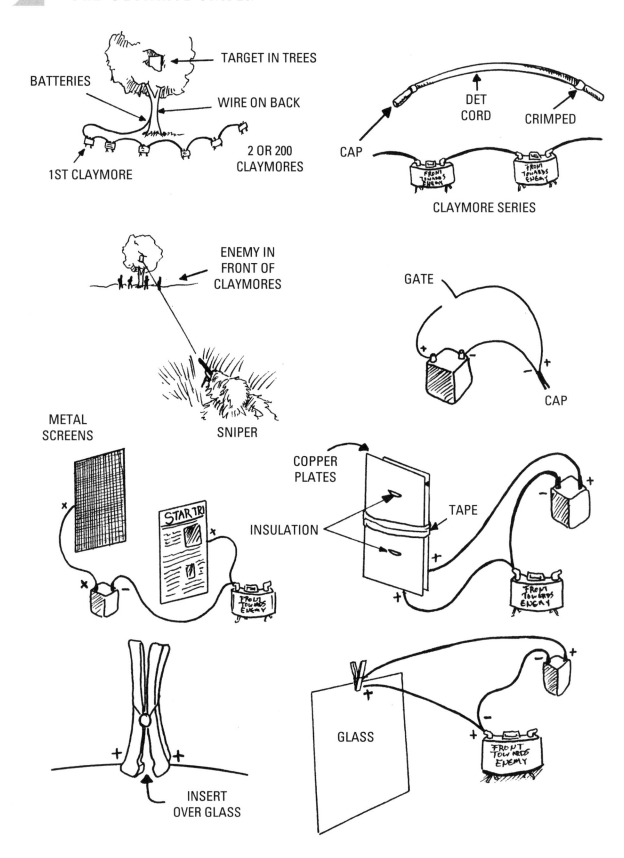

TARGET IN TREES

BATTERIES

WIRE ON BACK

1ST CLAYMORE

2 OR 200 CLAYMORES

CAP

DET CORD

CRIMPED

CLAYMORE SERIES

FRONT TOWARDS ENEMY

FRONT TOWARDS ENEMY

ENEMY IN FRONT OF CLAYMORES

SNIPER

GATE

CAP

METAL SCREENS

COPPER PLATES

TAPE

INSULATION

STAR TRI

FRONT TOWARDS ENEMY

FRONT TOWARDS ENEMY

INSERT OVER GLASS

GLASS

FRONT TOWARDS ENEMY

DETONATING EXPLOSIVES WITH RIFLE FIRE

Imagine their surprise. On 27 April 1941, two battalions of crack German parachutists descended on a critical British-held bridge crossing Greece's Corinth Canal. Linking the Greek mainland to the Peloponnesian Peninsula, seizure of this vital structure would allow quick passage for Panzer units and the overrunning of withdrawing British forces.

It seemed a perfectly executed textbook operation, with the Nazi paras simultaneously storming both canal banks, overwhelming anti-aircraft guns and security troops, then occupying the bridge itself before it could be demolished. German engineers instantly disconnected the detonator, and all seemed secure.

But none of the attackers noticed a British rifleman working his way to high ground, where he steadied his .303 Enfield and took careful aim at one of the yet intact dynamite charges. No one heard his shot, for it was masked by the louder roar of tons of explosives and the thundering crash of girders and concrete hundreds of feet into the canal. Yes, just imagine their surprise.

It has only been since World War II that explosives were made shockproof and became impervious to rifle fire. Prior to that, many explosives, and dynamite especially, contained enough unstable nitroglycerin to constitute a shock danger.

During World War II, the Allies perfected several powerful but shockproof explosives, among them plastic explosive and RDX. Also known as cyclonite, RDX is now the primary ingredient in so-called military dynamite, but it's diluted to generate the same blast effect and velocity as the true dynamite it replaced so that old blasting formulas remained constant.

The bottom line is that current military dynamite, unlike that used on the Corinth Canal bridge, cannot be detonated with rifle fire. So what's a clever sniper to do?

Much inexpensive civilian dynamite has stayed true to the original recipe and contains 40- to 60-percent nitroglycerin, and *this* will go up readily when a high-powered rifle bullet crashes into it. The clever sniper's challenge, therefore, is to scrounge civilian dynamite for long-range mayhem.

This same civilian dynamite can become your special long-range detonator for touching off otherwise stable, shockproof military explosives. Just layer your susceptible, civilian dynamite over the shockproof explosive, making a target for your fire. When the former goes up, its blast will sympathetically detonate the latter.

Test your scrounged dynamite live-fire to confirm that it's unstable enough to explode, especially at extreme long range where your bullet is losing velocity and energy.

FIRING FROM AN AERIAL PLATFORM

For Alaska State Trooper Jeff Hall this would be the test of a lifetime of marksmanship training and shooting drills. The Vietnam combat vet of the Army's 173rd Airborne Brigade and his partner, Troy Duncan, were among a dozen lawmen deployed 100 miles west of Fairbanks to pursue a mass murderer. Near Manley Hot Springs, a family riding ATVs had chanced upon a man disposing of two bodies—instantly he killed all three and was dumping their bodies when two more people arrived. They died next. The killer, Michael Silka, a wilderness drifter, then killed a trapper to steal his boat, bringing the death toll to eight, and raced away.

With Silka fleeing deep into the wilds, there was no time to waste. The Alaska troopers' tactical unit, the Special Emergency Response Team, put SWAT officers aboard two helicopters and two fixed-wings, searching rivers for the stolen boat. It was spotted beached on a tributary of the Zitziana River, 20 miles from the murder scene.

Hall's helicopter, a Bell Jet Ranger, was called in to provide cover while another chopper was to land a search team. As his Jet Ranger went into a treetop hover, Hall scanned carefully through his M16A1 open sights while

Aboard a hovering Coast Guard helicopter, a sniper takes aim with a Robar .50-caliber rifle.

Duncan viewed using a 3x optic on his M16. Both had 20-round magazines loaded with tracers. Over their shoulders, the E Detachment commander, Capt. Don Lawrance, also looked into the overhanging branches below but couldn't see a thing except Silka's boat.

The helicopter pivoted, and . . . *there he was, his rifle raised!* Duncan, Hall, and Silka fired simultaneously, missing. They fired again. Duncan fell back, shot dead by Silka's 30.06, and Lawrance, too, was hit by bullet fragments. The helicopter shifted; Hall saw Silka drop a fresh round in his Ruger and raise it. Hall fired into the swirling foliage, his burst shooting dead perhaps the worst mass killer in Alaska's history.

Jeff told me that harrowing story while I was in Alaska instructing a police sniper course. It's an excellent example because it contains the basic elements found in most law enforcement sniper engagements from aircraft, the primary one being *necessity*—there was no reasonable option but to use an aerial platform. The New Orleans Howard Johnson's incident cited in Chapter 1 equally was a case of necessity, when lesser measures failed to neutralize the rooftop gunman, Jimmy Essex.

Another component, as found in the Alaska case, is where the aircraft is a pursuit or observation platform that becomes a shooting platform, especially when the perpetrator fires at it. In 2004, Orange County, California, helicopter-borne deputies were searching for a dismounted gunman who'd shot two people near Irvine when the suspect, Jerry Larson, opened fire with a rifle, wounding the pilot. Their return fire killed Larson, effectively ending the incident.

The military approach to firing from an aircraft is that it's simply the best platform for

A helicopter-borne sniper, such as this U.S. Marshal, can halt a vehicle with accurate rifle fire.

Navy SEAL Master Chief Jim Kauber ready to fly a night interdiction mission over the Persian Gulf.

taking a shot in certain situations. For example, my friend, retired Navy SEAL Master Chief Jim Kauber, flew over the Persian Gulf at night in the late 1980s strapped to the outside of an Army OH-58 helicopter in order to interdict Iranian gunboats and mine layers. Outfitted with a Litton M845 night vision device on his M16, Jim was part of a then unacknowledged project, "Earnest Will." Kauber and his cohorts hunted in the darkness using the 58's mast-mounted FLIR system, struck with no warning, then disappeared before daylight. U.S. Special Operations Command credits these Gulf missions as "the first successful night combat engagement that neutralized an enemy threat while using aviator night vision goggles and forward looking infrared devices."

Realistic Missions, Realistic Assessments

Why use an aerial shooting platform? Because there's no terrain of equal or greater height than your target, like the Howard Johnson's shooter in New Orleans or the Texas Tower sniper. As well, there may simply be no other suitable approach, such as when a helicopter-borne force seizes an oil platform or conducts a vessel-boarding search and seizure on the high seas. Or you're escorting a heliborne force to provide covering fire for fast-ropers as they descend to a terrorist rooftop.

Realistically, given a helicopter's inherent movement and vibrations, a sniper cannot guarantee the same precision fire as when he's on the ground. However, a helicopter-borne sniper can place accurate, effective fire with considerably better discretion than a belt-fed machine gun, which is probably the only other small-arms alternative.

A Marine sniper perched in its door, a U.S. Navy Seahawk helicopter circles a ship in the Mediterranean during a vessel-boarding search-and-seizure exercise.

but your aircraft and aircrew, too. And he's not contending with aircraft movement and vibration to steady his aim.

On the other hand, it has been my experience that most hostiles on the ground do not appreciate how clearly—and at considerable distance—they can be observed and engaged from the air, a big plus on your side.

Optics, Weapons, and Ammo

More than anything, I think engaging from an aircraft is a target-acquisition challenge, so the first issue for consideration is your optic. Due to its limited field of view and the exaggerated visual effect of aircraft vibration, I'd gauge the least effective optic as the 10x fixed scope found on most military sniper rifles. Perhaps with a great deal of practice, a really fine shooter could master his 10x in a swaying helicopter, but most men find it extremely difficult. If you have a variable scope, crank it down to low magnification, both to enlarge the field of view and to reduce the visual disruption from aircraft movement and vibration. Better yet is a low-power scope, such as an ACOG, or the holographic EOTech sight.

When it comes to rifles, most shooters would agree that a bolt gun is the last choice because follow-on shots are almost a certainty, and the combination of small magazine capacity and slow reloading are real hindrances. I think you're much better off with an assault rifle, either 5.56mm or, even better, 7.62mm. The SASS or M14 variants fit this to a tee.

Finally, ammo. It's difficult to observe the impact of ball or match ammo from a hovering

Continuing your realistic assessment, respect that when you're hovering close enough to engage your foe—unless you're overmatching with a dramatically more powerful weapon—he is within range to engage you. Your sound and visual signatures are unmistakable, your position lacks cover or concealment, and, if you're in orbit, you're flying a predictable flight pattern. Further, it's not just you that's vulnerable to counterfire,

The most practical solution: a low-power ACOG scope and assault rifle ready to fire pure tracers, semiauto.

helicopter, even for a spotter using binoculars. The instant your engagement begins, nothing compares to the immediate feedback of tracer, which creates a closed loop for you to adjust your semiauto fire—*fire-observe-correct-fire*—repeated over and over, allowing you to finely adjust leads and holds until you're impacting perfectly.

Techniques That Work

First, it's most effective for the pilot and shooter to sit tandem, that is, the shooter behind the pilot. Why? That way both can look out the same side of the aircraft at the same general view of the target area, which simplifies communications and target descriptions.

As the shooter, you'll find more stability by being seated, but a tether offers more freedom of movement than a seatbelt. Do not use the airframe to steady your rifle since any direct contact will convey vibration. Instead, cushion it with your body or, as shown in the photo on page 258, rig suspension line or cargo straps for support.

As you near the target and the helicopter flares up to decelerate and then hover, it's critical for the aircrew to stay off the intercom so you can speak directly to the pilot—not through a crewchief or your spotter. Heeding your every call for an angle change, position adjustment, or other movement, the pilot and you work as a team. The most effective relationship is like that of a World War II bombardier who directed the pilot where to fly the plane during those crucial moments as he lined things up in the bombsight. *You are that bombardier, looking through the bombsight.* He is the aircraft commander, but he must realize that only by flying exactly the angles

This Marine sniper is wearing an aircrew helmet to communicate with the pilot, and his rifle is steadied by a rigged suspension line.

and speeds and hover that best enhance your shooting do you have a reasonable chance to make a shot and succeed in your mutual mission. That kind of rapport develops through practice, rehearsals, and experience.

Firing solely tracer, then, you place accurate fire into the target, instantly adjusting by observing your tracer. Incidentally, you'll all but eliminate the danger of ricochets if you fire at an acute angle—but in relative terms, that also makes your target thinner and smaller to hit.

Realize that there's no rule that says you're limited to one shooter. It's perfectly acceptable to put two or three snipers aboard the aircraft, provided there's sufficient space for them to fire without disrupting each other. If they've rehearsed or worked together before, they could probably share a single spotter.

Night could well be the best time for an aerial engagement since you can fire from a blacked-out helicopter and exploit American technology to the fullest. Employ a night vision scope, such as the PVS-10, but do not mount an IR laser illuminator on your helmet or you may inadvertently turn to the pilot and disrupt his vision. Instead, have your spotter "shine" the target using a handheld IR laser. Or you can wear night vision goggles and employ an IR wavelength laser aiming device on your rifle and fire nonvisible dim tracer.

Another Shooting Technique

Like many another SOG recon specialist who frequently overflew southern Laos low-level, on many occasions I engaged North Vietnamese soldiers from an aircraft. That was aboard helicopters and fixed-wing craft, with the latter most often O-1 Bird Dogs.

After several engagements, whether flyby shots or orbiting shots, I learned a shooting technique that proved accurate and effective. My weapon was a CAR-15, father to today's M4 carbine, and my ammo was pure tracer.

First, here's the unusual way to hold your weapon. Grasp the *top* of the forearm with your left hand and tuck your left elbow tight against your side. (This will vary a bit depending on the type of aircraft and door location.) The muzzle is now only a few inches left of your side, a bit higher than your waist. Your left hand is now "locked" against your side and will not move since it's the pivot point.

Grab the pistol grip with your right hand, but rotate it 90 degrees counterclockwise so the grip is pointing away from your body almost at chest level. In this position, you'll be able to watch your tracers much more clearly than when using sights. Now, holding the rifle firmly, fire a round semiauto, watch the tracer, then adjust by minutely pivoting. All adjustments come from the right hand. Shoot-adjust, shoot-adjust, shoot-adjust. Be concerned about just two things: clearly follow the track of your tracer all the way down, and fire a steady stream of semiauto tracer, minutely correcting with each shot. You're sort of "walking" your rounds, but actually you're firing much more precisely than a machine gun. Within three or four rounds, using this technique I could put a tracer right on top of an enemy soldier hundreds of yards away, even from the backseat of a moving O-1. As the photo on the next page demonstrates, Mike Buckland, who ran recon with me at CCC, could do it, too. This may be low-tech compared to some of today's techniques, but it works remarkably well and is quickly learned.

UNDERSTANDING AND EXPLOITING ECHO

Echoes are generated when sound waves reflect off such hard surfaces as hillsides, buildings, or large rocks, and can be very confusing, as demonstrated in Dallas when President John F. Kennedy was slain. To this day, some witnesses swear they heard gunshots from a grassy knoll as well as the building in which Lee Harvey Oswald concealed himself. Photos from the scene show motorcycle officers with guns drawn rushing the knoll, and even so-called experts argue about the total number of shots fired.

Any sound, including a muzzle blast, travels in all directions at a constant speed, about 650 mph at sea level. In flat, open country, such as desert or grassland, it's simple to identify where a sound originated since the noise reaches you directly. There's nothing to bounce off and cause an echo, so there's no confusion. It's when large objects are present that we get confused, because the sound of gunfire can reflect off these and make it seem to come from another direction.

This reflection can reduce your ability to detect enemy snipers, but you can also exploit it by selecting a hide having nearby surfaces that cause echoes and make it difficult to find you.

The most important point to remember when considering echoes is that the person being fired on *always* hears the *real* muzzle blast first, while the echoes follow. How quickly the echoes follow—and inspire confusion—is determined by the location of the surfaces off which the sound reflects. As the illustration on page 260 shows, the shortest distance the sound waves must travel is always from the sniper's location to the target—the echo off the rock must travel twice as far. There's a distinct pause between the shot and the echo, allowing the target an excellent likelihood of distinguishing between the echo and the real muzzle blast.

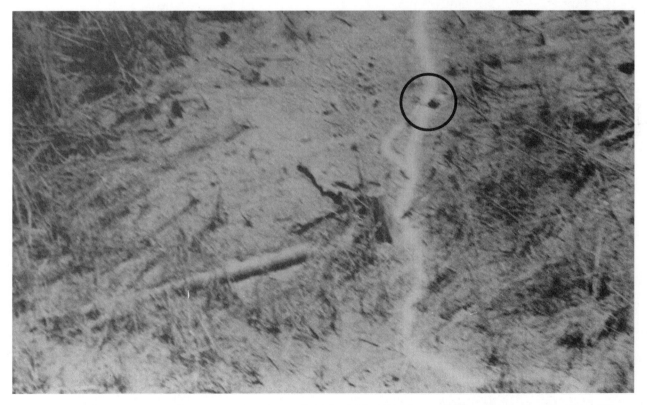

A North Vietnamese soldier collapses on a Laotian trail, hit by CAR-15 fire from a SOG man in an 0-1 Bird Dog. (Photo credit: Mike Buckland)

Now look at the next illustration. A short distance behind the target are two large rocks off which the sound bounces, reaching the target's ears at almost the same time as the real muzzle blast. This could confuse the target, but since the echoes are coming from his rear and not the same direction as the shooter, it probably won't fool him.

The most confusing echo, as illustrated at bottom right, has a hillside close behind the sniper that reflects his muzzle blast so that the echoes and real blast reach the target almost simultaneously *and* from the same general direction in which the shot was fired. If the sniper was well concealed, his target would probably find it impossible to locate him.

If you cannot plan your position in regard to echo effects, at least understand how it affects the sound of your muzzle blast so you'll know when it benefits you. And when in the countersniper role, remember: the sound of his real muzzle blast will reach you first. If you stay alert, you can "see" through echoes and correctly identify the enemy sniper's position.

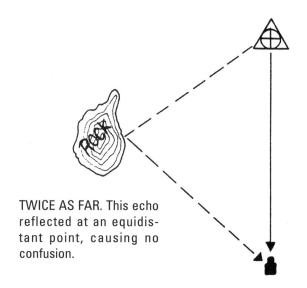

TWICE AS FAR. This echo reflected at an equidistant point, causing no confusion.

usually break up and splinter into tiny pieces upon impacting a firm surface. Military-type hardball ammunition will better withstand impact and likely retain more velocity and mass and thus more lethality.

Third, the likelihood of ricochet is affected by the angle of impact. Ricochets occur when a

RICOCHETING BULLETS

Bullets ricochet most reliably after striking a firm surface at a shallow angle of 10 to 20 degrees. Three factors affect this tendency to ricochet.

First is the hardness of the impact surface. The harder the surface, the more likely a bullet may ricochet. Hard surfaces include asphalt, steel, and cement, but don't forget we're also talking about vertical surfaces such as walls and the flat sides of heavy vehicles. Though softer surfaces like grass or dirt can generate a ricochet, the likelihood isn't as great.

Second, a ricochet depends upon the type of bullet. Soft-point and hollowpoint bullets

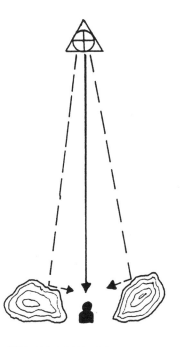

STILL NO CONFUSION. These echoes reflected off surfaces near the target.

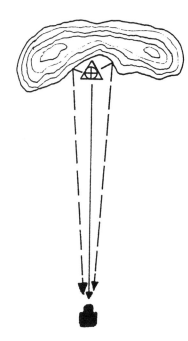

DECEPTION. Echoes that originate near the shooter confuse the enemy.

bullet hits a surface at a shallow angle—the momentum of the bullet is pushing it forward much more than downward. Usually, ricochets result when the bullet path is less than 30 degrees into the surface it strikes, causing it to glance off rather than penetrate the surface. Note the distinction: we're talking about the angle of your bullet's trajectory path, not the angle you're holding your rifle. After impact, a ricocheting bullet most likely tumbles but may continue flying tip-forward.

It's during your bullet's flattest trajectory—out to perhaps 350 yards—that a ricochet most likely would occur. Beyond this range, a 7.62mm bullet starts to plunge more sharply and lose the forward momentum required for ricocheting. Within this limited area, then—your muzzle to 350 yards—you should aim to hit a hard surface at less than 30 degrees to create a ricochet.

Planning a Ricochet

Planning a ricochet is wrought with uncertainty. You cannot plan exactly where the ricochet will go; a lot depends upon the angle and firmness of the round's impact point.

You probably cannot anticipate much beyond whether a bullet will ricochet up, down, right, or left. I can recall watching night tracer firing and observing one round flip skyward at 60 degrees; then another tracer, fired by the same weapon into the same approximate spot, careens into the horizon at 20 degrees. This variation resulted from the bullets impacting slightly different, although importantly, I recall that both rounds deflected up.

Generally, your ricochet will come off a surface at the same or a lesser angle than that which it struck, meaning if it impacted at 20 degrees, it will deflect no more than 20 degrees and probably less.

Ricochet Employment

A sniper employs ricochets to place rounds into targets that have too much cover to engage directly. In many circumstances, the concealed target will not even realize he can be hit by a purposely fired ricochet.

When you are facing an opponent who's employing effective cover, such as hugging a wall, crouching inside a concrete bunker, or lurking under a burned-out tank hull, carefully search the area to his front to see if there's a hard metal, asphalt, or cement surface to bounce a bullet off. This surface could be on either side, as well as below or even above him.

You may have to reposition yourself to ensure that your bullet strikes at less than 30 degrees. To increase the chance that a bullet ricochets at exactly the correct angle, fire multiple shots onto this hard surface, "walking" the bullets forward and bracketing the target.

You may choose to fire tracer rounds so your spotter can better assess results, though this would probably compromise your position.

Your spotter may not be able to determine whether you actually hit the target since it's concealed behind effective cover. Therefore when engaging a target with ricochets, you should fire a certain number of rounds—perhaps five—then cease the engagement unless continued target activity is apparent.

CHAPTER 9

HEAVY
RIFLE SNIPING

HEAVY RIFLE SNIPING

How can anyone exaggerate .50-caliber performance? Here's a bullet that, even at 1 1/2 miles, crashes into a target with more energy than Dirty Harry's famous .44 Magnum at point-blank. Appreciate the power of this cigar-size cartridge: the .50 caliber generates up to 25,000 ft-lbs. of muzzle energy, while the .308 M118LR tops out at hardly a tenth of that, just 2,626 ft-lbs., and even the .460 Weatherby Magnum yields "only" 8,095 ft-lbs.

Overpenetration concerns? One custom loader tested his ammo against simulated wooden frame houses and found that his solid bullets blew completely through six houses—not six walls, *six houses!*

Actually, the whole point of the .50 caliber is penetration, as it was developed originally to punch holes in the Kaiser's tanks in World War I. Fielded too late to see action, the Browning M2 heavy-barrel machine gun has served commendably in every subsequent conflict. Due to its flat trajectory and great antipersonnel range (2,700 yards), it was inevitable that some GI figured out how to rig a scope and employ it for extreme-range sniping, which began in the Korean War.

But until recent years, this long-range cartridge was not nearly as accurate as it was

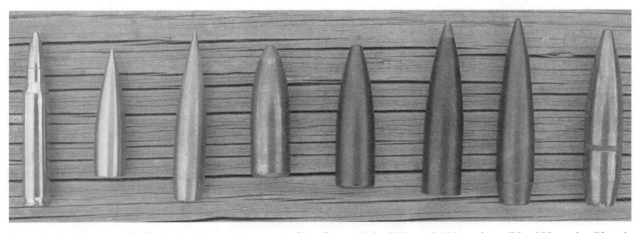

Relative bullet sizes (L-R): for scale, a .223 round; CheyTac .408 in 305- and 419-grain solids; 680-grain .50 cal. softpoint; ATP 680-grain flatbase .50 cal.; ATP flatbase 700-grain .50 cal.; ATP 700-grain rebated boat-tail; 750-grain ball. Dark rounds have been moly-coated.

powerful, and far more targets were missed than struck. Finally, the revolution in quality ammunition and precision rifle building caught up with this venerable cartridge. Today's cutting-edge heavy rifles are awesome powerhouses that deliver amazing, sniper-grade accuracy.

WORLD SHOOTING RECORDS

Think about how wide 2.6 inches are; that's the diameter of a beer can. Now consider how far 1,000 yards is—that's 10 football fields, or two-thirds of a mile.

Put them together—2.6 inches and 1,000 yards—and you have the incredible world-record five-shot group fired by the late Skip Talbot in 1999. A civilian gunsmith and rifle builder, Talbot used a modified .50 cartridge in his custom McMillan bolt action to shoot a group that measured a hair over 1/4 MOA—a phenomenal achievement. This grandfather of American long-range shooting died of a heart attack in 2005 while attending the national .50-caliber championships.

His legacy is the generation of technically oriented shooter perfectionists and long-range riflemen he inspired to squeeze ever more performance from the .50 cartridge. The Fifty

.50-CALIBER WORLD RECORDS
Smallest 5-Shot Groups @ 1000 Yards

Group Size	Shooter	Year	Rifle
2.600"	Skip Talbot	1999	Heavy Class
2.970"	Lynn McMurdo	2002	Light Class
3.064"	Paula Dierks	1999	Unlimited Class

Caliber Shooters Association, of which he was a founder and sometimes president, stands on the cutting edge of bullet and heavy rifle innovations, oftentimes several steps ahead of military and even manufacturer's research.

"I believe that the quality and performance of the .50 caliber guns we have coming up are going to be so accurate that they'll amaze you," he once prophesized to me. As you'll see, Skip was right.

CIVILIAN MATCH AND MILITARY AMMUNITION

The most accurate civilian match .50 caliber these men fire uses solid metal bullets—bronze or soft steel—turned on lathelike electric screw machines. "With machined steel bullets, you should be able to get the standard military sniper rifles down to less than 1 MOA at 1,000 yards," Talbot told me. Texan Dick Fisher shot a 9 1/2-inch group with an AMAC military sniper rifle, proving the compatibility of these advanced civilian loads and military weapons. (Fisher later told me he's even shot an amazing 3 1/4-inch 1,000-yard group.)

The advantage of a turned monolithic bullet is perfect concentricity so jacket deformities and variances simply don't exist. "The standard," one loader told me, "is reject any bullet that's not perfect." The downside is that these mono-

Champion .50-caliber shooter Skip Talbot cut this 4 1/2-inch world record group nearly in half to regain the title in 1999.

Heavy rifle match loads (L-R): .338 Lapua Magnum; .408 CheyTac (305 grain); .408 CheyTac (419 grain); .50-cal. Thunderbird bronze solid; .50-cal. with leaded steel solid; .50-cal with Hornady A-MAX 750-grain bullet.

lithic solids tend to wear out a match barrel's throat after about 2,000 rounds because there's no intervening soft jacket.

Dabco Professional Services markets four .50-caliber loads: a 750-grain centerless ground leaded steel solid; a 750-grain annealed bronze that is a reasonable compromise between efficiency and accuracy; a 700-grain copper lead with steel insert and hollowpoint, which delivers smashing energy but less penetration; and a 709-grain reload of military brass that imitates military trajectories.

The Bieber Bore Rider Bullet has a ballistic coefficient of .91—the highest I've ever heard claimed, which means it will slice through wind and space better than an F-15 fighter. Compare that to .30-caliber match bullets having a ballistic coefficient of .475 to .575! Truly amazing.

Thunderbird Cartridge Company of Phoenix, Arizona, is another producer of loaded .50-caliber match rounds, offering both leaded steel or bronze bullets machined to the highest of tolerances. These are the rounds my good friend

Dr. B.R.G. Kaplan fires through his rifle and has had nothing but good to say about. Thunderbird also markets flatbase and boattail match bullets for reloading.

Very high quality civilian match bullets are also produced by Hornady and Barnes. The Hornady bullet is a streamlined, silver-tipped 750-grain projectile offering both substantial mass and an extremely high ballistic coefficient of 1.050. J.D. Jones uses this bullet for his SSK .50-caliber Whisper suppressed rifle. Barnes produces two solid-copper .50-caliber X-Bullets, in 750 and 800 grains, with respective ballistic coefficients of 1.07 and 1.095. For several years, this excellent 800-grain projectile—designated its Long Range Solid—held the 1,000-yard world record.

Standard military .50-caliber ammo is not very accurate, but that's not surprising since machine gun rounds are intended to shoot a pattern, not a group. I've been told the U.S. standard for M2 .50-caliber ball is 12 inches at 600 yards, which is hardly the stuff of precision marksmanship.

U.S. military black-tipped armor-piercing rounds are fairly accurate because they retain their aerodynamic shape much better than ball, which tends to swell at its base during acceleration.

Another basic problem with conventional military ammo as a whole, one expert told me, is its heavy waterproofing of beeswax and lacquer. This makes for good shelf life and reliability in humid climates, but it causes inconsistent primer flash and variable pressure as the bullet separates from the case neck.

Scanning ballistic data for foreign cartridges, I found only one substitute load that approximates

.50-CALIBER COMBAT RECORDS

Born in the closing days of World War I, the .50-caliber cartridge came about when gunmaker John Browning was rushed to produce a heavy machine gun. To expedite things, he upscaled his already successful .30-caliber M1917 machine gun, proportionally scaling up its .30-06 cartridge and—*voila*, the .50 caliber!

Actually, this heavy machine gun was also the first .50-caliber sniper rifle, topped by a scope and fired single-shot during the Korean War. For the first time, an enemy could be engaged at such extreme range that he could not even hear the weapon's muzzle blast.

For lack of any other weapon that could reach the enemy soldiers he watched across Vietnam's An Lao Valley, legendary USMC sniper Carlos Hathcock similarly took the Unertl target scope off his Winchester M70 and put it atop a Browning .50 he'd selected for accuracy. Hathcock's resulting 2,500-yard shot, the longest known sniper kill of the Vietnam War, actually was part luck, he once told me. As he explained it, the flight time for so distant a shot was about 3 seconds, requiring that he aim where he reckoned the man would be rather than where he was. As luck would have it, his target—an enemy soldier squatting to fill his canteen—stood at the last possible second. If he hadn't, that 709-grain slug would have passed harmlessly over his head.

The author (R) with USMC sniping legend Carlos Hathcock, whose 2,500-yard record shot was exceeded only in 2002 by Canadian snipers in Afghanistan.

Gunny Hathcock's long-range record stood for 30 years, until Master Corporal Aaron Perry, a Canadian sniper from the 3rd Battalion, Princess Patricia's Light Infantry, scratched an al Qaeda fighter at 2,675 yards in Afghanistan's remote Shahi Kot Valley. The shooter, a young corporal from Newfoundland, benefited from his spotter lazing the target for an exact range. His rifle was a McMillan bolt action, firing high-grade Raufoss Mk 211 ammo he'd scrounged from his American allies.

Since that 2002 shot, there have been hundreds, perhaps thousands, of .50-caliber engagements in Afghanistan and Iraq, though none has yet surfaced that exceeds the Canadian record.

A Canadian sniper team in Afghanistan set a new world record for long-range sniping in 2002.

My good Special Forces friend Dr. B.R.G. Kaplan and his AMAC .50, which we fired extensively in the 1980s.

U.S. M2 ball ballistics, the British Mk 3Z, which is also a boat-tail and of identical weight and produces a muzzle velocity only 100 fps slower.

The good news is that American military snipers are no longer limited to such inconsistent .50-caliber loads. The first of these newer rounds, the SLAP—or Saboted Light Armor Penetrator—incorporates a .30-caliber, 415-grain tungsten penetrator enshrouded by a plastic sabot. It's available as a standard round, the M903, or a tracer version, the M962. Exiting the muzzle at a whopping 4,000 fps, it's undoubtedly America's flattest-firing small-arms projectile, while also offering considerable armored steel penetration—some 3/4 inch at 1,500 yards. The downside is that the SLAP round is not compatible with some rifles because its greater length will not allow it to chamber or can cause damage to the throat. I've also heard stories of plastic sabot bits gumming up muzzle brakes or being blown back on spotters. The bottom line: before firing SLAP ammo in your rifle, know for certain that it fits your chamber and is not a hazard to fire.

Thanks to the assistance of a SEAL sniper based in Bahrain, you'll find on page 269 all the comeups and MOAs needed to fire M962 SLAP tracer all the way to 2,000 yards. Note that I've listed the "book" MOA comeups beside his fine-tuned "actual" MOA comeups.

You should start with the book elevations; then, like the SEAL, fine-tune them precisely for your combination of rifle, scope, and

U.S. MILITARY .50-CAL. AMMUNITION

Type of Round	Marking	Muzz. Vel.	Max. Range
M2 Boattail Ball	No Marking	2930 fps	8140 yds
M2 AP	Black Tip	2930 fps	8140 yds
M8 AP/Incendiary	Alum. Tip or Alum. w/ Blue	3050 fps	7117 yds
M20 AP/Incendiary/Tracer	Aluminum Ring w/ Red Tip	3050 fps	7117 yds
M1 Tracer w/ Copper Jacket	Red/Maroon/Yellow Tip	2860 fps	6132 yds
M1 Tracer w/ Steel Jacket	Red/Maroon/Yellow Tip	3030 fps	5995 yds
M17 Tracer	Red/Maroon/Yellow Tip	3030 fps	5995 yds
M903/962 SLAP	Steel Tip in Amber Sabot	4000 fps	2500+ yds
Mk 211 Mod 0 Raufoss	Green Tip w/ Silver Ring	2918 fps	2500+ yds

M2 50-CAL. 709-GR. BT BULLET, MUZZLE VELOCITY 2,850 FPS
Distances in Yards/Trajectory in Inches

	100	200	300	400	500	600	700	800	900	1,000	1100	1200	1300	1400	1500
100	zero	-4.8	-14.6	-30.2	-52.2	-81.2	-118	-162	-218	-284	-363	-454	-561	-686	-831
200	+2.4	zero	-7.4	-20.6	-40.2	-66.8	-101	-143	-196	-260	-336	-425	-529	-653	-795
300	+4.8	+4.9	zero	-10.6	-27.7	-51.8	-83.3	-123	-194	-235	-309	-395	-497	-618	-758
400	+7.4	+10.2	+7.8	zero	-14.7	-36.2	-65.1	-102	-170	-209	-280	-364	-463	-581	-719
500	+10.	+16.0	+16.6	+11.7	zero	-18.6	-44.6	-79.0	-144	-180	-248	-328	-425	-540	-675
600	+13.4	+22.2	+25.9	+24.1	+15.5	zero	-22.9	-54.2	-116	-149	-214	-291	-385	-497	-628
700	+16.6	+28.7	+35.7	+37.1	+31.8	+19.6	zero	-28.1	-86.5	-116	-178	-252	-342	-451	-579
800	+20.1	+35.7	+46.2	+51.1	+49.3	+40.6	+24.5	zero	-55.0	-81.4	-139	-209	-297	-402	-526
900	+26.2	+47.9	+64.5	+75.5	+85.9	+77.2	+67.2	+48.8	zero	-20.3	-72.1	-137	-217	-317	-435
1000	+28.2	+51.9	+70.5	+83.6	+92.9	+89.3	+81.4	+65.0	+18.2	zero	-49.8	-112	-191	-288	-404
1100	+32.7	+60.9	+84.0	+102	+115	+116	+113	+101	+58.8	+45.2	zero	-58.1	-132	-225	-337
1200	+37.5	+70.5	+98.5	+121	+140	+145	+147	+140	+102	+93.6	+53.2	zero	-69.3	-157	-264
1300	+42.8	+81.1	+114	+142	+166	+177	+184	+182	+150	+147	+119	+64.0	zero	-82.7	-184
1400	+48.7	+92.9	+132	+166	+196	+213	+225	+230	+203	+206	+177	+135	+76.7	zero	-95.7
1500	+55.0	+105	+151	+191	+227	+251	+270	+281	+261	+274	+247	+211	+160	+89.3	zero

operating environment, which, like his dope, will vary somewhat.

I must also thank the same unnamed SEAL for providing similar comeup data on the M8 Armor-Piercing Incendiary (API) cartridge, which does double-service because it's ballistically comparable to our next new round, the Raufoss Mk 211 Mod 0.

Developed in Norway and manufactured under U.S. government contract by Olin-Winchester, the Raufoss is an exploding armor-piercing round containing a tungsten carbide penetrator. This sophisticated design incorporates a chain of tiny, split-second events that combine for awesome effect. During acceleration, an incendiary mix in the tip compresses slightly and forms a pocket of air. When that air pocket compresses on impact, it ignites the incendiary mix, and that sets off a tiny RDX explosive charge. Then the tungsten steel penetrator jolts forward, white-hot sparks of zirconium particles follow to flash-ignite fuel or

explosive vapors, while the bullet's soft jacket seals it against the impacted surface like a sloppy kiss. This would be impressive enough, but this 671-grain projectile's advanced design has also made it the most accurate military .50-caliber round in the inventory.

Please note: the Mk 211 Mod 0 is made in *two grades*, with the "A" grade offering better accuracy, firing on average a 3- to 4-inch group at 600 yards—1/2 MOA—from a test barrel, although the U.S. government considers a 6-inch group an acceptable standard. According to Norwegian data, the Raufoss round will penetrate up to 1/2 inch of armor at 1,100 yards. This Mk 211 Mod 0 has proved so popular among U.S. combat snipers that it's practically the only .50-caliber round they fire.

In 1999, the International Committee of the Red Cross (ICRC) unsuccessfully challenged combat employment of the Mk 211 Raufoss, claiming it violated the laws of war. Not only was this claim rejected, but on 14 January 2000, a

TRAJECTORY & MOA ELEVATION
M962 .50-Caliber
Saboted Light Armor Penetrator (Tracer)*
200 Yard Zero

Yards	Velocity	Trajectory	Book MOA	Actual MOA
100	3563	+0.1	—	—
200	3410	zero	zero	zero
300	3269	-3.1	1.00	1.00
400	3131	-9.5	2.50	2.50
500	2987	-19.4	4.00	4.75
600	2865	-33.2	5.50	5.25
700	2736	-51.2	7.25	7.00
800	2610	-73.8	9.25	8.75
900	2487	-101.6	11.25	10.75
1000	2368	-135.0	13.50	13.00
1100	2252	-174.6	16.00	15.25
1200	2139	-221.0	18.50	17.50
1300	2030	-275.0	21.25	20.25
1400	1925	-337.5	24.00	23.00
1500	1823	-409.4	27.25	26.00
1600	1726	-491.8	30.75	29.25
1700	1632	-585.7	34.50	33.00
1800	1543	-692.8	38.50	36.75
1900	1458	-814.6	43.00	41.00
2000	1377	-952.6	47.50	45.50

* SLAP ammo is not suitable or safe for some rifles.

TRAJECTORY & MOA ELEVATION
M8 .50-Caliber
Armor-Piercing Incendiary (API) *
200 Yard Zero

Yards	Velocity	Trajectory	Book MOA	Actual MOA
100	2594	-1.3	-1.5	-1.5
200	2443	zero	zero	zero
300	2297	-7.2	2.25	2.25
400	2157	-20.9	5.25	5.00
500	2022	-42.1	8.25	8.00
600	1843	-71.8	12.00	11.50
700	1770	-111.2	15.75	15.25
800	1653	-161.7	20.25	19.25
900	1543	-225.0	25.00	24.00
1000	1443	-302.7	30.25	29.00
1100	1342	-397.2	36.00	34.50
1200	1253	-511.0	42.50	40.75
1300	1170	-646.8	49.75	47.50
1400	1094	-807.8	57.75	55.00
1500	1025	-997.6	66.50	63.50
1600	964	-1219.0	76.00	73.00
1700	910	-1478.0	86.00	83.00
1800	861	-1777.0	98.75	94.25
1900	819	-2120.0	111.50	106.50
2000	782	-2512.0	125.50	120.00

* This round approximates the Raufoss Mk 211 Grade A trajectory.

U.S. Department of Defense review reconfirmed that the Mk 211 was legal to employ against both materiel and personnel targets. Propaganda generated by the ICRC claim has been sufficient that some American snipers in Iraq actually carry with them copies of the Department of Defense legal review.

More recently, research has begun on a new .50-caliber sniping round, an especially accurate projectile for antipersonnel use. Dubbed the XM1022, or Long Range Tactical Sniper Cartridge, its trajectory will parallel the Raufoss so a sniper can switch from one to the other and use the same BDC settings.

Earlier research on a depleted-uranium projectile has apparently gone by the wayside. I had a chance to examine one of these bullets, which had the same dimensions as a 709-grain slug, but it weighed twice as much. While that denser mass meant more momentum and better penetration, it also meant considerably more recoil to attain the velocity needed for long-range shooting.

LONG-RANGE ACCURACY

Like a test pilot exploring the limits of his flight envelope, Skip Talbot test-fired his .50 caliber at quite extreme ranges—up to 3,000 yards, the greatest credible accuracy experiment I've yet come across. Firing his custom civilian match rounds at an 8 x 10-foot

Barrier penetrators include (L-R) SSK's .50, black-tipped military AP round, Raufoss Mk 211, SLAP discarding sabot load, and solid leaded steel projectile.

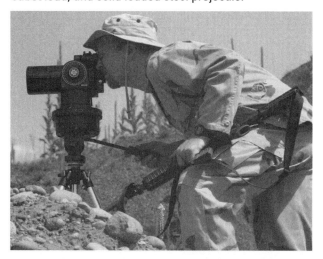

Extreme-range spotting may require the higher magnification of an astral telescope.

MOVING TARGET LEADS
.50-caliber M2 709-gr. BT Ball

Yards	Seconds in Flight	Walking (2 mph)	Running (6 mph)
100	.1081	3.81"	11.40"
200	.2213	7.78"	23.34"
300	.3396	11.94"	35.83"
400	.4638	16.30"	48.90"
500	.5955	20.93"	62.79"
600	.7340	25.80"	77.40"
700	.8788	30.89"	92.67"
800	1.0313	36.26"	108.78"
900	1.1943	41.99"	125.97"
1000	1.3677	48.08"	144.24"
1100	1.5504	54.51"	163.53"
1200	1.7412	61.22"	183.66"
1300	1.9450	68.38"	205.14"
1400	2.1621	76.01"	228.03"
1500	2.3907	84.05"	252.15"

panel, he scored many hits, about 85 percent of shots fired.

Interpreting these results, it means a rifleman armed with a .50 could readily hit parked enemy aircraft up to 9,000 feet—nearly 2 miles—away. The spotter would need an astral telescope to watch the impacts, but with some adjustment the team should be able to score hits against large point targets such as engines and cockpits.

I frequently fired an AMAC .50 at man-

UP/DOWN COMPENSATION FOR .50-CALIBER M2 709-GR. BT BALL
Inches of Compensation/Hundreds of Yards

Target Angle	100	200	300	400	500	600	700	800	900	1000
45 Degrees	0.6	2.7	6.2	11.4	18.5	27.6	38.9	52.7	69.4	89.6
60 Degrees*	1.1	4.6	11.5	19.5	31.5	47.2	67.0	90.0	118	153

* Maximum Effect

sized 55-gallon drums 1,250 yards away during demonstrations of M2 ball accuracy and penetration. I hit the drum about 70 percent of the time, while a couple of our marksmanship instructors did a bit better.

Dr. Kaplan, a master shooter and guest instructor at several sniper courses, once demonstrated how fast and easy he could hone in with his AMAC sniper rifle. Starting with the scope set for 400 yards, he fired just two spotter rounds, then put the third through a waist-high silhouette target 1,500 yards away. This was with Thunderbird civilian rounds.

Some of the most accurate civilian .50-caliber shooting involves the "free recoil" firing technique, by which the gun is heavily sandbagged, then fine-adjusted. At the instant of firing, only the shooter's finger touches the gun. Skip Talbot used the free-recoil technique to shoot his world record group, as do many benchrest shooting champions.

OPTICS FOR .50-CAL. SHOOTING

Most rifle scopes compatible with .308 rifles are not suited to their bigger .50-caliber cousins. First, many scopes cannot handle the greater Gs of heavy recoil, even though recoil is considerably dampened by a muzzle brake. It isn't that they're shaken apart, but their waterproof seals can crack, and the elevation and windage gears may slip.

Second, the greater distances of .50-caliber engagements imply higher magnification to achieve target clarity. This higher power also suggests a larger objective lens, so there's little or no decline in the exit pupil, which is the cone of light that reaches your eye. This can prove critical in low-light situations.

But most importantly, a .50-caliber scope needs more elevation—more Minutes of Angle—to coincide with the greater engagement

The Nightforce NXS 5-25x56mm has a superb reputation for heavy rifle sniping.

This special version of the USMC Unertl 10x scope has a BDC calibrated for .50-caliber trajectory.

TARGET KNOB SCOPES FOR .50 CALS.

Model	Maximum Elevation
Nightforce NXS 5.5-25x56	100 MOA
Nightforce NXS 3.5-15x50	110 MOA
Leupold Mark 4 M1 10x	90 MOA
Leupold Mark 4 M1 16x	140 MOA
Nikon Tactical 4-16x50	85 MOA
Burris Xtreme Tactical 3-12x50	90 MOA
Burris Xtreme Tactical 10x50	90 MOA
Swarovski PV 4-16x50 P	65 MOA
Zeiss VM/V 6-24x56	60 MOA
Zeiss Diavari V 6-24x72	63 MOA

Note: Not all Leupold or Nightforce tactical scopes are listed.

The 16x Leupold Mark 4 is the scope found on most U.S. military .50-cal. rifles, such as this Barrett M107.

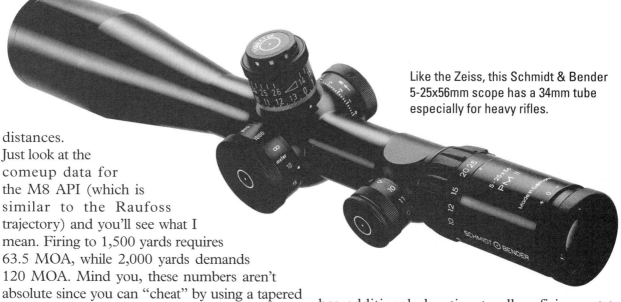

Like the Zeiss, this Schmidt & Bender 5-25x56mm scope has a 34mm tube especially for heavy rifles.

distances.

Just look at the comeup data for the M8 API (which is similar to the Raufoss trajectory) and you'll see what I mean. Firing to 1,500 yards requires 63.5 MOA, while 2,000 yards demands 120 MOA. Mind you, these numbers aren't absolute since you can "cheat" by using a tapered mount or shims and zeroing your rifle at 500 yards to increase your potential MOAs. But still, many of the scopes found in Chapter 3 simply cannot offer enough elevation to shoot much beyond 1,000 yards.

What about target knobs versus a BDC? The only BDC-fitted sniperscope commonly found on a .50 is a special version of the Unertl 10x that the Marine Corps uses with its Barrett Special Application Scoped Rifle. Although its elevation adjusts at 1/2 MOA clicks just like the version found on 7.62mm rifles, this .50 model has additional elevation to allow firing out to 2,000 yards. The Unertl's left side is marked ".50 Caliber."

Other scopes use 1/4 MOA target knobs, and with good reason. By the time you're shooting 1,500 yards, a .50-caliber bullet's arc is plunging so sharply that precision adjustments become critical. If you're a bit off with a 1/2 MOA scope, one click is now 7 1/2 inches—that's the finest you can adjust—while 1/4 MOA equates to 3 3/4 inches.

We've listed sniper-grade scopes offering the

Sporting an immense 72mm objective lens and 34mm tube, this Zeiss 6-24x scope was designed especially for heavy rifle sniping.

required elevation, but it's worth taking a closer look at some of them. The excellent Nightforce NXS scopes offer not just sufficient elevation but quality glass and high magnification, up to 25x.

I've fired the Leupold 16x a great deal on .50s and can say nothing but good about it. It's military-rugged and holds true to the elevation and windage settings. This scope is found on many U.S. .50-caliber rifles.

I've not fired the listed Nikon or Burris scopes, so I cannot offer much personal insight. However, I have fired Swarovski long-range scopes and found their optics excellent and adjustments true. The same can be said for Schmidt & Bender, whose 5-25x56mm scope was purposely designed for heavy sniper rifles. Quite impressively, it incorporates a 34mm tube, which both reduces distortion and yields extra elevation. It's available with either 1/4 MOA or metric adjustments.

Zeiss, too, has developed a special heavy rifle sniperscope, and like Schmidt & Bender, it sports a 34mm tube. However, this impressive piece of glass also has a 72mm objective lens, the largest I've ever seen on a quality scope, larger than some spotting scopes. It has an illuminated mil dot reticle, as do several of these .50-caliber scopes. It's hard not to like all these optics.

When it comes to spotting, heavier magni-fication comes in handy. I like at least a 30x spotting scope or it's difficult to see enough detail to prioritize extreme-range targets, although afternoon heat can cause mirage problems. Some .50-caliber sniper teams spot with an astral telescope—the kind normally used to search the night sky—and that works great, as long as you accept the considerable decline in field of view. It's usually bigger and heavier, too.

THE EXTREME-RANGE SHOOTING ENVIRONMENT

The importance of accurate range calculation is never so great as when shooting at extreme distances. The farther your bullet travels, the more its trajectory becomes a plunging arc, where even tiny errors grow into major significance. A range estimation error of only 5 percent means little at 400 yards, but at 1,500 yards that puts your .50-caliber projectile's impact point about 8 minutes long or short. Your bullet will sail a dozen feet over your target's head or thud harmlessly into the ground yards short of him. A long-range laser allows precision measurement, but for extreme distances that device must be aimed as carefully as a rifle, with keen awareness to avoid lazing beyond or before the target's actual location.

Wind estimation, too, gets tricky at extreme distances. Try to monitor the wind at three or four points between you and the target to ensure you don't overlook contradictory crosswinds. Observing falling rain or snow helps to identify such winds.

Correctly interpreting the effect of distant oblique winds becomes critical as well. For instance, when firing 709-grain M2 ball at 1,500 yards, a relatively mild 5 mph wind mistakenly judged to be coming across at 1:30 o'clock but actually crossing at 2 o'clock will cause a lateral compensation error of 18 inches—quite likely a complete miss.

Extreme-range shooting opens us to all sorts of ballistic concerns and factors that had seemed only esoteric at shorter distances. Due to your bullet's considerable time of flight, you must attune yourself to interpreting human visual cues to ensure that your target remains stationary long enough for the bullet to reach him. At 1,500 yards, a .50's flight time is 2.3 seconds, plenty of time for a sitting man to stand or a stationary man to take a step. In order to shoot where he is—not where he was—you must time your shot.

Time of flight also relates to the rotational speed of the earth. In a single day—one earth rotation—the planet turns approximately 25,000 miles at the equator, which equates to 1,042 mph, or 1,531 fps, with slightly less relative speed as you approach the poles. Your bullet's speed will vary a tiny amount, depending on whether you're shooting with or against the earth's rotation or angled away from the equator. It's a tiny, tiny amount, but its influence, too, grows with distance.

Likewise with the Coriolis effect. In 1835, Gustave de Coriolis, for who the effect is named, demonstrated that the Earth's rotation affects winds and ocean currents and even dictates whether your toilet flushes water clockwise or counterclockwise. Like a curveball leaving a pitcher's hand, your bullet is slightly affected by the Coriolis effect. It's not enough to matter at 1,000 yards or less, but its influence grows with range.

Theoretically, a headwind slightly increases drag on your bullet and thereby reduces its velocity, while a tailwind has the opposite effect. Thus, a headwind requires that you raise your elevation slightly, and a tailwind dictates that you lower it slightly. The formula for calculating the required compensation, according to 19th-century firearms authority W.W. Greener, is:

$$\frac{\text{Wind Velocity (MPH) x Distance (Hundreds of Yards)}}{4 \text{ (Math Constant)}} = \text{Yards of Range Change}$$

Using Greener's formula, let's calculate the compensation for a tailwind of 20 mph when engaging a target at 1,550 yards.

$$\frac{20 \text{ (MPH) x 15.5 (Hundreds of Yards)}}{4 \text{ (Math Constant)}} = \frac{310}{4} = 77.5 \text{ Yards}$$

Therefore, reset your elevation 77.5 yards closer, as if the target were at 1,422.5 yards, *but do so with caution.* Consider this: there's no variance in Greener's formula for a constant wind pushing on your bullet's full trajectory and a wind that affects it during only part of its flight. That's pretty substantial.

Air pressure matters, too, for the denser air at low altitude slows your bullet and the thinner air at high altitudes allows your bullet to fly faster. Then there's temperature, especially ammo temperature, because warmer gunpowder burns a bit faster than cooler gunpowder, with a resulting variance on muzzle velocity.

M2 .50-CAL. 709-GR. BT BULLET DRIFT IN A 10 MPH, 90-DEGREE CROSSWIND

Yards	100	200	300	400	500	600	700	800	900	1000	1100	1200	1300	1400	1500
Drift	0.5"	1.9"	4.2"	7.5"	12"	18"	25"	33"	43"	56"	69"	84"	101"	121"	143"

Nuances in up/down angles matter, too.

By now you're saying to yourself, how's a sniper to keep track of all these things without a computer? *Exactly!* That's what the long-range shooting specialists at CheyTac Associates realized, inspiring them to devise a special ballistics computer program for handheld PCs that takes into account all these meteorological factors, plus a dozen other considerations. Not only does their Advanced Ballistic Computer calculate the exact target knob settings to engage a target up to 2,500 yards away, it simultaneously keeps track of multiple ammo types for instantly switching the settings, say, from a SLAP round to a Raufoss Mk 211. Their programming has been tested against real-world results at the Department of Defense's Yuma Proving Grounds, using a Weibler high-speed radar. Because it is designed specifically for extreme-range shooting, I don't know of any other software that so perfectly fits the needs of heavy rifle sniping. When used in tandem with its cutting-edge .408 CheyTac rifle, this system offers incredible potential.

TACTICAL EMPLOYMENT

You can exploit an enemy's ignorance of your effective range and the long-range threat posed by a heavy rifle, especially when occupying a new position in those first few days on a stabilizing battlefield, before he appreciates the power of your optics and the reach of your bullets. This is prime shooting time.

On the other hand, when moving into established defensive positions, you may wish to just surveil and observe for a few days and record an elaborate range card before you fire your first shot. If your shooting is effective, the enemy soon will improve camouflage, shift his movement beyond your vision, and improve ballistic protection around his positions. By then it seems

.50-CALIBER BALL BULLET PENETRATION DATA
Distance in Meters

	200	600	1500
SAND (100-lb. Dry Wt./Cubic Ft.)	14"	12"	6"
CLAY (100-lb. Dry Wt./Cubic Ft.)	28"	26"	21"
CONCRETE	2"	1"	1"

.50-CALIBER ARMOR-PIERCING BULLET PENETRATION DATA
Distance in Meters

	200	600	1500
ARMOR PLATE (Homogeneous)	1.0"	0.7"	0.3"
ARMOR PLATE (Face-Hardened)	0.9"	0.5"	0.2"
SAND (100-lb. Dry Wt./Cubic Ft.)	14"	12"	6"
CLAY (100-lb. Dry Wt./Cubic Ft.)	28"	27"	21"

MAX ARMOR THICKNESS ON SELECTED SOVIET ARMORED VEHICLES
(measured perpendicularly)

	BMP	BMD	BTR-60	BRDM-2	BRDM	PT-76	ACRV	MTLB
HULL	0.8"	0.6"	0.4"	0.6"	0.6"	0.6"	0.6"	0.3"
TURRET	0.9"	1.0"	0.3"	0.3"	—	0.7"	0.8"	0.3"

SHORT-RANGE MEDIA PENETRATION BY .50-CAL. AP ROUNDS

Medium	Penetration @ 100 Yards
CONCRETE (solid)	9 inches
TIMBER (logs)	96 inches
STEEL (nonarmored)	1.8 inches
ALUMINUM	3.5 inches
RUBBLE (asphalt, soil, cement)	20 inches
TAMPED SNOW (19.9–24.9 lbs./cu. ft.)	77 inches
DRY SOIL	28 inches
WET SOIL	42 inches
DRY SAND	24 inches
WET SAND	36 inches
DRY CLAY	42 inches
WET CLAY	64 inches

An efficient muzzle brake reduces recoil but boosts the visual signature, especially on dusty, sandy soil.

impossible to find him, but your previous surveillance and range card data will enable you to engage his concealed positions for some time.

Due to their weight and bulk, .50-caliber rifles are not suited for direct assaults or classic sniper stalking. Indeed, U.S. Marine Corps and Army sniper teams outfitted with these heavy rifles typically have at least three men, and they're used almost exclusively in a support role for other maneuver forces. Although .50s are welcome support weapons for almost any kind of operation, they're especially useful for neutralizing enemy positions and crew-served weapons. It's their tremendous ability to penetrate bunkers and buildings that makes them so deadly, as reflected in the penetration data we've listed.

But also beware. The same efficient muzzle brake that makes recoil tolerable also produces a visible blast that begs for enemy counterfire and pulses a blast that can deafen you. A .50-caliber sniper needs to wear *double* hearing protection—ear plugs beneath earmuffs—which is absolutely critical when firing from inside a building or amid trees or rocks.

AWC System Technologies manufactures a special .50-caliber suppressor that addresses both these issues. Threaded to replace the muzzle brake, the AWC Turbodyne suppressor is 2 inches wide and a foot long, and it dramatically reduces the blast signature while also reducing sound so well that ear protection is not

The AWC Turbodyne suppressor reduces a .50's sound signature and blast well below that of a 30.06.

needed. Gemtech, too, manufactures a .50-caliber suppressor, the Stormfront, designed specifically for the Barrett M107 rifle.

Lacking such technological solutions, you'll have to resort to the tried and true—wear double hearing protection and, to avoid counterfire, displace after each shot.

Police Employment of Heavy Rifles

When I suggest to police audiences that their departments need at least one on-call .50, eyes roll toward the ceiling and a few muffled laughs are heard. But then I cite the modern urban environment, with skyscraper rooftops a half-mile apart and recall Austin killer Charles Whitman's ghastly record. If not a .50, what *can* reach such a gunman? Or how about the New Orleans sniper who barricaded himself for hours in a reinforced concrete shaft that proved impervious to hundreds of bullets fired over eight hours? The .50 caliber is well-suited to antihijacking and antismuggling roles, too, in which the law officer must disable aircraft, boats, or vehicles at moderate to great distances.

And penetration? I know of at least one case in which criminals crudely but effectively armored their vehicle, then shot one policeman to death and ran another down, the lawmen's guns having no effect. What happens when a crazy or terrorist commandeers heavy highway equipment or a bank armored car? I once helped a law enforcement agency photograph and analyze an anti-IRS revolutionary fringe hideout in a rural area, which contained log and earthen bunkers that easily could withstand ordinary pistol and rifle fire.

The heavy tempered and laminated glass in some modern commercial buildings, too, makes for very iffy penetration by .30-caliber weapons. In one imperfect 1991 hostage-rescue attempt, this fact contributed to the deaths of several hostages, which would not have been the case had the police sniper had a .50 caliber.

That's exactly what happened in Granby, Colorado, in June 2004. Marvin Heemeyer, 52, took several weeks to armor his 60-ton D5 bulldozer, surrounding the cab with cast concrete and welded steel shooting ports. He even installed an air conditioner and video cameras to monitor the outside. During an hour-long rampage, Heemeyer rammed 13 buildings, oblivious to hundreds of rounds fired at him by police and SWAT officers. Finally, after his dozer bogged down in a demolished hardware store, he shot himself. Inside the makeshift tank, police found a small arsenal of weapons, including one they most needed that day—a .50-caliber rifle.

The .50 caliber in police arsenals? You bet.

Undersheriff Glen Trainor fires 37 rounds of .40-caliber pistol ammo into makeshift "tank" in Granby, Colorado. Despite his courage, his shots could not halt the rampaging behemoth. (Photo credit: Mountain Power & Electric.)

The five-shot McMillan M1987/R: simple, solid, reliable—and very accurate.

McMillan's Combo .50 features fast takedown for convenient transportation.

AMERICAN BOLT-ACTION .50s

It has been the United States that has led the world in the development of .50-caliber, target-grade rifles for military and law enforcement snipers. When combined with match-grade ammunition and suitable optics, these weapons can produce 1 MOA accuracy, which means 10-inch groups at 1,000 yards, a very lethal size, or 20-inch groups at 2,000 yards, a wider spread that should still hit a silhouette target about 50 percent of the time.

McMillan entered the heavy gun arena in 1987 with its M1987 and M1987/R rifles, respectively single-shot and five-shot .50-caliber sniper-grade weapons. Intended for shooting in

excess of 1,500 yards, these relatively lightweight guns—25 pounds with optics—incorporate advanced muzzle brakes and sizable recoil pads to tame the potent .50-caliber recoil. These rifles are simple, solid, and reliable, with all the accuracy tunings found in lighter McMillan rifles.

The newer M88 McMillan uses the same five-round, fixed-magazine action as the M1987/R but adds a quick breakdown capability for easy backpack transportation, a design requirement reportedly generated by U.S. Navy SEALs. Also called the Combo .50, its highly adjustable stock disassembles at a joint just behind the trigger group.

Special attention is due McMillan's oversize

The hinged stock and shorter barrel on this Robar RC50F allows compact transportation.

These SSK man-packable .50s weigh 13 lbs. each and fire a round based on the .460 Weatherby. The lower version sports an integral suppressor.

Remington-style .50-caliber action since it has been incorporated in many custom .50s, including Skip Talbot's world record setter.

Robbie Barrkman, former gunsmith-in-residence at Gunsite and head of Robar Companies, uses the McMillan 700-style action in his hand-built .50-caliber sniper rifles. I've fired both his fine RC50, fitted with a fixed stock, and his RC50F, with a hinged, side-folding buttstock. Both these Robars and the McMillans are unmatched for accuracy and quality.

Offering his own approach to .50-caliber sniper rifles is the always innovative J.D. Jones, president of SSK Industries, famous for developing the Whisper family of subsonic, suppressed cartridges. To pack a .50's punch into a very handy 13-pound rifle, he blew out a .460 Weatherby Magnum case to .50 caliber, then loaded it with an excellent 750-grain Hornady Match bullet. I first fired this cartridge-rifle combo, called the Peacekeeper, at Ft. Bragg's JFK Special Warfare Center a few

years ago, and then later borrowed one for further testing at Gunsite. That weight really dampened recoil, allowing me to fire it off the shoulder, while the suppressor proved so effective that—although firing virtually an elephant gun—I didn't have to wear hearing protection. I was frankly amazed at how well Jones had made this roaring lion purr so gently.

FOREIGN BOLT-ACTION .50s

Having watched the United States develop .50-caliber rifles and the doctrine for their employment, many foreign countries are fielding or acquiring similar weapons. Some are of extremely high quality, but not all of them. Five years ago, by chance I was on an Eastern European rifle range the same morning that a crowd of military officers and defense officials were observing a demonstration of their country's new .50-caliber bolt-action rifle. With one glance, I could see that its designer hadn't

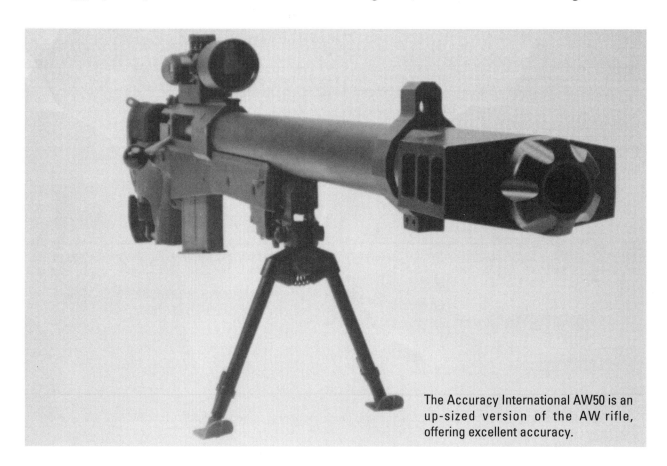

The Accuracy International AW50 is an up-sized version of the AW rifle, offering excellent accuracy.

U.S. Marine Scout-Snipers fire a French PGM 50 rifle during a visit to Djibouti on Africa's east coast.

The Russian KSVK .50-cal., a relatively new development, is primarily an antimateriel rifle.

the slightest idea of what makes a rifle accurate—he'd actually spot-welded the folding bipod and a carrying handle midway along the barrel (!) and incorporated a quick-release scope mount that was so flimsy it couldn't possibly hold zero under such pounding recoil. Fired at 500 meters, the demonstrator found it almost impossible to keep his slugs on a 4 x 4-foot panel. Despite that, his country went ahead and put it into production, later sending me a brochure that confidently proclaimed, "It is very accurate up to 2,000 meters."

By contrast, I can vouch that these next three foreign .50s *are* accurate weapons. The Accuracy International AW50 is an upsized version of Olympic Gold Medal champion Malcolm Cooper's earlier AW series sniper rifles. Unlike the earlier rifles, the AW50 incorporates a Picatinny rail, a fluted barrel (to reduce weight and improve cooling), and a folding buttstock and readily mounts an optional suppressor.

The Austrian firm Steyr recently added a bolt-action .50 to its weapon line, which includes such prestigious guns as the AUG and SSG rifles. A few years ago, Steyr was experimenting with a .60-caliber (15.2mm) that used a flechette projectile but apparently let that program fall by the wayside. The Steyr HS .50 is a conventional, single-shot rifle that features a hammer-forged barrel, Picatinny rail, and two-stage trigger.

The French-made PGM Hecate II is a skeletonized bolt action incorporating a five-

The French-made Hecate II is marketed in the United States by FNH.

round detachable magazine, match-grade fluted barrel, and two-stage trigger. Marketed in the United States by FNH—the conglomerate that includes Browning and Winchester—it's the standard heavy rifle for the French armed forces and a few foreign countries. I've not fired it, but people who have tell me it's on a par with the better .50s.

Beyond these are a host of Eastern European .50 calibers that undoubtedly offer great terminal ballistics, but I'm not so sure about accuracy. The absence of high-grade, match-quality .50 ammo in the former Soviet bloc—as essential to accuracy as the rifles themselves—leaves open the question of real precision. Thus, although the Serbian M-93 Crna Strela ("Black Arrow") uses a modified Mauser-style action and a free-floated barrel, I'm not sure that it's very effective past 1,000 yards. Likewise, the Russian KSVK .50-caliber rifle sports a free-floated barrel and appears to be of modern design; yet, one wonders, how accurate could it be considering the quality of the optic on it and military ball ammo that probably cannot shoot better than 4 or 5 MOA? Until these rifles are more extensively tested in the West, the jury remains out.

The Barrett M107, used throughout the U.S. military.

Marine snipers in Iraq firing the Barrett Special Application Scoped Rifle.

BARRETT SEMIAUTO .50s

America's only semiauto .50-caliber rifle is made by Barrett Firearms Manufacturing of Murfreesboro, Tennessee. Though several other semiautos have come and gone since Ronnie Barrett designed his original .50 in 1982, only his recoil-operated design has stood the test of time.

Today this 10-round, detachable-magazine rifle is found all around the world, the model varied for its user and application. Military engineers employ its countermine version to demolish mines from a safe distance. The USMC version, the M82A3 Special Application Scoped Rifle (SASR, pronounced "Sasser") was the starting point for the newest evolution, the M107 Long Range Sniper Rifle, developed in conjunction with snipers from the U.S. Army Special Operations Target Interdiction Course (SOTIC) at Ft. Bragg.

Interestingly, when the M107 selection process began, it appeared that only pinpoint-accurate bolt guns were considered, but further analysis revealed that every real-world target destroyed by a .50—from barricaded snipers in Bosnia to Scud missiles in Iraq—required several hits. To reduce engagement time and thereby reduce the counterfire threat to snipers, logic suggested, it's necessary to fire those rounds quick and depart—to "shoot and scoot." Thus a rifle offering fast follow-on shots and reasonable magazine capacity rose to the top—the Barrett.

It is now being fielded throughout the U.S. armed forces.

The M107 Long Range Sniper Rifle has a lengthy Picatinny rail running from the receiver across the forearm that can accommodate a night vision adaptive sight—like the Simrad—ahead of its Leupold daytime optic. The threaded muzzle on its match-grade-fluted barrel can mount either an efficient muzzle brake or a newly developed suppressor that reduces both recoil and sound signature. The M107 is considered capable of hitting individual personnel out to 1,500 meters and materiel targets to 2,000 meters.

When used in civilian competition, the semiauto .50 has not shot quite as well as its finely tuned bolt-action cousins. Current 1,000-yard, five-shot, semiauto world records, according to the Fifty Caliber Shooters Association, are held by Ed Brown with a group of 12.25 inches and Del Dimick with 12.75 inches. This equates to a 1.25 MOA, or 25 inches at 2,000 yards, pretty impressive by anyone's standard.

Initial M107 combat results from Afghanistan and Iraq have been extremely impressive. A U.S. Army sniper with the 325th Parachute Infantry Regiment reports he engaged an Iraqi with an RPG atop a water tower at a lazed distance of 1,400 meters. "The top half of the torso fell forward out of the tower and the lower portion remained in the tower," he told a debriefer. U.S. Army Lt. Col. Jim Smith reported, "Soldiers not only appreciated the range and accuracy, but also the target effect. Leaders and scouts viewed the effect of the .50 cal. round as a combat multiplier due to the psychological impact on other combatants that viewed the destruction of the target."

The Barrett rifle was used extensively by U.S. Marines assaulting Fallujah, Iraq, in 2004. The M107 won many engagements against hidden RPG gunners, snipers, and ambushers by punching through walls and barriers, with precision fire delivered over the heads of fellow Marines. I recently spoke with a USMC sniper who had nothing but praise for his SASR .50-caliber. Some of the lessons learned in Fallujah will influence heavy rifle sniping tactics and techniques for the next 20 years.

Barrett is now developing an even more advanced antimateriel rifle, based on this proven semiauto rifle. Chambered for a new 25x59mm cartridge, this man-portable gun more truly is an antimateriel weapon, not a sniper rifle. It's addressed below, along with 14.5mm and 20mm rifles.

In early 2006, Barrett fielded a new, cutting-edge, proprietary cartridge, dubbed the .416 Barrett, for which it is chambering updated versions of its M82A1M and M90 rifles. In its initial loading, this advanced, low-drag Barrett round features a 395-grain, moly-coated brass, match-grade bullet that generates a muzzle velocity of 3,300 fps. With a surprisingly high ballistic coefficient of 0.989, the new Barrett round is still supersonic at 2,000 yards and, according to Barrett's Dan Goodwin, fires groups measuring a mere 0.5 MOA. In addition to this step forward in ballistic performance, Goodwin notes, the new Barrett cartridge is "California legal" since it is not, by that states's definition, a .50-caliber round.

THE CHEYTAC .408 SYSTEM

The .50-caliber cartridge, developed almost 100 years ago, was not conceived or designed for accuracy, though recent decades of tweaking have improved it considerably. What if, instead, you began from scratch to design a modern cartridge that efficiently integrated all the breakthroughs in powder plasma physics, reduced drag bullets, and match-grade bullet manufacturing? Then, you fitted that new round to a rifle that incorporated what we better understand about rifle building—barrel harmonics, bedding, triggers, bolt faces, and such. And finally, you integrated this rifle and cartridge with a specialized ballistic program as sophisticated as anything produced by NASA for interplanetary probes, taking into account all the ways a bullet's trajectory is influenced.

That's the CheyTac .408.

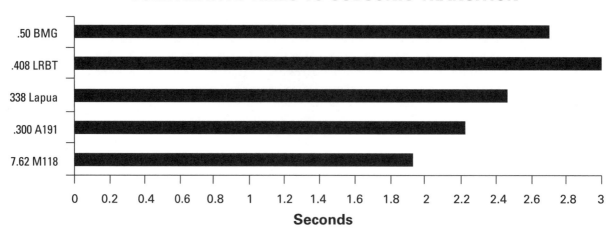

COMPARATIVE TIMES TO SUBSONIC TRANSITION

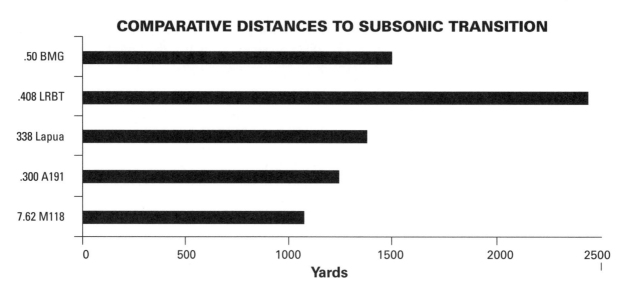

COMPARATIVE DISTANCES TO SUBSONIC TRANSITION

In July 2004, the company reports, a U.S. Marine sniper team fired an informal world record with this combination of cartridge, rifle, and ballistic computer, yielding a three-round group that measured 16 5/8 inches at 2,321 yards. Another Marine sniper from Quantico reports he scored a first-round hit against a target lazed at 2,460 yards, despite a moderate crosswind. A technician from the Army's Aberdeen Proving Ground—shooting into a crosswind of 10–17 mph—made a first-round hit against a 12-inch square target at 1,346 yards.

CheyTac fielded its revolutionary shooting system in 2002 after it was jointly developed by Lost River Ballistic Technologies and Tactical High Energy Impact Systems. This combination of physicists, bullet designers, gun builders, and a retired Special Ops sniper instructor began by developing the .408 cartridge and projectiles. The resulting two stream-lined (low-drag) bullets weigh 419 grains (3,000 fps muzzle) and 305 grains (3,500 fps). Machined from solid copper-nickel alloy, they're turned on a computer-controlled lathe for absolutely perfect consistency and a tip as sharp as a dart.

As shown in the data boxes above, the .408 projectile remains supersonic longer and farther

Supported by its Advanced Ballistic Computer (R), this CheyTac .408 M200 rifle is capable of amazing extreme-range shooting.

Using a more conventional Remington-style action and McMillan A-5 stock, the CheyTac M310 is also chambered for the .408 round.

seven-round magazine. The less elaborate—and presumably more economical—M310 is a single-shot bolt action, conventional in design and appearance. Neither of these rifles is claimed to outperform the other, with the company suggesting, "In the hands of a trained shooter, the CheyTac cartridge can hit a man-size target at 1.5 miles and beyond."

CheyTac recommends the Nightforce NXS 5-25x56mm scope as most compatible with its rifles and the .408 round.

As much as the bullet and rifle, it is CheyTac's Advanced Ballistic Computer that yields such incredible extreme-range accuracy. This software program, designed for a handheld PC, takes into account more variables than I've ever seen in ballistic software, including Earth rotation, impact area size, and spin drift. These theoretical values and formulas were calibrated against actual bullet flights monitored by sophisticated Doppler radar at the Army's Yuma Proving Ground to fine-tune the program. The result is that when punching in the data and lazing your target at 2,147 yards, the program doesn't print a chart with MOAs for 2,100 and 2,200 but tells you the exact target knob settings to actually hit at 2,147 yards. I believe this is precisely the kind of trailblazing technique and technology that will inspire the next advance in sniper weapon evolution.

than other sniping rounds, even the .300 WinMag and .338 Lapua Magnum. Further, it achieves this with considerably less report and muzzle blast than a .50 caliber, reducing the shooter's visual and sound signature. Because of superior retained velocity and its solid bullet, the .408 still achieves dramatic terminal effect despite being 30 percent lighter than its typical .50-caliber counterpart. Though the .50 generates 50 percent greater ft-lbs. of energy at the muzzle, beyond 700 yards the more streamlined .408 overtakes it, offering more impact energy. Company tests have shown its projectiles will penetrate Level IIIA body armor at more than 2,000 yards.

CheyTac offers two rifles chambered for this unique round. The M200 bolt-action, a skeletonized design, is scaled down from the earlier Windrunner .50 and features a Picatinny rail, butt adjustable for height and length, and detachable

THE HEAVIEST HEAVIES

The most powerful cartridge ever used for sniping is the Soviet 14.5mm, which is also the world's heaviest machine gun round, being about twice as massive as the .50-caliber Browning cartridge. The 14.5mm is slightly over 6 inches in length.

The Soviets developed the 14.5mm in the 1930s for their PTRS and PTRD antitank rifles. Today, it's fired by the KPV heavy machine gun as mounted on BTR-60 wheeled armored personnel carriers and BRDM-2 scout cars, while it's also found in Third World countries in the antiaircraft role on ZPU dual and quad mounts.

U.S. Army Col. Frank Conway used obsolescent Soviet PTRD antitank rifle actions in

The South African NTW 20mm
is a true antimateriel rifle.

1954 as the basis for his Aberdeen Proving Ground tests of experimental .50-caliber sniper rifles. According to Peter R. Senich's *Complete Book of U.S. Sniping* (Paladin Press, 1988), the fitting of quality U.S. barrels to these Soviet actions resulted in excellent accuracy, with claims of 10-inch groups at 1,000 yards.

But the 14.5mm cartridge itself was not employed in sniping until recent conflicts—especially Afghanistan—where terrain necessitated squeezing out ever greater range from sniper weapons. Pakistani custom gun makers reportedly hand-built 14.5mm sniper rifles with which the mujahideen played hell with Soviet occupation forces at ranges up to 2 miles. These custom rifles, however, were much too heavy and unwieldy for anything other than stationary employment. Some foreign forces may have found the 14.5mm performance interesting enough to conduct their own recent testing.

Russia now produces three 14.5mm rounds, the most suitable for sniping being the Type BS-41, a 994-grain armor-piercing/incendiary bullet having a muzzle velocity of 3,300 fps. This equates to 2.2 ounces, or about *twice* the weight of a typical 12-gauge shotgun slug, except instead of a blunt projectile exiting a shotgun at 1,600 fps, you have a twice-as-heavy aerodynamic missile screaming downrange at double that velocity.

The Soviet BZT 14.5mm is a 920-grain,

Heavy rounds include (L-R) .50-cal., .223 (for scale), immense Russian 14.5mm, CheyTac .408, 25x59mm Payload rifle round, and .338 Lapua Magnum.

armor-piercing/incendiary/tracer having a slightly faster velocity than the BS-41 load but less accuracy due to the inconsistency of its tracer burn. The other Soviet load, the Type ZP incendiary/tracer, too, lacks the accuracy of the BS-41. None of these bullets are boat-tail, nor are there any commercial bullets or loaded cartridges for the 14.5mm.

The Chinese manufacture 14.5mm loads similar to the Soviet BS-41 and BZT cartridges, while several other countries also make this round, including North Korea and Syria.

None of these loads are of sufficient quality to be called truly sniper grade, but when fired through decent rifles outfitted with good optics, you could expect enough accuracy to hit selected enemy positions at well over 1,000 yards and with sufficient energy to penetrate concrete and sandbag walls that would stop lesser bullets.

This field of antimateriel rifles has in recent years grown to include several 20mm guns. Though, like the 14.5mm rifles, they cannot offer the pinpoint precision of a sniper rifle, these weapons still offer considerable damage to materiel targets, with superior terminal performance because they can fire fused, exploding projectiles. The Croatian RT-20 saw service in that region's recent civil conflicts, while two designs have come out of South Africa, the NTW-20 and Aerotex 20x82mm. None of these designs has seen much use beyond their respective countries.

The Barrett 25x59mm Payload antimateriel, semiautomatic rifle is an entirely different matter. Employing a round originally intended for the next-generation Objective Crew Served Weapon, this development was thrust on Barrett to get a usable 25mm rifle fielded to U.S. Special Ops forces as quickly as possible. When this projectile matures, it will include advanced proximity and delayed fusing to allow rounds to detonate above a target or penetrate various barriers in sophisticated ways.

To accommodate the bulkier cartridge and its higher recoil, Barrett has completely redesigned its semiauto's upper receiver, although the lower remains similar enough for interoperability with .50-caliber rifles. Though not a sniper-quality weapon, the Barrett Payload rifle will offer better precision, greater range, and more effective terminal effects than any grenade launcher. And, of great value to a country at war, due to a tremendous effort by Ronnie Barrett and his employees, the Payload rifle will be in the hands of soldiers and marines much faster than the Objective Crew Served Weapon that may eventually replace it by 2010 or so.

Black Hills is the only U.S. loader of .338 Lapua Magnum ammo, in 250- and 300-grain loads.

The excellent Sako TRG-42, chambered for the .338 Lapua Magnum.

Accuracy International's AWM, one of the most accurate .338 Lapua Magnum rifles.

MEDIUM-WEIGHT SNIPING: THE .338 LAPUA MAGNUM

If you can imagine a cartridge that's halfway between the .300 Winchester Magnum and the .50-caliber Browning, then you've pretty well defined the .338 Lapua Magnum. It's made by shortening a .416 Rigby case 2/10 of an inch and necking it down to .338.

Purposely designed in the late 1980s as a long-range military sniping round, the .338 Lapua Mag was intended for bolt-action rifles that were still light enough for stalking and maneuvering. The importance of a barrier-penetrating sniper rifle being more compact and lighter than a .50 was quite apparent during countersniping operations in Sarajevo in the 1990s. In 1997, during a visit to the Beretta factory in Brescia, Italy, I discussed this subject with company officers, who'd learned from Italian special operations snipers that their .50s were simply too burdensome for the kinds of crawling, climbing, and stalking required to defeat Serbian urban snipers. Meeting this requirement called for a .338-class rifle, which also would achieve useful barrier penetration.

Performance is understandably very impressive with a muzzle energy of 4,880 ft-lbs., which is comparable to elephant rifles, and at 500 yards, its 2,193 fps velocity is 50 percent faster than such heavyweight rounds as the .375 H&H and .458 Winchester Magnum. This combination of great speed and heavy weight makes for especially lethal long-range shooting and good penetration against vehicles and aircraft—typical counterterrorist targets—as well as building materials.

The only American factory loads for the .338 Lapua Magnum are offered by Black Hills, including a 250-grain Sierra MatchKing (2,950 fps) or 300-grain MatchKing (2,800 fps), both obviously of match quality. Meanwhile, Lapua offers three bullets for the .338 Lapua Mag: a 250-grain Scenar Lock Base Match, a 260-grain hardball Forex tactical bullet, and the AP 485 armor piercing.

Some sniperscope BDCs are specially synched for the .338 Lapua Magnum, too. The Zeiss 3-12x56 Diavari VM/V 30mm scope has a .338 BDC calibrated to track this round out to 1,400 meters. Two Leupold scopes—the Mark 4 10x40mm LR and Mark 4 3-9x36mm—have BDCs for the 250-grain .338 Lapua, in increments of either yards or meters.

On this side of the Atlantic, only McMillan now builds a sniper-grade bolt gun chambered for the .338 Lapua, available with A-2, A-3, or A-4 stocks. This chambering is much more prevalent in Europe, where Sako has an upsized version of its TRG 22 sniper rifle—the TRG 42—in .338 Lapua Magnum. Accuracy International similarly has a larger version of its AW rifles—the AWM, for "Magnum"—for the Lapua round. The same Mauser SR93 chassis that accommodates the .300 Winchester Magnum also handles the heavier .338 Lapua. Other sniper-grade European .338 Lapuas include the Erma SR 100, the Blaser straight-pull LRS2 magnum, and FN's Mini-Hecate sniper rifle.

SNIPING WITH THE .50-CALIBER MACHINE GUN

Few snipers will ever get their hands on a .50-caliber AMAC, McMillan, or Barrett sniper rifle, but that doesn't mean you can't "reach out and touch someone" with the fabulous .50 round.

In Korea and Vietnam, American snipers made do with ordinary .50-caliber Browning machine guns, scoring individual kills out to 2,500 and 3,000 yards. How did they do it? The secret to .50-caliber machine gun sniping is simple: *consistency*, which begins with how you select your machine gun.

Selecting Your Gun

Start by examining several .50 calibers; the typical infantry battalion has six to 10 Brownings, so look at each of these.

More than anything else, find a traversing and elevating (T&E) mechanism that fits smoothly on a tripod's traversing bar, with crisp, well-defined clicks of elevation and windage. Here's where you'll get much of your consistency.

Next, pay close heed to how straight and true the bolt face is machined. Place a dummy round on the face to see how firmly and straight it's held; see if the round binds against the chamber or loads straight and smooth.

Following exact procedures from FM 23-56, adjust each gun's timing and headspace and *record* the precise rotations you used so you can reset the gun exactly the same each time you use it.

Now you're ready for test-firing.

The Proof's in the Pudding

Obtain an ample supply of black-tipped .50-caliber armor-piercing ammunition, enough so you can test-fire, zero, and tactically employ cartridges from the same lot. These AP rounds usually are more consistent and accurate than M2 ball ammo.

Test-fire the guns one at a time against a target that's at least 400 yards away. You don't need optics yet since you're just learning which gun shoots the tightest groups.

Set each gun for single-shot firing and sandbag it heavily so you can shoot it with free recoil, meaning only your trigger finger touches the gun. Use the T&E mechanism to adjust

aim, picking a concise aiming point that's proportional to the sight blade.

After confirming you're on-paper, shoot two five-shot groups at two clean targets, waiting long enough between shots so the barrel doesn't heat up. Manually load each round *exactly* the same as all others. After inserting a round, let spring power pull the retracting slide handle from your hand, then smartly slap it shut. Reconfirm your aim and adjust the T&E as needed before firing each shot.

A realistic accuracy goal is 10 to 15 inches at 400 yards, which equals 3 to 4 MOA. Granted, this isn't sniper-level performance, but it would be most exceptional to do much better. In a 1954 sniper application test of a Browning .50 fitted with 10x scope, the best five-round group was only 8 MOA, so I'm betting that you can do much better than the folks at Aberdeen Proving Ground.

So how bad is 3 MOA? At 1,000 yards it means you'll be firing 30-inch groups, or a pattern about twice the size of a human torso—you should score 50 percent of the time. And if the truth were known, the Korean and Vietnam War reports of .50-caliber sniping kindly omitted the fact that there were several misses for each hit. But the hits were well worth the misses.

Precisely Aiming Your .50 Caliber

Having tested and selected the best gun, your next step is to outfit it with optics, and here the challenge is primarily one of scrounging, for although the .50 caliber has a dovetail for a mount, the military doesn't provide the mating mount and rings. My best advice is to befriend a depot-level machinist, then guard his handiwork as if it were gold.

Despite mirage problems, you should use a 20x or larger scope so you can select targets at 1,000+ yards. Since you'll be firing free recoil—without your eye to the scope at the instant of firing—you won't actually need extended eye relief.

Unless your scope has a BDC with considerable elevation, you'll normally compensate

Fifty-caliber sniping began during the Korean War with jerry-rigged mounts and target scopes on the Browning M2.

for range by cranking the whole gun up on the T&E mechanism—that is, "holding" high. You must therefore zero the .50 at as great a distance as possible or you'll find yourself cranking the gun so high that the target's completely below your scope's field of view.

Now pay close attention: With practice and by keeping exacting notes, you can learn to compensate correctly for range and wind by counting clicks on your T&E mechanism. Although the T&E is not usually employed with such precision, the fact is that each elevation click—as shown on the elevating handwheel—is one mil. The reason you examined all your battalion's T&E mechanisms was to find the tightest, micrometer-like T&E so you could compensate with it reliably.

Recall that in our mil dot section, we noted that 1 mil equals 1 yard at 1,000 yards, which means one click up raises the point of impact 36 inches at that range. The traversing bar is marked in 5-mil increments, allowing precise windage compensation and moving target leads. (See more in the mil dot section in Chapter 4.)

You must ensure that the gun is properly balanced or it will cant when raising/lowering the T&E elevation. To prevent canting, focus your scope on a distant vertical line and adjust the gun's balance until you can raise and lower the T&E without the scope crosshair wandering from this line. Then sandbag it in place.

The T&E is also an excellent means for precision night fire at faraway point targets. Pick these in daylight and record their exact T&E location, possibly even going so far as to fire a few rounds and adjust with your spotter's assistance. You can then fire when there's visible nighttime activity or randomly to psychologically disrupt the enemy. Record these T&E adjustments on your range card for speedy reference in daylight situations, too. With practice, you can bring your gun to bear night or day—complete with proper compensation—in just a couple seconds.

Just as with any sniper rifle, for best results keep detailed, updated firing records on your .50 and its T&E mechanism.

CHAPTER 10

BINOCULARS AND SPOTTING SCOPES

BINOCULARS AND MINI BINOS

The most useful surveillance and spotting device in a sniper team is a pair of good binoculars. When properly focused and adjusted, a sniper can scan through "binos" for hours without eyestrain, and typically he will intersperse this with naked-eye observation and only employ a spotting scope when there's a target indicator worth investigating. Binoculars are the sniper team's real optical workhorse.

But binos also are the most effective twilight and night optical aid, because they have an exit pupil and a twilight factor significantly greater than those of a spotting or rifle scope.

The author with Leica 10x Geovid binoculars, which combine quality optics with a laser rangefinder.

Binocular Basics

Binoculars are described according to their magnification and objective lens size. For instance, 7x35 binos are 7 power with a 35mm front lens; 10x50s have 10x magnification and a 50mm objective lens. As with rifle and spotting scopes, the front/objective lens facilitates focus,

while the rear/ocular lens determines magnification and field of view.

Adjusting binoculars begins by setting the interpupillary distance, which only means setting the hinged tubes so each eyepiece aligns exactly with a pupil. Once you've found a comfortable angle, take a permanent alcohol marker and draw a thin line across the scale found at the hinge; unless you're exposed to certain hazardous chemicals and your head changes shape, you should never have to go through this process again.

But you'll have to refocus whenever someone else uses your binoculars, a process that's slightly different if you have central focusing between the tubes or independent focus on each eyepiece. With the latter, you focus the eyepieces only once, which is the "focus free" system now found on U.S. Army and Marine Corps Steiner binoculars.

To focus these eyepieces, pick a large object having lots of contrast and color that's about 100 yards away. Then, turn each eyepiece out as far as it can go; starting this way is *critical* or

Center-focused binoculars are slightly different since only the right eyepiece is adjustable. Begin by rotating the focus knob so the eyepieces are as far out as possible. Then rotate the right eyepiece as far out as it will go. Again using a distinct target 100 yards away, look through the left eyepiece while covering the right lens and focus by using the center knob. Be sure you're actually focusing and your eye isn't compensating. Now, cover the left lens and look through the right eyepiece, but *don't* touch the center focus knob while you adjust the eyepiece focus. When finished, mark that eyepiece with your permanent alcohol marker. From this point on, you'll use the center focus knob each time you adjust the binos, since both lenses are now in synch.

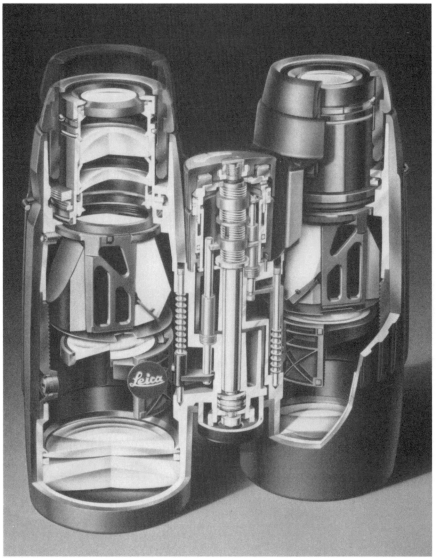

Why are they so darned expensive? The precision innards of a quality pair of binoculars look as complex as a fine timepiece.

STABILIZED BINOCULARS

By the 1990s, conventional binoculars evolved into a more sophisticated version that stabilized them for better image clarity. This technology had begun as a means to stabilize cameras and lenses, both for civilian cinematography and military aircraft targeting and acquisition. In 1995, I tested a pair of stabilized binoculars and found that, although they certainly worked, they were much too bulky and expensive for general sniper use.

Then in 1998, I tried a pair of Zeiss 20x60mm stabilized binoculars at the NRA

your eyes may compensate and make an out-of-focus image seem focused. Now, keeping both eyes open, cover one lens and focus the other eyepiece so it's crisp and clear. Brace yourself so there's minimal vibratory distortion. If you find yourself fine-tuning too much, start again with the eyepiece rotated all the way out and focus down. Then, reverse things and cover the other lens while focusing the opposite eyepiece. When you're done, take that alcohol marker and draw indicator lines on each lens for quick refocusing.

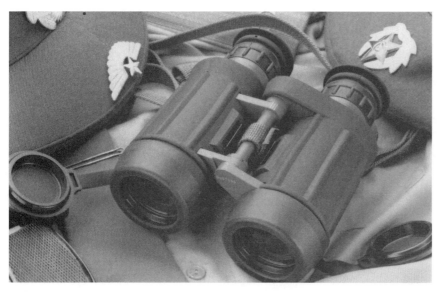

Surplus East German 7x40mm binoculars are rugged, compact, and a reasonable balance of size and capability.

These mechanically stabilized Zeiss 20x60mms are state-of-the-art.

Whittington Center, brought there by a German sniper team. According to Zeiss, these premium binoculars could distinguish a 15mm object at 1,000 yards. These were much more compact than earlier models, but the price was too steep for an old soldier.

A couple of years later I tried a pair of Canon stabilized binoculars, which were even more compact but worked admirably and at a price I could afford. I've used them for several years now and can attest to their quality and, most importantly, the quality of their image. Unlike earlier bulky gyro-stabilized devices, the Canon stabilizing system employs a tiny vibrating optical prism that pivots so fast that the image appears to remain stationary. Two seconds after pushing the activating button, any jerkiness smoothes out and you can distinguish dramatically finer detail. This stabilizing, floating sensation reminds me of watching combat FLIR footage of smart bombs falling on a target.

Standing (unsupported) with these 15x50mm Canons, I can see .223 bullet holes in a target 100 yards away—about as well as a 25x spotting scope on a tripod. Though these binoculars are a bit heavier than standard ones, I think they offer such enhanced optical capabilities that they can replace the spotting scope and tripod for a net reduction in bulk and

The author's 15x50mm Canon stabilized binoculars (left) offer such target clarity that they basically replaced both his spotting scope and binoculars while eliminating the need for a tripod.

Anchor binoculars to your eyebrows for steadiest hold and clearest focus. (Photo credit: Roger Kennedy)

weight. The only downside here, it appears, is that they aren't military-rugged, but I'm sure Canon could develop a version with heavier seals and a stronger body.

The U.S. Army already has a stabilized binocular, the 14x M25, so it's at least in the system, and it's possible for a sniper team to scrounge a pair.

Using Binoculars in the Field

Because they're hand-held, binoculars usually aren't steady enough to fully exploit their optical capabilities. This is operator error and easily solved. First, to minimize any movement or vibration between binos and your eyes, hold them so the tops of the eyepieces are actually in firm contact with the bottom of your eyebrows. It will feel a bit odd the first time you try it, but the results are impressive.

Additionally, though, think of your binoculars as a rifle in need of support for best results. Brace yourself and the binos along, on top of, or against some solid, stationary foundation like a wall or heavy tree. Just these two techniques will markedly improve long-range image resolution.

You can also improve image clarity by blocking light around the eyepieces with your fingers, as shown in the accompanying photograph. By blocking bright light, you allow your pupils to widen, or dilate, so they can recognize more detail in a magnified image.

When using binoculars, you must stay aware of the danger that reflected sunlight can compromise your location. This is a considerable danger for U.S. military Steiner binoculars with their mirror-like, laser-reflective coating. Without that coating, a flash of laser light—such as the range-finding laser on an Abrams tank—could cause blindness, so the coating is not without necessity.

The "fix" is the M22 KillFlash antireflection shield, the same kind of honeycomb filter the Tenebraex Corporation makes for sniperscopes. (In fact, the rifle scope version evolved from the binoculars version.) These cap-like covers slide over the binoculars lens tubes and work so well that, although only 2 1/4 inches long, they totally eliminate glint. They're available through supply channels in both the U.S. Army and Marine Corps.

ANTITANK BINOCULARS

I've dubbed especially large binoculars, such as the Steiner 15x80s and Bushnell 20x80s, as "antitank" to underline how bulky and heavy they are. They're simply too large for ordinary sniper team use.

Steady binoculars by pushing them against a solid surface, such as a tree or wall.

Improve image clarity by blocking light around the eyepieces.

Laser reflective coating on left lens easily compromises military Steiner binoculars unless—as on the right—it's covered with a KillFlash shield.

Antitank binoculars, such as these Steiner 15x80mms, are too heavy and bulky for most sniping situations but prove excellent for some surveillances.

But there's a lot to be said for glasses that can generate a twilight factor of 35–40 and be used at high magnification for long periods without the eyestrain that results from viewing through a spotting scope.

These oversize binos are excellent for surveillance work along borders, coast-lines, and airfields, where distances are long and observation may require hours or days. Some of my good drug interdiction friends on the Gulf Coast employ Steiner 15x80s—thoughtfully donated by an appre-hended cocaine smuggler—and they've proven particularly adept for night use.

But if there's a need to buffer vibra-tion with ordinary 7x or 10x binoculars, these 15x and 20x ones absolutely demand stability for good results. Bracing is essential, and what's even better is to mount them on a solid tripod; in fact, these biggies come threaded for tripod mounts.

MINI BINOS

At the other binocular extreme are the compact, pocket-size mini binos that have become extremely popular.

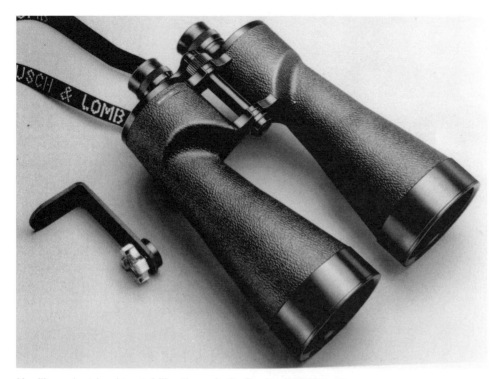

You'll need a tripod to stabilize these hefty Bushnell 20x80mms.

I think every sniper should have a pair of these handy and convenient binos, but only in addition to, *not* instead of, full-size binoculars. Since they're so compact, these mini binos can be in your pocket and go everywhere you do, instantly ready to check anything your eyes find curious. Instead of digging into your ruck for two minutes to retrieve full-size binos, you've placed optics to your eyes in 20 seconds.

The problem—indeed, the danger—

A handy pair of mini binos allows a sniper to quickly check targets in the middle of a stalk.

A compromised size but very high quality, the Swarovski 8x30mm binoculars pack a lot of capability in a small size.

impressive glasses are well suited to clandestine police and military operations, they can't quite replace their slightly larger brothers.

SPOTTING SCOPES

The most powerful optical device employed by a sniper team is its spotting scope. More so than any other optics, a quality spotting scope helps you deceive your opponent because you'll be able to detect and observe him far better than he can imagine. His ignorance makes him vulnerable.

Since it generates your thinnest optical field of view, you should use this scope as an *investigative* tool and not for ordinary observation and scanning. First, detect a target indicator using naked eyes or binoculars; then switch to your spotting scope to home in on the suspect location. The one optical aid that best enables you to detect a heavily camouflaged opponent is the spotting scope. But the physical effects of employing just one eye to look through a high-magnification lens—as well as its thin field of view—means you must use a spotting scope sparingly.

is that some misdirected soul may actually replace full-size binoculars with optically inferior minis. No matter the quality, not one of the minis comes close to the average exit pupils found on full-size binoculars, and twilight factors are worse yet. Simply put, mini binos are daylight optical systems and can hardly substitute for regular binoculars.

The problem with minis is that their small 20–25mm objective lenses just plain cannot gather much light. Think of it this way: the area of a circular lens increases faster than its diameter widens, meaning a 50mm lens has 2.8 times the light-gathering area of a 30mm lens. Set side to side, the best quality mini binocular will not look as bright as a merely adequate full-size binocular.

But confusing all this are several optics makers who've recently fielded compact binoculars that are larger than minis but not as big as full-size binos. The Swarovski compacts are truly nice pieces of glass and come very close to competing directly with full-size binoculars. While these

Roles and Capabilities

Several observation roles are best served by a spotting scope. When the sniper fires, his spotter's eye is glued to the spotting scope since its high magnification allows him to see the tiny visual effects of bullet impact, which aren't discernable through binoculars. When conducting practice fire on a range, that spotting scope will cut your time in half since you don't have to walk to the targets to assess your results. The spotting scope also is your best optical tool for reading mirage to learn wind speed and direction, which is no minor field task.

Much better than most binoculars, a spotting scope can enable you to actually see through glare or bright intervening light to find a target that could never be seen with naked eyes. Penetration of window reflection is an excellent example of a possible real-life scenario—and here you'll find that you can make out targets almost as if by magic.

But before you mistakenly conclude such magic can be applied to any situation, recall that your eye pupil is

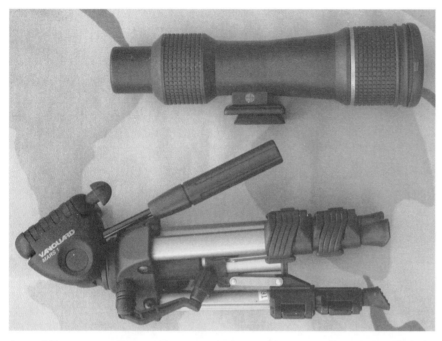

Leupold's compact 25x spotting scope, along with an equally compact Cabela tripod, doesn't take up much rucksack space.

Nearly indestructible, the Korean War–era M49 spotting scope is still in service today.

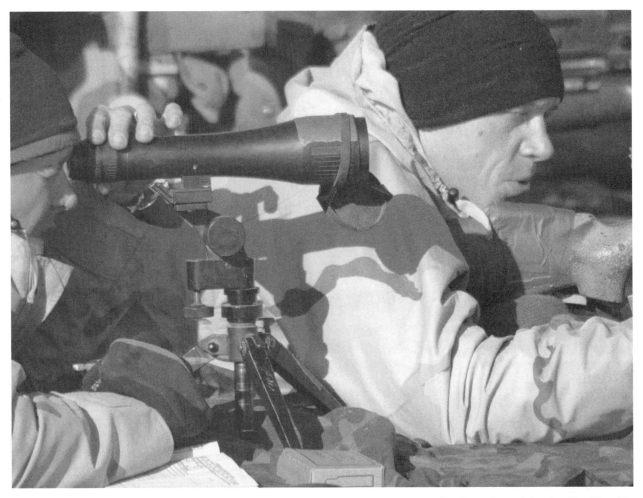

The U.S. Army's M144 spotting scope, shown here in Iraq, is a military-ruggedized version of Bushnell's Elite 15-45x60mm model.

about 6–7mm at night. What! There's not a single spotting scope that comes anywhere close to your pupil's night width—which is the optical trade-off we make when employing higher magnification. A spotting scope can only complement, not replace, binoculars.

And this underlines my earlier point: optics must be mutually integrated to be effective.

Zoom vs. Fixed Power

There are pros and cons to zoom and fixed-power spotting scopes, beginning with size and weight. The average fixed power is about 10 ounces lighter than the zoom scopes, and it's probably about an inch shorter. For these reasons, as well as the fact that they're less complicated, I generally find fixed-power spotting scopes more suited for sniping.

Earlier we observed that 30x is about the maximum magnification for a spotting scope, since higher powers become too readily disrupted by mirage. Considering this ceiling, it's questionable that you can exploit fully these zoom models, nearly all of which go well over 30x, some even to 60x. This doesn't mean the manufacturers are evil or making inappropriate products; it's just that these aren't best suited to sniping. Such higher magnification works just fine on a firing range or perhaps when scanning for game in mountain country.

Still, though, there's room for compromise. Some quality spotting scopes are convertible

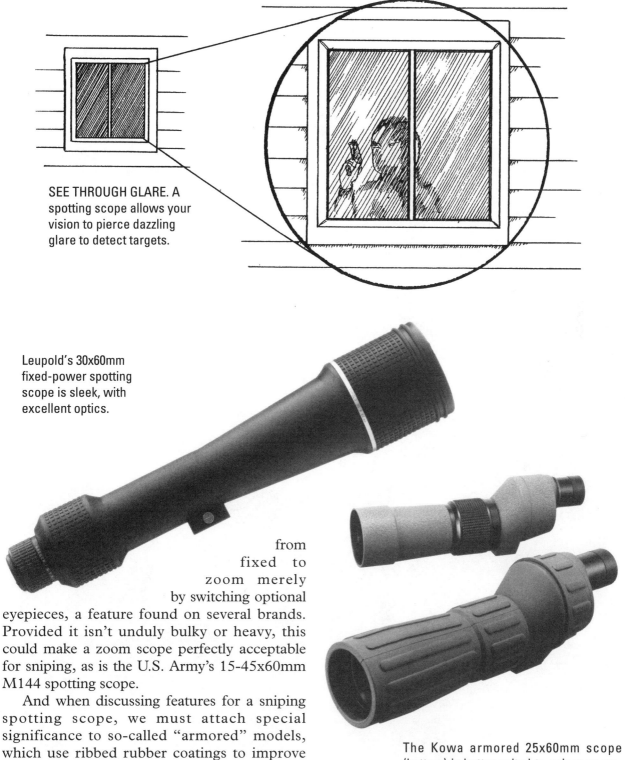

SEE THROUGH GLARE. A spotting scope allows your vision to pierce dazzling glare to detect targets.

Leupold's 30x60mm fixed-power spotting scope is sleek, with excellent optics.

from fixed to zoom merely by switching optional eyepieces, a feature found on several brands. Provided it isn't unduly bulky or heavy, this could make a zoom scope perfectly acceptable for sniping, as is the U.S. Army's 15-45x60mm M144 spotting scope.

And when discussing features for a sniping spotting scope, we must attach special significance to so-called "armored" models, which use ribbed rubber coatings to improve resistance to shock. For rugged field use, this is an absolutely essential feature.

The Kowa armored 25x60mm scope (bottom) is better suited to sniper operations than its unarmored version (top).

The military version of Leupold's 12-40x60mm spotting scope contains a mil dot reticle that synchs with magnification.

Antitank Spotting Scopes

Again emphasizing a special use by focusing attention on their disproportionate size, we're designating three zoom scopes as "antitank" optics.

The oversized Bausch & Lomb 15-60x60mm is simply too large (about 18 inches) and too heavy (48 ounces) for sniper field use, while the Swarovski 20-60x80mm is larger and heavier yet. But I still think every law enforcement agency needs at least one of these, or possibly a celestial telescope.

There are certain unusual tactical situations in which the great focal length and power of such scopes would be fully exploited—indeed, could prove crucial. Two situations that come readily to mind are a skyjack in which you must generate intelligence but cannot stalk close enough for ordinary observation, or a crazy rooftop sniper whose high-ground perch cannot be observed except from a hide atop a tall building blocks away.

A U.S. Marine Scout-Sniper surveils through a Leupold Mark 4 12-40x60mm zoom spotting scope, which incorporates a mil dot reticle.

usually the case that the higher you crank up the scope, the more it sways, so what you've gained in elevation you've lost in stability. But there are other ways to increase elevation.

During a real-world airfield surveillance operation, I was able to tape my spotting scope solidly to a 6-inch tree trunk right at my sitting eye level, with excellent results. But this only worked because my

Used by British SAS, the Swarovski CTC 30x75mm is simple in design but offers superb optics.

While a police sniper team wouldn't deploy with antitank optics to each incident, they still need to have these heavy optics one radio call away. On a more ordinary basis, these heavy scopes are useful for range firing and enable you to observe shot groups at even 200+ yards. But before their optical abilities seduce you, don't forget that these scopes are much too heavy and bulky for everyday field use.

Tripods and Mounts

Unlike normal binoculars or mini binos, you absolutely need a tripod to view clearly through a spotting scope. Even braced solidly against a tree, you won't be steady enough to resolve distant images when hand-holding a spotting scope.

My tripod preference is for simple ones because they're compact and lightweight. (Never forget that you actually have to hump all this gear!) Some tripods have highly adjustable knobs for elevation, windage, and scope angle and work fine, but they're too bulky for an already crammed rucksack.

Although I've used a videocam tripod for surveillance spotting, it's

When the spotting scope is on a tripod, look through it without touching it for best results. (Photo credit: Roger Kennedy)

Suspend a sandbag beneath a tripod to stabilize it solidly on uneven ground or during windy conditions.

attention was focused on a particular taxiway; once taped firmly in place, my scope was locked-in to just that spot.

Clamp mounts are available, too, by which you can attach your scope to an automobile window or a chair back and should be quite useful for law enforcement applications.

While earlier I advocated holding binocular eyepieces against your eyebrows for best results, now I must tell you exactly the opposite when using a spotting scope. Once it's focused on the intended location, *don't* touch it at all. Due to its high magnification, the tiniest vibrations will degrade the image in ways not readily noticed. The surest way to steady a tripod-mounted scope on a windy day or on uneven ground is to suspend a sandbag beneath its center. This also works great when using a tripod as a shooting rest.

And when using a spotting scope, be sure to rest your eye frequently and switch to binoculars from time to time to prevent eyestrain. By SOP, you should switch roles and optics with your partner on the hour to avoid straining your vision.

CHAPTER 11

SPOTTING AND TARGET DETECTION

INTRODUCTION TO SPOTTING

While a sniper obviously must be an excellent marksman, the most superb rifleman cannot take a shot unless first he finds a target—and most sniping targets intentionally avoid being seen. A sniper team devotes a quarter or even a third of its field time to surveilling and spotting through optical devices in a never-ending search for elusive quarry. This optical searching and scanning demands as much precision and attention to detail as does long-range shooting, and it begins by first understanding, then exploiting, these wondrous pieces of ground glass.

THE SPYGLASS

The handheld telescope, perfected by Dutch spectacle maker Hans Lippershey in 1608, proved as revolutionary a technological breakthrough to 17th-century warfare as code-breaking or spy satellites would become in our lifetime.

The sniper team's primary observation optic, binoculars, such as these U.S. Army–issue Steiners.

Imagine the tremendous tactical advantage afforded a frigate captain who, lifting a "spyglass" to his eye, detected an enemy's sailing fleet, still so tiny on the horizon that his own ships could not be seen by their keenest lookouts. The optically superior fleet held all the cards and deliberately played them.

So decisive was Lippershey's "instrument for seeing at a distance" that the Dutch government considered concealing its development "that the said instrument might be kept secret."

A modern sniper team's optics are no less wondrous or decisive an advantage, for when properly employed, just as in the days of fighting under sail, these devices allow you to fulfill a sniper's most fundamental requirement—"to see without being seen," both to detect targets and to develop intelligence.

Respect the tremendous advantage of optics versus an unaided human eye. I once staged a demonstration for students in which an optically equipped scout sitting totally in the open almost a mile away—and not detectable to our most

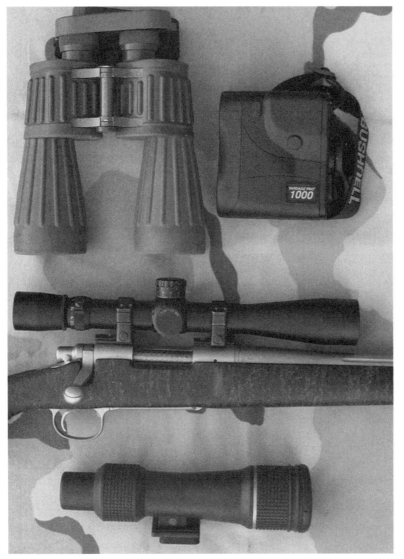

TEAM OPTICS. The sniper team integrates binoculars, rifle scope, spotting scope, and laser for effective observation.

eagle-eyed soldiers—described by radio my tiniest half-concealed gestures and motions. It was an unsettling demonstration because, gathered in this shaded treeline, we had seemed impervious to any observation. The students were properly impressed.

But I'd like to impress upon you as well that spotting integrates a whole field of related skills, to include detecting targets, assessing discovered targets for value and priorities, observing fire, and adjusting the sniper's shots. It's not just finding something; it's understanding what you've found, helping the sniper see it, supporting him as he engages, then adjusting his fire until he hits.

Understanding Lenses and Vision

The channel through which all visual images must travel to reach your brain is your eye. More precisely, light enters your eye through the pupil, an aperture that operates like a camera lens. The pupil dilates wide in limited light so you can make out more vague shapes, and it reduces itself automatically in glaring light to prevent damage to sensitive nerve tissue.

The most effective optical devices process gathered light into an image the same diameter as your eye's pupil; that is, from the eyepiece of a spotting scope or binocular, a circle of magnified light should emerge at least the same diameter as your pupil. This is a snap in daylight, since your narrowed pupil only measures about 3 millimeters across; virtually all full-size binoculars and spotting scopes achieve this.

But at dusk and at night, your pupil dilates, or widens, to gather more light, and many optical devices cannot produce a circle of light wide enough to fit a pupil, which is now 6 to 7 millimeters across. While you may not notice this shortcoming, it's profound and decisively dictates how much you'll see in low light. Therefore, the size of a device's light image—or "exit pupil"—is an important criterion and easily computed. Just divide the objective lens' millimeter diameter by its magnification. For example, a 7x35 binoculars has an exit pupil of 5mm, and a 20x60 spotting scope yields a 3mm exit pupil.

A slightly different way of rating optical

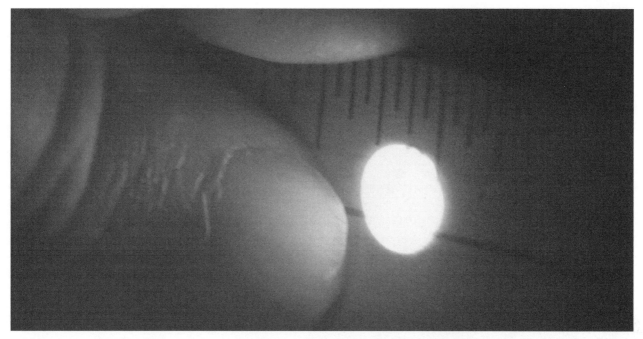

Shining a SureFire flashlight in a rifle scope's objective lens projected this circle of focused light 3 1/2 inches beyond the scope, exactly at correct eye relief. This circle of light—the exit pupil—widens as you reduce magnification and narrows when you increase magnification.

devices is called "relative brightness," which only requires that you square the exit pupil so that differences become algebraic and advantages more obvious, as shown here:

EXIT PUPIL	SQUARE	=	RELATIVE BRIGHTNESS
3	x 3	=	9
4	x 4	=	16
5	x 5	=	25
6	x 6	=	36
7	x 7	=	49

The third way to measure and rate light passage is the "twilight factor," which gives more weight to a device's low-light magnification and thus emphasizes the ability to resolve detail at dusk and in moonlight. This is an especially important rating for sniping observation. But to yield a valid comparison, you should *only* compare twilight factors for two devices having similar exit pupils or there's no significance in the rating.

To compute twilight factor, multiply the device's objective lens diameter by its power, then find this number's square root. Since both 7x35 and 10x50 binoculars have 5mm exit pupils, let's compare their twilight factors to determine which will allow better low-light resolution:

$$7 \times 35 = 245,$$
which has a square root 15.6 = Twilight Factor

$$10 \times 50 = 500,$$
which has a square root 22.4 = Twilight Factor

Thus, the 10x50 binos have a decisively superior twilight factor; indeed, a law enforcement agency once phoned me late one afternoon and asked what kind of binoculars to use that night for a drug case surveillance, 7x35 or 10x50, so now you'll understand why I recommended the latter. But I also asked the law officer if he'd be packing in somewhere or operating undercover, since the 10x50s are heavier and more difficult to conceal than 7x35s, criteria I cite because there are more considerations than merely numerical ratings.

Steiner's Night Hunter binoculars, the author's choice, provide excellent night viewing with an exit pupil of 7 and a twilight factor of 21.1.

My favorite all-around surveillance and spotting binoculars, Steiner 8x56mm Night Hunters, have an impressive twilight factor of 21.1, a rating that's itself considerably exceeded by 15x80 binos—but such immense binos are a third heavier and twice as bulky. Someone could also criticize my preference for Night Hunters, however, since they're heavier than 7x50 binoculars and don't have as much magnification as 10x50s.

Like so much of life, selecting optics involves compromises and balances, not just grasping at numerical ratings.

Quality More Important Than Numbers

Before considering any kind of rating—exit pupil, relative brightness, or twilight factor—realize that these say not one thing about lens quality; they reflect only lens sizes and magnification.

Low-quality grinding on third-rate glass results in shoddy optics that, no matter the impressive ratings, won't serve you well in the field. Quality lenses require precision grinding and microscopic coatings for surfaces so perfect that maximum light flows evenly and unhindered, with no visual aberrations, no distortions, and no reflection—glass clearer than crystal.

Using such excellent lenses allows high acuity; that is, being able to resolve distant images. We explained how to assess lens quality in the rifle scope section, so we won't repeat it here other than to urge you to use these same assessment criteria for all optics.

Don't be seduced by an oversized objective lens; it may claim to gather a lot of light, but if the device is poorly made, only a small amount of that light will reach your eye. The same goes for high magnification—if the focused image is too fuzzy to recognize the shape of a distant man aiming a rifle at you, what use is such high power?

Though the very best optics seem expensive, they yield results worth their cost. If your agency cannot afford the top of the line, at least strive for as much quality as possible, because saving money on optics is penny-wise/dollar-foolish when it comes to sniping gear.

Magnification

How powerful should your optical devices be? If 10x is good, won't 50x be better, and 500x better still? Don't fall for this bigger-is-better mentality; bigger usually also means heavier, bulkier, and of more limited application.

And as we'll cover more thoroughly in a moment, there's an inverse relationship between magnification and an optical device's field of view: the higher the power, the narrower the area you can see through it. It's because of such a highly restricted field of view and much too distant minimum focus range that you should *not* normally use celestial telescopes for spotting.

Another major limiting factor is mirage. Due to visual interference from shimmering heat waves, you'll have problems with a spotting scope of more than about 30x. With rifle scopes, the maximum magnification is about 12x before mirage seriously starts degrading images.

The upper limit on binocular magnification is dictated by how steadily one can hold them. With your body braced, you still can clearly resolve distant objects when using 10x or 12x binos. Any greater power and there's just too much unsteadiness in the human body to allow clear long-range viewing.

If your team has available both spotting scope and binoculars, the binos can be relatively lightweight 7x or 8x. However, in cases where no spotting scope's available, a team needs binos of at least 10x since they'll be employed not just to detect targets but also to observe and adjust the sniper's fire. But ideally, you should have several overlapping optical devices.

INTEGRATING OPTICAL SYSTEMS

A sniper team employs several viewing systems—naked eyes, mini binoculars, binoculars, rifle scopes, and spotting scopes—each possessing distinct optical qualities. Used alone, any one leaves visual gaps in depth or width or inappropriate magnification. But when properly integrated, with all optical systems employed in unison, a sniper team minimizes any shortcomings and effectively exploits optical advantages to the hilt.

Our most fundamental viewing system is only one power, the 1x system God gave us, our naked and natural eyes. Among the viewing systems available to snipers, naked eyes produce the widest possible field of view, an impressive 150+ degrees. Our eyes are extremely sensitive to even slight target movement; I've seen sniper students detect concealed foes who'd only shifted one boot some 300 yards away, so quick can a naked eye spot movement.

This wondrous human eye can process 60 distinct images per second, like a flickering motion picture. If you scan slowly enough that your mind has a chance to examine each of these framed images, your eyes can discern

much. But if you rotate your head faster than your brain can process such images, you'll see nothing—the so-called "blur" we frequently talk about but seldom define. While visually scanning, you must move your eyes slow enough that your brain can digest what you see.

Naked-eye observation is seriously disrupted by glaring light, which automatically causes the pupil to shrink, making anything near the light source difficult to see. The World War II movie cliché of enemy fighters diving out of the sun to achieve surprise was a well-founded exploitation of such visual masking. The American Indian and other native peoples simply but wisely enhanced their vision by blocking glaring light with a raised hand; you can do the same, or position yourself in shade to observe a sunny area.

Naked-eye vision also is degraded by staring too long at one spot, which is easily remedied by keeping your eyes correctly focused but slightly in motion.

In darkness and low light, human pupils nearly triple in size, but man's night vision still is much poorer than most animals, and it degrades with vitamin deficiency or smoking.

FUNDAMENTAL BUT EFFECTIVE. Block sunlight to see better detail in daytime.

Employing Optical Systems

The first consideration when integrating optical systems is the width of the area observed through each, called the "field of view." To generate the following field of view measurements at 100 yards, we averaged the listed widths for more than 70 optical devices. These are:

Naked Eye	1,000+ feet
Mini Binos	30 feet
Full Binos	30 feet
Rifle Scope	11 feet
Spotting Scope	7 feet

We've also illustrated below what these fields of view look like when focused against a target 100 yards away. With naked eyes we see the entire scene and probably would detect movement. As shown at the lower left, things are narrowed to roughly the size of the house when we employ binoculars. The rifle scope helps us see the window with much better detail. And when viewing through the spotting scope, the suspect's face can be seen in the lower right pane.

Another factor affecting field of view is the width of the opening you're looking through and how far back you are from it. As the illustration on the facing page depicts, the closer

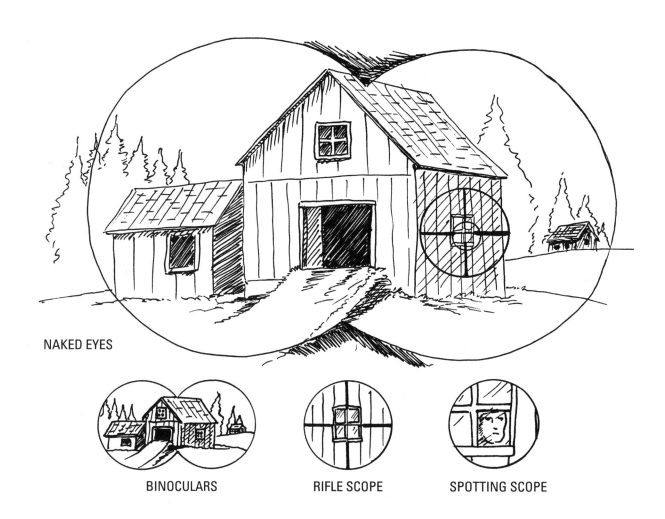

NAKED EYES

BINOCULARS   RIFLE SCOPE   SPOTTING SCOPE

Optical devices must be employed together and layered to effectively view a scene.

A position's field of view is wider when you're close to the opening (top) than when you must stay back from it (bottom).

you are to the opening, the wider the area you'll be able to observe. By pulling back, you narrow your field of view, but you probably also make it much more difficult for anyone to detect you.

Considering a sniper team's distinct optical capabilities, a strategy emerges for the wise, efficient employment of optical devices. Our first rule is, go wide to narrow; don't focus on a tiny area with a spotting scope unless you're examining something that you detected when using naked eyes or less powerful optics.

Next, both team members should not employ the same type of device at the same time; their optics should complement one another. This means that

when one's looking with naked eyes, the other is scanning with binoculars; when one's using the spotting scope, the other's using his rifle scope. Optical devices should be integrated so magnification and fields of view overlap, giving the team better viewing contrast and different visual perspectives.

Another rule for observing is that the sniper must use his rifle scope for spotting sparingly to avoid potential eyestrain. The sniper usually doesn't observe through his scope until he's investigating a target indicator found by his spotter; otherwise, he's using naked eyes and mini or full-size binos.

The spotting scope is used reservedly, probably only when a target indicator has appeared that's deserving of a much closer look. Remember that the spotting scope's field of view is much too limited for scanning large areas. As I once heard it put, it takes 10 times as long to scan an area in search of target indicators with a spotting scope than it does with binoculars.

Normally, only the spotter operates the spotting scope because it must be used while the sniper is firing, and there's no smooth way to exchange optical devices once a target is found. The only proper time to swap optics is when teammates rotate duties and weapons, usually every hour for military sniper teams.

Though this strategy is common-sensical, a great many sniper teams don't practice what they

Use the spotting scope, like this Bushnell Elite used by the U.S. Army, to more closely examine potential targets detected by binoculars or the naked eyes.

know to be "the best way." A couple of years ago, during a police sniper competition in Mississippi, a full-blooded Seminole lawman and his partner captured first place in an observation exercise. When pressed by friends for his winning technique, the Bureau of Narcotics investigator solemnly explained, "It's an old Indian trick."

Momentarily, when the others had wandered away, he turned to me, winked, and whispered, "Shoot! We just did it the way you're s'posed to."

Yes, the real secret is "do it the way you're s'posed to."

Splitting a Sector

After hasty and deliberate scans fail to detect targets, a sniper team begins detailed scanning, which requires meticulous, long-term optical searching.

To ensure their sector is properly covered, with optical systems matched against appropriate ranges and no duplication of effort, the sector is split in one of two ways, as we've illustrated.

The left panel shows how the sector is split in half along a linear landmark, such as a road or stream. The spotter, who's outfitted with higher magnification optics—full-size binoculars and a spotting scope—covers the farther sector. The sniper, optically equipped with a rifle scope and mini binoculars, scans the closer sector. When they rotate duties hourly, they'll swap optics and sectors, too, which both reduces eyestrain and keeps their perspectives fresh.

The second panel illustrates how a sector is divided according to likely target locations, again with the optically superior spotter taking the distant ones and the sniper taking the closer ones. For example, the spotter would surveil the distant farm, the recent earthworks on the upper right hillside, and the mid-sector farmhouse. The sniper, meanwhile, covers the bridge, the smoke vicinity, and the two earthwork berms just to their front. As with the half-sector division, they rotate optics and duties on the hour.

RANGE CARDS

The importance of a range card is only partly its value as a reference; I think the *process* of making one is equally or even more impor-

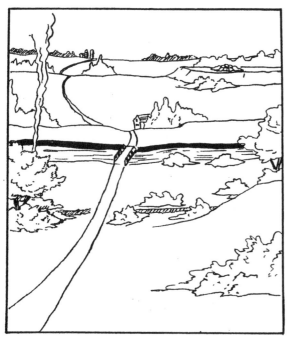

Splitting the sector in half.

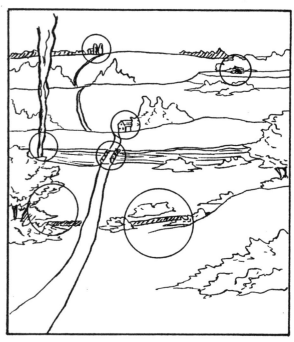

Splitting target indicators.

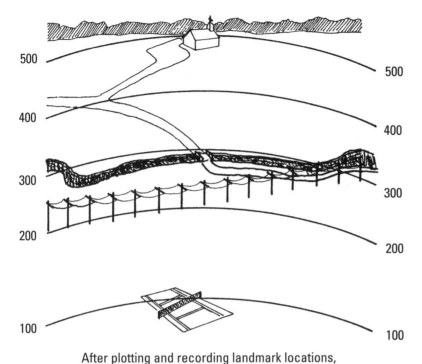

After plotting and recording landmark locations, estimate and record where each 100-yard arc should be.

using a laser rangefinder or splitting the difference between spotter and sniper estimates.

Then, log in BDC settings or moving target holds for each target. The final column, "Remarks," is the place to note some target detail, such as the tennis court's downhill angle and the church's uphill angle, requiring special compensation.

The small upper-right circle is for drawing an arrow to indicate wind direction and speed. Wind data should be reconfirmed at least every half hour. If you have multiple winds within the sector, draw them right in the sketch where they exist and indicate direction and wind speed. When-

tant because it forces you to examine your entire sector, select landmarks and likely enemy locations, make range estimates to each of these, then plot them along with trails and roads on the card.

A military range card should have at least 10 arcs across it, representing 1,000 meters—which realistically is the maximum range of the M24 and M40A3 snipers rifles in 7.62mm—but 1,200 or more meters if you're shooting a .300 Winchester Magnum or .50-caliber sniper rifle. Police range cards probably only need represent about 300 yards but should be the same size so they can record necessary details.

Filling Out a Range Card

First plot landmarks and distinct places you think targets may appear. In our sample, these include the edge of the woods, the church, the bridge, the tennis court, and the shallow ditch beside the road. These become targets and are logged in and numbered.

Next, estimate the range to each, either

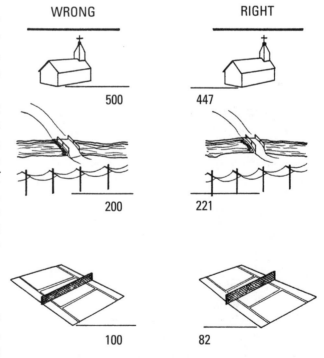

Fight the temptation to unthinkingly label major landmarks to the nearest hundred yards (left). Precisely estimate these distances before plotting them on the range card.

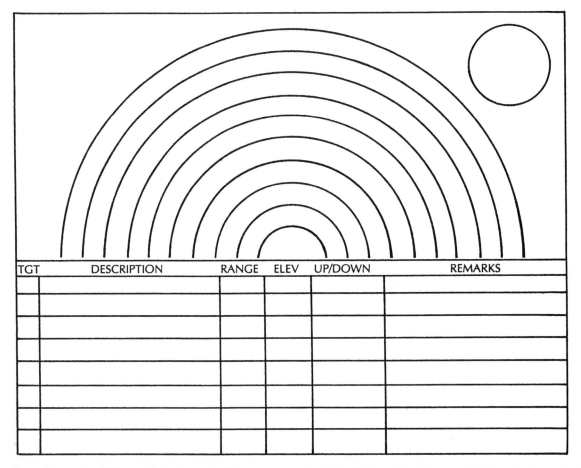

TGT	DESCRIPTION	RANGE	ELEV	UP/DOWN	REMARKS

ever entering wind data, use a pencil since you may have to change it.

Once finished, the range card is held by the spotter so he can read from it if the sniper needs data during an engagement. When your team is part of a larger unit's operation, give a copy of the range card to your next higher leadership so they can integrate it with their overall fire planning.

This range card should be prepared whenever you're in a hide for more than about five minutes without having seen any targets; it's an integral part of the detailed scanning process. Between bouts of optical scanning, both the sniper and spotter study the range card, eventually memorizing it.

We've included one blank range card form, which we'll allow purchasers of this book to reproduce provided they do not sell or duplicate it commercially, and only use it for official agency business. Please do not remove the source line.

OBSERVING AND ADJUSTING FIRE

. . . once the shot is fired, no individual rifleman, and I don't care how conscientious he is, can ever truthfully say whether or not he got his man. The rifle kicks up in your face and hides the aiming point, dust and dirt fly up around the target, and before your vision has cleared up, the target has disappeared. Whether shot or merely ducked, you cannot tell. Your observer often can.

Capt. H.W. McBride
British sniper, World War I

If there's a single, simple reason why a sniper

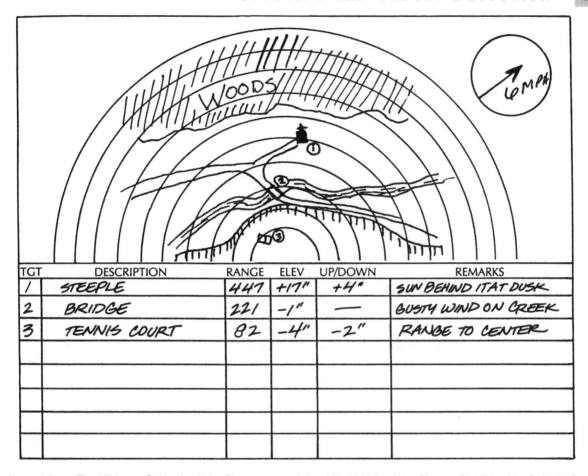

TGT	DESCRIPTION	RANGE	ELEV	UP/DOWN	REMARKS
1	STEEPLE	447	+17"	+4"	SUN BEHIND IT AT DUSK
2	BRIDGE	221	-1"	—	GUSTY WIND ON CREEK
3	TENNIS COURT	82	-4"	-2"	RANGE TO CENTER

absolutely needs a spotter, it is—as McBride declares—because the shooter's recoil prevents him from seeing whether he hit his target. If there's to be any chance of a follow-up shot, he must have a spotter tell him where his miss impacted.

Keen sniper teamwork is nowhere more apparent than when both are engrossed in an engagement. Too much attention has been paid the sniper and not enough to the spotter's contribution.

During a successful engagement, a spotter must be capable of the following:

- Talking the sniper into an obscure, barely visible target
- Watching while the sniper fires to determine the bullet's exact impact point, whether a hit or miss
- Adjusting the sniper's subsequent shot for a hit

These tasks are easily stated but every bit as difficult and critical as the sniper's shooting. They're so important that some senior snipers believe the spotter should be the team's most experienced man and the shooter the junior one.

Talking the Sniper into a Target

Imagine the dilemma. A new spotter detects a target through his binoculars or spotting scope, but he doesn't know how to direct the sniper to the spot without removing his eye—but if he removes his eye, he'll lose sight of the target. What's a spotter to do?

First, find a reference point or landmark within your field of view by seeing the larger perspective. Ideally you should keep the target in sight, but if there's nothing distinctive around it, you can try short pans right or left or tipping slightly up or down, very near the target. Keep

Talking the sniper into a target uses landmarks or reference points.

pivoting your optics back to the target so you don't lose sight of it.

If you're using a spotting scope, keep one eye focused through the lens on the target while the other eye examines the wider context and reference points.

The reference point you select should be simple, as we've used in the illustration. To describe Point A you'd say: "See that downed wire? Well, draw a line right through the pole it's hanging from and extend it until it just touches the woods. The target's 5 meters left of that point, between the two closest trees." To describe Point B: "From the road junction, come back east into the trees about 50 yards. See that opening? On the far side of the opening, at the base of the lone tree trunk." And for Point C: "Fifth fence pole north of the corner, at the north edge of the bush." (I'd hesitate to use compass directions while talking-in a sniper unless we were both familiar with the area and knew directions with certainty.)

Another talking-in technique, which can be used both for designating a target and adjusting

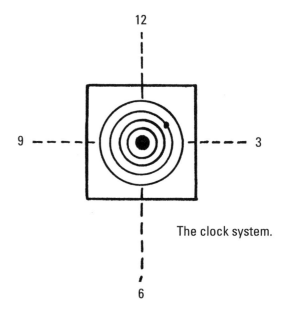

The clock system.

fire, is the clock system, illustrated over a bull's-eye target. Instead of a bull's-eye, however, the center could be a reference point near your concealed foe.

From the bull or reference point, right is 3 o'clock, left is 9 o'clock, straightaway is 12, and directly down or back toward you is 6 o'clock. In the illustration, you'd describe the bullet

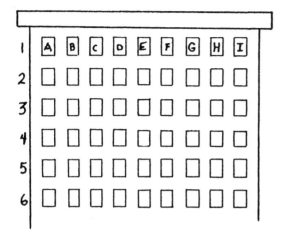

DESIGNATING A WINDOW. Count down from the top.

impact as "2 o'clock, 2 inches out." Were this a reference point, such as the lone pine tree in the center of the last illustration, and you wanted to designate Point C using the clock system, you'd say: "2 o'clock, 50 yards, at the far edge of the bush."

Note that we gave both a clock direction *and* an estimated distance—then for even more clarity described it as the "far edge of the bush."

Simpler than the clock system is directing the sniper to a target from a visual reference point using mils—but that's possible only if the spotter has a spotting scope containing its own mil dot reticle, such as the Leupold Mark 4. If he has mil dots, it's quick and easy for the spotter to announce, for example, "Three mils right of the corner telephone pole, and four miles up, by the fence." That's exact and precise. Those mil dots would come in handy for the spotter to help the sniper calculate his moving target leads or windage holdoffs, too.

One special problem I've encountered while surveilling is visual confusion about a target's exact location due to optical "depth of field"; that is, when viewed at a distance through an optical device, a deep area seems compressed on the same plane. You can overcome this by staying aware of the danger, but it really underscores the hazards of estimating range through an optical device unless it's designed for that purpose.

If you don't have to use an optical device,

one fast way of talking your sniper in is to describe the target's location in terms of fist widths, multifinger widths, or thumb widths—when your arm's fully extended—from a visible reference point. Again using the illustration's Point C as an example, "One thumb-width right of the road, next to the fence."

Our last talking-in technique, illustrated at left, is used in an urban area to designate a target in a particular window. We count floors *down* from the top of the building because many times the first floor may not be visible to us. To distinguish a particular window, we use alphabetical letters. Some SWAT units go so far as to assign a color code to each side of the building, too.

Observing Bullet Impacts

The five soldier figures in our illustration on page 318 depict ways of determining that a subject has actually been hit by a bullet.

The lower left figure typifies what's normally expected—visible blood splatter and obvious effects on clothing or equipment. Just above him, we see another subject hit through the left breast, but the only visible sign is the blood splatter that hit the wall behind him. You might also see the momentary reflection of blood spatter as it flies through the air behind him, which sometimes looks like a puff of smoke.

The man to his upper right is collapsing unnaturally. He's obviously not diving or controlling his fall; it's as if his body has liquefied. This effect can vary from a violent twisting due to bone impact to sliding passively straight to the ground.

On the far right, we may actually hear the audible "slap" of the bullet if the target's more than 200 yards but less than 400 yards away. The rifle muzzle blast dissipates by the time the bullet's gone 200 yards, but we won't hear a slap after about 400 yards.

The center and final example wouldn't be known to me if I hadn't seen it myself. This soldier's uniform is dusty, and the only way we know he's been hit is the dust that puffed just above his left pocket.

Bullet impact creates a variety of detectable effects.

But the complicated part is detecting misses. Unless there's a strong crosswind, misses usually are long or short of the target, with short hits typically the easiest to detect since their impact point is within your field of view. When you absolutely can see no sign of impact, the odds are that it went high.

Frequently, you'll be able to see the bullet trace or track as it passes through mirage near the target. This wisp of a trail—as illustrated at right—looks like a very thin jet contrail. Visible less than one second, the trace is created by the bullet's wake cutting through shimmering heat waves. Because the trace drifts at the speed of the wind, however, it's accurate only at the instant of the bullet's passage.

One late afternoon at Gunsite, while spotting for Eduardo Abril de Fontcuberta, a Spanish Foreign Legion officer and sniper advisor to the Spanish army, I observed the unusual phenomenon of actually seeing a flash of light off his bullet jackets as they neared the

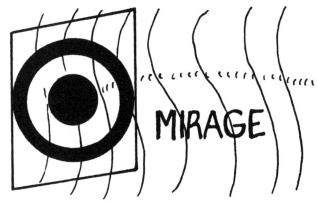

Bullet trace is visible in mirage.

target. This split-second twinkle of reflected light was possible because the sun was nearly setting and only about 20 degrees to the side of his bullet path. So it's possible to adjust from such a reflection, but only under these limited circumstances.

When it comes to adjusting fire, the cleverest real-world account I've come upon is from World War II, via a 1953 article in *American Rifleman*, in which a spotter put a precision rifleman's fire on a target that he couldn't even see. Using a 20x spotting scope, Robert Sears could discern a German machine gun firing away at 800 yards with such deadly effect that an infantry company could not cross a river. He had a competitive rifleman comrade fire (using ordinary open sights) at what he called a "reference target"—a rock the rifleman could see, though he could not see the machine gun nest. Observing that bullet impact, Sears announced a sight change to put it closer to the machine gun nest—pay close heed—*but had the rifleman fire again at the same rock*, which was the only thing he could see that far away. So, using his powerful 20x optic, Sears twice more adjusted the rifleman's rounds; then, still aiming at that rock, the rifleman put fire right atop the machine gun position, "either a hit or so close that the machine gunner went down in a foxhole."

That's about as slick as it gets.

Adjusting the Sniper's Fire

If the sniper missed, the spotter must tell him by how much, exactly describing the impact point. This is an important distinction: the spotter *doesn't* tell him how much to correct; he only gives him the raw data. The sniper interprets this data and decides how to adjust his scope or hold for a corrected follow-up shot.

The fastest, most easily understood way of describing to the sniper where his round impacted is via a mil dot reticle in a spotting scope because both spotter and sniper are using exactly the same yardstick. Second to that is the clock system, with the spotter giving first a clock direction then a distance in inches from the intended impact point. What needs to be clear, of course, is exactly what this point is; in most military sniping situations, it's center-chest. However, it's not so clear-cut for many police incidents, in which the sniper should probably announce his intended impact point just to ensure that his spotter understands.

TARGET DETECTION

Target detection is the first essential step in every sniping engagement. Without its success, there is no engagement. Unlike shooting on a range where targets are clearly marked and easily seen, your camouflaged foe purposely attempts to make himself and his position indistinct. While anyone can spot a conspicuous orange among many apples, your challenge is to find a brown or green object intentionally concealed among a whole field of brown or green. It's a major task involving advanced techniques.

Elsewhere we discuss the "wall of green" as the means for defensively detecting threats while under march. The techniques described here are applied while you're in a hide and offensively seeking targets. This target detection involves three levels of optically scanning for target indicators. Note that you're looking for *indicators* and not the targets themselves; such target indicators are the clues you follow up with intense observation until you find the enemy.

Before we delve deeper, I'll first share some important spotting insights born from hard experience.

Most Important Spotting Advice

1. *Your mind cannot detect something unless it has enough time to see it.* In order for your brain to recognize something, your eyes must linger on it long enough to register an impression. Rotating your head too fast creates an indecipherable blur. I've learned to pace my eye movement by consciously scanning from one point to another, then going back and doing it again half as fast, then repeating this yet again at one-quarter the speed. This slowest pace becomes the pace for all subsequent scanning. As a general rule, the smaller or more distant your potential target, the slower you should move your eyes.

2. *Your mind cannot find something unless it can visualize what you're looking for.* Inexperienced snipers watch for a whole human body in uniform carrying a weapon, which

they'll probably never find. No, you must "tell" your mind that you're looking for a grapefruit-size piece of a human target—perhaps the heel of a boot, half a face, one hand, a shoulder, a rifle muzzle. If you program your mind to look for whole men, you automatically filter out numerous smaller clues and fragments of humans. You should be so familiar with enemy gear that you can distinguish the shape of a canteen or edge of a helmet against an irregular, confusing background.

3. *Appreciate the significance of shadow.* Experienced soldiers prefer shadows for walking, resting, or locating their fighting positions. Stationary humans seek shadow naturally to get out of the sun, and most often it's in the protective umbrage of shadow that you'll find an enemy sniper. Optically penetrate shadows to find the enemy. Also, place yourself in shadow not merely for concealment but because your pupils will widen and you'll be able to see more clearly looking outward into a sunlit area. Our World War I sniping expert, H.W. McBride, advised paying special heed at sunrise and sunset, when shadows are longest and light pierces deepest into foliage.

4. *Patience is the key to successful target detection.* You may spend entire days scanning an area without detecting a single target, or you could spot several instantly. Your self-control should be such that your reaction is identical in both circumstances. Realize that patience is nothing but a form of self-discipline. Fight the temptation to engage the very first target you spot from a new hide; if the enemy is unalerted, take time to identify high-priority targets, then properly engage them first. The essence of successful countersniping is both outthinking and outwaiting your opponent while scanning the same areas over and over in search of him, trying to find significance in the most boring visual details.

5. *Human beings are creatures of habit and occupy or travel along predictable places.* Learn your enemy's doctrine and tactics so well that you can anticipate how he'd position himself on a particular piece of ground. See the battlefield as he would see it. Balance and adjust this against what you know of human nature: we like to stay warm, out of the wind, close to roads, and near habitation. Our final component of habit invites further elaboration, which we'll now cover under a concept called "natural line of drift."

Natural Line of Drift

I must thank my SOG Recon Company commander, Capt. Willie Merkerson, for teaching me about natural line of drift over a beer one night in the NCO club. (It was the closest thing to a classroom we had.)

My first step during mission planning was to take a grease pencil and "guesstimate" trail locations on my map, then decide which ones to avoid, which to approach only cautiously, and which to consider for ambushes. Applying what Captain Merkerson taught me, I was able to anticipate nine out of 10 hidden NVA trails in Laos and Cambodia despite the enemy's elaborate camouflage and clever diversions.

Having scribbled Merkerson's advice that night on a bar napkin, I've modified it but slightly over the years, and I'm now faithfully relaying it to you. Throughout history, man has preferred to travel across ground in habitual ways that save time and conserve effort by seeking the path of least resistance, which eventually became trails, paths, or roads. Man doesn't consciously plan this; he just sort of drifts into traveling certain ways across terrain. We've depicted these habits in the upper left of the illustration on page 321 to show that a human travels:

- Parallel to streams and rivers
- Along the long axis of ridgelines
- At the bottom of valleys
- Along the most direct, easiest route between two inhabited places
- By using the shortest, easiest route between known trails and roads and other natural lines of drift

Natural lines of drift.

As shown in the illustration's lower right, wartime tactical necessity generates additional natural drift habits so that foot soldiers:

- March through woods close enough to see the edge but far enough back to remain unseen
- Cross open areas at the narrowest, lowest point
- Cross streams and trails at bends
- Walk along a ridge's military crest, just below the top
- Occupy the highest points for observation but dig in at the military crest
- Bivouac near drinkable water

Applying this understanding of human nature allows you to see patterns the enemy doesn't notice himself and enables you to focus your surveillance at places the enemy most naturally will appear.

Hasty, Deliberate, and Detailed Scanning

I've identified three levels of visual scanning to be used when searching for targets: hasty, deliberate, and detailed, executed in that order so you always begin with the fastest and easiest technique.

But whichever you're conducting, I'd advise not to get too logical or too concrete too early. Allow yourself the latitude to "feel" something before looking closely at it, a kind of "What's wrong with this picture?" attitude.

Also, when using optical devices, "layer" your capabilities by one team member using, say, binoculars while the other employs naked eyes or his rifle scope.

And finally, readjust your binocular focus while scanning so it's crisp at exactly the range of each lateral sweep.

Hasty Scanning

Begin with this hasty scan, a quick naked-eye check from close to far, making visual sweeps from left to right and right to left. Start at the nearest terrain feature that could conceal a hostile and move all the way out to the maximum range of your rifle. You're also looking for close threats to your hide.

We've illustrated the hasty scan in the first of two scanning panels on the next page. Notice that you're looking at spots where an enemy most likely would be. Especially taking into account that he's a right-handed shooter, look for him at the low-left corner of each place having ground-level cover. Also apply what you know of natural line of drift, enemy tactics, and human logic. Where would *you* be if you were the enemy on this ground?

Perhaps you'd spend a minute or two doing a fast hasty scan.

Deliberate Scanning

The same panel illustrates deliberate scanning because you follow exactly the same procedures, only this time with binoculars.

One significant difference is that your visual sweeps are jerky and jump from likely locale to likely locale, but since you're now

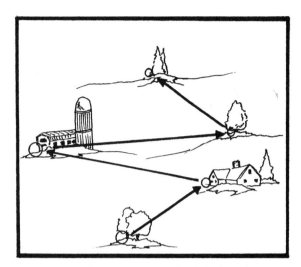

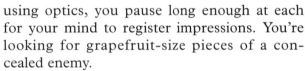

Hasty and deliberate scanning both look in the same places, but use binoculars for deliberate scans.

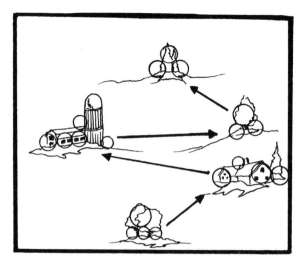

Detailed scans look at more places over a longer period and divide the sector between sniper and spotter.

using optics, you pause long enough at each for your mind to register impressions. You're looking for grapefruit-size pieces of a concealed enemy.

Roughly, I'd recommend spending three to five minutes doing a deliberate scan.

Detailed Scanning

If you failed to detect targets using a hasty or deliberate scan, you go on to the most thorough technique, the detailed scan. There's no time limit—this is the way you'll scan until you find a target or target indicator.

Now is when you employ all optical devices and formally divide the sector among you for long-term surveillance, as explained in another section. You're ready for the long haul.

As shown in the second scanning illustration panel, you look at every single place an enemy could be, over and over and over, recognizing that if he cannot be found where he's supposed to be, he must be somewhere else and therefore he can be anywhere. This means you look *everywhere.*

Pick limited areas and watch them intensely, use naked eyes and stay alert for movement in large areas, scan back and forth with binoculars, sketch his earthworks so you'll be able to tell tomorrow if he worked on it at night, practice

talking your partner in on a simulated target where a real one likely may appear, or use any other technique you can devise to stay alert and watch your sector. Keep your visual and mental edge.

Most likely, what you'll be finding now will be *indicators* of a target's presence rather than the target itself.

Target Indicators

Once spotted, you home-in on an indicator, with both sniper team members intensely surveilling that spot until you've found the target that generated the indicator. Again, program your mind to watch for grapefruit-size pieces of the enemy.

Indicators are evidence of the enemy's presence, which we've categorized according to the distinct ways they'll appear on the battlefield. These target indicators, as illustrated, include shine, movement, tactical sign, sound, smell, shape, contrast, and human sign.

Shine

Shine could be the reflection of sunlight off an optical device or, more frequently, the glistening of rain on a poncho or piece of equipment. Like shadows, shine is most prominent in the early morning or late afternoon

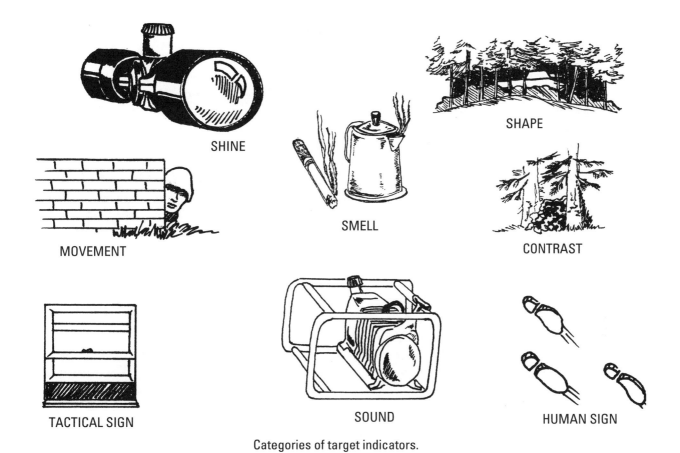

Categories of target indicators.

when slanted sun rays penetrate deepest into cover and foliage. Included in this category is the light of lanterns, flashlights, and campfires as well as the glow of cigarettes. In the last case, I'd watch especially closely just around dusk, when chain-smoking enemy sentries have their last daylight smoke and its glowing ember stands out.

Movement

Because of the way our brains process visual information, movement is the easiest and fastest indicator to spot. Recall that our minds process 60 images per second. This means an enemy must move so slowly that there's no visible change in 1/60 of a second, which is very unlikely.

To fully exploit your brain's ability to distinguish slight movements, hold your head very still, fix your eyes on a tiny spot in the middle of your field of view, "flush" all thoughts from your mind, and wait.

A related kind of movement is that of animals, especially birds, which may be flushed or attracted by a concealed enemy. A curious cow can compromise the cleverest camouflage. Understanding animal habits saved the life of Larry Predmore, a Minnesota woodsman and SOG comrade who detected an NVA counter-recon squad sneaking up on his team thanks to an owl. The owl had perched above him in daylight and kept looking back in the direction it had just left; Larry correctly interpreted this and a moment later drew a bead on a stalking NVA soldier's forehead.

The good guys won that encounter.

Tactical Sign

Our next category requires knowledge of the enemy and correct interpretation of clues.

You're looking for visible signs of how the enemy has modified the environment to facilitate his presence—things as simple as an open window on a cool or rainy day or as pronounced as a loophole cut into a wall. Other tactical signs could include exposed earth or berms from digging, stacked logs, sandbags, fire lanes cut through brush to improve sectors of fire, and commo wire strung through trees.

Sound

Sound target indicators can be as subtle as the "clunk" of equipment knocked about or as distinct as a rifle muzzle blast.

While going through a cycle at the U.S. Army's National Training Center at Fort Irwin, California, in the mid-1980s, I was surprised by how far the sound of generators carried in the night Mohave wind. The wind dramatically affects sound waves, making distant sounds seem close if it's blowing toward you, or deceptively lessening them when it carries them away from you.

When conditions are just right, you can even hear distant human voices or coughing that not only indicate the enemy's location but tell you how alert or lax he is.

A novel Soviet army technique from World War II was to lay a board on the ground and place an ear against it to hear distant vehicles, somewhat like listening to a railroad rail. This was especially effective near hard-surfaced roads and bridges or frozen ground.

Smell

Wind acts on scent like it does on sound, carrying it toward you or pushing it away from you.

Sometimes our SOG recon men could determine they were nearing a North Vietnamese base camp purely by the putrid smell of *nuoc mam* fermented fish sauce or the harsh aroma of Vietnamese tobacco. In another region or continent, it could have been the smell of coffee at dawn or the stench of a guerrilla band's unsanitary latrine.

The greatest problem with a sniper smoking,

I believe, is that he desensitizes his sense of smell and loses the ability to detect aromatic target indicators.

Shape

This target indicator is somewhat abstract. It means looking for something that doesn't fit, a shape that's contrary to its surroundings. In our illustration we show a few horizontal lines from a concealed tank, which is in the midst of vertical lines from trees and foliage.

Other shape indicators include a plain shape among much detail, something that looks regular in a sea of randomness, and straight lines amid curves. Sometimes this discernable shape is not the object or target indicator itself—which is well camouflaged—but its shadow, compromised by strong sunlight.

Contrast

Contrast is similar to shape, except here we're talking about conflicts in color and texture, which usually result from poorly prepared camouflage.

Contrast indicators include, as we've illustrated, leafy branches used as camouflage below a pine tree (meaning improper matching of natural camouflage), cut live camouflage foliage changing color or becoming limp as it dries, concentrating too much leafy foliage to conceal something, and outlines that are in conflict with shadows, which indicate use of camouflage nets.

Even the most superb camouflage is imperfect. Glass it with your optics, examine it in minute detail as the sun shifts and light changes angles, and you'll eventually penetrate it.

Human Sign

The section on tracking deals with human sign extensively, so we won't repeat it all here.

For target-detection purposes, all you need to remember is that man tends to be a messy beast who leaves tracks and trash in his wake, and the larger the enemy force the less concerned they are about concealing human sign. They may have perfectly prepared overhead camouflage,

USMC Scout-Snipers transmit a digital image on the Marine Air Ground Task Force Secondary Image Dissemination System (MSIDS).

but with a spotting scope you can find boot tracks leading into their fighting positions.

A related indicator is smoke from cooking or warming fires, sure signs of human—and enemy—activity.

The Importance of Patience

Ready for this? Sometimes there are *no* visible indicators, no quick and easy way to spot the enemy.

Then, like a cop checking the plates of every 2006 red Camaro in Kansas City for recent accident damage, you must thoroughly check every single potential location completely, boringly, repeatedly, until maybe hours or days later, you find one needle in the haystack. You need the self-discipline of patience.

Patience, patience, patience! The enemy will have to urinate in only an hour or two; insects may bite and bother him; the sun continuously shifts about like a great spotlight, illuminating now what had been shadow a moment before. Meanwhile, wind and sun degrade any foliage he cut for camouflage, and sweat washes cammo stick from his face and hands. He cannot stay motionless long before he gets cold or hungry or sleepy or uncomfortable. Conditions are changing constantly.

As the hours drag by and your eyes grow tired, never forget that your enemy is human, which means he's imperfect, and given enough time, he'll do something to make himself detectable.

THE SURVEILLANCE ROLE

Today in Afghanistan and Iraq, sniper teams often are being employed purely in a surveillance role. Due to their team's superior optics and observations skills—along with their ability to hide in plain sight—more so than other soldiers and marines, these scout-snipers are more likely to detect enemy forces emplacing improvised explosive devices (IEDs), smuggling people and weapons across borders, or many other hostile activities.

Most such surveillance missions are clandestine—that is, teams are infiltrated and operate to avoid any sign of their presence. Should they detect suspicious or hostile actions, instead of engaging they report it and vector in a reaction force so their presence is not compromised and they can continue to surveil the area. Interestingly, the U.S. Marine Corps recently equipped its Scout-Sniper teams with high-resolution digital cameras and an uplink device that connects to a military radio(shown on page 325). Practically real-time, these sniper teams can snap high-quality images of enemy activity and relay them miles to a headquarters for analysis, assessment, and action.

Given that the same position may be used again in the future—and it's best that the enemy never realize how information is being developed—it's essential that these clandestine sniper teams exfil just as carefully as they infiltrated. Whenever a reaction force achieves success, it's useful to let the populace believe that the enemy had been detected by a satellite, surveillance aircraft, paid informers—anything but a concealed sniper team.

PRACTICE FOR TARGET DETECTION

One simple technique for improving visual scanning skills is finding concealed words in those popular "word search" puzzles. We've prepared a sniping word puzzle to prove our point (see page 327).

Take one glance at it. You'll instantly notice that there's a letter missing, demonstrating how dramatically conspicuous anything different is. Target detection, however, involves the discovery of *inconspicuous* targets, not obvious ones. What this actually illustrates is how effectively a decoy or diversion can attract attention—indeed, your eyes were lured to a spot where there was absolutely nothing.

Applying target detection techniques, you start with a hasty scan, keeping your mind as unfettered as possible, almost letting instinct tell you when to look closer. You're scanning for subtle patterns that will cause you to take a second look without even being able to define what you think you see. You'll probably find about one-quarter of the words using a hasty scan, not even knowing which words are hidden in the puzzle.

After this, slow down and intensify your search, using a deliberate scan. This requires more analysis, actually examining the word list and looking for unusual letters or letter combinations so that your mind can watch for specific patterns. For example, you'll notice that only one word, "azimuth," has the letter Z in it, which is an infrequently used letter. Or you'll notice that both "medulla" and "McMillan" have double Ls, an unusual letter pattern. You'll actually scan each line right to left, bottom to top. A deliberate scan will help you find perhaps another half of the "target" words by mentally focusing on their visual distinctions while completely scanning the target area.

The remaining words are so subtle, so well blended, that only a detailed scan will detect them. You must carefully examine every single line and letter, using a well-planned scheme to ensure that you consider all possibilities from every direction and miss nothing. In the movie *The Day of the Jackal*, the French detective was able to trace a would-be assassin only by having his men search thousands of hotel registrations every single day. The sleuth's detailed scan is no different from yours: meticulous, patient, and demanding, focusing both intellect and instinct for your search.

```
T F I R D F O E N I L L A R U T A N
V R A B O R T H L H A N D K L A T S
A E N R F E M C Y L D W H R R S E E
E P R Y M C D T E O A T A O E M G P
P I B E J O N A M L C B M Y N T A O
O N O T G N I M E R F E T N I E L L
C S R S C I W C D E F I D I E L F S
S R E T T O P S U N C H R V T L U E
L A S C O N I B L O D H F L S U O S
A R I O H S A L L I A T T A O B M R
R R G L O R A E A M E H S U B M A E
E E H T R R V N A L L I M C M   C V
D I T E E T A C T I C S U A T I S E
E S T R N C E L A H R E K R A P Z R
F T C I R N O I T A S N E P M O C A
H S P I R H S P R E C I S I O N H S
T S D Y S D L E I F D E R N T O P S
R S I R R U B C D B D L O P U E L B
```

Alvin York	Bullet	Lead	Redfield	Spot
Ambush	Burris	Leupold	Remington	Spotter
Azimuth	Camouflage	Match	Reverse Slope	Stalk
Ball	Colt	McMillan	Rifle	Steiner
Barrett	Compensation	Medulla	Robar	Steyr
BDC	Decoy	Natural Line	Scope	Tactics
Binocs	Federal	of Drift	Sierra	Velocity
Boattail	H and K	Parker Hale	Sniper	Wind
Boresight	H S Precision	Recon	Spin	Yaw

Scanning Practice and Competition

I'm an advocate of word search puzzles because they help develop visual detection instincts quickly and don't require an elaborate outdoor tactical area, training aids, etc. But to be most realistic, they should employ words common to sniping or military or police work so that you're looking for patterns that already exist in your brain.

Select one word from our list, for instance, "spot." Time yourself and see how quickly you can find it. Now try a word consisting of nothing but indistinctive, common letters, such as "Sierra." Only use hasty scan techniques; don't get deliberate at all. With practice, you'll probably cut your search time in half.

You can get better with the added pressure of competition, in which perhaps four snipers compete to find a word, the winner gaining his comrade's undying respect and one "I-owe-you" brewski. I'd guess such competitions eventually will cut your time by another one-half.

Although they aren't unintelligent, some snipers won't experience any improvement. For unknown reasons, some people's brain pathways aren't wired to process visual images efficiently or quickly. Therefore, this word picking can help teammates assess their partner's strengths and weaknesses, though there's more to visual skills than just this exercise.

Visual scanning for subtle patterns is equally inherent to jigsaw puzzles, which also inculcate patience, an essential quality for any sniper. Indeed, assembling jigsaw puzzles is probably the best possible indoor exercise for developing a sniper's mental and visual skills. Combine this with dry-firing and you've got good training for a rainy afternoon.

A more concrete kind of indoor visual scanning practice can be accomplished using *Where's Waldo?* children's books, a concept we've modified in our illustration to "Where's Ivan?" How quickly can you detect the one figure carrying an SVD rifle? The drawings can be taped to a distant wall so you must employ binoculars or a spotting scope while scanning.

VISUAL INFORMATION RETENTION: "KIMS"

The ability to retain brief visual images is a critical sniping skill. Not only must a sniper record and report detailed intelligence, but he must remember exactly where targets are located or were last observed.

WHERE'S IVAN? Find the SVD-armed sniper.

During World War II, the American OSS intelligence agency trained its personnel to memorize an entire scene with a single glance so that with only one passing view of a railway yard, for instance, a spy still could report details about every Nazi train in the station.

This mental snapshot technique was made famous by Rudyard Kipling's novel *Kim*, in which his youthful hero plays it as a game. Called "Kim's Game," or just "Kim's," it has become so standardized in sniper training that it's equally known as the "Keep in Memory System" (KIMS,) which also spells the Kipling character's name. Whatever it's called, playing it is simple in concept and execution.

Take an ordinary blanket and a half-dozen commonplace items, such as a coin, a fired cartridge, a business card, eyeglasses, a piece of string, and a pencil. Lay them out randomly and cover them with the blanket.

Now, expose the items for two minutes and allow your fellow snipers to study them but not take any notes. Re-cover the items and then direct your audience to write notes in as much detail as possible, recording what they saw. They can even draw a sketch, depicting the relative sizes and spacing of the objects.

Now, ask them highly detailed questions. They probably all noted the coin's date, but how many wrote that it was facing the business card, which was about 5 inches away? And that string—which end was frayed and which end was cut?

To keep the mood competitive, it's excellent to allow a person who answers one question correctly to ask the group the next question—but in order to ask it, his own notes must record, say, that the business card had a phone number with an area code of 612. Or you can direct questions at people, with any wrong response eliminating a competitor and the final winner owed a brewski or relieved of policing brass from the range, etc.

To make KIMS even more challenging, increase the number of items displayed, reduce the amount of exposure time, or lengthen the time gap between observing and recording information. We've had our school cadre act out gunfight scenarios as a real-life kind of KIMS that was especially popular with students. It sometimes required observing through optical devices.

But just the blanket and trinkets technique works fine, too, and makes for an exercise that can be conducted anywhere with two minutes' preparation.

MILITARY SNIPER TARGET PRIORITIES

One of sniping's biggest illusions is that a sniper engages targets at leisure, for however long he wants, while the enemy cooperatively remains in the open like some splendid shooting gallery. Baloney!

Unless you stumble upon totally green troops or armed imbeciles, they'll vanish less than a second after hearing your first shot, instantly return fire, and do their utmost to kill you. A sniper must weigh his first shot because any subsequent shots will be against an alert enemy staying invisible and shooting back.

Your first shot *must* be your best, and for that reason you aim it at the most valuable target you can find, possibly even ignoring some initial targets in hopes that a better one will materialize. These are judgment calls based on a clear understanding of which targets are the most important—your *priority* targets.

Target Priorities

Day or night, in any situation, *your top priority always is your enemy counterpart*—a bad-guy sniper outfitted with an optically equipped rifle.

The enemy sniper is always priority one because, more so than any other hostile, he has the optics, training, ballistic performance, and perspective to eliminate *you*. If you're snuffed out, you can hardly accomplish any further sniping engagements; indeed, you will have yielded all local sniping capabilities to the enemy. On the other hand, by preemptively disposing of your foe, you'll be free to dominate the local long-range shooting environment.

Wrapped together with this top priority target is *any* enemy who can see you and poses a direct threat. Self-defense comes automatically.

Following this category, your priorities are leaders, crew-served weapons crewmen, and critical materiel targets, but not necessarily in that order. You'll have to reshuffle these to fit your situation or to coincide with the plans of the unit you're supporting.

For example, I would urge you to "decapitate" his leadership when the enemy's on the offense, because degrading his coordination and command will decisively affect his attack. When he's in the defense, however, I'd assign priority to crew-served weapons over leaders since the enemy will fight from where he is, and command and control won't affect the outcome nearly so much.

Leaders include both officers and noncommissioned officers, in that order. Understandably, you'd first engage the highest-ranking officer visible.

Other Priority Targets

Crew-served weapons include belt-fed machine guns, some antitank and antiaircraft weapons—such as the SA-7 Strella missile launcher illustrated at right—and belted grenade launchers like the Russian AGS-17. These are more important than the ordinary enemy rifleman because they more profoundly influence the battle—and, in some cases, you may very well be the only friendly with the optics to see them.

Materiel targets usually include things like radios, optical sights on mortars and artillery pieces, sensors, radars, laser designators, rangefinders on vehicles, and any kind of computer control boxes. Each materiel target demands that you place your bullet where it will do the most destruction; for instance, an antitank missile launcher is particularly susceptible to fire impacting the corrugated box containing its guidance system, while hits anywhere else have practically no effect. You

TARGET PRIORITIES

Always #1— the enemy sniper

Officers and NCOs.

Crew-served weapons and crews

Critical enemy equipment

must know the enemy's equipment well enough to target the Achilles' heel of each one.

Next on this priority totem pole are enemy personnel beyond the effective range of your non-sniper colleagues. This is because the 5.56mm bullet runs out of "oomph" at about 500 yards, but your 7.62mm can take out targets 500 yards farther.

The final target priority is very general, but it must be stated since it's sometimes misunderstood: *everything else*. When you're on your own deep behind enemy lines, perhaps you'll allow low-priority targets unhindered passage in hopes of seeing a higher-priority target later. But when you're supporting a unit, you cannot passively await a priority target while other friendlies are in heavy battle and desperately need your support.

The melee of battle can be an excellent sniping environment because the enemy is so preoccupied with other shooting that he won't distinguish the precision, long-range fire that's dropping his riflemen one after another. When the action is fast and furious, you engage as many enemy as possible.

But intertwined with target priorities is knowing how to recognize these targets when you see them. Recognition of enemy snipers is addressed in the countersniping section, and a special section explains how to engage materiel targets, so here we'll limit ourselves to recognizing leaders and detecting crew-served positions.

Recognizing Leaders

Generally, you can visually identify a leader by how he's equipped or attired, by how he interacts with those around him, and by his position in a tactical formation.

Our first leader-recognition illustration shows how to spot him by his uniform or gear. His uniform has elaborate epaulets—a sure sign of a leader—while a Sam Browne cross-strap supports the belt at his waist. This frequently encountered strap clearly discloses an officer since it's used to support the weight of a pistol. This strap is so blatant a sign of rank that I took to calling it a

"dummy strap" or "shoot-me strap" so students would recall this instant recognition feature. Stripes, decorations, and a just plain neater uniform also indicate a likely leader.

Also notice that around his neck, our leader has slung binoculars and in his hand he holds a map (likewise, he could carry that international symbol of authority, a clipboard). At a more subtle level, notice that he's older and wears glasses; combat is a young man's occupation, so whenever you see anyone who looks over 30, he's probably a leader. And finally, recognize what *isn't* there—almost every enlisted man and NCO carries a rifle and a rucksack, while any but the most junior officers aren't usually thus burdened.

The next illustration shows how to interpret interactions to identify a leader. During the 1982 Falklands War, the British SAS found that by promptly shooting those Argentines who appeared most agitated and shouted loudest,

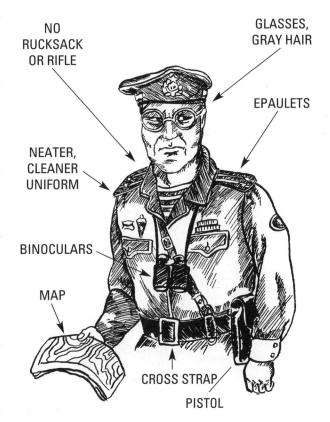

NO RUCKSACK OR RIFLE

GLASSES, GRAY HAIR

EPAULETS

NEATER, CLEANER UNIFORM

BINOCULARS

MAP

CROSS STRAP/ PISTOL

Detecting a leader by uniform and gear.

they'd effectively remove a unit's leadership. When you're shooting people, take the man who is waving his arms about, suggested Maj. Mike Norman to the 42nd Royal Marine Commandos. Due to Norman's suggestion, our first figure, on the right, is waving to the men about him and shows us even at long range that he's a leader.

But notice, too, that he's being followed by a radio operator, a sure sign that he's at least a platoon leader. However, since the next soldier is saluting him, I'd guess that he's probably a company commander and possibly even a battalion commander. An experienced army may wisely forbid saluting in the field, but you'll still see soldiers stop what they're doing or even jump to their feet when ranking leaders arrive.

The far-left soldier requires a more subtle interpretation—he's merely looking to his leader for direction, a sign that's often found in combat. We did not illustrate the last interaction example because it's another case of something you *won't* see: you won't see a leader performing some dirty or hazardous detail, but you may very well find a leader *watching* others while they do it.

The third leader-recognition category, his position in tactical formations, is depicted as abstract silhouettes so you'll consider it independent of other features like uniforms and equipment. The two highlighted silhouettes show where you'll most likely see a leader: at the middle of a file or column so he can control the formation but not so far forward as to be unduly in danger. Even peering through your spotting scope at a vague enemy 800 yards away, you should be able to distinguish where the middle of a formation is.

Then, concentrating your attention there, find one or two clues that clarify your target.

Detecting Crew-Served Positions

Once the action's started, it's simple to detect a crew-served weapon position. Just watch for green tracer, listen to the louder report of the PK machine guns, and notice the impressive backblast from RPGs and missile launchers. A machine gun's muzzle may also kick up dust.

But a sniper should be able to locate crew-served positions before firing starts so he can suppress or destroy the crewmen with well-aimed fire and ensure success for his comrades. It's not as hard as it would seem.

FOLLOWED BY RADIOMAN

SALUTING

LOOKING TO HIM FOR DIRECTIONS

WAVING ARMS, SHOUTING ORDERS

Detecting a leader by his actions.

it. You'll probably find antitank weapons positioned to the oblique, since these gunners prefer flanking shots, but machine gunners want to riddle a formation down its long axis, so they'll probably be nearly straight ahead, where the arrows point. If there's more than one potential spot, the enemy's probably using the one that gives better frontal protection and perhaps a concealed route for withdrawal.

Now, assuming you've come up with likely places for the enemy to put his crew-served weapons, how can you distinguish these positions from those of lesser weapons? Well, while surveilling through your spotting scope, you should be looking for what we've depicted in the illustration's center panel:

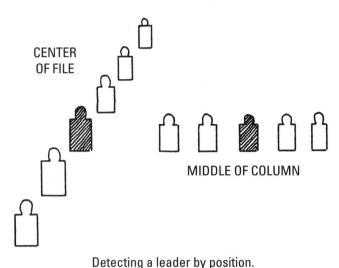

CENTER OF FILE

MIDDLE OF COLUMN

Detecting a leader by position.

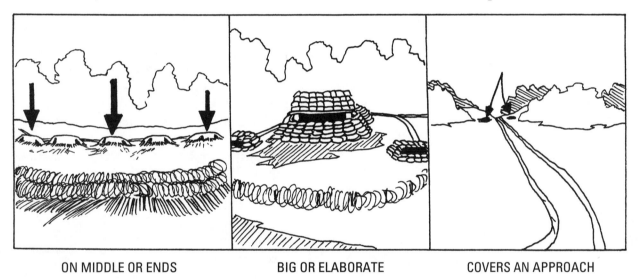

ON MIDDLE OR ENDS   BIG OR ELABORATE   COVERS AN APPROACH

Detecting crew-served positions.

As depicted in the left panel of the illustration above, the crew-served positions don't tend to be bunched up and probably will be found on the edges and/or center of an enemy platoon or company position. Not always, but a lot of the time.

In the far-right panel, you'll see another way to find a crew-served position, which is backtracking from the sector they should be covering, which in military terms is an "avenue of approach." Certainly *some* significant weapon is covering this road, and it's probably located at the spot that has the most complete overview of

- It's a larger position since it contains a larger weapon and several crewmen.
- It's visually different and may have an odd-shaped loophole or higher roof to accommodate the weapon.
- It's more elaborate, with heavier timbers, barbed wire, trimmed foliage for expanded fields of fire, etc.

Since your sniper team probably has the best optics in your unit, don't be surprised if your ability to find enemy crew-served positions becomes a component of every operation, for each objective. But before you get too confident, never forget that a wise enemy always employs at least a few dummy positions to divert fire from the real ones.

Other Engagement Considerations

After you've established a pecking order for the visible targets before you, you're ready to decide which to engage first, and here's where other considerations affect your judgment.

When targets are of equal value, you should first engage:

- The closer one, since it's a surer hit
- The one at your elevation, because up or down compensation may cause a miss
- The target *not* near a distant landmark, because the other target will be easier to find after he takes cover
- The stationary target, because it's more certain of a hit than a moving one
- The one near heavy cover first, because you can probably go back and find the foe who seeks thin cover

Where this process gets interesting is when the targets are not of equal value, leading to contentions like, "Do I engage the NCO who's 600 yards away and uphill, or the lieutenant who's only half-exposed at 500 yards?"

There are no pat "school solutions" to such judgments; you'll be the one in the thick of it, you'll be the one at risk, you know best your own abilities. You'll have to decide yourself.

POLICE SNIPER PRIORITY TARGETS

Just like his military counterpart, the law enforcement sniper designates target priorities, too, so he can engage suspects according to the threat they pose.

My greatest concern is that an officer who hasn't mentally prepared himself with realistic priorities may go for the first clear target which at that moment isn't much of a threat or can easily be taken by the entry team, while a mere 10 feet farther, and an equally attainable shot, is the guy who's shooting all the hostages.

We offer the following three categories of priority targets, which should be rearranged to fit each situation. How a suspect is armed and who or what he is should be addressed in your tac team plan so that the sniper team effec-

POLICE SNIPER JUDGMENTS. Is your priority target the man at the doorway with the pistol? Or to his right and behind glass, the suspect with the shotgun? Or visible in the back room and also behind glass, the suspect closest to the hostage?

tively supports other elements, especially the entry teams.

Most Dangerously Armed

The firearms danger varies with distance. At close range, the most dangerously armed foe has a shotgun, submachine gun, high-capacity pistol, or assault rifle. At moderate distances—say 100 to 200 yards—any rifleman or an optically equipped rifleman becomes a much greater threat than a shotgun-armed suspect. Beyond this distance, an optically equipped rifleman poses the greatest danger.

Most Dangerous Record of Violence

Should you have several potential targets visible, it only makes sense to cover more closely or engage first the one with an established record of murder, firearms assault, or violent acts due to mental instability or drugs. I'd consider, too, any suspect who has harmed a hostage or seems barely controlled by his comrades. This doesn't mean that another perpetrator won't pull a trigger first or that these others shouldn't be covered, too.

By Location, Greatest Threat to Friendlies

Suspects blocking or covering entrances, standing at critical junctures, or overwatching hostages may well be high-priority targets. In some especially complex hostage rescues, a hostile lookout could well be a fitting first target for "rapid incapacitation."

CHAPTER 12
RANGE AND WIND ESTIMATION

RANGE ESTIMATION TECHNIQUES

Incorrect range estimation is the biggest cause of long-range misses—more so than bad wind estimation, more so than jerking a trigger, more so than a poor hold or lead, more so than incorrectly computing up/down compensation. If you blow the range estimate, you've most likely blown the shot.

There are several reasons why. The biggest is that a bullet's trajectory—which is an arc—begins more and more to plunge at great distances so that a little error has a big effect. We've depicted the trajectory of a .308 Federal Match round below.

Notice that at 100, 200, and 300 yards, it flies a very flat path. Even if you made a great range estimation error—say, concluded the target was 300 yards away when it was really 200

yards—at close range, you'd probably hit your target just by aiming center-chest.

But let's say you mistakenly concluded a target was 600 yards away and it was only 500 yards—well, now the trajectory difference is about 3 feet. You see, at farther distances, the bullet plunges in an ever-steeper arc, and even minor errors become major.

Unfortunately, it's also at these greater distances that we most often and most understandably make range estimation errors.

But the other big problem with range estimation is that mistakes become *cumulative* and complicate all subsequent calculations for windage, moving target leads, and so on. And this can result in even short-range misses.

Look at the drawings in the sidebar on page 338, in which we consider the cumulative effect on a target that's merely 400 yards away. Despite

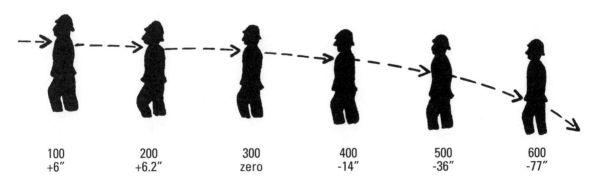

| 100 | 200 | 300 | 400 | 500 | 600 |
| +6″ | +6.2″ | zero | -14″ | -36″ | -77″ |

Due to a bullet's trajectory, range estimation accuracy becomes more critical with distance.

THE CUMULATIVE EFFECT OF RANGE ESTIMATION ERROR

Because several other aiming factors require increasing compensation with distance, they're very sensitive to any range error. Initial mistakes in range estimation, therefore, become cumulative, and even a moderate error can result in a total miss.

For our example, let's say that a target really is 400 yards away, but our sniper mistakenly has decided it's 300 yards away. We'll assume he's firing .308 168-grain Match and has a 300-yard zero. Note how his error compounds:

		400 yds	300 yds
1.	Compensation for Elevation/Range	14" High	Zero
2.	10 mph Wind Compensation	13" Left	7" Left
3.	Target Walking Left	17" Left	12" Left
4.	Target is 45 Degrees Up	14" Low	7" Low

So as we've shown in the illustration, just one fundamental range estimation error compounded and led to a complete miss.

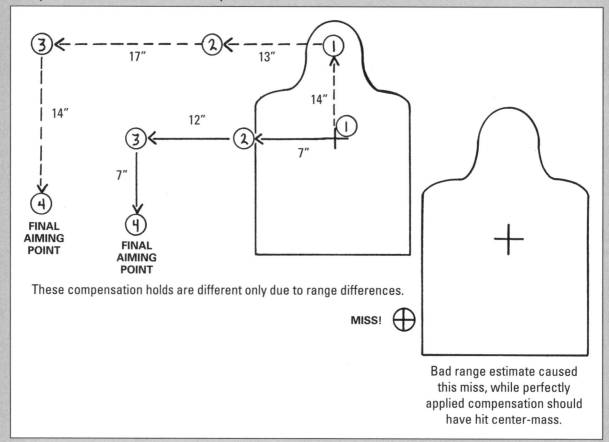

These compensation holds are different only due to range differences.

MISS!

Bad range estimate caused this miss, while perfectly applied compensation should have hit center-mass.

the sniper making every single computation correctly—except for the initial range estimate—he completely missed a relatively close target.

We're going to address a number of different devices and methods for range estimation, but as we cover these, keep in mind that you must practice them prone so that you learn to use them as you'll actually operate.

Through a Scope Reticle

Any duplex scope reticle has an inherent capacity for range finding. All that's needed is the precise reticle measurements.

Consider a Leupold Duplex reticle as found in a 3.5-10x rifle scope when set at maximum magnification. From edge to edge, the reticle's crosshair portion—the thinnest area—is 10 MOA wide. This represents 10 inches at 100 yards, then 20 inches at 200 yards, and so on.

At right we've illustrated how this reticle looks on a man. Note that we always rest the upper thick reticle on the top of his head, not at his feet. This is because it's far more likely to see a target's top than its base, especially at long range.

By the time he's at 600 yards, the target fills the entire thin reticle area. But beware: to be accurate, you always read range with your scope set on the *same* magnification.

We can thank FBI Special Agent Matthew Bowen Johnson for developing this technique while serving on the FBI Firearms Training Staff at Quantico. He is a fine rifleman and a genuine Southern gentleman. His technique works with any duplex-style reticle; all you need are the precise reticle dimensions.

Leupold took Special Agent Johnson's ranging technique a step further and inscribed a ranging ring alongside the zoom ring on its Vari-X III rifle scopes. All a rifleman has to do is zoom back and forth until the crosshair and a duplex edge bracket a 16-inch area, then read the distance off the zoom ring. It's not as precise as a laser, but it's more accurate than most eyeball techniques.

Some rifle scope makers, including Schmidt & Bender, put a vertical "step" rangefinder in their reticles for quick ranging. Here, the shooter

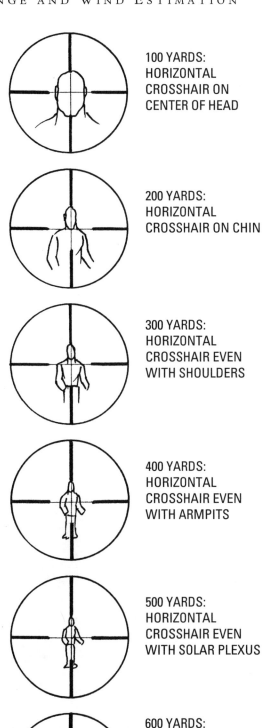

100 YARDS: HORIZONTAL CROSSHAIR ON CENTER OF HEAD

200 YARDS: HORIZONTAL CROSSHAIR ON CHIN

300 YARDS: HORIZONTAL CROSSHAIR EVEN WITH SHOULDERS

400 YARDS: HORIZONTAL CROSSHAIR EVEN WITH ARMPITS

500 YARDS: HORIZONTAL CROSSHAIR EVEN WITH SOLAR PLEXUS

600 YARDS: HORIZONTAL CROSSHAIR ON WAIST

Estimating range with a Leupold Duplex reticle, set on 10x.

Lower numerals on this Leupold Vari-X-III zoom ring synch with the reticle to calculate distances, set here at "6" for 600 yards.

paces needed to walk the width of your nail. That's his range in hundreds of yards.

If it takes just one pace, he's 50 yards away, two steps means he's 100 yards, and so forth, but only to a maximum of 200 yards. This is because you probably cannot accurately split the width of your thumb much finer than one-quarter.

Our next illustration shows a technique long used by the military. It's called the "football field" or "100-yard increment" method. To employ it, mentally divide the range into 100-yard increments by visualizing the length of a football field, or imagining the first 100 yards, then mentally laying it over and over the full distance.

When the distance gets greater than about 500 yards, or if any part of the ground is below your line of sight, the football field method

places a vertical scale over his human target to find the distance, applies holdover, and fires. This, too, is not very precise, but it's extremely fast and intended only for relatively close distances, under 400 meters.

Thumb and Eyeball Techniques

I must also thank FBI Special Agent Johnson for teaching me a range estimation technique that probably goes back to the days of the Kentucky long rifle.

As shown in the illustration on the next page, fully extend one arm and hold your thumb so the nail's just below your target and the target is at the very edge of the nail. Now, pretend that your quarry turned left and took whatever the number of normal

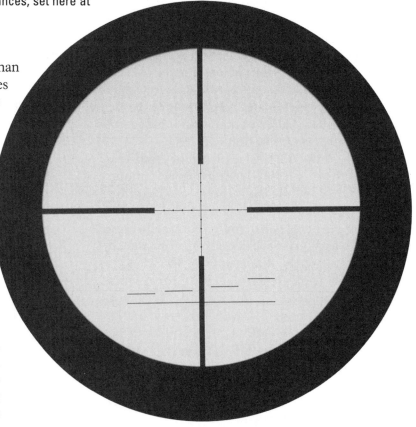

This Schmidt & Bender mil dot reticle includes a "step" rangefinder (bottom). Heights approximate an upright man at (L-R) 500, 400, 300, and 200 meters.

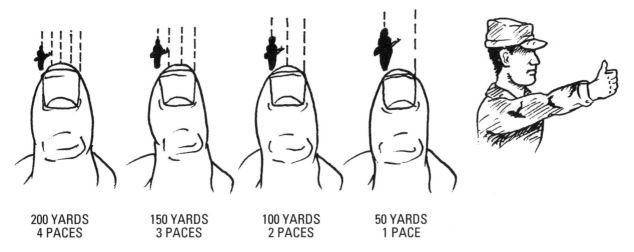

200 YARDS
4 PACES

150 YARDS
3 PACES

100 YARDS
2 PACES

50 YARDS
1 PACE

Thumb range estimation technique.

The football field/100-yard increment technique.

The half-distance technique.

becomes less and less accurate. Usually, it's better to divide the total distance in half, as shown next, then estimate just the closer half and double it. Not surprisingly, this is called the "half-distance" technique.

When using any range estimation technique—and especially when eyeballing—compare your results with those of your teammate and split the difference. Usually, this average is more accurate than either of your individual estimates.

The danger when using these eyeball methods is that in some situations our eyes can play tricks on us. These common visual confusions are seen in the illustration on page 342.

As depicted on the left side, a target will appear *closer* when:

- It's across a depression, most of which is hidden from view.
- You're looking down from high ground.
- You're looking along a straight line, like a road or railroad track.
- It's beyond a flat, uniform surface, like snow or sand, especially in bright sunlight.

On the right side, be warned that a target will appear *farther* when:

- It's small compared to its surroundings.
- It's on higher ground than you.

APPEAR CLOSER

ACROSS A HIDDEN DEPRESSION

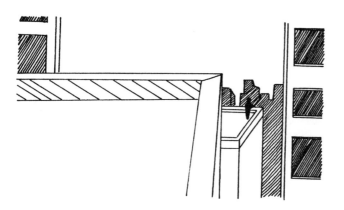

LOOKING DOWN FROM HIGH GROUND

LOOKING ALONG A STRAIGHT LINE

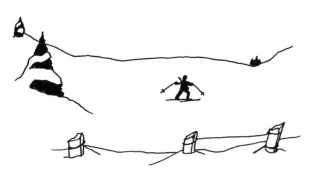

ACROSS FLAT, UNIFORM SURFACE

APPEAR FARTHER

SMALL TARGET, BIG SURROUNDINGS

LOOKING UP FROM LOWER GROUND

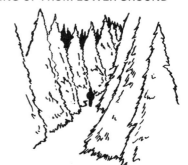

DOWN A NARROW SPACE

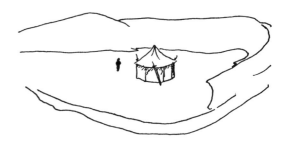

ACROSS A VISIBLE DEPRESSION

- The field of view is very narrow, such as along a trail.
- You're looking across a depression and all of it is visible to you.

Using a Map

When I tell students that one of the easiest and most accurate ways to estimate range is using a map, they typically seem to say, "Why, I could've thought of that."

This is so fundamental and so obvious, but very frequently it's the *last* method a sniper thinks of using—and it should probably be the first.

Clearly, the most direct approach is to plot your location and that of your target and simply measure the distance. That doesn't always work, though, because sometimes you're not sure of your target's location. In this situation, just look around until you see some prominent landmark that appears to be the same distance away and measure *this* range on your map. (Of course, beware of the visual pitfalls we covered a moment ago.)

A more exact range estimate can be ob-tained by using a GPS in unison with your map. Provided that there's distinctive terrain near the target, establish your exact location via the GPS. Plot this and the target location on the map, then measure it and you should have it. The Vector 21 system, as we'll see momentarily, takes this technique a step higher by integrating a GPS and laser to yield the most precise estimates obtainable.

Counting Fence Posts and Power Pylons

If you look closely around your operational area, you'll probably notice some kind of man-made feature emplaced at regular intervals that you can use for range esti-mation. The most frequently encountered are fence posts and power pylons or telephone poles. Any of these can be very useful, but take care that they really are positioned at a standard interval.

Since power pylons are so costly to erect, and most landowners don't like them, power companies tend to place them as far away from each other as they safely can—and this is usually

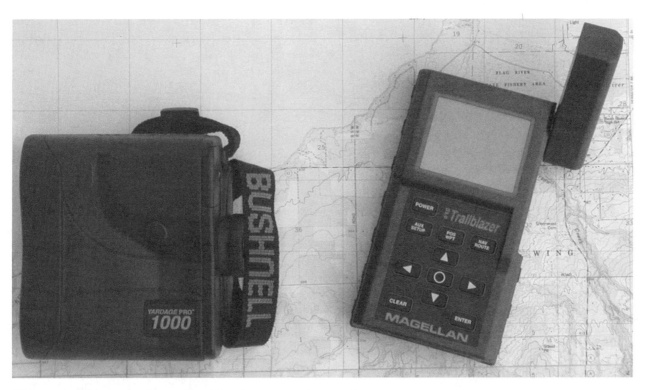

GPS, map, and laser can be used together for very precise ranging.

THE EFFECT OF
RANGE ESTIMATION ERROR

Because a bullet's trajectory starts as a gentle slant, then plunges more and more as it slows, long-distance range estimation is much less forgiving than short-range errors.

To help you appreciate this, we're providing data for .308 168-grain Match to show what a mere 10-yard range error does to bullet placement at various distances.

DISTANCE IN YARDS	BULLET DROP FOR 10-YARD ERROR
100–200	0.08"
200–300	0.61"
300–400	1.40"
400–500	2.40"
500–600	3.50"
600–700	4.80"
700–800	6.40"
800–900	8.20"
900–1000	10.20"

Now consider how easy it is to think a target's 750 yards away when it's actually 800—but this 50-yard error (not even 10 percent) would cause your bullet to hit 32 inches low, a miserable miss. Think about this when making range estimates.

a very set distance. Unless an extra one's been added for additional support at a river or on a hill, the distance should be fairly consistent.

On the other hand, fence posts will vary from landowner to landowner, and I'd hesitate to put much faith in consistent spacing. Still, though, it's worth checking.

Urban range estimation has its own opportunities and problems, which we'll cover extensively in the urban section.

LASER RANGING

Over the past decade I've used nine different laser rangefinders—and owned four—from three different manufacturers. I've field-tested them from the Arizona desert to the mountains of Alaska, the rarified air of the Rockies, and the forested mountains of Eastern Europe. Though lasers seem to be as temperamental an instrument as ever devised by man—you can range to 750 yards with one rated to 600, but cannot get 500 yards out of one rated for 800—I think I've finally figured them out.

I can thank Bushnell's top laser engineer, Tim Carpenter, for educating me along the way. He explained that a rangefinder uses a laser diode similar to a pen pointer, except it emits pulses of nonvisible wavelength light. Bushnell lasers, for example, have a wavelength of 905 nanometers (nm) in the infrared spectrum, while visible wavelength light measures 400 to 700 nm.

The laser diode emits light pulses of about 34–45 nanoseconds, which illuminate and reflect off a target, and this is optically detected by the rangefinder. This tiny reflection is amplified, then registered in multiple circuits containing a high-speed chronometer that measures the time it took for the light to reflect back. This time is converted to a distance, which appears in the device's liquid crystal display. Bushnell lasers are calibrated to read +/- 1 yard of a lazed target.

Interestingly, Carpenter explained, a laser rangefinder's maximum range is not determined by the laser's output. In fact, all Bushnell lasers—whether 600, 800, 1,000, or the latest 1,500-yard device—employ the same strength laser light emitter. The device's maximum effective range is determined by the quality of its receiver and its ability to measure milliseconds and sense tiny light reflections. The difference between economical units like Bushnell's and more expensive models also reflects lens quality and the ruggedness of construction. (Plus, the high-end lasers are installed in a pair of top-quality binoculars.)

View through the author's Bushnell Yardage Pro 1000 laser rangefinder, which measures in meters or yards.

Though Bushnell lasers use high-impact plastic rather than metal cases, it's worth noting that this also makes them lighter and more compact than the more expensive models. I guess it comes down to preference and pocketbook.

Interestingly, tests at Bushnell have revealed that scratched or dirty lenses do not degrade laser performance much.

Perhaps the least understood part of laser ranging is properly matching the beam's size to the object you're ranging. Many snipers don't get the maximum range out of their rangefinders because they imagine this beam is the size of a laser pointer beam. Wrong! Bushnell laser beams, for example, are 4 mils high and 2 mils wide. The closer your target is to these dimensions, the greater the likelihood that the beam will reflect off it to yield a range. For instance, at 500 yards this means a target 2 yards high and 1 yard wide, and double these dimensions at 1,000 yards. Thus, instead of ranging on a thin human—who's not even half the size of your beam—laze a wall 25 yards to his side, hopefully perpendicular to your beam.

Fundamentals for Lazing

Here are some insights for yielding a range measurement when initially it appears you cannot, as well as how to stretch your ranging to the maximum distance possible.

1. *Aim the laser as precisely and solidly as your rifle.* Not only is it essential that you laze the correct object, but I've found that steadying the laser increases the likelihood that enough light is reflected for the sensor to get a

reading. Optical depth of field for a distant target can visually confuse your aim, so laze several times for especially long-range targets to confirm the distance.

2. *Laze a suitably sized object.* As already noted, the laser beam at some distances is much larger than a human, so find a suitably sized object at the same distance and laze that instead. Usually, the larger the object, the better. At 1,000 yards, that beam is approximately the size of a car.

3. *Appreciate the effect of ambient light.* Bright sunlight or strong artificial light reduces your laser's maximum range because this extra, intense light overwhelms and somewhat confuses the laser's light sensor. Even waiting for clouds to block the sun can help, as can lazing into a shadow, but only marginally. The very longest ranging is achieved in overcast or at dusk. That's when I've had lasers range beyond their official maximum.

4. *Consider the lazed target's density.* The thicker and more impervious your target, the better. If you must laze foliage, go for the thickest clump of broad leaves rather than an equal area of pine needles, which may diffuse laser light. A solid cliff face is better yet. If you're lazing in grassland, don't laze at the grass but at a spot of exposed earth.

5. *Target reflectivity matters, too.* A shiny surface reflects laser light better than a dull surface. Look for wet leaves rather than dry ground. License plates work especially well, as does corrugated aluminum.

6. *The target's color influences its reflectivity.* A bright color usually reflects laser light better than a dark color. Alternatively, I've had difficulty lazing into fresh fallen snow, I think because the snow's microscopic crystals absorb and diffuse the light. Instead, find a clump of exposed earth or a tree in the snowy area and laze that.

7. *The shape of the target affects how well lazed light bounces off it.* Lazing onto a flat surface usually generates better reflection than on a concave or convex surface. For example, a flat rock the same width as a tree trunk should reflect more readable light because some of the light hitting the curved trunk will be deflected.

8. *The angle of your beam on the target surface affects reflection.* Related to an object's shape is the angle of your beam on it. For the best generation of reflected light, your beam should impact perpendicular, at 90 degrees, to the object's surface. Most of this light will bounce back toward you and the lazer's sensor.

All these factors dynamically interrelate to varying degrees, for varying effects. For example, during a visit to the U.S. Army Sniper School, I was on the Burroughs Rifle Range and lazed an old M113 Armored Personnel Carrier (APC) well beyond the maximum range of my 600-yard Bushnell laser. Still, it ranged instantly at 750 yards! But that APC was dull olive drab, and this was midday in full sunlight. How could that have happened? The extent to which bright light and a dull color affected the laser beam was dramatically more than countered by the APC's large, dense, flat surface, against which my beam had pointed perpendicularly.

Other Lazing Tips

Use caution when employing a laser after dark against an enemy outfitted with night vision equipment. Most infrared laser rangefinder beams can be seen in night goggles and weapon sights, dramatically compromising your location.

Lazing over water generates some unique considerations. Bushnell engineer Tim Carpenter has noticed that humid air absorbs laser wavelength light like a sponge. I've found that laser beams can bounce invisibly off water onto a distant object, then back, and yield an incorrect range. All it takes is a water-filled pothole for this to happen.

And finally, here's a useful visual demonstration I devised to help sniper students understand how various objects absorb, deflect, diffuse, or reflect laser light. Take a high-intensity SureFire flashlight and point it at a

Size comparison: an ammunition box, full-size 1,000-yard laser, and pocket-size 800-yard laser.

pine tree; see how diffused the light is? The same thing will happen to an IR laser beam. Now, point the SureFire at broadleaf bushes, especially wet ones, and see how much more it's illuminated by the beam. The same for a solid surface. And if the beam's wider than the object, you end up with wasted light, which reduces the maximum measurable range. This works wonders in helping students understand how to get the most out of their lasers.

Laser Rangefinders

Bushnell makes an entire family of laser rangefinders rated for distances from 400 to 1,500 yards. Their optical quality won't replace a team's binoculars, but they're economically priced, they work, and they belong in every police sniper's kit. Bushnell's 800-yard model really is pocket-sized and very handy. More than a few sniper teams in Iraq and Afghani-

stan—unable to obtain lasers from their supply system—are purchasing their own Bushnells.

Swarovski has long manufactured high-quality, compact laser rangefinders. Its current model, the Laser Guide 8x30, features superb glass and a greater range than previous models, all the way to 1,500 yards. Technically a monocular, this device is comparable to high-end compact binoculars, though its magnification is not as high as a team's typical binoculars. A few years back, Swarovski produced the world's first laser-ranging rifle scope, the LRS, which performed flawlessly for me. But the LRS's hefty price tag—recommended retail of about $3,500—precluded commercial success. Still, I'm confident that one day we'll see laser ranging integrated with a rifle scope.

Vectronix, the military optics marketing division of Leica, produces a high-end, compact laser monocular similar in size and optical

Compact with superb optics, this Swarovski Laser Guide 8x30mm can measure to 1,500 yards or meters.

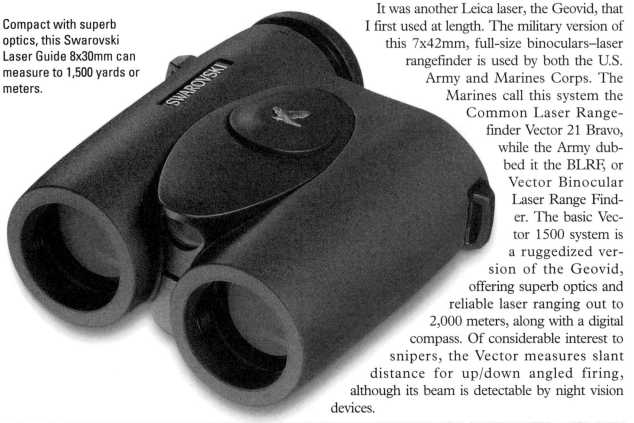

It was another Leica laser, the Geovid, that I first used at length. The military version of this 7x42mm, full-size binoculars–laser rangefinder is used by both the U.S. Army and Marines Corps. The Marines call this system the Common Laser Rangefinder Vector 21 Bravo, while the Army dubbed it the BLRF, or Vector Binocular Laser Range Finder. The basic Vector 1500 system is a ruggedized version of the Geovid, offering superb optics and reliable laser ranging out to 2,000 meters, along with a digital compass. Of considerable interest to snipers, the Vector measures slant distance for up/down angled firing, although its beam is detectable by night vision devices.

Swarovski's LRS Laser Ranging Scope integrated a digital laser rangefinder with a quality rifle scope.

quality to the Swarovski. This PLRF, or Precision Laser Range Finder, allows lazing out to 2,000 meters, giving it the range for .50-caliber rifles but, at 6x, probably not enough magnification. One version, the PLRF-15, transmits a 1,550 nm wavelength beam, rendering it invisible even to Generation III night vision devices.

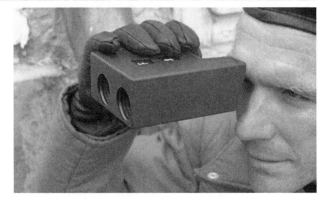

The Vectronix PLRF laser ranging monocular can laze to 2,000 meters.

The more advanced Vector IV ranges to 4,000 meters while using an IR wavelength laser beam that's invisible to night vision devices. It, too, measures slant distances.

The most elaborate version, the Vector 21, issued to artillery forward observers and Special Ops teams, integrates all these capabilities with a GPS and small PC, allowing this device not only to determine the distance to a target up to 10,000 meters away but to calculate its location so precisely that a GPS-guided bomb can be plopped virtually atop it. When fitted with a compatible AN/PVS-14 night vision device, the Vector 21 can operate in total darkness.

WIND: INVISIBLE BUT DECISIVE

A distinguished rifleman once told me, "A plinker studies trajectory tables; a master studies the wind." His point was well taken.

While accurate range estimation is absolutely essential, most long-range shooters learn to judge distances and compensate correctly. They know it's important, so they do it.

But that leaves the other great factor of long-range accuracy—wind estimation—and here is

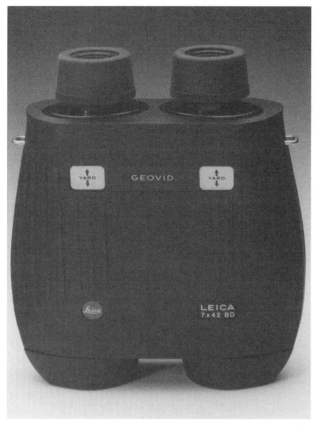

Full-size Leica Geovid 7x42mm binoculars are both great glass and an excellent laser rangefinder.

U.S. Marines in Iraq with Designated Marksman Rifle and Vector laser ranging system.

The most sophisticated Vector system integrates a GPS, laser, compact computer, and night vision device.

The U.S. Army's GVS-5 laser ranges out to 10,000 meters—which is also this device's approximate cost in dollars.

where far too many shooters fall down. Because wind is invisible, they don't appreciate how much it can affect a bullet in flight. I'll give just one example.

Consider a 10 mph wind; that's fairly gentle, not enough to seem a problem. But by the time a .308 168-grain bullet has traveled just 400 yards, this moderate crosswind has pushed the bullet 13.6 inches—enough that if you were aiming center-chest, it's drifted completely off-target. And recall this is a "gentle" wind and the range only 400 yards.

Yes, wind is important. It's also important to law enforcement snipers because some missions may require firing through tricky winds, especially across an airport or between urban rooftops.

Because there are considerable overlaps between wind estimation, effects, and proper compensation, we're going to address all three in this section

rather than scatter this information throughout the book. First, let's appreciate wind effects.

Understanding the Wind

The flow of air is wind, and it travels as a current, just like water currents. The best way to understand what wind does is to imagine it's water, which we can visualize.

When looking down a narrow gorge or across an open valley, imagine water is flowing past and try to visualize how water flowing in the direction of the wind would be affected by the foliage and terrain around you.

We've illustrated this below to show that a rural wind flowing across high, flat ground will not have any impediments; it consistently blows or gusts equally and everywhere across that ground. Just below the ridge, we see the wind splitting, as if it were a water tributary flowing from the top of the hill. It's been split obliquely by the trees and terrain and, similar to water, seeks the path of least resistance. Finally, at the bottom, an entirely contradictory wind is blowing into our sector through a gorge. Undoubtedly it entered at a direction very

Rural winds vary with topography and elevation and seem contradictory until you watch them closely.

RELATIVE WIND EFFECTS

Soon after publication of *The Ultimate Sniper* in 1993, I received letters critical of how I'd explained wind effects and their required compensation. Having never seen other than the stylized illustrations in military manuals, the writers insisted I had it wrong and, for instance, a 45-degree wind was 1/2 value, not the 3/4 value I'd described. (Though that's incorrect, it would seem logical since 45 is half of 90, or half of a full-value wind.) So that you can see exactly what these values are, here's the multiplier factor table used by Sierra Bullets, which verifies my original data.

Wind Angle to Bullet Path	Required Multiplier
0 Degrees	0.000
5 Degrees	0.087
10 Degrees	0.174
15 Degrees	0.259 *
20 Degrees	0.342
25 Degrees	0.423
30 Degrees	0.500 **
35 Degrees	0.574
40 Degrees	0.643
45 Degrees	0.707 ***
50 Degrees	0.766
55 Degrees	0.819
60 Degrees	0.866
65 Degrees	0.906
70 Degrees	0.940
75 Degrees	0.966
80 Degrees	0.985
85 Degrees	0.996
90 Degrees	1.000 ****

* 1/4 value
** 1/2 value
*** 3/4 value
**** Full value

similar to that of the higher winds but turned around as it passed down the gorge.

The presence of such contradictory winds is far more frequent than most people realize. We sensitize sniper students to their presence by posting crepe paper streamers every 100 yards on our 1,000-yard known-distance range. They're initially surprised to find that winds at the distant firing line are steady and left to right, while mid-range winds are gusting and right to left.

It's only by looking closely that they notice the firing line overlooks an expanse of flat, open ground—which causes the steady wind— while there's a service road that cuts through thick woods at mid-range—hence an opposite, gusty wind.

Your challenge as a sniper is to learn where to look to detect evidence of winds so that you can determine exactly the directions of any winds in your sector. Having determined direction, you then must estimate wind speed, which equally demands attention to minute details.

Estimating Wind Speed

The most important thing for you to realize when estimating wind is that the wind direction and speed at your location may be irrelevant.

Here's what I mean. Think back about times when you've found shelter from a brisk wind by getting below a ridge or 20 yards back into the woods. You were comfortable, but the conditions at your spot did not reflect those around you. No matter how perfectly you estimated the wind where you were, it would not reflect wind at your target or the wind between you and the target.

And these are exactly the winds of interest to you: first, the wind at the target; then, the wind between you and the target; and, only last, the wind at your location. You and your spotter must examine the entire area to determine wherever you have distinct winds—as cited above—then estimate the speed of each and note whether it is steady or gusting.

Wind gauges can be used only at your own location, but they're still worth having because knowing the exact wind speed where you are helps to make a correct estimate of other winds. A yachter's wind gauge is compact and inexpensive (less than $20), but it requires a bit of experience to interpret accurately.

By contrast, Kestrel electronic wind gauges require no special training or particular experience to operate—other than ensuring that the aperture for the miniature propeller is directed into the wind correctly. These wondrous gadgets—costing $100 or less—have contributed greatly to the long-range shooting revolution, helping solve the last remaining challenge: systematically "doping" the wind. So useful have these become that the Kestrel 4000 is a required component of the CheyTac extreme-range shooting system. That model also measures humidity, temperature, and atmospheric pressure.

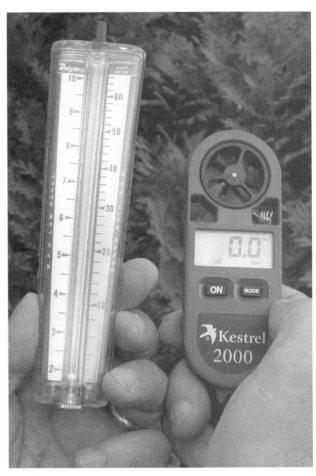

The Kestrel 2000 electronic wind gauge rendered obsolete earlier mechanical instruments, like this yachting wind gauge at left.

THE POINTING METHOD. Divide the angle by four.

| FELT SLIGHTLY ON FACE | LEAVES AGITATE CONTINUOUSLY | BLOWS AROUND LOOSE PAPER | SMALL TREES SWAY |

Estimating wind speed by effects.

WIND ESTIMATION WITH A LASER

A couple of years ago, a friend with the Defense Department told me about research under way at Los Alamos National Laboratories to design a laser that could measure wind not just where you were but at a distance as well. Checking the Internet, I found that the Israeli Atomic Energy Commission's Yavne Soreq Research Establishment also is looking into laser wind measurement. This is, however, raw, basic research, and I doubt we'll see a usable device anytime in the next decade.

But that got me to thinking—with so precise a ranging instrument, isn't there some way that a laser can be employed to more accurately calculate wind than the old-fashioned "how it feels on your face" or tossing a cloth to the ground?

Here's what I came up with.

Turn exactly into the wind. Carefully find a point before you—directly into the wind—where you can see some visual effect(s) that a gust of wind has reached that spot. This could be a rustling of leaves, lifting of a string, swaying of a branch—anything that tells you exactly when the wind has reached that spot. Now, laze a point within this area to see where, exactly, is 100 yards or 100 meters. At this exact point is a particular leaf or some tiny item susceptible to wind that you can see being affected.

Working with your spotter, here's how you do it. The *split second* that you see this item affected by the wind, call, "Now!" and your spotter begins timing. When that same gust of wind reaches you—you feel it on your face or see it affect something beside you—call, "Stop!" He now has an exact time that it took that gust of wind to travel 100 meters or 100 yards to your position. Now, just look at the chart I prepared and you'll know the exact wind speed. Let's say your spotter timed it as 17 seconds, and the spot you'd lazed was 100 yards away. On the chart, that translates to 12 mph.

What's most interesting about my technique is that it also can work anywhere between you and the target, provided there are items out there that are visually affected by the wind and you can determine the wind's angle, as well as a lateral distance of 100 meters or yards.

Here's how this works. Observing a wind at 800 yards, carefully determine how it's laterally crossing your front. Using binoculars or a spotting scope, select two points along this wind line where wind-induced movement can be detected—rustling leaves, etc., just as you did near your own position. Then, very carefully pick two points exactly 100 yards or meters apart for timing the wind's crossing, again calling it out to the spotter.

The first time I tried this, it was a bit confusing to ensure that I was timing a single gust, but with some practice it works better than anything except an electronic wind gauge.

WIND TIMING AND SPEEDS

100 Yards (seconds)	100 Meters (seconds)	Wind Speed (mph)	100 Yards (seconds)	100 Meters (seconds)	Wind Speed (mph)
200	220	1 mph			
100	110	2 mph	18	20	11 mph
67	73	3 mph	17	18	12 mph
50	55	4 mph	15	17	13 mph
40	44	5 mph	14	16	14 mph
33	37	6 mph	13	14.5	15 mph
29	32	7 mph	12.5	13.7	16 mph
25	27	8 mph	11.5	13.0	17 mph
22	24	9 mph	11.0	12.0	18 mph
20	22	10 mph	10.5	11.5	19 mph

I have a Kestrel 2000 that I use primarily to check my wind estimates yielded from old-fashioned estimation techniques. (A "de-liar" I call it.) What's wonderful is that this instrument gives you an honest yardstick for gauging all the contributing winds, too. Carefully measuring the wind around me on my Kestrel and watching the local effects, I then look for similar effects downrange to help gauge those winds.

Even if you have gauges available, however, you still must learn other wind estimation methods in order to read distant winds. Our four-panel illustration on page 352 shows ways in which the effects of wind can be read to indicate wind speed. A 3–5 mph wind is felt lightly on your face; a 5–8 mph wind causes leaves in trees to agitate continuously; an 8–12 mph wind will raise dust and blow around loose paper; and a 12–15 mph wind causes small trees and bushes to sway.

The key is to look for the most extreme wind effect when using this method. Start by checking whether any small trees are swaying and then work downward.

While observing these distant wind indicators, be sure to note exactly the direction of wind. I have seen sniper students carefully and correctly discern a distant wind, only to mistakenly call it oblique when it actually was a full crosswind.

The pointing method, also shown on page 352, requires that you drop a handkerchief or balled-up piece of paper from the height of your shoulder. To determine wind speed, point to where it landed and estimate the angle between your arm and body. Then divide this angle by four to learn the wind speed. In our illustration, the angle is 60 degrees; dividing by four yields 15, which means the wind speed is 15 mph.

You also can estimate wind by noticing how it lifts a flag—as taught in several military manuals. But this technique is inconsistent because modern flags often are made of ultralight materials, needing minimal breeze to stay astir.

Mirage

Most long-range competitive riflemen use mirage for "doping the wind"—their jargon for estimating wind direction and speed. This isn't the kind of mirage that produces an imaginary oasis or any other nonsense. No, in reading mirage you employ an optical device—your spotting scope—to detect the way heat waves shimmer above the earth. When examined through a spotting scope, this mirage tells you wind direction and speed with great accuracy.

To see mirage, lay prone and focus your spotting scope on your distant target. Now, rotate the focus ring and you'll see that as the target becomes blurry, the heat shimmer you may have hardly even noticed becomes very clear. Disregard the target and tune the focus for this shimmer—the mirage.

Mirage is most easily seen by focusing at a point about halfway to your target and is most distinct against a dark background. You may find that you must tip the scope down a bit closer to the earth for the best perspective.

We've illustrated four views of mirage on the facing page to show how it's affected by wind. On the left, mirage is rising straight up—"boiling," as shooters say—which indicates no wind at all.

The easiest way to understand what hap-

A Marine Force Recon operator reads mirage in Iraq's western desert to calculate wind direction and speed.

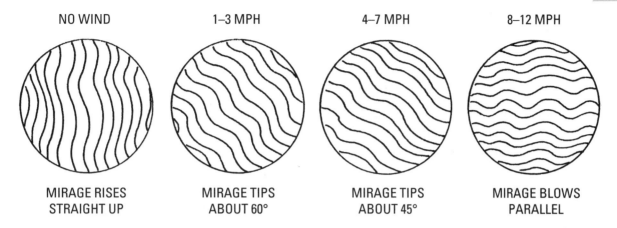

NO WIND	1–3 MPH	4–7 MPH	8–12 MPH
MIRAGE RISES STRAIGHT UP	MIRAGE TIPS ABOUT 60°	MIRAGE TIPS ABOUT 45°	MIRAGE BLOWS PARALLEL

Estimating wind with mirage.

pens in the other views is to imagine mirage as smoke rising through a chimney. As wind speed increases, it pushes the smoke flatter and flatter until it's blowing straight to the side. A slow wind of 1–3 mph pushes the mirage so it rises at about 60 degrees; next, a medium wind of 4–7 mph turns the mirage to 45 degrees; and on the right, an 8–12 mph wind pushes the mirage so it travels straight on its side. Mirage usually is an accurate indicator of wind speed only up to 8–12 mph, but some experienced long-distance shooters claim they can estimate speed up to 20 mph by closely analyzing the wavy mirage pattern.

To learn the wind direction, just rotate the spotting scope right or left until you encounter boiling wavy lines, which tell you the wind is coming from that side. If there's no boil, it is coming from the opposite side.

For fine-tuning, you should combine mirage with other observations to determine if a wind is oblique or a 90-degree crosswind, etc. These distinctions will matter when computing how to compensate for wind.

Repositioning and Other Solutions

The best way to adjust for a problem wind is to totally concede and surrender—just pick up and move so that by repositioning your hide, you neutralize or minimize the effect of the wind. For police snipers especially, who usually have many options in hide selection and a foe who's in a fixed position, repositioning may be the best way to minimize a fast crosswind.

Once the wind is head-on (12 o'clock) or at your tail (6 o'clock), you can shoot in a gale with very little effect. Indeed, a .308 bullet fired in a 30 mph headwind suffers only a slight decline in velocity, which causes it to impact a tiny 1.75 inches low at 600 yards. Had it been a 30 mph tailwind, it would've hit a bit high. But had you fired into a 30 mph crosswind, your bullet would have been pushed 99.9 inches off point of aim!

Military snipers, too, would do well to relocate to neutralize a hefty crosswind. But reducing the distance, the other way shown on page 356 for minimizing wind, may be too dangerous for military snipers. It's very practical for police, however.

If you can stalk forward to within 100 yards of your quarry, again you will have almost eliminated the effect of wind. When firing a .300 Winchester Magnum 200-grain bullet, even a 60 mph full crosswind pushes the bullet just 3 inches laterally at 100 yards. With a tamer wind speed of 20 mph, a .308 would experience just 1.6 inches of drift at 100 yards.

But many times you'll not have the option of relocating, and that's when traditional compensation for wind comes into play.

Determining Wind Values

In order to interpret and apply wind com-

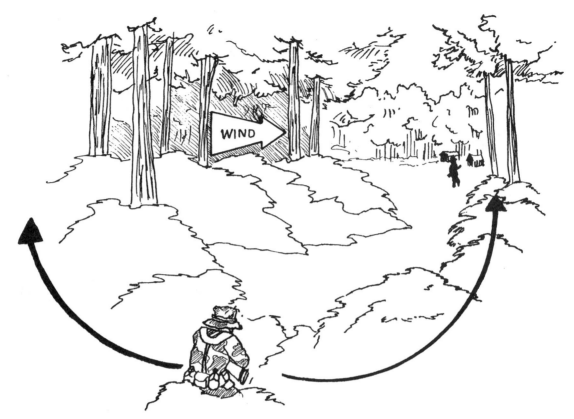

Minimize wind effect by repositioning directly up or downwind (L) or reducing the distance (R).

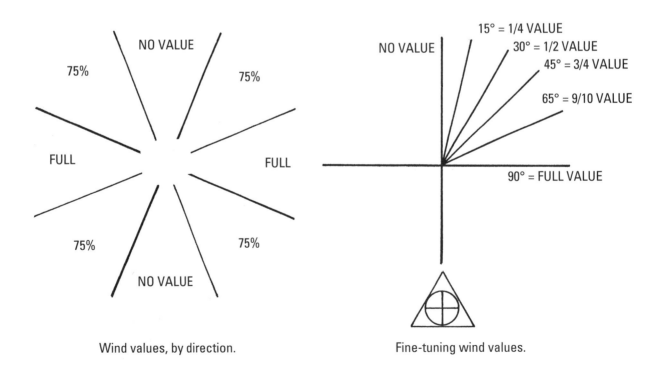

Wind values, by direction.

Fine-tuning wind values.

pensation correctly, you have to determine the angle of the wind, because how the wind flows across the bullet will determine the amount of drift.

As our illustration on page 356 shows, a tailwind or headwind will have no value; they have essentially no effect on a bullet's flight. A direct crosswind, which blows from the right or left 90 degrees into the path of the bullet, is called a "full" wind because the full effect of the wind is experienced.

Here, though, please pay close attention: an oblique wind of 45 degrees, from right or left, has not a one-half value but a *three-quarters* value. It has a 75-percent effect, even though the angle is only halfway between no effect and full effect.

Most shooters initially have trouble getting this straight in their heads. The effect is not proportional because of the aerodynamics of a bullet in flight. Just remember that halfway between full and zero effect is three-quarters.

As seen in the next illustration, benchrest shooters use even finer values and split the wind for exact aiming. I've included this to give you a better feel for how quickly the wind has an effect once a bullet is other than at tail or head. Once it's just 15 degrees right or left, already a quarter of the wind value must be used when compensating.

Shooting into the Wind

To shoot accurately into a wind, compensate by holding or aiming in the direction the wind is coming from. This is shown in the illustration on this page. As the bullet travels downrange, it drifts into your target. In order for this to work, however, you must know exactly how far to compensate.

We've prepared detailed ballistic tables at the end of this chapter that show the wind drift for the most popular military and police sniping loads, to include:

- .308 168-gr. BTHP Match/M118LR 7.62mm
- .300 WinMag 190-gr. BTHP Match
- .223 69-gr. BTHP Match

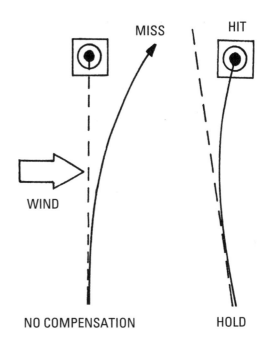

Wind compensation requires holding into the wind, letting it drift your bullet into the target.

Although several wind speeds are listed, the most important, I think, is 10 mph because, once memorized, it's easiest to compute in your head. Just about anything can be divided or multiplied when you start with a factor of 10.

Looking at the tables, note that compensation doubles as wind speed doubles. This means that the necessary compensation for a 20 mph wind is twice that of a 10 mph wind, and 5 mph is half that of 10 mph. But the differences in distances are *not* proportional: compensation for 600 yards is much more than twice that of 300 yards. This is because the farther the bullet goes, the more it slows down and the worse the effect becomes. In a way, this is similar to how a bullet starts to plunge at long range, when its path becomes a sharp arc.

But now, at last, we're ready to bring together ballistic data and wind values and compensation. It's really quite simple.

First, determine the direction of the wind in respect to a line between you and your target. For sake of illustration, let's say it's 90 degrees,

NEAR VS. FAR WIND

When faced by multiple crosswinds, doctrinally you should time your shot so one wind is calm and the bullet passes through the other, which is the only one you compensate for.

Does it make any difference which of these winds is the one you shoot through? Absolutely, and our drawing shows why.

Assuming both winds are of equal velocity, the near wind has more time to push the bullet sideways and will cause it to be much farther off target than a far wind. Therefore, you should shoot when the near wind is calm and compensate for the far wind.

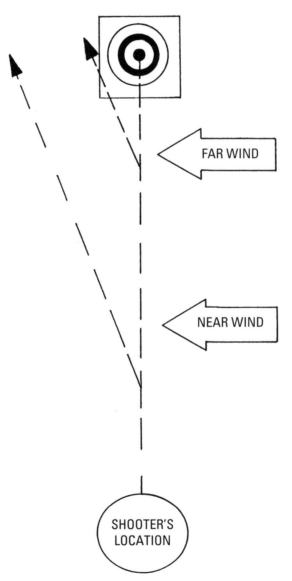

and, as already seen, that would make it a full wind. Next, consulting with your spotter, determine the speed of that wind; we'll say that you agree it's 5 mph. Finally, you both expertly estimate your target is 600 yards away. You're using Federal .308 BTHP Match.

Looking at the table on the page 359, you find that the required compensation is 16.1 inches. The compensation on all the tables reflects a full value.

Since your scope has an adjustable windage knob, you dial in the equivalent of 16.1 inches at 600 yards; since 1 MOA equals 6 inches at that range, you rotate it 2.75 MOA into the wind. And because your scope has 1/4 MOA positive clicks, this means you turn it 11 clicks.

Having made the adjustment, you aim dead-on, let off a good shot, and score a perfect hit. If your scope lacked

a windage knob, you would have looked at the target, determined that 16.6 inches is the width of a fit man at the hip, and held this far into the wind, aimed, and engaged, again with perfect results.

But what about other than full-value crosswinds? Just factor in the value when determining the compensation. Let's try another example.

You and your spotter agree the wind is 15 mph, coming on at a 45-degree oblique, and the range is 800 yards. Again you're using a Federal .308 Match round. The table says full compensation would be 96.1 inches, but we will only use 3/4 of that because the wind is oblique at 45 degrees. Three-quarters of 96 inches, you compute in your head, is 72 inches.

So, if you have a windage knob you realize that 1 MOA equals 8 inches at 800 yards;

WIND DRIFT DATA
.308 168-gr. BTHP Match/M118LR 7.62mm
Distance in Yards

	100	200	300	400	500	600	700	800	900	1000
5 mph	0.4"	1.5"	3.7"	6.8"	11.1"	16.1"	23.5"	32.0"	42.1"	53.8"
10 mph	0.8"	3.1"	7.4"	13.6"	22.2"	33.3"	47.1"	64.1"	84.2"	107"
15 mph	1.2"	4.6"	11.1"	20.4"	33.3"	49.9"	70.6"	96.1"	126"	161"
20 mph	1.6"	6.2"	14.8"	27.2"	44.4"	66.6"	94.2"	128"	168"	215"
30 mph	2.4"	9.3"	22.2"	40.8"	66.6"	99.9"	141"	192"	253"	322"

WIND DRIFT DATA
.300 Winchester Magnum 190-gr. BTHP Match
Distance in Yards

	100	200	300	400	500	600	700	800	900	1000
5 mph	0.3″	1.2″	2.8″	5.0″	8.2″	12.1″	17.1″	23.3″	30.5″	39.0″
10 mph	0.6″	2.4″	5.5″	10.1″	16.4″	24.2″	34.2″	46.6″	61.1″	78.0″
15 mph	0.9″	3.6″	8.3″	15.1″	24.6″	36.3″	51.3″	69.9″	91.6″	117.0″
20 mph	1.2″	4.8″	11.0″	20.2″	32.8″	48.4″	68.4″	93.2″	122.2″	156.0″
30 mph	1.8″	7.2″	16.5″	30.2″	49.2″	72.6″	102.6″	139.8″	183.2″	234.0″

WIND DRIFT DATA
.223 69-gr. BTHP Match
Distance in Yards

	100	200	300	400	500	600	700	800	900	1000
5 mph	0.5"	1.8"	4.3"	8.2"	13.5"	20.5"	29.5"	41.1"	54.5"	70.0"
10 mph	0.9"	3.7"	8.7"	16.3"	27.0"	41.3"	59.5"	82.2"	109"	140"
15 mph	1.4"	5.5"	13.0"	24.5"	40.5"	61.8"	89.0"	123"	163"	210"
20 mph	1.8"	7.4"	17.4"	32.6"	54.0"	82.6"	129"	164"	218"	280"
30 mph	2.7"	11.1"	26.1"	48.9"	81.0"	124"	188"	247"	327"	420"

therefore, you divide 72 by 8, which equals 9, and you click off 9 MOA on your scope at 1/4 MOA increments, or 36 clicks. On another scope, you'd hold into the wind what you estimate to be 72 inches from your target—about the height of a man.

Where shooting into the wind gets tricky is when it's gusting or you must deal with several winds.

Old-time shooters will tell you *not* to wait for pauses during a steady wind, that you'll have much better results shooting into a predictable wind than hoping a short calm lasts long enough for your bullet to reach the target.

Strong gusts require timing your shot, and the spotter helps by telling you when to fire. With his eyes free and able to look around, he should be able to assess when it's best to shoot. When faced by two winds, try to time your shot so it's fired during the slower or the least gusting or the farther wind so there's less effect and a more predictable outcome. (This is getting pretty complex, but the reason you prefer shooting through a farther wind is that there's less remaining flight time to be affected by the wind.)

When shooting in mountains or urban areas, don't be concerned by updrafts; where they exist, these winds are very shallow and your bullet will pass through too quickly to make much difference.

The role of the spotter is very important in a windy area because direction and speed may change with no warning. In the case of 90-degree winds, he should watch for changes in speed. If you have head or tailwinds, he watches closely for any shift in direction, from being no factor into having an effect.

USMC Wind Adjustment Method

For those of you having a boundless desire for ever more information, we've included an old U.S. Marine Corps method for computing sight changes when firing in the wind. The USMC has been using this windage adjustment method since the days of the 1903A3 Springfield. Ever sensitive to the feelings of my Marine brethren, I include it here lest they say I didn't know about it.

After determining wind direction and speed, use the following formula:

$$\frac{\text{Range in 100 yds. x speed in mph}}{15 \text{ (math constant)}} = \frac{\text{MOA}}{\text{Windage}}$$

For instance, your target is 300 yards away, and there's a 10 mph wind:

$$\frac{3 \times 10 = 30}{15} = 2 \text{ Minutes of Angle}$$

Now just click in the 2 Minutes of Angle in the direction of the wind and aim dead-on. This is a great formula—*except* it's only accurate at 500 yards or less. When your target is farther, the mathematical constant must increase, as shown below:

600 Yards:	Divide by 14
700 Yards:	Divide by 13
800 Yards:	Divide by 13
900 Yards:	Divide by 12
1,000 Yards:	Divide by 11

CHAPTER 13

CAMOUFLAGE FOR SNIPING

CAMOUFLAGE

The word camouflage evolved from a French verb meaning "to play a practical joke"—in other words, to fool your foe. Part art and part science, camouflage employs visual trickery to exploit vulnerabilities in how human eyesight and the brain process visual information.

The key is understanding how the brain and eye work together. For instance, the human mind automatically scans scenes anticipating something that's different, not something that looks like everything else. The better you look like everything else, the more likely an eye will sweep right past you.

An object's edges are much more important visually than its interior because eye and mind readily define an object by its outline or shape, as illustrated on page 362. Notice that both the white and the black silhouettes have distinct edges that define a human shape. But the middle silhouette uses dark splotches to irregularize the edges and confuse the object's actual outline. Dark colors—

CAMOUFLAGED TO THE MAXIMUM. Australian soldiers guard this captured Turkish sniper at Gallipoli, 1915.

not light ones—create the illusion of empty space and false edges.

The first photo on page 362 shows how to apply this principle by having your partner break up your body's outline with black spray paint on your shoulders, arms, and hips. In SOG we'd do this a half-hour before boarding helicopters while wearing our complete field gear—rucksack and all—and found it very, very effective. Not only does this irregularize your outline but it blends together your clothing, weapon, webgear, and rucksack, which brings us to our next point.

Solid-colored clothes don't conceal you nearly so well as do camouflage patterns that break up your outline. The next photograph proves this by showing how much less distinct the jacket is compared to the black pants.

This shows, too, that your camouflage must be consistent to be effective. Don't mix patterns or different-colored clothes or you'll create a visual contrast that *attracts* attention. This also

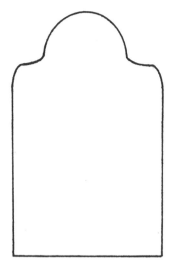  

LESSON ONE. Outline defines an object, so effective camouflage (center) uses dark colors and irregularity to obscure and disrupt the outline.

Spray paint ordinary jungle fatigues to perfectly match your surroundings or just to break up your outline.

The distinct outline of black pants (bottom) highlight the wearer, while the woodland pattern blends much better into the surroundings.

requires camouflaging everything equally, so you must burlap-wrap your spotting scope if you're in a Ghillie suit, and your boots need draped material, too. Indeed, I've often seen poorly camouflaged boots compromise otherwise perfectly concealed sniper students. The heels also reflect sunlight off their shiny, worn rear edge.

Recognize that nature prefers randomness and curves, while straight lines and symmetry instantly shout, "*Man!*" You must fight the urge to "balance" camouflage, whether coloring your face or tying burlap to your rifle; keep it as irregular and random as possible—the occasional clump is more "natural" than the evenly spaced and uniform. Nature blends different colors and textures; it doesn't balance them.

Appreciate also that the eye is easily fooled by depth, that something that looks three-dimensional due to shading and dark coloring is far less suspicious than flat, painted two-dimensional surfaces. If your enemy thinks he's looking *through* you, you can't really be there.

The Concept of Fade Distance

A human with normal 20-20 vision can distinguish a 1-inch object at 100 yards if it's in stark contrast to its surroundings. This translates to 1 MOA, meaning 2 inches at 200 yards, 6 inches at 600 yards, etc. This determines an object's "fade distance." When an object is smaller than 1 MOA, human eyes won't be able to resolve it enough to distinguish it from its environment.

Therefore, the sniper's challenge is to keep every aspect of himself and his gear so well broken up that nothing's distinctly visible. Since your ballistic advantage dictates that you avoid engagements of less than 400 yards, this means your camouflage must break up or conceal any portion of you or your gear larger than 4 inches.

Ah, but if it were only so easy! What about unplanned encounters at less than 400 yards? And of far greater relevance, what happens when your enemy uses optics, which means

he'll be glassing your area with magnification and he can see much smaller than 1 MOA. In fact, a 20x spotting scope brings you 20 times closer than do naked eyes, so he can be 500 yards away—where a naked eye cannot resolve smaller than 5 inches—but with his scope he can resolve to 1/10 of an inch. From personal experience, I've found such computations only theoretical since the combination of mirage, scope vibration, and lens quality degrade resolution enough that realistically one can only make out 1/2 inch or so at 500 yards. Still, the optical threat is serious.

And *this* is why snipers use Ghillie suits, because your concealment must be so good that even with optics an enemy cannot resolve your image sufficiently to see you. The fuzziness of a Ghillie suit's frazzled burlap strips makes your figure too indistinct to be resolved except at very close distances.

When you're not wearing a hot G-suit, appreciate that even though American digital camo patterns have tiny, irregular splotches measuring less than 1 MOA, your rucksack and various pouches and webbing add sizable contrast that is larger than 1 MOA. Therefore, it's worthwhile to break up your outline with add-on paint, drape a few pieces of burlap here and there, stay in the shadows, and keep natural foliage between you and the enemy. Such practices can make even marginally useful camouflage effective.

In the context of fade distance, the importance of matching surrounding colors cannot be overstated. To the degree that your camouflage shades mimic local coloration, you degrade the eye's ability to distinguish it at "book" distances. A black 1-inch square against a white backdrop is visible at 100 yards, but a leaf-green, 1-inch square amid many similarly colored leaves is hell to find. Ensure you make yourself hell to find.

And what about when you don't even have camouflage clothing? Recall that traditional German field gray, American olive drab, and British khaki uniforms were solid colors but still allowed wearers a degree of concealment, a point especially important to law officers who sometimes must deploy without the opportunity to don mottled camouflage gear. Provided the color is dull and generally fits the surroundings, such plain uniforms typically fade into indistinction at about 300 yards due to how the eye perceives colors and shapes.

Blending with Your Surroundings

A moment ago we touched on the important relationship between color and size; our general rule is, the closer your colors match those around you, the tougher it becomes to visually resolve your shape. But it's more than just coloration.

To match his environment effectively, a sniper must develop a keen appreciation for colors, textures, foliage shapes, density, and depth. Look around you—I mean *really* look around and take time to notice details. Recognize that a sniper's slice of the woods is mostly 18 to 24 inches above the ground since that's where you'll low-crawl, shoot prone, or lie in a temporary hide.

Notice what's around you. Pine needles have a different texture and visual depth than do leafy plants. Dried leaves on the forest floor have a distinct pattern and color. Wild grass grows in vertical clumps that average about a foot wide. The dark sides of leaves face the sun while the lighter bottoms face the forest floor.

Shadows are more stark in pine woods than in a walnut grove.

Each time your surroundings change a bit, you must change your camouflage to match it. The best technique for this is to use a pattern that generally fits your area, then enhance it

An Army sniper adapts his Ghillie suit to the current locale by adding foilage.

Like a sore thumb, this team's leafy camouflage sticks out among these pine needles.

with bits of distinct natural foliage as you move from one area to the next. While in this treeline, attach oak leaves to your uniform; when you crawl forward into the meadow, replace the leaves with clumps of grass, and so on. The key is updating whenever you enter different surroundings, which reminds me of an incident in the fall of 1971.

I was flying backseat in an OV-10 armed FAC (forward air controller) bird over the Ho Chi Minh Trail when the pilot and I simultaneously noticed a long line of leafy clumps down the middle of a major road. We knew the North Vietnamese trained their soldiers to squat motionlessly if caught in the open by an airplane. We flew past, not hinting we'd seen anything, but in fact we knew we'd just seen a 2-mile line of marching soldiers. Had these men taken one sideward step so their leaves fit the overlapping jungle, they would have been home free.

As it was, we went into orbit just over the horizon and 10 minutes later inserted the first of more than 50 air strikes. We cancelled other CCC/SOG (Command and Control Central/Studies and Observation Group) operations for two days just to keep bombing them, achieving what must have been one of the highest cross-border BDAs (bomb damage assessments) in all of 1971—and all because their camouflage didn't fit their surroundings.

When it comes to an imperfect color match, I go along with the advice of Don Helmeke, the designer of today's camouflage nets for the U.S. Army and Marine Corps. "I'd rather be dark and be wrong," he told me, "than be light and be wrong." We'll probe this deeper when discussing facial camouflage, but already it should be noted that dark colors appear to recede to human vision and don't attract nearly the attention that bright colors do.

SEASONAL COLOR VARIATIONS

Sensitizing yourself to your surroundings includes developing an appreciation for dominant field colors, which are more complex than merely green in summer and white in winter. In the Northern Hemisphere, for example, these are the dominant field colors, by season, which should be the basis for your camouflage.

SEASON	BASIC BACKGROUND COLORS
Early Spring	Brown, black, dark greens
Late Spring	Bright greens, brown
Summer	Dark greens, bright greens
Late Summer/ Early Fall	Dark greens, brown
Fall	Brown, yellow, black, green
Late Fall/ Early Winter	Brown, black, gray, some white
Early Winter	White, gray, brown
Winter	White, some gray, some brown
Late Winter/ Early Spring	Brown, white, some gray

Try this yourself: look at a scene and pick out the darkest object and the brightest object. Without fail, it's faster to find the latter because it's lighter color seems to advance toward you. This natural inconspicuousness of dark shades is why I repeatedly recommend that you exploit shadows.

Movement detection is quite similar. The human mind instantly keys on even tiny movements; you can be wearing the most perfect G-suit, but an enemy observer can detect you when you move. He may not know *what* you are, but he'll sure know *where* you are, and that's just as deadly.

While you obviously should try to keep some foliage to your front, what's not commonly understood is the usefulness of keeping foliage to your back, too. Provided your coloration is similar to this backdrop, it does wonders for cloaking your presence. During World War I,

Capt. H.W. McBride found he could stand still with a tree trunk to his back and be invisible to Germans 500 yards away—just wearing his ordinary khaki uniform.

More commonly understood but related is the need never to skyline yourself, which means walking along a ridge with the sky behind you. You should stay just below the ridge and move along what's called a hill's "military crest."

The last general point I'll make on camouflage concerns the growing belief in "total invisibility," which is a myth. A sniper aspires to be *undetectable*; it's impossible to be invisible. Maturely facing this reality allows you to make informed judgments and compromises and not to foolishly bet your life on a well-made Ghillie suit.

Another aspect of this maturity is respecting that even minimal camouflage can save your life by complicating an opponent's aim, causing his shots to be near misses instead of mortal hits.

Cops Need Camouflage, Too

Police snipers have been the most resistant to using any kind of camouflage, perhaps because they see it as symbolic of a military/offensive attitude when, legally, they must operate defensively.

While every law enforcement sniper may not need a full-fledged G-suit, his success is just as much dependent on operating without detection as is his military sniper counterpart's. When he's conspicuous, a suspect can engage a police sniper, but of equal concern is that his visible presence may signal that an operation is about to be undertaken or a decision has been made to rescue hostages.

While a police sniper's camouflage may not be as elaborate as a military sniper's, it still must accomplish the same goal: make him undetectable.

I've known of several police departments that imaginatively exploited their snipers' stealth and camouflage. When crack dealers made a municipal park inhospitable for local children in Albuquerque, New Mexico, tactical team snipers slipped in before daylight, lay in hiding all day, and then radioed the deals they saw unfolding. Other uniformed officers appre-

Pembroke Pines, Florida, police detective Earl Feugill in the Ghillie suit he wore to foil the robbery of a fast-food restaurant.

hended the perpetrators, who never realized they'd been observed by hidden snipers. In another instance, Pembroke Pines, Florida, police detective Earl Feugill, a tactical team sniper, donned his Ghillie suit and hid in nearby bushes to observe a fast-food restaurant that had been robbed several times. Sure enough, he apprehended the culprits—friends of an employee who merely slipped in a back door to carry away their loot. In this case, however, the sniper himself arrested the perpetrators—and wouldn't you like to have seen their faces? "They were quite surprised," Feugill, a former Marine, told reporters.

MAKING A GHILLIE SUIT

The finest sniping camouflage yet developed is the Ghillie suit, first employed by British Lovat Scouts snipers during their great countersniper offensive of World War I. They'd come upon this garb in their native Scotland, where gameskeepers wore Ghillie suits to

World War I American Doughboy snipers in France, attired in "sniper robes."

The author's one-piece Ghillie suit (R), and a two-piece suit from Custom Concealment.

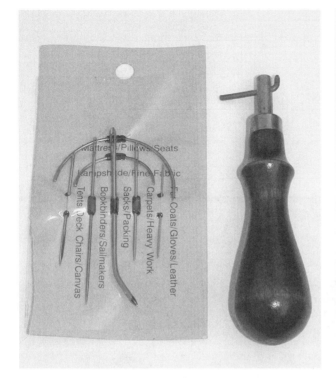

Ghillie suit construction is easier with large carpet needles and even a leather working tool.

The U.S. Army–issue Ghillie suit kit includes four shades of burlap in both rolls and cut cloth.

TIPS FOR CONSTRUCTING YOUR GHILLIE SUIT
(See illustration, page 369)

UPPER LEFT: Ghillie suit components include a basic garment, 2-inch-square netting, tent screening, and burlap. It's assembled with only a carpeting needle, stout thread, and silicone cement, such as Shoe-Goop. In the military, most often the base garment is mechanic's coveralls; Nomex pilot's coveralls can be used, but they tend to be hotter. You can make a two-piecer from ordinary BDUs.

TOP CENTER: Turn the garment inside out so pockets are inside and still accessible. You may even add pockets or pouches if your one-piece coverall lacks them. Some snipers Shoe-Goop a nylon handgun holster here.

UPPER RIGHT: You can add a pouch at the lower back, while nylon screening is excellent high on the back for maximum ventilation and along the underarms and inside the thighs.

CENTER LEFT: Remove your glove's trigger finger and be sure to camouflage boots elaborately to complement the suit.

CENTER: Burlap strips hang similarly from either one- or two-piece suits.

CENTER RIGHT: Glue inner-tube rubber, heavy canvas, or Naugahyde to the knees and elbows for reinforcement. Put thin sponges underneath for padding.

BOTTOM LEFT: Similarly attach about 15 inches of netting to the hat, tie burlap strips, and create a drape to hang smoothly across your scope. Cut out the hat's center and glue screening for ventilation.

BOTTOM MIDDLE: As Ranger Weber did, you can mount a 2-quart canteen or CamelBak water carrier and sip from it while prone.

BOTTOM RIGHT: The netting covers only the back, with an inch or two of excess. It's sewn on with heavy thread and anchored about every 4 to 5 inches. Cut burlap strips 10 to 12 inches long and 2 inches wide, then tie at least one strip to each square.

capture clever poachers. As the legendary pistolero Jeff Cooper pointed out to me during a visit to his Gunsite Ranch, "Ghillie" in old Scottish means "man"—so a Ghillie suit literally is a Scottish man suit.

Description

A G-suit is a one- or two-piece uniform to which you attach hundreds of dull-colored cloth strips—usually burlap or jute—and create such subtle texture and diffuse coloration that you can blend completely into outdoor surroundings.

A properly made Ghillie suit so well conceals its wearer that it never fails to impress first-time viewers. As a standard practice, our instructors leisurely lectured about camouflage, then casually introduced a G-suit-attired sniper, who rose from the ground like some bog monster only a few feet away. Students needed no further convincing.

The front of a Ghillie suit is kept relatively smooth to facilitate low crawling; only the back contains draped burlap. For stowing, I roll my G-suit up with the burlap backing inside for a tight, neat package and secure it with cinch cords.

Since a quality G-suit requires 40 to 60 man-hours of tedious work, commercially made ones are not cheap—at least the ones worth having. I saw a catalog ad for a G-suit that cost $50 and unsurprisingly learned it was an old pair of coveralls with cloth strips glued on it. Sniper purists insist that each sniper must make his own suit, but some people have little time but an adequate budget, so it makes sense to put up $600 or more for a G-suit, which is what a good one costs. My own G-suit is a one-piece, but I also have a two-piece from Custom Concealment, based in Zanesville, Ohio. They offer a good variety of styles and colors, including weapon covers and chaps, and they're truly well made. Dave Mallery in Portland, Oregon, produces high-quality suits, too, but the last time I checked he had more business than he could handle.

Coloration and Materials

My Ghillie suit is green and forest-oriented, while the other one we've pictured is brown and grassland- or desert-oriented. My G-suit actually contains six colors and three different textures, which were spray painted to tone down light spots and blend it all together. Just one sleeve probably contains 200 to 300 burlap strips.

My suit uses hand-tied netting, made from ordinary string, to hold the burlap in place. I did it this way just to prove it could work effectively. Otherwise, most of our students use nylon hammock material as netting. Either way, the resulting squares should be no more than 2 inches wide.

The Sniper Cape

In situations where it's too hot or you're short of materials for a full-fledged G-suit, you may get by with a sniper cape, which is an abbreviated version that conceals just the sniper's head and body above his waist. The ones I've seen were simple pullovers made from army camouflage netting. Known humorously as an "ape cape," this half-size Ghillie-like concealment is popular in the 100+ degree temperatures of the Middle East and Southwest Asia.

I also know civilian police snipers who've made sniper capes rather than G-suits and keep them stowed with their alert gear just in case.

Ghillie Hats and Veils

The camouflaged hat is as important as the G-suit itself because it's the highest part of the prone sniper and must blend into the suit and camouflaged rifle.

Netting identical to the G-suit is sewn to the hat, so about 15 inches of it hang across the front and rear. The sniper ties burlap to these squares, just like the G-suit; this creates a drape that will hang smoothly from the top of his head right across the scope for an uninterrupted, indistinguishable silhouette. My hat includes layers of tinted mosquito screening in front to allow better observation than burlap.

Ghillie Suit Limitations

While providing excellent camouflage, Ghillie suits have limitations, too, the biggest one being stifling heat from layers of thick

Sniper capes cover just the head and shoulders. They work well when it's too hot to use a full Ghillie suit.

As important as the G-suit itself, the hat's camo drapes completely across the scope for a smooth, continuous flow.

burlap. Because of this, you should wear it only during a stalk, and drink plenty of water to prevent heat exhaustion.

A G-suit is hot, bulky, heavy—murderously heavy when wet. Due to these limitations, I consider using a G-suit the exception rather than the rule. When there's plenty of foliage around, I'd advise *not* using a Ghillie suit; during fall and early spring, though, a G-suit probably is essential.

Capt. H.W. McBride, who called a Ghillie suit a "sniper robe," warned about being too bold when wearing one, because a sniper "is apt to be pretty much up against it if anything goes wrong." I don't disagree—everybody practices stalking forward for a shot, but I don't see enough practice of what to do *after* the shot—

FIRE DANGER. A burlap strip from the author's Ghillie suit is consumed in seconds.

and it's what happens after the shot that gets snipers killed. Have you ever tried running 500 yards in a Ghillie suit?

Another problem not usually addressed is the fire danger. A Ghillie suit is like an old Christmas tree waiting for a spark, and exactly that happened to one of my former instructors, Ranger Weber, during a field exercise. All it took was one spark from a smoke grenade to turn him into a human torch; he escaped injury by only the thinnest of margins. If he wasn't a PT nut strong enough to tear his way out of his G-suit, he very well could have burned to death.

This is why you should use Velcro fasteners instead of buttons or zippers on your G-suit—and it's why I *urge* you to treat your G-suit with a fire retardant. The only such treatment I've ever found is Burn Barrier FPR, available from Fire Retardants, Inc. (formerly Minnesota Fire-Chem) of Chaska, Minnesota. This liquid works on burlap and is applied by spraying or dipping. Some tests have found it "mildly irritating to exposed skin . . . and corrosive to metals," but it's also listed as nontoxic, provided you don't drink the stuff. Spray it on as a mist, using at least one quart per G-suit. To ensure you've used enough, remove a couple strips and try to light them. When properly applied, FPR will prevent the burlap from flaming, although it may char or smolder.

POPULAR CAMOUFLAGE PATTERNS

All camouflage patterns are not created equally. Some are more effective than others, some evolved from genuine research, some are nothing more than commercial hype, and some are so bad they can get you killed.

Military and Police Patterns

The current U.S. Marine Corps digital camouflage uniforms have, in my opinion, the finest camouflage pattern ever developed. Whether the brown/tan desert version, or the green/brown woodland style, this pattern works superbly both at close and long ranges.

At close range, the pattern's many tiny pixel

The best camo pattern ever devised, the author believes, is this USMC digital scheme.

Great uniform, questionable camo pattern—the U.S. Army's latest combat uniform.

points break up the wearer's outline effectively, almost three-dimensionally, blending him into his surroundings. Farther away—as we reach fade distance—these tiny pixels meld into larger blobs that create an irregularity to obscure and disrupt a Marine's outline. For the first time ever, here's a pattern that works really well, both close up and far away.

I wish I could say the same for the U.S. Army's digital pattern, found on its latest Army Combat Uniform, or ACU. Although the ACU itself is extremely well thought out, its camouflage designers began their slide down the slippery slope when it was decided that one universal shade must work worldwide, for every terrain, every coloration, every season, literally every environment. Inevitably, when you design

a camouflage pattern to work everywhere, it won't work really well *anywhere*.

Although the ACU's digital concept offers the same potential for effectiveness as the Marine pattern, it's too light-colored—sort of a gray/tan/beige—for just about any setting except the desert. (In a wooded, green setting it will stick out like the proverbial sore thumb.) Still, since tan desert and brown mountains dominate Southwest Asia, where the U.S. Army will be engaged for the immediate future, this pattern will prove acceptable.

Second only to the latest Marine digital patterns, the most effective all-around pattern is the U.S. Army's woodland BDU. The randomly splotched, four-color woodland pattern blends well in all but desert and winter settings, while its

MILITARY/POLICE PATTERNS. (L-R) woodland, plain olive drab, "urban" (Snowflage), black, and tiger stripes.

special IR-absorbent cloth helps conceal wearers from some high-tech surveillance systems.

Plain olive drab, as found on Vietnam jungle fatigues, wasn't bad coloration, but it left the wearer's silhouette intact. To be more effective, this pattern needs spray painting.

Tiger stripes, another Vietnam favorite, reminds me of fishing lures, half of which, my father once noted, are colored to catch fishermen rather than fish. This is a sexy pattern, but it's polarized with the black stripes oriented only horizontally. What happens when real shadows are vertical?

To fully appreciate the danger, recall that prisoners used to wear horizontal-striped uniforms so guards could confirm their presence by glancing through vertical cell bars. I doubt there's been a sexier pattern, but tiger stripes can get you killed. The colors are great; polarization is bad.

Black BDUs, very popular for entry teams, suffer from the same shortcoming as olive drab, but black makes for an even more distinct outline that can compromise a sniper. I once argued this with a Chicago-area police sniper whose entire tac team wore black, he said, because it "intimidated" bad guys. This particular cop was a "know-it-all," so my words were wasted; I hope they aren't wasted with you.

Understand: in order to be "intimidated," a bad guy has to *see* you—and if he can see you, he can shoot you. Intimidation works against a

gunman who wants to be talked out, but it's begging for death from a determined man who wants to kill someone, especially a police sniper.

Black's not a bad color for entry teams, where they gain a short advantage by startling and intimidating hostiles, especially when wearing helmets and gas masks. But it's a terrible color for stealth and infiltration. What does a shotgun-armed bad guy call two black-attired cops sneaking toward him in daylight? Skeet.

We proved the inferiority of black uniforms during a SWAT competition in Gulfport, Mississippi, when *every single* black-attired competitor was detected during an observation exercise. It made believers out of everyone. Enough said.

The only overall worse pattern is the gray-white-black combination that's sometimes promoted as "urban camouflage." It's so bright that it highlights the wearer in all conditions except snow—but here's the irony. When originally developed, this pattern was called Snowflage and was not intended to blend with concrete and other urban elements. Use it in snowfields, not on city streets. The military woodland pattern is much more effective in urban settings.

Reality Hunting Patterns

Some real camouflage breakthroughs have come from private-sector developments, which have fielded an incredible array of patterns.

CIVILIAN REALITY PATTERNS. (L-R) Treebark II with leaves, Realtree, Mossy Oak, Mirage, and Marshland.

They're called "reality patterns" because they attempt to duplicate actual foliage.

Leading this pack was Treebark, introduced in 1979 by a keen-eyed hunter, Jim Crumley, who took the time and effort to match his pattern with predominant colors and textures he saw in North American woodland. He's since added Corn Stalk, Treebark II, and another variation with leaves.

Realtree followed in 1985, the outgrowth of computerized study by Bill Jordan, a serious Georgia bowhunter whose pattern includes more leaf shapes and shades than did Treebark. Jordan defined six distinct foliage patterns, which he integrated into Realtree, with three varieties now available for brown, gray, and snow backdrops.

Invented by Toxey Haas, Mossy Oak indeed seems most in synch with oak forests and has become very popular among deer hunters. It's available in gray-oriented Bottomland, limb-studded Tree Stand, and leafy Full Foliage. Mossy Oak has a bit more contrast and larger shapes than Realtree.

Mirage pattern presents realistic leaves against green (spring) or brown (fall) backgrounds for an almost 3D effect.

The next step in stark realism is Cattail, a marsh pattern designed in 1986 by Larry Sanburg, which is similar to another yellow grass pattern, Delta Marsh. While these are fine for duck hunters, such patterns have a "right-side-up." As soon as you're "right-side-down" you stick out like the proverbial sore thumb.

With any of these reality patterns, just recognize that the more specific its design, the more restricted its application.

Abstract Camouflage Patterns

ASAT (All Season—All Terrain) camouflage attempts to solve the limited application of some patterns by trying to be general enough for any situation. Designed by Stan Starr Jr. and Jim Barnhart, ASAT was introduced in 1986.

A roughly similar abstract pattern is Treeline, which uses a mesh of linear shapes to create an indistinct, all-terrain pattern. But unlike ASAT, Treeline has an excellent winter version called Skyline.

We've included plain gray among the abstract patterns because at moderate distances it blends reasonably well in urban or rural areas, day or night. This wouldn't be my first choice, but it works. Were I an undercover cop, I'd make it a point to wear gray streetclothes whenever possible.

Our last abstract pattern isn't really abstract, but plain olive drab jungle fatigues make an outstanding base which you can embellish with black, brown, green, or yellow spray paint to fit an amazing array of foliage. When I was tasked a decade ago with surveilling a large Western cattle ranch for rustlers, I painted this very shirt to fit that area's grasslands perfectly.

The civilian ASAT pattern is very effective, especially at medium and long distances.

Mesh Pullover Suits

Perhaps the handiest pieces of police sniper camouflage are the mesh pullover suits made in Realtree brown or gray. These can be compressed into a beer-mug-sized space for convenient storage and be donned in less than a minute. Further, its mesh allows good ventilation in summer.

These mesh suits won't hold up as long as regular-weight camo suits, but the cost is so reasonable and the benefits so obvious that long-term wear is an irrelevant concern.

HATS, FACES, AND VEILS

Probably the part of a sniper's body most readily detected is the head because it contains his primary sensors—his eyes—and snipers often must lift or turn their heads to see. Improper camouflage only amplifies this problem.

There's so much "bad poop" floating around about facial camouflage and headgear that it's scary. Hopefully we'll put some of this misinformation to rest.

ABSTRACT PATTERNS. (L-R) Treeline, painted jungle fatigues, and plain gray.

Realtree mesh suits can be worn over other clothes and provide instant camouflage.

A Sniper's Headgear

While the Kevlar helmet allows unparalleled protection from small-arms fire, the sniper's need to avoid detection normally outweighs ballistic protection. Even when camoed, this helmet adds much bulk to the head, making any movement much easier to spot. When operating with a larger unit, however, the sniper should wear a helmet to blend in with non-snipers and to protect himself from the fire they're likely to attract.

The BDU or Ranger cap is smaller, and its bill adds shadow over the wearer's eyes, improving his vision in sunlight and making his face a bit more difficult to see. But its squarish outline is too well defined for me.

The baseball cap, worn by many police SWAT teams, is even more defined since it's not crushable like the BDU cap. Further, I've never seen a police baseball cap that wasn't black or blue rather than camouflage-patterned.

The traditional watch cap, in black or navy blue, sometimes is worn as cold-weather Special Operations headgear, but its utility is based on warmth, not concealment. An identical cap, but white or mottled to resemble local coloration, is much better.

Camouflage cloth scarves—usually olive drab triangular bandages—add a touch of "devil-may-care" piracy, but they aren't very effective concealment.

No, the best concealment headgear I've found is the humble jungle hat, in a pattern that matches your other clothing. Its crushable shape and all-around bill soften and diffuse the head's outline, while it gives plenty of shadow and many convenient tie-downs for burlap or natural foliage.

Veils and Masks

Today's sniper veils evolved from the World War II Japanese sniper practice of wearing a mosquito net to shade and disrupt his face's outline. You can use mosquito netting the same

None of this headgear works well for sniping since all create a distinct, head-size silhouette.

way today or acquire commercial sniper veils. The best veil I've seen was cut from a piece of heavy Treebark netting I bought in a fabric store for about $2.

But a problem common to all these veils is that they limit your peripheral vision and add a confusing netted layer between your eye and your scope. Therefore, my inclination is toward Spandoflage, the stretchable head masks. Introduced to me by an old friend, the St. Paul Police Department's rifle instructor, Sgt. Darryl Schmidt, these Spandoflage head masks come in five different patterns compatible to nearly any season or camouflage coloration. Due to its elasticity, be careful to snip only about 1/4 inch when cutting eyeholes. Spandoflage still isn't as effective as correctly applied camouflage paste; it's just fast to put on. (More on camo paste below.)

A black Nomex hood or balaclava is popular in some police tactical teams and military Special Operations units. While there's no question it's sexy, let's face it: this solid, distinct

BEST HEAD COVERING. The irregular shape and bill and the anchor points for attaching camo make the jungle hat the best sniper headgear. It works ideally with a Spandoflage headnet.

VEILS. Spandoflage (L) allows unobscured viewing through a rifle scope, which the author thinks makes it superior to veils, such as the one at right.

hood highlights you as nicely as a target's black bull's-eye. I wish Hollywood could convince low-lifes and terrorists to always wear black hoods; it would make our shot placement so much easier.

Facial Pastes and Sticks

No veil or Spandoflage can substitute for correctly applied facial coloration. When used properly, a camoed face doesn't look like it's been painted; it no longer looks like a face at all.

Here are the basics for applying coloration. First, realize that the human eye sees dark colors as receding, or going away, but it interprets light colors as advancing, or sticking out toward the viewer. Therefore to trick the eye, reverse the high and low points of your face, using dark or light colors.

The concave, inward places—around the eyes, inside the ears, the inward folds of the chin, and beside the nose—color these *light* so they look like they're advancing/protruding.

Next, make *dark* the naturally protruding places—the nose, chin, cheeks, and forehead—and they'll look receding.

You'll find it much easier if you apply light colors first, because you can be sloppy and later fix it up when you add the darker shade. Also remember that nature isn't symmetrical, so *don't balance* the right and left sides of your face. Just let an irregular pattern emerge on its own, and only tie it all together as you finish. Make sure you finish and cover everything, including eyelids, moustache, nostrils, behind the ears and neck, and so on. *Nothing* is left flesh colored.

And talking about flesh colors, black snipers should follow these steps and use the same shades and techniques. Attempts I've seen to exploit natural dark skin tones didn't camouflage as well as covering it with camouflage shades.

Military camouflage sticks work well but sometimes become so tacky that you've got to mix mosquito repellent with them before you can spread them. My preference is civilian paste, which is much faster and easier to apply and available in more colors. If this is your preference, too, just be sure not to apply it too thick or it becomes shiny and reflects light.

When no paste or stick is available, you can burn cork or use ordinary barbecue charcoal to

Pastes, sticks, and compac shown here are used by most U.S. military and police snipers.

Wrong facial camo (L) highlights face and is symetrically balanced, while face at right is perfectly camouflaged.

SNIPER GLOVES. Top to bottom: green cotton; most popular snug-fitting aviator gloves with Nomex and leather; Spandoflage; and cotton with silicone nubs.

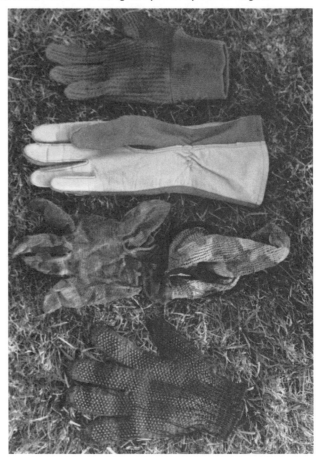

at least darken your face as a poor but minimal alternative. But no matter what you use, employ the buddy system to inspect it and fix it when sweat and toil wear it off.

SNIPER GLOVES

Many snipers wear gloves for warmth and to protect fingers from insect bites and thorns. If you don't wear gloves, your hands must be camouflaged with as much detail as your face.

Solid black gloves create the same distinct outline problems as headgear, while tan or green solids can be acceptable if they fit the background and match your clothes.

Treebark and Realtree pattern gloves work fine, but Spandoflage gloves seem too thin to last long in a field environment.

Many snipers (including the author) prefer Nomex pilot's gloves because of their snug,

Excellent Ghillie suit and positional camouflage, but this sniper's uncamouflaged rifle compromises his location.

Much better. This sniper has camouflaged his rifle and immersed himself in natural foilage.

comfortable fit. You can tone down the green-gray color with spray paint.

For any of these gloves, remove the trigger finger material and glue or sew the cut edges to prevent further unraveling.

POSITIONAL CAMOUFLAGE

Where snipers and police on surveillance details tend to let camouflage standards slip is when it comes to concealing a position.

The first rule in effective positional camouflage is to improve what nature already put there rather than to artificially create concealment. Therefore, try to locate your hide in a natural dip that has good shadows and adequate foliage. One trick is to pull bushes slightly and tie them in strategic locations with clear fishing line rather than cut foliage, which soon droops. This also works to create shadow. Just be sure the leaves' lighter bottoms don't get turned up.

Sod can do wonders for concealment. Cut it from behind your position and use it to cover exposed earth or add background. And if you must dig, scatter the dirt widely instead of leaving a visible berm. Be sure to sterilize your position when you abandon it.

Modern camouflage nets are effective because they allow light to shine through and create shadows, giving visual depth to a position. Normally used to conceal vehicles and large pieces of equipment, it's worth scrounging a few pieces of camouflage netting for positional camouflage. The same goes for nylon screening or cheesecloth, that sheer, see-through cloth. No only do these help cut the sun's glare when you're in a stationary position, but they also reflect light so your adversaries cannot see you under or behind it, creating a sort of shooting blind.

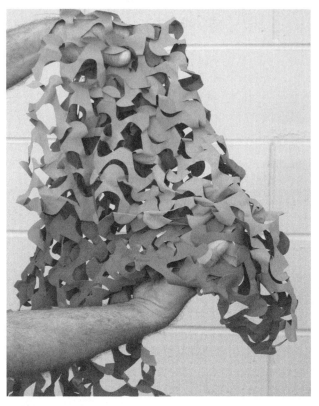

Military camouflage netting enhances a sniper team's position.

Cheesecloth screening at this USMC sniper post atop the embassy in Kabul, Afghanistan, reflects the bright sun, making it difficult for countersurveillance or countersnipers.

CAMOUFLAGING YOUR EQUIPMENT

Your weapon and webgear should be camouflaged in the same general pattern, colors, and texture as the rest of you. It all blends together. Let's start by talking about rifles.

Robar, the maker of the excellent SR-90 sniper rifle, has developed a permanent polymer coating that completely covers all metal and synthetic surfaces in exact camo patterns. Robar's Polymax coating reportedly is hard and durable and not only conceals but protects surfaces from moisture and rusting.

Two other sniper rifle builders—McMillan and H.S. Precision—offer their wares with pattern-perfect camouflaged stocks, suitable for desert, winter, or woodland environments. The quality here is excellent, too.

Although not frequently encountered prior to 9-11, today many U.S. military sniper rifles are

This Special Forces sniper has wrapped his rifle, scope, and bipod for effective, consistent camouflage.

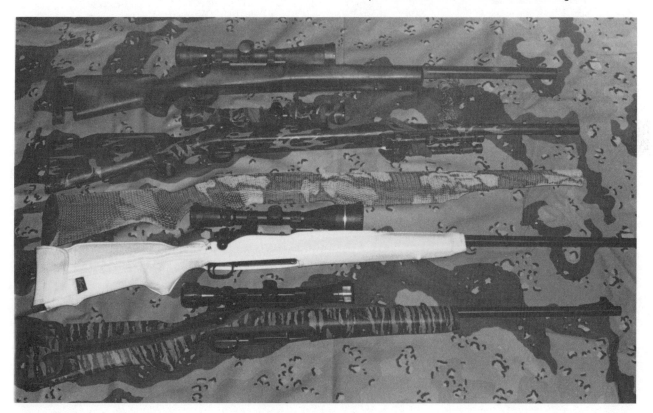

RIFLE CAMOUFLAGE. Top to bottom: a painted M24 Sniper Weapon System; the author's taped Remington 700; a Spandoflage gun sock on a shotgun; winter-white chap on a Winchester 70; Realtree chap on the author's Sako target rifle.

painted in camouflage colors, ranging from dark shades for northern areas to desert tans for Iraq and Afghanistan. Most of this painting has been done at depot-level, applied by technicians who properly degreased and prepped surfaces, and used the correct kinds of oil-based, matte paints.

Should you be in a military unit or law enforcement agency that frowns on painting a weapon, you still can modify its color without "damaging" your rifle. Simply cover it with an appropriately colored tape intended for bows or guns, available through archery stores and sporting goods catalogs. Many military PXs sell camouflage duct tape, but *beware*: check this

This Army sniper team's spotting scope (center) is as well camouflaged as the snipers.

Eagle's sniper drag bag has plenty of loops for tying burlap strips.

If you cannot paint your rifle or optics, another option is to cover it with camouflage tape.

tape to make sure it doesn't harm metal surfaces and won't melt on a hot barrel. Some of it's even reusable.

If you tape, make *sure* you don't compress the barrel against the forearm, which would degrade the free float. Instead, tape the barrel lengthwise and tape the forearm separately. I then tie on random burlap strips as the final effect. Be sure to reverify the zero after taping; my zero always shifts when taping and untaping my Remington.

When camouflage tape's not available, wrap your weapon with torn-up strips from old fatigues, thereby matching your clothes with your rifle's color pattern. I actually prefer to wrap my rifle scope and spotting scope with cloth, which is easier to apply and remove than tape. You can either tape or sew the ends.

And when it comes to wrapping your rifle scope, be sure the cloth or tape doesn't interfere with the zoom or focus rings or BDC and windage knobs. If you're concerned about reflections off the objective lens, install a sun shade/hood or KillFlash filter rather than draping cheesecloth, which would reduce resolution and brightness.

Although a great deal of attention is paid to painting and camouflaging the sniper's rifle, some other critical gear often isn't camouflaged at all—but it should be. I'm talking about spotting scopes, tripods, and bipods. Many a time I've seen a perfectly painted rifle, but hanging under its forearm is a pure black Harris

bipod. Or, while in position, both sniper and spotter lie there, practically invisible, and there's a totally uncamouflaged spotting scope. These should have similar camouflage—color and type—as all the other gear, or they become target indicators that an enemy sniper can use to locate you. Paint them, wrap them with colored cloth or tape, string some burlap that's the same size and style as your Ghillie suit. Make them as well camouflaged as everything else.

Webgear and rucksacks are probably the easiest items to camouflage since there are so many loops and ties to attach burlap, and spray paint absorbs so readily into the material. Just apply paint and strips and tape as needed to make a camouflage having the same pattern, colors, and texture as everything else.

One special touch I use is sewing on a piece of military camouflage screen to the back of my webgear and to my rucksack, keeping it fairly close so it doesn't snag on brush. This improves camo considerably when you're lying prone or low-crawling.

THE FLIR THREAT

In 1968, many years before anyone even heard of it, our covert actions unit had FLIR—Forward Looking Infra-Red—viewing systems aboard our MC-130 aircraft. These were virtually the world's first FLIRs, used by our planes to fly covert night jumps and resupply missions into North Vietnam. It was a tremendous advantage being able to see *through* the foliage, night or day, which helped foil a number of attempts by the enemy to play our captured agents back against us or to lure our teams and planes into traps. Yes, FLIR was a great technological advantage.

The problem today is that the FLIR genie is out of the bottle. Many countries—both friendly and not so friendly—have FLIR or similar thermal-imaging technologies that can be used against Special Ops and sniper teams. The latest handheld thermal imager weighs only 1 pound—and that's counting the battery! What's a sniper team to do?

Before looking at solutions, let's consider more closely what thermal imaging is and does. A FLIR is a sort of video camera, but it doesn't see visible light; it senses minute differences in temperatures and assigns various shades to them according to what's hottest and coolest. This results in ghost-like images that look reversed, like a photographic negative. What's most impressive is that FLIR can "see" through thin foliage as well as rain and snow—and those capabilities can be just as important in daylight as in darkness.

That would sound like the end of the world to a sniper if there were no means to counter it, but there are. I'm not going to be too specific (bad guys can read, too), but I think it's obvious that if you can change your external body

FLIR sensor unit in nose of a USMC helicopter. Thermal-sensing technology today is used throughout the world.

FLIR images of armed soldiers in thin foilage. Note brightest thermal images from exposed faces and hands.

Anti-FLIR cream is applied to flesh to reduce body heat signature.

A British sniper demonstrates an anti-FLIR Ghillie suit.

Viewed through a FLIR, a sniper wearing a special Custom Concealment Ghillie suit (upper right) is largely devoid of a heat signature.

temperature or make it close to the temperature of things around you—think of it as another way of camouflaging yourself into your surroundings—then the FLIR won't be able to distinguish you. There's a true story about a Marine sniper gunny at Quantico who purchased an item at a flea market for $2 and used it to hide from a multimillion dollar thermal detection system—with several congressmen watching. Yes, FLIR can be fooled.

A thermal detection-resistant Ghillie suit has been developed in Britain that vents and deflects body heat to reduce the wearer's thermal image. I'm not sure how effective it actually is. On this side of the Atlantic, Custom Concealment makes two Ghillie suits specially modified to enhance their resistance to thermal detection. Examining FLIR photos of demonstrators wearing these suits, I don't think there can be any question that the heat signature has been reduced, and quite a bit.

An even more novel approach has been that of a Greek defense contractor, Intermat Group SA, which developed an antithermal cream. Applied to exposed parts of the body—face, arms, and hands, where heat is registered by a FLIR most easily—the dense cream blocks heat dissipation, thereby reducing the wearer's thermal signature. This is a serious product from a serious manufacturer that already makes paints and specialized coatings for helmets, uniforms, and vehicles to reduce their detection by IR systems. They may actually have something, since all the FLIR images I've seen are brightest at the very spots that this cream would cover.

Overall, I wouldn't be too concerned about FLIR since it is more of a future threat than it is a current one. And if the day comes that an enemy uses FLIR against us, we'll already have the techniques and the technology to counter it.

CHAPTER 14

STALKING AND MOVEMENT

STEALTH

Barraged by constant mental diversions in music and television, seeking instant gratification, compelled to live at a hectic pace or fall behind socially or economically, today's youth is conditioned to be impetuous, impatient, and inattentive. Consider by contrast the pace and focus required for operating behind an enemy's lines.

In SOG operations, our Special Forces recon teams penetrated heavily patrolled North Vietnamese Army base areas in Laos, Cambodia, and North Vietnam. At any instant, a single six-man team was pursued by well-trained trackers, sometimes with dogs; had likely hides swept by platoon-size enemy patrols; evaded dozens of squad-size ambushes along trails, streams, and roads; and bypassed lone concealed "watchers" who'd fire signal shots if they spotted a team. Standing by at a nearby camp was up to a battalion-sized (400+) reaction force, ready to deploy the instant a Green Beret team's presence was confirmed.

To help you appreciate the scale of this challenge, understand that we never had more than about 15 to 18 teams of six

A sniper must develop an attitude—a philosophy—of stealth.

389

SOG Recon Team New Hampshire slips across a Laotian river in an area teeming with North Vietnamese soldiers. (Photo credit: Will Curry)

or eight men each in the field—but opposing them were 40,000 (yes, forty *thousand*) troops dedicated to security along the Ho Chi Minh Trail road system.

Since many of our recon men—including yours truly—were products of the instant gratification/rock 'n' roll era, it's obvious that young people can adapt to this most dangerous environment if they learn to practice *patience*, *slow down* in everything they do, and do it all *deliberately*. These habits are the epitome of stealth and will make you a successful sniper.

Here's what I mean by slow down. In an entire day (10 hours) of movement in especially dangerous country, my team sometimes traveled only 500 meters. That works out to 50 meters per hour, or just over one step per minute.

Within that one minute, you scan the view to front and sides; carefully eyeball any place an enemy soldier could lurk; examine the ground where next you'll place your foot; pause; smell;

listen; use your left hand to lightly push a vine aside; with one toe delicately test the ground, and perhaps deftly slide a dry leaf to one side; slowly shift your weight to the forward foot; ease the vine behind you and make sure it didn't catch on webgear or rucksack, etc. Then repeat it all to bring the trailing foot alongside the other one. Stealth becomes an attitude, a way of life.

In other words, you virtually immerse yourself in tiny, deliberate actions—continuous actions that occupy mind and body and keep you focused on the here and now. Your goal is practicing perfect attention to detail while making absolutely no noise. If you so much as rustle a branch, your silent teammates will strangle you—which is nothing compared to what the enemy will do if your team's detected.

At a normal pace, it would take perhaps five minutes to walk that 500 meters; using deliberate stealth, however, you take *150 times* longer, which means by both slowing down and actively planning your every step, it could be said that you are 150 times more alert, quiet, and careful than a guy just "diddybopping" through the woods.

You apply this standard—this special stealth consciousness—to your every action while behind enemy lines. You constantly look for ways to do each thing more quietly, more invisibly, and with less chance of its being detected. For instance, when you cross a stream you learn never to lift your feet above the water, instead gliding your boots along the bottom. And you cross at a curve, through thick shadow, after silently watching and listening for 10 minutes.

You're so close to your teammate that you need never talk in a normal voice; you whisper. But most of the time hand signals are the only communication, and even this simplifies over time as you learn to understand each other so well that even a glance or raised eyebrow conveys an entire message. This is perfect mental synch; it's almost ESP.

Stealth also means exploiting bad weather, the kind of inclement cold and wet that we SOG troopers called "Special Forces weather." Human beings understandably seek protection from the elements, leaving it easier for you to roam. This is especially true at the start of a cold snap, or early in winter, or on a night of heavy rain following many pleasant nights—*before* the enemy's adapted to the change in weather. The third day of rain, for example, is far less an opportunity than was the first night. And a midwinter snowstorm is not nearly as likely to reduce enemy surveillance as did the season's first blizzard.

Inclement weather also helps mask noise so that you can move faster without detection. A downpour creates continuous leaf rustling in jungle and woods. Lightning flashes alert you to coming thunderclaps, which make five-second windows for short dashes—and conveniently reduce the enemy's night vision temporarily. Wind gusts, too, can cover short spurts of noisy movement.

In addition to providing exploitable darkness, night also provides excellent stealth opportunities if you understand human metabolism. I'm not sure that science has yet explained why, but it's long been recognized that most human beings become groggy, least alert, or sleep deepest from about 2:30 through 3:15 A.M. If you must travel at night, realize that a one-hour stalk conducted at 10:00 P.M. is much more dangerous than one commencing at 2:30 A.M. And even if your goal is to be in a hide and ready to fire by dawn, it doesn't automatically follow that you must move into your hide during the last hour of darkness. I'd want to be there several hours early and just lie there quietly alert, or even get some sleep before show time.

In dealing with stealth, I cannot overemphasize shadows. They're your best friend and worst enemy. On the one hand, shadows conceal your movement when you go out of your way to stay inside their friendly grasp. If, however, you err and step from a shadow into a sunbeam, the effect is similar to

Never step on or through a sunbeam!

stepping into a spotlight, with a much magnified likelihood of being spotted. Even slight movement in an isolated sunbeam can be detected by the human eye because it contrasts vividly against its background. And the shadow your body could generate may magnify this danger because afternoon or early-morning shadows are up to three times your body size.

Think of the isolated sunlight and moonlight you see in woods as natural spotlights that you must always sidestep. Also recognize that shadows closest to such bright patches are the darkest and most concealing because an observer's eyes will contract according to the brightest light in his field of view.

Finally, realize the tremendous advantage you have while operating behind enemy lines. The danger to you is constant, so you know you must practice stealth continuously. Your enemy, however, only appreciates his true situation when he actually encounters you—and if you're very stealthy, that encounter is one round fired at great distance.

CROSS-COUNTRY MOVEMENT

Snipers cannot possibly stalk continuously. Not only would they never arrive anywhere traveling at a snail-paced low crawl, but the physical demands of stalking would soon exhaust them. And snipers cannot march great distances while in Ghillie suits since they'd eventually become heat casualties instead of an effective fighting force.

Reality is that a sniper team compromises by adjusting its mode of movement to the situation and available concealment. A team only stalks while moving into or out of a hide, while closing with a target of opportunity, or while evading the enemy. The rest of the time, which is *most* of the time, the team's moving cross-country in search of hides and shooting opportunities or returning to friendly lines.

Perhaps I can better distinguish stalking and cross-country movement by comparing a sniper to a crocodile. As a croc, you generally swim steadily and invisibly beneath the water, raising your eyes every so often to see if there are pickings worth slipping ashore. When, at last, you spot an isolated sheep resting obliviously in the noonday sun, you deliberately and silently stalk a short distance from the water, seize your unalerted quarry, then rush back beneath the concealing waves.

A nearby shepherd may scream, throw stones, and run to the water's edge, but it is too late. You have plucked your prize and disappeared into terrain where he dares not pursue you. And so with the sniper.

Planning Movement

The most fundamental thing to understand about sniper team movement is that the team plans its route so it avoids enemy contact until it wants to begin engagements. Therefore, while planning the mission, the team studies its map, paying special heed to natural lines of drift— places where humans naturally prefer to walk, such as along ridgelines, down the long axis of valleys, etc., as we examined in the target detection section. It was by studying lines of drift that I was able to anticipate North Vietnamese roads and trails about 80 percent of the time, despite their elaborate, expert camouflage efforts.

By avoiding lines of drift, you reduce the likelihood of chance contacts with traveling enemy. If you must cross a natural line of drift, it's done perpendicularly and at as remote a place as possible, perhaps even under cover of darkness.

On the other hand, these natural lines of drift, as natural routes for human movement, make excellent places to hunt your foe.

If your area of operations has little water, you can count on encountering enemy wherever water is found, and you thus choose to seek or avoid him by planning your route toward or around water. This was equally true for Cambodia's eastern wasteland—one old SOG haunt—as it is today for Iraq's western desert.

While route planning, you always prefer traveling through "bad" terrain having good concealment, such as swamps and thickly wooded hills, especially if it has no inherent military value, which means it does not overlook a critical road junction or sit astride a key bridge, etc. Not only does this terrain make chance contact less likely, but should you be detected, enemy pursuers cannot move through such difficult terrain faster than you should be able to outrun them.

The Wall of Green

During your march, you practice several smart habits to improve the likelihood of preventing or surviving chance encounters with enemy patrols. The first smart habit, as urged in Maj. Robert Rogers' Standing Orders is, "See the enemy first." (Rogers led British Rangers on the American frontier during the French and Indian Wars, for which he drew up his famous Standing Orders, still respected and practiced in Special Operations units today.) To accomplish this, I highly recommend an old trick from my youthful squirrel-hunting days, which saved my life several times in Southeast Asia, a concept I've dubbed the "wall of green."

Simply put, the wall of green is the detectable "wall" of foliage beyond which you can't see. Assuming you're in North American wooded terrain, it would be the leafy, irregular "screen" at the far edge of your field of view, in some spots only 50 yards deep and at others perhaps up to 200 yards deep. This is shown in the adjacent illustration.

To exploit the wall of green, first you scan the zone between you and the distant wall until you're comfortable that there's no threat within it. Once satisfied, focus your mind and eyes on its distant, semicircular edge. Now, with each step you take, this irregular wall of green will push forward a bit and you scan each new bit, step after step, bit by bit, keeping your senses focused as far forward as possible. Whenever a potential threat appears on the edge of this wall of green—such as an open area, road, or any sign of habitation—stop for five minutes, just listening and watching.

If you're doing it correctly, you should spot an unalerted enemy before he sees you, so it's then your decision whether to engage, bypass, or surveil him. *You* keep the initiative; it's your option.

Incidentally, though green may not be

WALL OF GREEN. Focus your attention as far forward as you can see (top), and when you walk, keep pushing this attention as far as possible (bottom).

present, the wall of green concept works on any terrain. For instance, in relatively flat land or desert, stay keenly aware for movement or activity at the farthest edges of your vision, which, just like in wooded terrain, will grow and shift as you advance.

Exploiting Cover During the March

The second habit is making it a practice to meander a bit in your walk so that you keep a tree to your front as much as possible, both for cover and concealment. If not trees, these could also be termite mounds in central Africa, basalt rocks in a Mideast desert, or telephone poles in downtown Dallas.

Whenever you pause—and that should be frequently—you make sure you're behind suitable cover/concealment, within its shade, preferably occupying the side opposite the direction of greatest danger, which means putting yourself on the downhill side of trees on a hillside, on the deep forest side of trees near the edge of a woodline, or on the side opposite any natural line of drift.

And during cross-country movement, unlike during a stalk, the spotter leads and the sniper follows. This is because the spotter's armed with a high-capacity M16, preferably mounting an M203 grenade launcher, which is much more effective during a chance enemy contact.

STALKING

It was hunting experience that Maj. Robert Rogers had in mind in 1756, during the French and Indian Wars, when he penned the third of his famous Standing Orders for his band of Rangers: "When you're on the march, act the

Having stalked without detection along a river bank, Soviet Red Army snipers creep forward to engage German forces.

way you would if you was sneaking up on a deer. See the enemy first."

Invisibility, sneaking, creeping, seeing without being seen—these are the ingredients of modern sniper movement, yet they are identical to techniques used by hunters and warriors since we abandoned cave dwellings. All that's different now is that stalking is a cohesive doctrine, a true methodology that's as much learned as instinctive.

And it's the toughest subject for would-be snipers to master in training. In both the Army and Marine sniper schools, the inability to complete stalks without detection washes out more students than any other subject or skill. Part of this challenge is physical because a lengthy stalk can demand low-crawling hundreds of yards, but I think it's more so a combined problem of technique, camouflage, and route selection. Which isn't saying that the failing students were sloppy or inattentive, but that under intense optical observation by their instructors, the slightest—*and I mean slightest*—error is detected. As they learn, stalking is difficult, demanding, and—in combat—dangerous.

The Doctrine of Stalking

Stalking is, simply put, the invisible movement of a sniper who's positioning himself to take a shot, withdrawing after taking a shot, or evading enemy soldiers. In any other situation a sniper is merely moving cross-country, which we address separately.

There are three components of stalking doctrine, easy to understand but a challenge to employ well in all circumstances. First, correctly executing movement techniques; second, selecting a good stalk route divided into separate "legs"; and, third, matching the best movement technique to each of these legs. Let's look at movement techniques first.

While conventional troops or police entry teams advance in three- to five-second rushes, a sniper *never* rushes except while fleeing. Remember, a sniper isn't assaulting, he's slipping

GySgt. Jim Owens (L), USMC Scout Sniper Instructor School NCOIC, intensely observes stalking sniper students at Quantico.

into position with the intention of never being seen. So to stay invisible, a sniper moves using two kinds of walking and four variations on crawling, each with a specific application in mind.

A sniper *walks upright* while moving through thick woods or other adequate masking, when there is concealment from all but close-range detection. This allows for faster, easier movement.

When foliage is more irregular or perhaps less than head-high, a sniper advances at a *crouching walk*. He still moves steadily but with a bit more physical effort than walking upright.

The *high crawl* is similar to how a man moves when carrying a child "horse-back." His elbows are locked and he supports himself on hands and knees. We've illustrated this and other crawling techniques. Note that his head is waist-high for decent observation, and he can raise himself even higher with minimal detectable movement. This is the fastest kind of crawl, with the best observation.

The *elbow crawl* is necessitated by still shorter foliage and results in considerably slower movement. While performing this crawl, the sniper's elbows are on the ground for a much lower silhouette. He moves by lifting arms and legs.

The *low crawl* is employ-

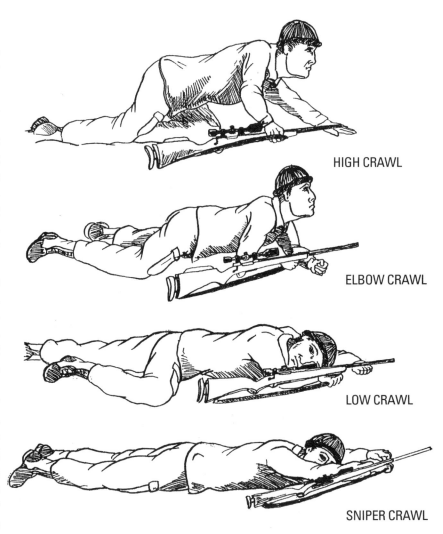

HIGH CRAWL

ELBOW CRAWL

LOW CRAWL

SNIPER CRAWL

When concealment or foilage is suitable, the sniper team advances on foot, upright.

ed when available concealment is shorter still. Now the sniper's belly is right on the ground, as are his complete arms and legs, and he never lifts them while moving. Movement has become very slow and physically strenuous.

The *sniper crawl* is the lowest, slowest movement technique, used not only when concealment is sparse but when movement must be so slow that there's no visible action to detect. He creeps along, only 4 inches per move, using just fingers and toes to propel himself. Note how he keeps his arms outstretched and stays so low that his head is turned to one side.

Note, also, that during all crawls the sniper grasps his rifle by the sling and keeps it propped above his hand so the bore doesn't drag through dirt and the scope and action are protected. Alternately, the rifle could be carried in a drag bag and tethered to the sniper.

Assessing the Terrain

A sniper's life depends on detecting and exploiting minute variances between different kinds of foliage and terrain. You must develop an "eye" for assessing opportunities and dangers in shadow, sunlight, grass, bushes, bare ground, and so on.

During World War II, Russian snipers stalked across open fields behind a camouflage screen like this.

When considering a stalking route, look *closely* at the ground before you to detect the slight folds and rises and gullies that otherwise seem insignificant and go unnoticed by the enemy. Let me give an example.

I once conducted an infiltration exercise for a rural police SWAT unit preparing to raid a simulated clandestine drug lab. The bad guys had all the obvious approaches covered. We suggested that the police infiltrate through a field of 12-inch-tall alfalfa, but their raised eyebrows instantly said, "It can't be done." So we had them take a closer look at that "flat" field, and only then did they notice several natural depressions of 6 to 10 inches, which—when added to the height of the alfalfa—allowed 18 to 22 inches of concealment, plenty for a man to low-crawl.

The entire five-man entry team invisibly low-crawled 100 yards across that alfalfa field, despite intense, optically assisted surveillance. Their very satisfied team leader, Mike, afterward wiped heavy perspiration from his face and declared, "No hood would've *ever* thought we could cross that 'open' field."

My point exactly.

Putting It All Together

Thus far, you've seen six optional means for movement: walking, crouch walking, high crawling, elbow crawling, low crawling, and sniper crawling. And you realize that you must pay keen heed to the concealment (protection from enemy view) and cover (protection from enemy fire) afforded by surrounding foliage and terrain. Even slight advantages are exploited to the maximum.

To plan your stalk, view the prospective area from a concealed position, as our sniper is doing at the top of our stalking illustration on page 399. Prior to arriving at the edge of these woods, he had been walking

A nearly invisible sniper student pauses to plan the next leg of his stalk.

Our illustration has three legs. In the first, the sniper switches from his initial crouch walk to a high crawl as he exits the woods at the top and advances through the waist-high bushes.

When he reaches the end of the bushes, he must begin low-crawling to stay below the knee-high meadow grass. This, the second leg of his stalk, will be the most time-consuming since it's long and all low-crawling. The exact spot where he exits the bushes to begin crawling was carefully selected so he wouldn't have to push any foliage aside but rather could exploit a natural gap, preferably covered by shadow.

The final leg, through the head-high bushes at the bottom, is accomplished with a crouch walk, and special care is taken as the sniper and spotter ease up to the lower side so they don't "spook" any enemy activity. From here, finally, they'll select their exact hide location.

In the real world, as in our example, you usually won't know the exact hide location until you're actually on the prospective ground and personally eyeballing it.

Some Stalking Tips

While stalking, the sniper leads and the spotter follows, traveling along the same exact path so there's less detectable sign left in grass and brush, and they don't become separated while low-crawling. Since he's in the lead, the sniper can modify their route if he sees a better hide position. Meanwhile, since he's trailing, the spotter "sterilizes" their backtrail, removing or erasing any evidence of their passage.

Stalking, especially if you're crawling, is physically draining. Not only does hurry endanger you, but it wears you down and easily leads to heat exhaustion or heat stroke. If you're low-crawling even 150 yards per hour, you're probably traveling too fast.

When selecting the route, try to have each leg end in brush tall enough so you can at least sit up, rest, drink water, and glass ahead of you. It also gives you a chance to readjust your Ghillie suit and possibly change your next leg based on your updated assessment.

erect and heading cross-country. Now, realizing his likely hide will be at the bottom of the illustration, at the far edge of the next wooded area, he plans how to stalk forward.

He divides this stalk route into separate, short legs, with each leg having a single type of concealment, and during which he must use one single type of movement technique. A stalk could have one leg or 10 legs—it's all dictated by available cover/concealment.

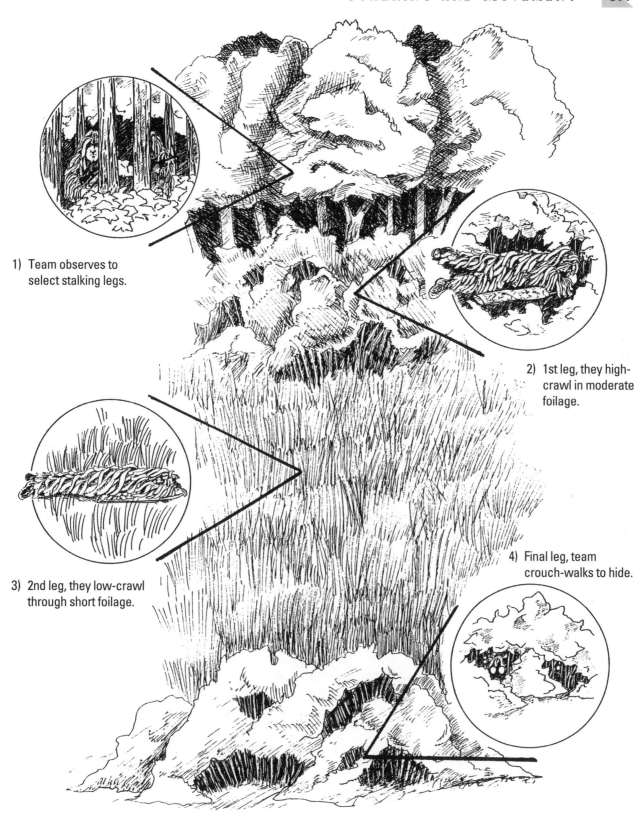

1) Team observes to select stalking legs.

2) 1st leg, they high-crawl in moderate foilage.

3) 2nd leg, they low-crawl through short foilage.

4) Final leg, team crouch-walks to hide.

WOODLAND STALKING. Divide your route into "legs" and match the best movement technique to each leg.

WRONG! Don't poke your entire head above concealment (L);
keep it low and on its side (R) and move very slow.

Because you don't want to lift your head while low-crawling, you can use the sun's location to stay oriented while on your leg. Know the exact compass direction you must travel so you can check it about every 10 minutes—but without lifting your head. Wind direction, too, can be used to keep oriented, again rechecking it about every 10 minutes in case it shifts.

Should you absolutely have to lift your head, move it so slowly that movement cannot be detected. What does this mean? The human mind processes 60 visual images per second, which is why television broadcasting uses 60 frames per second. The significance is that an enemy's eye can "see" something that moves enough that it changes visible position in 1/60 of a second. So you have to lift or turn your head so slowly that there's no visible difference in just 1/60 of a second. Given that you normally turn your head 90 degrees in less than a second, this means turning so slowly that it seems you're thinking about moving more than you're actually moving. I'd guesstimate taking about 15 to 25 seconds.

To further minimize detection, lift only the side of your head for a flatter, less distinct silhouette. And do so *slowly*.

When assessing the threat of detection, the only safe assumption while stalking is that your location is under continuous surveillance by an optically equipped foe ready to engage you the instant you get sloppy.

CHAPTER 15

THE SNIPER'S HIDE: THE FFP

THE SNIPER'S HIDE

It was the British who dubbed a sniping position a "hide," forever confusing ordinary soldiers into thinking some poor deceased sniper has been skinned out by trophy-seeking enemies. But in fact if you're haphazard in selecting a hide, or sloppy while operating one, you'll likely lose your personal hide, too.

USMC snipers operate a rooftop firing position and surveillance post in Iraq.

Though generically this term—"hide"—applies to any sniper firing position, the U.S. military more formally calls this a Final Firing Position, or FFP. Until it is occupied by the sniper team, this FFP is only a TFFP, or Tentative Final Firing Position. That's because theoretically, until the sniper team is actually in it and can eyeball it, they aren't certain that it will prove suitable. No matter whether it's called a hide or FFP, though, it all begins with a careful selection process.

The exact spot you select for a hide is affected by several considerations, the first and prime one being, "Does it allow me to cover my sector?"

No matter how invisible your hide is or whatever other superb qualities it may have, if you cannot see and shoot into the area desired, it's unsuitable. Since you most frequently will be firing prone, it becomes difficult to find a place that allows long-range observation from ground level.

While a superior may assign you a sector, he should not tell you where to locate your hide since he won't understand the exacting needs of a hide position. You need the leeway to pick the best spot yourself.

Selection Considerations

Beyond the need to see and shoot into a desired area, hide considerations vary with the situation and involve trade-offs and compromises.

We've illustrated the ideal hide on page 403 to show what you'd have if everything were perfect. First, before you is a deep, open sector having several natural lines of drift. The most likely places for targets to appear are far enough that you have a ballistic advantage; you're a bit

Snipers sometimes conceal themselves in destroyed vehicles or, as here, a destroyed amphibious aircraft, where a Japanese sniper fought U.S. Marines. He had no route for escape or displacement.

This World War I German sniper's firing position is a cast iron tree that perfectly duplicates a real tree in "no-man's-land" and will be switched with it during darkness.

uphill, but not so much that it complicates range estimation and trajectory compensation; many likely hide locations are around you, making the one you use inconspicuous; ridges and fingers create frontal protection from small-arms fire; there's a water obstacle—a creek—to your front, which delays any attempt to rush you; adjacent hillsides will cause confusing echoes; the wind is head-on or tail-on, meaning it has no crosswind effect; the sun's behind you or over your shoulder and causing you no glare but making countersurveillance difficult; and there's a handy "back door" with plenty of trees for a covered withdrawal.

I'm sometimes asked by students, "Which is more important, cover or concealment?" My answer is *both*, but if I could choose only one, I'd probably go with concealment in a temporary hide, which is abandoned after just one shot, and cover for a permanent hide, which may be used considerably longer for a determined defense. But these become "iffy" things and depend on your specific situation.

Consider Enemy's Perspective

The best hides also take into account how the enemy will view your area. As the next illustration shows, most soldiers have a subconscious tendency to pay closest attention to threats at their left oblique. This is caused by habitually reading papers and books starting at the top left corner, as well as the fact that most people are right-handed and can shoot fastest and easiest to their left front. If you have the slightest doubt, talk to a grouse hunter.

In addition to an enemy's left front, you don't want to position yourself to his immediate front since that's the direction he's probably best prepared to fire into. The more you are to his right oblique, the more he must coordinate or maneuver before he can return fire.

We've shown an urban area (page 404) to illustrate still other hide considerations, taking into account the enemy's perspective. As shown, resist the urge to locate in the closest possible hide; he may prep that site with a recon-by-fire before you've fired a single shot. The highest

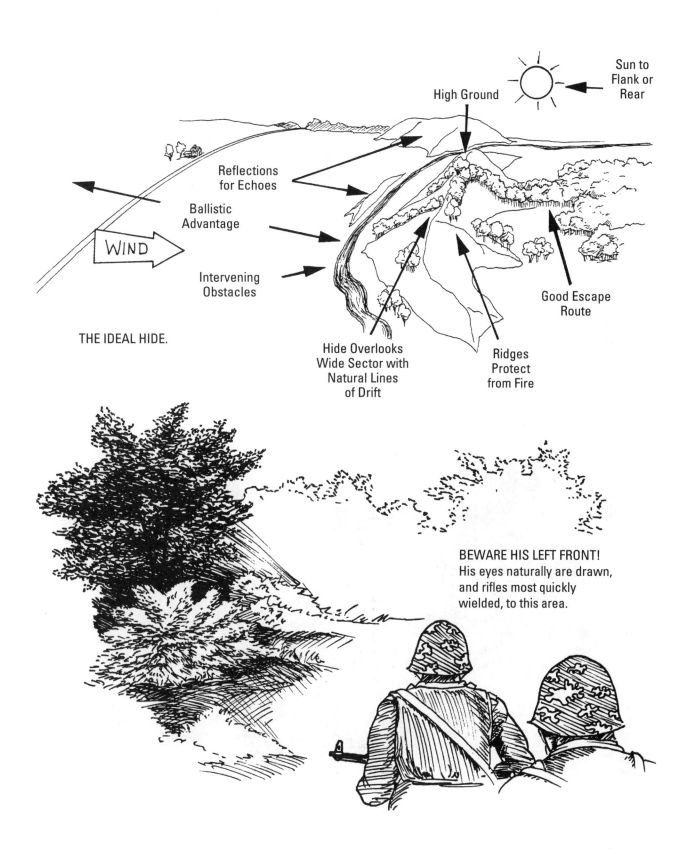

High Ground

Sun to
Flank or
Rear

Reflections
for Echoes

Ballistic
Advantage

WIND

Intervening
Obstacles

THE IDEAL HIDE.

Good Escape
Route

Hide Overlooks
Wide Sector with
Natural Lines
of Drift

Ridges
Protect
from Fire

BEWARE HIS LEFT FRONT!
His eyes naturally are drawn,
and rifles most quickly
wielded, to this area.

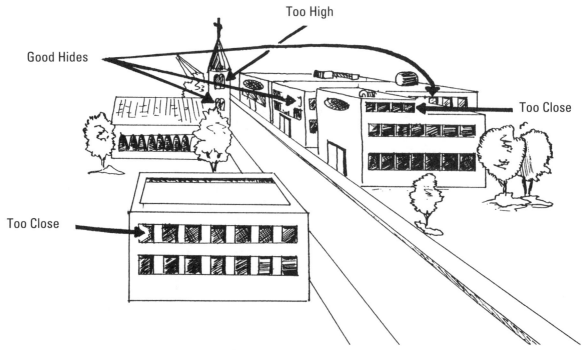

Too High

Good Hides

Too Close

Too Close

HIDE SELECTION. Don't be conspicuous.

Ditches make outstanding temporary hides, offering cover, concealment, and a protected route for withdrawal.

point in the church steeple is equally obvious, as is a facing window from the first building on the right. But the other two sites are especially usable, not just because they're less noticeable but they are also roughly aligned with conspicuous locations that the enemy mistakenly will fire into rather than into your hide.

This is an important lesson: *never* locate in the "best" location; position your hide so it *seems* that you're using the "best" location.

Temporary Sniper Hides

We've illustrated an assortment of temporary hides on page 406, discussed thoroughly in an accompanying explanation. What they all have in common is an attempt to be invisible and to exploit whatever protection there is from small-arms fire. Probably the best temporary hides are the edges of ridgelines, ditches, and creek beds because they offer excellent small-arms protection and excellent cover for your withdrawal.

Most often you'll use temporary hides when conducting independent operations or while supporting a unit in the offense. In the latter case, the enemy should be so preoccupied with the primary assault that he won't pay much attention to you, making it unlikely that you'll face effective counterfire.

A temporary hide can be placed in a tree, which was popular during the Civil War. The single greatest shortcoming of a tree hide is that there's usually not enough room for both spotter and sniper, and a wind may sway the tree. Hardwood trees tend to be more stable than softwoods, and you'll find better stability close to the trunk. Ideally, you should position yourself so the trunk is before you so it provides protection from fire. The most effective tree hides are placed well back into a grove instead of along an edge.

One special tree hide is a "Machan," a comfortable seat made of ropes or webbing, originally used by tiger hunters in India. As shown in the illustration, wide webbing works well and can be rolled up and carried compactly in your rucksack. Thin webbing, such as that used in a

Exploiting the slight rise of an Iraqi railway as an FFP, Marine snipers Sgts. Adam Scheele (L) and Sean Little prepare to engage a distant target.

TEMPORARY SNIPER HIDES

A sniper exploits the best hide position from which he can place fire into his target or assigned sector of fire. It could include a bunker with overhead cover (upper left), using a rucksack for support. Or he could take cover under a vehicle, keeping the engine block above him and a wheel before him, staying in shadow, and not extending his muzzle beyond cover (upper right). He could choose a tree hide (center), but this isn't usually his first choice since wind will sway it, he cannot displace quickly down the trunk, nor is there protection from small-arms fire—not to mention separation from his spotter. In the lower right, he has placed his hide just beyond a ridge finger—a truly excellent site because he has protection and can take a shot, then pull back and displace safely behind the ridge. The bottom hide has a log for frontal protection (but he's careful not to let anything touch his barrel), and he has scraped the earth to a depth of 18 inches for even better cover.

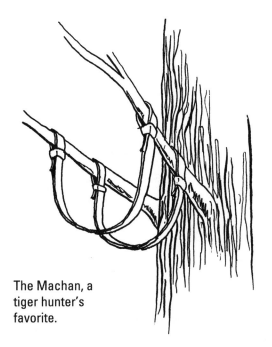

The Machan, a tiger hunter's favorite.

JOINT RESPONSIBILITIES

Compare Wind Estimates
Compare Range Estimates
Observe Half of Sector
Keep Position Sterile
Stay Packed & Ready to Displace
Improve Partner's Camouflage
Stay Alert to Close-Range Threats

SPOTTER RESPONSIBILITIES

Prepares Range Card
Talks Sniper into Detected Targets
Ranks Visible Targets by Priority
Times Sniper's Fire Between Wind Gusts
Observes & Adjusts Sniper's Fire
Updates Wind Estimates
Monitors and Operates Team Radio
Engages Close-Range Threats
Sketches & Records Intelligence

SNIPER RESPONSIBILITIES

Determines Target Priorities
Engages Selected Targets

rappel seat, can stop blood flow and numb your legs in just a few minutes, while a properly made Machan historically was occupied for an entire night. Interestingly, Japanese snipers during World War II sometimes literally tied themselves into trees.

Permanent Sniper Hides

A wise military axiom is, "The longer you're there, the deeper you dig." This applies to snipers as much as any other soldier, for the longer you're in a fixed position, the more aware

This belly hide has been improved with overhead cover.

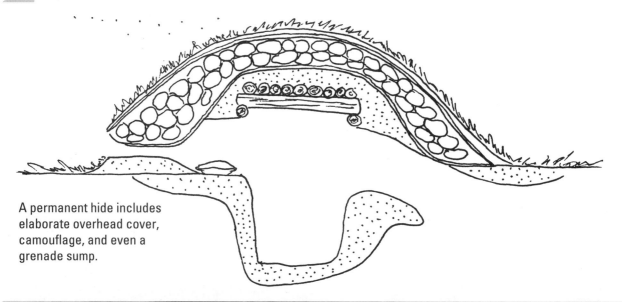

A permanent hide includes elaborate overhead cover, camouflage, and even a grenade sump.

This permanent Israeli sniper post overlooks a hot spot of terrorist activity in Jenin.

Lay a wet cloth or canvas below your muzzle to prevent blast from kicking up dust.

the enemy becomes of your presence, and the more fire he can bring to bear against you.

So, when accompanying a unit that starts a hasty defense, a sniper prepares his simplest permanent hide, known as a "belly scrape," shown in the illustration on page 407.

How deep do you dig it? Cartoonist Bill Mauldin once had his character Willy grunt to his buddy, Joe, "I wuld'a dug deeper, but muh buttons kept gittin' in duh way." If you're directly under fire, as a minimum a belly scrape must allow you to lie flat and not be hit.

If you remain there a few hours, you'd better start placing overhead cover above you or enemy mortars and artillery will be your ruin. Respect the fact that about two-thirds of wartime casualties are caused by indirect fire fragmentation and blast, not bullets.

By now you're building a full-fledged permanent hide, with 3 feet of overhead cover, a sump for grenades to roll into, and even water drainage. And you've prepared a dummy hide to draw fire away from your real position.

If you're there still longer, you start working on an alternate position, which allows you to move into it but still shoot into your assigned sector of fire. Then you build a supplementary position so you can fire into another sector. And if there is more time, you begin digging a trench between these positions.

And throughout this work, you and your partner take turns, with one man digging while the other covers. Incidentally, the covering man will be the sniper, since he's most rested and can engage a target faster than the other man.

Occupying a Sniper Hide

You and your partner should be close enough to speak in a whisper or touch one another at night. There's enough space for all your gear, and it's so well camouflaged that even optically assisted enemy surveillance will not detect you. You've left any trash or wreckage in place and moved not a thing in any visible way.

You trimmed a few branches and pieces of

Natural Dummy Hide

Actual Hide

Straight Lines (Board) Added to Haystack

The dummy hide.

Sometimes an FFP offers observation far beyond a rifle's maximum range, like this position in eastern Afghanistan.

grass in the hide so you could turn and even move a bit without touching any foliage. Your barrel doesn't protrude from the foliage; you pruned just enough leaves to allow firing without any visible muzzle blast. And you even put an 18-inch square of wet canvas below the muzzle to prevent any dust from being kicked up.

So that you could shoot prone, you shoved some dirt aside or filled a sandbag. Perhaps you had to lay a flat rock beneath your bipod legs for better stability in soft soil. To keep your minds active, you and your spotter simulate engagements, with him detecting a target and talking you into it. On the hour, you rotate the responsibilities we've listed in the box on page 407.

Note that the spotter is much busier than the sniper—indeed, in a hide it's the sniper who is somewhat resting so that his mind and body are better prepared for shooting.

DUMMY SNIPER HIDES

It's wise always to give the enemy a target for his wrath, a false position to take the counterfire that's certain to come.

The enemy usually will have a fair idea of where your shot originated, probably to within 20 or 30 degrees. Depending on how terrain and weather affect your muzzle blast, he'll likely guess your distance to within 100 or 200 yards. Within such a sector, he'll instantly shoot up any obvious sniper hide, hence my repeated warnings about being inconspicuous.

But the corollary to blending in is to ensure there's something else nearby that will divert his fire away from you. Capt. H.W. McBride, the World War I sniper, usually located his hide beside or below a natural dummy position. He wrote at length of a barn that the Germans repeatedly blasted, but it was well above and to his rear. The only advice I add is to make sure you're not too close or a long or short round might hit you.

If there's no natural dummy position, you must construct one, which doesn't need to be very elaborate. Just a few straight lines in the midst of foliage can do the trick, such as

stacking a few logs or scraping together an ankle-high berm. And recognize a long-known aspect of deception: it's far easier to reinforce what your opponent thinks already than it is to get him thinking something entirely different.

Recall, too, that there's nothing like a bit of movement to attract attention. During World War II, a Japanese sniper would jerk a distant bush with a string to divert fire, a tactic that caused his opponents not to cooly conclude a bush was moving but to declare excitedly, "There he is!" On a more subtle level, Captain McBride often tied a piece of red cloth to nearby barbed wire because it invariably drew German observers' attention away from his hide.

Anticipate how the enemy will view your area, how he will scan it, what he'll see. And remember that, psychologically, he needs the gratification of returning your fire.

SURVEILLANCE HIDES

In addition to providing long-range, precision fire, the continuous, parallel mission of both police and military snipers is intelligence gathering. They are especially well suited for this role due to their excellent optics and special observation training as well as their ability to operate invisibly in an opponent's rear.

Some sniper team operations are devoted purely to reconning an area, which implies

The SAS hide. From the front, there is no visible sign of its occupation. It's so low that you low-crawl into it.

walking and exploring, or surveilling, which involves covert observation from a fixed location. Such surveillance is conducted from a hide, but it's slightly different from a sniping hide since you don't intend to fire from it, and clear observation is the overwhelming criteria for selecting its location.

When abandoning a surveillance hide—just like a sniper hide—be sure to erase any sign of your presence.

We've illustrated three distinct types of surveillance hides, but no matter which design is used, it should be so well camouflaged that an opponent can pass within 10 feet and not detect it.

The SAS Hide

This hide has been used by the British SAS along Northern Ireland's southern border to detect IRA gunrunners and suspects crossing from the Irish Republic.

The spiderhole.

The igloo hide, showing how it's hollowed out.

It's very effective because it's placed in knee-deep foliage that seemingly is too short to conceal a team. The team cuts natural camouflage and carefully drapes it or ties it to create an 18-inch-high cover, beneath which the team crawls into position. Do *not* add a poncho roof because when wet it will reflect light and even dry it creates a dangerous silhouette.

The SAS hide is positioned to exploit existing shadow and preserves natural foliage as much as possible.

The Spiderhole

When there's not enough concealment above the ground, go below it. Not only does a spiderhole provide concealment, but it protects you against small-arms fire.

Concealment of displaced dirt is a major consideration; throwing it over a wide area usually is the best solution. The hole should be kept small to produce minimal dirt and to hold down construction time.

The spiderhole cover is superbly camouflaged and fits flush. In Vietnam, where Communist Vietcong guerrillas frequently employed spiderholes, it was almost impossible to spot one until you actually stepped into it.

The Igloo Hide

This hide works well in dense foliage that is all but impassable for a walking man. The snipers low-crawl into the foliage from the

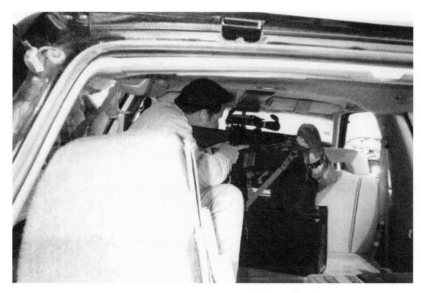

A law enforcement sniper practices firing from a vehicle hide at the McMillan Sniper School. (Photo credit: McMillan Sniper School)

reverse side, dragging rucksacks behind them and carefully obscuring tracks or scrapes that could compromise their presence.

They thin out the foliage just enough to sit and observe their front, probably about 1 or 2 meters inside the woodline. I personally used an igloo hide for three days during a real-world remote airfield surveillance and found it worked well.

POLICE SNIPER HIDES

The only significant difference between a police hide and a military sniper hide is the distance to the target.

Law enforcement snipers usually occupy a hide no more than 100 yards away, which coincides with the typical police zero distance. By positioning the same distance as his zero, a police sniper all but eliminates any trajectory compensation and pretty well neutralizes any crosswind.

A tendency I've seen among too many police snipers, however, is locating much too closely to their suspect. This is caused, I think, by an understandable concern about not being able to see, or to engage accurately, their target.

They'd rather be criticized for occupying a conspicuous hide than run the danger of blowing a shot. I'm a great advocate of reducing risk, but you must realize that you may *increase* risk inadvertently if you're detected. Not only might a foe fire on you, but a criminal or crazy may misinterpret your mere presence as a death warrant and initiate aggression against hostages. Less dramatically but of equal concern, if a perpetrator detects a police sniper, he quite likely will block this view or draw shades or move, which will preclude a subsequent sniper shot.

Law enforcement hides could be well over 100 yards away if suspects are armed with rifles, they have optics, any closer hides are too obvious, or the sniper must relocate to avoid a significant crosswind. Still, though, a 100-yard hide tends to be the ideal, especially should the officer have to take a head shot, which becomes very difficult much beyond this range.

In some instances where no suitable cover or concealment exists for a police sniper, he may employ a vehicle hide. After modifying an automobile or a van as a concealed sniper's shooting platform, this vehicle is driven to the incident and deliberately left parked where the police sniper can best achieve an engagement.

MANTRACKING

MANTRACKING

By now it should be clear to you that a sniper team's operating environment demands independent and immediate action since external support may not be available or is too distant. This is just as true for police sniper teams as military ones. Indeed, several police sniper team missions, such as clandestine drug lab recon and remote airfield surveillance, require skillful interpretations of signs of suspect activity, both to develop intelligence and to enhance officer survival, while tracking is the essence of any police cordon and search operation. Most police departments have integral K-9 teams, but would a dog be available? Could a dog even be employed without compromising your presence?

As a minimum, any sniper should be able to determine the number of people in an opponent's party, estimate their direction of movement, learn when they passed this point, interpret what they were doing at this location, reasonably anticipate where they are going and when they'll get there, and follow their trail so long as required.

Put Yourself in Your Quarry's Mind

Consider the dynamics of *who* your quarry is and *what* he's attempting to do. He acts differently if he's fleeing you than if he doesn't think anyone's on his trail; he shows less caution in a body of 20 than a party of four; he travels slower and more carefully en route to an objective than on his return; he walks faster during the day than at night; he moves more deliberately over unfamiliar ground than in his own backyard; he chooses his route differently if he's an urban creature rather than rural born; his tactical use of terrain will say much about how experienced and well-trained he is; his route will make more sense if he's using a map than if he doesn't have one; he probably follows natural line of drift unless he's afraid or following a rigid predetermined route; he will bypass difficult terrain if he is an obese or middle-aged man in poor condition; he might sleep during the day and move at night, or vice versa; and so on.

Consider, then, these dynamics: *who* he is versus *what* he's up to. By examining what he is doing, you can gradually fill in the unknowns about who he is. By considering what you already know about who he is, you simplify your search for his sign and can more easily discern where he is going. Like a crossword puzzle, each conclusion in one area suggests new conclusions in the other. Taken to its ultimate, the truly gifted tracker learns to "see" his surroundings through his quarry's eyes. He isn't following him; he anticipates his quarry's next move and "heads him off at the pass."

But first you must learn the fundamentals.

Tracking Fundamentals

When you think about tracking, undoubtedly you visualize following footprints—so let's start by talking about footprints.

If you observe your own foot as it touches

TRACK VARIETIES

Shapes, sizes, and gaits tell much. Thinner width and shorter steps tell you the left tracks were made by a woman. The next set to the right were made by a man. The middle set of tracks, again a man's, show he was running since his toes scraped more earth and the gait stretched. Deeper impressions and longer scrapes on the tracks second from right disclose that he was carrying a heavy load. The last set on the right indicates deception and danger—this man is walking backward but dragging dirt in his true direction.

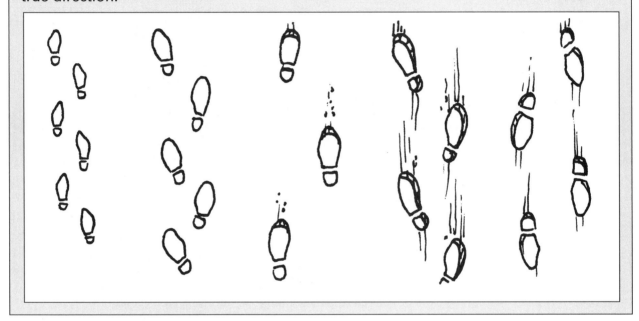

the ground, you'll notice that first your heel comes into contact. It's the heel that presses heaviest into the ground and, due to its sharp edge, it's more likely than any other portion of your foot to *leave a mark*.

Your toe is the last portion of the foot to leave the ground, and usually its tip drags a bit of earth with it. This is of great significance, for no matter how evasive your quarry may be, this dirt scrape always shows the true direction of movement.

We've shown this on the far right of our first illustration, in which you can see that an attempt to walk backwards would fail because the earth is dragged in the true direction. You also see that a man's footprints (second from left) tend to be larger and point straight ahead or to the sides, while a woman's tracks (far left) usually are thinner and somewhat pigeon-toed.

Being often smaller of frame, women have shorter legs and therefore a shorter stride.

If a person is running (third from left), his stride is longer and his toes press deeper than a normal pace. And finally, when carrying a heavy load, a man's prints will show longer and more pronounced toe drags, as seen second from right.

There are two techniques for estimating the number of persons in a party: the "stride method" and the "36-inch method." These are depicted in the illustrations on the next page.

The first shows the stride method, where you must identify one particular set of tracks, which is called the "key print." Then, in an especially soft spot in which all other tracks also are visible, draw a line behind the heel of one key print and another line through the opposite

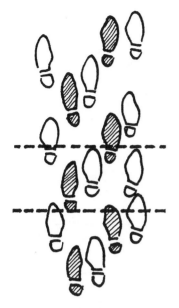

STRIDE MEASUREMENT. Identify one set of tracks, key print.

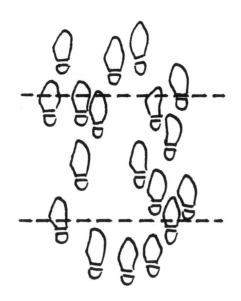

36-INCH METHOD. Select a spot with clear tracks, divide total footprints by two.

key print foot's next instep. Now, count the number of whole footprints in the box you've drawn, only once counting the whole key print track. The total number of whole tracks is the number of persons in the party, which in our example would be three persons.

The 36-inch method, illustrated next, is less exact and used when you cannot find a key print. To do this, randomly line-out a 1-yard length of tracks, count all tracks and parts of tracks inside your box, and divide by two. This will be the number of persons in the group, which in this case is six.

And the number is very important for your interpretation of who they are and what they're up to. For example, if there are only two men, they could be an enemy sniper team, an artillery forward observer team, or an enemy observation post. By closely focusing on where they're going and how they move tactically, you should be able to learn which they are. Sheer numbers can tell you a lot more: 8 to 11 soldier tracks suggest an infantry squad, meaning they will have assault rifles and perhaps a rocket-propelled grenade launcher, giving you a notable ballistic advantage for engaging them at

400 yards or more. But 30 or more prints imply a platoon, which would have two medium machine guns, and since these fire full-size 7.62mm rounds, you would have no advantage—just the need to be more careful when you engage. Since a platoon usually prefers to move through wider forested cover than would a squad, you can anticipate where they'd cross an upcoming stream just by looking at the density of adjacent foliage.

By now I hope you're grasping what I mean about interconnecting knowledge of your opponent with what you can see in his tracks.

Detecting Sign

The biggest problem with tracking is that seldom can you find actual, complete tracks. Even if your opponent isn't wary of being followed, it's unusual for the ground to be so soft and open that a long series of whole footprints can be seen.

What you'll actually find is a host of human-activity indicators collectively called "sign," meaning faintly visible clues of human footprints, handholds, passage, litter, and body waste.

Most sign, depicted in the series of panels on page 418, is usually evidence of walking because that is the way in which our bodies constantly touch the area around us, but any other way we come in contact with our environment can leave sign, too, such as branches twisted or pulled where we climbed uphill or cobwebs torn when we passed between bushes. I will comment only upon those types of sign that need special explanations, the prime one being flattening.

As U.S. Border Patrol Agent Jack Kearney correctly notes, man is the only creature other

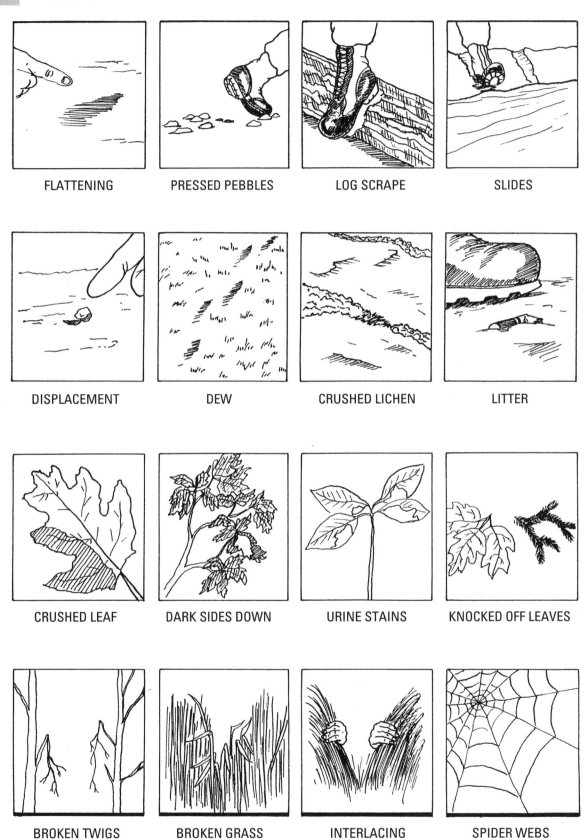

FLATTENING   PRESSED PEBBLES   LOG SCRAPE   SLIDES

DISPLACEMENT   DEW   CRUSHED LICHEN   LITTER

CRUSHED LEAF   DARK SIDES DOWN   URINE STAINS   KNOCKED OFF LEAVES

BROKEN TWIGS   BROKEN GRASS   INTERLACING   SPIDER WEBS

Even if you must walk backward or look over your shoulder, keep tracks between you and the sun for best shadow.

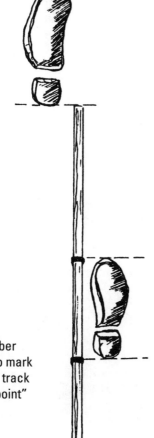

PACE STICK. Wrap rubber bands or cut grooves to mark the heel and toe of one track so the stick's tip can "point" to the next heel.

than hooved animals that actually *flatten* soil in distinct ways. When examined closely, you can see whether the ground is merely pressed or scraped or distinctly flattened. If no hooved beasts are around, any small, flat spot confirms at least one man's presence. No matter how faint the indentation, usually *flat means man*.

Nature has a way of interlacing vegetation so that man's best attempts to put it back to where it was cannot be perfect. Interlaced vegetation in its undisturbed state is not bent or twisted or otherwise noticeably in contention.

Likewise, the undersides of leaves, which are usually a lighter color, naturally prefer to face the ground so that the darker side can gather light. The more unnatural such leaves appear, the fresher this sign probably is.

Slide marks on ravines, hillsides, and stream banks are usually easy to spot and a fast way to check for crossings.

Along cliffs and rocky areas, the only sign you may see will be crushed lichen. Because it's sparse, your quarry may not think it significant when he steps on it.

While many would-be trackers could easily spot dislodged stones and sticks or broken twigs

Holding the pace stick over one track, pivot its tip to find the next one.

OPERATING A TRACK DETECTION BARRIER

For many years, Israel's northern border with Lebanon was constantly threatened by infiltrating terrorists who slipped across in remote areas at night. The problem continued even after Israeli security forces erected a fence and patrolled the area.

Finally, after many techniques and technologies were tried, an effective means was developed to detect and hunt down infiltrators. Along the southern side of the fence, Israeli military engineers scraped a simple dirt road, which a modified truck passes over each morning with a special brush-like drag to sweep and smooth the soil. The road is too wide for infiltrators to leap across, so inevitably they must step on it—leaving behind fresh tracks. Whenever such tracks are discovered, special tracker teams immediately are flown in to hunt down the infiltrators. Except for one incident when an infiltrator flew across in a motorized hang glider—only to be shot down and killed—the barrier has proven quite effective.

sign location, as shown in the top illustration on page 419. At times this may cause you to walk beyond the sign and look back over your shoulder or even walk backwards. The best times of day for spotting sign by means of shadow is early to mid-morning, and mid- to late afternoon.

Should you be in forest or jungle so thick that sunlight cannot reach the floor, you can make shadow by holding a flashlight at low angles and sweeping the beam back and forth across the area you think could contain sign.

Following His Trail

Invention of the tracking stick can be credited to U.S. Border Patrol Agent Jack Kearney, whose tracking skills and accomplishments remain legendary. Kearney's book, *Tracking: A Blueprint for Learning How*, is probably the best yet written on the subject. David Scott-Donelan's *Tactical Tracking Operations* (Paladin Press, 1998) is also recommended.

(Mentioning Kearney obliges me to plug the U.S. Border Patrol, with which it has been my privilege to work. When it comes to survival, tracking, and just plain woodsmanship, these

and branches, it is the exceptional man who sees the tiny pebble pressed deeper into the ground.

Urine stains and feces are in the same category as litter—if you find it at all, it indicates an opponent lacking tactical discipline. Urine stains in snow are well known; dried urine tends to leave a shiny glaze on leaves. Human feces are soft and damp when fresh and the same color throughout; with age, the outside crusts and grows darker.

Detecting sign is a lot easier said than done, especially any sign related to footprints, unless you know how to use sunlight to your best advantage. Here the rule is simple: to yield the most contrasting shadow on scrapes or indentations, position yourself so the sun is on the other side of the

The spotter covers while the sniper tracks.

are federal law enforcement's premier experts. They're a hardy lot of real pros.)

As shown in the illustrations on page 419, Kearney's tracking stick is simple in design but clever in application. It's only a thin, yard-long pole on which you mark the length of your quarry's foot, then the distance from one print's toe to the next print's heel. These lengths are marked using either twisted rubber bands or by cutting notches.

Now, with this bit of information, you can pivot the stick from one track you've detected to indicate very closely where his opposite heel should set down next. His stride should average about 20 inches forward and 8 inches to one side. By using the tracking stick to "point" at possible sign locations, you can focus your attention so precisely that you'll find tiny indentations or scrapes or drags that show where a foot has touched.

While one of you is busy using the tracking stick or otherwise searching for sign, the teammate should be nearby overwatching and providing security. Remember this: only *one* man tracks at a time; the other secures. The tracker should have the sniper rifle, while the security man carries the assault rifle/M203. To provide effective overwatch, the security man may position himself behind, to one side, or even in front of the sniper/tracker, his only concern being the need for good observation and fields of fire and not disrupting sign as he walks.

To stay fresh and alert—both to keep the tracker sensitive to sign and the security man keen to enemy threats—the tracker and security man should rotate duties periodically, perhaps on the hour or when either man feels the need for a change. When they swap duties, of course, they also swap weapons.

And talking about security, don't underestimate your foe. He could be attempting to draw you into an ambush, so don't be too quick to follow his tracks into an open area. Glass the open area with optics, estimate where the tracks must exit on the opposite side, then circle around the edge until you again cut trail.

Periodically pause and study your map, which is really a fabulous crystal ball. If you stare at it long enough and hard enough, with what you know about your quarry and can discern about how he's traveling, eventually you'll anticipate his future moves. Examine the map for likely routes, his probable destinations, the routes you would use to make an "end run," and where to position yourself to ambush him.

Whether he realizes he's being followed or not, a serious opponent still may attempt evasive moves, which aren't usually very effective. These evasions could include:

- Brush dragged on trail, which works swell in the movies but in real life looks exactly like what it is
- Walking backward, which, as we've already noted, still results in earth tossed or pushed in the true direction of movement
- Walking in streams, which means you must focus your attention on the banks where he exits from the water
- Hopping from rock to rock or staying on a hard surface, which must end somewhere, so focus your search where it gets soft again
- Varying his compass direction, such as heading northwest then northeast, and you respond by averaging his deviations, determine he's still heading generally north, and circle back and forth until you pick up the trail

If you lose his trail, don't get emotional. Take a break, drink some water, pause, think. What about natural line of drift? Study the map. What does your teammate think? Sometimes it's best to back off because you may be too close to the forest to see the trees—literally. Back away and use naked eyes and optics to scan around for sign that may have been too slight or general to be noticed up close.

Aging, or "How old is it?"
In order to project where your opponent is *now*, you must be able to estimate when he made the sign you have found.

Fortunately, nature degrades or "ages" all

sign in ways we can observe; it's up to you to interpret this aging correctly. Footprints and other sign age due to the actions of rain, sun, and wind, but not the same way every time or every place. You must sensitize yourself to how quickly nature degrades sign at your location and for your time of year or time of day.

One technique you should use frequently is to test ground resistance and dampness near tracks by pressing the ground with your own foot as if taking a normal step. Is your track as pronounced, as deep, and as clear as the sign? If not, look closer and see how the conditions must have changed since the sign was made. How long did it take the earth to change like this?

Be especially aware that footprints in soft soil can be just as old as those on firm ground but too easily can be misread as fresher since they're better defined. The way to test this, again, is pressing your own foot beside the sign.

The most often cited yardstick for measuring aging is knowing when the last rain fell—but this could have been days ago. You need a more exact estimate.

How crisp are the edges of your track compared to the sign? Is direct sunlight touching the sign? How long has it been in sunlight? Can you see shade differences where the moisture has left the sign's tiniest edges? How quickly are the edges of your track drying? Notice how the sign is collapsing just enough into itself that the sides are becoming rounded? How long did this take?

Notice how just a few fine grains of sand have blown into the track—when did the wind start gusting? And this footprint is over a fresh vehicle track—recall that you heard that vehicle pass only 15 minutes ago. A leaf blew into this track off that walnut tree. When did the wind shift northeast so this could happen?

In a swamp, where tracks have water standing in them, is the water muddy or clear? Usually the stirred-up mud will settle in less than an hour.

When temperatures hover near freezing, it's easy to misestimate aging because the process becomes skewed by freezing and thawing. I remember one wintry Minnesota deer hunt when my party thought we'd found the "Great Buck Burial Ground," an area absolutely overrun with multiple sets of "fresh" hoof prints. Actually, a lone buck had meandered about a new clearcut for a few days, laying muddy tracks over semifrozen tracks. Instead of spreading over a wide area, we concentrated at one spot and so overscented the scene that not even the singular buck showed up.

Blood Trails

A special category of tracking and aging estimation regards blood trails.

You can find tiny drops of blood on leaves and ground where they fell freely, or wide smears and streaks left secondarily on tree trunks, rocks, etc., where the subject placed his hands or leaned his body. To ascertain the subject's condition, our greater interest is in free-flowing blood.

Gushes of free-flowing blood imply arterial wounds, while steady, free-flowing blood suggests a serious nonarterial wound. Although the amount of blood usually is indicative of the wound severity, this isn't always true; some serious gunshot wounds may cause only slight external bleeding. While hunting big game I've found pencil-tip size blood drops generated by internal injuries so severe that I later found during field dressing that the entire chest cavity had been sloshing in blood.

It's not unusual to find blood spatter caused by your round exiting through the subject; you'll find it just beyond where he was at impact, from the ground to as high as 6 feet. If you don't find any spatter at all, you probably missed or only "dinged" him—or you're not really looking in the right spot.

As you begin following the blood trail, the kind of blood you find can tell you a lot about the wound's location and type. Pink, frothy, bubbly blood suggests a lung wound. If you find steady, dripping blood, it's most likely a hit to the trunk. Thick, gelatinous blood would probably be from a head wound. And any mixture of blood with smelly clear or yellowish liquid implies a stomach wound.

The freshness of blood, at least for a short period, is easily recognizable. Truly fresh blood is a very bright ruby red that soon becomes brown from sun and wind. From personal experience, I'd guess it takes about 30 minutes to an hour, above freezing, for this color shift to happen. When it does, the blood trail becomes much more difficult to follow.

One technique I've used when following a blood trail was to post my partner where I last saw a tiny blood drop while I fanned out looking for the next drop. When I did, I'd stand fast and he'd go forward looking for the next one, and so on, leapfrogging.

Don't ignore the great danger you're in while following a blood trail. Your quarry probably no longer has any illusions about mortality and appreciates his situation. He'd just as soon inflict one final casualty to "square things" for his own demise. Therefore take plenty of time and, whenever you approach cover in which he may be lying, circle it, listen, watch, glass the site, and operate only with the greatest caution. If tactically feasible, recon his likely location with hand grenades.

Overtaking and Engaging

It's easy to pronounce that after identifying your opponent's trail, you merely move fast enough to overtake and engage him. But this is easier said than done and brings to mind the largest body of hostile tracks I've ever come across.

In May of 1970, my SOG recon team, RT California, and several other C&C RTs were thrust deep into Cambodia amid the U.S. invasion. My team inserted just north of the town of Snuol in search of major enemy units fleeing west from a Cambodian border sanctuary known as the Fish Hook.

On our second day on the ground, we made a truly startling discovery: on the edge of a large rubber plantation we cut a fresh, 5-yard-wide cross-country human trail of more footprints than were countable, heading northwest toward Kratie. It looked just like a cattle drive. I reported an estimated regiment-plus, certainly more than a thousand enemy, and began the pursuit. The eight of us—four Americans and four Montagnard tribesmen—advanced as quickly as we dared, knowing that such a force had a rear guard of several platoons at least. How could we advance quietly

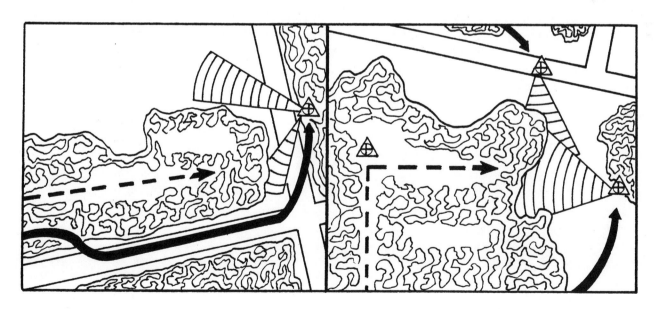

Pursuing tracker team shifts to high-speed route (road), makes an end run, and ambushes enemy.

Tracker team directs two other teams to intercept enemy.

and cautiously and yet overtake a briskly moving force several hours ahead of us? Answer: we couldn't.

I tell this story to make a point: the glib, axiomatic "doctrinal" solutions look fine, but that doesn't mean they're realistic. If you must move slowly enough to detect your foe's tracks or to remain invisible, you just plain won't ever catch up to him. So what can you do?

First, you can increase your pace by "jump tracking," which means quickly advancing from any noticeable sign to the most distant bit of sign, in a sense advancing by the largest leaps you can make. You slow down only when it's hard to find another bit of sign.

You must stay quiet as you advance on your quarry, because the first confirmation you'll have of his exact location will be hearing him at close range, which isn't really where a sniper team wants to be. Therefore, at some point when you can see the sign is becoming *very* fresh, you'll want to shift into a higher gear.

When shifting into higher gear, you slip laterally from his direct rear and take a faster route parallel to his direction of movement, then circle in front of him to find a suitable hide from which to ambush him. We've illustrated this technique on page 423.

However, the fastest and most effective way to locate and engage a traveling enemy is to employ several sniper teams in unison, with one team on the enemy's backtrail and the others ahead, quickly cutting back and forth along his direction of movement, searching perpendicular creek banks and ditches and soft ground for fresh sign. This, too, has been illustrated. This joint effort is coordinated by radio, modified with each new piece of information, until one team is positioned for an engagement. This technique is especially suitable for counterrecon operations and against Spetsnaz-type units.

To estimate your opponent's pace, use the U.S. Army's "official" planning factor for the movement rate of dismounted soldiers: 2.2 miles per hour. Add a bit if your opponent is rested and marching along a flat trail or road; cut his estimated pace if he's heading uphill, he's tired, or it's night.

We haven't covered everything there is to know about mantracking, but if you become proficient with just these techniques you'll be ready for most sniping situations. Remember to try to see your environment as your opponent sees it.

And in case you're wondering: about two hours after we started tracking that North Vietnamese unit, we were extracted by helicopter so an immediate B-52 strike could go in. What, if anything, the bombers hit, I don't know to this day. That's reality, too.

CHAPTER 17

BASIC OFFENSIVE AND DEFENSIVE TACTICS

AN INTRODUCTION TO SNIPING TACTICS

The weakest link in American military sniping has been at the commander and operations officer levels, because our combat arms basic and advanced courses don't address the subject, nor do our manuals effectively integrate sniping into larger unit operations.

If battalion S3s do not employ sniper teams properly, you should hardly be surprised since there's no graphic symbol for a sniper team. How can it be employed if it cannot be depicted on a map? Other systematic, institutional problems exist.

The first step in strengthening this link and giving sniping the tactical legitimacy it deserves is to refine the subject in terms operations officers and commanders understand.

Sniping Graphics

The symbol I developed for a sniper hide is

A Special Forces sniper team takes up a rooftop position to cover a helicopter landing.

identical to that of an observation post—a triangle—so it's automatically understood that trained observers with optics occupy this position. But to instantly distinguish its sniper role, I've inserted a circle and crosshair inside it. Graphically, this describes perfectly what's present here. The sniper hide symbol can be in a friendly unit position, all alone on a distant hilltop—wherever there's a sniper hide, or Final Firing Position (FFP).

Next, we must depict an independent sniper team's assigned operational area, and I've come up with two. First, there's the "sniper skirmish line," which is only a modification of the existing scout screen, an uneven, two-headed arrow. The sniper version is distinguished by our circle and crosshair in its center. My definition requires that the team maneuver and shoot no more than 2 kilometers on either side of the line, which is enough space for it to stalk, find and occupy hides, engage enemy, evade, and repeat the process. Given its

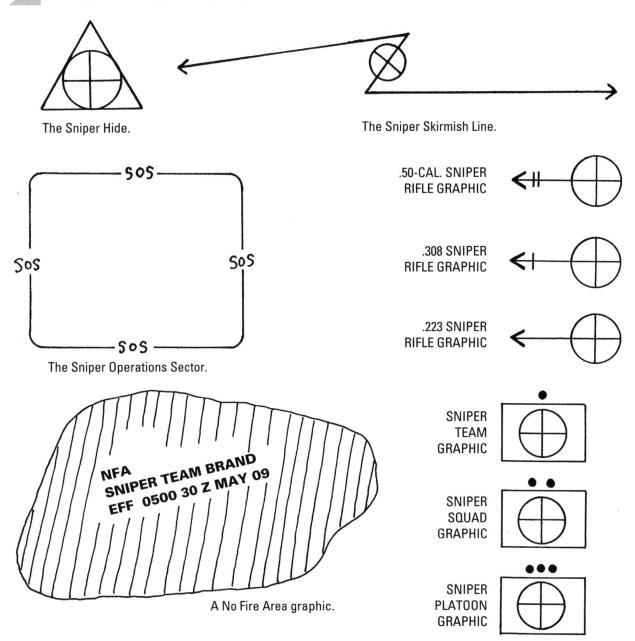

The Sniper Hide.

The Sniper Skirmish Line.

The Sniper Operations Sector.

.50-CAL. SNIPER RIFLE GRAPHIC

.308 SNIPER RIFLE GRAPHIC

.223 SNIPER RIFLE GRAPHIC

NFA
SNIPER TEAM BRAND
EFF 0500 30 Z MAY 09

A No Fire Area graphic.

SNIPER TEAM GRAPHIC

SNIPER SQUAD GRAPHIC

SNIPER PLATOON GRAPHIC

shape and concept, a sniper skirmish line probably would be on a larger unit's flank or it could parallel a linear terrain feature like a road or valley.

The second operational area graphic I've dubbed the "SOS," for "sniper operations sector," which is a circular or squarish area at least 2 kilometers wide, with breaks in the line for the insertion of "SOS" in capital letters. This encircled area belongs to the sniper team;

no other element may maneuver through it or call fire into it without team approval.

The "NFA" or "no fire area" graphic, which already exists, has special utility for sniper teams. Outlined in red, an NFA designates terrain in which no fire may be placed without the approval of the listed unit—our sniper team. It's a safe haven you can rush into and hunker down safely while friendly aircraft or artillery forward observers shoot hell out of the rest of

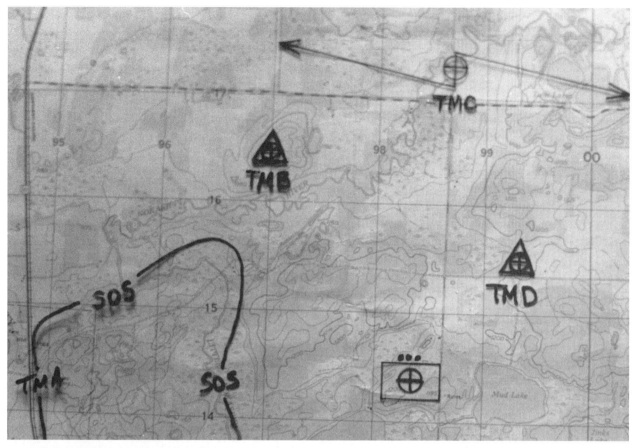

SNIPER GRAPHICS. Here's how they look plotted on an operational map.

your sector. By designating an NFA, you expedite fire coordination should a strong enemy suddenly appear.

Weapon and Unit Graphics

We've developed a light sniper weapon (5.56mm) graphic identical to that of a light machine gun, except we've added our familiar circle and crosshair to it. The medium (7.62mm) sniper rifle graphic adds a hatch mark in the symbol's center, just like other medium weapon graphics. And our heavy (.50-caliber) sniper weapon graphic places a second hatch mark, but we can see it's a sniper weapon because of the circle and crosshair at its base.

The symbols for a sniper team, squad, and platoon, too, are derived from long-established graphics. All we've done is insert our circle and crosshair in the center.

Sniper Planning Parameters

For greatest effectiveness, sniper teams need a coordinator at battalion level to understand and coordinate their efforts into the unit's overall operations. Too frequently their contribution is an afterthought, a last-minute add-on mission to keep them busy instead of exploiting their capabilities to the maximum.

At battalion level is a designated sniper employment officer—an NCO or a commissioned officer—who acts as the liaison and planner for snipers and sniping operations. To use teams effectively, he must first realize that snipers most often will be used to support a larger element's operation. Name a mission—as we will in the coming pages—and there's an excellent sniper contribution.

In those instances where sniper teams operate independently, however, that planner

Independent sniper team patrols happen mostly while a parent unit is in the defense.

must realize these men are too few to seize or hold ground. Instead, the sniper's role is to inflict maximum casualties on the enemy while also observing and reporting key intelligence.

This sniper employment officer should never dictate where the team's hide will be, since its suitability cannot be gleaned from a map. Instead, he should designate the *sector of fire*, then let the team find the best hide position for covering it.

Independent team missions should not be vague "roam around and see if you can shoot something" assignments. As a minimum, the team is directed to destroy, suppress, or harass the enemy.

A destroy mission suggests inflicting maximum casualties by specific priorities, which may change from mission to mission.

When directed to suppress, the team uses fire to prevent the enemy from firing his weapons effectively and/or to seek cover and stop maneuvering, which technically means to "fix" him as well. The commander isn't concerned that you fail to inflict a single casualty as long as the enemy is suppressed and fixed. It is thus implied that your volume of fire is probably greater and less focused than during a destroy mission.

A harass assignment may be the least gratifying to the sniper team, but it can contribute dramatically to the parent unit's mission success. Your duty is to deny the enemy sleep, to disable his leaders, to cause him to abandon wounded men, to keep him constantly on edge and at a high-alert status, to wear him down psychologically in preparation for your unit's mass attack, or to limit his advance against your unit. A harass mission implies longer duration for your fire to have some effect.

But no matter what your specific mission, your automatically assumed secondary one always is recording and reporting key intelligence for which you are especially suited given your optics and view of the battlefield.

Sniping Mission Planning Considerations

Traditionally, independent sniper patrols and operations involved only a two-man sniper team, although several such teams may have been operating in mutual support. However in Iraq, where terrorists have specially targeted American sniper teams, their composition has been beefed up, with as many as four men: two snipers, an extra M16-armed rifleman, and a SAW machine gunner. The trade-off is a larger potential signature and, of course, the need for a larger hide to conceal them.

We've illustrated how a typical independent sniper team mission unfolds on page 429. First, the team departs friendly lines in company with a larger patrol, which disguises its departure; another way would be leaving after dark. Second, at a certain predetermined point, the team goes its separate way, taking care to obliterate its tracks. Next, the team finds an area with potential targets and suitable hides, so it caches its excess gear and stalks forward. After an engagement, as depicted in the last panel, they displace to another hide or return to the cache site, retrieve their gear, and return to friendly lines. Their return probably would be after dark, at an exact passage point designated before the operation and which utilized preplanned recognition signals.

For clarity in orders, the team should be given a specific time it will depart friendly lines (a "line of departure" time), a time at which it will land in an LZ ("landing zone" time), or a time by which it must be in position and ready to engage, an NLT ("no later than" time).

A SNIPER MISSION. The team accompanies a friendly patrol, goes its own way, then conducts a separate operation.

They need specific guidance on when and when not to engage if it's a mission factor. For example, they could be told to observe only until a certain time, or to report the sighting of certain enemy activities immediately instead of engaging, or not to engage certain targets without permission, or, during surveillance missions, not to engage an enemy of less rank than, say, a field-grade officer.

And finally, they should know what it takes for a mission complete—perhaps a certain number of engagements or a certain number of days. I think it's a bad idea to declare a mission's accomplished by inflicting a certain number of casualties, not because it's ghoulish but because it leads to exaggerations or undue risks by men who want a hot shower and decent meal.

OFFENSIVE SNIPING OPERATIONS

The first phase in most offensive operations is a "movement to contact," in which a friendly unit advances either to attack a predetermined objective or to seek and engage an unlocated enemy. To keep this in context, we've drawn a cyclical graphic that shows how a movement to contact leads to the offense, which eventually subsides into the defense, until you're rested and resupplied and ready for another movement to contact.

During a movement to contact, there's a role

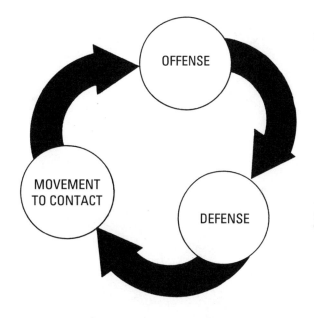

The Operations Circle.

for snipers in the advance, on unit flanks, with the main body, or covering the unit backtrail. The data box on page 430 details missions and priorities for each of these roles.

Sniping During a Hasty Attack

When a unit first clashes with the enemy while under way, it mounts an immediate or hasty attack in hopes its forward momentum will carry it through. There's no pause for planning

SNIPER TEAM ROLES DURING A MOVEMENT TO CONTACT

LOCATION	TEAM'S ROLE	TARGETS/PRIORITIES
Advance Guard	Early Warning; Route Recon; Surveillance of Objective	Identify and Engage Crew-Served Weapons
Flank Guard	Parallel Unit March; Surveil for Threats	Detect, Report, and Engage Threats
Main Body	React to Enemy Contact; Help Unit Move Forward	Enemy Snipers and Crew-Served Weapons
Backtrail	Countertracker and Countersniper	Enemy Snipers and Trackers

Supporting a hasty attack. Crew-served weapons are a suitable target, probably more valuable than leaders.

or coordination; the unit just executes SOPs as modified by the commander's verbal orders.

Ideally, this is a situation where a sniper has the leeway that Hiram Berdan's Civil War sharpshooters did—free to place himself at "any part of the line where in his own judgment he could do the most good."

The sniper's top-priority target should be enemy leaders who, in such a clash, frantically direct their soldiers as the fluid situation shifts back and forth. Their loss is felt immediately.

Wherever friendly soldiers are gaining ground, that's where I'd be, supporting their advance with precision fire at leaders especially

During an offensive, like the British attack into Basra, Iraq, sniper teams stay just behind the lead elements.

but at crew-served weapons, too. I'd be camouflaged no more heavily than other soldiers, but with my Ghillie suit in my ruck, I'd still have the option of stalking forward invisibly.

Snipers During a Deliberate Attack

Unlike a hasty attack, a deliberate one employs a detailed plan and usually follows a preparation phase that could last several days. A deliberate attack almost always is focused on a specific piece of ground or objective and may encompass intermediate objectives and integrate supporting attacks with the main one.

I think the best sniper mission in a deliberate attack is to surveil the objective continuously well before the assault, with the team relaying, then updating, intelligence to planners. This information should include precise data about enemy positions and strengths.

When the assault is mounted, the sniper team's surveillance hide becomes a shooting hide, and crew-served positions are its priority target since the enemy will fight from fixed locations and leadership won't change things much. Due to the team's protracted surveillance, it can readily engage particularly

Supporting a deliberate attack.

important enemy weapons such as the shoulder-fired antiaircraft missile we've illustrated because it already knows their location.

But snipers also could mount an effective diversion or supporting attack alone by pinning enemy forces at another nearby objective. Or the team could position itself on the enemy's rear or flank to help isolate the objective and prevent its reinforcement or relief. Of course, these tasks require suitable hide locations.

And certainly snipers can support the main attack, which we've phased into three segments in the illustration above. First, the sniper team fires in support of assaulting troops, then it rushes forward to a suitable hasty hide, and finally it helps repel any enemy counterattacks.

During an advance, snipers occupy hasty hides, like this Iraqi ditch.

Snipers Supporting an Air Assault

A heliborne air assault should land friendly forces directly on or very near their objective, so close that they can rush to it on foot quicker than the enemy can reinforce it.

It's because the first lift of landing troops must be prepared to let loose with a wicked, massive fusillade of fire that snipers should not be on that lift; every aircraft seat, I think, is needed for machine guns and assault rifles. But the second lift certainly should include snipers, and their priority target would be enemy antiaircraft weapons crews until the landing's complete.

Sniper teams could be inserted clandestinely to overwatch positions prior to the main landing, but their presence at that point makes for very difficult coordination should it become necessary to place air or artillery strikes around the first lift.

When conducting independent operations, however, helicopters prove particularly suitable for inserting sniper teams.

Snipers in Support of River Crossings

As with any other assault, snipers support a river crossing with fire rather than cross with the attacking troops. Snipers are especially well equipped for supporting river crossings due to the great reach of their rifles, which is much farther than any friendly small-arms weapon other than a .50-caliber machine gun.

But to gain this maximum range, the team must find a hide with sufficient elevation and may find that, paradoxically, it must be well back from the river's edge in order to shoot to maximum range.

Once a beachhead is established, sniper teams can cross the river, but realize that the water's movement will preclude any aimed fire until they've reached shore.

SNIPING DURING AMBUSHES

An ambush is the surprise engagement of an unalert enemy moving through or temporarily halted at a place selected by the ambusher. The

SUPPORTING A RIVER CROSSING. Snipers overwatch from high ground, then cross when a beachhead is seized.

enemy unwittingly chooses the ambush time while his ambusher chooses the location, usually along a trail or road behind enemy lines.

The ambusher plans his fire for a narrow space called a kill zone, with the engagement triggered by the victim's passage into it. A correctly planned and executed ambush results in total destruction of any enemy inside this kill zone.

Sniper Support of Ambushes

As in the case of raids, a sniper team supports friendly ambushes with precision long-range fire. But because other elements tend to prefer ambushing at close range, the sniper rifle may not be suited for placing fire in the kill zone. Even for short-range or near ambushes, however, the sniper can effectively contribute by engaging distant reaction forces or enemy fleeing the kill zone as part of a flank security element.

Independent Sniper Ambushes

Independent ambushes seem a natural for snipers because most sniper actions are very similar surprise engagements of an unalert enemy from concealment. The basic difference is that an ambush singularly focuses on a small spot—the kill zone—while a sniper otherwise scours a large sector for targets.

Ambush preparation begins by selecting the kill zone you intend to cover, then searching for suitable hides—not the other way around. A kill zone should cause the enemy to bunch up naturally, lack nearby cover to escape your fire, and yet be open enough for your long-range observation and shooting. A good example is a narrow footbridge across open water, or perhaps a desert trail at the base of a steep hill. Ideally, there should be natural obstacles like a stream or fences between the kill zone and your hide to delay the enemy should he react by attempting to rush your position.

Also, as we've illustrated, a sniper team should conduct far ambushes only, which use only fire to inflict damage. The other type, a near ambush, includes an assault through the decimated enemy and the search of bodies and seizure of wounded personnel. Not only is a sniper team too small to attempt an assault, but they're at a tremendous ballistic disadvantage at close range.

As a rule of thumb, if you really want to inflict damage, two sniper teams should be allocated for each anticipated squad of enemy. Less than this ratio results in too slow a rate of precision shooting, enabling many enemy to escape your fire. Instead of destroying them, you're only harassing them.

Breaking In Novices

There's no better means to introduce a novice sniper to his craft than through a well-planned ambush, particularly one that stacks the odds in his favor so there's maximum opportunity and minimum risk.

The ideal situation I've devised is targeting an enemy signal unit's wire repair party, of which those of us in SOG dispatched more than a few. To set these guys up, just find an enemy landline wire and follow it until it passes through an excellent kill zone. Find a suitable hide to cover this spot. Then, at about 0400 the next morning, cut the wire in the kill zone, go back to your hide, and await the dawn arrival of three to four sleepy signalmen. Shoot the one with his arms on his hips, a sure sign of being in charge.

One variation of this ambush technique is to lure an enemy patrol into a sniper kill zone by leaving suspicious footprints in a place where they're sure to be found and followed.

A "near" ambush (upper left) is dangerous for a sniper and doesn't exploit his ballistic advantage like a "far" ambush (lower right) does.

"Why this wire is cut!" A well-placed ambush, such as that of a wire repair team, makes a good introductory engagement for a new sniper.

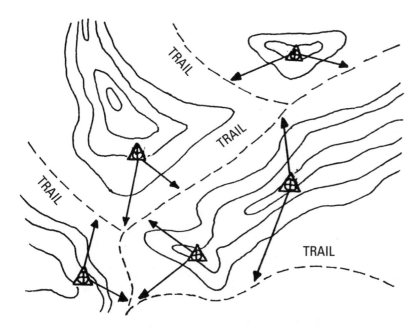

WOLFPACKING. This sniper area ambush has overlapping fields of fire, inflicting both casualties and confusion.

Wolfpacking: The Sniper Area Ambush

An outstanding sniper tactic for both conventional and counterguerrilla operations is the coordinated ambush of trails and roads across a large area by multiple sniper teams, a concept I've named "Wolfpacking." A Wolfpack consists of at least three or as many as nine sniper teams—a battalion's entire sniper platoon.

Ideally, these teams have almost interlocking kill zones so the enemy will stumble into another sniper team's fire when it flees one team's ambush or tries to maneuver against it.

Reaction forces rush into the area, only to become the target of ambush themselves, but confusingly from a direction that isn't where the earlier fire originated. Meanwhile, the original sniper ambush team is displacing to another hide or escaping scot-free.

A well-planned Wolfpack area ambush leaves the enemy not just bloodied but confused as to what exactly happened and fearful that it could happen again. The key to a Wolfpack mission's success is stalking into hides without detection.

Tank Ambush Techniques

During the mid-1980s, our military sniping school was honored by the visit of several Swedish army officers interested in gathering information about sniping. They politely observed our demonstration and asked suitable questions

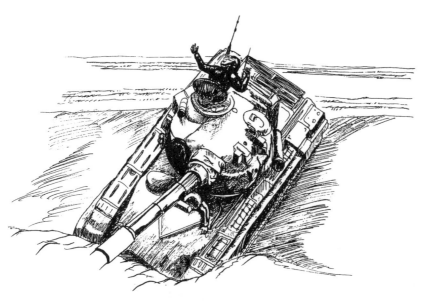

TANK AMBUSH. After eliminating the driver, engage the commander—
who probably doesn't understand what's happening.

while viewing an equipment display, but their eyes didn't really light up until we started talking about ambushing tanks, apparently one of their favorite subjects.

Snipers can ambush tanks? You bet. Or more precisely, snipers can stop tanks by shooting tankers. Here's how it's done.

Understand that tank crewmen prefer to travel "unbuttoned" with hatches open and heads exposed, which allows considerably better visibility than peering through vision blocks and periscopes.

Even though their heads are out, the roar of diesels and the muffling effect from helmets prevents these tankers from hearing a lone rifle shot. Therefore, when your crosshairs find that lead driver's head, other tankers won't understand why he suddenly ran off the road.

His tank commander, after fruitlessly attempting to reach the driver by intercom, might crawl out of the turret to investigate, and here's where you drill him, too. This continues until the other tanks button up and race away or commence counteraction with dismounted enemy infantry.

Such a tank ambush works best where there's a narrow chokepoint, like a defile, so that halting one tank blocks other tanks. A moderate curve is useful, too, since the driver will slow while taking it, making for an easier shot.

We've also explained in the section on shooting under special conditions how a sniper can trip a series of claymore mines with rifle fire.

SNIPING IN THE DEFENSE

As our operations cycle graphic showed, combat flows from offensive operations, intended to destroy the enemy and gain ground, into defensive operations, which hold ground and grind an opponent down while preserving

With sufficient height, this Marine sniper can engage distant mortar crews attempting to bombard his unit's position.

the size and capabilities of our own forces. The defense is a temporary measure to allow essential resupply and rest, or to shift air, artillery, and logistical support to another sector, where its concentration facilitates another unit's offense.

Interestingly, it's usually the defense that finds the most aggressive sniping because it's now, with your unit occupying stationary positions, that you launch independent sniper forays behind enemy lines. And when a sniper's not "snooping-shooting-and-scooting" on his own, he finds himself part of an integrated, cohesive unit defense.

The Deliberate Defense

The term "deliberate" implies stronger resistance, detailed planning, and more time conducting a defense—which can be as short as the few days typical for North Africa in 1942, to many months, which was the case in Korea a decade later when United Nations forces dug in on the 38th Parallel.

A deliberate defense usually is oriented on "avenues of approach" (AAs) such as roads, trails, or passable open ground. Due to his rifle's inherent capabilities, a sniper normally is focused on the AA most suited to dismounted

infantry rather than armor. And because his rifle is not effective at short range, the sniper needs at least 100 yards of clear ground before him; lacking this, the team should be shifted to another sector or pulled back for a more fitting role, such as counterrecon or manning an observation post.

Since appropriate frontage widths expand and contract according to terrain, I won't cite any specific width as appropriate for a sniper team. Instead, a team's frontage is planned according to the size of the unit it reasonably can be expected to cover, which I'd say is a squad's front as a minimum and a platoon frontage maximum.

When it comes to positioning snipers, the sniper team's employment officer, company commander, or battalion sniper coordinator assesses AAs and assigns each team a sector of fire—and here we must again make the important distinction: the superior assigns the *sector* but the sniper team selects the actual hide position. This way, the resulting hide reflects all the peculiar needs and capabilities of a sniper rifle and matches these to a specific piece of ground far more thoroughly than if the leader tried to decide it all himself. Your sector of fire could dictate that you locate your hide well

A leader designated the sniper team's sector of fire (circle), but it's up to the team to select its hide location.

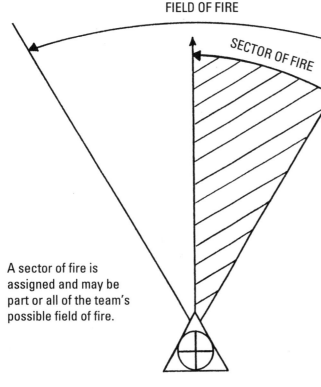

FIELD OF FIRE

SECTOR OF FIRE

A sector of fire is assigned and may be part or all of the team's possible field of fire.

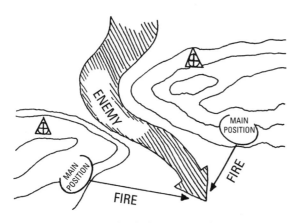

REVERSE SLOPE DEFENSE.
Sniper teams surveil the frontal slopes.

forward of the unit's main position, right on the main defensive line, or even to its rear and overlooking the front.

In those inevitable cases where your assigned sector of fire overlooks an armored AA, examine the approach minutely to determine where antiarmor fire will be so withering that enemy vehicles seek cover to halt and dismount infantry. Here's a place to plan sniper fire. Using common sense, anticipate the routes his infantry will follow from these dismount points during an attempted assault on your antitank weapons, where he'd put crew-served weapons to support this maneuver, and so on. Equally anticipate how the enemy would approach dismounted in darkness, and plan fire for engaging with both NODs and available light.

So long as you're in the defense, continue to improve your hide until eventually you've built primary, secondary, and supplementary hides all linked by trenches and each containing cached ammo, food, and water, with nearby dummy hides to draw away fire.

The special "deliberate defense on a reverse slope," first employed by Germans on the Russian Front during World War II, avoids direct fire from enemy tanks and artillery by conceding front slopes and arraying defensive positions on their back sides.

The reverse slope defense is most effective against an armored enemy on the move who wanders deeply into your fire before he realizes his predicament. It's more like an enormous ambush than a traditional defense. The most practical sniper contribution is to employ teams as early warning on the front slope, where they'd also prevent or delay dismounted enemy from passing over the top. Their hide, of course, must be dug deeply and invisibly.

Integrating Defensive Fields of Fire

The challenge in any deliberate defense is integrating fire so sniper teams at dispersed locations adequately cover all their important approaches and sectors yet saturate none and still synchronize their shooting. Clear responsibility and balanced fire are your goals.

The battalion employment officer uses commonsensical techniques to ensure that fire is integrated among individual teams and within platoon and company sectors, with special emphasis on tying in abutting company sectors of fire. On the facing page we've illustrated four simple ways to integrate fire, as shown in the four panels, left to right.

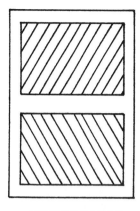

SPLIT INTO NEAR
AND FAR SECTORS

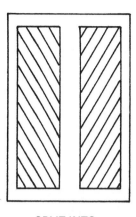

SPLIT INTO
ADJACENT SECTORS

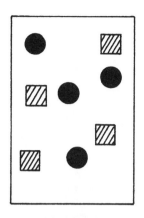

DIVIDED BY
TYPES OF TARGET

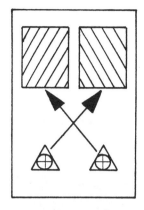

EXCHANGING
SECTORS AND
FIRING OBLIQUELY

Integrating sniper team fire.

First, one team covers the nearer sector; another team covers the deeper one, with the sector split by a linear landmark, such as a road or power line. Next, we've divided the area into side-by-side sectors, again using a linear demarcation landmark.

In the third panel, we divide targets instead of dividing a sector, with one team engaging leaders (squares), while the other's responsible for crew-served weapons (circles). And the final panel shows two sniper teams shooting across each other's fronts in a shallow sector, giving each team maximum range by shooting obliquely while also inducing great confusion on the enemy.

These are all *primary* sectors of fire; each team also has a secondary in which it shoots if nothing's happening in its primary, or some action such as a smokescreen disrupts sniper rifle fire.

And when it comes to staking out a sector, you can try an Afrikaner rifleman's trick from the Boer War. Position painted rocks at exact paced-off or lazed distances for precise range estimates against advancing enemy infantry. It proved so effective in southern Africa that veteran British troops approached painted rocks only with the greatest caution.

And at what range does a sniper engage an approaching enemy when he's in a deliberate defense? As a rule, I'd say you should fire to the maximum range of your rifle, which realistically means 1,000 yards, but this should be addressed specifically in unit plans so an early engagement doesn't contradict your commander's intent.

Sniping in a Hasty Defense

A hasty defense is prepared quickly, perhaps even under fire right where you are or after a fast dash to nearby defensible terrain. It usually evolves from a meeting engagement or when repelling an unexpected enemy attack while under way. It is the most fluid of defensive situations.

According to Captain McBride, a sniper's number-one hasty defense mission is to deny the enemy control of no-man's-land, the unoccupied territory between opposing forces. In more contemporary terms, the sniper supports his temporarily halted unit by preventing the enemy from advancing, fleeing, reconning, or positioning itself to observe and adjust artillery. Dominating all terrain within your rifle's effective range should be done automatically by SOP each time your unit's forced to pause and assume a hasty defense. Without specific instructions, friendly sniper teams immediately occupy high ground and begin engaging targets until the enemy no longer dares to move or show himself. Concurrently, you prepare a belly scrape hide

These U.S. Army snipers are defending a major road against sudden attacks by RPG rocket teams.

and begin rotating duties with another sniper team to take turns shooting and improving your hides.

At least until the situation clarifies itself, your teams use the clock system to split the front among them. Assuming three teams are with a company, one covers 8–11 o'clock, the second 11–2 o'clock, and the third 2–5 o'clock.

Conducting a Delay with Snipers

A delay is a defensive operation in which ground is traded for time, with an advancing enemy slowed or temporarily halted, usually by a weaker force. The classic example is the Battle of Thermopylae, the 480 B.C. delay of a 100,000-man Persian army by King Leonidas of Sparta and his 300 royal guards. Their spirited defense of a mountain pass so narrow that only 10 men could advance at once bought enough time to mobilize the Greek army and prepare an ultimately successful defense.

The key to Thermopylae, or any effective delay, is finding terrain that naturally reduces the enemy's width and speed so that your limited fire has an effect. An enemy restricted by a bridge, causeway, paddy dike, narrow trail, or mountain pass can be delayed dramatically by properly employed sniper rifle fire.

By properly I mean maneuver at least three teams in unison, along the same narrow avenue of approach, then retrograde using backward leapfrogs. When the enemy attempts to maneuver against one sniper hide, he's engaged from another while the first team displaces. The enemy diverts its maneuver to the second hide, only to be engaged by the third team, and so on. The enemy's advance is made more difficult by the emplacement of mines and booby traps where he'll likely maneuver when trying to bypass or flank a hide.

When backed up by skillfully directed artillery on top of terrain exploited to the maximum, I think three to five sniper teams could slow even a reinforced company's ad-

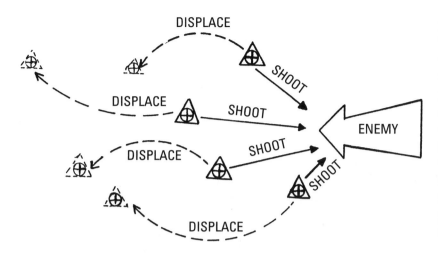

A DELAY BY SNIPERS. Multiple sniper teams phase ambushes along a single avenue of approach.

vance to only a couple of kilometers per day, enough time for their parent unit to prepare an elaborate deliberate defense.

BREAKING AN ENGAGEMENT

How many rounds does a sniper fire in a single engagement? I'll give you some food for thought.

Ordinarily you can count on only one shot per engagement, not just because your targets will disappear and aggressively react, but a second or third round could very well pinpoint your location. Think about it: your first round surprises the enemy, but they still learn your general direction and distance; a second shot has their every eye and ear turned your way; and a third? Well, it can only raise your insurance premiums.

Your first target is critically important since in most cases it's the *only* target you'll have. Within a half-second of your shot, the enemy will already have disappeared from view. One-quarter of a second later, they'll be blasting away in hopes of hitting you. Five more seconds and they'll be calling for artillery or mortars. As the rounds begin falling, they'll dispatch a maneuver force to sweep you up.

Don't underestimate the intensity and volume of enemy counterfire. A Soviet-style platoon having 22 AKs and three PK machine guns, even when spraying haphazardly in your direction, packs a lot of firepower. Assuming each man fires one magazine and the machine gunners let loose with only a half-belt apiece, that's still 740 rounds, all ripping your way in probably less than five seconds.

If your hide is even slightly conspicuous—say they guess you're in a particular shadow that's 20 feet deep and 6 feet wide—and you're hunkered down "safely" behind sandbags and firing through only a 6-inch-wide loophole, you're still likely to have big problems. Mathematically, even with them randomly firing into this general area, it means 6.1 rounds will enter that narrow 6-inch loophole and ruin your day. (And that's firing just one magazine apiece and excludes other weapons they'd likely employ, such as AGS-17 grenade launchers or heavy machine guns, not to mention indirect fire.)

On the other hand, if your hide is more than 600 yards away, it becomes very difficult to detect you. It's possible you could catch a sizable enemy unit in the open and, like Carlos Hathcock, the USMC's renowned Vietnam sniper, engage them at leisure for two days from a single hide. Perhaps the enemy's green or demoralized, or it's just a single squad, or the terrain decisively favors you. These are judgment calls.

When you're firing in support of a friendly unit in the attack, the enemy defenders will be so preoccupied with those visible attackers that they'll barely notice your sniper fire. The same is true when you're firing in support of a unit's defense; the enemy is so fixated on other fire and actions that he cannot respond effectively to your shooting.

MAJOR POLICE MISSION LIST

HOSTAGE RESCUE

BARRICADED SUSPECT

SKYJACK

BUS AND TRAIN HIJACK

HIGH-RISK WARRANT SERVICE

MOVING VEHICLE INTERDICTION

COUNTERSNIPER

COUNTER WMD/SEIZURE

CORDON AND SEARCH

SMALL VEHICLE ASSAULT

DIGNITARY PROTECTION

WITNESS PROTECTION

OVERWATCH OF DRUG BUY

CLANDESTINE DRUG LAB RECON/SURVEILLANCE

SAFEHOUSE RECON/SURVEILLANCE

REMOTE AIRFIELD RECON/SURVEILLANCE

MARITIME AREA RECON/SURVEILLANCE

BORDER SURVEILLANCE

But when it's just your team operating behind enemy lines? Any shot taken after the first one stacks the odds against you. Remember: "He who shoots and runs away, lives to shoot another day."

QUICK REACTION FORCES

As learned in Iraq, it's essential to support sniper teams with a Quick Reaction Force (QRF), usually platoon in size that, as its name implies, can immediately respond when a team is suddenly attacked by a numerically superior force. To be effective, this cannot be a contingency plan but an organized QRF that's ready to go and can reach an endangered team's location faster than it can be overrun—typically, for planning purposes, no more than 15 minutes. Ideally, the QRF is backed up by helicopter gunships.

Of equal concern, however, is not falling for the age-old tactic of a foe attacking an isolated detachment to lure a reaction force into a large ambush—which also has happened in Iraq. The best way to avoid this is to have the QRF not use the most obvious route and be preceded by a security vanguard.

POLICE SNIPING MISSIONS AND OPERATIONS

This section is purposely brief, not because there isn't much to learn about law enforcement sniping operations, but because I cannot disclose much here without placing both law officers and possible hostages in jeopardy. Some bad guys can afford the price of this book, so I'd just as soon keep them guessing as to how exactly a police tac team would handle them.

These details will be disseminated at a future point when I'm assured a confidential supplement to this manuscript can be kept out of hostile hands. It's the least I can do for the many police and special operations snipers who've shared their tricks of the trade and SOPs with me.

But by listing these specific missions, and emphasizing that there's at least as much sophistication to them as to military operations, it will encourage police snipers to analyze their roles with new insights. Keep in mind that each of the following major missions has beneath it a host of subtasks and special skills and considerations.

One question I've encountered several times from law enforcement snipers is, "How many snipers should be targeted against a suspect?" I once flippantly replied, "Ideally, 1,238." After the student chuckled, I made my real point: *as many snipers as you can conceal within range of the suspect*, taking into account available cover and concealment and backstop, if that's an issue. In an ideal setting, such as an open-air option, I'd suggest four sniper teams, one for each primary direction to boost the odds of a clear shot, and have at least one more sniper ready for a follow-up shot if required.

CHAPTER 18

SNIPING IN AN URBAN ENVIRONMENT

SNIPING IN AN URBAN ENVIRONMENT

Whether Stalingrad, Hue, or Fallujah, modern combat has featured fighting in urban areas. This environment is not unusual, but it's unique enough that it requires grouping in this single chapter all our urban sniping information.

The specialized information you see here—such as urban range estimation techniques and urban stalking—supplement what was covered on these subjects elsewhere but cannot replace it. You need to know both the general and these specialized techniques.

Urban Movement Techniques

Whether you're a police or military sniper, avoid moving toward danger along open, predictable routes. If you must move quickly, at least use less expected approaches such as backyards, alleys, and rooftops. When you absolutely must advance along a street, do so on the *left* side so you can quickly duck into a doorway or behind a building corner and return fire with your rifle on your right shoulder.

When time isn't so pressing, you should actually

A rubbled urban environment, whether Stalingrad or here, Grozny, creates an ideal physical setting for sniper concealment.

go *through* urban cover, as we've illustrated on page 444. This means exploiting sewers and subway tunnels below ground, transiting through large buildings rather than going around them, and even using demo to blow holes from one adjacent building to the next, a technique the Germans called "mouseholing" at Stalingrad.

An excellent urban movement technique when you're overwatching advancing friendly troops is leapfrogging, which requires at least two sniper teams, though we use three in our next illustration. One team is in a hide and covering the troops (the rooftop team), while another is abandoning a hide (the water tower), and a third team just behind the troops (entering the storefront) prepares to occupy a hide. Should a threat be detected or the troops come under fire, one team engages and tells the other two teams where to position themselves to best support the action.

Urban stalking is just as carefully planned and meticulously executed as its rural counterpart, but your selected route and movement technique must fit your urban surroundings. It's still a matter of dividing the route into distinct legs, as our sniper has done in the stalking illustration on page 446, with his ultimate destination being a suitable hide location.

At street level, a U.S. Army sniper advances cover to cover in Iraq's northern city of Mosul. Note SAW machine gunner watching the sniper's 6 o'clock.

Urban Sniper Hides

Especially in older cities, you'll find houses and commercial buildings so closely packed that ground-level hides reduce your observation and fields of fire to less than 100 yards—often too short for a military sniper but quite acceptable to a police sniper provided he's well concealed. When the military sniper improves his field of fire by occupying high ground, it's this same issue of conspicuousness that he must consider. Firing from a lone church steeple fools no one.

When selecting an urban hide, avoid using a room with many windows since this gives the enemy too many angles to look into your lair and may allow too much flying glass from mortar and

UNDERGROUND,
use sewers, subways.

SURFACE LEVEL,
go through buildings.

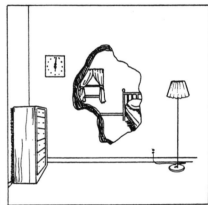

ABOVE GROUND,
go through walls.

URBAN MOVEMENT ROUTES.

LEAPFROGGING. One team (roof) covers the advancing squad while another displaces (tower) and a third (storefront) prepares to occupy a hide.

An optically equipped Squad Designated Marksman covers fellow Marines in Fallujah.

artillery fire. It should be several stories below the roof so there's overhead protection, too. As our illustration on page 447 (lower left) shows, build a shooting platform by removing a door from its hinges and supporting it on concrete blocks with sandbags for even more stability and ballistic protection. Notice that the room's outer wall has been inconspicuously lined with sandbags and a glass panel removed so it looks like the window's still closed. As a final touch, our sniper tore out a piece of drapery cheesecloth lining, which he's hung from the ceiling; behind this he'll be invisible to even the most intense observation.

Sgt. Neal Terry, an Albuquerque police sniper instructor, extensively fired match-grade, hollowpoint .308 bullets through typical household metal and nylon screens and found there was no appreciable decline in performance. His bullets hit at the same point of impact as with no screening—which told him that he could leave screens in place to better conceal his presence behind a screened window or door.

Another clever urban hide we've illustrated on page 447 (upper right) similarly has the sniper team heavily sandbagging an interior, but this time it's a seemingly innocent attic, with your firing port appearing to be only a missing shingle.

Dummy hides are particularly quick to prepare in an urban area, and echoes are such a prominent feature that your dummy hide can seem quite real.

Urban Shooting Positions

In addition to employing all the standard shooting positions—prone, squatting, sitting, kneeling, and offhand—an urban environment's uniqueness requires a sniper to consider some other body positions and kinds of support.

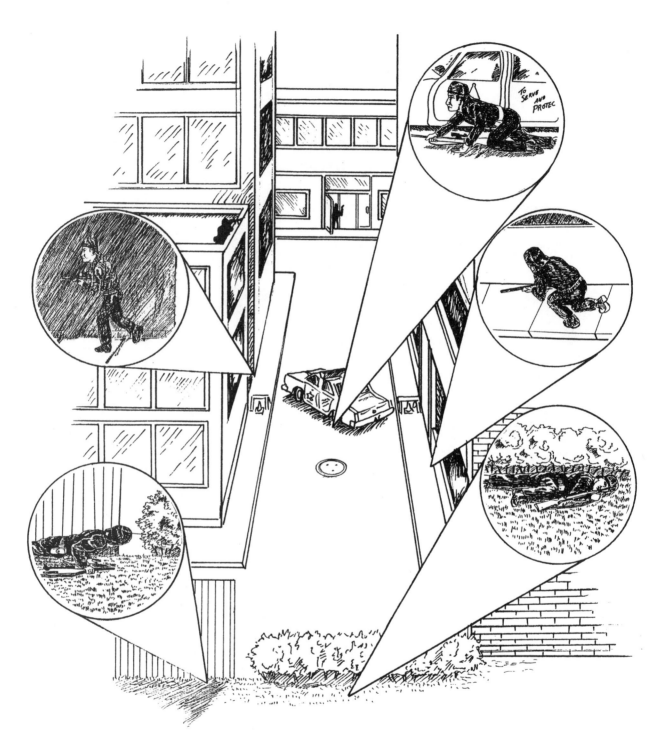

URBAN STALKING. A sniper uses the same techniques used in woodland stalking, dividing his route into legs and matching an appropriate movement style to each leg.

Textbook perfect, this U.S. Marine sniper in Fallujah, Iraq, is well back from the opening and off to one side, all but impossible for a hostile to detect.

AN ATTIC HIDE. The sniper's loophole is disguised by removing shingles.

Seek an FFP at least equal to surrounding buildings. But if you position much higher, you won't be as able to see and shoot into windows on facing buildings.

THE URBAN HIDE. Note especially the removed window pane, door/platform, and cheesecloth screen.

For quick urban support, lean back into a building or wall, shifting about 40 to 55 percent of your weight against it.

An Albuquerque police SWAT sniper demonstrates the effectiveness of cheesecloth, even just duct-taped over an open window.

An urban area's abundance of man-made structures and lack of trees can make it hard to stabilize an offhand shot. To solve this, I developed a body position in which you plant your feet firmly and lean back into a wall or building, shifting about 40 to 50 percent of your weight against the structure. It's quick to assume and noticeably superior to an unsupported shot.

We've already covered the shooting platform, but realize that you can improvise a support of any height with a little imagination. At the McMillan Sniper School, students learn to fashion supports from scraps of wood and duct tape, as shown in an accompanying photo. It's well worthwhile to keep a roll of tape in your rucksack.

Another useful urban support is a line or cord or strap, nailed or tied in place. What's especially flexible here is that you can install it for the ideal height you need whether firing prone, sitting, or standing. And it can be rigged in those places where it would seem it's impossible to find support.

The "urban prone" position was made famous by the Los Angeles Police Department's SWAT team, whose officers shot and killed an AK-armed suspect using this firing position. To assume the urban prone, lie beside a parked vehicle, almost parallel to it, and place your rifle underneath it. If you're a right-handed shooter, it will feel more natural to lie on your left side but you won't be able to get your rifle as low and probably won't be able to get clearance beneath a compact car. Lying on your right side initially feels a bit odd and may attenuate recoil somewhat, but it's more stable and you can get your rifle closer to the ground. Support it by propping the forearm's side with your left hand.

Here's where it's a bit tricky and requires some live-fire practice before employing it real-world. While lying on your side, your scope's vertical crosshair becomes the horizontal, and vice versa. In essence, because your scope is no longer above your bore, your windage has become your elevation and your elevation has become your windage.

This sniper student improvised an excellent support with just duct tape and scrap wood. (Photo credit: McMillan Sniper School)

Where there's no support, hang a line, cord, or straps to improve stability.

Lying sideways in an urban prone position allows a sniper to fire below a parked vehicle.

A U.S. Army sniper employs a tripod to cover a dangerous urban neighborhood in Iraq.

To a small degree, your bullet will impact right or left—depending on whether you're lying on your right or left side—and if you need holdover, you will use what had been your vertical crosshair and has now become the horizontal crosshair. Again, you should practice this before attempting it real-world. (And use caution: a tank full of gasoline is not far from your muzzle!)

Urban Spotting and Target Detection

Urban spotting is especially complicated because you're virtually surrounded by target indicators: straight lines abound, as do manmade cover and concealment, and so forth. If you try to surveil all target indicators intensely, you'll go buggy.

To distinguish a hostile in this confusing maze, watch for even slight *movement*, which requires using naked eyes and binoculars extensively until movement's detected. Only then do you switch to your spotting or rifle scope.

Urban locations worthy of special surveillance include roof edges, where any movement skylines the individual; open windows or doors, indicating a possible shooter inside; the edges of walls, hedges, and buildings, where a bad guy may peek or shoot; and any high ground that commands the area.

The spotting section explained a system for directing your partner to a particular window, but buildings, too, need a quick reference system for brief communications. The best way I've found is using slang terms that best distinguish each building from surrounding ones, such as the glass house (all glass), the mansion (Greek column facade), the gray whale (long, dark building), and the blockhouse (concrete block and few windows).

Aside from spotting for your own shooting, your optical surveillance capabilities will prove valuable to your commander and operations planners, too. During offensive urban operations, they'll particularly benefit from your detection of:

- Crew-served weapons positions
- Tactical command and control posts
- Obstacles and likely mine locations
- Fighting positions and trenches
- Fields of fire covered by enemy weapons
- Weapon and visual dead space
- Routes and locations with cover/concealment

When your unit is in the defense, your optics enable you to report the approach of enemy, his concentrations, direction of movement, special weapons, etc.

A SUPERB URBAN SNIPER

USMC Sgt. John Place (R) receives the Silver Star for his gallantry in the Fallujah fight, where he accounted for 32 enemy insurgents in 13 days. The award was presented by the 1st Marine Division commander, Maj. Gen. Richard Natonski.

While fighting in Fallujah, the U.S. Marines heavily employed sniper teams, with one courageous young Marine sniper demonstrating skill and technique on a par with the best snipers in Marine history. In one 13-day period of April 2004, Sgt. John Ethan Place scored 32 confirmed kills while engaging insurgents who fought the Marines of Echo Company, 2nd Battalion, 1st Regiment, 1st Marine Division.

The 1st Division commander, Maj. Gen. Richard Natonski, while presenting the Silver Star to the 22-year-old sniper, said his unerring fire had so unnerved the enemy that insurgent negotiators pleaded to have Place and his fellow snipers withdrawn while the talks were under way. "It's hard to believe," Major General Natonski said, "that one individual could have had such an impact on our combat operations."

Urban Range Estimation

More so than any other operating environment, a laser rangefinder works at its peak in an urban setting. The widespread presence of solid structures and reflective surfaces with squared, perpendicular sides makes for reliable, long-range lazing to a device's maximum range. But this setting also contains plenty of aspects that lend themselves to fairly accurate range estimation using eyeball and manual techniques, too.

Unlike rural areas, urban ones contain regularly spaced or standard-sized yardsticks you can use when estimating range. The most fundamental is what I call "the standard block," which recognizes that many urban areas have city blocks of consistent dimensions. Discover these dimensions and your range estimation becomes a snap. To be truly accurate, you also must know the widths of standard two-lane and four-lane streets.

Another urban yardstick is parking meters, which usually are spaced at very precise intervals, as are sidewalk slabs in downtown areas. When combining the standard block with counting parking meters, you'll be able to estimate distance to an accuracy of +/- 1 yard!

The toughest urban (and mountain) range esti-

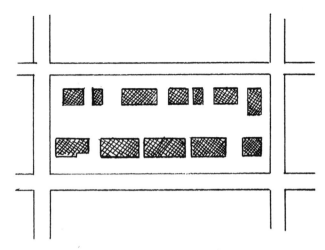

"STANDARD" CITY BLOCK. Many urban areas have regularly sized blocks.

mate is an uphill or downhill one, and the solution comes from a Greek mathematician named Pythagoras. He discovered that you could exactly compute the side of a triangle opposite a right angle by squaring the other two sides, which yielded the square of the third side. Confused? Look at our illustration.

The Pythagorean theorem—A squared plus B squared equals C squared—requires that you square A, which is the desired height above ground, then add it to the square of B, which is the distance to the house. Take the result and determine its square and you'll have the distance for C. Let's try it once.

The building is 100 feet tall, which we'll convert to 33.3 yards, and multiple it by itself to equal 1,108.89. Now, the distance from the building base to the house is 175 yards, which times itself is 30,625. Combining A and B, (1108.89 + 30,625) equals 31,733.89, and to find C we find it's square. Thus, C is 178.1 yards.

Urban Wind Effects and Estimation

Urban winds are confusing, contradictory, and especially difficult to see in a downtown area. As our illustration shows, among a city's major buildings the wind will vary direction and speed,

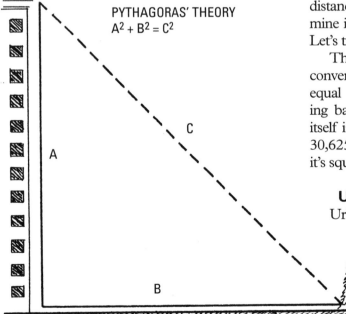

PYTHAGORAS' THEORY
$A^2 + B^2 = C^2$

winds to blow down the long axis, parallel to the street. Where these "canyons" meet—at street intersections—contradictory winds create considerable confusion. Therefore, when possible, avoid shooting through a major urban intersection on a windy day unless your shot is so close that it won't drift much.

Be very sensitive to wind passing through porous buildings such as parking ramps, and the strange twisting wind that can emerge when one short building is surrounded by tall ones.

Determining wind direction is tough, too, unless flags or other moveable materials are present. One alternative we've shown is to watch how smoke rises from chimneys, but this may not help you for ground-level winds (look for blowing loose paper there). Another wind indicator is mirage, which in an urban area can be optically observed on a flat roof edge even on cold days.

A police sniper friend suggests that tactical team SOPs require that 18-inch lengths of police line tape be hung in the vicinity of an incident, and that identical 18-inch streamers be hung all over the department's firing range. He reasons that you can learn to read the wind from these range streamers, then apply it when the unobtrusive ones are hung at the scene. This seems a good solution for locales lacking any means of detecting wind, provided your fellow officers can post enough streamers.

Incidentally, while there are updrafts in major downtown areas, I've learned that they tend to be

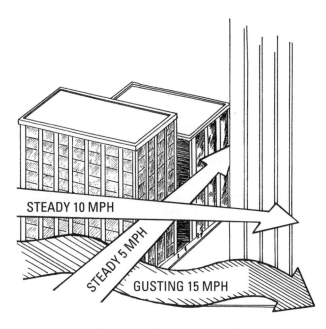

STEADY 10 MPH

STEADY 5 MPH

GUSTING 15 MPH

Urban winds vary in speed, direction, and intensity by elevation.

gusting perplexedly at one level, then blowing steadily at another.

To figure this out, realize that winds become steadier with elevation. Gusting may prevail at ground level, but rooftop winds tend to be steadier. Next, recognize that downtown streets actually are man-made canyons, and, just like mountain country, this terrain causes low- and medium-level

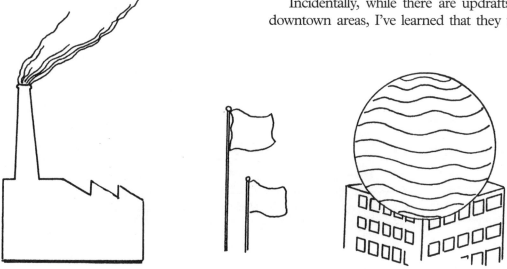

URBAN WIND INDICATORS. Smoke, flags, and rooftop mirage.

very shallow—only a few yards—and should not affect your bullet long enough to influence its flight.

Urban Sectors of Fire

We've already noted how narrow streets and short strips between buildings make urban fields of fire so shallow that a sniper cannot exploit his weapon's ballistic advantage. But as we've shown in the illustration below, an *oblique* or side-facing sector of fire not only increases your range by three or four times, it places your fire at an odd angle that the enemy will have great difficulty returning or maneuvering against. In essence, you'll be shooting across the front of several enemy elements, which makes for a slow, coordinated, and probably ineffective enemy reaction.

Another way to confuse the enemy as well as engage him with effective fire is by firing when he thinks he's safely behind cover. This requires that your hide be high enough for you to see into dead space and, to be most effective, that you hold your fire until the enemy has taken shelter there in the false belief that he's escaping danger. Just realize that the higher you place yourself in a building, the more dead space you will have created beneath it that you cannot see or cover. You give up short-

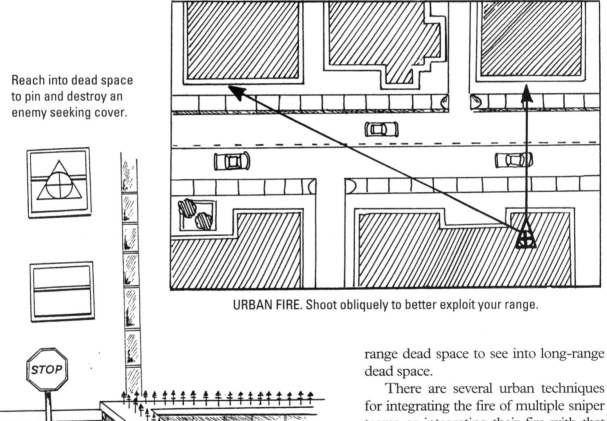

Reach into dead space to pin and destroy an enemy seeking cover.

URBAN FIRE. Shoot obliquely to better exploit your range.

range dead space to see into long-range dead space.

There are several urban techniques for integrating the fire of multiple sniper teams or integrating their fire with that of infantrymen using M16 rifles and M60 machine guns. Our illustration at right shows one sniper team on a building's fifth floor, which, due to their elevation, will cover a sector that extends 100 through 500 yards before them. Picking up the sector at 500 yards is another team, positioned on the tenth floor, which shoots out to 1,000 yards.

POLICE BEWARE! A higher-level gunman can see and shoot over cover, too.

Our other illustration on page 456 shows how a sniper team's fire supplements that of other weapons by reaching beyond the range of M16s and M60s. All these fire simultaneously to give the enemy grief out to 1,000 yards and in a balanced way.

Urban .50-Caliber Sniping

The tremendous barrier penetration capability of the .50-caliber round—especially the Raufoss explosive projectile—makes it well suited for urban sniping, where a barrier of some kind is seemingly everywhere and often impervious to other small arms.

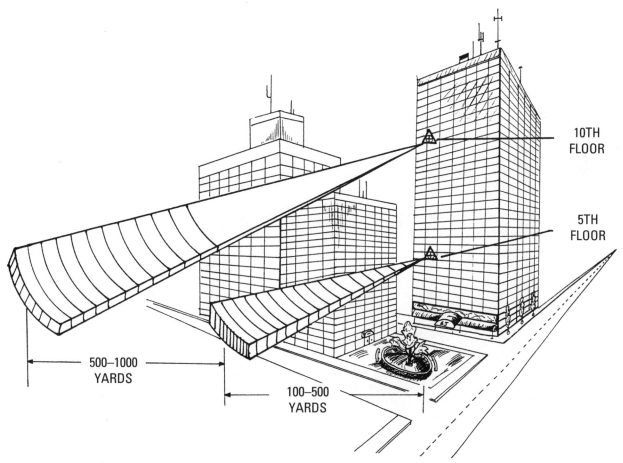

Integrating sniper fire between two teams at different heights.

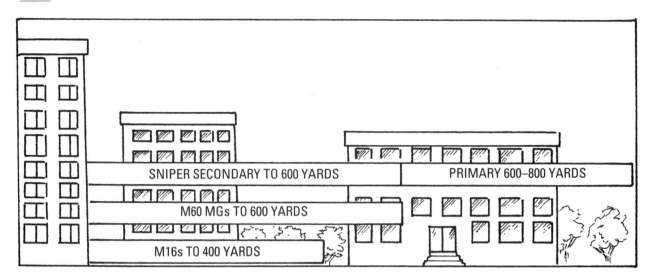

Integrating fire between snipers, infantry, and M60 machine guns.

A Marine sniper prepares to fire a .50-caliber Barrett in Fallujah, where it proved crucial in rooting out barricaded insurgents.

HIGHEST STORY GUNS CAN HIT WITH DIRECT FIRE

Ground Range	T-80 Tank	BMP/BMD 73mm	122mm SP Howitzer
100 Meters	8 Stories	10 Stories	30 Stories
300 Meters	10 Stories	60 Stories	90 Stories
500 Meters	15 Stories	97 Stories	150 Stories

The downside of a .50-caliber rifle, however, is its considerable weight and bulk, which precludes most fast movement or stalking. Thus, it makes more sense to employ a .50 in a support role, a bit back and preferably on higher elevation than the fighting being supported. In most instances, in this support role the .50 won't engage to its maximum range because intervening buildings will block its fire by creating dead space.

In this support role, the sniper most likely won't displace after firing only one or two shots, though he should always be ready to reposition if enemy counterfire makes his position untenable or the advance of friendly troops requires his advance, too. Ideally, .50-caliber-equipped sniper teams are deployed in pairs for mutual support, which not only helps confuse the enemy by offering muzzle blasts from more than one location but also allows covering fire when one gun must reposition.

Inside their final firing or overwatch position, the sniper team is especially careful to tape down or remove items that could be visibly affected by the big gun's muzzle blast, such as curtains and window shutters. And in such a contained area, the sniper and spotter must wear double hearing protection—*earplugs under earmuffs*—or hearing damage is a certainty.

In Iraq, and especially during the Fallujah offensive, .50-caliber rifles played an important support role, offering such a tremendous ballistic effect that it discouraged the enemy and raised the morale of supported troops.

The Greatest Threat

Ask veterans of World War II streetfighting what proved the deadliest threat and they won't cite a machine gun or rifle—they'll tell you it was self-propelled guns that could withstand small-arms fire and directly blast away at your position.

With their mobility, armor protection, and heavy guns, tanks, too, are deadly, while the recent growth of cannon-packing armored personnel carriers cannot be ignored, either. All these can smash the most heavily sandbagged position with direct fire—it's just a question of bringing their guns to bear. In an urban area, the relevant information becomes, how high can these weapon systems elevate their guns?

I computed the answers, as displayed above, and was surprised to see how steeply these guns elevate and how high they can reach even at short ranges. My conclusion: have an alternative hide ready at a lower level so the instant tanks and self-propelled artillery appear, you can get down low enough that intervening buildings mask your hide.

CHAPTER 19

COUNTERSNIPING TACTICS AND TECHNIQUES

THE ULTIMATE COUNTERSNIPER ENGAGEMENT

In modern history there's never been a battle so dominated by snipers as was Stalingrad, the 1942 high-water mark of German conquest in Russia. With aggressive attackers pitted against determined defenders, this most bitter urban contest of World War II would see the ultimate sniper encounter in history.

By October 1942, the Germans had seized nine-tenths of the city, which artillery had so reduced to rubble that the Reich's weary soldiers called the fighting "Rattenkrieg," or the "War of the Rats." Combatants on both sides tunneled, scurried, and hid in the ruins of once enormous industrial plants and whole blocks of collapsed apartment buildings. It was a sniper's haven, the Beirut of its era.

The premier Soviet sniper at Stalingrad was Vassili Zaitsev, a broad-faced Siberian who had been a hunter and shepherd in the Ural Mountains. In his first 10 days of shooting, Zaitsev killed 40 Germans. When his tally neared 100, he received the Order of Lenin and became the focus of a Soviet propaganda campaign as the living epitome of Russian resistance.

With the sniper death toll climbing more steeply every day, and with German soldiers becoming ever more fearful of these Russian

Vassili Zaitsev (L), Hero of the Soviet Union, in overwhite camouflage smock with two fellow snipers on the Eastern Front.

marksmen, it was inevitable that Berlin would strike back. Dispatched directly from the Fatherland was the commandant of the Wehrmacht Sniper School at Zossen, a Major Koning. His target: the deadly Russian premier sniper, Vassili Zaitsev.

The German army had been the first to field specially trained snipers during World War I, and so highly regarded were the Reich's World War II snipers that the army created three special Eagle Badges to honor them for having killed 20, 40, or 60 enemy personnel. Though there remains no record of Major Koning's decorations, quite likely his shoulder displayed this coveted Eagle Badge.

Shortly after Koning's secret arrival, his presence was compromised by a cocky German POW who boasted that soon Zaitsev would die. Now alerted, the Russian sniper devoted himself to finding this German stalker.

After several days of inaction, two experienced Russian snipers suddenly were shot by a German armed with a telescopic sight. This was the calling card Zaitsev had been expecting. "Now there was no doubt," he concluded when his sniper comrades were lost. "They had come up against the Nazi 'super-sniper' I was looking for."

Focusing his search along a narrow front, he and

Using a quality 7.92mm Mauser rifle topped by an excellent scope, Germany's World War II sniper was technically superior to his Soviet counterpart. Note the Eagle Badge on this sniper's sleeve, which was awarded to German snipers for having killed 20, 40, or 60 enemy.

his spotter, Nikolai Kulikov, finally observed the top of a German helmet creeping along a trench. Dare he shoot, Zaitsev asked himself. "No! It was a trick: the helmet somehow or other moved unevenly . . ."

The next day they returned to the area before dawn, this time with a Communist political officer who wanted to witness this historic encounter. At one point, the commissar excitedly proclaimed that he could see the German and raised himself "barely, literally for one second," Zaitsev said. Then, *crack!*—a bullet struck him. Though the commissar laid in the open writhing in pain, his wound was not serious.

Zaitsev, keen to the tactics of German snipers, unemotionally continued to search with his binoculars, ready to fire if the German compromised himself by engaging the medics who now retrieved the commissar. Purposely wounding rather than killing, Zaitsev thought. And with less than a second of exposure? "That sort of firing, of course, could only come from an experienced sniper," he realized.

To test this, Zaitsev slid a glove over a plank and slowly exposed it. *Bang!*—a bullet smacked through it. The Russian could see that the shot must have come from somewhere in a particular rubble pile. But it was too late to do anything about it that day.

The ever-patient Zaitsev returned before dawn and lay motionless all morning because the sun's angle could reflect light off his scope. By late afternoon, the sun had shifted to his back, exactly reversing the reflection danger. Having his spotter raise a dummy's head inside a helmet, at last he saw a glimmer of scope glare from beneath a boilerplate. *Bang!* The German shattered the dummy's head. Instantly Zaitsev fired, too, but it was no decoy he hit. The contest was over; the Reich's supersniper, Major Koning, lay dead.

Zaitsev eventually was credited with 242 kills at Stalingrad. By the end of the war, he personally had accounted for 400 Germans and was declared a Hero of the Soviet Union.

COUNTERSNIPING TECHNIQUES

The best countersniper weapon we have is a friendly sniper team—*you*.

As a trained, equipped sniper, you think like your foe does, see your surroundings—complete with dangers and opportunities—like he does. You're equipped with great optics similar to his; and you have a weapon capable of reaching him. Essentially, you're the "thief" needed to catch a "thief."

Equally, though, you're also the most knowledgeable countersniper expert in your unit and the commander's key adviser on the subject. How your entire unit—whether military or a police tac team—reacts depends on what you tell them and help teach them. It's no small responsibility.

But what is a sniper? In terrorist and criminal situations, any law officer will tell you that a sniper is any concealed gunman firing a rifle. In most military situations, though, a sniper should be a specially trained enemy rifleman using optical sights—if you want to be technical. But when your unit is pinned down and taking significant casualties, your commander won't care if the invisible rifleman has a sniper's union card or not. He wants him neutralized—now.

Recognizing His Presence
While such distinctions may not seem so important to others, it's important to you because a

genuine sniper is always your priority target, and knowing one is present will cause you to spend more time overwatching your unit and hunting this dangerous foe.

Your first countersniper duty is educating your fellow soldiers about enemy snipers, to develop an awareness so you'll be contacted instantly if a real sniper appears. Teach them to be especially alert for:

- Hits attained from more than 400 yards away
- Several killed or wounded with only one shot apiece
- Hits on personnel exposed for a few seconds, or only partially exposed, or hit only in the head
- High proportion of leaders and crew-served weapons members hit
- Discovery of fired, unlinked 7.62x54mmR brass

After thus educating them, teach them a few key features to watch for so they can recognize enemy snipers, as shown in our illustration below.

Special camouflage (including face masks, smocks, or Ghillie suits) is a strong indicator that a soldier is a sniper. If one or two men are seen maneuvering alone on the battlefield, they're likely a sniper team or artillery forward observers, both of which are worthy of your immediate attention. And unusual optics such as a spotting scope, rifle scope, or binoculars would indicate the same option—they're either FOs or a sniper team.

Weapon recognition is obviously important: you should be notified instantly when an enemy bearing a bolt-action rifle is spotted. Be sure to alert your men to similarities between the SVD rifle's hollow buttstock and that of the PK machine gun (and both have flash suppressors, the only Soviet weapons that do). The lengthy SVD barrel, though, is an easily detectable recognition feature.

Another recognition feature can be found at a Soviet sniper's waist, where he carries a distinctive SVD pouch containing three 10-round magazines and optical accessories. It's usually found on his right side. (Why this emphasis on Soviet snipers? See "The Opposing Sniper" section below.)

Finally, any enemy detected on high ground

A SNIPER'S PRESENCE is indicated by (clockwise from bottom left) unusual rifles, SVD pouches, enemy on high ground, unusual camouflage, specialized optics, and small teams operating alone.

with a very wide or deep field of fire, especially when it's a solitary or small position, likely is a sniper team in a hide or artillery FOs.

If you're fortunate enough to detect such an enemy before he has fired, *don't wait* to engage him. As a kind of tactical preventive medicine, eliminate him as soon as possible.

Offensive vs. Defensive Threat

Unfortunately, too many people in the sniping community think the only dignified way to counter a sniper is with a one-shot kill from long range—which I heartily dispute. The problem is that overfocusing on this one-shot solution limits and delays effectively dealing with an armed opponent who may be harvesting more lives with each passing minute.

You need a host of assorted countersniper techniques so you immediately can match a workable one to any situation you encounter. Before covering these techniques, though, consider what exactly you are trying to accomplish.

An unimpeded enemy sniper, invisible and free to roam and shoot when and where he wishes, is an *offensive* threat since he is the hunter and we his quarry. Any large or small action you take is geared toward reducing his abilities to see, shoot, or move. That is, any technique must contribute to turning him from an offensive threat into a defensive threat—deprived of the initiative, robbed of observation, unable to move, and capable of firing only in self-defense. Actually shooting him is just one of many options, although your ultimate goal always is his total elimination.

Therefore, merely disrupting his ability to take aimed shots could be useful, just as causing him to cease firing or flee may be enough to suit your situation. For military snipers, it's important not to fall into the rut of "escalation" in which you think you must attempt and fail the least violent techniques before the others can be employed. On the other hand, police snipers may be obligated to limit collateral damage and must consider bystanders in any deadly force situation.

Whether a police or military sniper, though, in any countersniper situation you will follow two steps: first, locate the sniper, and second, act upon him.

Locating the Sniper

When we say "locating" the sniper, it doesn't mean pinpointing his exact location with a single glance. Recall that, like you, he will attempt to exploit available concealment and use any trick he can to stay invisible, from preparing dummy positions to masking with echo. You could be lucky and observe him immediately, but this is unlikely.

Realistically, you'll probably start your search by narrowing his possible positions—that is, analyzing the situation enough that you can reduce him to several likely hides or a relatively narrow sector, in either case small enough that you and your teammate and perhaps other observers can intensely and continuously optically surveil these likely locations.

In order to have adequate observation, you'll probably surveil from well to the rear and/or above those under fire. You should avoid crawling forward into his field of fire because you may become pinned down. You easily could find that you must observe from one location, then go to another hide to engage him. Or, as Soviet snipers did during World War II, you could use a small periscope, the size of a musical flute, to safely peer from behind cover to search for the sniper.

As you consider his potential hides, keep in mind the criteria you use for your own hides: it should be inconspicuous; have good observation and fields of fire, concealment, and cover; and have a means for invisible withdrawal. I would pay especially close heed to shadows, inside which a truly professional sniper usually prefers to lurk.

While observing, watch for slight movement, reflection, and dust kicked up by muzzle blast—all the things previously covered under target detection.

There are some tricks for narrowing down his host of likely hides, first among them called the "back azimuth" technique, as shown in the adjacent drawing. Find one of his bullet holes through a porous material such as wood, insert a rifle rod or any dowel, and look back down it to determine the direction the bullet traveled. By observing whether the bullet path was flat, slightly descending, or

The rifle rod technique indicates direction and distance to the shooter.

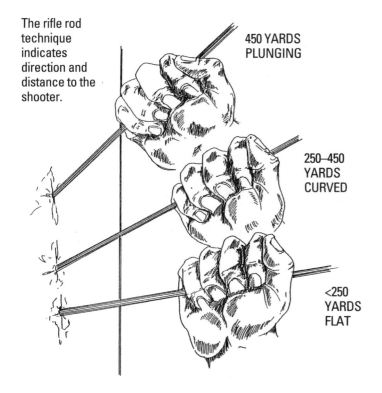

450 YARDS PLUNGING

250–450 YARDS CURVED

<250 YARDS FLAT

The rifle rod technique literally points to the concealed gunman.

plunging, you can also learn how far away the sniper is. I used this technique about 10 years ago while investigating a stateside shooting and it worked perfectly. Since this technique requires that you enter his field of fire, *be careful!* You must conceal yourself or mask yourself with smoke while inserting the rod.

A variation on this back azimuth is called "triangulation," depicted in our next illustration. Back azimuths from *two* separate locations are plotted on a map for a more exact fix, with their intersection marking the sniper's location. Triangulation can also work with the mere *sound* of the sniper's muzzle blast, provided you are relatively certain the sound is true and not an echo. When using either technique, be sure to convert from the magnetic north of your compass to the grid north on your map for plotting the azimuth accurately.

Sound also is involved in our next technique, called "crack-bang." Recall that high-power rifle bullets travel supersonically, creating a sonic boom, which causes a loud (and unforgettable) "crack!" if it passes anywhere near you. A second or two later you'll hear the distant "bang!" from the rifle muzzle. Since the muzzle report sound travels at a measurable speed—1,100 feet, or roughly 300 yards per second—you can approximate his distance by timing the gap between the crack and the bang. Practice this: count to five so that you count "one-two-three-four-five" in one second. This one-second five count starts when you hear the crack and stops when you hear the bang. Each numeral equals that many hundred yards: i.e., "two" is 200 yards, "four" is 400 yards, etc. Don't forget that what you are timing is the *gap* between the crack of the bullet overhead and the sound reaching you from the muzzle. Both these speeds and times are reflected by your count, even if it seems a bit confusing at first. In live-fire exercises, with students safely in a pit listening to bullets pass overhead, we've had a shooter's location correctly estimated to within 25 yards merely by matching crack-bang for range finding with the muzzle report for direction. But the big limitation on this technique, as explained in

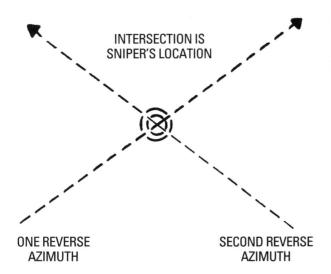

ONE REVERSE
AZIMUTH

SECOND REVERSE
AZIMUTH

Triangulation traces two
back azimuths to find the gunman.

the adjacent sidebar, is its maximum accuracy range of only 500 yards.

Decoy: Sniper vs. Sniper

On the next page we've illustrated some decoys that you can use to provoke or lure the sniper into firing when and where you are best prepared to detect and engage him. No matter which decoy you use, preparations should usually be done outside his vision or in darkness so you're surveilling intensely and ready to fire when the hostile sniper first sees the lure.

The decoy can simply be an apparently valuable piece of equipment "mistakenly" left in the open, such as a radio, which in this case is an unserviceable one. Or position a mocking sign toward enemy lines, but draw the lettering so small that ordinary riflemen cannot read it—only an optically equipped sniper can.

Various kinds of helmets or heads on broomsticks can be effective if the decoy seems to be acting consistent with the situation and conveys "life" through realistic animation. Conveying such life is a special challenge—be clever, original, and even a little off the wall.

Whatever decoy you use, though, do not forget

CRACK-BANG CALCULATIONS

The crack-bang technique works because we can accurately calculate the time difference between a supersonic bullet reaching a certain point and the slower speed-of-sound bang that catches up with it—but only to 500 yards.

So you will appreciate its limitations, we're providing the data below. We've designated 500 yards as the maximum practical distance because beyond that, the time difference becomes too thin for accurate estimation. You cannot slice a second much thinner than 1/5 without using instruments instead of your ear to measure it. Note that the bullet slows down while the "bang" remains constant at the speed of sound, about 1,100 fps.

Bullet Travel Times vs. Sound Travel Times

Distance	Bullet/ Crack	Report/ Bang	Difference
100 yds	.12	.27	.15
200 yds	.25	.54	.29
300 yds	.39	.81	.42
400 yds	.54	1.08	.54
500 yds	.70	1.35	.65

Maximum Practical Distance

600 yds	.881	.60	.72
700 yds	1.07	1.90	.83
800 yds	1.28	2.20	.92
900 yds	1.50	2.40	.90
1000 yds	1.75	2.70	.95

(Bullet data is for .308 168-gr. HPBT Match)

DECOY. Credit your foe with having intelligence and judgment, requiring a real effort to fool him.

A PROVOCATIVE LURE. This target is overwatched by a sniper team awaiting an incensed rifleman's shot. Ingeniously, the lettering is small enough that only an optically equipped sniper can read it.

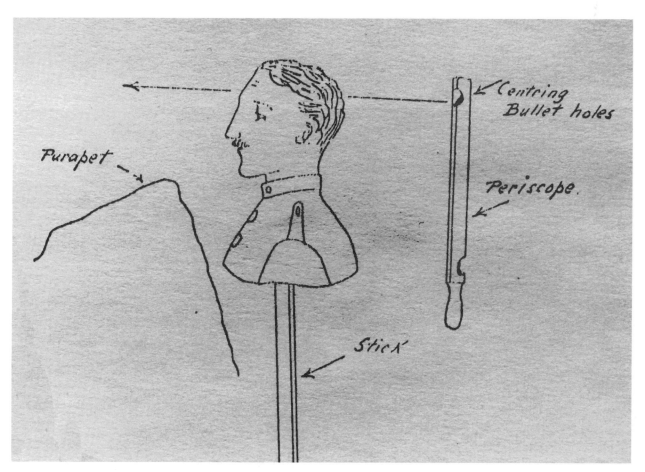

This World War I papier-mâché head not only drew fire but allowed back-azimuthing to the sniper by peering down the resulting bullet path through a periscope. To work, the head must be fixed in place, not held in the air.

that your opponent is a breathing, thinking human being with intelligence and determination just like you. If you were hunting a mere mallard duck, having a brain the weight of a bar pretzel, you'd cleverly camouflage your boat, lure him on with lifelike decoys and a realistic call, and stay motionless until the last possible second. Your sniper opponent deserves no less.

And beware of decoys yourself. You could encounter them during lulls in fighting, when lines have stabilized and there's enough time for such handiwork. If you've recently had several successful engagements in a somewhat limited area, you can expect some kind of response, to include decoys. Because it's so complicated to simulate human movement realistically, however, the enemy probably could operate only one credible decoy at a time. You must ask yourself, "Does it make sense for this activity to be happening here, in this kind of situation?"

Finally, like any con, if a shooting opportunity seems too good to be true, it probably is.

Engaging the Sniper

In an ideal world (or classroom setting), it's fine to preach the one-shot solution for eliminating your opponent. Problem is, this is more feasible in the classroom than in the real world.

I once shot a North Vietnamese soldier in the foot (and never heard the end of it from friends) because it was the only shot I had. He and a comrade were hunkered down behind a mahogany log ripping away at me with AK-47s. Had I hesitated for even an instant, these words would be written in Vietnamese by a middle-aged ex-soldier living in Hanoi.

Remember that a high-powered rifle wound in any part of the body is a serious wound, and even a hit to your foe's leg, shoulder, or foot probably will cause him to cease firing and could even kill him. It's not neat or fast, but it works. To paraphrase Gen. George Patton, "I'd rather fire a shot at a partially exposed sniper now than wait for a totally exposed sniper later." Enough said.

Now here's a tough question: you have only one shot, so which do you engage, the enemy sniper or his observer? Answer: whichever one you're most certain of hitting, because either survivor could grab the rifle and continue firing—but he'd probably flee. Of course, this assumes both team members are qualified snipers, which may not always be the case.

A slight step beyond merely wounding him is subjecting his likely hide to a "recon by fire," as the troops are attempting in the illustration below. Perhaps you've narrowed his positions to three or four; firing five rounds into each hide takes only a few minutes and, unless the hide is in heavy cover, should result in at least a wound. Your spotter intensely surveils each hide while you're firing, watching for the slightest indication of his presence.

If his likely hides are in thick cover, you fire tracer ammo while several other riflemen—perhaps an entire platoon—add fire to the spots thus designated. This reinforced recon by fire retains a degree of selectivity but adds devastating firepower. It's fast, relatively controllable, and simple, probably the most effective countersniper technique available when you're working with conventional infantry.

During a protracted criminal sniping incident, such as the New Orleans Howard Johnson's siege, after lesser techniques have failed, this reinforced recon by fire would seem a reasonable, proportional use of deadly force, provided bystanders have been evacuated and there's not a backstop problem. I would recommend perhaps 10 riflemen with

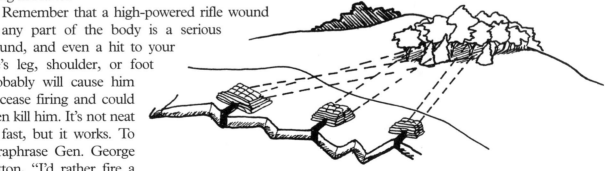

RECON BY FIRE. Limited fire is placed on specific possible sniper positions.

AR-15s or 9mm submachine guns placing fire at several small points designated by your tracer, and each rifleman would fire a predetermined number of rounds. (This assumes the sniper's holding no hostages or you have reason to believe hostages are protected from your fire.)

If your unit is under way, a more passive yet fairly effective self-defense technique is employing smoke, either to blind the sniper or to mask friendly forces. To distinguish these, fire smoke projectiles in front of the sniper's likely hide using grenade launchers or mortars and you've temporarily blinded him. On the other hand, you can throw smoke grenades near you, *wait a few seconds* for smoke to build, then use it to mask your movement.

The SWAT team in our illustration below is masking its rush from cover to cover with smoke grenades and wisely planning its route along straight lines such as walls so it doesn't get disoriented in the smoke. Should any gaps exist, they'll know the number of paces before encountering the next straight line. If there are no straight lines, they could use a compass, but they'd plan to arrive at something that blocks their path so they don't go too far. Their destination should have good cover and conceal them from the sniper.

Don't hesitate to pop several smokes if needed. On the other hand, unless there was some covering fire, I would hesitate to dash through smoke in front of a sniper having a high-capacity weapon such as an AR-15, with which he could fire wildly and maybe be lucky enough to hit my men.

Our next illustration shows a much more violent technique, but it has a long history of effective employment: the "mad minute." During a mad minute, your entire unit opens up with all weapons, upon signal, expending a designated number of rounds. Typically this would mean one or two magazines alongside one or two belts of machine gun ammo. In early 1969, I participated in a company-size mad minute targeted at suspected enemy infiltrators in our wire. It was an incredible experience that instantly reinforced our morale and absolutely scared the hell out of the local water buffaloes. And perhaps this is where a mad minute is especially valuable—in restoring

MASKING WITH SMOKE. Allow smoke to build, and know where you're going.

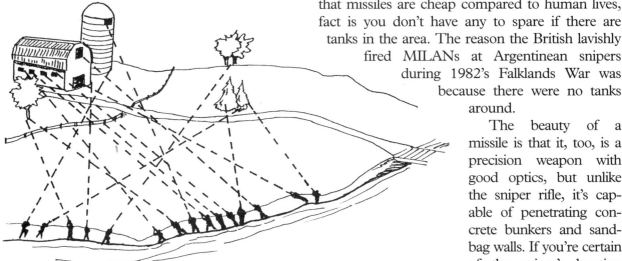

MAD MINUTE. All personnel fire a set number of rounds at any possible sniper location.

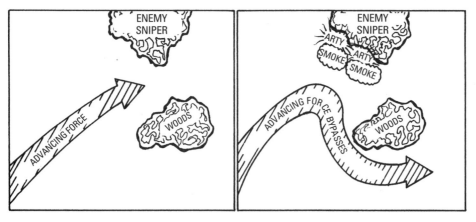

PINNING AND PASSING. Suppress and pin the sniper, then bypass him.

that missiles are cheap compared to human lives, fact is you don't have any to spare if there are tanks in the area. The reason the British lavishly fired MILANs at Argentinean snipers during 1982's Falklands War was because there were no tanks around.

The beauty of a missile is that it, too, is a precision weapon with good optics, but unlike the sniper rifle, it's capable of penetrating concrete bunkers and sandbag walls. If you're certain of the sniper's location and can describe it to the missile gunner correctly, you should be able to scratch one sniper for each missile. Most likely, only an officer, probably a company commander, could authorize firing a missile at a "mere" sniper—and that's the way it should be.

In contrast to fire, though, you can employ maneuver against the sniper. Maneuver can be basic and simple, such as having your entire unit merely bypass the sniper and continue on its way while your team makes a very deliberate stalk against him. To prevent the sniper from moving, you may choose to pin him with indirect fire—mortars or artillery—dropping smoke or high explosive or a combination of these rounds. I've dubbed this technique "pinning and passing." Use this type of maneuver when your unit's not pinned down by the gunman.

If a sizable portion of your unit is pinned and the sniper is inflicting ever more casualties one by one, your only option may be what I call "3-2-1, RUSH!" Within this, there are two options. If he's

confidence and depriving the hidden enemy of the psychological advantage.

It's important to realize that a mad minute is only employed when you have no idea of the enemy's location. If you knew, you'd focus your shooting somewhat and it would become a recon by fire.

When the sniper has inflicted a significant number of casualties or seriously delayed your unit's forward movement, it's time to let loose with the most expensive weapon found in an infantry company—an antitank guided missile. While it's easy to say you wouldn't hesitate to use a missile or nearby, your men actually rush his position. If he's farther away and it would take so long to assault him that he could hit many men, you instead rush to cover. Once they start running, your men will stop for nothing—pausing to help a fallen comrade, while admirable, will only allow the sniper to hit yet another man.

Critical to success in this maneuver is acting simultaneously. A piecemeal dash of only a squad at a time will only give the sniper better shooting opportunities. Launch the rush with an unmistakable loud signal, such as the commander detonating a hand grenade.

All the techniques we've considered can be used separately or in a variety of combinations. Mix them together—be flexible enough to adapt.

But it's important that you realize, as well, that any and all of these techniques could be used against you. Think through how you would react, how you would minimize their effect, how you would "shoot today and run away, so you can shoot another day."

THE OPPOSING SNIPER

With the Soviet Union dissolved and gone, why put any particular focus on the Soviet sniper? Is it worth studying Ivan and his distinctive SVD rifle? It is, and here's why.

Recall that throughout the 1970s and 1980s, Soviet SVD rifles and Communist Bloc instructors appeared in most Mideast countries, perhaps half the nations of Africa, and several in Latin America. While you may not encounter a Soviet sniper today, you could face snipers equipped and trained in Red Army doctrine. By combining this knowledge with what we already know of Western snipers, it should prepare us for countersniper operations against nearly any foe in the world.

Doctrine and Perceptions

Like all things in the Soviet Red Army, the sniper has been employed in sufficient numbers to overcome his individual quality shortcomings. As Stalin used to say, "Quantity has a quality of its own."

This is not to diminish the Red Army sniper's abilities—his achievements during World War II

speak for themselves. But the sniper concept as taught in the former USSR is not the same as that taught at Quantico or Fort Benning; the Soviet sniper's role is not precision fire but long-range *aimed* fire. This implies that he selects and actually engages distinct targets, in contrast to other Soviet infantrymen who merely chatter away on full auto.

Doctrinally, his job is to compensate for his AK-74-wielding comrades who have ballistic shortcomings beyond 400 meters. He's outfitted with a semiauto 10-shot weapon for a relatively high sustained rate of aimed fire—five rounds per minute—and he should score hits, but his do-all and be-all is not one-shot kills.

Despite this lower level of marksmanship expectations, though, he's still intended to be a cut above the rest, mastering, a Russian captain wrote in 1982, "the art of observation and concealment, accurate fire, and skilled tactical actions."

Selection and Training

Simply said, the Soviet sniper is the best shot in his platoon, based on an assessment after he arrives at his unit.

Most likely, prior to his induction the sniper was a member of his neighborhood DOSAAF (Voluntary Society of Assistance to the Army, Aviation, and Navy) shooting club and ideally should have been an accomplished competitive rifleman. The Soviet civilian marksmanship training/competition system, which includes DOSAAF, is first-rate, having produced world and Olympic shooting champions.

In addition to having DOSAAF experience, the sniper candidate is "physically fit and hardy with sharp vision and hearing, a good memory and quick reactions," according to Col. R. Minin, "honored master of sport, honored USSR coach in rifle shooting." Experienced hunters, the colonel says, are also of special interest.

After selection, the sniper candidate attends a division-level sniper school with all the candidate snipers from his regiment. This four-week course is conducted twice a year for each regiment, meaning some six division-level cycles per year, or a very steady training program.

At the start of the school, the novice is matched

with an experienced sniper who can help coach and train him, presuming there are enough course graduates in his unit and they are available for a refresher sniper course. Apparently, all the soldiers are treated as students by the course cadre, and even the qualified snipers must shoot the final record fire as a kind of recertification. This two-man team exists in training only, not in their unit; it's a "training buddy" kind of relationship.

Out of about 200 hours scheduled training, 88 are devoted to marksmanship, 43 to tactical training, political training for 16 hours, engineer tasks for 10 hours, physical training for 11 hours, land navigation for 9 hours, and various tests 12 hours.

Course content is predictable, with the first week spent on marksmanship fundamentals and an introduction to the SVD. The other weeks are logically divided into general blocks on operations in the defense and offense.

What I've found most interesting in studying the Soviet sniper training program is their concept of marksmanship and their primitive attitude about accuracy. This is quite apparent in their practice and qualification courses of fire.

For example, in both practice and record fires, students almost never shoot more than 700 meters, and the sniper typically has 15 to 30 seconds to locate and engage a target—standards considerably easier than their Western counterparts. And to make target detection simpler, the Soviets fire simulators near the daylight targets and highlight night ones with IR light. Furthermore, in order to pass a go/no-go final record fire, the sniper need only score 50 percent hits! (If fired as a team, 70 percent is needed to pass.) There is no induced stress during firing.

But what I find most surprising is the lackadaisical way tracer and ball ammo are fired interchangeably, even in their qualification shooting. This means the Soviet program does not know or place enough emphasis on precision shooting to appreciate the significant trajectory variances between Soviet Type D 185-grain boat-tail ball exiting the muzzle at 2,720 fps and T-46 149-grain flatbase tracer, with a muzzle velocity of 2,850 fps. This underscores my earlier point about the Soviet concept being long-range aimed fire, not precision shooting.

"While Invisible, I See and Destroy"

Before concluding dangerously that the Soviet-era sniper is a pushover, recall Vassili Zaitsev at Stalingrad, who killed more than 400 Germans with his sniper rifle. Or how about the naval infantryman Filipp Yakovlevich, who shot 346 of the Reich's warriors in the Caucasus.

The Germans frequently cursed "Slav cunning," as they called the perfectly executed fieldcraft and tactics of their Russian tormentors. This is not far removed from my belief that the best snipers are "close to the earth"—men who feel best in the outdoors and hunt other men with the natural talent that some men display when throwing a baseball or riding a surfboard. With a sizable segment of its society still on farms or roughing it in a Siberian wilderness every bit as untamed as Alaska, Russia has many men close to the earth, and such men don't need the most advanced sniper weapon in the world to engage their quarry.

German Major Koning's 7.92mm Mauser rifle and superb scope certainly were superior to Zaitsev's Mosin-Nagant, but this didn't determine the outcome of their duel. The Soviet army sniper's motto, dating back to World War II, emphasizes fieldcraft, not marksmanship: "While invisible, I see and destroy."

The Soviet sniper could probably apply this "cunning" more often if he were allowed to operate independently as a two-man team. This is not the way Russian snipers are organized, however, and it is not the way they operate, either.

Organization and Tactics

As illustrated, each motorized rifle, airborne, and air assault platoon in the Soviet army was authorized one SVD-equipped sniper, who's found in the First Squad. It's this same First Squad where the platoon leader is assigned, meaning the sniper purposely has been kept near him for instant directions so the sniper can quickly support platoon operations.

Interestingly, the platoon's shoulder-fired SA-7 antiaircraft missileman, the other platoon-level special weapon, is in another vehicle, meaning that the "wise men" who determine the Red Army's organization think it's more important to have the sniper rather than the SAM close to the platoon's senior leader.

MOTORIZED RIFLE PLATOON

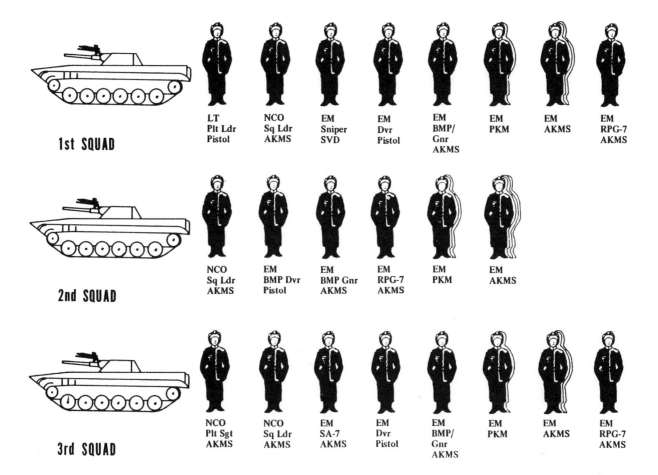

1st SQUAD

| LT
Plt Ldr
Pistol | NCO
Sq Ldr
AKMS | EM
Sniper
SVD | EM
Dvr
Pistol | EM
BMP/
Gnr
AKMS | EM
PKM | EM
AKMS | EM
RPG-7
AKMS |

2nd SQUAD

| NCO
Sq Ldr
AKMS | EM
BMP Dvr
Pistol | EM
BMP Gnr
AKMS | EM
RPG-7
AKMS | EM
PKM | EM
AKMS |

3rd SQUAD

| NCO
Plt Sgt
AKMS | NCO
Sq Ldr
AKMS | EM
SA-7
AKMS | EM
Dvr
Pistol | EM
BMP/
Gnr
AKMS | EM
PKM | EM
AKMS | EM
RPG-7
AKMS |

During a platoon attack, with its three BMPs or BTR-60s or BMDs fanning out roughly abreast, the First Squad vehicle—which contains the sniper—will not lead the "V" formation but will hang back a bit. The idea is to "test the waters" with the Second Squad's vehicle but be close enough to provide supporting fire when it takes fire.

Generally, during offensive operations the sniper supports his comrades by engaging targets that generate such fire that the advance could be hindered or halted. The platoon leader's goal, transmitted to his nearby sniper, is to maintain the momentum of the attack. Unsurprisingly, the sniper's targets may be crew-served weapons, leaders, forward observers, and enemy snipers.

That the Soviets truly intend to have their snipers fire in the midst of armored attacks is verified by their shooting exercises, several of which include firing from the deck of a halted vehicle or shooting over the top while the BMP or BMD is under way or pausing for quick halts. It's possible the Chinese or North Koreans could train similarly, but there's no Western army I know of that does so. And again, this firing on the move is contrary to precision shooting.

The sniper will dismount his vehicle beside his fellow soldiers but undoubtedly will hang back a bit to shoot over them in support. To make his hasty hides more difficult to detect, he may carry a sort of camouflage fan made of burlap and bent wire, as we've illustrated on page 472.

When it comes to defensive operations, the Soviet sniper is more akin to his foreign counterpart in that he takes considerable effort to build a well-camouflaged hide with good fields of fire. He builds a thick earthen berm to his front and fires

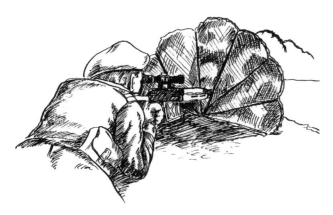

CAMOUFLAGE SCREEN. Fashioned from wire and burlap, it folds up like a fan for compact carry.

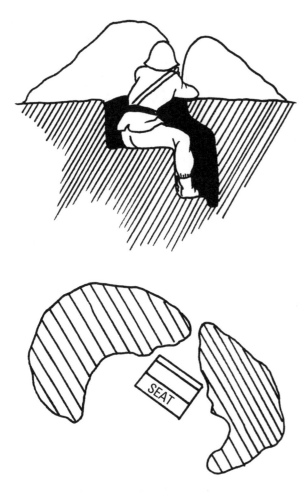

SOVIET SNIPER'S POSITION. Note the parapet protecting his front while he fires to the oblique.

obliquely, as shown, making it more difficult to detect and engage him.

But unlike Western snipers, the Soviet sniper seems to spend his entire time with his unit right in its position. He is not a member of a sniper team, lacking a trained spotter for independent operations. It seems that his superiors are too rigid to allow the kind of snoop-and-poop-and-shoot missions frequently done by Western snipers.

This rigidity, I should warn, only applies in peacetime. Never forget that necessity dictates in war and that all doctrine and tactics are subject to change once the bullets start flying. During World War II, Soviet snipers were organized into two-man teams and independent platoons; in Afghanistan, mujahideen riflemen became such a bloody menace that Soviet airborne units issued triple the normal number of SVD rifles, and some companies created special antisniper squads of three to five SVD riflemen.

Other Sniper Threats

Where two-man spotter-sniper teams most likely exist in Russian forces would be in Spetsnaz elements, but they'd be employed primarily on special assassinations and deep-penetration raids. Sniper teams also likely exist in GRU Special Operations units, as well as within Razvedchiki (scout) units.

Beyond Russia and among the incorrigible Communist regimes, detailed information is scant. North Korea remains a distinct threat and maintains many snipers in the Light Infantry Brigades and Special Purpose Units of the VIII Special Corps. Ambush and infiltration is their most basic doctrine.

North Korea has a serious marksmanship training program, which I personally witnessed during a very rare visit to that closed land in 1979. At the Children's Palace in Pyongyang, I saw photos of mere tots firing .22 bolt guns at—you guessed it— American "bogeymen," and they were shooting surprisingly well. One incontrovertible indicator of the quality of their marksmanship is that the Olympic Prone Free Rifle Shooting record is held by Ho Jun Li of North Korea.

The Chinese bullpup version of the SVD, designated the Type 88 sniper rifle.

According to unclassified references, the North Korean army continues to employ the ancient Mosin-Nagant rifle for sniping, which I find remarkable. Pyongyang manufactures its own military hardware, to include AKs, machine guns, and even Scud missiles; it's well capable of producing moderate-quality sniper rifles such as the SVD or a Mauser variation. Or it could go to its immediate northern neighbor, China, and obtain either.

Indeed, China surprised many analysts in 1985 when it began manufacturing the SVD as its Type 85 sniper rifle, despite its ideological fallout with the USSR. And in 1990, the Chinese began exporting Mauser-action bolt guns—and having seen one, I'm favorably impressed at the quality of machining, fit, and finish. There can be no doubt that Beijing could produce quality bolt-action sniper rifles whenever desired.

On the other hand, I've found Chinese ammo to be among the worst I've ever fired. Their 9mm ball is atrocious, and the 7.62x39mm is only a bit better. If this is what they're sending overseas to yield badly needed foreign currency, could they produce true match-grade sniper rifle ammo? I don't think so. (Some alleged Chinese match recently arrived in the United States, but I doubt that it measures up to our standards.)

Cuba's armed forces gained considerable experience in Africa during the 1970s and 1980s fighting in Ethiopia and Angola. While Cuban units certainly have SVDs, it should also be recalled that Fidel Castro has a reputation for buying small arms that personally interest him—and it must be remembered that during his own guerrilla

days in the Sierra Madre Mountains, Castro's favorite weapon was a scoped, bolt-action rifle; I think it was a Winchester M70 in .30-06.

Therefore, it's possible some Cuban snipers use contemporary bolt guns—and this is almost a certainty when it comes to sabotage and terrorist units affiliated with the Cuban Communist Party's Americas Department, which would employ foreign weapons to enhance deniability. The Cuban DGI intelligence service, working in tandem with the Americas Department, similarly provides deniable foreign weapons to foreign terrorists, and it's likely these would include sniper weapons.

When it comes to terrorist snipers, topping our list for sophistication and quality gear would be the Irish Republican Army's gunmen. Many British soldiers—most likely several dozens—have been shot by IRA snipers in Belfast and Londonderry or down south along the rural borderlands. Their tactics are simple: elaborate preliminary planning, a good hide, excellent operational security, then a quick escape and concealment of the weapon.

While IRA snipers occasionally may use hunting rifles, most often they snipe with scopes atop American AR-15s and purloined British 7.62mm NATO assault rifles. Even at several blocks, either of these certainly will do the job.

Peru's Sendero Luminosa ("Shining Path") guerrillas also use snipers in hit-and-run attacks, but they make up for their lack of sophistication and mediocre weapons with a "native cunning" reminiscent of Russia's World War II snipers. Sendero's snipers usually support a larger operation, such as a raid or ambush, although they could be used in an assassination targeted against a specific person. They don't seem to run free-roaming, snoop-shoot-scoot kinds of sniper missions.

Lebanon's various Shiite groups employ snipers in Beirut, but they have appeared to be sprayers of bullets, not precision riflemen.

The PLO has sent some of its fighters to Soviet, Eastern European, and friendly Arab military schools, including sniper courses. While the Israelis captured some SVDs and Romanian FRKs during their 1982 Lebanon invasion, I am unaware of any PLO soldiers operating explicitly as snipers, either against the Israelis or rival revolutionaries.

Curiously, Islamic countries, most notably Iraq and Iran, have not placed much importance on sniping, and there was not much about sniping reported during their eight-year war, which, during its stalemated, trench-warfare phase, should have been an ideal sniper setting. Nor was there much Iraqi sniping activity reported during the Persian Gulf War.

This is curious, since the Mideast's desert tribesmen have a tradition of long-range shooting that's not apparent today. Perhaps it's an indicator that, like so much of the world, these people, too, are becoming so urbanized that they've forgotten the skills they had when they were "close to the earth."

THE SVD SNIPING SYSTEM

The SVD was the first military rifle ever designed from scratch as a sniper weapon. Introduced in 1967, the SVD was the brainchild of a

The SVD rifle and its variants have been manufactured in the hundreds of thousands and can be found throughout the world.

SVD BASIC DATA

Cartridge: Russian 7.62x54mm Rimmed
Weight: 9.5 lbs. (4.31 kg)
Overall Length: 48.2 inches (122.5 cm)
Barrel Length: 24 inches (62 cm)
Rifling: 4 grooves, 1:10 rt-hand twist
Capacity: 10 rounds, detachable magazine
Max Rate of Fire: 30 RPM
Aimed Rate of Fire: 3–5 RPM
Scope Type: PSO-1 with IR detection
   capability
Scope Data: 24mm objective lens,
   4x, 6-degree field of view
Exit Pupil Measurement: 6
Compatible Passive Night Scopes:
   • NSP-3: 2.7x, 7-degree field of view,
      range of approx. 300 yards
   • PGN-1: 3.4x, 5.7-degree field of
      view, range of 400–500 yards

---

sporting rifle designer, Yevgeniy Dragunov, and carries his name in its official nomenclature, "Snayperskaya Vintovka Dragunova" (Dragunov Sniper Rifle).

Mr. Dragunov crafted the SVD along the lines of a sporting rifle, yielding a graceful but deadly appearance that added to its mystique. Using molded fiberglass in its hollowed, one-piece butt and pistol grip, this was the first Russian weapon to employ such high-tech materials now commonly found in AKs and PK machine guns.

While externally resembling the AK family of weapons, the SVD uses a markedly different action. Since its cartridge is much longer than AK rounds, Dragunov determined that a long-stroke bolt would travel so far during recoil that its rearward shifting momentum would push the shooter completely off target. To alleviate this, he created a short-stroke bolt akin to American M1 and M14 rifles, which use an intervening piston and carrier to reduce bolt travel. The result was a smoother, shorter recoil for improved shooting, but as a result, few parts were interchangeable with AK rifles and PK machine guns.

The former East German regime produced the SVD under license, while a Chinese version, the Type 85, appeared seven years ago. Although the Romanian FPK is cosmetically similar, it's not a true SVD, only a modified RPK machine gun with doubtful accuracy.

The SVD is issued with four magazines and a special pouch for carrying the PSO-1 scope while detached, an extra scope battery and reticle bulb, and a cleaning kit. By the book, a Soviet sniper carried 140 rounds of ammo as his basic combat load.

Shooting the SVD

Although I've seen magazine articles claiming that the SVD "easily" achieves one-shot kills at 1,000 yards, this merely proves you shouldn't believe everything you read in gun magazines.

After personally test-firing this rifle, I found the Dragunov adequate to hit man-sized targets through about 600 yards, with accuracy comparable to my old '03A3 Springfield, but nowhere near as deadly as today's specially tuned Western sniper rifles. I received the same assessment from Special Ops friends.

Firing good quality Norma 180-grain boat-tail, our SVD produced about 2 MOA accuracy and became tough to keep on target beyond 500 yards. According to U.S. Army data published by *Jane's*, the SVD has a 90 percent chance of hitting its target at 300 yards, 80 percent at 500, 60 percent at 700, and only 50 percent at 800. By 1,000 yards, the SVD hits a silhouette only 20 percent of the time.

All those who fired our SVD were impressed by its light weight and surprisingly easy handling for so long a rifle. One peculiarity to the SVD is its gas regulator, normally kept at position "1" but turned to "2" should the rifle begin cycling sluggishly. This only means that, despite carbon buildup at the gasport, the weapon can keep firing. The best solution, of course, is to keep it clean.

Accurizing an SVD?

I found the Dragunov trigger better than that of any AK I'd fired and similar to a good M1 Garand—smooth in takeup, crisp at release, with about a 4-pound trigger pull. The Dragunov trigger isn't adjustable for weight or length of

The SVD rifle, fired here by an Eastern European sniper, requires a higher magnification scope than the PSO-1 to yield greatest effectiveness.

pull, and it uses a twisted coil spring, which cannot be tuned.

Other SVD features work against accurizing, the most notable being its thin barrel, which, due to the way it's attached, cannot be free-floated easily and disrupts vibrations during firing. There's no provision for attaching a bipod, and I can almost see a Soviet soldier clipping an RPK machine gun bipod near the muzzle in the misbelief it will improve his shooting.

Compared to Western-tuned assault rifles like H&K's PSG1, Springfield Armory's M1A, and D&L Sports' AR-15s, the Dragunov distinctly takes a backseat. Though manufactured to higher standards than AKs, the SVD's performance is well below that of accurized rifles produced decades after it was designed.

The PSO-1 Rifle Scope

Ever since its adoption, the SVD has been topped with the PSO-1 rifle scope, with copies made in East Germany, China, and Romania, while the Yugoslavians make a derivative scope for their M76 sniper rifle.

The PSO-1 has a relatively narrow (6 degree) field of view, and its 24mm objective lens is substantially narrower than Western sniperscopes. But with only 4x magnification, it still generates an exit pupil of six.

The PSO-1's Bullet Drop Compensator uses the center inverted V as its aiming point; to shoot at 1,100, 1,000, and 1,300-meter targets, the BDC is set at 1,000 and the respective Vs underneath it are employed for higher holds, as shown in the reticle illustration at right. But since it's adjustable only in 100-meter increments, even slight BDC calibration error results in subtle inaccuracies at all distances.

The scope's rangefinder is simple and effective, just a curved scale representing a height of 1.7 meters, or 5 feet 6 inches, which its designers considered an average man's height. Hold this scale so it brackets your target, as shown on page 477, and it

yields a reading from 200 through 1,000 meters. Beyond about 700 meters, though, that scale becomes so thin that its accuracy is doubtful.

One novel PSO-1 feature is its battery-powered reticle illuminator, which makes the crosshair more visible in low-light shooting situations.

Another low-light feature is its special infrared filter, which can detect or use IR light for night shooting. However, IR illumination is obsolete in the West because it compromises the IR source's location; further, friends who've used the SVD extensively tell me this IR filter almost never works.

The passive night scope normally associated with the SVD is the NSP-3, a device comparable to first-generation Starlight scopes and having a range of about 250 meters. I obtained a video of Russian Spetsnaz training, recorded in December 1990, in which a Dragunov was shown with a second-generation PGN-1 night scope. The PGN has a 3.4 magnification and a respectable range of

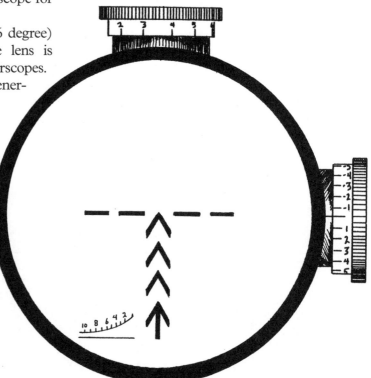

The PSO-1 reticle contains a rangefinder and elevation "hold" arrows. The center arrow works with the BDC to 1,000 meters, after which the shooter uses arrow tips below to aim 1,100, 1,200, and 1,300 meters.

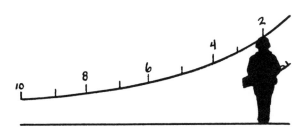

PSO-1 range finder tells your range to a 5'6" man by placing the scale over his standing figure. Numerals are hundreds of meters.

400 to 500 meters, putting it on a par with the American AN/PVS-4.

Like the SVD rifle it tops, the PSO-1 scope is an adequate but not fabulous device. The glass is of moderate quality, and I saw no tinted reflection from the objective lens—implying there is none or very minimal lens coating. With a magnification of just 4x, it becomes difficult to see a man beyond about 600 yards.

For overall workmanship and design, I'd rate the PSO-1 as comparable to the Korean War-era U.S. M84 scope, but it is so far below that of modern Western rifle scopes that any comparison becomes ridiculous.

The SVD's 7.62x54mm Rimmed Round

The Russian 7.62x54mm is the only rimmed military cartridge now in use worldwide. Developed in 1891, it's a product of the same era that produced two ballistically similar venerable rounds, the .303 British Enfield and U.S. .30-06 Springfield.

Originally chambered for the Model 1891 Mosin-Nagant, this 54mm-long round is *not* interchangeable with the AK's 7.62mm cartridge, which is only 39 millimeters in length. Today's 7.62x54mm primarily serves as the PK machine gun round, and most cartridge styles are loaded for this weapon, not the SVD.

While all these rounds can be fired in the sniper rifle (see box, next page), only the boat-tail ("streamlined") bullets provide suitable accuracy, and the silver- or white-tipped 149-grain LPS round provides the best performance, I was told by a Special Ops expert.

The Soviets did not supply snipers with match-grade ammo for the SVD, which partially explains its mediocre performance, although it's well within Russian capabilities to produce match rounds. After the 1976 Winter Olympics, I was able to examine some special Soviet biathlon ammo that a U.S. competitor brought back, which reflected the highest state-of-the-art technology.

Today, a variety of match-grade 7.62x54R ammo is available for the SVD, the SV-98, and their predecessor, the Mosin-Nagant rifle. Silver-tipped Russian and Czech 147-grain loads perform similarly and were intended for the SVD. The Czech ammo, packed in 20-round pastel green boxes—

Match loads in 7.62x54R include (L-R) Sellier & Bellot 174-grain; Russian Wolf 200-grain; Russian competition load in 200 grain; and Russian and Czech silver-tipped loads of 147 grain. Only the S&B uses a BTHP bullet.

7.62MMx54 RIMMED CARTRIDGE, 185-GR. BT BULLET
WIND DRIFT IN 90-DEGREE CROSSWIND
(Inches at Hundreds of Yards)

	100	200	300	400	500	600	1000
5 mph	.31	1.27	2.96	5.44	8.29	13.09	41.91
10 mph	.61	2.55	5.91	11.07	17.57	26.19	86.83
15 mph	.92	3.82	8.88	16.31	25.88	39.29	125.75
20 mph	1.23	5.12	11.84	21.79	35.14	52.39	167.66

This data may slightly exaggerate SVD performance.
It was generated by adjusting established Norma loads and Sierra tables.

ADJUSTED 7.62x54MM BALLISTIC INFORMATION

Distance (yds)	Muzzle	100	200	300	400	500	600	1000
Velocity (fps)	2700	2537	2380	2228	2082	1942	1808	1348
Energy (ft-lbs.)	2994	2595	2272	1991	1854	1518	1344	747
Drop (inches)	0.0	-2.3	-10.3	-23.9	-44.7	-73.6	-111.3	-387.3
Bullet Path (inches)	-1.5	+2.0	zero	-8.0	-23.1	-46.2	-78.2	-331.4

RUSSIAN 7.62x54MM RIMMED ROUNDS CURRENTLY IN PRODUCTION

Round Type	Tip Marking	Style	Wt.	Muzz. Vel.
Type D Heavy Ball	Yellow	Boat-tail	185-gr.	2720 fps
Type LPS Light Ball *	White/Silver	Boat-tail	147-gr.	2842 fps
Type T-46 Tracer	Green	Standard	149-gr.	2842 fps
Type B-32 API	Black & Red	Boat-tail	155-gr.	2842 fps
Type BS-40 API	Black & Red	Standard	188-gr.	2636 fps
Type BZT API-T	Purple & Red	Standard	142-gr.	2875 fps

* The LPS is the best-performing round for the SVD rifle.

unmarked but for a wide silver stripe—is mildly corrosive due to the caustic mixture in its primer. Packaged in a bright yellow and blue box is Russian "Extra" competition-grade ammo, which uses a 200-grain ball bullet and a brass case. A similar commercial 200-grain load is distributed by Wolf Ammunition. Lapua of Finland produces true match-grade ammo in this caliber, as does the Czech company Sellier & Bellot, with both loads employing Sierra-style HPBT bullets.

Combining our assessment of rifle, scope, and ammunition, we can conclude that the SVD is as good as the man shooting it out to about 600 yards and adequately fulfills the role for which it was designed—to place aimed fire at man-sized point targets beyond the range of AKMs and AK-74s. The SVD does this job well, and in the hands of a superior marksman—particularly one employing good fieldcraft and tactics—it is a deadly sniper rifle.

RUSSIA'S NEW SNIPER RIFLE

As many sniping authorities—including me—

Russia's SV-98 bolt action replaces the SVD rifle. Though it resembles the AW, it is of entirely different design. (Photo credit: Valery Shilin Guns Club)

forecast more than a decade ago, Russia finally replaced its SVD semiauto sniper rifle with a modern design bolt action, capable of accuracy on a par with Western sniper rifles. Though Russia no longer is an avowed enemy of the West, its sniper rifles have such a long record of ending up in the hands of actual and potential enemies that it's worth examining in a countersniper context.

The Russian SV-98 suspiciously resembles the Accuracy International AW in both stock profile and its action's squared-off shape, but it differs in too many ways to conclude that it's a reverse-engineered copy of that fine weapon. Like the AW, the SV-98

The SV-98's porro-prism scope increases magnification to 7x, but it's still not as powerful as most Western sniper scopes. (Photo credit: Valery Shilin Guns Club)

This Czech police sniper fires a modern, high-quality copy of the 1891 Mosin-Nagant at the 1998 European sniping championships. Note the adjustable cheekpiece.

has a 10-round, detachable magazine that fits flush with the stock, and it employs a through-the-stock pistol grip, while its bipod fits to the stock almost identically to the AW.

Yet in the most fundamental way, it's different: instead of a clamshell stock that attaches to a full-length aluminum skeleton, the SV-98 employs a fairly conventional stock and action. The action is bedded inside its laminated wood stock with a thermal bedding technique that's apparently unique to this rifle and the earlier Russian target rifle from which it evolved, the Record-CISM.

Like the Record-CISM, the SV-98 is capable of sub-MOA, sniper-grade accuracy when using match-quality ammunition, of which a variety is now available. Apparently there's also a new military load for the SV-98—known as 7N14—that incorporates a 152-grain boat-tail bullet.

Unfortunately, the SV-98 is mated to the PKS-07 scope, a 7x optic that just cannot compare with 10x or larger magnification for long-range engagements or precision shot placement at closer ranges. Interestingly, the PKS-07 scope is of step-down, porro-prism design, a kind not seen on sniper rifles since the American Warner-Swasey musket sight in World War I—unless you consider the AN/PVS-10 a porro-prism scope.

Of equal interest with this weapon is what it portends for Russian military sniper employment. The SV-98 signals a shifted emphasis on shot placement and away from volume of fire. In order to place shots accurately, the sniper will need a spotter to detect targets at longer distances and to adjust the sniper's fire. Essentially, I think Russian snipers will go back to their World War II tactical roots and operate more like Vassili Zaitsev—and more like today's Western snipers.

MOSIN-NAGANT BASIC DATA

Cartridge: Russian 7.62x54mm Rimmed

Weight: 11.3 lbs. (5.1 kg)

Overall Length: 48 inches (122 cm)

Barrel Length: 29 inches (72.6 cm)

Rifling: 4 grooves, 1:10 rt-hand twist

Capacity: 5 rounds, fixed magazine

Max Rate of Fire: 10 rpm

Aimed Rate of Fire: 3–5 rpm

Scope Types: 3.5x PU or 4x PE

Reticle Type: Adjustable post

Obsolete but with a distinguished record, the Soviet 1891-30 Mosin-Nagant sniper rifle with 3.5x PU scope.

THE MOSIN-NAGANT SNIPER RIFLE

Although now obsolete, the Mosin-Nagant Model 1891-30 sniper rifle may yet be encountered on Third World battlefields. This World War II Soviet rifle was the North Vietnamese Army's primary sniper weapon during the Vietnam War.

Distinguished by its lengthy barrel and turned-down bolt, the Mosin-Nagant fires the same 7.62x54mm rimmed cartridge as the SVD sniper rifle, making it ballistically comparable to the American .30-06.

High-quality versions of the Mosin-Nagant were produced in Finland and the Czech Republic, which I've personally examined and found to be quite nicely made, with a smooth action and excellent fitting of wood to metal. The triggers, too, are honed and as good as those on the best Mauser sniper rifles. These high-grade Mosin-Nagants are still in service in the hands of Eastern European SWAT officers.

The military model Mosin-Nagant is outfitted with a 3.5x PU or 4x PE scope, both of which use an adjustable centerpost instead of crosshairs and are claimed to be effective out to 800 meters—which seems a bit of an exaggeration. I've been told these reticles are adjustable in 1 MOA increments to more than 1,000 meters.

I once examined a Mosin-Nagant and 4x PE scope that had been taken off a dead North Vietnamese by U.S. 173rd Airborne Brigade troopers. Its absolutely perfect condition said a lot about the enemy sniper's meticulous maintenance, and I was surprised by the action's buttery smoothness. This was no off-the-rack rifle but a tuned weapon almost akin to an American match-grade firearm, but I didn't have a chance to test-fire it.

While not as sophisticated as current Western sniper rifles, the Mosin-Nagant still sent many thousands of Germans to their graves in World War II. And thanks to generous Soviet arms aid to regimes and rebels throughout the Third World, it may still be encountered even in the 21st century.

CHAPTER 20

COUNTERSNIPING IN IRAQ

Many countersniping experiences and lessons have emerged from Iraq, where U.S. and coalition forces are fighting a resourceful, dedicated sniper adversary. In addition to gleaning experiences from Iraq veterans, we've incorporated into this chapter dozens of U.S. military reports, media articles, and even Iraqi insurgent accounts involving 16 terrorist sniper engagements against U.S., British, and Polish forces.

NOT A CAREFULLY AIMED SHOT. This masked Iraqi terrorist sniper fires at U.S. forces and appears about to flee.

A PROFILE: THE IRAQI SNIPER

Before analyzing the Iraqi insurgent sniper's other attributes, keep in mind that he's a terrorist first, who's capable of any kind of act to further his cause without regard to law or ethics or what a Westerner would consider morality. An inseparable seam connects him to his comrades who bomb public places and kill helpless hostages with little remorse. Every day he violates the Laws of Land Warfare by wearing civilian clothes, assassinating civilians, continuing to shoot incapacitated soldiers and marines, escaping sniping incidents in ambulances, purposely firing behind a human shield of women and children, and operating from mosques. Expect no quarter from him and do not be surprised by his outrages.

Explaining his motivation, one Iraqi sniper told the *London Sunday Times*, "When I snipe at my target and watch him drop, I feel elated—dizzy with ecstasy. I fall on the ground, shouting to God, calling *Allah akbar*, for God is indeed great. When their snipers kill one of us, we go to heaven as martyrs. But when we kill them they go to hell."

Based on the threat they pose, I've categorized Iraq's insurgent snipers into three classes: the "potshot sniper," the "trained marksman," and the "one shot-one kill"sniper.

The potshot sniper is a relatively untrained civilian who has acquired a scoped rifle. His zealotry exceeds his ability, although he's reasonably deadly at 100 to 200 yards—about two city blocks—close enough that he doesn't need to master range estimation, wind compensation, etc., to hit targets. Reminiscent of the Hitler Youth snipers who fought in the closing days of World War II, he got started with as little as a couple hours of instruction. Someone else may even have zeroed his rifle for him, but all he needs to know is how to hold the crosshairs on his target. Most potshot snipers will be captured or killed before they learn enough to be called snipers, although experience alone eventually will elevate some to that level. Very roughly, I'd estimate this category constitutes half the snipers in Iraq.

Above him is the trained marksman, probably a former military or sport shooter who knows how to fire a rifle competently, but he's not sniper-trained and lacks sniper experience. He can hit dinner-plate-sized targets accurately at 200 to 400 yards, or smaller and partially exposed targets at closer ranges. If he absorbs his experiences, he can be as deadly as a school-trained sniper in a few months. The trained marksman comprises perhaps 40 to 45 percent of insurgent sniper ranks.

The smallest category is that of the school-trained, fully qualified, one shot-one kill sniper, or those with enough experience from Chechnya or elsewhere that they've previously qualified on the job. They represent 5 or at the most 10 percent of enemy snipers. One of Iraq's more accomplished snipers—allegedly with 23 kills—told a British interviewer that he learned his skills via the Internet and by playing videogames—which I don't

A rooftop Iraqi sniper takes aim at distant U.S. forces. After firing, he'll flee, conceal his rifle, and blend into the populace.

believe for a second. Do you just suppose that he attended a sniper course, perhaps outside Iraq, which he would never have admitted to a foreign journalist?

All these snipers watch U.S. forces and study their tactics and techniques. They understand what a Quick Reaction Force is and how it operates and have learned to fire and flee before a QRF can contain them for a cordon and search. Repeatedly, I found Iraqi insurgent media boasting that American cordons were not in place fast enough to prevent a sniper's escape.

ARMAMENT AND EQUIPMENT

Iraq's snipers have a plentiful supply of Soviet SVD sniper rifles or the Iraqi-built version, the al Kadesih rifle. Despite being captured by the thousands in 2003, Saddam Hussein's internal security and special operations units earlier had cached stockpiles of such rifles, enough to sustain the current level of sniping. An indicator of the al Kadesih's prestigious image is that Saddam had hundreds—possibly thousands—of them gold-plated for

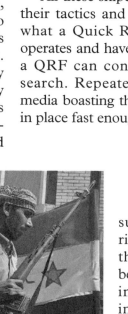

A uniformed Iraqi Army sniper with the al Kadesih version of the SVD sniper rifle.

THE AFGHAN SNIPER

Though allied forces have encountered a few snipers in Afghanistan, the enemy sniper effort there has not been anywhere near the scale of Iraq. Partially I think this is explained by terrain and typical engagement distances.

The fight in Afghanistan is largely in mountainous country, away from urban areas and their shorter engagement distances. The Afghan Taliban, when they choose to fight, normally prefer to engage at 1,000 or more yards with mortars and heavy machine guns, rather than AKs or rifles. As well, I think culturally the Taliban—whose members boast of their ignorance and rejection of the modern world—may lack the education, sophistication and inclination to learn the ballistics and optical adjustments required for long-range rifle shooting.

In Afghanistan, a Northern Alliance sniper scans the horizon for targets.

This isn't to say that their ideological cousins, the al Qaeda terrorists, have no use for sniping. It has been documented that al Qaeda formally instructed snipers, confirmed by Nizar Trabelsi, a detainee at Guantanamo Bay's Camp X-Ray who told FBI agents he'd personally observed three-man teams in training. However, these teams were recruited and trained for attacks overseas, particularly inside the United States. Their graduation exercise simulated assassinating a U.S. Senator on a golf course. By early 2002, al Qaeda and its sniper teams had abandoned Afghanistan, leaving the Taliban behind to continue the fight against the Americans.

In February 2005, the FBI apprehended Mohammed Kamal Elzahabi, a Lebanese citizen, in Minneapolis, Minnesota, who admitted he'd been a sniper in Chechnya and had been an instructor at al Qaeda's Khalden sniper training course in Afghanistan. Where his graduates are today is anyone's guess.

---

presentations. These gold rifles have become the war's most sought after GI souvenir.

Depending on the source, the al Kadesih is comparably accurate—or slightly less accurate—than its Russian SVD cousin, probably in the realm of 2 MOA. I cannot say for certain because I've not test-fired the al Kadesih. But clearly, this rifle in many ways is identical to the SVD, its most distinctive difference being the absence of a cheekrest. Some magazines have a palm tree stamped on them and are not interchangeable with the SVD. I've not come upon a single incident of an Iraqi sniper using a bolt-action rifle, although one boasted to a journalist that he was purchasing a quality European bolt-action rifle.

Still in their protective wraps, these captured Iraqi al Kadesih sniper rifles will never reach a "muj's" hands.

An American armorer deactivates a gold-plated al Kadesih sniper rifle so it can legally be brought home as a war trophy.

The Iraqi sniper's maximum effective range is limited by the capability of his optics. The obsolescent Soviet-style PSO-1 scope found on most Iraqi sniper rifles has a fixed 4x magnification, keeping his well-aimed shots to 400 yards or less. Beyond that range, a talented marksman can hit a human torso, but he won't be making precision shots.

Further, because he lacks a spotter and spotting scope, the Iraqi sniper cannot effectively adjust his fire like a Western sniper. I've not come upon a single Iraqi sniper engagement that involved a night weapon sight,

so I doubt that they have them—however, there have been shots fired in well-illuminated areas after dark.

As a rule, the Iraqi sniper does not have a radio, but sometimes he communicates via a cell phone—which, if you think about it, is much less incriminating if he's stopped by security forces. Likewise, he carries no gear beyond his rifle and perhaps one spare magazine, both to remain flexibly mobile and to keep it simple to discard incriminating evidence when he must blend back into the population.

While on an operation he often wears a black balaclava, a practice perhaps influenced by similarly attired Palestinian terrorists. Partially this ski mask generates a mystique, but more practically it also conceals his identity so he cannot be identified by Iraqi bystanders. Some Iraqi snipers further hide their identities behind a nom de guerre or code name.

THE CHECHEN INFLUENCE

While some Chechen fighters have infiltrated Iraq, in the area of sniping their influence has exceeded their numbers. During much of the past decade, Islamic radicals have fought Russian forces in the breakaway Chechnya Republic and learned a great deal about urban warfare, especially during battles in the country's capital, Grozny. Their combat achievements have been significant, including

Unconcerned about the civilians that surround him, a Palestinian masked sniper fires at Israeli troops, much as some Iraqi snipers have done.

THE EMERGING .50-CALIBER THREAT

Despite a U.S. protest, in 2005 the Austrian Interior Ministry issued an export license to famed gun maker Steyr to sell 800 .50-caliber sniper rifles to Iran. These high-quality, single-shot, bolt-action Model 50 HS rifles have an effective range of 2,500 meters, comparable to quality American .50-caliber bolt guns.

In 2005, Iran received some 800 high-quality Steyr 50 HS rifles, despite the country's history of arming terrorist groups.

"We asked the Iranians to give us a certificate stating that the end user of the weapons would be the Iranian police," an Austrian government spokesman explained, adding that the Iranians "would use it to protect the country's borders and to combat drug trafficking." That's not exactly how Iranian Defense Minister Ali Shamkhani saw it, telling reporters, "Now our snipers can target the enemy in their armored personnel carriers and concrete bunkers."

Iran, which has long supported such major terrorist organizations as Hezbollah and recently was caught smuggling an entire shipload of weapons to terrorists, insisted that the .50-caliber rifles were not intended for use in Iraq, despite its lengthy border with the neighboring country.

Chechen influence is suggested by this Iraqi terrorist video, which shows an SVD-armed sniper teamed up with RPG and AKs as a fighting group.

the January 2000 sniper killing of Maj. Gen. Mikhail Malofeyev, the commander of Russian forces in northern Chechnya.

Chechen snipers affiliated with al Qaeda have become respected as subject experts and readily share their experiences, and perhaps even conduct schools for allied combatants such as the Iraqi insurgents.

It was the Chechens who first organized hunter-killer teams ("fighting groups") by combining snipers with RPG rocketeers and machine gunners for roving hit-and-run attacks—a tactic mimicked by Iraq's insurgents and quite likely inspired or instructed by Chechen veterans. Some Iraqi terrorist videos have featured an SVD-armed sniper alongside insurgents with RPGs and AKs—similar to a Chechen hunter-killer team—and such squads have been encountered in Iraq's more rebellious neighborhoods.

Although not seen in Iraq, five-man teams—with one sniper and four AK- or machine gun-armed gunmen—have been fielded by the rebels in Chechnya's rural areas. The sniper would stalk forward perhaps 500 meters—or lie in ambush that far forward—and fire one well-aimed shot. Hearing this, his comrades would open fire to divert attention and provide

A Russian sniper in Chechnya, alert for possible Chechen gunmen.

covering fire for the sniper to escape from responding Russian forces.

Given their expertise, it's possible that some of Iraq's best insurgent snipers—the one-shot, one-kill types—have been trained or advised by Chechens. Or some may actually be Chechens.

SNIPER AMMUNITION

The availability of quality ammunition could be a limiting factor for insurgent snipers. The most abundant 7.62x54R ammo is low-grade ball rounds intended for firing in PK machine guns, which lack consistency and, thus, accuracy.

However, a sniper has such a low expenditure rate that it doesn't require much ammunition to keep him supplied. An Iraqi urban sniper could operate for an entire year with the contents of a single ammo can. As is well known, before the 2003 invasion, Saddam had his elite units and internal security forces—the nucleus of the insurgency—cache ammo and weapons specifically for continued fighting. This fact, along with the availability of quality ammunition in neighboring countries, suggests that ammunition supply is not a significant problem for snipers. When snipers eventually are found to be firing chiefly ordinary ball ammo—and one-shot kills decline—it will be a strong intelligence indicator that the larger counterinsurgency effort is achieving success.

SNIPER ATTACKS ON AMERICAN UNITS

At some time, probably every American combat unit in Iraq must contend with an enemy sniper, but too often their counteraction does not eliminate their attacker.

Montana National Guardsmen assigned to

Collapsed on the pavement after being hit by sniper fire, USMC GySgt. Ryan P. Shane (L) and an unidentified Marine were shot while attempting to rescue a third Marine in Fallujah. (Photo credit: USMC photo by Cpl. Joel A. Chaverri)

Task Force Liberty manning a listening post at Al Huyway Jah had a single sniper shot narrowly miss a man. Though they returned fire and rushed the sniper's suspected firing position, they found nothing. As usual, an NCO noted, "there are three other ways out of [his firing location] besides the side facing our trucks. He fired one shot, which left him plenty of time to get away from us before we engaged him." Especially, the Guardsmen were frustrated by the lack of cooperation by Iraqi bystanders. "As usual, no one heard the sniper shot but heard the rip of the .50 returning fire," reported one infantryman.

Recalling his predeployment countersniper training in Germany, a 1st Infantry Division soldier told *Stars and Stripes*, "You could see the window open, you see the rifle and then you see the guy leaning out of the window." He shook his head. "Here it's not like that. They are very well hidden."

When a sniper inflicts casualties and escapes unscathed, it can affect morale. After losing a fellow Marine to a sniper at a traffic control point, a young Marine confided to a *Washington Post* reporter, "Having a sniper out there scares the hell out of me. He's a pretty good one, too. Only three shots and he got one of ours."

Here are some examples of the kinds of snipers American forces must deal with.

The Opportunistic Neighborhood Sniper

The neighborhood sniper operates mostly near where he lives, which usually is one of the more dangerous neighborhoods of Ramadi, Baghdad, Tikrit, Fallujah, or a dozen other Sunni triangle towns. Like kicking over a rock and finding a rattlesnake, U.S. forces encounter him when they penetrate his neighborhood. He sees the Americans as a convenient, opportunistic target right in his own backyard.

Limited by his optics—a 4x PSO-1 scope—he cannot selectively place a shot beyond 400 yards, but urban dead space reduces that further, to about 250 yards or less. He occupies a temporary hide atop a building of perhaps three or four stories—at least as high as the buildings around him. Lacking a spotter and his spotting scope, the sniper will search for a target with his rifle scope. If he's a potshot sniper, he may expend his entire 10-round magazine before he flees; with more experience, he'll carefully place one shot so he's certain of a hit, then flee.

His opportunistic target could be a GI at the open hatch of a Bradley Fighting Vehicle, a dismounted patrol, perhaps a soldier standing beside a temporarily halted HMMWV. If a military supply route (MSR) passes his neighborhood, the sniper may well take to engaging these, too, when presented the opportunity.

This neighborhood sniper knows the area well and has planned his escape route, often using a rope to descend a building's back side, beyond the sight and counterfire of those he's engaged. Early in the war these snipers sometimes left behind their rifles, but SVDs and al Kadesih rifles are growing harder to replace; more likely he'll carry his rifle a short distance, then ditch it in a preplanned hiding place. Operating against such a potshot sniper in 1969, I spotted him within 30 seconds of his shot, but already he'd hidden his rifle, which I never found—that's how quickly such a shooter knows he must discard his weapon.

Iraqi "neighborhood" snipers, such as this one, opportunistically engage U.S. forces when they appear.

The Vehicle-Borne Hit-and-Run Sniper

Another kind of opportunistic engagement has been experienced at American traffic control points (TCPs). While U.S. servicemen are stopping and searching vehicles, a civilian automobile halts 300 or more yards away—far enough for a sniperscope to offer an optical advantage. While the driver remains at the wheel, a sniper takes aim across the car's hood or top, fires one or two fast shots, then the car speeds away and immediately disappears into traffic.

The troops operating the TCP take cover, so rarely do they even approximate a vehicle description. Unless a helicopter is already airborne and in radio contact with the TCP, it's impossible to intercept the sniper's vehicle. This kind of sniper might be apprehended during a routine vehicle search that also discovers his rifle—but he's just as likely to melt back into the populace. Because the insurgents use radios or cell phones to alert their comrades whenever they spot a TCP, U.S. forces have begun running "flash" TCPs, set up with no warning for short periods of time, in hopes of ensnaring vehicles carrying contraband.

The Last-Stand Sniper

Another type of insurgent sniper is one who has decided to occupy dominant terrain with no possibility of escape and die with his boots on, so to speak. Like suicidal Japanese snipers in World War II who tied themselves in trees and let Marines advance beyond them before opening fire, this sniper climbs into a minaret—the tower beside a mosque from which a mullah calls the faithful to prayer—where he intends to make his last stand. He will take with him as many enemies as possible.

The most determined kind of sniper—though likely not the most tactically adroit—the last-stand sniper is always ready to die, which yields its own kind of effectiveness. No matter the accuracy of counterfire, he cannot be forced from his position or suppressed—he can only be

When a determined Iraqi sniper atop a Fallujah minaret held up a Marine infantry company, tank fire brought down the entire tower.

killed. On several occasions in or near Fallujah, such to-the-death snipers have held up U.S. forces for extended periods until, finally, antitank weapons or tank main guns blasted them from their barricaded FFPs.

The Targeted Sniper Attack

The insurgent's best snipers are employed in carefully planned attacks against somewhat fixed targets, such as a soldier at a guard post, security personnel outside a public building, or a GI manning a guard tower at a U.S. base.

We know that these operations involve their finest shooters because with uniformity, these are one-shot kills—usually head shots—carefully placed to bypass the victim's body armor. These usually are "shoot and scoot" attacks, but if the sniper's first shot misses he may linger for a second shot. This pattern is clear with quite a number of incidents. In some instances, the sniper has been supported by a video cameraman who recorded the attack for later broadcast on Arab television or insurgent Web sites.

Typical of these targeted sniper attacks were two incidents in Ramadi on 8 and 17 August 2004, which each killed a U.S. Marine. In both instances, they were manning a well-established observation post, and the victim was killed with a single shot to the head. The second victim was atop a seven-story building, not a very simple shot. The earlier victim, at Outpost Ghetto, was safely behind a 5-foot sandbag wall when he paused momentarily at a narrow opening to speak to a fellow Marine. That's all it took.

To succeed, such deliberate attacks are preceded by reconnaissance and surveillance to confirm the target's location, select FFPs, and determine stalking and escape routes. The best counter, it appears, is tactical awareness of this recon/surveillance stage and being alert to the presence of suspicious observers—if they're clumsy enough to appear suspicious.

Because these deliberate attack snipers are not committed to a particular town or neighborhood, I've dubbed them "floaters" who probably are centrally controlled by regional or city-level insurgent leaders.

Targeting U.S. Snipers

There can be no question that Iraqi insurgents have especially targeted U.S. snipers. Besides being the number-one priority on an Iraqi terrorist Web site (see sidebar, page 492), American snipers are despised for their effectiveness, so detested that insurgent propaganda frequently accuses them of heinous offenses such as killing women and Muslim holy men—crimes so despicable that any punishment is justified.

Though most often these are opportunistic attacks, some appear to be focused on particular U.S. snipers. On 2 September 2004, one of the U.S. Army's finest rifle shots, a Specialist 4th Class who'd previously been with Ft. Benning's Marksmanship Training Unit and aspired to make the U.S. Olympic rifle team, was ambushed near Kirkuk. After his vehicle was halted by a roadside bomb, the veteran sniper stepped from his vehicle and was shot dead by an enemy sniper's bullet to his head. He was slated to return to Ft. Benning to be an instructor at the U.S. Army Sniper School.

Indeed, there has been at least one incident where an American soldier was targeted for assassination and, according to the Iraqi sniper who took the shot, he was paid the equivalent of $5,000 for killing him. This same sniper was also tasked to kill a particular U.S. Army officer, which he claimed to have accomplished.

There have been a number of other incidents where Marine and Army snipers have been killed by insurgent snipers, usually picked off individually while operating in support of platoons and companies. Perhaps more troubling has been the growth of larger Iraqi countersniper operations intended to wipe out entire American sniper teams.

The first of these I've come upon occurred on 18 April 2004, in the al Rashid District, near the Baghdad airport. A three-man sniper team from the 1st Cavalry Division led by 1st Lt. Eric Johnson had waited for darkness to occupy an overwatch position in a building under construction. While observing from the fourth-floor rooftop for insurgents planting bombs

IRAQI SNIPER TARGET PRIORITIES

Iraqi terrorists often communicate via the Internet, posting messages and setting up temporary Web sites to convey information. In May 2005, an Iraqi terrorist Web site suggested seven "duties" or target priorities for that country's insurgent snipers. Here is a literal translation of that posting, provided by the U.S. Army:

7 Duties of a Sniper

1. Target enemy snipers and surveillance teams.
2. Target commanders, officers and pilots, "that is, to target the head of the snake and then handicap the command of the enemy."
3. Assist teams of mujahideen infantry with suppressive fire. These teams may include RPG brigades or surveillance teams.
4. Target U.S. Special Forces, "they are very stupid because they have a 'Rambo complex,' thinking that they are the best in the world. Don't be arrogant like them."
5. Engage specialty targets like communications officers to prevent calls for reinforcements. Likewise, tank crews, artillery crews, engineers, doctors, and chaplains should be fair targets.
   — a tank driver was shot while crossing a bridge, resulting in the tank rolling off the bridge and killing the rest of the crew
   — Killing doctors and chaplains is suggested as a means of psychological warfare
6. Take care when targeting one or two U.S. soldiers or [Iraqi] agents on a roadside. "A team of American snipers [may be] waiting for you. They [may be] waiting for you to kill one of those agents and then they will know your location and they will kill you."
7. In the event of urban warfare, work from high areas and assist infantry with surrounding the enemy, attacking target instruments and lines of sight on large enemy vehicles, and directing mortar and rocket fire to front-line enemy positions.

along nearby Highway 8, Lieutenant Johnson noticed civilian vehicles converging. "Cars were pulling up without lights, scooters were coming in and out, and 20 to 30 military-aged Iraqis appeared," he recalled. As Johnson told his radioman to call for a Quick Reaction Force, the arriving Iraqis suddenly opened fire, attempting to overrun the snipers. Johnson was shot three times—through one lung, his back, and his left arm. Friendly forces arrived, compelling the attackers to withdraw. Johnson was medevacked back to the States and survived.

Two months later, in Ramadi, 20 miles west of Baghdad, a similar sudden assault by two dozen insurgents succeeded in overrunning a Marine sniper position. These four Marines, too, had been on a surveillance mission, but the aggressive attack and heavy fire was more than they could repel. The insurgent attackers stripped their bodies, then videotaped them for foreign propaganda distribution.

The next such incident again took place in Ramadi on 4 November 2004. This time an eight-man Marine sniper element was crossing a darkened street at 2:30 A.M. when, with no warning, a remote-controlled bomb detonated, killing two and seriously wounding several others, including the sniper platoon sergeant. The Marines had been en route to a surveillance position.

The most publicized attack on American snipers came in August 2005, when two Marine sniper teams—six men—were ambushed and killed near Haditha, 140 miles northwest of Baghdad. In this case I received a copy of the terrorist videotape that recorded the ambush, so I was able to derive considerable detail. Initially, the Marines advanced as two three-man teams through head-high sand dunes, about 25 meters apart. Then an insurgent pickup truck rolled to a stop at a nearby farmhouse, apparently within sight of the Marines, who probably did not notice a 120mm mortar pulled out and set up. When all was ready, it appears that insurgent machine gun fire pinned the Marines atop a sand dune, then the mortar pounded them with high-explosive rounds until all were incapacitated. It's not clear in the videotape, but I suspect a final assault by insurgents ended the fight. Later, the masked insurgents videotaped a stripped body, then laid out a display of captured gear and weapons beneath palm trees, including two M40A4 sniper rifles.

What all these incidents have in common is that they were not chance contacts. The insurgents executed planned attacks or ambushes and knew where the sniper teams were positioned or could accurately anticipate their routes. Clearly these teams were compromised.

The cause could be operational security—OPSEC—meaning the Americans had unwittingly telegraphed their punches or repeatedly used the same positions or routes. Equally, though, the cause could have been penetration by hostile intelligence, a major problem we faced in my old covert warfare unit, MACV-SOG. In the Studies and Observations Group and the 5th Special Forces Group as a whole, there was such a continuing shortage of interpreters that Vietnamese nationals often were hired without proper vetting—and some were

Despite serious wounds, 1st Lt. Eric Johnson's sniper team fought off mass attackers in Iraq. Other teams have not been so fortunate.

enemy agents. The simplest, most reliable way for a hostile intelligence service to penetrate American military units is to dangle an English-speaking interpreter before them. We had 14 Special Forces SOG teams vanish behind enemy lines and another 10 overrun and annihilated, some due to compromise by enemy moles. Interpreters are essential, but I urge readers, *deny interpreters advance knowledge of operations, and keep them away from operational maps and planning meetings.*

PASSIVE COUNTERSNIPER MEASURES

American forces in Iraq are practicing all the passive countersniper measures cited in Chapter 19, plus, as fitting, those learned in Sarajevo. (See sidebar, page 495.)

Unlike previous conflicts, however, U.S. military personnel are also benefiting from body armor that protects wearers from even the powerful 7.62x54mm sniping round. Several GIs have survived solid hits from this bullet—I'm aware of at least three—and come away with little more than an ugly bruise. It's heavy, it's hot in Iraq's summer heat, but it genuinely works.

Modern Kevlar helmets, too, have saved a number of lives and have proved more effective than the old steel pot ever was. U.S. Army SSgt. Chad Chapman would have been another one-shot kill for an Iraqi sniper, but the bullet struck his Kevlar helmet, knocking him unconscious with no lasting effect. At least two other GIs have survived similar hits to Kevlar helmets.

ACTIVE COUNTERSNIPER MEASURES

As with passive measures, U.S. forces are employing all the active countermeasures cited in Chapter 19. Additionally, dismounted patrols are run through areas in which a sniper could approach or stalk toward a U.S.

Living proof that body armor works, USMC LCpl. Richard Guillenavila shows where a sniper's bullet struck his protective vest.

Fragments of the 7.62x54mm bullet intended to take the life of Lance Corporal Guillenavila.

This ACOG scope saved the life of USMC Sgt. Todd Bowers by stopping a sniper's bullet in Fallujah. The scope was a gift from his father.

COUNTERSNIPING LESSONS OF SARAJEVO

During much of the 1990s, the city of Sarajevo, Bosnia, was the scene of unrelenting sniping by Serbian gunmen. Hidden in carefully selected dominant terrain in the surrounding hills or inside modern concrete buildings, these concealed riflemen took an almost daily toll of men, women, and even children to challenge the division of Yugoslavia into independent states.

Riddled by sniper fire, a NATO vehicle is halted along a Sarajevo street.

NATO and UN forces provided security assistance, to include countersnipers, who learned much from this protracted urban fight. Here are their most important lessons:

1. **Intelligence support is critical, to include:**
   a. *Dead Space Analysis:* Tracking bullet impacts and lines of fire helped identify safe routes and hazardous ones. This analysis also provided clues to likely Serbian Final Firing Positions, which could then be intensely observed.
   b. *Periodic Photography:* Regularly photographing buildings and high ground likely to be used by Serb snipers helped detect subtle changes, such as removed windows, firing ports cut in walls, and shifted barrier materials.
   c. *Pattern Analysis:* Detailed assessment of each sniping incident contributed to a larger mosaic that provided useful clues for future sniping incidents, such as times, locations, and methods. This analysis was best accomplished by directly involving countersnipers in the process to help interpret the raw data.
2. **Passive measures are as useful as active measures:**
   a. *Identify Safe Routes:* Shift civilian and military traffic away from the snipers' direct fire to streets and alleys and areas into which snipers cannot observe or fire.
   b. *Install Screens to Block Sniper Observation:* Along hazardous routes or locations within the snipers' field of fire, erect screens to block his observation. Such screens are not ballistically protective, composed usually of canvas or plywood.
   c. *Employ Armored Vehicles:* Even lightly armored personnel carriers and fighting vehicles offered sufficient protection against sniper fire.
3. **Barrier penetration is absolutely essential:**
   a. *Sniper Positions Heavily Barricaded:* Serb snipers deeply embedded themselves in rubbled buildings and/or elaborately positioned concrete blocks, timbers, and sandbags around their positions.
   b. *7.62mm and .300 WinMag of Limited Application:* Although accurately placed, counterfire shots from standard sniper rifles often could not penetrate well-constructed Serbian firing positions. However, accurate fire usually had a suppressing effect.
   c. *Need for Overmatching:* Only heavy rifles—.338 Lapua Magnum and .50-caliber rifles—could penetrate Serb barriers with reasonable consistency.
   d. *Rifle Weight and Bulk Matters:* Many NATO countersnipers preferred the .338 Lapua Magnum over the .50-cal. because it was lighter and easier to manipulate while climbing, running, and stalking.

installation, while dominating terrain is denied enemy snipers by occupying it or keeping it under surveillance.

Much more so than the past, surveillance has become aerial. Both the Army and Marines are employing small unmanned aerial vehicles—UAVs—to search rooftops and likely sniper positions. The scale of this effort is astounding—more than 1,000 UAVs are currently in use in Iraq and Afghanistan, according to the U.S. Defense Department, looking for roadside bombs, snipers, and a host of other threats.

Despite all these roving eyes in the sky, however, most countersniper engagements still result from the tried and true—U.S. snipers intensely surveilling for their Iraqi foes. I've

U.S. Marines ready an unmanned aerial vehicle (UAV) in Fallujah to fly reconnaissance in support of the Marine assault and to watch rooftops for Iraqi snipers.

To obscure sniper observation, U.S. Marines in Ramadi burn a large smoke bomb.

With a SAW machine gunner alert to return fire, a Marine raises a dummy head to attract sniper fire in Fallujah.

Hoping to attract a hidden sniper's shot, a U.S. Army sniper raises a cleverly designed decoy head in Iraq. (Note .50-caliber sniper rifle in background.)

been quite impressed by the quality of lures and decoys fashioned by American counter-snipers, as good as those waved over the trenches in World War I to attract fire from Hun sharpshooters.

And the same old-fashioned techniques still work. A 1st Cavalry Division sniper, SSgt. Jeff Young, exploited the shifting rays of the setting sun to pinpoint an Iraqi sniper. "We got lucky when the sun was going down," he told *Stars and Stripes*. "It hit his scope at the right angle and we got a glare in our direction so we engaged it."

Another Army sniper, Sgt. Randall Davis, twice defeated opposing snipers, engaging them from a rooftop in Samarra. Firing an M25 Designated Marksman Rifle, he patiently outwaited an Iraqi sniper who had fired on Americans three days earlier. When the Iraqi finally reappeared, Davis' keen eyes picked him out of the shadows where he stalked. As the Iraqi raised up to fire his SVD rifle, one shot from Davis and it was over. In the second case, Davis eliminated an Iraqi sniper with a 750-yard shot with a Barrett .50-caliber M107, thanks to his team's high-quality optics.

USMC Abrams tanks blast an insurgent sniper's position in Fallujah.

Marine snipers, too, have taken their toll of Iraqi gunmen. In Fallujah, Sgt. Sean Crane detected an Iraqi creeping along a rooftop, then saw him slide down a palm tree and pause for his rifle to be handed down to him. From more than two blocks away, Crane's shot hit the Iraqi's leg, then an immediate follow-up shot dropped him. Scratch one Iraqi gunman, the Marine's 11th kill.

It's that kind of steady, patient, meticulous, day-in/day-out effort that's necessary to win the sniper war in Iraq.

HIGH TECHNOLOGY IN THE COUNTERSNIPER FIGHT

The countersniper fight can be assisted by some surprisingly advanced technologies, though it's still too early to estimate their potential contribution in Iraq.

Countersniping involves two sequential steps: first, find the sniper; second, engage him. Each step is now being addressed by cutting-edge devices.

The first step, finding the sniper, uses sensing technologies that either acoustically locate his rifle's muzzle blast or acquire a reflection off his optics. Acoustic-signature technology employs a number of sensitive microphones linked to a computer, which pinpoint a muzzle blast by multiple reverse azimuths. Posted discreetly on buildings and light poles, these wireless, cigarette pack-size sensors hear the shot, then relay it to the computer, which instantly compares all these versions of the sound to calculate where the shot originated. The principle is the same as the "crack-bang" technique discussed in Chapter 19—timing the difference between hearing a bullet's "crack" and the "bang" of its muzzle blast. Linked to a GPS, the computer precisely calculates data from several sensor locations, then spits out a fairly exact location.

Originally developed to "fingerprint" Soviet submarines entering the North Atlantic by analyzing the cavitation noise of their propellers, accoustic signature technology is damned impressive—but I'm skeptical about how well its current configuration will perform real-world. In the midst of heavy fighting in Fallujah, can it single out one sniper's muzzle blast? Will it merely cause snipers to become "shoot-and-scoot" practitioners who displace so quickly that they're gone before there's time for counteraction? An earlier acoustic gunfire sensor system, developed by Honeywell, was tested a decade ago in Atlanta during the 1996 Olympics—and it was already claimed that it "worked." If it was truly effective, we'd see it heavily employed in Iraq, and it hasn't been. I suspect that despite earlier claims, it's still in development and probably is being further tested, perhaps on a discreet basis in Iraq.

The other major sensing technology does work and actually has a deployable system. The USAF BOSS—Battlefield Optical Surveillance System—is the latest evolution of a laser-based acquisition technology that I first heard about some 20 years ago, when the Soviet Union was developing a similar system. Just as radar operates by emitting a radio wave that reflects back to disclose an aircraft, the BOSS emits a brilliant flash of laser light that reflects off any optical lens—a rifle scope, spotting scope, night vision goggle, antitank weapon sight, etc. A BOSS sensor detects this reflection, then pinpoints its location by computer analysis. Instead of just relaying this location, the BOSS takes the further step of automatically directing a visible laser beam to the spot to "designate a threatening individual." Although the official BOSS description correctly notes that this laser "will not harm eyes," in fact, similar U.S. and Soviet devices developed in the 1990s were not only capable of that but were intended to "detect and neutralize a sniper's optics"— meaning his eyesight.

More portable versions of this laser "neutralizing" device—the U.S. Army's Stingray and LCMS (Laser Countermeasure System)—were so close to fielding in 1995 that they were addressed in a U.S. Army field manual. This technology is more advanced than most people realize, for Stingray already had been installed in some Bradley Fighting

USAF BOSS (Battlefield Optical Surveillance System), a mobile countersniper system, uses a laser to detect and "illuminate" hostile snipers.

Vehicles, which a manual noted "can be set to scan a specific sector and then [automatically] engage and neutralize all telescopes and night vision devices it detects."

After careful reconsideration, the U.S. government decided not to deploy a weapon that inflicted casualties by blinding enemy soldiers. (An opinion I share.) Thus, today's BOSS offers the detection and acquisition capabilities but not the blinding laser—and that, alone, can be quite useful. As now mounted on a HMMWV, the system is too bulky and heavy to achieve much in most Iraqi neighborhoods, but a more portable version installed on rooftops or perhaps towers could have some usefulness. The director of the Defense Advanced Research Projects Agency, Dr. Anthony Tether, in announcing that laser-based antisniper systems were deploying to Iraq, realistically assessed their effectiveness. "They're not going to be 100 percent solutions," he said, "but when you're in a situation where you have no solutions, even a 25 percent solution is going to be great."

Indeed, before you get too enthused, keep in mind that this technology detects optical reflections, not snipers. In a major urban area you'd still have to determine what exactly the BOSS detected—an Iraqi kid playing with a kaleidoscope, a pretty girl looking at her face in a makeup compact, or an SVD-armed sniper aiming at you.

The next generation of gunfire-detection technology offers considerably improved capabilities, with IR sensors that literally track a bullet's flight and special laser radars that read atmospheric pressure disturbances created by a bullet's passage. Both the Army and Marine Corps have prototypes that incorporate these technologies, in tandem

From a laptop computer inside this HMMWV, a Marine can so precisely control the TRAP 250's .50-caliber that he can hit a soda can at 100 meters.

with acoustic sensors and GPS locators. The Army Research Laboratory is even installing these countersniper systems on small radio-controlled robots, and I'd speculate that helicopter-mounted ones aren't long in the future. Some of these prototypes probably will find their way to Iraq.

High-Tech Engagements

Something that's here right now and deployed to Iraq in 2005 is a very capable, remote-controlled firing unit for optically equipped rifles, including the USMC's Designated Marksman Rifle, the Stoner SR-25, and the Barrett .50 caliber. Manufactured by Precision Remotes, the TRAP 250 System incorporates a stabilized cradle and video link that allows a remote operator to minutely

The TRAP 250 laptop computer view through a Unertl scope, with video zoomed to 80x.

2004/12/20

USMC Designated Marksman Rifle atop a Force Protection Cougar vehicle. The TRAP 250 System also can be pintle-mounted or installed on a standard machine gun tripod.

manipulate the rifle and aim with impressive precision using an ordinary laptop computer.

The TRAP 250's cradle is compatible with standard U.S. military pintle mounts as well as machine gun tripods, allowing it to be ground- or vehicle-mounted. Its sensitive, micrometer-like adjustments and 0.1 MOA resolution allow the operator to place a shot with considerable accuracy. During demonstrations, the company consistently shoots soda cans at 100 meters with the unit.

Already the TRAP 250 has seen combat service with explosive ordnance disposal (EOD) teams, where its precision fire has disabled Iraq mines. The USMC has a newer version that mounts atop the Force Protection Cougar vehicle, while the U.S. Army has incorporated it on a remote-controlled robot under the SWORDS (Special Weapons Observation Reconnaissance Detection System) program. A number of SWORDS units have just deployed to Iraq, where they'll be tested in the most unforgiving environment of all—real combat.

The day will come, I am sure, when all these sensing and acquisition and firing systems will be integrated, but I think they will supplement—not replace—the human countersniper. Because, always remember, the enemy sniper is a living, breathing, thinking human who will adapt to changing situations and new technologies. Ultimately, it will take another living, breathing, thinking human to outwit and eliminate him: you, the countersniper.

CHAPTER 21

SPECIAL SNIPING OPERATIONS

COUNTERING ROADSIDE BOMBERS

Since the capture of Baghdad by U.S. armed forces in 2003, more Americans have been killed by roadside bombs in Iraq than any other method. It's the greatest threat faced by Coalition forces and war on the cheap for the insurgents; once an improvised explosive device (IED) is in place, it requires only one man to detonate it, making this an economical way to fight U.S. forces.

Probably the most effective counter to roadside bombings is the employment of sniper teams in a clandestine surveillance role. Due to their optics, their stealth, and their superb camouflage, U.S. Army and Marine sniper teams have discovered, prevented, or acted on numerous attempts to implant and detonate IEDs along major roads and highways. And each time they've disrupted such an attack, they've saved several—even dozens—of U.S. lives.

This is a specialized sniper surveillance role because teams must infiltrate areas frequented by Iraqi civilians and remain fixed in thin concealment for days at a time. From insertion, while observing, and right through exfiltration, these counter-IED teams must not be detected,

An Israeli sniper overwatches a traffic control point in Israel, watching for threats to soldiers and for terrorist suspects bypassing the TCP.

both for their own security and to ensure that the insurgents are killed or captured while attempting such nefarious deeds.

The first challenge is infiltrating without detection, most readily accomplished in darkness or as a stay behind when a platoon-size American patrol passes through or sets up security for an adjacent traffic control point (TCP) roadblock. Exfiltration is equally important because the surveillance position may be used again—and it's always useful to leave the enemy guessing on how he was detected.

Initial selection of this position can result from aerial photos, a visual recon aboard a helicopter, or even a drive-by amid an ordinary-looking convoy or vehicular patrol. To plan an effective infil, the team should have a clear destination in mind.

While the team's in place, they're heavily camouflaged. To avoid compromising their location, they may forego directly engaging the enemy and instead radio for a Quick Reaction Force or helicopter gunship attack.

Along some busy highways it's simply impossible to infiltrate without being noticed by civilians—in which case, don't kid yourself about operating clandestinely. Assume your presence is known and subject to compromise, which means you should be on good defensive terrain even though you'll attempt to be inconspicuous.

One trick to help conceal your team's presence is to employ friendly Iraqis disguised as "muj" to stage a demonstration within sight of your position. (In MACV-SOG we often put our indigenous soldiers in enemy uniforms to confuse our foes.) Have two fake insurgents halt their car, brandish SVDs or RPGs, shout at some local civilians, then drive off. In only a few seconds you will have convinced the locals that no U.S. snipers are anywhere within shooting range. (To be really clever, the fake insurgents can even demand to know if the civilians have seen any Americans.) Of course, make sure your "muj" are not engaged inadvertently by other U.S. forces.

Counter-IED surveillance missions are long and difficult. "We'll be going for two, three, four days at a time in the baking sun in 113-degree weather," explains USMC Sgt. Willis Davis. "And if it's 113 degrees outside, it gets to be 145–150 inside a Ghillie suit." The payoff, though, is well worth it to such dedicated snipers.

Navy Petty Officer 3rd Class Jeff Pursley, a medic operating with a Marine sniper team, helped foil a roadside bombing in August 2004. Along a dangerous stretch of highway nicknamed "IED Alley," his team observed two vehicles halt at night to plant a bomb inside the stripped remains of a car. While the insurgents unrolled detonation wires, the sniper team leader, Sgt. Joshua Clark, had the Marines stalk forward and engage at close range, forcing several insurgents to flee and capturing one.

USMC Sgt. Willis Davis (L) and his assistant team leader, Cpl. Joseph Piner, surveil an Iraqi highway on the lookout for insurgents planting IEDs.

This Marine sniper team, Navy Petty Officer 3rd Class Jeff Pursley (front) and Cpl. Olen Thyssen, disrupted an IED attack along a major Iraqi highway.

Four months earlier, another Marine sniper team, led by SSgt. Steve Reichert, also operating in darkness, spotted a dead animal just ahead of an advancing Marine patrol. From atop an oil storage tank, Reichert studied the carcass with a spotting scope and reported, "I could see the slight reflection of wires coming out of the animal." As he radioed a warning, insurgent ambushers opened fire and pinned the Marine squad. The deadliest fire came from a distant 12.7mm machine gun, a target so far away that Reichert turned his own .50-caliber rifle toward it and fired. The shot missed, but his spotter helped him correct windage and elevation. Reichert's second shot—an explosive Raufoss slug—hit the gunner, which the Marine Corps credited with winning the firefight. When a lieutenant later measured the distance, it was determined that Reichert had scored his hit at 1,614 meters—more than 1 mile.

Precision sniper fire resolved another IED incident, this time involving an Illinois Army National Guard sniper, Sgt. Bruce Hartman, near Baghdad. When a suspicious parked car

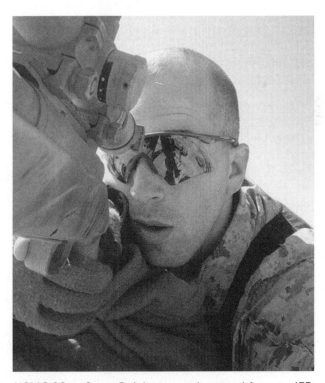

USMC SSgt. Steve Reichert saved a patrol from an IED and hit an insurgent machine gunner more than a mile away.

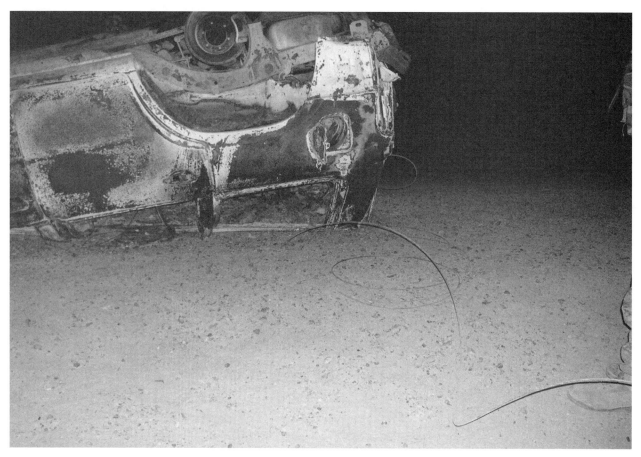

A Marine sniper team spotted insurgents planting an IED in this abandoned car. Note electrical wire rigging it for remote detonation.

was noticed along a busy highway, Hartman's squad leader, SSgt. David Jensen, examined it through binoculars. On the dashboard he spotted a cell phone—the insurgent's favorite means for remote detonation—wired to a large package on the front seat. It was no sweat for the superb marksman, Hartman, who fired two shots—one to blow out the window and a second to destroy the cell phone. Afterward an EOD team destroyed the car in place.

COUNTERING LONG-RANGE ATTACKS ON U.S. INSTALLATIONS

Sniper teams have also proven themselves adept at interdicting insurgent mortar teams and RPG rocketeers and heavy machine gunners. Particularly, the insurgents have

attempted to exploit darkness to approach American installations and inflict casualties from so great a distance that they can fire a few rounds and safely escape. Typically these attacks by fire originate at 500 or more yards from a U.S. position, far enough that counter-fire is unlikely to hit the fleeing attackers.

To counter this, sniper teams insert clandestinely or depart their bases under the cover of darkness. Depending on the terrain and potential enemy firing positions, the sniper teams occupy a suitable overwatch position or patrol any approaches to the base.

U.S. Army Sgts. Daniel Osborne and Cyrus Field demonstrated what snipers can do against such attackers when they were targeted against an insurgent .50-caliber machine gun that repeatedly attacked a U.S. base near Baghdad.

From a four-story roof, they spotted the machine gunners firing some 800 yards away and—using night vision devices—simultaneously fired their M24 rifles. Two Iraqis fell at the machine gun and two others turned to run. Osborne and Field ran their bolts and again fired simultaneously, and the last two insurgents fell. In less than 10 seconds they'd dropped all four gunners, and not one of them was farther than 15 yards from the machine gun.

On 9 June 2004, a four-man sniper team from Charlie Company, 3rd Battalion, 153rd Infantry, after hiding for a full day, spotted insurgents firing a 60mm mortar into an American installation, Forward Operating Base Dakota. The snipers killed two of the three gunners, then recovered the mortar, a quantity of ammo and a loaded RPG-7 launcher. Likewise, U.S. Army Spec. 4 Ryan Cannon, with the 82nd Airborne Division, could barely make out an insurgent mortarman in the darkness, some 500 yards away, about to drop

a round in his tube. Then the Iraqi puffed on a cigarette, just enough glow to make him out, and—*bang!* Another indirect fire attack stopped dead.

Some of these sniper engagements have evolved into much larger affairs. Air Force General Richard B. Myers, Chairman of the Joint Chiefs of Staff, told Pentagon reporters about a U.S. sniper team that wounded two insurgent mortarmen, then followed their blood trails to a nearby compound. A Quick Reaction Force captured 12 insurgents inside, which inspired a larger search that netted two trucks loaded with more than 1,500 rockets, apparent truck bombs in the final stage of assembly.

DISARMING BY FIRE

A tactic first employed in 1993 in Mogadishu uses snipers to enforce a public weapons ban. In Somalia, this meant sanitizing the streets of pickup trucks carrying Soviet 12.7mm heavy

Sgt. Herbert Hancock (L) and teammate Cpl. Geoffrey Flowers watch for suspicious activity from an Iraqi rooftop.

machine guns, called "technicals," along with anyone carrying an RPG or any other crew-served weapon. American snipers from all services—Army Special Forces, Marines, and Navy SEALs—demonstrated that within a few days, precision fire could effectively clear the streets of such heavy weapons. In one case, a sniper firing a .50-caliber Barrett with Raufoss exploding ammo even destroyed a ZSU-23-4 tracked antiaircraft gun. Maj. Gen. Carl Ernst, the commander of U.S. forces in Somalia, was so impressed by this performance that he inspired a major expansion of sniper training and improved sniper weaponry throughout the U.S. Army.

In Iraq this mission has similarly proved itself. In October 2004, the entire sniper platoon from the 1st Battalion, 23rd Marine Regiment, was sent into the town of Hit to rid it of heavily armed insurgent gangs who'd taken over the streets. Not only were they attacking U.S. vehicles but indiscriminately shooting by-standers and detonating IEDs along congested streets.

"They were all out in the open doing whatever they wanted to," said Sgt. Herbert Hancock, the platoon's chief Scout-Sniper. "They were in control of that side of the city, rerouting traffic, threatening to kill people, and terrorizing people."

The Marines began by targeting masked gunmen in a traffic circle. Sgt. Milo Afong shot the first insurgent, but instead of fleeing, more terrorists streamed into the area. The Marine snipers were ready for them.

For the next 45 minutes it was like the shootout at the O.K. Corral, a wild gunfight decisively won by the snipers. "At first they were fighting us out in the open and behind cars," recalled Cpl. Steven R. Johnson. "That wasn't working for them so they got up in the buildings and tried to set up concealed positions and shoot at us."

The fighting went on for several days, but eventually the masked thugs had to give up the streets—or die.

The Army's 4th Infantry Division similarly targeted an arms bazaar in downtown Tikrit after repeated warnings that the sale of military weapons had to cease. Teams of snipers engaged Iraqis carrying automatic weapons, killing three. Though the tactic was criticized in the press, it ended that black market's sale of weapons and ammunition to the insurgents.

SNIPERS IN RAIDS

A raid is characterized by a stealthy approach, surprise assault, aggressive execution, great violence, short duration, and rapid withdrawal. The raiding force is executing a carefully thought-out plan, one they have rehearsed, perfected, and memorized. It's similar to an ambush, except a raid's objective is fixed, and the attacker selects both the location *and* the time of action. By implication, a raid's target always is an enemy installation far enough behind his lines that he does not anticipate an attack.

Because the assault element needs the heavy firepower of submachine guns and assault rifles, sniper teams usually are assigned to the security element, which is responsible for sealing off the objective and preventing both its reinforcement and the escape of enemy personnel.

The utility of snipers supporting the assault element and the raid itself will be dictated mostly by terrain, which determines whether there are clear fields of fire for a sniper weapon. If the terrain is suitable, snipers may support the assault by placing precision fire into key targets within the objective. Remember that a sniper team doesn't generate a heavy volume of fire and therefore should not be assigned tasks more fittingly accomplished by machine guns.

A sniper's targets should be distant, small, and unalert to best exploit the capabilities of his rifle during a raid. A perfect scenario is a sniper-initiated assault, in which the synchronized fire of multiple snipers neutralizes gate guards at an enemy base just as a hidden assault force rushes them. Or snipers could eliminate an enemy observation post or perhaps a border guard checkpoint. These also are excellent situations for suppressed sniper rifles.

Since there are few other lightweight, hand-carried weapons effective out to 1,000 yards that a

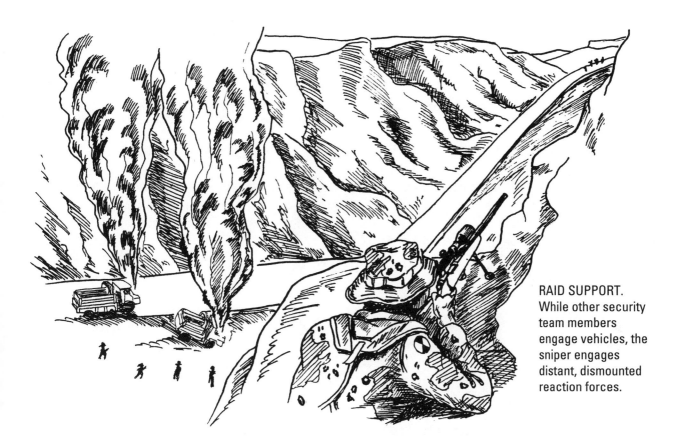

RAID SUPPORT. While other security team members engage vehicles, the sniper engages distant, dismounted reaction forces.

raiding force would carry along, the value of a sniper rifle must not be underestimated. I can recall the harrowing action of Tyrone Adderly, a Special Forces acquaintance from Fort Bragg who was a security team member on the Son Tay Raid against a POW camp deep inside North Vietnam. Adderly, who received the Distinguished Service Cross for his heroism, had to let a truckload of enemy reaction troops approach to within 250 yards before he finally could hit it with a light antitank weapon (LAW) rocket. Think about how much better it would have been to have nailed that truck driver with sniper fire at three times that distance, then drill his comrades as they cowered around the vehicle.

I guess the lesson is, you'll only have as much capability on a raid as you carry in with you, which isn't as obvious as it seems. And remember that a raid is dependent on security and surprise for success; if your approach is compromised, the tactical advantages dramatically shift to the enemy.

COUNTER REVOLUTIONARY SNIPING

It was El Salvador that I had in mind while preparing this section, although this information applies equally to Peru, the Philippines, Nepal, or any country suffering from internal shadows that prey on public and governmental vulnerabilities.

What distinguishes this sniping environment is the presence of noncombatant civilians, among whom your foe blends both in hopes your overreaction will drive the populace into his arms and, in a baser sense, to let him hide behind the public's skirt.

The revolutionary is a cynical, manipulative pragmatist to whom all manner of misdeeds become justifiable if they propel his campaign. Having fought these types, I have no illusions about their romantic quest and glorious goals, ad nauseam. These most dangerous men and women are not to be underestimated.

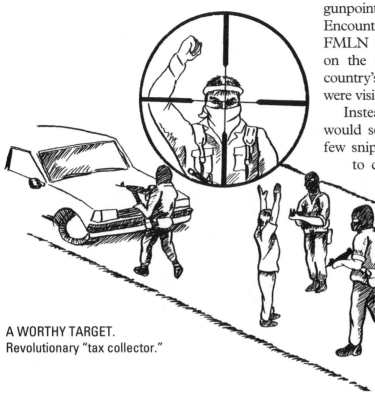

A WORTHY TARGET.
Revolutionary "tax collector."

Sniping: A Measured, Balanced Response

Sniping is an ideal means for countering revolutionary warfare because it's controllable, proportional, and extremely precise, and the sniper is as invisible as the guerrilla himself.

The sniper's exacting fire can reach into the midst of civilians and exorcise the terrorist, as surely as the hands of a skilled surgeon remove cancer from a vital organ. I can think of no other technique or weapon that so perfectly can separate the revolutionary foe from his innocent shields, which deprives him of protective cover and concealment.

Recognizing that political and tactical realities limit the effectiveness of conventional units in a low-intensity conflict, I think each infantry battalion needs a company of small teams trained to infiltrate, stalk, surveil, observe, shoot with exacting precision, then withdraw invisibly—an entire company of snipers that works in tandem with other units.

Typical Sniper Missions

Can there be a more fitting sniper target than a revolutionary "tax collector" who halts cars at gunpoint and deprives passengers of their wallets? Encountered frequently in El Salvador, such FMLN roadblocks were erected time after time on the same stretches of highway outside the country's capital, except when Salvadoran troops were visibly present.

Instead of a conventional show of force, it would seem far more productive to infiltrate a few sniper teams and allow these tax collectors to continue their trade. It's simple to determine the priority target: whoever pockets the purloined money is the one in charge.

Another roadside place worth covering is about 1 mile from any national police checkpoint, where unsavory types abandon cars or leave buses to avoid having their credentials checked and baggage searched.

Contraband smugglers delivering ordnance and weapons from Nicaragua plagued El Salvador, with some coming overland on burros, but most often they were transported across the Gulf of Fonseca. Small boats and dugouts delivered the contraband to beaches along the southern coast, a perfect place for night sniping with quality NODs. Guerrilla lookouts and patrols could warn of approaching conventional forces in time for the boats to be turned away, but sniper teams bypass such security and still reach the landing beaches.

This is equally true for Northern Ireland's borderlands along the Irish Republic, rural forests and fields that have concealed IRA weapons smuggling for generations. While conventional forces may patrol these lands, they'll never see a thing. Only small teams of cleverly infiltrated men stand any chance of encountering gunrunners.

One SAS infiltration technique practiced in Northern Ireland and taught at the USMC sniper school is called "stay behind," and it works well when you must insinuate men into a place that has no possible approach providing cover and concealment. In a stay behind, you intermigle the sniper team(s) with other soldiers, a larger unit ostensibly

Smuggling interdiction on a lonely beach.

conducting a search or sweep through the area. At some point, your snipers disappear into a ditch, beneath a house, or onto a roof and stay behind while their comrades depart.

This team remains invisibly in place for up to several days and either exfiltrates in darkness or joins a subsequent staged sweep. This technique works well for inserting police officers on counternarcotics operations, too.

Our final example of employing snipers in a counterrevolutionary role employs them in unison with conventional forces sweeping through a village controlled by revolutionaries. Well before the sweep, multiple sniper teams infiltrate and occupy hides overlooking likely escape routes that a guerrilla cadre will travel when the approaching military force is spotted. You can identify senior cadre because they'll carry the lightest loads and usually appear the neatest and cleanest in their group.

UNCONVENTIONAL WARFARE SNIPING

It's the sniper's capability to place shots exactly over great distances that makes him valuable in an unconventional warfare environment, with his

STAY BEHIND. This sniper team slipped away from a passing patrol and will stay behind.

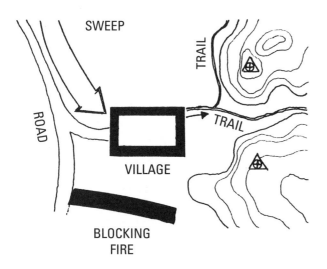

Ambushing fleeing guerrillas.

long-range fires making life miserable, if not hazardous, deep behind an enemy's lines. We've identified several specialized sniping applications that can harvest fruitful results in this theater of special warfare.

Raids by Fire

In a sense, some of Britain's greatest aces of World War II were in the SAS, not the Royal Air Force. Hundreds of Nazi warplanes were destroyed by SAS ground raids against German airfields in North Africa, a mission for which Col. David Sterling had specifically founded his commando force in their distinctive sand-colored berets.

Armed with Bren guns and satchel charges, Sterling's desert raiders could inflict damage only at close range. Their amazing early successes declined, however, when the enemy beefed-up airfield perimeter defenses.

But such installation defenses would not prevent aircraft destruction by today's .50-caliber sniper rifles, which can reach out nearly 2 miles and—as world-record shooter Skip Talbot learned—place shots consistently into targets the size of fighter cockpits and transport engines.

All that's needed to accomplish a raid by fire is line-of-sight high ground that overlooks an important enemy installation, which by no means is limited to airfields. Seaports, refineries, munitions dumps, missile parks, major headquarters—any localities having valuable targets vulnerable to .50-caliber fire are suitable objectives.

And most high-tech counterbattery radars, sensors, and airborne surveillance platforms would not detect a threat so small as a three-man .50-caliber sniper team. Imagine the enemy's confusion trying to figure out even *what* was hitting their valuable planes, much less where it was coming from.

Jackaling: Shadowing an Enemy Force

This tactic was practiced by Viet Cong guerrillas early in the Vietnam War and directed primarily against South Vietnamese units but eventually American ones, too.

A two-man guerrilla team followed a conventional unit from a safe distance and, perhaps every other day, crept close enough to shoot one soldier. These

RAIDS BY FIRE. High-performance aircraft are especially vulnerable to long-range .50-caliber fire.

"jackals," as I've named them, carefully avoided even visual contact and evaporated immediately after firing their one shot, only to inflict another casualty several days later. In the course of a 60-day operation, a single jackal team would have killed or wounded nearly a platoon of soldiers.

When operating as jackals, a sniper team must be careful to parallel instead of follow its quarry to avoid ambush. The most effective Vietnam War counter-tactic was to leave carefully hidden stay-behind teams along the unit's backtrail and flanks, but even this didn't yield satisfactory results.

Jackaling is fairly terrain dependent since the sniper team must have adequate foliage or other concealment available.

Instigating Fratricide

The slickest sniper tactic I've ever personally witnessed was the night a lone Communist rifle-man slipped between our compound in Vietnam's Central Highlands and a tiny Vietnamese army guard post at a bridge a mile away.

Exploiting the natural confusion of darkness, the rifleman fired a couple of rounds at the guard post and then turned his rifle toward our perimeter and let loose a few shots. Sure as hell, one of our indigenous security men shot back, and since the distant bridge was directly in line, his bullets caused our allies to start throwing rounds our way. It escalated in seconds to a full-scale shoot-out, under cover of which the anonymous rifle-man slipped safely away. For 10 minutes we exchanged fire, and only the great range kept anyone from being seriously hurt.

A similarly instigated fratricide incident in Italy during World War II, launched by a British special operations unit known as Popski's Private Army, led to heavy fighting between two German units, complete with the loss of tanks and many casualties. Again, it was done in darkness, and here we can observe the components to make this trick most effective.

First, initiate it under the cloak of darkness, which inspires confusion and makes recognition most difficult. Second, expect greatest success against units that have just moved into new positions and don't clearly understand who and what are to their front and flanks. Our Vietnam fratricide was soon stopped because we realized there was a friendly position in the direction of fire.

Third, fratricide is far more likely when the two enemy units are of different languages or different components or at least different major organizations. This makes speedy confirmation difficult and slow—and of less concern to the soldiers.

And finally, the two enemy units should be within effective small-arms range of each other, perhaps a maximum distance of 700 yards, so their exchange of fire inflicts casualties.

While instigated fratricide can induce significant casualties, the long-term animosities it creates between allied units may ultimately be of much more significance.

ESCAPING A PURSUING ENEMY

"Nothing in life is so exhilarating as to be shot at without result."

Winston Churchill

As a former SOG recon man whose team repeatedly escaped a numerically superior foe bent on our destruction—especially an enemy supported by bloodhounds and native trackers that sometimes outnumbered us 25 to 1—I must admit that the subject of evading pursuit is close to my heart.

Virtually all these tactics and techniques have proven effective real-world, tested either by myself or other SOG troops who lived to tell the tale. But I have to caution that no matter how clever or aggressive you think you are, survival against these odds eventually passes into the hands of the Creator. The best solution is to remain undetected in the first place.

Getting an Initial Lead

When the enemy's breathing down your neck,

Time-delay explosives and grenades confuse and divert pursuers.

pursuing so close that the slightest pause will have him all over you, there's little option but to run hell-bent.

You've got to knock him back at least enough to gain time for some counteraction. To get this initial lead, toss a few hand grenades, even if it's tossing them back over your shoulder without slowing enough to see what's back there.

To break this terrifying "they're-right-on-my-ass" pursuit, I modified fragmentation grenades by replacing their 5-second pull fuzes with nonelectric caps and slow-burning time fuze and a fuze lighter, which we've illustrated. Depending on the mission, my men carried two to five such grenades, as well as time-delay claymore mines.

Wrapped mummylike in time fuze, such a grenade detonated anywhere from 30 seconds to 10 minutes after being tossed and, in essence, created a minefield to our rear. These explosions caused the enemy to turn away from us, thinking we'd split, or if a grenade detonated really close, he'd think somehow we'd drawn him into a booby trap or mine. Either way, the confused enemy screeched to a halt.

The U.S. Army adopted a similar device, the M86 Pursuit Deterrent Munition, a 1-pound mine that spews seven monofilament lines, each 6 meters long. Contact with a line causes a preliminary explosion, which bounces the mine up about 1 meter, where it finally detonates and throws a very deadly fragmentation pattern. I haven't personally tested this mine, but it's my understanding that, like my old mummy-wrap grenades, you just pull a pin and toss the M86, with no need to pause for emplacement.

If the enemy's not too close, use a pull-wire

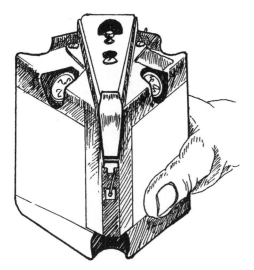

The U.S. Army's M86 Pursuit
Deterrent Munition.

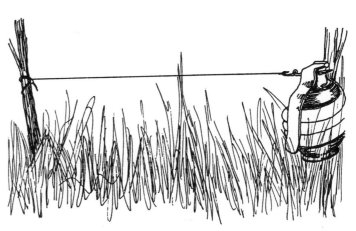

Tripwire booby traps delay the enemy, but you
must have a decent lead to emplace one.

booby trap fitted to a hand grenade, which can be emplaced in about a minute. The sniper should emplace the mine while the spotter covers him with his M16.

Creating False Impressions

Assuming you have a few seconds to think, start your evasion by heading in a direction *away* from, or at least *oblique* to, the way you truly intend to head. Having seen the frenzy of excited, armed pursuers running as if they were a pack of hounds, my dime-store psychiatry tells me some kind of group mentality takes over, and all of them do what they think everyone else is doing or expects them to do.

This means they don't coolly analyze the situation, weigh all the options, and so on. No, in a contagious, mentally infectious way, they all assume the next guy knows what's going on, so that *first impression* sticks with them. If you initially run north, they'll run north automatically and not veer from that direction unless compelled to. Don't let them see you again. Once out of sight, you exploit terrain, cover, wind, weather, diversions, and whatever else you can to mislead them as to your direction, pace, and location.

One SOG friend likened evading the enemy to practicing jujitsu: if the enemy comes on fast, sidestep and slowly slip away; if he advances slowly and deliberately, you run like hell. The game is run then creep,

creep then run. A steady pace and consistent compass heading is certain to bring disaster.

Other Evasion by Maneuver

On page 516 we've illustrated five evasion techniques used by SOG teams to escape pursuers. The most fundamental technique is to run like hell seemingly in a straight line, shown in the upper left, only to slow and veer away, then finally disappear in an entirely different direction.

An especially fitting evasion technique for a small two-man sniper team is illustrated upper right, which is to simply stay hidden in as tiny a spot as possible, then creep away when things calm down.

Center left we have phased ambushes, in which you pause just long enough to hit one or two enemy, then take off again. Your pursuers will seek cover when you shoot, pause, return fire, maneuver a bit, and only realize you've taken off when you don't shoot anymore. To be most effective, pause to shoot only when the terrain temporarily favors you, such as when you reach the top of a rise and can shoot, then disappear across it.

The next technique, shown center right, was frequently employed against native trackers and bloodhounds, a maneuver we called "the button-hook." It's simply doubling back and ambushing your own backtrail.

The final evasion technique can inflict consider-

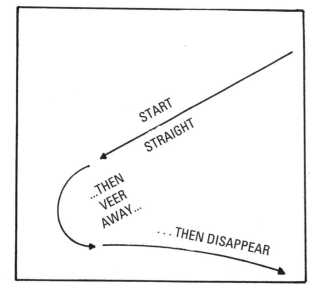

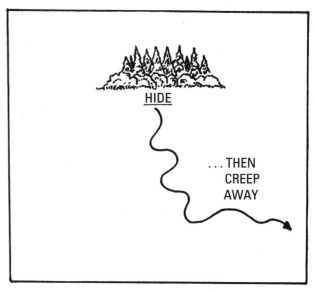

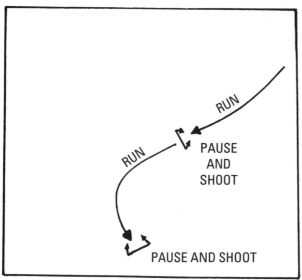

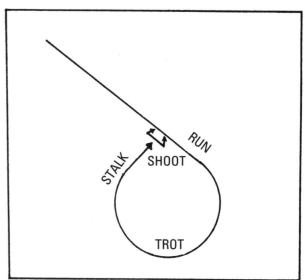

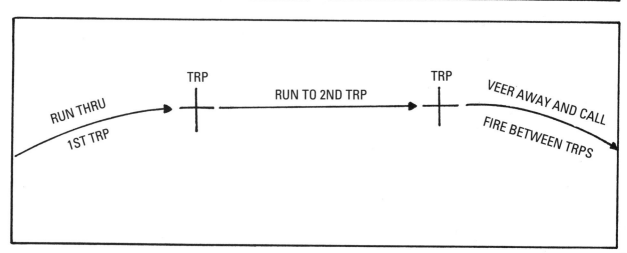

able casualties, and I used it myself with tremendous effect. A TRP is a "target reference point," meaning artillery has been registered for that exact spot and all the ballistic data has been computed in advance by the fire direction center. It's the fastest way to use artillery.

With the enemy in pursuit, you run through the first TRP—we'll say it's a trail junction—and alert the artillery by radio, telling them to prepare to fire. You make a beeline for the next nearby TRP—say a hilltop—then veer dramatically away and have the artillery shoot hell out of the space between the two TRPs. Air bursts are particularly devastating against this unprotected enemy; they'll forget about you once these rounds start bursting.

A slight variation uses two smoke grenades instead of TRPs and an airstrike instead of artillery. This works really well since the fighters can strafe and bomb on a long axis and you're still safe even if their ordnance impacts long or short.

CHAPTER 22

NIGHT SNIPING OPERATIONS

NIGHT SNIPING OPERATIONS

The night belongs to whoever wants to use it and understands how best to exploit it. It's an environment boundless with opportunities for sniping.

The most basic feature of night is darkness, which, in addition to cloaking the sniper, lends itself to surprise, facilitates deception, and induces confusion. Beyond his difficulties in detecting you, your foe will encounter great problems in coordinating any counteractions should he discover your presence. Typically he will react not with maneuver but with fire, because controlling troops in the dark is a task wrought with danger. Further, he faces incredible problems discerning between foe and friend in the darkness.

Imagine the confusion trying to figure out what's happening. I once personally observed a North Vietnamese antitank rocketeer fire an RPG into a U.S. compound. His position was covered with an M60 machine gun, loaded and ready to rip. But it was night, and his backblast looked too small to be an RPG; also, his position was in the midst of what recently had been friendly ground. In the precious minutes it took to figure it all out, he got away clean.

U.S. Army Special Forces snipers atop a Baghdad roof prepare to engage insurgents at night.

Everything takes longer in the dark: decisions, reactions, movement, relaying messages—just everything. And all the hand and arm signals in the world are useless because no one can see them.

When you're behind enemy lines at night, identification of friend or foe for you is very simple: they're *all* bad guys. However, your foe has to figure out exactly who you are, should he even detect you. But in recent years, the spreading use of night observation devices (NODs) is making this a much more dangerous environment.

Avoiding Night Detection

There are some techniques to make yourself more difficult to detect at night. Merely by staying behind leaves and shrubbery, you'll avoid being seen by passive, handheld NODs.

But thermal and IR technologies *can* read your heat signature even in foliage. While there are ways to fool these state-of-the-art devices, I won't disclose them here.

However, the Special Forces SOTIC (Special Operations Target Interdiction Course) sniper handbook reports you can evade enemy ground surveillance radars by moving very slow and staying among radar-reflective clutter. An enemy having too much faith in technology would hardly expect you to infiltrate though a sector "covered" by radar, making this approach all the more effective.

To hone your ability to sneak through ground radar, you should work with a friendly battalion radar surveillance element and practice slipping through their system.

Night Camouflage

Among current U.S. military uniforms, I think the most effective night camouflage is provided by the Marine Corps' dark shade digital pattern. After that, the classic woodland pattern found on Army BDUs is efficient, as is the computer-generated checkered black-and-green desert night pattern developed a decade ago.

Gray is a decent night color, especially for police who may have to "blend" in among civilians during an infiltration. But gray reflects light somewhat and can be silhouetted.

Black BDUs are worn by many police tac teams, but at night they define the wearer by silhouetting him. This isn't a problem if it's really dark, but by the time it's this dark, almost any color or pattern would work.

Probably the best solid night color is olive drab—called "loden" by yuppies—because it's less distinct than black and absorbs most of the light that strikes it.

A full-fledged Ghillie suit is not really needed at night. You can make yourself sufficiently invisible with just a head-and-shoulders sniper cape that breaks up your outline as you walk and that you can drape across yourself while prone.

Night Sniper Movement and Stalking

A police sniper, too, must be concerned about remaining invisible during night movement, especially in rural areas while reconning a suspected clandestine drug lab or surveilling a remote airfield, for instance.

NIGHT CAMOUFLAGE PATTERNS (L-R): woodland, black, olive drab, desert night, and gray. (Photo credit: Roger Kennedy)

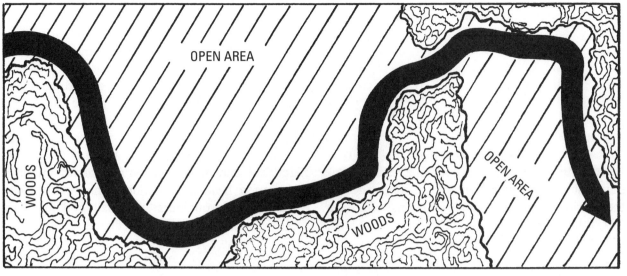

Exploit open areas for fast movement, but stay near wood lines.

Any humans seen moving about at night in a rural area attract attention because they don't belong there. Even if a suspect doesn't detect you, a nosy neighbor could. The best bet is to be invisible, and this starts with route selection. You should avoid skylining yourself along a ridge, stay away from natural lines of drift, and give yourself extra time.

Your en route rally points must be carefully selected because only the most prominent landmarks are easily found in darkness. Provided it's in line with your compass direction, you can use a star or constellation to guide your movement, but since these rotate in the night sky, you must recheck and adjust the one you're guiding on about every 10 minutes.

Traveling through moderately thin growth should be sufficient concealment against even NODs. For more speed you can walk through open areas, but stay close to the edges—even if it means walking in a wide circle—so you can duck into cover quickly if necessary. I guarantee you, you do not want to get caught in the middle of a large open area at night.

At times you may be steered by a friendly surveillance radar vectoring your team toward enemy forces that the radar unit detected. A radar operator may want to "walk" you into an open area because it's easier for him to track you, but carefully consider the tactical situation before venturing into an open expanse. It's your behind, not the radar operator's, that's on the line.

As our illustration on page 522 shows, try to travel with the moon to your back, which illuminates the area in front of you but masks you with glaring moonlight if someone tries to spot you from the opposite direction. To keep this straight in your mind, think of the moon as the sun; you'd want the sun at your back when approaching a foe, wouldn't you? Notice how in this same illustration our sniper holds his rifle close to his body so it won't rustle against foliage, and he extends his left arm to feel his way through brush and obstacles.

Each sniper should sew "cat's eyes" into the back of his hat. These luminous tape strips glow just enough for you to keep track of the man you're following in the dark but aren't visible at more than about 10 paces. Two 1-inch-high strips are sewn so there's a half-inch gap between them; when you're just the right distance behind your partner, you'll see two strips, but if you start slipping too far back, you'll notice them meld together into one image. Stay close enough in total darkness that you can communicate with whispers.

For recognition at greater distances, U.S. forces employ glint or glow tape that reflects IR light and can be detected at considerable distances with a night vision device or FLIR. The newer glow tape, attached to shoulders or a helmet as a small square or stripes, reflects back so brilliantly that it resembles the glare of an arc welder. So sophisticated has this ID tape become that the newest version reflects back as a half-degree beam toward the IR light source, leaving it undetected elsewhere.

Another means of night signaling is provided by M276 Dim Tracer ammunition. Distinguished by a green tip and pink ring, this IR tracer round is visible only to night vision and thermal devices, so a sniper can fire it to designate a target or otherwise indicate a location in darkness, without detection—except for his muzzle blast.

Light and Discipline

More than anything else, your night movement can be detected by generating noise or emitting some kind of light. I recall that while training at the Army National Training Center in the Mojave Desert, we could detect a glowing cigarette a mile away, and even a red filtered penlight was visible at twice that range.

Because we've been spoiled by a century of electrical light, it takes a special effort not to use light or to use it only in such a way that it cannot be seen. If you must em-

Keep the moon to your rear and your rifle close to your body.

Its Velcro cover removed, the "glint" patch on this soldier's helmet allows overhead gunships to identify him in the dark.

ploy light—say, to check your map—do it under a poncho you've already tested for light leaks.

Foolishly smoking cigarettes at night during World War I led to a superstition that persists to this very day: third man on a match. When British soldiers huddled together at night in the trenches, they frequently shared hard-to-find matches. From the German trench, a sniper would notice the glow of the first man lighting his cigarette and thus learn the Tommies' general location. By the time the second man's cigarette glowed, the enemy sniper was searching through his scope. When the third man used the match, the German snuffed him out.

Sound, too, is a problem since it travels farther and can be heard more clearly in the cool of night, requiring that you ensure all your gear is taped, tied, or wrapped to make it silent. Your slow movement, too, generates no noise.

Your team can exploit sound masking, such as wind rustling leaves or jets passing overhead, to accelerate movement. An ideal situation would be masking your night shots with thunderclaps and lightning.

Should you suddenly be illuminated by a light, *freeze*—unless it's very close, less than 50 yards—since a stationary image is probably 10 times harder to spot than a moving one. At very close range, of course, run for cover. But in either situation, be sure to protect your shooting eye's night vision by closing it when light suddenly appears.

If you have any advance warning—such as hearing a mortar fire an illumination round or seeing approaching headlights—get into thicker cover and get down. And don't lift your face into the light.

You could have a spotlight intently searching for you, with no alternative but to extinguish it with rifle fire. Aim for its center, and use your "weak" eye so you're still capable of firing in low light after it's been shot out. Fight smart.

Night Sniper Hides

There's a tendency for snipers to overextend themselves in the darkness; that is, to occupy a hide that may be excellent for night engagements but becomes extremely dangerous by daylight.

Evaluate your night hide in this respect, and be ready to relocate well before dawn into thicker, safer cover. An excellent temporary night hide would be in a ditch or creek bed from which the sniper can take a shot then withdraw without having even once exposed himself directly to small-arms fire.

And when it comes to overextending yourself, don't operate your hide both day and night or you'll wear yourself out. You should either sleep during the day and shoot at night, or shoot in daytime and rest at night—*unless* there's some kind of actual or likely enemy activity that's worth losing sleep to observe, or your orders specifically require day and night surveillance. Otherwise, remember: a fatigued sniper makes dumb, deadly mistakes.

Natural Night Vision

If we didn't have two eyes, we'd be in big trouble because this overlapped vision helps compensate for the natural blind spots in each human eye. Blind spots? Absolutely. In daytime it's easy to find the blind side in your vision. Look at our special black illustration below and cover your right eye while focusing your left eye on the X. Now, move the book back and forth. At about 18 inches, the crawling silhouette disappears because there's a spot inside your eye receptors that lacks light-sensitive cells.

This is called your "day blind spot," but your night vision also suffers because the eye's most sensitive area is out of line with your normal field of view. When you look directly at something in the dark, you will not see it as well as when you look slightly to its left. This is called left-of-center vision, which is shown on page 524. By focusing about 5 to 10 degrees left of a spot, your eyes will see what's there more clearly.

I thought this technique was fairly well known; however, a few years ago I was discussing night operations with a friend, a retired CIA paramilitary operations officer, and it was all new to him. But

Close your right eye and look at the "X" with your left, moving this image back and forth. At about 18 inches, the sniper at left will disappear.

Left-of-center vision.

photo receptor cells for darkness, requiring about 30 minutes in a dark room. During this period, a special chemical that's normally bleached out by daylight will accumulate in your eyes, boosting your light sensitivity 10,000 to 100,000 times. Due to oxygen depletion from carbon monoxide in his blood, a heavy smoker will attain only about 80 percent of his potential night vision.

Once accustomed to darkness, you must protect this vision because exposure to light bleaches these chemicals, requiring time for your eyes to readjust again. If you must use a light, make sure it's red filtered because the red wavelength has the least effect on these light-sensitive chemicals. But keep even red light as dim as possible.

Because you'll be using red light, don't mark your map with red since it becomes invisible in the filtered light. And make it a habit to protect your shooting eye. If you must look in the direction of bright lights or use a white light, close your shooting eye.

Night Spotting

In daylight a sniper cannot observe his own fire because recoil disrupts his vision. This problem compounds in darkness because muzzle flash also temporarily washes out his night vision. Thus, a spotter's role increases when the sun goes down.

Ideally, night observation is easiest when the moon is to your back, illuminating the sector in front of your hide. You'll probably find

this is commonly known in Special Forces, which conducts most operations at night. This night blind spot is large enough to hide a man at 75 feet and a tank at 300 yards.

Related to the night blind spot is the tendency for your eyes to "wash out" a night image by staring directly at it. A sniper overcomes this vision shortcoming by keeping his eyes active; scanning up, down, right, left, and in circles. When he notices something deserving a closer look, he uses left-of-center vision, offsetting his gaze by about 10 degrees. These techniques are especially critical when using a spotting or rifle scope, since you're employing just one eye.

Night vision itself is the sensitizing of

Silhouette your foe with the moon.

binoculars, with their wider field of view and overlapping vision, more effective than a spotting scope.

If the moon is to your front or side or there's any urban light reflected in the sky, try to silhouette your foe by positioning yourself on slightly lower ground. We've illustrated this to show that even dropping prone on relatively flat ground can silhouette an opponent who's otherwise invisible.

The ability to detect night targets using your other night sense—hearing—is done by cupping your hands behind your ears, an old Indian technique. This transforms your head into a sort of parabolic antenna. Rotate your head slowly and you'll be able to detect distant sounds with clarity and accuracy. You should practice estimating sound distances in the dark.

And when it comes to making night distance estimates, beware when estimating the range to a light source. Typically, you'll think it's farther away than it actually is.

Your night target priorities are the same as in daylight—snipers, then leaders, then crew-served weapons crewmen—except in the presence of enemy night vision systems. Then your number-one night target becomes any soldier with a weapon NOD or wearing NOD goggles. If you think about it, this is similar to day priorities since these likely will be snipers and leaders. You'd also shoot out IR vehicle lights to blind drivers.

The difficulty, however, is identifying priority targets at long range in darkness. Uniform features and badges of rank cannot be seen; weapons and equipment may be only vague shadows. So the best recognition feature likely is a target's activity combined with his position in a formation.

Available Light Shooting

During our sniper school, our first night fire is always with available light and students employing their ordinary daytime optics. It's not as sexy as high-tech NODs, but the students gain tremendous respect for their abilities to engage targets with "only" a scoped rifle. The optics portion of the spotting chapter addressed the ability of quality lenses to transmit light, so we won't rehash all that material. But recall that your eye pupil dilates to 7mm in total darkness, and

about 6mm on the average night, and that your scope is most effective when it produces a cone of light of this diameter.

Yes, an exit pupil of about 6mm is best for low-light shooting, and you should adjust your zoom scope's magnification to achieve this. The effect is the same as dilating your pupil to let more light enter or opening up a camera's F-stop for low-light photography. For night shooting, set your scope at the following power:

Objective Lens Diameter		Best Night Power
56mm	set at	9x
50mm	set at	8x
44mm	set at	7x
40mm	set at	6x

This also shows why some scope makers use ever larger objective lenses to allow higher magnification without reducing relative brightness.

When adjusted properly, your optics will disclose more detail than is visible to your naked eye. Our students are surprised to be able to engage balloons accurately at 200 yards under a half-moon using only daytime optics. One tip, though, is not to aim too long or focus your eye on a target too intensely or it fades from view.

Also, light of any kind in your field of view diminishes your ability to see targets. The effect of such light can be minimized by relocating your hide so the light is to your side or back.

Even in total darkness, you still can hit targets accurately 100 yards away with a daytime scope by having your spotter illuminate it with a four-cell flashlight or a SureFire. With practice, you can hit head-size targets with only 1 second of illumination, which we've done many times in demonstrations. This technique is well suited to police and counterterrorist operations.

Any extra light you can bring to bear will pay big dividends at night. Vehicle high-beam headlights generate enough reflective glare to see all the targets on a range, and, during a search for a hostile in a wooded area, this can help you spot him optically before he spots you.

Diversions and Deceptions

Every time a sniper fires in darkness, he also creates a muzzle flash that tells the enemy, "Shoot here!" Bolt-action rifles lacking any kind of flash suppressor generate a particularly conspicuous flame at night.

In an urban hide, the muzzle flash will fill the room and look like someone just took a photograph, it's so bright. Friends who've experimented with wet bandanas draped over the muzzle tell me these dampen the flash and claim it does not degrade accuracy, but I haven't tested this myself.

Another technique is to mask the flash by having your muzzle well back into foliage. Similar results are achieved in an urban hide by draping dark curtains in front of the windows, which you emplace after sunset. Leave a narrow hole for aiming and for your bullet to exit.

As a rule of thumb, much more so than in daytime, I think you should fire only one shot from a hide at night, then displace or withdraw. The odds of having that muzzle flash detected are just too great, especially if you attempt a follow-up shot.

I've already plugged the need for dummy positions to fulfill the enemy's psychological desire for retaliation. At night this becomes much easier because it's so simple to simulate a muzzle flash. The claymore mine firing device can be unwound and placed up to 50 feet away; at the instant you fire, your spotter detonates the cap, which bangs and flashes dramatically.

The same can be achieved by removing a smoke grenade fuze and attaching a pull wire to its ring. Just be aware that your pull cord can become tangled, there's a two-second delay before it flashes, and there's no "bang." A truly insidious sniper, however, does the same thing, but with a brilliant tripflare. Not only will the enemy fire at this dazzling light, but the more he looks at it, the more he'll burn out his night vision, and the easier it becomes for you to disappear.

Something a bit more subtle is to expose an IR chemlight in a dummy position, again using a pull cord so that enemy NOD-equipped riflemen have something to shoot at, too.

If you want to fire in darkness but lack NODs, you can use a World War I German trick, called a "fixed rifle." All you do is sandbag a rifle firmly so the crosshairs are dead on a point that you're sure will have activity after dark, such as a bunker slit or window. Long after sunset, when there's a hint of activity, pull the trigger and who knows? As a minimum the enemy will conclude you can see him, and this has psychological effect at least.

But whether firing for deception, with NODs, or just available light, the challenges and special techniques for night shooting are so significant that we recommend 40 percent of practice shooting take place in darkness.

GENERATIONS OF NIGHT VISION DEVICES

The first electro-optical devices that improved observing and shooting at night were introduced by the United States in the closing days of World War II. When a target was illuminated with a nonvisible infrared spotlight, a shooter could look through a compatible IR night vision scope and hit reliably to nearly 100 yards. Problem was (aside from bulk and weight), anyone on the battlefield with an IR-filtered viewer could see the spotlight as clearly as a white light beam. Through most of its post–World War II history, the Soviet army relied on assorted IR devices despite this substantial vulnerability, while American night technology went in a profoundly different direction in the 1950s.

Nazi Germany, too, had developed IR devices late in the war, as well as a completely new technology that had not even reached prototype stage, the cascade image tube. The U.S. Department of Defense contracted with RCA to continue this research, which in 1958 resulted in a new, passive viewing technology that intensified available light. No IR spotlight was required because this device boosted available light by about 20,000 times to make faint images visible. Within a few years, the U.S. Army fielded the AN/PVS-2—the Starlight scope—the world's first passive night sight, which was used extensively in the Vietnam War. Thus, the Starlight scope and other passive viewing systems of that era are considered Generation I (Gen. I) devices.

The AN/PVS-4 night vision device is ballistically compatible with assault rifles, not sniper rifles.

AN/PVS-7 monocular goggles offer Gen. II+ night viewing.

DISTANCE TO SEE A 6-FOOT MAN IN DARKNESS

Device	Full Moon (0.1 lux)	Half Moon (0.001 lux)	Quarter Moon (.0005 lux)	Starlight (.0001 lux)	Overcast (.00001 lux)
Eyes	250 yards	150 yards	50 yards	<20 yards	<10 yards
Gen. II	675 yards	590 yards	530 yards	330 yards	100 yards
Gen. III	800 yards	750 yards	700 yards	500 yards	200 yards

By the mid-1970s, the U.S. Army's Night Vision Laboratory had perfected a better imaging tube with enhanced clarity, resulting in the AN/PVS-4 night weapon sight. This boosted available light by about 50,000 with finer clarity, much like a digital image improves with more pixels per inch. Like many a veteran who used the PVS-2 in combat, I was overwhelmed by the improved image of the PVS-4, which became the yardstick for a Generation II device. The first U.S. night vision goggles—the AN/PVS-5s—actually are Gen. II devices because they incorporate the newer intensifier technology (though miniaturized) found on the PVS-4.

Generation II+ and III devices arrived during the late 1980s and 1990s, found in such night sights as Litton's Models 845 and 938 and AN/PVS-7 goggles.

To put these capabilities in perspective, the comparative data on the previous page from ITT Night Vision contrasts how far you can see a 6-foot man in low-light conditions.

From my experience, I'd say these figures exaggerate sniper engagement distances by about 25 percent because merely being able to make out a human figure against a contrasting background is not as visually difficult as picking out a tactical target and placing your crosshair on him. Still, the Gen. III possibilities are impressive, allowing engagements at distances compatible with sniper rifle capabilities.

LASER POINTERS AND ILLUMINATORS

Paralleling the evolution of night vision devices has been a family of supporting laser pointers and illuminators. While I believe that visible-light lasers have almost no utility as day weapon sights, IR-wavelength lasers—not visible to unaided eyes—are a tremendous aid to shooting and signaling at night.

The U.S. military uses two types of IR wavelength laser weapon sights, the AN/PAQ-4 and AN/PEQ-2, mounted atop and on the forearm side of assault rifles, particularly the M4 carbine. The PAQ-4 is purely an aiming device, projecting a 0.5 mil IR laser beam that the shooter can see while wearing night vision goggles. Though it looks similar—about the size of a paperback book—the PEQ-2 is both a weapon sight and a laser illuminator. When used to aim, the shooter sets the PEQ-2 beam to 0.5 mil and output power on low so it doesn't glaringly overwhelm his goggles. To illuminate a target, he widens the beam to 10 mils and increases power to 24 milliwatts. This intense nonvisible spotlight helps identify targets as far as 2,000 meters away, allowing engagement by night vision devices—but just like IR lights in the early days, it can be seen by anyone with a night vision device.

Used in tandem with night vision goggles, the AN/PEQ-2 laser aimer projects an otherwise invisible dot for night shooting.

The next generation of laser aimers—the Integrated Laser White Light Pointer (ILWLP)—adds a SureFire-style intense flashlight to this device.

When installed on an M4 or M16, these laser sights usually are zeroed at 300 yards so the shooter can aim center-mass and achieve hits all the way to 400 yards. At 100 yards, this zero puts the bullet 4 inches high, almost the same at 200, dead-on at 300, and 12 inches low at 400 yards. The laser is bright enough that the shooter can see it at up to 660 yards, though he must use holdover after 400 yards.

Related to these IR laser weapon sights is the Ground Commander's Pointer-Infrared, a much more powerful invisible laser—100 milliwatts—used primarily to direct helicopter gunships and attack aircraft at night. About the size of a candy bar, its adjustable beam looks like something out of the *Star Wars* movies to anyone wearing goggles or looking through a night weapon sight. Of great relevance to snipers, as I demonstrated in the video *Advanced Ultimate Sniper*, this pointer's beam can illuminate a gunman hidden in the deep shadows of a dark room or beneath an overhanging rock who would not otherwise be visible to a sniper using even a Gen. III night sight.

This Ground Commander's Pointer-Infrared projects a powerful invisible laser beam to illuminate targets for night weapon sights.

IMAGE-INTENSIFYING NIGHT WEAPON SIGHTS

Because night sights are evolving in several directions, I'm addressing them by how they operate, beginning here with night-only, sole-purpose, stand-alone night scopes like the AN/PVS-4. Except for specialized, high-magnification sights for snipers, this class of night vision device has almost completely given way to day/night units, modular systems, and night vision adaptive units, covered momentarily.

The prime examples of the specialized sniping scopes are the NVEC Raptor, a 6x weapon sight with a 100mm objective lens, and the similar-performing ITT F2000. This combination of high magnification, a large objective lens, and Gen. III image tube makes for target clarity at true sniping distances—1,000 or more yards, depending on ambient light. They're especially compatible with .50-caliber sniper rifles.

The downside of these excellent devices is that they are night-only scopes, and contrary to some claims, you probably won't retain a precise long-range zero if you remove, then remount them. Once this kind of night sight is mounted and zeroed, for best results designate that weapon a night engagement rifle and leave it alone.

DAY/NIGHT SNIPING SCOPES

To solve this problem of switching from day scopes to night sights with attendant rezeroing requirements, a new class of sniper scopes has been developed that puts both capabilities in a single device.

ITT addresses this need with its Modular

This Gen. II+ weapon sight's 100mm objective lens works well with a McMillan .50-caliber rifle.

The Gen. III F2000 night sight from ITT offers the magnification and image clarity required for sniper-grade shooting.

Day/Night Weaponsight F7201, which has an interchangeable ocular lens unit. One is for daylight; the other is a compact Gen. III ocular adapter for night firing. You use the same scope, the same windage and elevation, and the same zero for both modes. I've tried this scope and found it works great, but it's not military ruggedized so I doubt it will stand up to harsh field conditions. For civilian law enforcement I think it would be just fine.

The other device, the U.S. military AN/PVS-10 day/night sniper scope, *is* ruggedized, and it's now in use by both the Army and Marine Corps. Built on contract by Northrop, ITT, and NVEC, the PVS-10 has an 8.5x and a 12.2x version, although most of the units reaching the field are the lower-magnification model. It's intended to replace the U.S. Army's Leupold Mark 4 M3A scopes and Marine Corps' Unertl 10x scopes.

Compact and high quality, the Leitz Gen. III night weapon sight.

The good news is that this device does all that its designers said it would. The bad news is that it has not been very well received in the field. I've spoken with a number of snipers and military sniper instructors who find significant faults with the PVS-10, to include weight (5 pounds), bulk (twice the size of a daylight scope), a decline in magnification (8.5x versus 10x), and so many adjustment knobs that it's a challenge to keep it tuned.

The great majority of snipers I've spoken with would rather continue to use their daytime Leupold and Unertl scopes, simply adding on a Simrad night adapter for nighttime firing—which brings us to our next category of night weapon sights.

The AN/PVS-10 day/night scope is being used by both Army and Marine snipers.

A USMC sniper practices firing from a hovering helicopter using an AN/PVS-10 day/night scope.

NIGHT VISION ADAPTIVE UNITS

Developed in Norway and now manufactured in Florida under license, the Simrad is a night vision adapter that attaches to a sniper scope's objective lens. Originally produced as Gen. II devices and now Gen. III, the Simrad KN203 and KN253 FAB convert a daytime scope to a high-quality, night-capable viewing system. Snipers really like the Simrad because it employs the excellent lenses of their daytime scopes, which they believe are superior to the AN/PVS-10. Further, they point out, when using the PVS-10 they must carry its bulk and weight (5 pounds) everywhere, on every mission. Depending on the model, the

The Simrad night sight converts a variety of optics into night-capable viewing systems.

The Simrad KN200P is especially popular with U.S. Army snipers.

Mounted atop a Barrett M107, this Simrad KN203FAB night adapter allows a daytime Swarovski scope to fire in darkness.

on a Picatinny rail extension over the barrel so it's directly in-line with the daytime scope. By contrast, the Simrad attaches above the scope on a special mount that replaces its front, upper ring. Employing an AN/AVS-6 tube housing, the UNS is Gen. III, weighs 2 pounds, and is powered by two AA batteries.

Both the Simrad and the UNS are being considered for the U.S. Defense Department's requirement for a Long Range Sniper Rifle Night Sight, which will be used with the Barrett M107 .50-caliber rifle.

MODULAR NIGHT VISION SYSTEMS

The concept behind a modular system is that you can take one basic device and—by adding or removing lenses, adapters, and mounts—employ it

UNS (Universal Night Scope) from Knight's Armament fits in-line on a Picatinny rail to convert a daytime scope for night firing.

Simrad adds 2.5 or 3.5 pounds, but they only mount it for specific night missions.

The Simrad also offers greater flexibility because marginal lighting conditions—like dawn, dusk, or nighttime city lights—and sudden bright lights, such as headlights and flares, do not degrade its image. The sole downside to the Simrad is that its porro-prism, step-up design optically shifts the daytime scope's reticle up about 4 MOA, which is corrected by similarly shifting the elevation. Snipers don't find that significant.

Still, even this issue is addressed by another night vision adapter, the UNS—Universal Night Scope—from Knight's Armament. The UNS fits

The Gen. III PVS-14 night vision device allows many daytime optics—from spotting scopes to laser rangefinders—to see in the dark.

as a monocular goggle, a weapon sight, laser range-finder, you name it. The best example is the AN/PVS-14, often seen mounted on M4 carbines for night viewing with daytime optics or suspended from soldiers' helmets for night observation. The PVS-14 is sometimes employed with laser range-finders, while Northrup Grumman even makes a 5x afocal lens to convert it into an assault rifle weapon sight. Displaying Yankee ingenuity, some GI snipers in Iraq have extended the stocks on their M24s and attached the PVS-14 to their Leupold's ocular lens for night firing. It works, but you have to be careful about recoil.

THERMAL SCOPES AND FUSION TECHNOLOGY

Not many years ago, thermal viewers weighed hundreds of pounds and required special coolants to operate. Thanks to miniaturization, thermal viewers have become compact and light enough to use as weapon sights—and not only for night. As explained in the FLIR section (see Chapter 13), thermal imaging penetrates thin foliage, smoke, fog, rain, and snow. Since thermal imagers measure heat instead of intensify ambient light, they operate with equal efficiency no matter the available light conditions.

The U.S. military is acquiring the PAS-13 family of thermal weapon sights, with a considerable impact on long-range shooting. The Light Thermal Weapon Sight (LTWS), intended for the M16 and M4 carbine, weighs only 3 pounds and

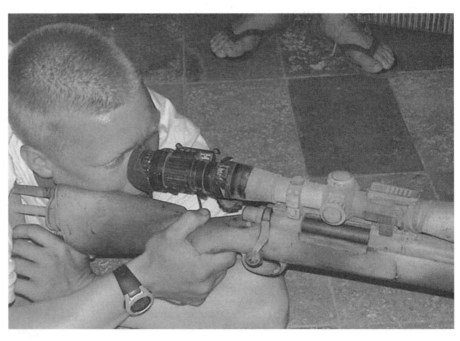

This GI in Iraq jerry-rigged a day/night scope by attaching an AN/PVS-14 to his daytime M3A scope.

An FBI SWAT officer patrols New York harbor, his machine gun mounting a thermal weapon sight.

Though these goggles resemble PVS-7s, they're actually thermal.

These PAS-13 thermal weapon sights are compatible with assault rifles or long-range sniper rifles.

Though still inferior to Western night vision devices, newer Russian night sights are improving in quality.

allows engagements to 550 meters. The Medium Thermal Weapon Sight (MTWS), a 5-pound device, is compatible with 7.62mm rifles, allowing engagements to 1,100 meters. The 6-pound Heavy Thermal Weapon Sight (HTWS) is intended for .50-caliber weapons, with a maximum viewing range of 2,200 meters. All these PAS-13 sights are now arriving in Iraq and Afghanistan.

Like anyone who has used one, I've been properly impressed by handheld thermal viewers and weapon sights—but they can be fooled with a bit of ingenuity. The next generation of night vision devices addresses this by fusing thermal imaging with Gen. III+ image intensification in a single unit. Already ITT has delivered prototype goggles to the Army that fuses both technologies in a unit that's no larger than AN/PVS-7s, proving

that it's within the capabilities of current technology. I think the bigger question is, with night sights that already cost five times as much as a quality sniper rifle, will we be able to afford such wondrous night vision devices?

CHAPTER 23
SPECIAL SNIPING ENVIRONMENTS

SPECIAL SNIPING ENVIRONMENTS

America's War on Terror finds U.S. troops combating foes in a variety of environments—from Iraq's parched western desert to Afghanistan's Hindu Kush mountains and the steamy jungles of the Philippines. Were war to erupt on the Korean Peninsula, snow and cold would be components of fighting there.

Afghanistan combines winter and mountain shooting environments, challenging this U.S. Army 10th Mountain Division sniper.

Each of these terrains and climates offers such distinct challenges and opportunities that it's worth taking a closer look at how they affect sniping.

Sniping in the Desert

Everything in the desert is farther or greater than in other environments. Movement rates are faster; how far you must roam to find the enemy is greater; visibility is farther; and shooting distances are longer, too. Because of this, many spotters prefer to carry the ballistically superior 7.62mm M21 or M25 system rather than a 5.56mm M16 or M4 carbine.

Just as in snow country, the desert's harsh, glaring light may be overwhelming when you look through your scope. To improve target clarity, reduce the amount of light entering your objective lens with a homemade aperture, easy to fashion out of tape and cardboard. Be sure to color it to match your camouflage.

Dust is a never-ending problem. As our troops have found in Iraq, desert sand contains powder-fine granules—finer than powdered sugar—that adhere to lubricated weapon components. The best treatment is a dry lubricant like Smooth-Kote and its related cloth applicator, Tuf-Cloth, which molecularly bond to metal, leaving a layer of molybdenum disulfide particles that lasts a long time. If you don't have these products available, use the absolute minimum of lubricant and wipe off your bolt, chamber, receiver, and magazine twice daily. Also put a piece of tape across your muzzle to keep sand out. (This shouldn't affect your zero, but be sure to test that this is so before going into the field.)

Range and wind estimation is particularly difficult in trackless desert country. With few visible objects or terrain features to establish perspective or scale, the "naked eye" range estimation techniques we covered in Chapter 12 don't work well. A laser rangefinder is essential for desert shooting.

In both snow country and desert, improve target clarity by installing a field-expedient aperture to reduce glaring, harsh light.

Likewise, the GPS has proven itself a perfect tool for desert navigation—but you still need a compass and map.

Wind direction, an old desert hand tells me, is sometimes discernable by looking at how it sculpts sand drifts, as we've illustrated at right. Interestingly, the same approach can be used in winter by studying snowdrifts.

Mirage has a ubiquitous presence, which is handy for estimating wind through a spotting scope. But that same mirage is a significant impediment to long-range observation and aiming. One solution is to plan your shots for dawn and early morning, before the sun has warmed

Featureless desert terrain lacks landmarks for navigation and range estimation, making a laser rangefinder essential.

Look to how wind drifts sand to find its direction.

Water is a special concern. The amount of water you carry most likely will determine your mission's duration. You could extend its length if you cached extra water at an insert LZ or vehicular dropoff point. However, so little water is found out there that to get near natural sources for it means you'll encounter people and possibly enemy forces. Remember: in the desert, where there's water, you'll find people.

Desert Camouflage

In the daytime desert sun, a Ghillie suit is too hot for most situations. Sniper capes and small, positional camouflage nets are much cooler and—provided you're reasonably camouflaged—almost as effective.

the desert enough to radiate shimmering heat waves. Another is to locate your Final Firing Position on high ground so you're looking and firing downward through the mirage—where it's thinner—rather than straight through it.

In most cases, you must be as mobile as the enemy you may encounter and/or have a Quick Reaction Force available. To be caught on foot in flat desert country free of natural obstacles—such as wadis or boulder fields—is to beg for trouble. If not a HMMWV, a sniper team needs all-terrain vehicles or even motorcycles, which they use to infiltrate during darkness. During daylight, the team surveils or engages targets, with their vehicle hidden nearby. This is a fitting method for sniper teams interdicting weapons smugglers and infiltrators along Iraq's western border with Syria, giving them both the mobility they need and a low-signature to avoid detection.

Desert country's sparse foliage does not lend itself to stalking or to evasion after taking a shot. Careful route selection—to exploit gullies and wadis and folds in the land—is the best solution. Obscuring your backtrail to preclude hostile trackers is a never-ending requirement. Equally, by SOP you should buttonhook several times per day, doubling back in a wide circle to overwatch your backtrail, just to see if anyone's following you.

ANORAKS. These handy pullover jackets provide warmth in the desert's cool night wind.

DESERT CAMOUFLAGE PATTERNS. (L-R) Six-color, brown Realtree, tan, night desert checkered, and three-color. (Photo credit: Roger Kennedy)

In Chapter 13 we already discussed the excellent Marine Corps digital desert pattern, so to that we'll add the Army's three-color pattern. The presence of pink in three colors is especially effective because, although desert coloration is dominated by brown shades, sunlight diffuses and reflects pink across desert sands, a fact exploited by both British and German desert camo in World War II. The newer Army Combat Uniform's universal digital pattern, I believe, is inferior to the three-color camo because it's too gray, although it's not so bad that it won't work.

Plain tan or khaki isn't bad either, especially when it's enhanced with spray paint or local natural camouflage. When you tie the colors to your specific area, the results are always better.

We've included brown Realtree mesh as a desert candidate because once the sun's down, bright daylight patterns too readily reflect light and silhouette the wearer. Even if you can acquire only a darker jacket, this added touch will greatly enhance night concealment.

Finally, one of the most useful pieces of desert clothing is the anorak, a hooded pullover jacket whose warmth is most welcome at night. Ideally, your anorak should be reversible, like those issued to Special Ops units, with daytime camo on one side and a night pattern on the other.

Sniping in Winter

What distinguishes the winter environment are snow and cold; snow primarily affects movement, while cold affects the operation of equipment and condition of personnel. Beyond these fundamentals, realize that everything takes longer in winter—whether moving cross-country, cooking chow, or loading your rifle. Rifle maintenance and operation are much more critical because some lubricants thicken and even freeze at subzero temperatures. I can recall stories from Korea of GIs urinating on their frozen M1s to keep them operating. During World War II, German forces in Russia found that only sunflower oil remained liquid in bitter cold.

Once the temperature falls below +10°F, the U.S. Army advises to lubricate the M24 sniper rifle with Lubricant Arctic Weapon (LAW) but only lightly. The dry molybdenum lubricant Smooth-Kote is even better than LAW in subzero cold since it cannot freeze or become gummy. If you don't have LAW or Smooth-Kote, I don't think you should use *any* lube in bitter cold—wipe the bolt and especially the lugs *totally dry* to keep the weapon from freezing shut.

A related problem is the weapon's "sweating" when you take it back and forth from a heated area to the outdoors, which may freeze your bolt, too.

Moonlight reflecting off snow allows excellent available-light shooting and dramatically increases the range of night sights.

When shooting from skis, use the poles for support. Note how the wrist straps are interlocked.

In deep, soft snow, support your rifle with snowshoes.

The long-accepted solution here is to *keep the rifle outdoors* once it's accustomed to that temperature, under guard if there's threat of any theft.

Carrying your weapon in and out also fogs the scope lens, a very dangerous problem for police in winter since they may await action in vehicles or heated shelters. Real-world, this happened to one of my law enforcement sniper graduates; when his SWAT team cornered a cop killer on a rural farm, he was warming up in a squad car and deployed with a rifle he couldn't possibly fire. It took about 15 minutes for the lens to clear, but eventually the murderer surrendered—and my former student had learned quite a lesson.

Observation becomes much easier in winter because foliage loses its leaves and light reflects off the snow, making for a bright scene day or night. In fact, there's so much light that glare can

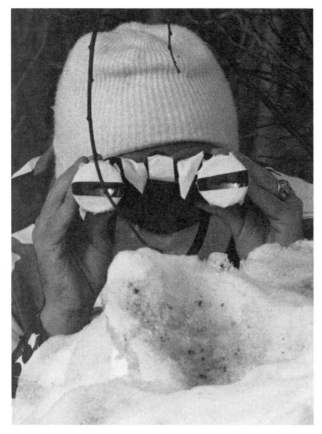

Reduce glaring light by partially taping binoculars or spotting scope objective lenses. (Photo credit: Brad Hopkins)

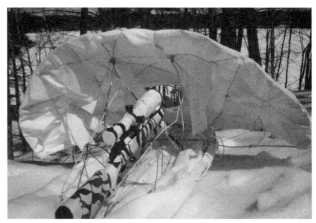

This Russian-style shooting sled's white screen conceals the sniper, who stalks forward by pushing with his feet.

5.56MM BALL PENETRATION OF SNOW
(single rounds)

Loose Snow (11.2–13 lbs./cu. ft.)	46 inches
Packed Snow (17.4–23.7 lbs./cu. ft.)	28 inches

7.62MM NATO PENETRATION OF ICE AND SNOW
(5-round bursts)

Loose Snow	144"
Frozen Snow	64"
Packed Snow	60"
Frozen Soil	19"
Ice-crete *	15"

* Water and soil aggregate

degrade your vision, which can be improved by partially taping the objective lens of your spotting scope, binoculars, or rifle scope to reduce the amount of entering light. Leupold even makes special screw-on aperture disks to reduce light passage into its rifle scopes.

Tactics and techniques are largely determined by the long-range observation, impassibility of snow, and impact of cold and wind that characterize winter. As Finnish ski troops demonstrated in their 1940 Winter War with the USSR, superior cross-snow mobility allows you to cut an enemy to shreds, and this is particularly true for snipers who nip at an enemy's heels, then disappear. I recall one clever Finnish tactic: attacking a foe with the bitter wind to your back so your enemy must face the wind to aim at you and, in only a few seconds, his eyes water and he loses his vision. It's as effective as coming out of the sun.

As a rule, any vehicle light enough to drive over the snow is vulnerable to rifle fire, despite the fact it may appear armored. I'm thinking in particular of Russian and Chinese GT-T Model 1970 tracked vehicles; although they look like personnel carriers, they're only made of sheet metal.

We're discussing winter camouflage separately, so I'll only add that proper clothing will make or break you. An outer layer of wind-resistant material is essential, as are layers of insulated clothes that you add or remove according to the heat your activity produces. What's *not* correctly understood,

Chemical hand warmers and wool mitts help maintain trigger sensitivity.

WRONG. Bottoms should be white, like the ground.

however, is that you should heavily overdress while lying motionless in your hide to retain body warmth. And you must keep your shooting hand warm or your trigger finger will lose its sensitivity.

Winter Camouflage Patterns

Rarely is snow so deep and terrain so feature-less that pure white totally dominates a winter scene. Be just as keen eyed when assessing varied winter coloration as during summer.

Add some green if you're in pine woods, black and gray shadows to match rocks, yellow lines for standing corn stalks, etc. I've noticed that subtle gray-blue stripes can really enhance white camouflage.

Fight the mistaken inclination to wear only a white parka. As our illustration above shows, this *highlights* you because the ground is white and leafless trees are dark, exactly the opposite of the way you're dressed. Also, make a special effort to keep white clothing clean to keep it effective.

Military Overwhites and Expedient Clothing

To avoid the expensive duplication of issuing both summer and winter uniforms, most armies use overwhites, simple oversized white garments worn over regular uniforms in winter.

German army overwhites are reversible, with pure white on one side and pine bough highlights on the other. The pants are held up by adjustable suspenders, while both parka and pants have plenty of zippers and surprisingly good workmanship.

My U.S. military overwhites, which I've high-lighted a bit with gray and black, are not so elabo-rate and rely more on elastic and tie-downs than zippers. Still, they're adequate.

Commercial paper overwhites should be stan-dard equipment for all snowbelt police tactical teams. They're cheap, compact to store, and the easiest way to be ready. Look for those made of Du Pont's Tyvek paper, which is particularly resistant to tearing.

The long-time winter standby, a white bed-sheet parka, can do the trick, but make sure it drapes low enough to cover your legs or you'll only highlight yourself.

WINTER PATTERNS. (L-R) Brown and white parka, West German army overwhites, Snowflage, U.S. Army overwhites with spray-painted highlights, and Skyline.

Sometimes while lying prone in a smooth snowfield, I've found it especially effective to toss a white sheet across myself to blend in even better with the snow's surface. The edges of my 6 x 6-foot sheet are weighted with lead sinkers sewn into it to keep it in place.

Civilian Winter Camouflage

A number of years ago, an investigator friend asked me to surveil a site where a murder victim's body was to be dropped in a few hours. We'd had heavy snow two days earlier, and I had no over-whites in the closet. Desperate, I rushed to a local Sears and bought an oversized lab worker's jacket and a pair of white painter's overalls. It was expedient as hell, but it worked great.

Also shown are three civilian winter patterns, the most effective in my experience being Skyline with its hints of blue-gray shadows. The black-gray-white Snowflage-pattern BDUs, sometimes promoted as "urban camouflage," blend much better into a winter environment than a city one.

And finally, there's a mottled white-brown pattern that looks interesting but seems to have very limited application—how often do you see such orange-brown shades in winter?

Camouflaging Face and Head

Don't make the mistake of coloring your flesh with white cammo paste or you'll conceal telltale signs of frostbite. Instead, wear a white ski mask or gray-white Spandoflage.

The U.S. Army has long used the white Extreme Cold Weather Mask, which both conceals your face and protects your flesh from stinging winter winds.

Tracks and Hides in Snow

Plan your winter marches—whether by ski, snowshoe, snowmobile, or plain foot—realizing that you'll leave tracks through the snow. You should stay inside woodlines, travel along snowdrifts that cover your passage with shadow, and exploit snowfalls and strong winds that mask your tracks.

Occupy low hides that blend into the background, which should be the most difficult to detect. You can create a dummy hide merely by leaving visible tracks and exposed earth.

Sniping in Mountain Country

Mountain sniping is characterized by frequent high-angle uphill or downhill shots, long-distance shots across chasms, and terrain that lends itself well to stalking and concealment. With many ridgelines and jagged fingers, this environment should afford you plenty of protection from enemy small-arms fire, too. Also, the many sound reflective surfaces found in mountains readily generate confusing echoes, which you can exploit to great effect by how you position your hide.

Maybe my judgment's colored by memories of elk hunting in Colorado, but I'd feel much better in mountain country with the superior range and wind-bucking advantages of a .300 Winchester Magnum than with a .308/7.62mm. I think the various .50-caliber sniper rifles are too bulky and heavy for day-to-day operations in difficult mountain terrain, but they'd fit the bill perfectly for some special raids and ambushes.

And talking about winds, they get really tricky in canyons and valleys, similar to how we've already illustrated them for major urban areas. Usually the closer you are to the bottom of a steep valley, the more likely the wind is to follow its long axis, while wind direction and speed will vary with altitude.

Altitude may affect your bullet's trajectory significantly enough that we're featuring this in its own section. (See page 547.)

American sniper and Special Ops teams working Afghanistan's Hindu Kush Range of the Himalayas have coined a new term—"acoustic dead space"—meaning you can be slightly on one side of a high ridge yet not hear gunfire a quarter-mile away on the reverse slope, which is important if an adjacent team is being attacked or Taliban lookouts are signaling each other with rifle fire. Be aware of this.

A longtime Special Forces friend just back from Afghanistan told me, "John, you can't believe the terrain we're fighting in." Indeed, some of these mountains are a third higher than the Colorado Rockies, with narrow defiles and steep cliffs—all devoid of trees. SSgt. Matthew Blaskowski, an Army Scout-Sniper wounded in the remote Arghandab Valley, told Army interviewers his unit was "surrounded by walls, steep cliffs." From atop them, Taliban shooters poured fire on the Scout-Snipers, Blaskowki recalled. "It was a very uncomfortable feeling."

At times, Afghanistan's immense valleys and mountains seem so deceptively empty of human presence that you wouldn't know where to begin to look for the enemy. Keep in mind that these guerrillas aren't flying around, and they can't rappel up and down those mountains. Natural line of drift analysis (see Chapter 11) and careful map studies can provide clues to the age-old goat trails used by a dozen generations of smugglers and today's al Qaeda and Taliban. Identify those natural lines of drift and you'll find them and can engage them.

Immense valleys and vast visibility in Afghanistan demand long-range optics and weapons.

There's a temptation with such apparently unlimited visibility—often measurable in miles—to forgo facial camouflage, but that's a mistake. Keep in mind that the American Indian referred to his Caucasian adversaries as "pale faces" because that was a major target indicator. Even at long range, in the right lighting pale flesh can stick out.

Probably the greatest advantage American snipers have over the Taliban and al Qaeda fighters is their optics, which our teams are using to the maximum. It's having an effect because these foes have largely fled across the border into Pakistan or the most remote mountain valleys of an already remote country.

Sniping in Jungles

An unfortunate misimpression generated by several recent books is that sniping was widely practiced during the Vietnam War. I don't wish to diminish the honor and achievements of Vietnam snipers, but we must realistically recognize that a jungled environment is not normally suited to long-range engagements.

The usefulness of sniping is dictated by terrain, and Vietnam's triple-canopy jungle did not generally lend itself to sniping. The major exceptions were the devegetated northern hill country of I Corps, where legendary USMC snipers Chuck MaWhinney and Carlos Hathcock operated, and the Mekong Delta, where the 9th Infantry Division's Adelbert F. Waldron III performed admirably.

The vast, *vast* majority of contacts with enemy personnel occurred at close range, usually about 50 yards or less, due to Vietnam's thick vegetation. In such conditions, you're at a disadvantage if you're armed with a scoped rifle and your enemy has a large-magazine assault rifle. As a (humble) survivor of many firefights during three years in Vietnam, I can think of only one instance where I would have preferred to have had a scoped rifle.

But sniping still has utility in jungle country, provided a sniper's properly employed in terrain where he can exploit his superior optics and ballistic advantage. Just taking a sniper along for an operation in thick jungle—as can happen too easily—is the height of foolishness.

Assuming you're deployed in an area where there's adequate observation and fields of fire, though, certain aspects of the jungle can be exploited to great effect. First, unlike any other terrain, jungle foliage absorbs sound well, making it tough for the enemy to detect your muzzle blast location. Second, jungle concealment is excellent, and you won't need a hot Ghillie suit to be invisible. And third—and I have no doubt this is why I'm alive today—the enemy may attempt to chase you through thick jungle, but the lush greenery quickly swallows you, making pursuit extremely difficult.

Cross-country jungle travel is slow and physically demanding for a sniper

Sparse foliage in Afghanistan's lowlands makes for difficult stalking. Thus, sniper teams maneuver in darkness and exploit folds in the land.

team, which dares not march along a trail. The quickest way to get killed is using trails behind enemy lines.

Compared to other operating environments, range estimation seems to be least troublesome in the jungle because there's plenty of physical perspective and terrain features. Likewise, winds don't tend to blow nearly so fast and confusingly through thick foliage as in desert or mountain country.

And finally, I'd advise you to quietly open your bolt each morning before dawn and wipe the chamber free of any water condensation that gathered during the night. If you don't do this, that thin layer of moisture could screw up the headspace and cause your weapon not to fire, or it could freeze the bolt lugs if you are able to shoot. I've personally seen bolt guns jam due to such condensation, which is easily prevented.

Sniping in the Rain

I've yet to come across any information about the effect of a bullet passing through rain or hail, although this environment must have some ballistic impact.

What we *do* know, however, is that even a single drop of rain in your muzzle can cause a bullet to deflect, which in benchrest shooting is called a "rain shot." Glenn Newick, the national benchrest shooting champion who authored *The Ultimate in Rifle Accuracy*, cites this problem, although he doesn't quantify it.

Another competitive rifle shooter, Geza Nagy, similarly tested the effect of water drops entering a rifle muzzle. A few drops gradually opened his groups. A few more drops and his bullets didn't even hit the target frame—less than a half-teaspoon of water, he discovered, had blown a tiny fracture in his rifling.

To prevent this, I suggest taping your bore, an old SOG practice that protects against crud and mud, too. Although you should test this, I don't think one small piece of tape will affect barrel harmonics enough to shift the zero.

While elsewhere we cite rainfall for visually concealing and sound masking your movement, in some instances this can facilitate shooting as well. The cleverest shooting environment I can imagine

is a night thunderstorm in which you exploit the lightning flash to see and engage, while the following thunderclap conceals the sound of your muzzle blast. Now that's devious.

ALTITUDE AND BULLET BALLISTICS

You're about to launch an important operation in Afghanistan. Being a diligent sniper, just before boarding your 160th Special Operations Aviation Regiment Chinook, you walk across the Kabul airfield and verify your zero. Beautiful! Nuts-on!

That Nightstalker chopper soon inserts you atop a ridge, where you and your teammate spot an al Qaeda fighter, hardly 400 meters downhill.

You fire. And you miss.

But you did everything right, from your zero to

Afghanistan's thin mountain air flattens bullet trajectory and so limits Blackhawk ceilings that most missions are flown by Chinooks.

TEMPERATURE EFFECTS ON TRAJECTORY, .308 MATCH, 200-YARD ZERO
Distance in Yards

Deg. F.	Muzz. Vel.	100	200	300	400	500	600
-10	2400 fps	2.8"	Zero	-11.0"	-31.6"	-63.7"	-109"
+25	2500 fps	2.5"	Zero	-10.0"	-28.8"	-58.0"	-100"
+59	2600 fps	2.2"	Zero	-9.1"	-26.4"	-53.1"	-91"
+100	2700 fps	2.0"	Zero	-8.3"	-24.2"	-48.8"	-84"

TEMPERATURE EFFECTS ON M118 SPECIAL BALL VELOCITY
Temperature (F)

- - - - - - FASTEST ROUND

———— AVERAGE VELOCITY

- · - · - · - SLOWEST ROUND

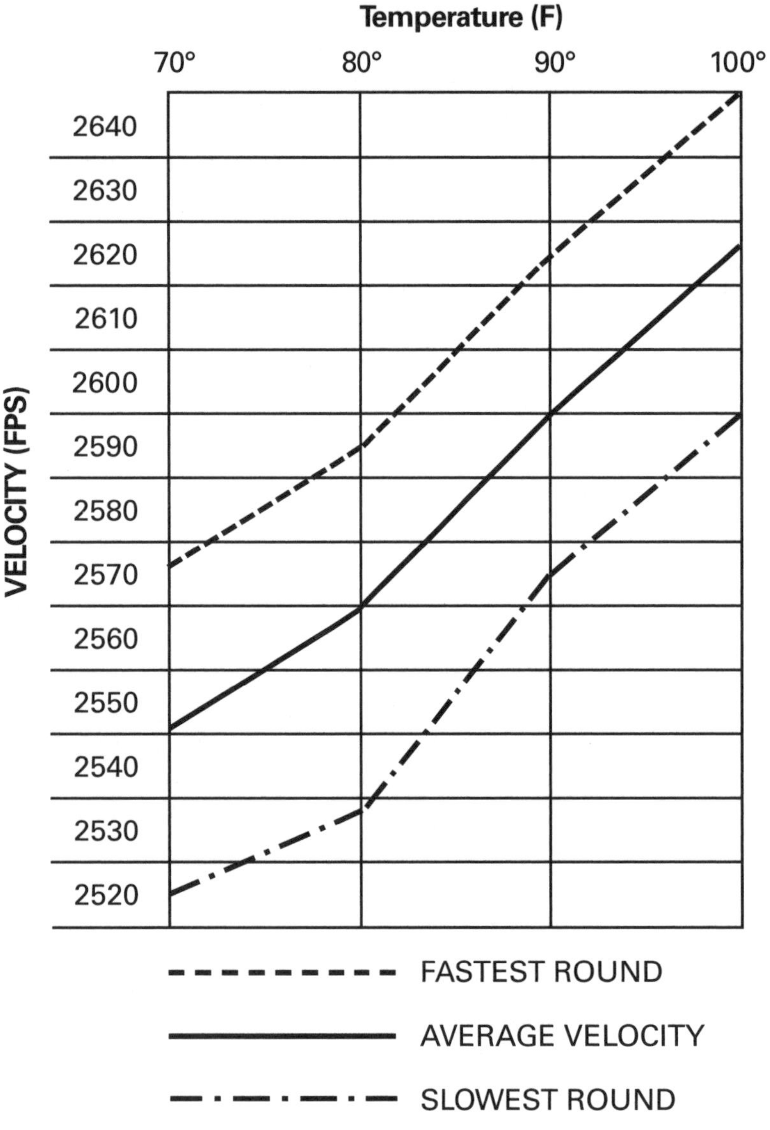

the perfectly lazed range to the precise compensation you applied. But you still missed.

The reason was the change in altitude. You had zeroed your rifle at the Kabul Airport, elevation 5,931 feet above sea level, and attempted to engage the al Qaeda fighter on a 15,000-foot ridgeline, some 9,000 feet higher. The problem is not that gravity decreases when you're farther from the center of the earth; it's that the air becomes thinner and there's less drag, causing your bullet to fly faster with a flatter trajectory.

It has long been known that jet fighters attain their greatest speeds at high altitude because they zip easier through thinner air, but few riflemen realize this principle applies to their bullets, too. And if the altitude is high enough, it will throw your Bullet Drop Compensator completely out of synch with your trajectory, no matter if you rezero, because the BDC is designed for the M118LR bullet's sea level trajectory.

There are special ballistic formulas to compute these effects, but having looked at these three-step algebraic beasts—which change slightly according to humidity, barometric pressure, and temperature—I've concluded that the only practical solution is to forget about computations and just plain rezero your rifle, then test it at 100 yard/meter distances to see how close the BDC is to true.

Although it's not truly precise, there is a general rule of thumb when compensating for a change in altitude: you should add or subtract 1 MOA for each 5,000 feet of elevation change. But this will vary with the distance you're shooting. Army tests have shown, according to *Hatcher's Notebook* (a shooting ballistics bible), that M1 boat-tail bullets fired through the Garand rifle required 8 MOA additional elevation when fired at sea level, compared with those fired at 10,000 feet, for a range of 1,000 yards.

If at all possible, you should rezero for the altitude at which you'll operate and test-fire at assorted distances to fine-tune your BDC or target knob settings.

TEMPERATURE AND BULLET TRAJECTORY

The rate at which gunpowder burns varies with temperature. The colder it is, the slower it's consumed and the less velocity it imparts on a bullet.

This velocity, in turn, determines your bullet's trajectory, and here's where it gets important. When the temperature changes enough—getting your powder either hotter or cooler than when you zeroed your rifle—the bullet will depart from zero and impact higher or lower than your point of aim.

We've been able to compute these effects by crunching several kinds of data to show you how significantly it can affect your shooting. This data is *not* ironclad or perfect, but it's very close. Note that 59°F (15°C) is the industry standard when computing ballistics.

At 300 yards or less, the differences are worth noticing but not very dramatic. At 500 and 600 yards, however, trajectory changes can determine hits and misses, and these temperature swings can occur in a single day in the desert. I recall 59-degree dawns and 100-degree noons in the Mojave. Mountain temperatures may vary as much as 25 degrees in a day, too.

For several years I've wrestled with various ways to calculate compensation for a change in tempera-

ture—including some dating back to the 19th century—and found most rules of thumb too general to be called precise. The sole exception, which I've tested and verified to be pretty consistent, is the following, which best applies to a .308 round:

- When the temperature changes 20 degrees, apply 1 MOA at 300 yards.
- When the temperature changes 15 degrees, apply 1 MOA at 600 yards.
- When the temperature changes 10 degrees, apply 1 MOA at 1,000 yards.

Obviously, if it's an increase in temperature, your bullet's flying faster/flatter so you lower your sight; if the temperature falls, your bullet travels slower, so you have to raise your sight. The logic behind this method is that the temperature change will first be felt at the greatest distance—because that's where even a slight change will matter. By contrast, it will take quite a temperature change to matter at only 300 yards. If you study the adjacent table titled "Temperature Effects on Trajectory," you'll find that its data is consistent with this technique.

We recommend that you reconfirm your zero when there's a temperature change of 20 degrees or more. And when operating in an area that experiences wide daily temperature fluctuations, you must test-fire, record results, and apply them to your shooting. To facilitate this, make an inexpensive clip-on thermometer, available at backpacking stores, a part of your basic equipment.

Having been convinced that cartridges perform differently at different temperatures, you should agree that a new challenge arises: keeping the cartridge/powder temperature consistent from round to round. Therefore, in winter make sure you don't carry any reload ammo close enough to your body that it gets warm, and don't chamber a follow-up round until the chamber has cooled.

Likewise, in summer don't fire rounds that have been lying in direct sunlight until they've cooled. The closer you can keep your ammo to the temperature it was when you zeroed your rifle, the fewer complications you'll have.

APPENDIX I

GLOSSARY OF SNIPING AND MARKSMANSHIP TERMS

ALTERNATE POSITION: A backup position selected by a sniper to which he can displace and still shoot into his original sector of fire. A sniper should have several alternate positions. (See Primary Position and Supplementary Position.)

AVENUE OF APPROACH (AA): A road, path, or open area across which the enemy could advance toward you, depending on whether he's mounted or dismounted. Snipers should cover dismounted avenues of approach.

BACK AZIMUTH DETECTION TECHNIQUE: A technique to identify an enemy sniper's position by inserting a cleaning rod or dowel into his bullet hole, noting the angle of trajectory to estimate the range, then recording its reverse azimuth to determine the direction from which the shot was fired. (See Triangulation Detection Technique.)

BACKSTOP: Any material through which your rifle's bullet will not pass, located behind your target's location so that bystanders, hostages, and other friendly forces will not be endangered by friendly sniper fire.

BALLISTIC ADVANTAGE: A concept whereby a sniper should seek engagements only when he's at least 400 yards away from his quarry and beyond the effective range of enemy riflemen. Although he's not out of danger, he has a much higher probability of surviving enemy countersniper fire.

BALLISTIC COEFFICIENT: A rating system based on a bullet's weight, shape, and ability to retain velocity. The higher the rating— expressed in decimal points—the higher the bullet efficiency at long range. For instance, the Federal 55-grain 5.56mm BTHP rating is .206, while Federal's 7.62mm (.308) Match 168-grain is .484—meaning the heavier bullet will perform better at extended ranges. However, identical-weight bullets of the same size will have different ballistic coefficients if they are of different styles: a 180-grain 7.62mm round nose has a ballistic coefficient of .205, while the same weight 7.62mm boat-tail's coefficient is dramatically better, at .535!

BALLISTICS: For purposes of marksmanship, knowledge of data concerning the trajectory, velocity, and energy of bullets.

BASE: See Mount.

BEANBAG: An old sock or small cloth bag filled with a dry material, such as sand, and placed below a rifle butt's heel so it can be squeezed to lower or elevate the rifle for precise aiming.

BIPOD: A two-legged support attached to the rifle forearm for better stability. It should *never* be attached to the barrel.

BOAT-TAIL BULLET: An aerodynamic bullet design shaped like a boat, with a pointed tip and gradually tapered to a flat base. Boat-tail bullets have better long-range accuracy than other bullet designs.

BODY ARMOR: Various kinds of vests designed to protect wearers against injury from fragmentation and small-arms fire.

BORESIGHT: An optical device inserted in a rifle muzzle to tentatively zero a rifle scope by setting its crosshairs coaxial to the rifle's bore. This greatly speeds subsequent live-fire zeroing. Also called a "collimator."

BULLET DROP: The ballistic measurement of how far a bullet drops, at 100-yard intervals, were the barrel pointed perfectly parallel to the earth. A baseline trajectory used for computing other ballistic data.

BULLET DROP COMPENSATOR (BDC): A knob mounted atop a rifle scope by which the shooter can adjust elevation without rezeroing the weapon so that he can fire quickly at varying distances and aim directly at the target instead of "holding." Some Bullet Drop Compensators use internal cams to synchronize adjustments for specific bullets at specific distances.

BULLET TRACE: Also called "bullet track," this is a tiny but visible wisp of trail left through mirage by a bullet's shock wave.

CALLING A SHOT: The practice of "calling" where your shot impacted just after firing but prior to observing it through a spotting scope. It develops a keen, almost subconscious ability to accurately "know" if your shot was dead-on, right/left, or up/down purely by how it "felt" when fired.

CANTING: Turning or dipping the barrel slightly right or left, usually as the result of a bad sight picture or improperly mounted scope. This results in bullet trajectory obliquely departing from point of aim as distance increases.

CATASTROPHIC BRAIN SHOT: A special one-shot kill to the brain stem or neural motor strips that kills so instantly that body reflexes cannot react. Used in hostage rescue situations. (See Immediate Incapacitation.)

CENTERFIRE AMMUNITION: Ammunition that detonates by striking an exposed primer in the center of the cartridge base. All military and big-game rifles use centerfire ammunition.

COLD BARREL ZERO: As distinct from where a series of bullets may impact after a rifle's barrel has warmed, the cold-barrel zero applies *only* to the exact impact of the very first round, which could be several inches different. Police and counterterrorist forces zero their weapons for the cold-barrel zero. (See Zero.)

COLLIMATOR: Another name for a boresight.

COMEUPS: Expressed as full MOAs or 1/4 MOAs, you must "come up" in elevation to go from one range to another range, usually in 100-yard increments. For example, to go from 100 yards to 300 yards you must come up 5.25 MOAs, or 21 1/4 MOA clicks, but only if you're firing Federal Match .308 168-grain. Comeups are calculated for a particular round, so the MOA increments are not the same for military 7.62 Match, for example, as for Federal .308 Match.

CONCEALMENT: Natural or man-made features, such as bushes or ditches, that offer concealment from observation but not always protection from fire. An ideal route to a sniper's hide should have both cover and concealment. (See Cover.)

COUNTERSNIPING: Various techniques and tactics to eliminate a sniper, or at least limit his effectiveness, ranging from blinding him with smoke to firing a wire-guided missile at him. The most natural and flexible countersniper system is a friendly sniper team operating in a countersniper mode.

COVER: Natural or man-made features—such as buildings or thick trees—that offer protection against small arms but not always concealment from observation. An ideal route to a hide should have both cover and concealment. (See Concealment.)

CUTTING SIGN: Tracking term meaning to cut back and forth across a quarry's likely route until discovering "sign" of his passage. (See Sign.)

DECOY TARGET: A countersniper technique that attracts an enemy sniper's fire so as to locate his position and eliminate him.

DOMINANT EYE: The ability of one eye to focus more intensely than the other, causing the second eye to compensate by misaligning itself slightly. For best marksmanship performance, a sniper should determine his dominant eye and use this eye for aiming.

DOPING THE WIND: A competitive shooter's term, meaning to estimate the wind accurately and adjust sights for correct compensation.

DRAG BAG: A heavily camouflaged rifle case dragged behind a low-crawling sniper in a Ghillie suit so he has both hands free for picking his way through brush.

ENERGY: The amount of potential energy a bullet can deliver at various distances is expressed in foot-pounds. A foot-pound is the amount of energy required to lift 1 pound, 1 foot.

ENGAGEMENT: One shot or a series of shots fired by a sniper from one hide during one short period.

ENGAGEMENT SEQUENCE: A standard series of steps a sniper takes from the instant he detects a target until he fires. This is practiced to ensure that the sniper has taken into account range and wind and prepared himself for a likely one-shot kill.

EXIT PUPIL: The cone of clear vision created at the rear of an optical device, such as a spotting scope. It is measured by dividing the objective lens diameter in millimeters by the magnification. For example, 50mm divided by 10 power equals an exit pupil of 5. To match the size of human eye pupils in low light, an exit pupil should measure 5 to 7. (See Relative Brightness and Twilight Factor.)

EXTERNAL BALLISTICS: That portion of a bullet's travel after it exits a muzzle but before impacting a target. (See Internal Ballistics and Terminal Ballistics.)

EYE RELIEF: The distance between a shooter's dominant eye and the rear (ocular) scope lens from which he can clearly see the entire scope field of view. It's usually about 3 or 4 inches.

FEINT: The deceptive technique of creating the impression that you are where you are not or that you intend to travel a route that you actually will not use.

FIELD OF FIRE: An area relatively free of obstructions into which a sniper can fire, ideally up to the maximum range of his weapon. A superior could further limit this by designating within it a sector of fire. (See Sector of Fire.)

FIELD OF VIEW: The angular measurement of how wide an area can be observed through an optical device. Spotting scopes have a very narrow field of view, rifle scopes a wider field of view, and binoculars an even wider one.

FINAL FIRING POSITION (FFP): The U.S. military term for a sniper's hide, the concealed position from which he engages a target within a field of fire. Ideally, the FFP also incorporates ballistic protection (cover) and suitable terrain over which to withdraw or displace after firing. (See Hide.)

FLEETING TARGET: A target that only exposes itself for a few seconds, then disappears and reappears. For both police and military snipers, this is the kind of activity a target most often will display.

FLUTED BARREL: A barrel on which thin grooves have been cut along its outside, long axis. It allows for a greater external surface for cooling while also creating better rigidity.

FOLLOW-THROUGH: A shooter's continuous concentration and nonreaction after firing a shot so he develops a mental and physical habit of no disruption whatsoever at the instant of shooting.

FRANGIBLE BULLETS: A bullet design intended to completely fragment on impact and thus impart 100 percent of energy into the target. The most commonly seen type is the Glaser Safety Slug, manufactured as both rifle and pistol cartridges. While devastating on soft targets, prefragmented ammo has almost zero penetration of even thin cover such as wooden doors and thus has limited usefulness for sniping. Also called "prefragmented ammunition."

FREE-FLOATED BARREL: A barrel that does not touch the rifle's forearm, for better accuracy. The barrel "floats" freely, unimpeded, with a 1/8-inch clearance recommended.

FREE RECOIL: The technique of heavily sandbagging a rifle and touching it only with your finger when firing to improve consistency.

GHILLIE SUIT: An elaborately camouflaged coverall originally used by Scottish gameskeepers to catch poachers, adopted for use by snipers. In a well-made Ghillie suit, a prone sniper is virtually invisible, even in thin cover.

GLASS BEDDING: Applying liquid fiberglass or epoxy between a rifle's action/receiver and the stock for the snuggest possible fit. This eliminates any "play" between action and stock. Quality sniper rifles incorporate glass bedding.

GOOSE NECKING: The undesirable practice of stretching one's head up above the rifle cheekrest (and thereby losing the stockweld) in order to see through a scope. Corrected by using a different buttstock, installing a strap-on cheekrest, or using an adjustable cheekrest. (See Stockweld and Turkey Necking.)

GROUND SURVEILLANCE RADAR VECTORING: Using friendly radar to detect enemy forces in darkness, then maneuvering night vision-equipped friendly snipers either into position to engage the enemy or around the enemy if his forces are too numerous. (See Remote Sensors.)

HARDBALL BULLET: Also called "full metal jacket" or "metal case," this bullet design uses a hard metal covering over a lead core so the round does not expand on impact, as required by the Geneva Convention. All military ammunition is hardball.

HIDE: The temporary or permanent position a sniper occupies to engage a target. A hide should have excellent concealment and cover, good observation, fields of fire, and a "back door" through which the sniper can invisibly displace to another hide position after engaging. Depicted on a map as a triangle with a scope crosshair inside. (See Final Firing Position, Primary Position, and Surveillance Hide.)

HIGH-POWERED RIFLE: A term that distinguishes more powerful rifles from .22-caliber rimfire weapons. All big-game and military rifles are high-powered rifles.

HOLD: Compensating for wind or elevation by purposely aiming high/low or right/left instead of changing the setting on your scope. This is the fastest means of engaging multiple targets at assorted distances. (See Kentucky Windage and Tennessee Elevation.)

HOLLOWPOINT BULLET: A bullet design in which a cavity has been reamed in the tip so that on impact it expands dramatically, increasing the delivery of energy to a target, similar to softpoint bullets.

IMMEDIATE INCAPACITATION: The desired effect of a bullet fired during a hostage-rescue operation so that the subject instantly is incapable of firing a weapon or otherwise endangering anyone. (See Rapid Incapacitation and Catastrophic Brain Shot.)

INFRARED (IR) SCOPE: A night observation device that needs an infrared light for illumination. These infrared lights can be detected by other IR optics as well as Western Starlight-type night vision devices, making them very dangerous to use. Since the IR devices generate detectable energy, they are called "active" devices, while Starlight ones generate no detectable energy and are called "passive" devices.

INTERNAL BALLISTICS: A bullet's acceleration and travel in a rifle's chamber and barrel. (See External Ballistics and Terminal Ballistics.)

KENTUCKY WINDAGE: A vintage American frontier term, meaning to hold rifle sights right or left of a target to compensate for the effect of a crosswind. (See Tennessee Elevation.)

LEAD: The side width of the human body—which this book finds to be 12 inches—used to estimate how far a sniper should lead a moving target. For example, at 500 yards a sniper must aim two leads ahead of a walking man and four leads ahead of a running man.

LEADE: The smooth, unrifled gap in a rifle's bore between the chamber and the start of the rifling. A sniper-quality weapon should have a leade that's so short the bullet need not "jump" into the rifling since this degrades accuracy.

LIGHT-GATHERING ABILITY: The misstated ability of a lens to gather available light, an important factor for dusk/dawn and night shooting. What it actually refers to is light *transmission* through the lens, which is determined by how wide the objective lens is, how finely ground is its surface, and the quality of its lens coating. (See Twilight Factor.)

LOCK TIME: The amount of time between the sear releasing the firing pin and its striking a cartridge's primer. Short lock time is desirable for a precision rifle so that there's no time for weapon movement after the shooter pulls the trigger. Lock time typically is .0022 to .0057 of a second.

LOT or LOT NUMBER: One batch of ammunition made up at the same time and using the same run of subcomponents. A sniper uses ammunition of the same lot number to enhance consistent performance.

MACHAN: A comfortable "tree seat" developed in India for tiger hunting that uses straps and ropes lashed between tree branches.

MAD MINUTE: A countersniper technique first used in World War I in which all of a unit's weapons are fired simultaneously for 1 minute at any possible position a concealed enemy could use. (See Recon by Fire.)

MATCH-GRADE AMMUNITION: Ammunition manufactured to much closer tolerances than regular ammunition to produce rounds that consistently perform to the highest of standards. (See Premium-Grade Ammunition.)

MAXIMUM EFFECTIVE RANGE: The greatest distance at which a weapon can inflict casualties, based on *both* the energy of a bullet and the weapon's inherent accuracy.

MIL: An angular measurement equal to 1/6400 of a circle, or 3.375 Minutes of Angle. The mil is a handy measurement since it subtends 1 yard at 1,000 yards and therefore facilitates range estimation.

MIL DOT: A tiny dot of very exact angular width in some scope reticles, such as the M3A1 Leupold, and used for range estimation. *Beware*: the M3A1's mil dot is actually 3/4 mil in diameter; it's the distance from center of dot to center of dot that is 1 mil.

MILITARY CREST: The area along a ridgeline just below its actual crest, preferred by military units for occupation or movement because soldiers and positions will not be silhouetted against the sky.

MINUTE OF ANGLE (MOA): An angular width normally used to describe shooting and scope adjustments since 1 Minute of Angle almost exactly equals 1 inch at 100 yards (1.047 inches), 2 inches at 200 yards, 3 inches at 300 yards, etc. When a shooter says he has a "half-minute rifle," he means it will shoot 1/2-inch groups at 100 yards. Scope adjustments are similarly described, so that a 1/4 MOA scope requires four "clicks" to move the impact 1 inch at 100 yards, two clicks to move the impact 1 inch at 200 yards, etc.

MIRAGE: In shooting terms, the reflection of heat waves from the earth's surface, which may obscure long-range visibility, but also allows a sniper to estimate wind speed by observing mirage through his spotting scope.

MOUNT: Also called a "base," this is the intermediate adapter that connects a scope to a rifle. Quality bases should be of machined steel and use hex screws for a snug fit. Scope rings attach the scope to the base, and these, too, should use hex screws.

MUZZLE BRAKE: A recoil-reducing device attached to the barrel that deflects blast down and/or backward to "pull" the rifle slightly forward. While it definitely reduces recoil, it also accentuates the more visible effects of muzzle blast, thereby increasing the chance of being detected by enemy observers.

MUZZLE CROWN: Polished, smoothly finished rifling at the muzzle, done during manufacture to ensure the unimpeded, consistent exit of bullets. Some muzzles have a recessed crown to reduce the chance of "dinging" any rifling edges during normal use.

MUZZLE ENERGY: A bullet's kinetic energy measured in foot-pounds as it exits a rifle muzzle. Since this is based on a bullet's weight and velocity, energy decreases significantly as the bullet slows and typically is charted in 100-yard increments during its entire flight.

MUZZLE VELOCITY: A bullet's speed when it leaves a rifle's muzzle, in feet per second (fps). This speed declines significantly during flight and thereby causes a reduction in kinetic energy and energy transmitted on impact.

NATIONAL MATCH: A term applied to ammunition and certain firearms to distinguish them as having been modified for higher-precision shooting. For rifles and pistols, this means expert gunsmiths have fine-tuned them for match-type accuracy.

NATURAL LINE OF DRIFT: Based on human nature and terrain, this is the route human beings most naturally would take from one place to another. Usually this means humans will walk parallel to streams, down the middle of valleys, and along ridgelines. In wartime, this would include enemy soldiers walking slightly inside woodlines and crossing danger areas at the narrowest possible points.

NIGHT OBSERVATION DEVICE (NOD): Any of many night vision sights and scopes that intensify available light to "see" in darkness, which caused them initially to be called "Starlight" scopes. Also termed "passive" devices since they don't need infrared light or any other detectable energy.

NO FIRE AREA (NFA): An artillery fire planning term, meaning an area in which no fire may be placed without the permission of the unit that created it. Used by sniper teams to create safe havens in their area of operations. With the team's okay, forward or aerial observers can call artillery or airstrikes on sudden targets in the NFA without time-consuming coordination. (See Sniper Operations Area and Sniper Skirmish Line.)

OBJECTIVE LENS: The front/forward lens of an optical device. (See Ocular Lens.)

OCULAR LENS: The rear/back lens or "eyepiece" of an optical device. (See Objective Lens.)

OPERATION ORDER (OPORD): A written order following a five-paragraph format that addresses situation, mission, execution, service support, and command and signal. A commander issues an OPORD to subordinates to ensure that all are executing his common plan, with internal coordination.

ORDINATE: The maximum height above a horizontal surface that a bullet rises while in trajectory to a target. For example, the ordinate of a Federal .308 Match round that impacts a target at 300 yards is 7.23 inches.

PARALLAX: The tendency for scope crosshairs to shift and change the point of impact if the shooter moves his head. Not a problem with new quality scopes of about 10x or less, but can be a problem above 10x unless the scope has an adjustable objective lens.

PERMANENT WOUND CHANNEL: The path of permanent tissue damage left by a bullet, usually an inch or two in diameter. When this channel passes through vital organs or nerve tissue, significant injury or death results. (See Temporary Wound Cavity.)

POINT-BLANK RANGE: Exploiting the flat phase of a particular bullet's trajectory so a shooter can hit targets with almost no high or low holds. For example, Federal .308 Match does not begin plunging until 400 yards; therefore, by setting his scope at 300, the shooter can ignore correct range estimation and holds, instead aiming dead-on at all ranges to 300, and yet never miss by more than about 7 inches—an acceptable standard for hunters but *never* for a sniper.

POSITIONAL SHOOTING: The correct practice of firing from the standing, kneeling, sitting, and prone positions for maximum stability and best accuracy. A sniper prefers firing prone supported since it's the most stable position.

PREFRAGMENTED AMMUNITION: See Frangible Bullets.

PREMIUM-GRADE AMMUNITION: Commercial rifle loads of closer tolerance and therefore closer to true match-grade loads than typical ammunition. Federal Premium, Winchester Supreme, and Remington Extended Range rounds are three examples. While a sniper prefers match-grade ammo, he may be outfitted with a weapon—such as .243 or 7mm Magnum—for which match-grade ammo is not available. (See Match-Grade Ammunition.)

PRIMARY POSITION: The hide a sniper initially uses in a deliberate defense, from which he can engage targets in an assigned sector of fire. The sniper also should select "alternate" and "supplementary" positions to which he can displace after firing from his primary position. (See Alternate Position and Supplementary Position.)

RANGEFINDER: An optical/mechanical device to determine the range to a target. The four basic types are a parallax lens, which is focused until the target is clearly visible and results in a distance readout; mil dots or special lines in a scope's reticle, which allow the user to calculate range by measuring the height or width of an object at or near the target; a simple height scale in a scope reticle, such as found on the SVD rifle's PSO-1 scope; or a laser measuring device, which employs an invisible beam that reflects off the target.

RAPID INCAPACITATION: Term used by the FBI to describe the need for a bullet to disable a suspect quickly so he no longer can resist apprehension or pose a threat to arresting officers. (I have added to this concept "Immediate Incapacitation" to distinguish hostage-rescue situations in which a suspect must be neutralized instantly.)

RATE OF TWIST: Term to describe rifling by the distance in inches a bullet passes in the barrel during a single rotation. A 1:7 twist means a bullet rotates once for each 7 inches it travels. A .308 sniper rifle typically has a 1:10 or 1:12 rate of twist, with the latter preferred.

RECOIL LUG: A wide, heavy steel lug attached below the barrel at the front of the receiver through which recoil is transmitted to the rifle stock. The contact between lug and stock *must* be true and snug to ensure the action and barrel do not twist during recoil.

RECON BY FIRE: A countersniper technique in which friendly snipers fire several rounds into the most likely enemy sniper hides in hopes of hitting him by chance. Typically, this will result merely in suppressing the sniper or causing him to move, but it will not eliminate him. Depending on the situation, a commander could have all unit weapons join in the recon by fire. (See Mad Minute.)

RELATIVE BRIGHTNESS: Term describing the ability of an optical device to transmit light. Relative brightness is computed by squaring the exit pupil so that an exit pupil of 5 results in a relative brightness of 25. (See Exit Pupil and Twilight Factor.)

RELEASE POINT: The point along a route at which a subelement or accompanying group leaves the main body to follow its own route. For instance, a sniper team initially could accompany a squad for security or to deceive any observers, then separate invisibly at the release point.

REMOTE SENSORS: Remotely monitored sensors emplaced by hand, air, or artillery. Of interest to snipers because such sensors can be used to maneuver them into an engagement of enemy at night or in areas not otherwise observable by friendly forces. (See Ground Surveillance Radar Vectoring.)

RETICLE: Another word for "crosshair," the post, dot, or intersecting lines in a scope with which a shooter aims.

RIMFIRE AMMUNITION: Usually found only in .22 rounds, a cartridge that has an internal primer detonated by a firing pin striking the cartridge's rim. By contrast, military and big-game rifles use centerfire ammunition.

RIMLESS CARTRIDGE: A high-powered rifle cartridge whose base is no wider than the cartridge's side, a design that facilitates feeding into the chamber. U.S. and NATO military rounds are rimless.

RIMMED CARTRIDGE: A cartridge—most often .22 caliber—whose base is wider than its side, a design that simplifies extraction. Although long obsolete for military use, the Soviet SVD's 7.62x54mm cartridge is rimmed, the only such military round in use today.

ROUND-NOSE BULLET: A bullet design that presents the maximum width of the bullet to a target on impact, which imparts greater "knockdown power" or energy. Because of their blunt design, round-nose bullets tend to lose velocity quickly and drift in crosswinds, with a resulting decline in long-range accuracy. Usually found in civilian hunting rounds with a softpoint nose.

SCOPE: An abbreviated term for "telescopic sight." Rifle scopes can be divided into two basic types, fixed-power and zoom, each of which has pros and cons.

SECTOR OF FIRE: An assigned area into which a sniper places his fire. Usually, this is a portion of a wider field of fire, but in some cases the sector of fire could be as wide as the sniper's entire field of fire. (See Field of Fire.)

SHOOTING PLATFORM: A bench or table constructed so a sniper can fire prone through an upper-story window from deep inside a room.

SIGN: Tracking term meaning any indicator of human activity, from a footprint to a candy wrapper. A tracker follows sign, not necessarily tracks. (See Cutting Sign.)

SILENCER: An obsolete term for a suppressor, no longer used because no device totally silences a firearm. (See Suppressor.)

SNIPER: A specially trained marksman equipped with quality optics and a target-grade weapon who employs stealth and fieldcraft to engage targets at ranges greater than those of the conventional rifleman. Due to his equipment and observation training, the sniper is an excellent intelligence source. (See Spotter.)

SNIPER DATA CARD: A detailed record of ballistic data, developed and periodically modified, on the performance of a particular sniper rifle while used by a particular sniper. This detailed record enables the sniper to know his weapon intimately, allowing him to understand its performance in all weather conditions, at all ranges, and against a variety of targets.

SNIPER DEMOLITION AMBUSH: A remote-controlled, command-detonated ambush using a series of claymore mines aligned along a route likely to be used by the enemy. The sniper detonates the claymores using a single long-range rifle shot.

SNIPER OPERATIONS SECTOR (SOS): A sector assigned exclusively to a sniper team for independent operations and marked on maps by a thick border with "SOS" on each side. The sector's usually about a 3- to 5-kilometer square, large enough for the team to stalk, hide, engage, and evade. (See No Fire Area and Sniper Skirmish Line.)

SNIPER RANGE CARD: A detailed sketch of a sniper team sector of fire, including all prominent terrain, likely enemy avenues of approach, cover the enemy may use, and dead space, with range estimates so the sniper can engage targets quickly.

SNIPER SKIRMISH LINE: An assigned line on a map showing that a sniper team may maneuver up to 1 kilometer from it while stalking, hiding, shooting, and evading. Depicted as a jagged line ending in arrows, similar to a reconnaissance screen. (See Sniper Operations Sector and No Fire Area.)

SNIPER TEAM: Usually a two-man team of qualified snipers, with one man acting as spotter while the other snipes, and rotating responsibilities. Team composition could vary by mission and MTOE (Military Table of Organization and Equipment).

SOFTPOINT BULLET: Also called "dum-dum" bullets, this design uses an exposed lead tip that expands on impact, thus increasing the amount of energy delivered to the target for far more damaging effect. It is outlawed by the Geneva Convention for combat use but legal in domestic counterterrorist and criminal situations. Softpoints frequently are preferable because they more quickly dissipate energy and fragment, lessening danger to bystanders.

SOG: Using the cover name "Studies and Observation Group," this was the U.S. military's top-secret unconventional warfare task force during the Vietnam War, composed mostly of U.S. Army Green Berets used in cross-border intelligence forays and raids into Laos, Cambodia, and North Vietnam.

SPOTTER: A trained sniper and member of a two-man sniper team who helps the sniper detect and identify targets, then adjust his fire on the target. He's also responsible for close-range security. Spotter and sniper duties rotate. (See Sniper.)

SPOTTING SCOPE: A single-lens scope, usually of 20 power or greater and used with a tripod for long-range observation, adjusting the sniper's fire, and reading mirage for wind speed and direction.

STALKING: The ability to move silently and invisibly, which incorporates camouflage, selecting the best route to a hide, physical fitness, and self-discipline. A sniper must be a master stalker.

STOCKWELD: The habitual placing of a shooter's cheek at the exact same spot on his stock, shot after shot, so that his eye relief and scope picture become consistent. By "welding" his eye to one spot, a rifleman improves consistency and therefore accuracy.

SUBTENDS: The amount an angular measurement equals at a given range. For example, 1 Minute of Angle subtends 3 inches at 300 yards.

SUPPLEMENTARY POSITION: A sniping hide to which the sniper may displace after firing from his primary or alternate positions. Unlike the alternate position, the supplementary one does not allow firing into the sniper's primary sector of fire; from a supplementary position, he shoots in a different direction/sector of fire. (See Alternate Position and Primary Position.)

SUPPRESSOR: A device that uses baffles and fine meshing to dissipate and slow the escape of gases from a weapon muzzle and thereby reduce the normal muzzle report. (See Silencer.)

SURVEILLANCE HIDE: A hide selected and prepared for observation only, and therefore its field of view and concealment are the most important selection criteria. Used by both military and law enforcement sniper teams, in the case of the latter especially for the surveillance of remote airfields, clandestine drug labs, and borderlands.

TARGET DETECTION: A series of observation techniques the sniper team uses to pick out concealed or obscured targets.

TARGET IDENTIFICATION: The sniper's ability to identify a detected target and thus determine the target's priority. For instance, knowledge of enemy uniforms and formations enables the sniper to identify leaders.

TARGET PRIORITY: The declining order in which a sniper engages targets so that he shoots the most important ones first. Target priority will vary according to day and night and the situation. An enemy sniper is always a friendly sniper's first priority target.

TEMPORARY WOUND CAVITY: The dramatic expansion of soft tissue that results from a bullet's passage, sometimes 10 inches or more in diameter. This phenomenon is impressive but only temporary and does not usually cause rapid incapacitation or death. (See Permanent Wound Channel.)

TENNESSEE ELEVATION: To compensate or "hold" high or low to hit targets beyond or short of a rifle's zero—the trajectory correlation to Kentucky Windage. (See Kentucky Windage.)

TERMINAL BALLISTICS: That part of a bullet's flight when it strikes and passes through a medium until all energy is depleted, and deals extensively with wounds. (See Internal Ballistics and External Ballistics.)

THROAT: Inside a rifle's bore, the entrance to the rifling, just forward of the chamber and leade. Although it's commonly said that a rifle's bore loses accuracy or wears out after a certain number of rounds have been fired, it's primarily the throat that degrades due to the heat, flash, and pressure of firing.

TRACKING: One of two techniques for engaging moving targets. The shooter swings with and ahead of the target, holding an appropriate lead for the target's speed and range. (See Trapping and Leads.)

TRAJECTORY: The arched path a bullet follows from a rifle's muzzle until it hits the ground. The steepness of this arch varies depending on the angle at which the shooter holds the rifle—and this, of course, will vary according to how far away his intended target is located.

TRAPPING: One of two techniques for engaging moving targets. In this technique, the shooter picks a point ahead of the target, holds steadily on the point, then squeezes off a shot when the target arrives there. (See Tracking and Leads.)

TRIANGULATION DETECTION TECHNIQUE: A countersniper technique used to determine an enemy sniper's location. It involves pinpointing the enemy's direction of fire from two separated locations and plotting these on a map so as to identify a point through triangulation. Friendly snipers then scan this area for likely sniper positions until he is located and eliminated. (See Back Azimuth Detection Technique.)

TURKEY NECKING: The undesirable practice of stretching your neck forward or back in order to see through your rifle scope properly. Corrected either by lengthening the buttstock or changing the scope eye relief. (See Stockweld and Goose Necking.)

TWILIGHT FACTOR: A means of measuring an optical device's low-light resolution *and* magnification, which is probably a more useful way for comparing scopes, binoculars, etc., for night use. Measured by multiplying the objective lens diameter by the device's power, then computing this figure's square root. For a 10x scope having a 40mm objective lens: 40 x 10 = 400, which has a square root and twilight factor of 20. (See Exit Pupil and Relative Brightness.)

VELOCITY: The speed at which a bullet travels, in feet per second (fps). The combination of velocity and bullet weight determines a round's kinetic energy.

WALL OF GREEN: The maximum distance you can see in a rural area, depending on thickness and breaks in the vegetation. This roughly jagged, semicircular "line" is where you focus mind and vision while walking in order to detect hostiles before they detect you.

"WHAT IS IT?" DECOY: A curious object placed in a location covered by fire to lure inquisitive enemy soldiers into a sniper's sights. The object could be the guts of a damaged radio, a flag, etc. To be most effective, this ambush technique should draw the enemy into a spot he doesn't think could be hit by long-range fire and have no indicators of any hostile presence. Decoys are best emplaced during darkness. (See Decoy Target.)

WIND DRIFT: The lateral distance a bullet drifts in a crosswind, measured in inches at various distances. Some bullet shapes, such as round nose, are more susceptible to wind drift, but others, like boat-tail, are less affected.

YAW: The twisted, unstable departure of a bullet from its horizontal axis or trajectory, which results from perhaps nicking a branch or grazing a bone. These wild centrifugal forces debilitate accuracy, but the tumbling bullet inflicts buzzsaw-like damage in flesh.

ZERO: The adjustment of an optical or open sight so that a bullet precisely hits a target at a given distance. Police usually zero their rifles for 100 yards.

CURRENT
U.S.-BASED
TRAINING PROGRAMS

STATESIDE SNIPER TRAINING COURSES

American Small Arms Academy

P.O. Box 12111
Prescott, AZ 86304
928-778-5623
www.chucktaylorasaa.com

Chuck Taylor's American Small Arms Academy offers a seven-day, military-oriented sniper course, at the end of which students are shooting to 600 yards. The final three days are spent in the field, shooting an assortment of tactical exercises.

Badlands Tactical Training Facility

408 North Simpson
Grandfield, OK 73546
580-479-5559
www.badlandstactical.net

Oklahoma-based Badlands Tactical has a four-day basic and five-day advanced course, oriented toward law enforcement snipers. At the end of the basic course, students are firing to 600 yards, while the advanced course features tactical subjects along with advanced shooting techniques.

Blackwater USA

P.O. Box 1029
Moyock, NC 27958
252-435-2488
www.blackwaterusa.com

Blackwater is a major contractor to the U.S. government for paramilitary security officers and services, most notably in Iraq. Two sniper courses of five days each are offered at its 6,000-acre facility, with emphasis on tactics and fieldcraft in addition to marksmanship. Blackwater also conducts a nontactical, precision rifle series of three courses, each lasting three days, with students firing at 600 and 1,000 yards during the more advanced phases.

Crosshairs, Inc.

260 Hurricane Road
Keene, NH 03431
603-357-2604
www.crosshairs.org

Crosshairs has seven different sniper courses, clinics, and workshops, including basic, intermediate, and advanced sniper classes of five days each. The content is distinctly focused toward law enforcement sniping, and instructors have a police tactical background.

Front Sight Firearms Training Institute
P.O. Box 2619
Aptos, CA 95001
800-987-7719
www.frontsight.com

Front Sight offers two long-range shooting courses, Precision Rifle I and Precision Rifle II, with firing out to 1,000 yards in the advanced phase. According to course descriptions, these are long-range shooting classes, not tactical courses.

Gunsite Academy, Inc.
2900 W. Gunsite Road
Paulden, AZ 86334-4301
928-636-4565
www.gunsite.net

Founded by Jeff Cooper nearly a half-century ago, Gunsite is undoubtedly America's oldest professional shooting school. During the late 1990s, I was one of Gunsite's Precision Rifle adjunct instructors and helped shape the courses. Today's curriculum includes two five-day courses and a five-day sniping field exercise, during which students fire to 800 yards and apply the full gamut of sniping fieldcraft and tactical skills.

At the McMillan Sniper School, Special Ops snipers fire from "Little Bird" helicopters into an abandoned movie set.

McMillan Sniper School
P.O. Box 14481
Scottsdale, AZ 85267
602-690-2550
www.sniperschool.org

The McMillan Sniper School is an offshoot of the McMillan rifle company, which builds high-quality sniper weapons. The school's five courses benefit from realistic live-fire training at a sizable former movie set in the Arizona desert. Most phases last two or three days, plus a special 11-day course designed to prepare U.S. military snipers for combat in Iraq and Afghanistan. Instructors include a cross-section of state, federal, and local police and military snipers.

National Rifle Association
Law Enforcement Activities Division
11250 Waples Mill Road
Fairfax, VA 22030
703-267-1640
www.nra.org

The NRA offers a week-long Precision (Scoped) Rifle Instructor Course at a number of locations around the United States. This is a "train-the-trainer" course, which prepares law enforcement students to return to their agencies and instruct fellow officers in scoped rifle shooting.

National Tactical Officers Association
P.O. Box 797
Doylestown, PA 18901
800-279-9127
www.ntoa.org

The NTOA is the nation's premier SWAT officers professional organization. In addition to an annual conference and occasional work-shops, NTOA offers a Basic Sniper and an Advanced Sniper course, each lasting five days, open to bona fide law officers. All instructors are experienced police snipers.

Precision Rifle International
19898 Keenan Cut Off Road
Montgomery, TX 77316
936-587-5371
www.precisionrifleinternational.com

Founded in 2001, Precision Rifle International conducts assorted sniper courses, primarily one week in length, and includes .338 and .50-caliber weapons in its curriculum.

SIGARMS Academy
18 Industrial Drive
Exeter, NH 03833
603-679-2003
www.sigarmsacademy.com

An offshoot of the prestigious firearms company, SIGARMS Academy offers three five-day Tactical Marksman Observer courses, with the full variety of military and police sniping subjects, from Ghillie suit construction to ballistics, marksmanship, and assorted fieldcraft. The basic course is sufficiently fundamental that students need no prior experience with a scoped rifle.

The Site–Firearms Training Center
P.O. Box 27
Bourbonnais, IL 60914
815-244-2815
www.shoot-at-the-site.com

The Site's Precision Rifle One and Precision Rifle Two courses are distinctly directed toward law enforcement snipers. The basic course focuses on rifle marksmanship and related fieldcraft, while the advanced course incorporates marksmanship into tactical shooting situations. Students fire to 600 yards.

Small Arms Training Academy
D&L Sports
P.O. Box 651
Gillette, WY 82717-0651
307-686-4008
www.dlsports.com

Dave Lauck's D&L Sports is a custom firearms builder, especially of AR-15 based rifles and .45-caliber pistols. Among his training academy's many courses is a three-day Practical Precision Rifle class that takes place on an 1,800-yard range. He also hosts a major annual three-gun competition that includes firing to 1,000 yards.

Snipercraft, Inc.
472 Lakeside Circle
Ft. Lauderdale, FL 33326-4103
954-389-0829
www.snipercraft.org

Snipercraft's founder, Derrick Bartlett, is a Miami-area police sniper and author of several instructional books. In addition to its major annual conference and police sniper competition, Snipercraft offers three five-day courses: a basic class, an advanced class, and a "train-the-trainer" police instructor class. There's also a two-day sniper supervisor course.

Storm Mountain Training Center
Rt. 1, Box 60
Elk Garden, WV 26717
304-446-5526
www.stormmountain.com

Storm Mountain offers two Long-Range Rifle courses, plus three levels of sniper training courses. Sniper courses are five days long, and rifle courses last three days. Basic courses enable students to fire more than 500 yards, while advanced phases extend shooting to 900 and 1,000 yards.

TACFIRE
2426 East Main Street
Ventura, CA 93003
805-652-1345
www.tacfire.com

The curriculum at TACFIRE includes two week-long Precision Rifle courses, offered to bona fide police snipers. The first course has students firing to 600 yards, while the advanced course extends firing to 1,000 yards.

Thunder Ranch
96747 Hwy. 140 East
Lakeview, OR 97630
541-947-4104
www.thunderranchinc.com

Clint Smith's Thunder Ranch moved to Oregon in 2003 and now offers an Urban Precision Rifle course among its many firearms classes. This three-day police sniper course emphasizes relatively short-range engagements that typify realistic urban situations.

Yavapai Firearms Academy
P.O. Box 27290
Prescott Valley, AZ 86312
928-772-8262
www.yfainc.com

A noted firearms authority, author, and former Gunsite instructor on pistol, shotgun, and rifle, Louis Awerbuck prepares tailored sniper training based on specific requirements from host agencies. His classes take him across the country, with instruction given on-site at the host agency's facility.

MILITARY SNIPER SCHOOLS

U.S. Marine Corps Schools
In addition to its well-known Quantico sniper school, the Marine Corps has division-level sniper training courses at Camp Pendleton, California, and Camp Lejeune, North Carolina, plus independent courses on Hawaii and Okinawa.

USMC Scout Sniper Instructor School
Weapons Training Battalion
Marine Corps Combat Development Command
Quantico, VA 22134-5040

This is the USMC's highest level sniper training school, founded by GySgt. Carlos Hathcock in 1977. The nine-week Quantico school produces instructors for all other Marine sniper training courses. Students also come from other military services, federal agencies, and even foreign countries. Sniper school cadre assist the design and testing of U.S. sniping-related items, from camouflage to weapons to ammunition.

U.S. Army Schools
Like the Marine Corps, the U.S. Army operates a number of sniper courses separate from its Army-wide sniper school. For example, the 1st, 5th, and 10th Special Forces Groups operate independent Special Operations Target Interdiction Courses that train students from a variety of military units.

U.S. Army Sniper School
Company C, 2nd Battalion, 29th Infantry Regt.
Ft. Benning, GA 31905

In addition to its instructional role, the Ft. Benning sniper school is the U.S. Army's receptacle for lessons learned and a test bed for new sniping weapons and gear. This five-week course is the active Army soldier's sole means for earning the Bravo-Four sniper certification. In addition, the school hosts an annual military sniper competition that draws competitors from throughout the U.S. military and several foreign countries. Five years ago, I was honored to be the U.S. Army Sniper School's graduation speaker.

A U.S. Army Sniper School instructor demonstrates a rooftop firing position.

National Guard Sniper School
Camp Joseph T. Robinson
North Little Rock, AR 72199

Co-located at Camp Robinson with the Guard's Marksmanship Training Unit and home to the annual Winston P. Wilson Matches, this is the course I cofounded with Lt. Col. Gary Schraml at Camp Ripley, Minnesota, in 1983, which moved to Arkansas a decade later. Other than Ft. Benning, this is the only school authorized to award the Army's B-4 sniper certification. The course is conducted in two two-week phases to better fit Reserve Component schedules. In 2003, its cadre traveled to Iraq to conduct a sniper course for American forces.

Special Operations Target Interdiction Course
Company D, 2nd Battalion,
1st Special Warfare Training Group
Ft. Bragg, NC 28307

This is an advanced course, with the prerequisite that students already be sniper-qualified. Emphasis is placed on Special Ops roles and environments along with extreme-range shooting using advanced heavy weapon systems. Most graduates are destined to assignments throughout the Special Ops community.

U.S. POLICE SNIPER TRAINING COURSES

Many major metro police departments, such as Dallas and Los Angeles, along with state-level law enforcement agencies, conduct or sponsor sniper schools. As well, several FBI regional offices host or support police sniper courses, as do a number of federal law enforcement agencies, with some assisted by the Department of Homeland Security. Information on these courses can be obtained by contacting them. Here are the three longest established federal courses for police snipers:

Federal Law Enforcement Training Center
Firearms Division
1131 Chapel Crossing Road
Glynco, GA 31534

This is a week-long, advanced scoped rifle course, which integrates realistic scenarios with shooting. Two days of the Precision Rifle/ Observer Training Program (PROP) are devoted to long-range shooting at nearby Ft. Stewart, Georgia. This training is offered twice per year, with classes limited to 12 students.

U.S. Department of Justice—FBI
Firearms Training Unit
FBI Academy, Building 9
Quantico, VA 22135

The FBI's two Observer/Sniper Courses, each a week in length, are open only to bona fide law officers, with priority given to FBI students and those from other federal agencies. Due to their co-locations, there's considerable cross-fertilization between the FBI courses, the FBI Hostage Rescue Team (HRT), and the Marine Corps Scout Sniper Instructor School. The FBI school has a reputation for incorporating cutting-edge tactics, procedures, and gear into its curriculum.

U.S. Department of Energy
Central Training Academy
Kirtland Air Force Base
Albuquerque, NM 87117

Operated by a civilian contractor, Wackenhut Services, Inc., the Central Training Academy's program is oriented toward tactical team operations, with priority to Department of Energy security students, although any bona fide police officer may apply. Dates and course lengths vary, but typically this is a two-week course, taught at least annually.

OVERSEAS SNIPER TRAINING

Under the Foreign Military Assistance Program, U.S. military sniper instructor teams often teach foreign military and police sniper students at overseas locations. Additionally, the State Department's Bureau of Diplomatic Security offers specialized SWAT sniper and countersniper training, instructed by American police experts. Foreign police and military students also are permitted to attend U.S. military sniper schools, with proper coordination. To arrange a school or obtain a slot in a U.S. school for foreign personnel, contact your local U.S. Embassy. Some private trainers, such as the McMillan Sniper School, conduct tailored foreign sniper courses at overseas locations.

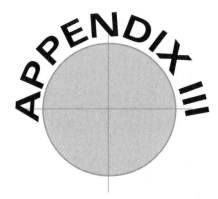

REFERENCES

BOOKS AND MILITARY MANUALS

Advanced Tactical Marksman, Dave M. Lauck, Paladin Press, 2002.

The Art and Science of Visual Illusions, Nicholas Wade, McMillan Co., 1983.

The Art of Deception in Warfare, Col. Michael Dewar, David and Charles Publishers, 1989.

The Art of the Rifle, Jeff Cooper, Paladin Press, 1999, 2002 (color edition).

The Art of War, Sun Tzu (translated by Samuel B. Griffith), Oxford University Press, 1982.

The Australian Guerrilla: Sniping, Ion L. Idriess, Paladin Press, 1978.

The Best of Precision Shooting (Vol. II), Precision Shooting Magazine, March 1987.

Blasters' Handbook: A Manual Describing Explosives and Practical Methods of Using Them, E.I. Du Pont & Co., 1942.

Bolt Action Rifles, Frank de Haas, Follett Publishing Co., 1971.

The Book of the Rifle, Jim Carmichael, Outdoor Life Books, 1985.

Browning Machine Gun Caliber .50 HB, M2, FM 23-65, U.S. Army, May 1972.

Camouflage, FM 5-20, U.S. Army, May 1968.

Care and Use of Individual Clothing, FM 21-15, U.S. Army, February 1985.

CIRT Training Manual (two volumes), Critical Incident Response Team, St. Paul Police Department, 1988.

The Complete Book of U.S. Sniping, Peter R. Senich, Paladin Press, 1988.

The Complete .50-Caliber Sniper Course, Dean Michaelis, Paladin Press, 2000.

The Conduct of Antiterrorist Operations in Malaya (3rd ed.), British Royal Army, 1958.

Counter Sniper Guide (pamphlet), U.S. Army Marksmanship Training Unit, Ft. Benning, GA, July, 1967.

Dismounted Patrolling (Ranger), U.S. Army Infantry School, 1985.

Explosives and Demolitions, FM 5-25, U.S. Army, February 1971.

Extended Ballistics for the Advanced Rifleman, Art Blatt, Pachmayr Books, 1986.

Gun Digest Book of Scopes and Mounts, Bob Bell, DBI Books, Inc., 1983.

Handgun Stopping Power: The Definitive Study, Evan Marshall and Edwin Sanow, Paladin Press, 1992.

Hatcher's Notebook, Maj. Gen. Julian S. Hatcher, Small Arms Technical Publishing Co., 1932.

How to Track and Find Game, Clyde Ormond, Outdoor Life Books, 1975.

The Infantry Sniper, (coordinating draft), FM 7-999, U.S. Army, September 1987.

Jane's Infantry Weapons, 1988–1989, Ian V. Hogg, ed., Jane's Information Group, 1989.

Lectures on Sniping and the Use of Telescope and Optical Sights, Lt. Col. P.W. Richardson and Capt. H. Lattey, 1916.

Light Infantry Company Operations, FC 7-14, U.S. Army, February 1985.

Marine Sniper, Charles Henderson, Berkley Books, 1986.

Night Operations, FM 31-36 (test), U.S. Army, April 1968.

NRA Firearms Fact Book, 3rd Edition, National Rifle Association, 1989.

The Official Soviet SVD Manual (translation), James F. Gebhardt, Paladin Press, 1999.

One Shot—One Kill: American Combat Snipers, Charles Sasser and Craig Roberts, Pocket Books, April 1990.

Operator's Manual, M-24 Sniper Weapon System, TM 9-1005-306-10, U.S. Army, June 1989.

Patrolling and Tracking, Australian Military Forces, 1959.

The Police Sniper: A Complete Handbook, Burt Rapp, Loompanics Unlimited, 1988.

The Ranger Handbook, U.S. Army Infantry School, May 1972.

Ranger Training and Ranger Operations, FM 21-50, U.S. Army, January 1962.

Ranger Unit Operations and Training, FC 7-85, U.S. Army Infantry School, April 1985.

Rifle Marksmanship, FM 23-71, U.S. Army, December 1966.

A Rifleman Went to War, Capt. H.W. McBride, Small Arms Technical Publishing Co., 1935.

SEAL Sniper Training Program, U.S. Navy (Paladin Press), 1992.

Sierra Bullets Reloading Manual, Hayden, Hull, Almgren, and McDonald, The Leisure Group, Inc., 1974.

Silencer History and Performance, Vol. I, Alan C. Paulson, Paladin Press, 1996.

Silencer History and Performance, Vol. II, Alan C. Paulson et al., Paladin Press, 2002.

Small Arms Design and Ballistics (two volumes), Col. Townsend Whelen, 1954.

Small Arms Lexicon and Precise Encyclopedia, Col. Chester Mueller and John Olson, Shooter's Bible Press, 1968.

Small Arms of the World (8th ed.), Joseph E. Smith, Stackpole Books, 1964.

Small Arms of the World (12th ed.), Edward C. Ezell, Stackpole Books, 1983.

Sniper Training, FM 23-10, U.S. Army, 1994.

Sniper Training and Employment, TC 23-14, U.S. Army, October 1969.

Sniper Training and Employment, TC 23-14, U.S. Army, June 1989.

Sniping, USMC Fleet Marine FM 1-3B, USMC, 1975.

Sniping in France, Maj. P. Hesketh-Pritchard, Helion & Co., 2004 (reprint edition).

Special Forces Operational Techniques, FM 31-20, U.S. Army, December 1965.

Special Forces Operations, FM 31-21, U.S. Army, June 1965.

Special Operations Sniper Training and Employment, U.S. Army John F. Kennedy Special Warfare Center, February 1988.

SWAT Training and Employment, Steven Mattoon, Paladin Press, 1987.

The Tactical Marksman, Dave M. Lauck, Paladin Press, 1996.

The Tactical Rifle, Gabriel Suarez, Paladin Press, 2003.

Tactical Tracking Operations, David Scott-Donelan, Paladin Press, 1998.

Telescopic Sights, Maj. Gen. J.S. Hatcher (pamphlet), National Rifle Association, 1961.

Tracking: A Blueprint for Learning How, Jack Kearney, U.S. Border Patrol (Ret.), Pathways Press, 1986.

The Ultimate in Rifle Accuracy, Glenn Newick, Stoeger Publishing Co., 1989.

Unit Rifle Marksmanship Training Guide, FC 23-11, U.S. Army Infantry School, August, 1984.

U.S. Army Special Operations Target Interdiction Course: Sniper Training and Employment, Paladin Press, 2000.

U.S. Marine Corps Scout/Sniper Training Manual, Marine Corps Education and Development Command, Lancer Militaria, 1988.

With British Snipers to the Reich, Capt. C. Shore, Lancer Militaria, 1988.

MAGAZINE ARTICLES

"Police Sniper Training," Maj. John Plaster, *FBI Law Enforcement Bulletin*, September 1990.

"Selection of a Police Countersniper," Sgt. John Gnagey, *FBI Law Enforcement Bulletin*, April 1984.

RECOMMENDED PERIODICALS

Law and Order, Hendon Publishing Co., 130 N. Waukegan Rd., Suite 202, Deerfield, IL 60015 www.hendonpub.com/lawmag

Police Marksman, Police Marksman Association, P.O. Box 241387, Montgomery, AL 36124-1387 www.policemarksman.com

Precision Shooting, 222 McKee Street, Manchester, CT 06040 www. precisionshooting.com

Shooting Sports USA (monthly competitive shooting magazine), National Rifle Association, 11250 Waples Mill Road, Fairfax, VA 22030 www.nra.org

S.W.A.T. Magazine, 3025 North Valley View Drive, Prescott Valley, AZ 86314 www.swatmag.com

The Tactical Edge, National Tactical Officers Association, P.O. Box 797, Doylestown, PA 18901 www.ntoa.org

Tactical Response, Hendon Publishing Co., 130 N. Waukegan Rd., Suite 202, Deerfield, IL 60015 www.trmagonline.com

Very High Power, Fifty Caliber Shooters Association, P.O. Box 111, Monroe, UT 84754-0111, www.fcsa.org

RECOMMENDED ORGANIZATIONS

Fifty Caliber Shooters Association, P.O. Box 111, Monroe, UT 84754-0111
www.fcsa.org

International Association of Law Enforcement Firearms Instructors, 25 Country Club Road, S-707, Gildford, NH 03249
www.ialefi.com

National Rifle Association, 11250 Waples Mill Road, Fairfax, VA 22030
www.nra.org

National Tactical Officers Association, P.O. Box 797, Doylestown, PA 18901
www.ntoa.org

Police Marksman Association, P.O. Box 241387, Montgomery, AL 36124-1387
www.policemarksman.com

SNIPER-RELATED WEB SITES

www.americansnipers.org

www.snipercentral.com

www.snipercountry.com

www.snipersparadise.com

www.sniperworld.com

www.ultimatesniper.com

ABOUT THE AUTHOR

John L. Plaster

Maj. John L. Plaster, USAR (ret.), served three 1-year tours in Southeast Asia with the top-secret Special Forces covert operations unit, MACV-SOG. Qualified as a Green Beret weapons and communications NCO, he led strategic intelligence-gathering teams deep behind enemy lines in Laos and Cambodia on the Ho Chi Minh Trail. Plaster was wounded once and decorated four times for heroism. Leaving Vietnam as a staff sergeant, due to his extensive combat experience he received a direct commission as a reserve officer.

Combining what he'd learned of stealth, stalking, and camouflage with his postwar experiences as a competitive shooter, in 1983 he cofounded a Reserve Component sniper training program, which quickly became a major national school, instructing hundreds of students from all military services and many law enforcement agencies, including the FBI and U.S. Customs Service. He went on to be a precision rifle instructor at the prestigious Gunsite Training Center, a lecturer for American Special Operations schools, and twice served as Chief of Competition for the U.S. and European military and police sniping championships. In addition to authoring several books—and receiving the Bernal Diaz Award for the best nonfiction military history of 1997—he's designed a specialized sniper rifle stock and other shooting equipment.

In 1998 he was honored as the Special Forces Association's "Man of the Year," and in 2004 was inducted into the Air Commando Association's Hall of Fame. Major Plaster has appeared in a dozen documentaries for the *History Channel*, the *Discovery Channel*, and British television and continues to work on books and firearms-related research.